Database Management Systems

Database Management Systems

Designing and Building Business Applications

GERALD V. POST
Western Kentucky University

Boston Burr Ridge, IL Dubuque, IA Madison, WI New York
San Francisco St. Louis Bangkok Bogotá Caracas Lisbon
London Madrid Mexico City Milan New Delhi Seoul
Singapore Sydney Taipei Toronto

Irwin/McGraw-Hill

A Division of The ***McGraw-Hill*** *Companies*

DATABASE MANAGEMENT SYSTEMS: DESIGNING AND BUILDING BUSINESS APPLICATIONS

This book is printed on acid-free paper.

2 3 4 5 6 7 8 9 DOW/DOW 9 3 2 1 0 9

ISBN 0-07-289893-3

Vice president and editorial director: *Michael W. Junior*
Senior sponsoring editor: *Rick Williamson*
Developmental editor: *Christine Wright*
Marketing manager: *Jodi Fazio*
Project manager: *Margaret Rathke*
Production supervisor: *Scott M. Hamilton*
Designer: *Kiera Cunningham*
Supplement coordinator: *Rose M. Range*
Compositor: *York Graphic Services, Inc.*
Typeface: *10/12 Garamond Book*
Printer: *R. R. Donnelley & Sons Company*

Library of Congress Cataloging-in-Publication Data

Post, Gerald V.
Database management systems : designing and building business applications / Gerald V. Post.
p. cm.
Includes index.
ISBN 0-07-289893-3
1. Database management. 2. Database design. 3. Business—Databases. 4. Management information systems. I. Title.
QA76.9.D3P675 1999
005.74—dc21 98-21687

www.mhhe.com

To my wife, Sarah, for her support, stories from the real world, and the world's best chocolate chip cookies. The Pet Store case is named in memory of her mother.

G.
V.
P.

Preface

A TALE OF TWO WEB SITES

The Orinoco Music Company is proud of their Web site. The graphics are cool, the audio clips are hot, and initial excitement in the press has brought record numbers of potential customers to the site. Orders are coming in through the Web order form. After a few weeks, some problems arise. Clerks are making mistakes in copying the orders from the Web form into the company's existing mail order system. Customers are canceling orders because many of the shipments are backordered—they are complaining that if they had known the item was not in stock, they would never have ordered it. After a couple of months, the press begins to downgrade the site—noting that the graphics are old and they cannot get audio clips for the new bands. Because of the expense of constantly changing the site, Orinoco Music is thinking about removing the site and returning to a basic company-information site.

Customers have been flocking to the new Web site for Salt Peanuts Music Company. In the month since the site was activated, orders have almost doubled—in terms of the number of customers and in the value of each order. Reviews of the site have noted the limited use of graphics, but they rave about the service provided. In particular, customers can constantly see if an item is in stock. With a couple of clicks, they get background information on any artist and can play short clips from any song. Once customers place an order they can use the UPS tracking system to see when it will arrive. Customers can also call sales representatives who have instant access to all of the customer data. But everyone's favorite feature is that the system tracks individual purchases and suggests similar groups. These selections are based partly on expert opinions, but are primarily driven by grouping sales. Customers can see what products are bought by groups of similar customers. Everyone is happy with the system. Company managers like it because it increases sales. Customers like it because they have instant access to the information they want. Recording artists like it because it gives everyone access to the music and increases sales.

What, you might ask, does this tale of two Web sites have to do with database management systems? The difference between the two Web sites is that the Salt Peanuts Music Company's site is built on a database management system that integrates the company's data and enables them to create a more complete, interactive site. This text will teach students what they need to know about database management systems and how they can be used to solve similar business problems.

INTRODUCTION

While databases are often created and maintained by information technology professionals, more often in today's businesses management professionals in all disciplines are designing and creating their own database applications. Virtually every area of management uses databases: marketing professionals to analyze sales data, human resource managers to evaluate employees, operations managers to track and improve quality, accountants to integrate data across the enterprise, and financial analysts to analyze a firm's performance. That is why it is so important for business students to understand how database management systems are used to design, build, and run a modern database application.

This text is targeted at the primary business database course at the junior level. Students from any business major should understand the material. Although the text favors the database management approach over traditional programming techniques, students will find it easier if they have taken an introductory programming course. This text supports the learning process through clear exposition, many examples, exercises, and sample databases. Although some students might learn how to build an application through a general lecture or discussion, most require examples and hands-on practice supported by comments from a knowledgeable instructor.

GOALS AND PHILOSOPHY

The goal of this text is straightforward: At the end of the text, students should be able to evaluate a business situation and build a database application. The text focuses on the use of relational database technology for building applications as it is what students will encounter in businesses today.

Before they begin building relational databases, students need to master three specific areas of knowledge: database design, SQL, and programming. Databases must be carefully designed to gain the strengths of the DBMS approach. That is why the heart of this text focuses on the two topics crucial to building successful databases: database design (normalization) and SQL (queries). These two topics—standardized across all major database systems—must be covered carefully and thoroughly, particularly because they can be difficult for students.

Database design is the foundation for building applications. A well-designed database can simplify building, maintaining, and expanding an application. An important strength of relational database design is its flexibility. A properly designed database can be expanded to meet changing business conditions. On the other hand, if the design is weak, building an application will be substantially harder and more time-consuming. It is often better to throw away a poorly designed database and start over, than to try fixing or expanding it.

SQL is a powerful, standard query language that is used for virtually every step of application development. One of its greatest strengths is its availability in many different products. Once students learn the foundations of SQL, they will be able to retrieve data from almost any major database system. Many queries in SQL are relatively simple, so the foundations can be learned rapidly. Yet SQL can also be used to answer complex questions.

Another area of knowledge students need to build solid business applications is programming skills. Some applications and some database systems require detailed programming skills. However, in many cases, programming is used sparingly. It can be used as a glue to combine various components or add new features that make the application easier to use.

Most applications experience trade-offs among database design, SQL, and programming. The weaker the design, the less you rely on SQL and the more programming you will need to build the application. Because programming code is more likely to create errors and is harder to change, application developers should rely on proper database design and the power of SQL.

Database designs and queries are relatively standardized across hardware and software platforms, but details and application development depend on the specific DBMS. Microsoft Access has been chosen as the platform for demonstrating application development in this text because of its market dominance, similarity to other packages, availability, and ease of use.

DATABASE DESIGN AND THE UNIFIED MODELING LANGUAGE

For several years, entity-relationship diagrams have been the predominant modeling technique for database design. However, this approach causes problems for instructors (and students) because there are several different diagramming techniques. This text helps solve these problems by incorporating the Unified Modeling Language (UML) method, instead of traditional entity-relationship (ER) diagramming, as the modeling technique for database design. This change will be most apparent in the replacement of the ER diagram notation and terminology with the parallel concepts in UML class diagrams.

UML class diagrams, although very similar to ER diagrams, are superior in several ways. First, they are standardized, so students (and instructors) need learn only one set of notations. Second, they are "cleaner" in the sense that they are easier to read without the bubbles and cryptic notations of traditional ER diagrams. Third, they provide an introduction to object-oriented design, so students will be better prepared for future development issues. Fourth, with the rapid adoption of UML as a standard design methodology, students will be better prepared to move into future jobs. In late 1997, many of the systems design organizations adopted UML as a standard method for designing systems. UML has the support of major authors in systems design (e.g., Booch, Rumbaugh, and Jacobsen) as well as being supported by the major software development firms like IBM, Microsoft, Oracle, and Sterling. In addition, students should have little difficulty transferring their knowledge of the UML method if they need to work with older ER methods.

The basic similarities between ER and class diagrams are (1) entities (classes) are drawn as boxes, (2) binary relationships (associations) are drawn as connecting lines, and (3) n-ary associations (relationships) are drawn as diamonds. Hence the overall structures are similar. The main differences occur in the details. In UML the multiplicity of an association is shown as simple numerical notation instead of a cryptic icon. An example is shown in the following two figures.

UML also has provisions for n-ary associations and allows associations to be defined as classes. There are provisions for naming all associations, including directional names to assist in reading the diagram. Several situations have defined icons for the association ends, such as composition (rarely handled by ER), and subtypes (poorly handled by ER).

More details of the UML approach are shown in Chapters 2 and 3. Only a small fraction of the UML diagrams, notation, and terminology will be used in this text. You can find the full specification on the Web at http://www.rational.com/uml/.

ORGANIZATION

The organization of the text follows the basic steps of application development: design, queries, applications, administration, and advanced topics. Some instructors might prefer to teach queries before database design, so the initial chapters are written with that flexibility.

The introduction motivates the students and relates database applications to topics the students have likely seen in other classes. In particular, the chapter emphasizes the strengths of the database approach.

The section on database design has two chapters: Chapter 2 on general design techniques (systems techniques, diagramming, and control) and Chapter 3, which details data normalization. The objective is to cover design early in the term so that students can get started on their end-of-term projects.

Queries are covered in two chapters, with the foundations in Chapter 4 and advanced topics like subqueries in Chapter 5. Although the two chapters could be

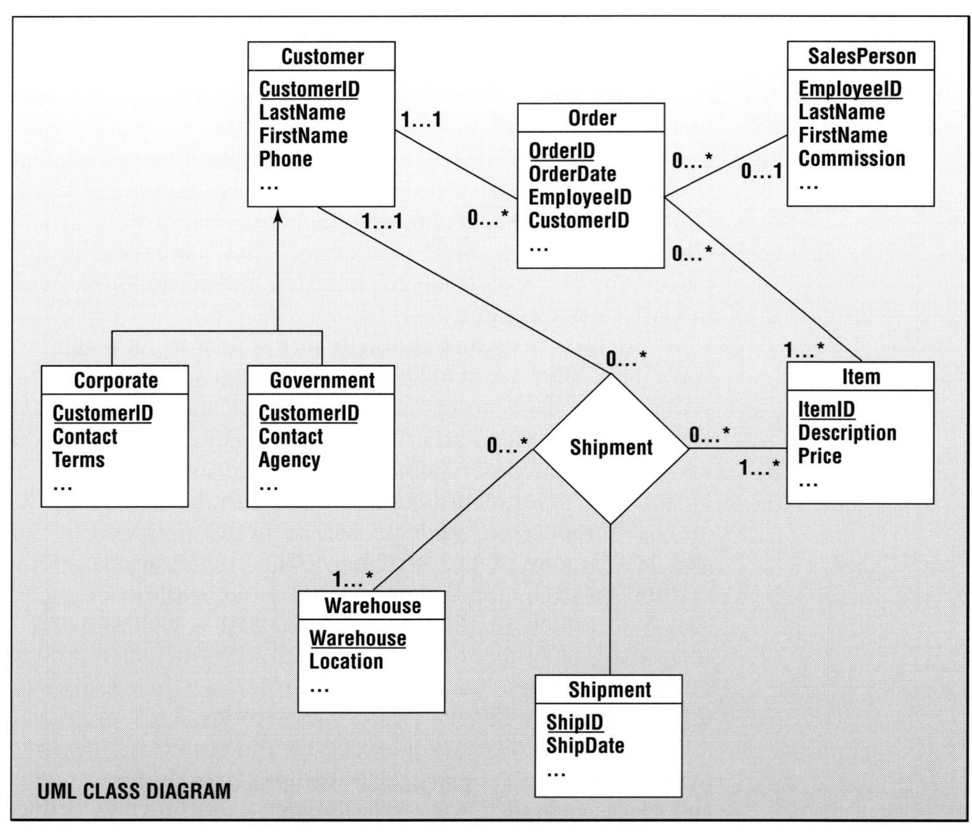
Customer
CustomerID
LastName
FirstName
Phone
...
Order
OrderID
OrderDate
EmployeeID
CustomerID
...
SalesPerson
EmployeeID
LastName
FirstName
Commission
...
1...1
0...*
0...*
0...1
1...1
0...*
1...*
0...*
Corporate
CustomerID
Contact
Terms
...
Government
CustomerID
Contact
Agency
...
Item
ItemID
Description
Price
...
0...*
Shipment
0...*
1...*
1...*
Warehouse
Warehouse
Location
...
Shipment
ShipID
ShipDate
...
UML CLASS DIAGRAM

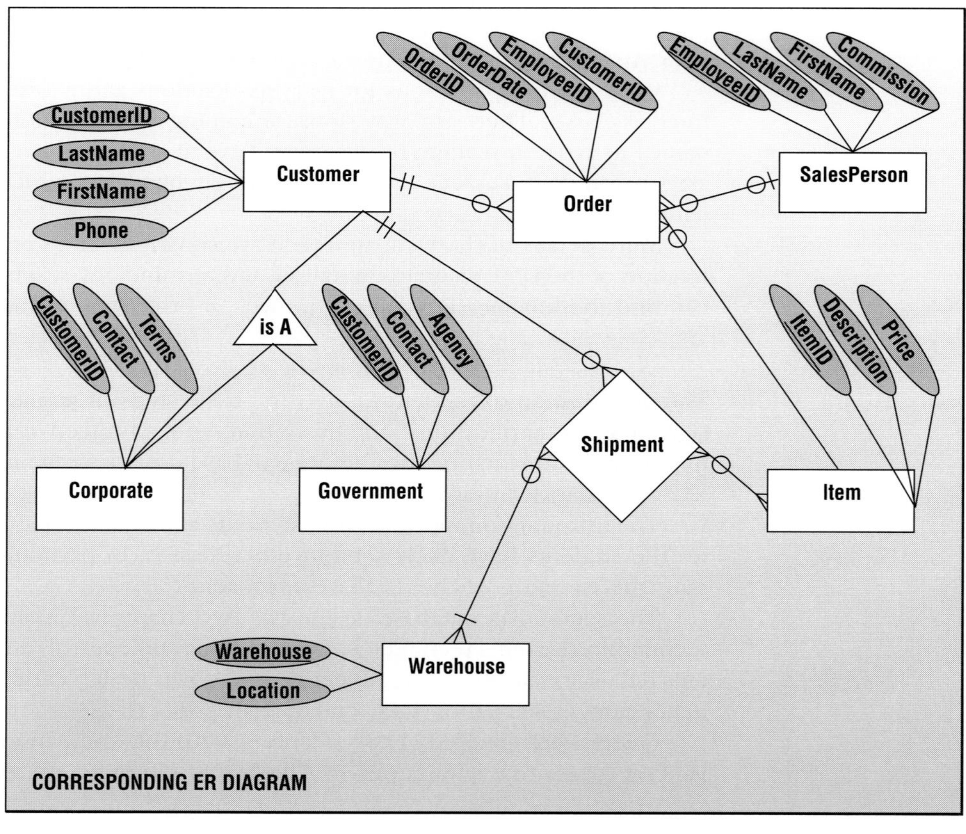
OrderID
OrderDate
EmployeeID
CustomerID
EmployeeID
LastName
FirstName
Commission
CustomerID
LastName
FirstName
Phone
Customer
Order
SalesPerson
CustomerID
Contact
Terms
is A
CustomerID
Contact
Agency
ItemID
Description
Price
Shipment
Corporate
Government
Item
Warehouse
Location
Warehouse
CORRESPONDING ER DIAGRAM

CHAPTER 1: INTRODUCTION
PART 1: SYSTEMS DESIGN
Chapter 2: Database Design
Chapter 3: Data Normalization
PART 2: QUERIES
Chapter 4: Data Queries
Chapter 5: Advanced Queries and Subqueries
Appendix: SQL Syntax
PART 3: APPLICATIONS
Chapter 6: Forms and Reports
Chapter 7: Calculations and Data Manipulation
Appendix: Introduction to Programming
Chapter 8: Application Development
Appendix: Database Applications in Visual Basic
PART 4: DATABASE ADMINISTRATION
Chapter 9: Physical Design and Performance
Chapter 10: Database Administration
PART 5: DISTRIBUTION AND INTEGRATION OF DATA
Chapter 11: Distributed Databases and The Internet
Appendix: Introduction to Oracle PL/SQL
Chapter 12: Object-Oriented Databases and Integrated Applications
Appendix: Database Projects

combined, the split provides for a second set of end-of-chapter material (particularly exercises).

Part 3 describes the development of database applications, beginning with the essentials of form and report development in Chapter 6. Chapter 7 provides a foundation in writing programs in a database environment. It focuses on Microsoft Access, but the general concepts can easily be applied to other systems, such as PowerBuilder. Chapter 8 discusses application-finishing concepts like transactions, menus, toolbars, and help files.

Part 4 examines various topics in database administration. Chapter 9 investigates aspects of physical design and database performance including indexes, clustering, and choice of storage methods. It focuses on understanding database options to improve application performance. Chapter 10 examines management issues emphasizing planning, implementation, and security.

Part 5 expands applications into larger solutions. Chapter 11 covers several issues involving distributed databases and discusses developing databases for use over the Internet. It describes how to integrate a database with Microsoft Windows NT Active Server Pages. Chapter 12 introduces the topic of integrating data objects across applications, such as using a database in a groupware environment to share spreadsheets or driving a word processing report system with a database application program. Chapter 12 also describes the use of object-oriented databases and SQL3.

Additionally, three chapters have appendixes that discuss programming concepts that are more technical. The appendix to Chapter 7 introduces programming using Microsoft's Visual Basic for Applications, which underlies Microsoft Access.

The appendix to Chapter 8 briefly describes how to create database applications in the stand-alone product Microsoft Visual Basic. The appendix to Chapter 11 introduces programming concepts in Oracle's PL/SQL, which is similar to the proposals for SQL3.

PEDAGOGY

The educational goal of the text is straightforward and emphasized in every chapter: By the end of the text, students should be able to build business applications using a DBMS. The text uses examples to apply the concepts described in the text. Students should be encouraged to apply the knowledge from each chapter by solving the exercises and working on their final projects.

Each chapter contains several sections to assist in understanding the material and in applying it to the design and creation of business applications:

- **What You Will Learn in This Chapter.** A series of questions that highlight the important issues.
- **Overview.** A student's perspective of the chapter contents.
- **Chapter Summary.** A brief review of the chapter topics.
- **A Developer's View.** A short summary of how the material in the chapter applies to building applications.
- **Key Words.** A list of words introduced in the chapter. A full glossary is provided at the end of the text.
- **Additional Reading.** References for more detailed investigation of the topics.
- **Web Site References.** Some sites that provide detailed information on the topic. Some are newsgroups where developers share questions and tips.
- **Review Questions.** Designed as a study guide for the exams.
- **Exercises.** Problems that apply the concepts presented in the chapter. Most require the use of a DBMS.
- **Projects.** Several longer projects are presented in an appendix at the end of the text. They are suitable for an end-of-term project.
- **Sample Databases.** Two sample databases are provided to illustrate the concepts. Sally's Pet Store illustrates a database in the early design stages, whereas Rolling Thunder Bicycles presents a more finished application, complete with realistic data. Exercises for both databases are provided in the chapters and called out with icons.

FEATURES OF THE TEXT

1. Focus on modern business application development.
   - Database design explained in terms of business modeling.
   - Application hands-on emphasis with many examples and exercises.
   - Emphasis on modern graphical user interface applications.
   - Chapters on database programming and application development.
   - Appendixes on programming and development details.
2. Hot topics.
   - Description and use of the unified modeling language (UML) for modeling and system diagrams. This new standard will soon be required for all designers.

- In-depth discussion of security topics in a database environment.
- Development of databases for the Internet and intranets.
- Emphasis on SQL 92, with an introduction to SQL3.
- Integrated applications and objects in databases.

3. Development examples in Microsoft Access and Visual Basic.
4. Applied business exercises and cases.
   - Many database design problems.
   - Exercises covering all aspects of application development.
   - Sample cases suitable for end-of-term projects.
5. A complete sample database application (Rolling Thunder Bicycles).
   - Fully functional business database.
   - Sample data and data generator routines.
   - Program code to illustrate common database operations.
6. A second database (Sally's Pet Store) for comparison and additional assignments.
7. Lecture notes as PowerPoint slide show.

END-OF-TERM PROJECTS

Several projects are described in the appendix at the end of the text. These cases are suitable for end-of-term projects. Students should be able to build a complete application in one term. The grading focus should be on the final project. However, the instructor should evaluate at least two intermediate stages: (1) a list of the normalized tables collected shortly after Chapter 3 is completed and (2) a design preview consisting of at least two major forms and two reports collected shortly after Chapter 6.

Some instructors may choose to assign the projects as group assignments. However, it is often wiser to avoid this approach and require individual work. The project is a key learning tool. If some members of the group avoid working on the project, they will lose an important learning opportunity.

INSTRUCTIONAL SUPPORT

An Instructor CD-ROM is available to adopters and contains the following:

- A test bank prepared by G.W. Willis of Baylor University with multiple choice, short answer questions, and short projects is available for use with the Irwin/McGraw-Hill electronic test bank software.
- Lecture notes and overheads are available as slide shows in Microsoft PowerPoint format. The slides contain all the figures and additional notes. The slides are organized into lectures and can be rearranged to suit individual preferences.
- Several databases and exercises are available. The instructor can add new data, modify the exercises, or use them to expand the discussion in the text.
- Sally's Pet Store database application is provided in Microsoft Access format and is used extensively in the text to illustrate topics. The Pet Store example is in an earlier stage of design than Rolling Thunder for two main reasons. (1) Students can compare the applications and gain insight

into the development process. (2) Students can be given assignments to provide additional features to the Pet Store application.

- The Rolling Thunder database application is available in Microsoft Access format. It is a self-contained application that illustrates many of the concepts and enables students to examine many aspects of a complete database application, including the code that drives the application.
- An Internet site for direct contact with the author: http://www.mhhe.com/business/mis/post.
- An Internet site for contact with the publisher: http://www.mhhe.com.

SUPPLEMENTAL BOOKS

The purpose of this book is to show students how to design and build business applications. To illustrate the concepts, several examples and applications use existing DBMS. Most examples are based on Microsoft Access; a few use Oracle and Microsoft SQL Server. However, to learn to use these tools in-depth, students may wish to read a supplementary book that explains the detailed features of a particular database system.

Irwin/McGraw-Hill has many supplemental books that can be bundled with this book as a package. Books are available to help students learn the details of Access, Oracle, and Visual Basic.

ACKNOWLEDGMENTS

Creating a new approach to teaching database management required the efforts and support of many people. The database class can be a difficult course to teach but one of the most enjoyable. It requires considerable dedication by instructors to develop methods to teach the material. The dedication of the reviewers who shared their time and expertise to improve this book is greatly appreciated. They are: Susan Athey, Colorado State University; Gerald C. Canfield, University of Maryland; Connie W. Crook, University of North Carolina-Charlotte; Tom Farrell, Dakota State University; John W. Gudenas, Aurora University; Thomas Hilton, Utah State University; Chris Jones, University of Washington; Bhushan Kapoor, California State University-Fullerton; John C. Malley, University of Central Arkansas; Bruce McLaren, Indiana State University; Rajesh Mirani, University of Baltimore; Hsueh-Chi Joshua Shih, National Yunlin University; and G. W. Willis, Baylor University.

Feedback from students has refined the teaching methodologies and improved the text. I am particularly indebted to the "students" at the 1997 National Computer Educators Institute. Their dedication, camaraderie, and professionalism are an inspiration to all instructors. Their input led to several improvements in the text. Thanks to Lou Adelson, Clarion University; Kellie Keeling, University of North Texas; Alyson Livingston, Tarrant County Jr. College; Scott Lord, Bainbridge College; Donald Musselman, James Madison University; Beth Paver, Grand Rapids Community College; Doug Stoddard, Clovis Community College; and Ben White, Bainbridge College.

It is always a pleasure to work with the staff at Irwin/McGraw-Hill. Rick Williamson's guidance and support were crucial to producing this text. Christine Wright's dedication and humor kept the project on track. The entire staff made my job much easier and more enjoyable. I am also grateful to G. W. Willis of Baylor University for assistance in preparing the instructor supplements.

Brief Contents

Contents

PART 5 *Distribution and Integration of Data 381*

Database Management Systems

CHAPTER 1

Introduction

WHAT YOU WILL LEARN IN THIS CHAPTER

OVERVIEW

Miranda: *My uncle just called me and said his company was desperate. It needs someone to build an application for the sales team. The company wants a laptop system for each salesperson to enter orders. The system needs to track the order status over time and generate notices and weekly reports. My uncle said that because I know a lot about computers, I should call and get the job. His company is willing to pay $4,000, and I can work part-time.*

Ariel: *Wow! Sounds like a great job. What's the problem?*

Miranda: *Well, I know how to use basic computer tools, and I can program a little, but I'm not sure I can build a complete application. It could take a long time.*

Ariel: *Why not use a database management system like Microsoft Access? It should be easier than writing code from scratch.*

Miranda: *Do you really think so? What can a database system do? How does it work?*

INTRODUCTION

Do you want to build computerized business applications? Do you want to create business applications that operate in multiple locations? Do you want to conduct business on the Internet? Do you want to enable customers to place orders using the Web? If you are going to build a modern business application, you need a database management system.

A modern database system is one of the most powerful tools you can use to build business applications. It provides many features that represent significant advantages over traditional programming methods. Yet database systems are complex. To gain the advantages, data must be carefully organized. To retrieve data and build applications, you need to learn to use a powerful query language. Once you understand the concepts of database design, queries, and application building, you will be able to create complex applications in a fraction of the time it would take with traditional programming techniques.

A **database** is a collection of data stored in a standardized format, designed to be shared by multiple users. A **database management system (DBMS)** is software that defines a database, stores the data, supports a query language, produces reports, and creates data entry screens.

Some of the most challenging problems in building applications arise in storing and retrieving data. Problems include conserving space, retrieving data rapidly, sharing data with multiple users at the same time, and providing backup and recovery of the data. Initially, programmers used to solve these problems for every application they created. Today, however, the DBMS already provides some of the best solutions to the problems.

APPLICATION DEVELOPMENT WITHOUT A DATABASE

Most programs need to store data that can be retrieved later. Most programming languages have the ability to create and store data in separate files. COBOL programs make extensive use of basic files. For many years these traditional files were the only way to store data. Even today many applications are written using traditional files.

FIGURE 1.1 Common problems with using files. The problems arise because the data is defined within individual programs. Each program may have a unique file structure. All file operations have to be redefined for each application.

- Uncontrolled duplication
  - Wastes space
  - Hard to update all files
- Inconsistent data
- Inflexibility
  - Hard to change data
  - Hard to change programs
- Limited data sharing
- Poor enforcement of standards
- Poor programmer productivity
- Excessive program maintenance

Except for small applications, using traditional files to store data can cause several problems. The basic problems with the file approach are summarized in Figure 1.1. The main cause of these problems arises from defining the data files within individual programs. For example, if an application needs customer data, the program must define a customer file and contain all the code to create the file, store the data, and retrieve the data as it is needed. Each programmer is free to create files as needed and to store data in any format. This flexibility can be nice for some problems, but it can create serious complications when a company creates multiple applications. Highly structured organizations with excellent planning methodologies can ask programmers to follow comprehensive standards when they create files. If all programmers follow the standards and if everyone documents the programs and files, then it is possible to share data across applications.

Integrated Data

Even when everyone builds applications and files carefully, problems still arise as the systems get larger and more complex. Consider the small example in Figure 1.2, which shows two human resource programs: one for payroll and one for benefits. The payroll program uses two files (Pay History and Employee). The benefits program uses three files (Benefits, Employee, and Employee Choices). The programmers who de-

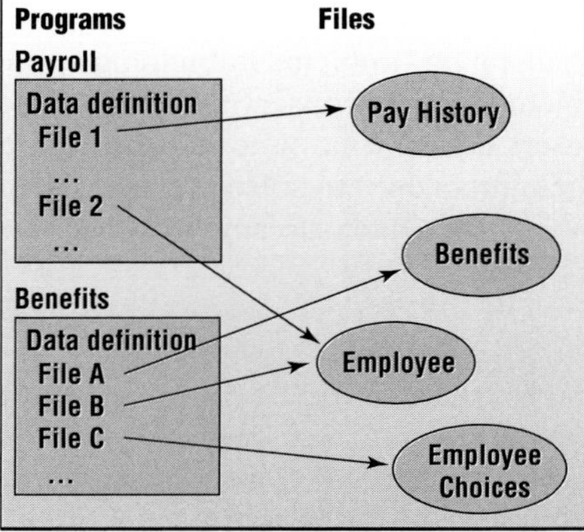

FIGURE 1.2 Intertwined files. If programmers change the payroll program and alter the Employee file, they must find and update all other programs that use that file. This process is time-consuming, expensive, and error prone.

veloped the benefits application arranged to share the Employee file from the payroll application. Otherwise, it would have been necessary to duplicate the employee data, which would waste space and make it difficult to keep the two files consistent.

As they stand, these two systems are fine. The real problems arise when the business changes and the applications have to be modified. Say that the company agrees to reimburse some of the employees for their cell phone usage. As indicated in Figure 1.3, the programmers modify the payroll program and add CellPhone data to the Employee file. Unfortunately, they are not aware that the benefits program also uses the Employee file. When the benefits program is run at the end of the month, it crashes because the internal definition of the Employee file no longer matches the data stored in the file. Of course, the programmers should have changed the benefits program when they altered the Employee file. That is the heart of the problem. How were the programmers supposed to know that the benefits program referred to the Employee file? The system could contain thousands of programs and files. Can programmers check every possible program? And not make any mistakes? Even if a company keeps good documentation, as the applications get larger, more complex, and more integrated, program changes become exceedingly difficult and time-consuming. An alternative is to create separate files for every application; however, then the data is duplicated, and when an employee moves, personnel data has to be updated in four or five different files.

Repeating Development Tasks

Every business application has several common features in terms of using and sharing data. In particular, programmers have to solve problems involving efficiency, security, and concurrency. All of these problems and solutions are complex. Without a database system, the code to handle them has to be rewritten for every application and every program.

Consider the issue of efficiency. What percentage of all programmers knows the advantages and drawbacks of the various ways to store and search data? Even if everyone knows the answers, how much time does it take to rewrite basic search techniques for every application? Likewise, how many programmers truly understand all the components needed to build a security system from scratch? Even small tasks like backup and recovery can be difficult to program—but they are absolutely critical to a successful application.

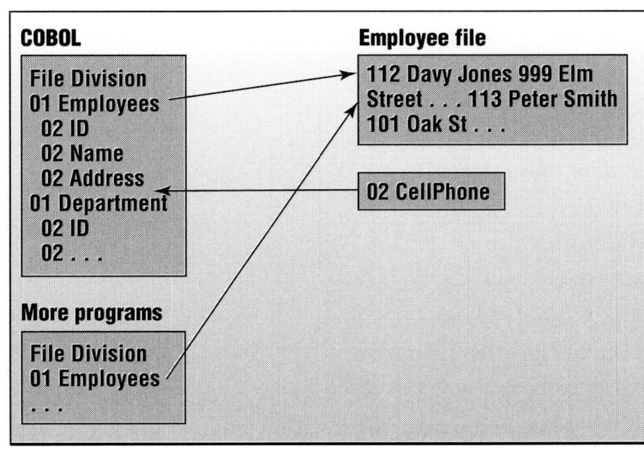

FIGURE 1.3 Altering a program and file. To add a new element to the data file, the programmer has to first expand the file. That entails writing a program to copy the old file into a new structure and add space for the new data. Next, the original program has to be rewritten to include the new data and recompiled. Then every other program that uses the file has to be rewritten.

ADVANTAGES OF THE DATABASE MANAGEMENT SYSTEM APPROACH

Many business applications need the same features (efficient storage and retrieval of data, sharing data with multiple users, security, and so on). Rather than re-create these features within every application program, it makes more sense to purchase a database management system that includes these basic facilities. Then developers can focus on creating applications to solve business problems. The primary benefits provided by a DBMS are shown in Figure 1.4.

First, the DBMS stores data efficiently. As described in Chapters 2 and 3, if you set up your database according to a few basic rules, the data will be stored with minimal wasted space. Additionally, the data can be retrieved rapidly to answer any query. Although these two goals seem obvious, they can be challenging to handle if you have to write programs from scratch every time.

The DBMS also has systems to maintain data consistency with minimal effort. Most systems enable you to create basic business rules when you define the data. For example, price should always be greater than zero. These rules are enforced for every form, user, or program that accesses the data. With traditional programs, you would have to force everyone to follow the same rules. Additionally, these rules would be stored in hundreds or thousands of separate programs—making them hard to find and hard to modify if the business changes.

The DBMS, particularly the query language, makes it easy to integrate data. For example, one application might collect data on customer sales. Another application might collect data on customer returns. If programmers created separate programs and independent files to store this data, combining the data would be difficult. In contrast, with a DBMS any data in the database can be easily retrieved, combined, and compared using the query system.

Focus on Data

With the old programming-file method, developers focused on the process and the program. Developers started projects by asking these kinds of questions: How should the program be organized? and What computations need to be made? The database approach instead focuses on the data. Developers now begin projects by asking, What data will be collected? This change is more than just a technicality. It alters the entire development process.

Think about the development process for a minute. Which component changes the most: programs (forms and reports) or the data? Yes, we collect new data all the time, but the structure of the data does not change often. And when it does change, the reason is usually that we are adding new elements—such as cellular phone numbers. On the other hand, users constantly need modifications to forms and reports.

FIGURE 1.4 Advantages of a DBMS. The DBMS provides a solution to basic data storage and retrieval problems. By using a DBMS to handle data storage problems, programmers can concentrate on building applications—saving time and money in developing new systems and simplifying maintenance of existing applications.

- Minimal data redundancy
- Data consistency
- Integration of data
- Sharing of data
- Enforcement of standards
- Ease of application development
- Uniform security, privacy, and integrity
- Data independence

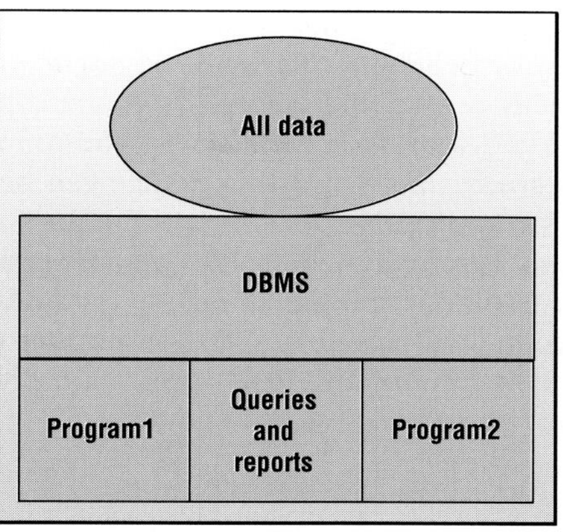

FIGURE 1.5 DBMS focus on data. First, define the data. Then all queries, reports, and programs access the data through the DBMS. The DBMS always handles common problems such as concurrency and security.

As shown in Figure 1.5, the database approach concentrates on the data. The DBMS is responsible for defining, storing, and retrieving the data. All requests for data must go through the database engine. Hence the DBMS is responsible for efficient data storage and retrieval, concurrency, data security, and so on. Once the data structure is carefully defined, additional tools like the report writer, forms generator, and query language make it faster and easier to develop business applications.

Data Independence

The other important feature of focusing on the data is the separation of the data definition from the program—known as **data independence.** Data independence enables you to change the data definition without altering the program. Similarly, data can be moved to new hardware or a completely different machine. Once the DBMS knows how to access the data, you do not have to alter the forms, reports, or programs that use that data. You can alter individual programs without having to change the data definitions.

There are exceptions to this idealistic portrayal. Obviously, if you delete entire chunks of the database structure, some of your applications are not going to work properly. Similarly, if you make radical changes to the data definitions—such as changing phone number data storage from a numeric to a text data type—you will probably have to alter your reports and forms. However, a properly designed database rarely needs these radical changes.

Consider the problem of adding cell phone numbers to an Employee table. Figure 1.6 shows part of the data definition for employees. Regardless of how many forms,

FIGURE 1.6 Adding cellular phone numbers to the Employee table. Adding a new element to a table does not affect existing queries, reports, forms or programs.

Field Name	Data Type	Description
Employee ID	Number	Autonumber . . .
Taxpayer ID	Text	Federal ID
LastName	Text	
FirstName	Text	
. . .		
Phone	Text	
. . .		
CellPhone	Text	Cellular

reports, or programs exist, the procedure is the same. Simply go to the table definition and insert the entry for CellPhone. The existing queries, forms, reports, and programs will function exactly as they did before. Of course, they will ignore the new phone number entry. If you want to see the new values on a report, you will have to insert it. With a modern report writer, this change can be as simple as dragging the CellPhone item to the appropriate location on the form or report.

The focus on data and careful design enable database systems to avoid the problems experienced with traditional programming-file methods. The consolidation of common database functions within one application enables experts to create powerful database management systems and frees application programmers to focus on building applications that solve business problems.

Data Independence and Client/Server Systems

Increasingly powerful personal computers developed over the past 10 years have opened up new methods of designing and building business applications. The most important of these is the client/server model. Database management systems have played important roles in creating client/server systems. In a simple client/server approach, the data is stored in a DBMS on a centralized computer. The decentralized personal computers run a front-end application that retrieves and displays data from the server.

The power of data independence is that the client-side applications are essentially independent from the database. Developers can create new applications without altering the database. Similarly, they can expand the database or even move it to multiple servers, and the applications remain the same. Users continue to work with their familiar personal computer applications. Developers retain control over the data. The DBMS can monitor and enforce security and integrity conditions to protect the data yet still give access to authorized users. Chapter 11 discusses the use of database systems in a client/server model in more detail, including building client/server systems on the World Wide Web.

COMPONENTS OF A DATABASE MANAGEMENT SYSTEM

To understand the value of a DBMS, it helps to see the components that are commonly provided. This basic feature list is also useful when you have to evaluate the various products to determine which DBMS your company should use. Each DBMS has unique strengths and weaknesses. You can evaluate the various products according to how well they perform in each of these categories. A DBMS is evaluated based on the database engine, data dictionary, query processor, report writer, forms generator, application generator, communication and integration, and security.

Database Engine

The **database engine** is the heart of the DBMS. It is responsible for storing, retrieving, and updating the data. This component is the one that most affects the performance (speed) and the ability to handle large problems (scalability). The other components rely on the engine to store not only the application data but also the internal system data that defines how the application will operate. Figure 1.7 illustrates the primary relationship between the database engine and the data tables.

With some systems the database engine is a stand-alone component that can be purchased and used as an independent software module. For example, the Microsoft "jet engine" forms the foundation of Access. However, the main files for this engine can also be used with programs such as Visual Basic or an Excel spreadsheet.

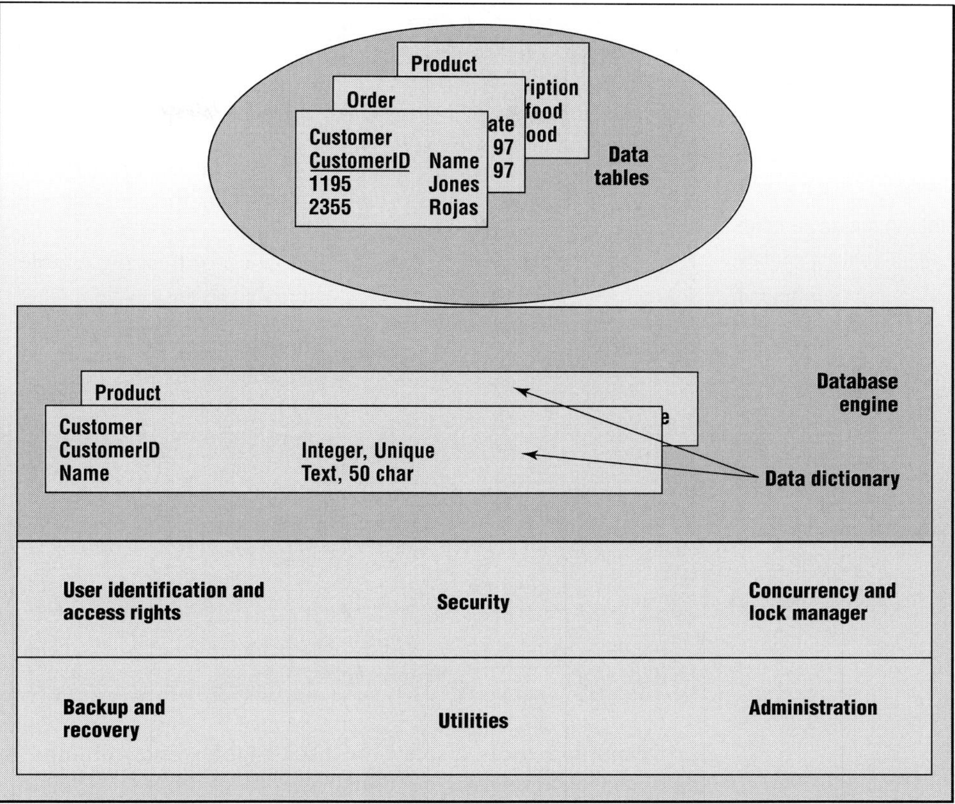

FIGURE 1.7 Database engine. The engine is responsible for defining, storing, and retrieving the data. The security subsystem of the engine identifies users and controls access to data.

The database engine is also responsible for enforcing business rules regarding the data. For example, most businesses would not allow negative prices to be used in the database. Once the designer creates that rule, the database engine will warn the users and prevent them from entering a negative value.

As shown in Figure 1.8, the database engine stores data in carefully designed tables. Chapters 2 and 3 explain how to analyze business documents and convert them into the proper tables.

Database performance is an important issue. The speed of your application depends on the hardware, the DBMS software, the design of your database, and on how you choose to store your data. Chapter 9 discusses some popular programming methods, for example, indexing, that improve the performance of a database application.

Data Dictionary

The **data dictionary** holds the definitions of all of the data tables. It describes the type of data that is being stored, allows the DBMS to keep track of the data, and helps developers and users find the data they need. Most modern database systems hold the data dictionary as a set of system tables. For example, Microsoft Access keeps a list of all the tables in a hidden system table called MSysObjects.

These tables are used by the system, and you will rarely need to use them directly. The DBMS should provide other tools that help you examine the structure of the database. For example, Microsoft Access displays a list of tables from the main database window. By clicking on a table, you can display a list of the columns. Other

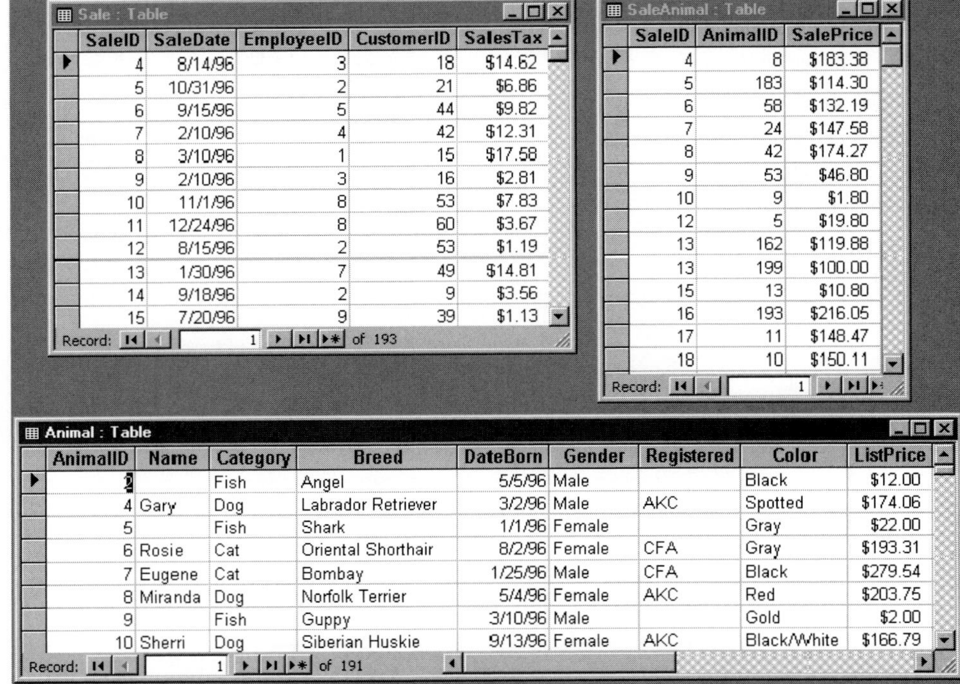

Sale : Table

SaleID	SaleDate	EmployeeID	CustomerID	SalesTax
4	8/14/96	3	18	$14.62
5	10/31/96	2	21	$6.86
6	9/15/96	5	44	$9.82
7	2/10/96	4	42	$12.31
8	3/10/96	1	15	$17.58
9	2/10/96	3	16	$2.81
10	11/1/96	8	53	$7.83
11	12/24/96	8	60	$3.67
12	8/15/96	2	53	$1.19
13	1/30/96	7	49	$14.81
14	9/18/96	2	9	$3.56
15	7/20/96	9	39	$1.13

Record: 1 of 193

SaleAnimal : Table

SaleID	AnimalID	SalePrice
4	8	$183.38
5	183	$114.30
6	58	$132.19
7	24	$147.58
8	42	$174.27
9	53	$46.80
10	9	$1.80
12	5	$19.80
13	162	$119.88
13	199	$100.00
15	13	$10.80
16	193	$216.05
17	11	$148.47
18	10	$150.11

Record: 1

Animal : Table

AnimalID	Name	Category	Breed	DateBorn	Gender	Registered	Color	ListPrice
2		Fish	Angel	5/5/96	Male		Black	$12.00
4	Gary	Dog	Labrador Retriever	3/2/96	Male	AKC	Spotted	$174.06
5		Fish	Shark	1/1/96	Female		Gray	$22.00
6	Rosie	Cat	Oriental Shorthair	8/2/96	Female	CFA	Gray	$193.31
7	Eugene	Cat	Bombay	1/25/96	Male	CFA	Black	$279.54
8	Miranda	Dog	Norfolk Terrier	5/4/96	Female	AKC	Red	$203.75
9		Fish	Guppy	3/10/96	Male		Gold	$2.00
10	Sherri	Dog	Siberian Huskie	9/13/96	Female	AKC	Black/White	$166.79

Record: 1 of 191

FIGURE 1.8 Database tables in Access. Tables hold data about one business entity. For example, each row in the Animal table holds data about a specific animal.

programming tools display the list of tables and columns within each table. Many database systems provide similar graphical tools.

Query Processor

The query processor is a fundamental component of the DBMS. It enables developers and users to store and retrieve data. In some cases the query processor is the only connection you will have with the database. That is, all database operations can be run through the query language. Chapters 4 and 5 describe the features and power of query languages—particularly standard SQL.

Queries are derived from business questions. The query language is necessary because natural languages like English are too vague to trust with a query. To minimize communication problems and to make sure that the DBMS understands your question, you should use a query language that is more precise than English. As shown in Figure 1.9, the DBMS refers to the data dictionary to create a query. When the query runs, the DBMS query processor works with the database engine to find the appropriate data. The results are then formatted and displayed on the screen.

Report Writer

Most business users want to see summaries of the data in some type of report. Many of the reports follow common formats. A modern **report writer** enables you to set up the report on the screen to specify how items will be displayed or calculated. Most of these tasks are performed by dragging data onto the screen. Professional-level report writers enable you to produce complex reports in a short time without writing any program code. Chapter 6 describes several of the common business reports and how they can be created with a database report writer.

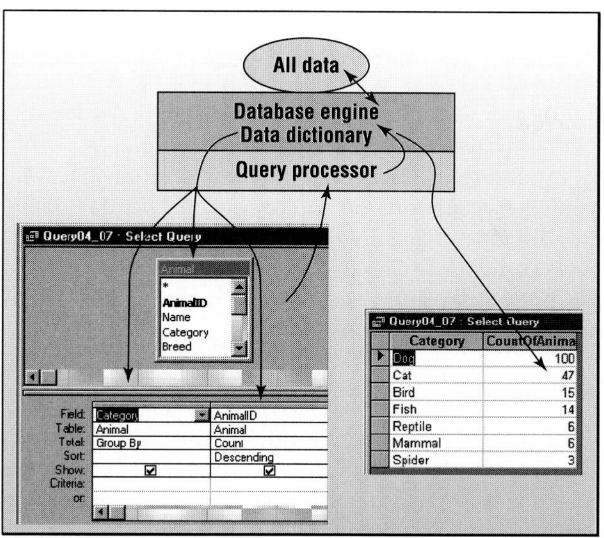

FIGURE 1.9 Database query processor. The data dictionary determines which tables and columns should be used. When the query is run, the query processor communicates with the database engine to retrieve the requested data.

The report writer can be integrated into the DBMS, or it can be a stand-alone application that the developer uses to generate code to create the needed report. As shown in Figure 1.10, the developer creates a basic report design. This design is generally based on a query. When the report is executed, the report writer passes the query to the query

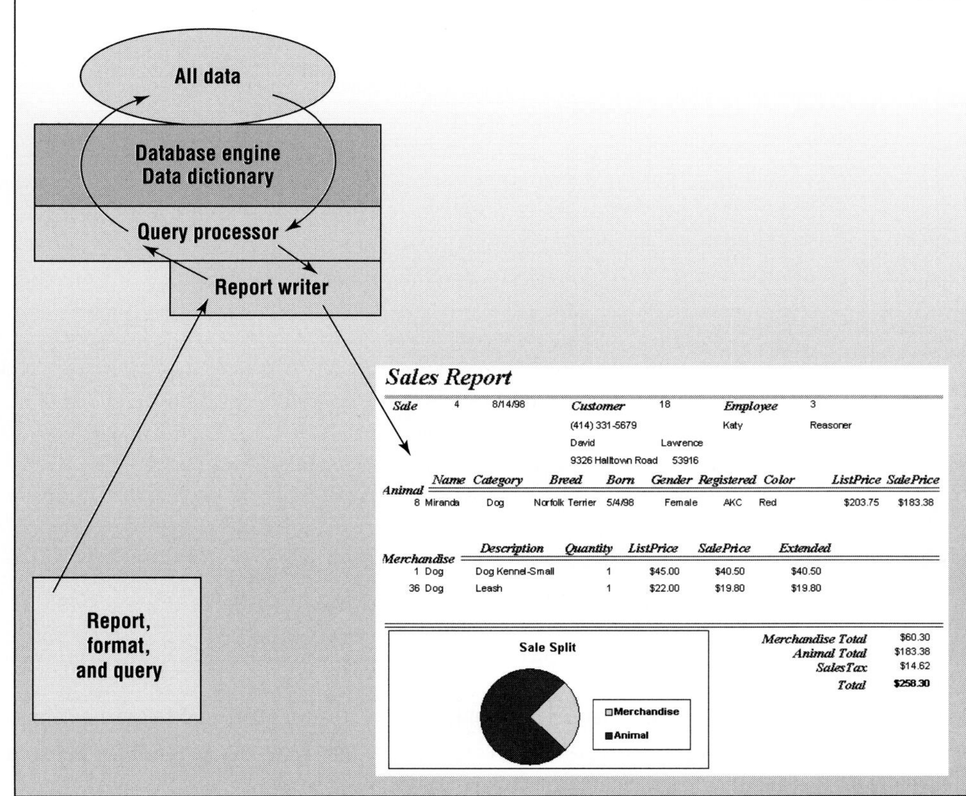

FIGURE 1.10 Database report writer. The design template sets the content and layout of the report. The report writer uses the query processor to obtain the desired data. Then it formats and prints the report.

processor, which communicates with the database engine to retrieve the desired rows of data. The report writer then formats the data according to the report template and creates the report complete with page numbers, headings, and footers.

Figure 1.11 shows the report writer that Oracle (a DBMS vendor) provides in its Developer 2000 system. The report writer generates reports that can be distributed and run by other users. This report writer is much like Microsoft Access; in both products you set up sections on the report and display data from the database. The report writer includes features to perform computations and format the columns. You also have control over colors, you can place images on the report (e.g., logos), and you can draw lines and other shapes to make the report more attractive or to call attention to specific sections.

Forms Generator

A **forms generator** or input screen helps the developer create input forms. As described in Chapter 6, the goal is to create forms that represent common user tasks, making it easy for users to enter data. The forms can include graphs and images. The forms generator enables developers to build forms by dragging and dropping items

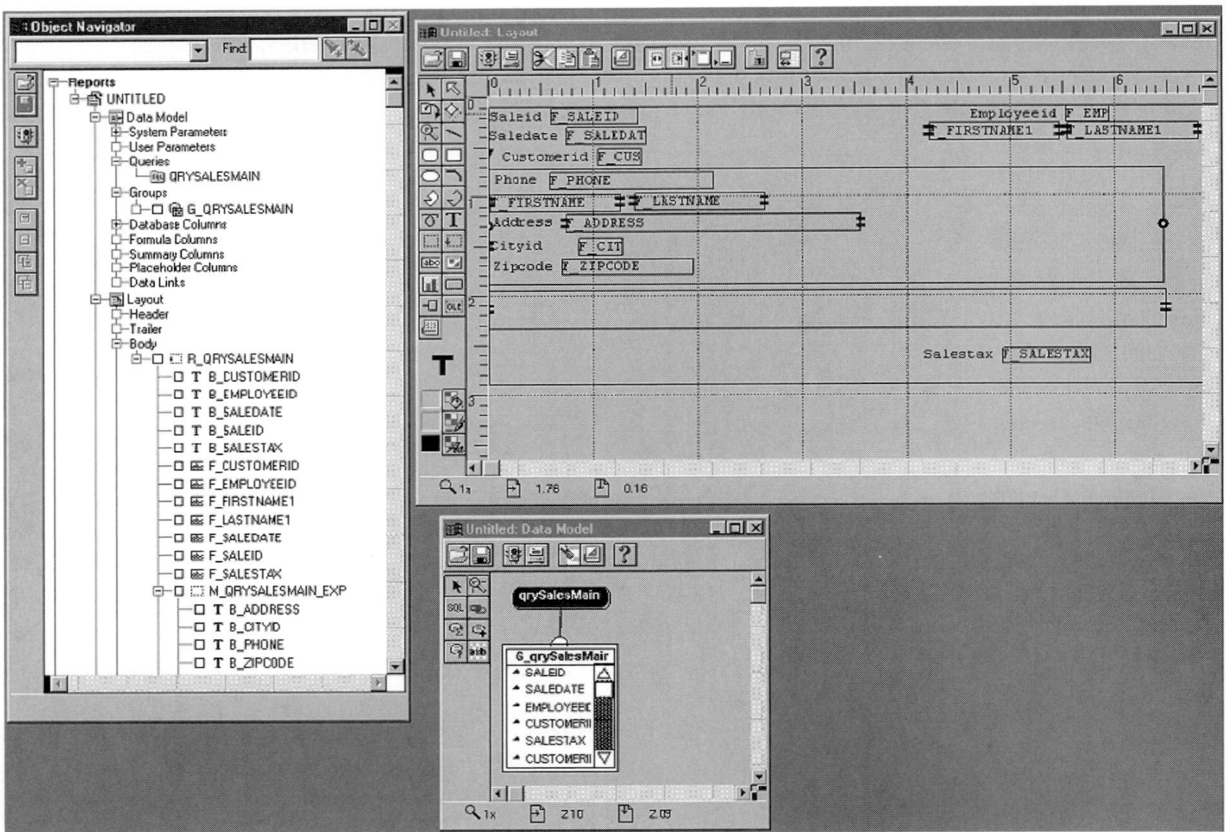

FIGURE 1.11
Oracle Developer 2000 report writer. The Data Model is used to create a query and select the data to be displayed. Then Developer 2000 creates the basic report layout. You can modify the layout and add features to improve the design or highlight certain sections.

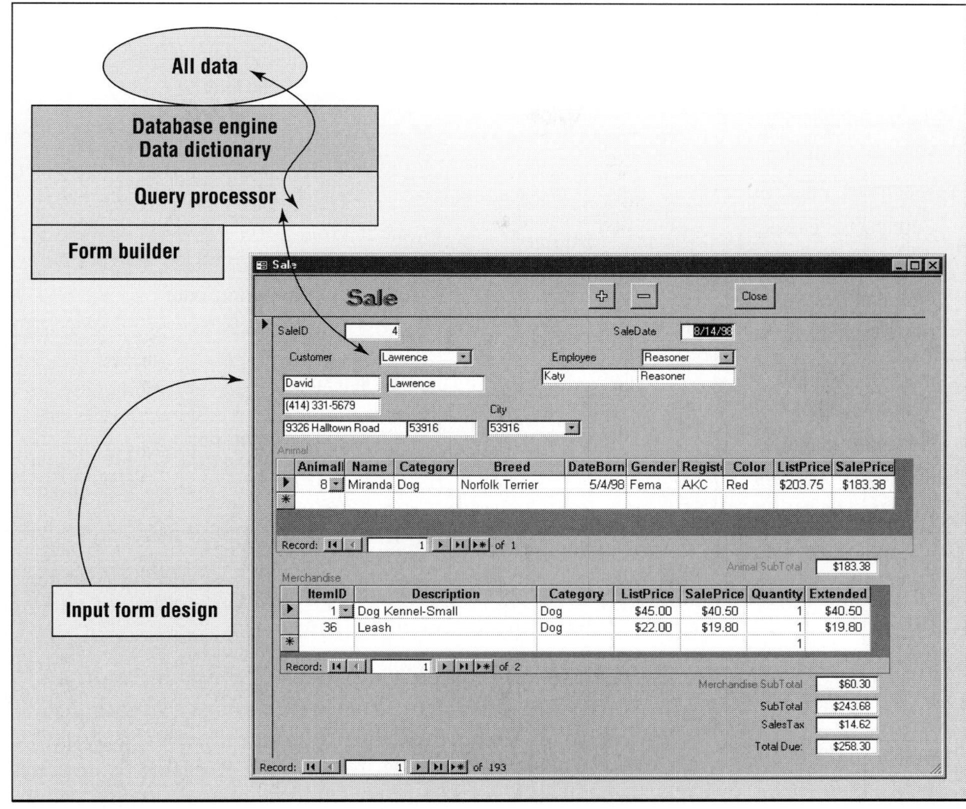

FIGURE 1.12 Database form. A form is used to collect data. It is designed to match the tasks of the user, making it easy to enter data and look up information. The query processor is used to obtain related data and fill in look-up data in combo boxes.

on the screen. Figure 1.12 shows that forms make heavy use of the query processor to display data on the form.

Chapter 7 points out that most applications still need some traditional programming. However, these programs tend to be short subroutines that are embedded on the forms. Again, the purpose of the coding is to make the application easier to use and to protect the data.

Many database systems also provide support for traditional, third-generation languages (3GL) to access the database. The issues in writing programs and accessing data through these programs are directly related to the topics discussed in Chapter 7.

Application Generator

An application is a collection of forms and reports designed for a specific user task. It is the final package that you are trying to create. The Pet Store database that accompanies this text shows the start of an application. The Rolling Thunder database is a more complete application. Applications can be small and consist of a few input forms and reports, or they can be large, complex systems that integrate data from several databases with hundreds of forms and reports.

A good DBMS contains an **application generator,** which consists of tools that assist the developer in creating a complete application package. As discussed in Chapter 8, popular development tools include menu and toolbar generators and an integrated context-sensitive help system.

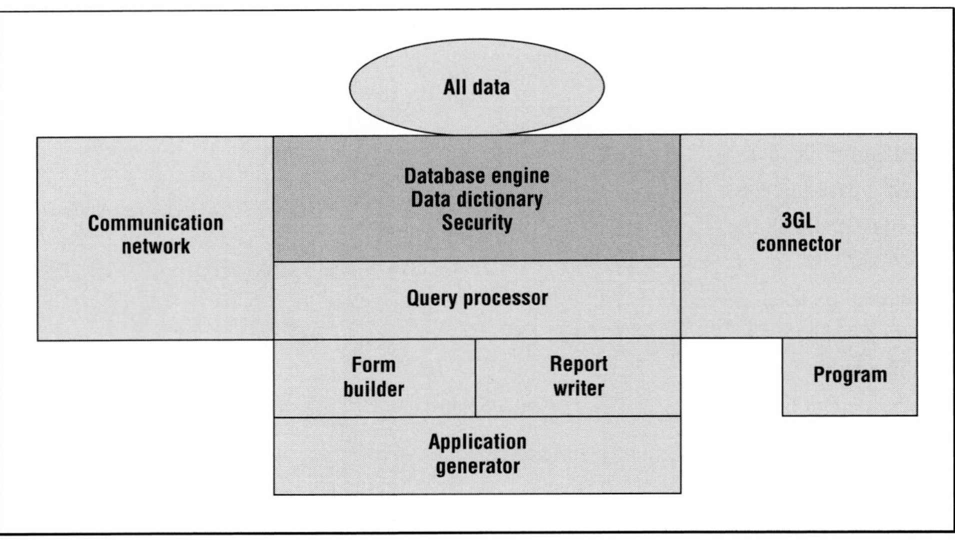

FIGURE 1.13 Database components. The communication network connects the database on different machines. The 3GL connector enables developers to access the database while using traditional programming languages. The application generator helps build a complete application with menus and help files.

Communication and Integration

Some database systems provide special communication and integration utilities designed to store and use data in several databases running on different machines, even if they are in different locations. Modern operating systems and independent networks, including the Internet, have made it easier to connect databases running in different locations. Nonetheless, some database systems do a better job of using these tools and support connections to share data globally.

Chapters 11 and 12 discuss some of the issues and complications that arise in building distributed database applications. Chapter 11 also describes some of the basic features of creating an Internet Web site that relies on a database to collect and retrieve data.

Figure 1.13 shows how a modern DBMS has additional components to share data with other machines across communication networks. The 3GL connector provides utilities that connect traditional languages (COBOL, C++, etc.) with the database engine. Developers can use the power and flexibility of these languages and still use the query processor to retrieve and store data in the database.

Security and Other Utilities

Because a primary goal of a database is to share data with multiple users, the DBMS must also be responsible for establishing and maintaining security access controls. Chapter 10 describes how individuals or groups of users can be granted specific privileges and how their actions can be restricted to specific areas of the database.

Security is a complex issue with databases running on personal computers, since most personal computer operating systems have few controls. The DBMS has to take responsibility for more aspects of security. In particular, it must identify the user and then provide or limit access to various parts of the database.

Various administrative utilities are provided by the DBMS and discussed in Chapter 10. Common features include backup and recovery, user management, data storage evaluation, and performance-monitoring tools.

LEADING COMMERCIAL DATABASES

Some of the leading database systems include DB2, Oracle, Ingres, SQL Server, and Informix. Tools from IBM, Oracle, and Ingres are available for a variety of platforms, from large to midrange to personal computers. The Informix database system is also available for various hardware platforms but is primarily designed to run on computers using the UNIX operating system. Products for network file servers are also available from Microsoft (SQL Server), Sybase, and IBM (DB2/400). Many database packages are available for personal computers, but most of the vendors recommend that their use be limited to small applications. Popular packages include Microsoft Access, Paradox from Borland, and Lotus Approach.

This list includes only a small fraction of the database systems available. Many applications have been running successfully for years on other systems. Additionally, software vendors are introducing new database systems on a regular basis.

Choosing a database management system is an important task. In some cases an organization will already have chosen to standardize on software from one vendor, and as the application developer, you will have little choice. Other times you will have to choose the DBMS before you begin developing the application. In these situations you will have to carefully evaluate the features, compare the strengths and weaknesses, negotiate pricing, and learn to use the specific tools of the new system.

BRIEF HISTORY OF DATABASE MANAGEMENT SYSTEMS

Developers quickly realized that many business applications needed a common set of features for sharing data and began developing database management systems. Developers gradually refined their goals and improved their programming techniques. Many of the earlier database approaches still survive, partly because it is difficult to throw away applications that work. It is worth understanding some of the basic differences between these older methods. The following discussion simplifies the concepts and skips the details. The purpose is to highlight the differences between these various database systems—not to teach you how to design or use them.

The earliest database management systems were based on a hierarchical method of storing data. The early systems were an extension of the COBOL file structure. To provide flexible access, these systems were extended with network databases. However, the relational database approach originated by E. F. Codd eventually became the dominant method of storing and retrieving data. Recently, the object-oriented approach has been defined. In some ways it is an extension of the relational model. In other ways it is different. However, it is so new that systems based on the concept are still evolving.

Hierarchical Databases

The **hierarchical database** approach begins by claiming that business data often exhibits a hierarchical relationship. For example, a small office without computers might store data in filing cabinets. The cabinets would be organized by customer. Each customer section would contain folders for individual orders, and the orders would list each item being purchased. To store or retrieve data, the database system must start at the top—with a customer in this example. As shown in Figure 1.14, when the database stores the customer data, it stores the rest of the hierarchical data with it.

The hierarchical database approach is relatively fast—as long as you only want to access the data from the top. The most serious of the problems related to data storage is the difficulty of searching for items in the bottom or middle of the hier-

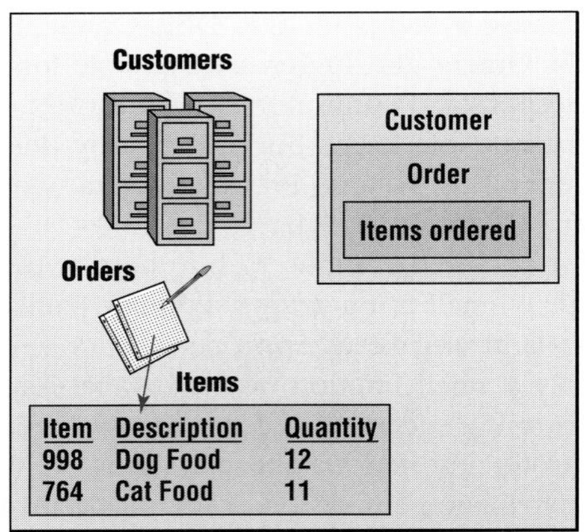

FIGURE 1.14 Hierarchical database. To retrieve data, the DBMS starts at the top (customer). When it retrieves a customer, it retrieves all nested data (order, then items ordered).

archy. For example, to find all of the customers who ordered a specific item, the database would have to inspect each customer, every order, and each item.

Network Databases

The **network database** has nothing to do with physical networks (e.g., local area networks). Instead, the network model is named from the network of connections between the data elements. The primary goal of the network model was to solve the hierarchical problem of searching for data from different perspectives.

Figure 1.15 illustrates the Customer, Order, and Item data components in a network model. First, notice that the items are now physically separated. Second, note that they are connected by arrows. Finally, notice the entry points, which are indicated with arrows. The entry points are predefined items that can be searched. In all cases the purpose of the arrows is to show that once you enter the database, the DBMS can follow the arrows to find and display matching data. As long as there is an arrow, the database can make an efficient connection.

Although this approach seems to solve the search problem, the cost is high. All arrows must be physically implemented as indexes or embedded pointers. Indexes are described in Chapter 9. Essentially, an index duplicates every key data item in the associated data set and associates the item with a pointer to the storage location of the rest of the data. The problem with the network approach is that the indexes

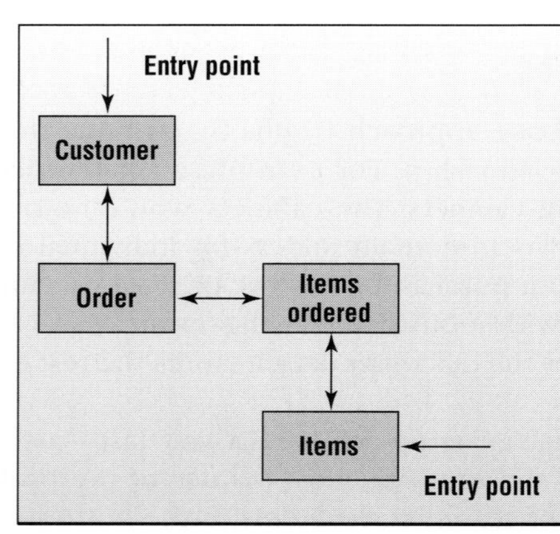

FIGURE 1.15 Network database. All data sets must be connected with indexes as indicated by the arrows. Likewise, all entry points (starting point for a query) must be defined and created before the question can be answered.

FIGURE 1.16 Relational database. Data is stored in separate sets of data. The tables are not physically connected; instead, data is linked between columns. For example, when retrieving an order, the database can match and retrieve the corresponding customer data based on CustomerID.

Customer(CustomerID, Name, . . .
Order(OrderID, CustomerID, OrderDate, . . .
ItemsOrdered(OrderID, ItemID, Quantity, . . .
Items(ItemID, Description, Price, . . .

must be built before the user can ask a question. Consequently, the developer must anticipate every possible question that users might ask about the data. Worse, building and maintaining the indexes can require huge amounts of processor time and storage space.

Relational Databases

E. F. Codd originated the **relational database** approach in the 1970s, and within several years three elements came together to make the relational database the predominant method for storing data. First, theoreticians defined the basic concepts and illustrated the advantages. Second, programmers who built database management system software created efficient components. Third, hardware performance improved to handle the increased demands of the system.

Figure 1.16 illustrates how the four basic tables in the example are represented in a relational database. The key is that the tables (called "relations" by Codd) are sets of data. Each table stores attributes in columns that describe specific entities. These sets are not physically connected to each other. The connections exist through the matching data stored in each table. For example, the Order table contains a column for CustomerID. If you find an order that has a CustomerID of 15, the database can automatically find the matching CustomerID and retrieve the related customer data.

The strength of the relational approach is that the designer does not need to know which questions might be asked of the data. If the data is carefully defined (see Chapters 2 and 3), the database can answer virtually any question efficiently (see Chapters 4 and 5). This flexibility and efficiency is the primary reason for the dominance of the relational model. Most of this book focuses on building applications for relational databases.

Object-Oriented Databases

An **object-oriented (OO) database** is a new and evolving method of organizing data. The OO approach began as a new method to create programs. The goal is to define objects that can be reused in many programs—thus saving time and reducing errors. As illustrated in Figure 1.17, an object has three major components: a name, a set of properties or attributes, and a set of methods or functions. The properties describe the object—just as attributes describe an entity in the relational database. The "methods" are the true innovation of the OO approach. *Methods* are short programs that define the actions that each object can take. For example, the code to add a new customer would be stored with the Customer object. The innovation is that these methods are stored with the object definition.

Figure 1.17 also hints at the power of the OO approach. Note that the base objects (Order, Customer, OrderItem, and Item) are the same as those for the relational approach. However, with the OO approach, new objects can be defined in terms of existing objects. For example, the company might create separate classes of customers for commercial and government accounts. These new objects would contain

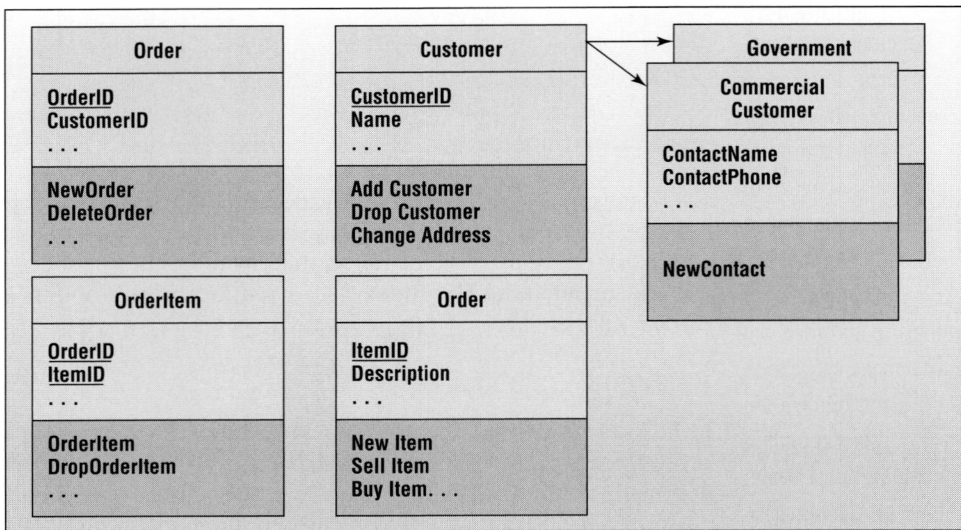

FIGURE 1.17 Object-oriented database. Objects have properties—just as relational entities have attributes that hold data to describe the object. Objects have methods that are functions the objects can perform. Objects can be derived from other objects.

all of the original Customer properties and methods and also add variations that apply only to the new types of customers.

The OO approach is fundamentally altering the way programmers create applications. Some of these changes are explored in Chapters 7 and 8. As an application developer, you will be using DBMS software that was created with an OO approach. Hence you will use the objects, properties, and methods that have already been defined.

On the other hand, OO databases are less common, and the foundations are still being developed. Chapter 12 discusses some of the features of OO database systems. Probably the greatest difficulty with OO databases is dealing with different types of computers. Transferring data from one computer to another is usually not too difficult, as long as the data items are basic text and numbers. Transferring complex objects like images and video can be challenging or impossible for different types of hardware. Storing and transferring methods or program segments is even more difficult. If a programmer creates an object and associated methods on a large IBM computer, the methods will work on that computer. However, if an employee wants to use a personal computer to access the database, how can the code for the method run on the personal computer? Most of the current approaches to this issue suffer from performance and security problems.

These are just some of the issues faced by companies developing an OO database management system (OODBMS). The OO approach has the ability to provide powerful components. It also might provide the means to create hardware independence, where databases and software can run unchanged on any platform.

APPLICATION DEVELOPMENT

If you carefully examine Figures 1.12, 1.13, and 1.14, you will notice that they all have essentially the same data sets. This similarity is not an accident. Database design methods described in Chapters 2 and 3 should be followed regardless of the method used to implement the database. In other words, any database project begins by identifying the data that will be needed and analyzing that data to store it as efficiently as possible.

The second step in building applications is to identify forms and reports that the users will need. These forms and reports are based on queries, so you must create any queries or views that will be needed to produce the reports and forms as described in Chapters 4 and 5. Then you use the report writer and forms generator to create each report and form as described in Chapter 6.

The next step is to combine the forms and reports into an application that handles all of the operations needed by the user. The goal is to create an application that matches the jobs of the users and helps them to do their work. Chapter 7 describes how to improve your forms and reports. Chapter 8 discusses how to add the special features (menu, switchboards, help system, etc.) that create a polished application.

The next step is to determine whether there are ways to improve the database. By controlling the way the database stores and retrieves individual sections of your database, you can fine-tune the performance. Chapter 9 discusses some of the common techniques used to improve performance.

When the application is designed and while it is being used, several database administration tasks have to be performed. Setting security parameters and controlling access to the data is one of the more important tasks. Chapter 10 discusses various administration and security issues.

As an organization grows, computer systems and applications become more complex. An important feature in modern organizations is the need for users to access and use data from many different computers throughout the organization. At some point you will need to increase the scope of your application so that it can be used by more people in different locations. Distributed databases discussed in Chapter 11 are a powerful way to create applications that remove the restrictions of location. The Internet is rapidly becoming a powerful tool for building and implementing database applications that can be used by anyone around the world. The same technologies can be used for applications that are accessed only by in-house personnel. Systems that use Internet technology but limit access to insiders are called **intranets.**

Applications are also becoming more complex. Users are demanding the integration of data from databases, spreadsheets, and word processors. These demands constitute a move from **transaction processing** to **decision support systems (DSS).** Transaction processing applications focus on collecting data and producing basic reports. A DSS application typically requires more analysis, computations, and experimentation by the user. Users need applications that can retrieve data from the database, format it and transfer it to a spreadsheet to perform complex analyses. The results and graphs from the spreadsheet are transferred to a word processor or publishing package for integration into a final report. Automating these steps within your application makes for impressed, happier users—and more jobs for you.

SALLY'S PET STORE

A young lady with a love for animals is starting a new type of pet store. Sally wants to match pets with owners who will take good care of the animals. One of her key objectives is to closely monitor breeders to make sure that they take good care of all of their animals and that baby animals receive proper care and attention so they will become friendly pets. A second objective is to develop long-term relationships with customers. She wants to help them choose the best type of animal for each situation and to make sure the customers have all of the support and information they need to properly care for the animals.

Sally realizes that meeting these two objectives requires her to collect and monitor a large amount of data. After taking an information systems course in an MBA program, she realizes that she needs a database to help her collect data and monitor the operations of the store.

At the moment Sally has only one store, but she dreams of expanding into additional cities. She wants to hire and train workers to be "animal friends," not salespeople. These friends will help customers choose the proper animal. They will answer questions about health, nutrition, and pet behavior. They will even be taught that some potential customers should be convinced not to buy an animal.

Because the workers will spend most of their time with the customers and animals, they will need technology to help them with their tasks. The new system will also have to be easy to use, since little time will be available for computer training.

Even based on a few short discussions with Sally, it is clear that the system she wants will take some time to build and test. Fortunately, Sally admits that she does not need the complete system immediately. She has decided that she first needs a basic system to handle the store operations: sales, orders, customer tracking, and basic animal data. However, she emphasizes that she wants the system to be flexible enough to handle additional features and applications.

Details of Sally's Pet Store will be examined in other chapters. For now, you might want to visit a local pet store or talk to friends to get a basic understanding of the problems they face, and how a database might help them.

ROLLING THUNDER BICYCLES

The Rolling Thunder Bicycle Company builds custom bicycles. Its database application is much more complete than the Pet Store application and provides an example of how the pieces of a database system fit together. This application also contains many detailed forms that illustrate the key concepts of creating a user interface. Additionally, most of the forms contain programming code that handle common business tasks. You can study this code to help you build your own applications. The Rolling Thunder application has a comprehensive help system that describes the company and the individual forms. The database contains realistic data for hundreds of customers and bicycles.

One of the most important tasks at the Rolling Thunder Bicycle Company is to take orders for new bicycles. Several features have been included to help nonexperts select a good bicycle. As the bicycles are built, the employees record the construction on the Assembly form. When the bicycle is shipped, the customers are billed. Customer payments are recorded in the financial forms. As components are installed on bicycles, the inventory quantity is automatically decreased. Merchandise is ordered from suppliers, and payments are made when the shipments arrive.

The tasks performed at Rolling Thunder Bicycles are similar to those in any business. By studying the application and the techniques, you will be able to create solid applications for any business.

SUMMARY

One of the most important features of business applications is the ability to share data with many users at the same time. Without a DBMS sharing data causes several problems. For example, if data definitions are stored within each separate program, making changes to the data file becomes very difficult. Changes in one program and its data files can cause other programs to crash. Every application would need special code to provide data security, concurrency, and integrity features. By focusing on the data first, the database approach separates the data from the programs. This independence makes it possible to expand the database without crashing the programs.

A DBMS has many components. Required features include the database engine to store and retrieve the data and the data dictionary to help the DBMS and the user locate data. Other common features include a query language, which is used to retrieve data from the DBMS to answer business questions. Application development tools include a report writer, a forms generator, and an application generator to create features like menus and help files. Advanced database systems provide utilities to control secure access to the data, cooperate with other software packages, and communicate with other database systems.

Database systems have evolved through several stages. Early hierarchical databases were fast for specific purposes but provided limited access to the data. Network databases enabled users to build complex queries but only if the links were built with indexes in advance. The relational database is currently the leading approach to building business applications. Once the data is defined carefully, it can be stored and retrieved efficiently to answer any business question. The object-oriented approach is a new technique for creating software. Advances are still being made in defining and creating object-oriented databases. An object consists of properties that describe it and methods that it can perform.

Regardless of the type of database implemented, application development follows similar steps. First identify the user requirements, determine the data that needs to be collected, and define the structure of the database. Then develop the forms and reports that will be used and build the queries to support them. Next, combine the various elements into a polished application that ties everything together to meet the user needs. If necessary, distribute the database across the organization or through an Internet or intranet. Additional features can be provided by integrating the database with powerful analytical and presentation tools, such as spreadsheets, statistical packages, and word processors.

A DEVELOPER'S VIEW

For Miranda to start on her database project, she must first know the strengths of the tools she will use. At the starting point of a database project, you should collect information about the specific tools that you will use. Get the latest reference manuals. Install the latest software patches. Set up work directories and project space. For a class project, you should log on, get access to the DBMS, make sure you can create tables, and learn the basics of the help system.

KEY WORDS

application generator, 13
data dictionary, 9
data independence, 7
database, 3
database engine, 8
database management system (DBMS), 3
decision support system (DSS), 19
forms generator, 12
hierarchical database, 15
intranet, 19
network database, 16
object-oriented (OO) database, 17
relational database, 17
report writer, 10
transaction processing, 19

REVIEW QUESTIONS

1. What data problems tend to arise in application development?
2. What are the advantages of the DBMS approach to application development?
3. What are the basic components of a DBMS?
4. Why is the relational database approach better than earlier methods?

Member(MemberID, LastName,FirstName, Address, DateJoined)

332	Ant	Adam	354 Elm	5/5/84
442	Bono	Sonny	765 Pine	8/8/72
553	Cher		886 Oak	2/2/85
673	Donovan	Michael	421 Willow	3/3/71
773	Moon	Keith	554 Cherry	4/4/72
847	Morrison	Jim	676 Sandalwood	5/5/68

Round(MemberID, PlayDate, Course, Score)

442	6/4/98	9:00am	Blue	98
332	6/4/98	1:00pm	Gold	87
442	6/5/98	7:00am	Blue	99
673	6/6/98	8:00am	White	89
847	6/6/98	10:00am	Gold	74
442	6/7/98	3:00pm	Blue	97
553	6/8/98	2:00pm	Gold	82
773	6/10/98	9:00am	Blue	68
332	6/10/98	9:00am	White	87
442	6/11/98	11:00am	Blue	99

Report

332 Adam Ant		
6/4/98	Gold	87
6/10/98	White	87
	Average	87.00
442 Sonny Bono		
6/4/98	Blue	98
6/5/98	Blue	99
6/7/98	Blue	97
6/11/98	Blue	99
	Average	98.25
553 Cher		
6/8/98	Gold	82
	Average	82.00

5. What are the main features of an object-oriented design?
6. How is an object-oriented approach similar to the relational approach?
7. How is an object-oriented approach similar to a hierarchical approach?

EXERCISES

1. Create a new database with the two tables shown in the figure. Feel free to add more data. Be sure to set a primary key for the underlined columns. Next, create a query that includes every column in the two tables. Create a report based on this query similar to the one shown in the figure. Hint: Use the wizard to create the report.
2. Read the documentation to your DBMS and write a brief outline that explains how to
   a. Create a table.
   b. Create a simple query.
   c. Create a report.
3. Interview a manager, a friend, or a relative and describe a situation that could use a database. Identify basic data that would be collected and possible reports to be produced.

4. Find a recent reference that compares at least two DBMS software packages. List the major strengths of each package. Describe the basic features (query, report writer, etc.) for each package.

5. Find three "databases" that limit the way they can be searched. Explain why the limitation is a problem and describe how it might be solved. Sample: using a telephone book to find a name when you know the phone number.

6. Search the Internet and find three Web sites that use a database system to provide information to users. From the perspective of the user, briefly explain the value of the database approach.

7. Using Internet resources, select a DBMS vendor, identify the components needed, and estimate the cost of purchasing a complete system for use on a medium-size project. The database will include at least 100 primary tables and approximately 800 megabytes of data storage. The system will be used by at least 20 users at the same time—most of whom use personal computers attached to a central server.

Sally's Pet Store

8. Download and install the Pet Store database or find it on your local area network if it has already been installed. Print out (or write down) the list of the tables used in the database. Use the Help command to find the version number of Microsoft Access that you are using.

9. Visit a local pet store and make a list of 10 merchandise items and five animals for sale. Enter this data into the appropriate Pet Store database tables.

10. Create a mailing label report that lists the customers who live in Kentucky (KY). First create a query that includes the Customer and City tables. Then use the Report Wizard to create a label report based on that query.

11. Outline the basic tasks that take place in running a pet store. Identify some of the basic data items that will be needed.

Rolling Thunder Bicycles

12. Download and install the Rolling Thunder database or find it on your local area network if it has already been installed. Using the BicycleOrder form, create an entry for a new bicycle.

13. Use the Rolling Thunder Help system to briefly describe the firm and its major processes. Identify the primary business entities in the company.

14. How does the application relate the receipt of merchandise (from suppliers) to the purchase order?

WEB SITE REFERENCES

Site	Description
http://www.microsoft.com/access/	Microsoft Access
http://www.microsoft.com/sql/	Microsoft SQL Server
http://www.oracle.com	Oracle
http://www.cai.com/products/ingres.htm	Ingres
http://www.sybase.com	Sybase

http://www.software.ibm.com/data/db2/	IBM DB2
http://www.acm.org	Association for Computing Machinery
news://comp.databases	Questions and sometimes answers on many topics and subtopics
http://www.amazon.com	A very large bookstore

ADDITIONAL READING

Gatlin, A. J., and J. P. Mueller. *The Complete Microsoft Certification Success Guide.* 2nd ed. New York: McGraw-Hill, 1997. [An introduction to certification on Microsoft software.]

Jones, E., and J. M. Jones. *Access 97 Answers: Certified Tech Support.* Berkeley: Osborne, 1997. [One of many books on Access. Spend some time at your local (or electronic) bookstore and choose your favorite.]

Litwin, P., K. Getz, and M. Gilbert. *Access 97 Developer's Handbook.* San Francisco: Sybex, 1997. [One of many books on Access.]

PART 1

Systems Design

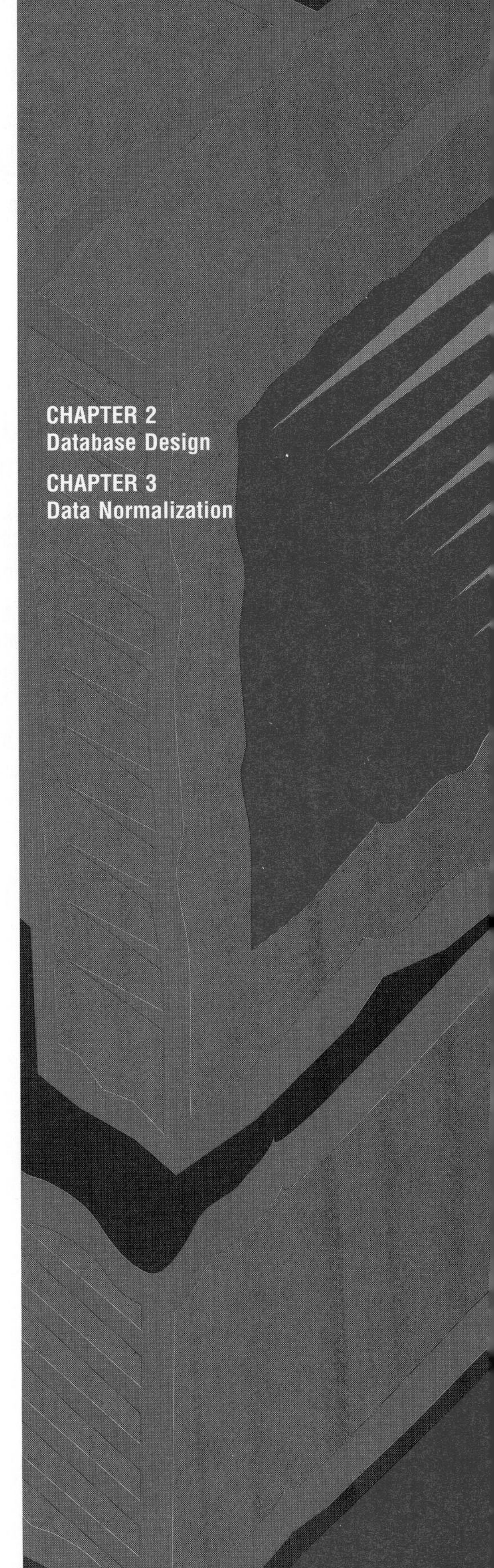

To create a useful application, you must first understand the business and determine how to help the users. In a database context, the most important issue is to identify the data that must be stored. This process requires two basic steps. In Chapter 2 you will design a logical (or conceptual) data model that examines business entities and their relationships. This logical data model is displayed on a class diagram and specifies the various business rules of the company.

The second design step is to create an implementation model of how the data will be stored in the database management system. This step usually consists of creating a list of nicely behaved tables that will make up the relational database. Chapter 3 describes how to create this list of tables and explains why it is important to define them carefully.

CHAPTER 2

Database Design

WHAT YOU WILL LEARN IN THIS CHAPTER

- Why are models important in designing systems? 28
- What is a feasibility study? 29
- What is a class diagram (or entity-relationship diagram)? 33
- What is an object? 33
- What are events, and how are they described in a database design? 48

OVERVIEW

Miranda: *Well, Ariel, you were right as usual. A database management system seems like the right tool for this job.*

Ariel: *So you decided to take the job for your uncle's company?*

Miranda: *Yes, it's good money, and the company seems willing to let me learn as I go. But, it's only paying me a small amount until I finish the project.*

Ariel: *Great. So when do you start?*

Miranda: *That's the next problem. I'm not really sure where to begin.*

Ariel: *That could be a problem. Do you know what the application is supposed to do?*

Miranda: *Well, I talked to the manager and some workers, but there are a lot of points I'm not clear about. This project is bigger than I thought. I'm having trouble keeping track of all the details. There are so many reports and terms I don't know. And one salesperson started talking about all these rules about the data—things like customer numbers are five digits for corporate customers but four digits and two letters for government accounts.*

Ariel: *Maybe you need a system to take notes and diagram everything they tell you.*

INTRODUCTION

The goal of any information system is to add value for the users. To achieve this goal requires answering two important questions: Who are the users? and How can an information system help them? Both of these questions can be difficult to answer and usually require research and interviews.

Before spending large amounts of money on a project, most organizations perform a feasibility study to provide initial answers to these two questions. Organizations are particularly interested in evaluating benefits in three key areas: (1) reduction of costs, (2) increase in sales or revenue, and (3) competitive advantage or long-term benefits.

Completing a project on time and within the budget is a challenge. Small projects that involve a few users and one or two developers are generally straightforward. However, you still must carefully design the databases so they are flexible enough to handle future needs. Likewise, you have to keep notes so that future developers can easily understand the system, its goals, and your decisions. Large projects bring additional complications. With many users and several developers, you need to split the project into smaller problems, communicate ideas between users and designers, and track the team's progress.

As explained in systems analysis and design courses, there are several formal methodologies for designing systems and managing projects. Details can be found in any systems development textbook. Recently, several attempts have been made to speed the development process, known as **rapid application development (RAD).** Steve McConnell's book, *Rapid Development: Taming Wild Software Schedules,* pre-

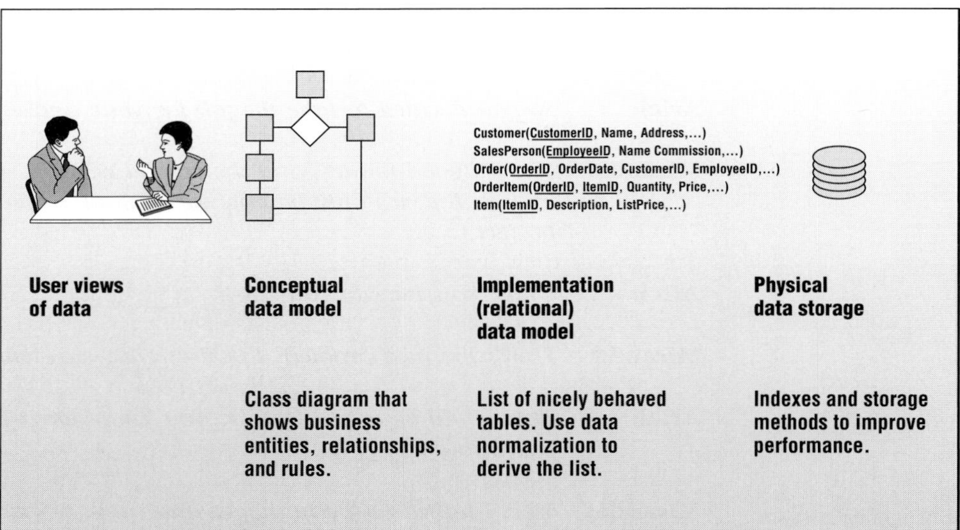

FIGURE 2.1 Design models. The conceptual model records and describes the user views of the system. The implementation model describes the way the data will be stored. The final physical database may utilize storage techniques like indexing to improve performance.

sents an excellent analysis of the importance of design, how development time can be reduced, and when it cannot be reduced. Development of database applications can take place within any of these methodologies.

An important step in all of these methodologies is to build models of the system. A *model* is a simplified abstraction of a real-world system. In many cases the model consists of a drawing that provides a visual picture of the system. Just as contractors need blueprints to construct a building, information system developers need designs to help them create useful systems. As shown in Figure 2.1, conceptual models are based on user views of the system. Implementation models are based on the conceptual models and describe how the data will be stored. The implementation model is used by the DBMS to store the data.

Three common types of models are used to design systems: process models, class or object models, and event models. Process models are displayed with a **collaboration diagram** or a data flow diagram (DFD). They are typically explained in detail in systems analysis courses and are used to redesign the flow of information within an organization. Class diagrams or the older entity-relationship diagrams are used to show the primary entities or objects in the system. Event models such as a sequence or statechart diagram are newer and illustrate the timing of various events and show how messages are passed between various objects. Each of these models is used to illustrate a different aspect of the system being designed. A good designer should be able to create and use all three types of models. However, the class diagrams are the most important tools used in designing and building database applications.

Database applications can be part of a larger project, which require formal project management techniques to control costs and monitor progress. Alternatively, database projects can be shorter, independent projects developed by a small team working closely with users to rapidly build a new system. The project management controls and system design methodologies will be different in these two approaches. However, certain fundamental database design techniques will be the same. This book focuses on the database design elements and leaves the system and project management issues for systems development textbooks.

THE FEASIBILITY STUDY

Ideas for information systems can come from many sources: users, upper management, information system analysts, competitors, or firms in other industries. Ideas that receive initial support from several people might be proposed as new projects. If the project is small enough and easy to create, it might be built in a few days. Larger projects require more careful study. If the project is going to involve critical areas within the organization, require expensive hardware, or require substantial development time, then a more formal **feasibility study** is undertaken.

Feasibility studies are covered in detail within systems analysis texts. However, because of their unique nature, it is helpful to examine the typical costs and benefits that arise with the database approach.

The goal of a feasibility study is to determine whether a proposed project is worth pursuing. The study examines two fundamental categories: costs and potential benefits. As noted in Figure 2.2, costs are often divided into two categories: up-front or one-time costs and ongoing costs once the project is operational. Benefits can often be found in one of three categories: reduced operating costs, increased value, or strategic advantages that lock out competitors.

Costs

Almost all projects will entail similar up-front costs. The organization will often have to purchase additional hardware, software, and communication equipment (e.g., expand a local area network). The cost of developing the system is listed here, including the cost for all additional studies. Other one-time costs include converting data to the new system and initial training of users. Database management systems are expensive software items. For example, for larger projects, the cost for software like Oracle can easily run several million dollars. You will also have to purchase "maintenance" upgrades of the software at least on an annual basis.

Hardware and software costs can be estimated with the help of vendors. As long as you know the approximate size of the final system (e.g., number of users), vendors can provide reasonably accurate estimates of the costs. Data conversion costs can be estimated from the amount of data involved. The biggest challenge often lies

FIGURE 2.2
Common costs and benefits from introducing a database management system. Note that benefits can be hard to measure, especially for tactical and strategic decisions. But it is still important to list potential benefits. Even if you cannot assign a specific value, managers need to see the complete list.

Costs	Benefits
Up-front/one-time costs	**Cost savings**
• Software	• Software maintenance
• Hardware	• Fewer errors
• Communications	• Less data maintenance
• Data conversion	• Less user training
• Studies and design	**Increased value**
• Training	• Better access to data
Ongoing costs	• Better decisions
• Personnel	• Better communication
• Software upgrades	• More timely reports
• Supplies	• Faster reaction to change
• Support	• New products and services
• Software and hardware maintenance	**Strategic advantages**
	• Lock out competitors

in estimating the costs of developing the new system. If an organization has experience with similar projects, historical data can be used to estimate the time and costs based on the size of the project. Otherwise, the costs can be estimated based on the projected number of people and hours involved.

Once the project is completed and the system installed, costs will arise from several areas. For example, the new system might require additional personnel and supplies. Software and hardware will have to be modified and replaced—entailing maintenance costs. Additional training and support might be required to deal with employee turnover and system modifications. Again, most of these costs are straightforward to estimate—as long as you know the size of the project.

Unfortunately, information system (IS) designers have not been very successful at estimating the costs. For example, in January 1995 *PC Week* reported that 31 percent of new IS projects are canceled before they are completed. Additionally, 53 percent of those that are completed are 189 percent over budget. The greatest difficulty is in estimating the time it takes to design and develop new software. Every developer is different with large variations in programmer productivity. In large projects, where the staff members are constantly changing, accurately predicting the amount of time needed to design and develop a new system is often impossible. Nonetheless, managers need to provide some estimate of the costs.

Benefits

In many cases benefits are even more difficult to estimate. Some benefits are tangible and can be measured with a degree of accuracy. For instance, transaction processing systems are slightly easier to evaluate than a DSS since benefits generally arise from their ability to decrease operations costs. A system might enable workers to process more items, thus allowing the firm to expand without increasing labor costs. A database approach might reduce IS labor costs by making it easier for workers to create and modify reports. Finally, a new IS might reduce errors in the data, leading to improved decisions.

Many benefits are intangible and cannot be assigned specific monetary values. For instance, benefits can arise because managers have better access to data. Communication improves, better decisions are made, and managers can react faster to a changing environment. In addition, the new system might enable the company to produce new products and services or to increase the sales of ancillary products to existing customers. Similarly, firms might implement systems that provide a competitive advantage. For example, an automated order system between a firm and its customers often encourages the customers to place more orders with the firm. Hence the firm gains an advantage over its competitors.

When information systems are built to automate operations-level tasks and the benefits are tangible, evaluating the economic benefits of the system is relatively straightforward. The effects of improving access to data are easy to observe and measure in terms of decreased costs and increased revenue. However, when information systems are implemented to improve tactical and strategic decisions, identifying and evaluating benefits is more difficult. For example, how much is it worth to a marketing manager to have the previous week's sales data available on Monday instead of waiting until Wednesday?

In a database project benefits can arise from improving operations—which leads to cost savings. Additional benefits occur because it is now easier and faster to create new reports for users, so less programmer time will be needed to modify the system. Users can also gain better access to data through creating their own queries—instead of waiting for a programmer to write a new program.

Database projects can provide many benefits, but the organization will receive those benefits only if the project is completed correctly, on time, and within the specified budget. To accomplish this task, you will have to design the system carefully. More than that, your team will have to communicate with users, share work with each other, and track the progress of the development. You need to follow a design methodology.

DESIGNING SYSTEMS

Information systems are complex, constantly changing, and expensive to create and maintain. Building a useful system requires that you understand and communicate with the user. It often requires organizing and controlling a team of developers. System designs are models that are used to facilitate this communication and teamwork. Designs are a simplification or picture of the underlying business operations. The design models also record the fundamental features, assumptions, and restrictions present in any business.

Identifying User Requirements

One challenging aspect of designing a system is to determine the requirements. You must thoroughly understand the business needs before you can create a useful system. A key step is to interview users and observe the operations of the firm. Although this step sounds easy, it can be difficult—especially when users disagree with each other. Even in the best circumstances, communication can be difficult. Excellent communication skills and experience are important to becoming a good designer.

One of the most important tasks in designing a database application is to correctly identify the data that needs to be stored. As long as you collect the data and organize it carefully, the DBMS makes it easy to create and modify reports. As you talk with users, you will collect user documents, such as reports and forms. These documents provide information about the basic data and operations of the firm. You need to gather three basic pieces of information for the initial design: (1) the data that needs to be collected, (2) the data type (domain), and (3) the amount of data involved.

This basic information is used to create a model of the data. A **class diagram** displays the key elements and associations. The class diagram is used to communicate with users and with other designers. It presents a visual picture of the data needed by the system. The initial goal is to identify the business entities or objects and describe how they are related to each other.

Designing Systems with the Unified Modeling Language (UML)

If a program is small enough so that you can visualize it completely in your mind and you will work alone, you might get by without using a design methodology. In real life most projects are considerably more complex. You will need to communicate with users, share designs with other developers, and split the project into smaller components. Experience has shown that the only way to accomplish these tasks is to follow a design methodology.

When a project is approved, you need to create a detailed business design. The business design is a logical model of the new system. It describes the business com-

FIGURE 2.3
Primary UML diagrams. The class diagram is the most important for database design. Collaboration diagrams are useful to show processes, and you might create sequence diagrams to help build forms and understand the timing of various events.

Primary Types of Diagrams	Function
Class diagram	Shows the static model of things that exist and their relationships.
Use case diagram	Shows how actors will use the functionality of the system.
Sequence diagram	Represents an interaction or set of messages exchanged among objects. Specifically shows interaction over time.
Collaboration diagram	Shows the interaction and links among objects. Does not show time as a separate dimension. It is a process diagram.
Statechart diagram	Shows the sequence of states that an object goes through during its lifetime in response to stimuli.
Implementation diagram	Shows the structure of the code or of the run-time modules.

ponents and how they are related. From this design, you can develop the physical model—define databases, develop applications, and write procedures. Once the application is developed and tested, it can be implemented.

Several design methodologies have evolved over the past 20 years. Any standard systems analysis and design textbook will describe the choices and their strengths and weaknesses. However, one of the drawbacks of having so many methodologies is that each organization may use a different methodology, so it takes time to train new workers. The problem has been exacerbated by the introduction of new features and changes to various diagramming techniques. For example, entity-relationship diagrams were a common method for designing database applications. The base concept of an entity-relationship diagram is to show how various business entities (e.g., customers and orders) are related. However, there are at least three major variations of the entity-relationship diagram—each with its own notation and embellishments. Complicating the process even further, **object-oriented programming (OOP)** created the need for a new methodology.

These factors have led to a renewed interest in systems design. Recently, Grady Booch, Jim Rumbaugh, and Ivar Jacobson, leaders in OO design, combined their initial methodologies into a new system known as the **Unified Modeling Language (UML)**. This methodology has been adopted by most of the leading software-development companies (including IBM, Microsoft, Oracle, Rational Software, and Sterling Software) and by several standards groups. Although UML was designed to emphasize OO concepts, it is a complete system and encompasses all aspects of systems design. Many of the leading tools will eventually rely on UML to design and build systems, so you should learn to use its terms and techniques.

UML is too large to cover completely in this book. Only the portion that deals with database design will be presented and used here. For reference, Figure 2.3 lists the primary types of diagrams available. This text will concentrate on the class diagram, but in large projects you will probably use collaboration diagrams to describe business processes or activities and sequence diagrams to highlight timing of the events. You may also see and use other diagrams in other courses. In any case you should check out the primary UML Web sites for additional information and documentation.

CLASS DIAGRAMS

The DBMS approach focuses on the data. In many organizations data remains relatively stable. For example, we collect the same basic data on customers today that we collected 20 or 30 years ago. Basic items like name, address, and phone number are always needed. Although we might choose to collect additional data today (cell phone number and Internet address), we still utilize the same base data. On the other hand, the way we accept and process sales orders has changed over time, so forms and reports are constantly being modified. The database approach resolves this problem by focusing on defining the data correctly. Then the DBMS makes it easy to change reports and forms. The first step in any design is to identify the things or entities that you wish to observe and track.

Classes and Entities

It is best to define a few terms before illustrating the models. The basic definitions are given in Figure 2.4. Note that these definitions are informal. Each entry has a more formal definition in terms of Codd's relational model and precise semantic definitions in the UML. However, you can develop a database without learning the mathematical foundations.

An **entity** is some item in the real world that we wish to track. We describe that entity by its **attributes** or **properties.** For example, a customer has a name, address, and phone number. From UML, a **class** is the descriptor for a set of objects with similar structure, behavior, and relationships. That is, a class is the model description of the business entity. Class descriptions can also contain **methods** or functions that can be performed by the class. For example, a Customer class might contain a method to add a new customer. Methods are functions that you will have to create to perform some task. In a true object-oriented system, the functions would be defined within the classes. However, existing relational databases do not handle this process very well, so you will probably have to write separate programs to perform the functions. For now, be sure to identify and record any calculations that will be needed. An **object** is an instance or particular example of a class. For example, Joe Jones could be a Customer object. The object would contain specific data about one person or thing in the class. An association is a relationship among two or more classes.

To design a database, you must understand the difference between classes, properties, and associations. Your solution depends on how the business deals with the

FIGURE 2.4
Basic definitions. These terms describe the main concepts needed to create a class diagram. The first step is to identify the business entities and their properties. Methods are less important than properties in a database context, but you should identify important functions or calculations.

Term	Definition	Pet Store Examples
Entity	Something in the real world that we wish to describe or track	Customer, Merchandise, Sale
Class	Description of an entity that includes its attributes (properties) and behavior (methods)	Customer, Merchandise, Sale
Object	One instance of a class with specific data	Joe Jones, Premium Cat Food, Sale #32
Property	A characteristic or descriptor of a class or entity	LastName, Description, SaleDate
Method	A function that is performed by the class	AddCustomer, UpdateInventory, ComputeTotal
Association	A relationship between two or more classes	Each sale can have only one customer

entities and what data needs to be collected. For example, consider an employee. The employee is clearly a separate entity because we always need to keep detailed data about the employee (date hired, name, address, and so on). But what about the employee's spouse? Is the spouse an attribute of the Employee entity, or should he or she be treated as a separate entity? If the organization only cares about the spouse's name, it can be stored as an attribute of the Employee entity. On the other hand, if the organization wants to keep additional information about the spouse (e.g., birthday and occupation), it would be better to create a separate Spouse entity with its own attributes.

Associations and Relationships

An important step in designing databases is identifying associations or relationships among entities. Entities are usually related to other entities. Similarly, attributes within an entity can be related to other attributes. **Associations** or **relationships** represent business rules. For example, it is clear that a customer can place many orders. But the relationship is not as clear from the other direction. How many customers can be involved with one particular order? Many businesses would say that each order could come from only one customer. Hence there would be a one-to-many relationship between customers and orders. On the other hand, some organizations might have multiple customers on one order, which creates a many-to-many relationship.

Associations can be named—UML refers to the **association role**. Each end of a binary association may be labeled. It is often useful to include a direction arrow to indicate how the label should be read, as shown in Figure 2.5. For example, a customer places an order.

UML uses numbers and asterisks to indicate the **multiplicity** in an association. As shown in Figure 2.5, the asterisk (*) is read as "many." So each customer can place many orders. Some older design methods used multiple arrowheads or the letters *M* and *N* to represent the "many" side of a relationship.

Correctly identifying relationships is important to properly designing a database application. Remember that the relationships are determined by the business rules—so it is important to carefully talk with the users to identify these relationships. When you collect forms and reports from users, you want to go through them and identify the initial entities—such as customer, order, and product. Then talk with the users to determine how the business handles the relationships between these entities.

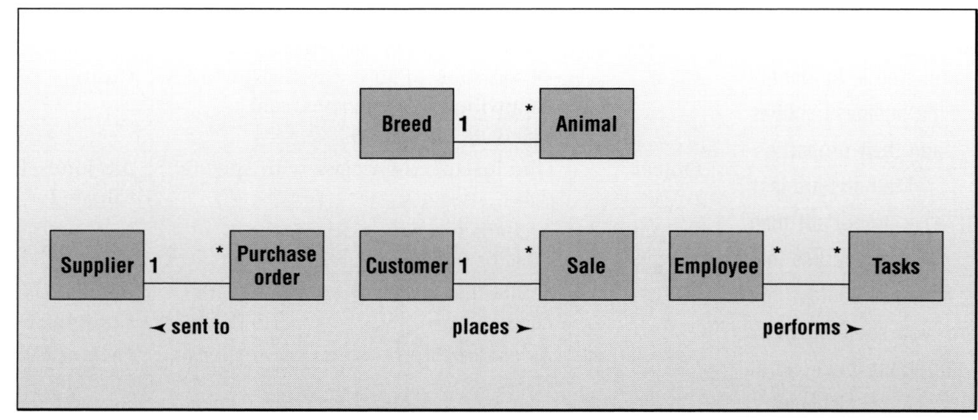

FIGURE 2.5 Associations. Three types of relationships (one-to-one, one-to-many, and many-to-many) occur among entities. They can be drawn in different ways, but they represent business or organizational rules. Avoid vague definitions where almost any relationship could be classified as many-to-many. They make the database design more complex.

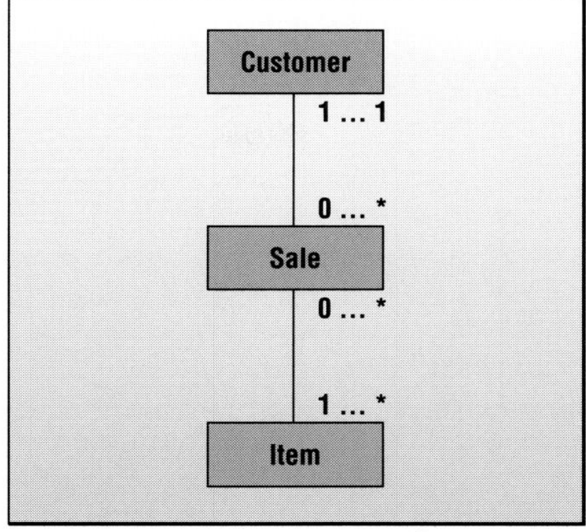

FIGURE 2.6 Class diagram or entity-relationship diagram. Each customer can place zero or many orders. Each order must come from at least one and no more than one customer. The zero (0) represents an optional item, so a customer might not have placed any orders yet.

Class Diagram Details

A class diagram is a visual model of the classes and associations in an organization. There are many options for drawing these diagrams, but the basic features that must be included are the class names (entities) in boxes and the associations (relationships) connecting them. Typically, you will want to include more information about the classes and associations. For example, you will eventually include the properties of the classes within the box.

There are several options for describing associations. One of the most important design issues is the multiplicity of the relationship, which has two aspects: (1) the maximum number of objects that can be related and (2) the minimum number of objects, if any, that must be included. As indicated in Figure 2.6, multiplicity is shown as a number for the minimum value, an ellipses (. . .), and the maximum value. An asterisk (*) represents an unknown quantity of "many." In the example in Figure 2.6, exactly one customer (1 . . . 1) can be involved with zero to many (0 . . . *) sales.

Sometimes a relationship requires both of the entities to exist. For example, what happens if you have an order form that lists a customer, but there is no data on file for that customer? There is a referential relationship between the order and the customer entities. Business rules require that customer data must already exist before that customer can make a purchase. This relationship can be denoted by specifying the minimum value of the relationship (0 if it is optional; 1 if it is required).

Be sure to read relationships in both directions. For example, in Figure 2.6, a customer can place from zero to many sales orders. That is, a customer is not required to place an order.

Moving down the diagram, note the many-to-many relationship between sale and item (asterisks on the right side for both classes). A sale must contain at least one item (empty sales orders are not useful in business), but the firm might have an item that has not been sold yet.

Association Details: N-ary Associations

Many-to-many associations between classes cause problems in the database design. They are acceptable in an initial diagram like Figure 2.6, but they will eventually have to be split into one-to-many relationships. This process, and the reasons for it, are explained in detail in Chapter 3.

In a related situation, as shown in Figure 2.7, entities are not always obvious. Consider a basic manufacturing situation in which employees assemble components

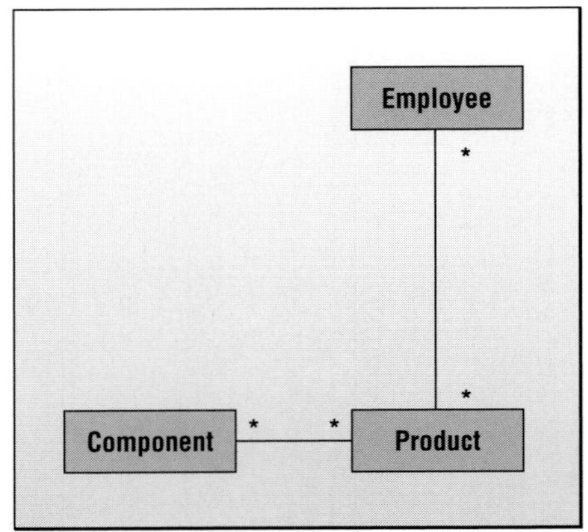

FIGURE 2.7 Many-to-many relationships cause problems for databases. In this example many employees can install many components on many products, but we do not know which components the employee actually installed.

into final products. At first glance, it is tempting to say that there are three entities: employees, components, and products. This design specifies that the database should keep track of which employees worked on each product and which components go into each product. Notice that two many-to-many relationships exist.

To understand the problem caused by the many-to-many relationships, consider what happens if the company wants to know which employees assembled each component into a product. To handle this situation, Figure 2.8 shows that the three main

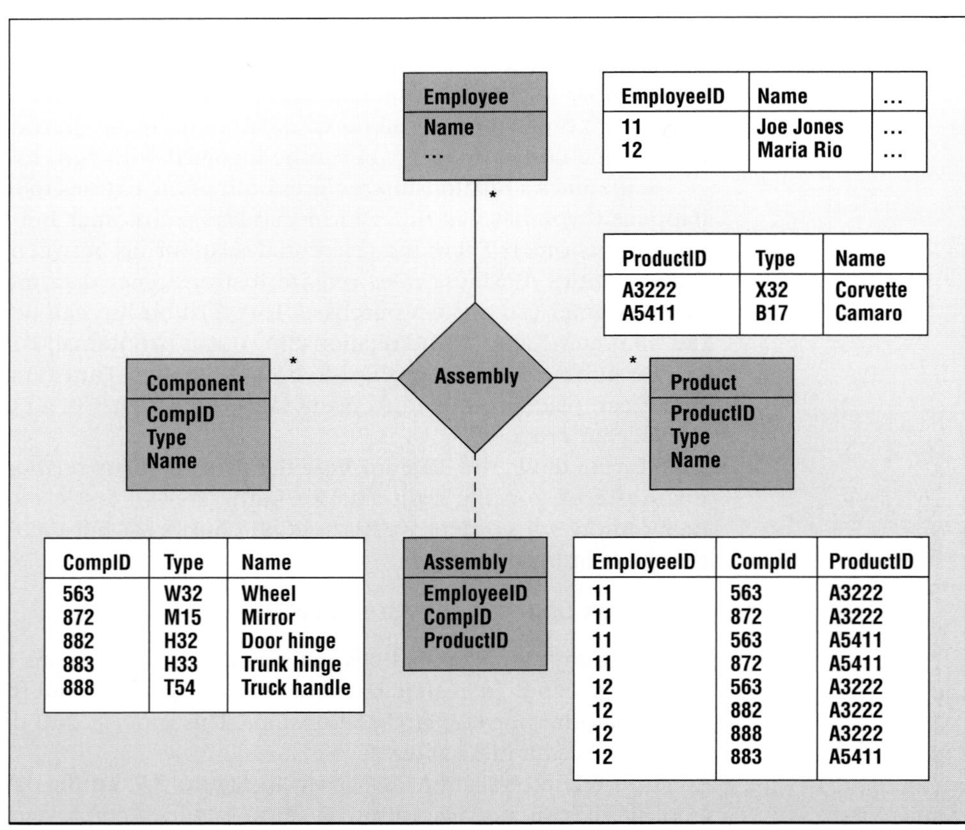

EmployeeID	Name	...
11	Joe Jones	...
12	Maria Rio	...

ProductID	Type	Name
A3222	X32	Corvette
A5411	B17	Camaro

CompID	Type	Name
563	W32	Wheel
872	M15	Mirror
882	H32	Door hinge
883	H33	Trunk hinge
888	T54	Truck handle

EmployeeID	CompId	ProductID
11	563	A3222
11	872	A3222
11	563	A5411
11	872	A5411
12	563	A3222
12	882	A3222
12	888	A3222
12	883	A5411

FIGURE 2.8 Many-to-many associations are converted to a set of one-to-many relationships with an n-ary association, which includes a new class. In this example each row in the Assembly class holds data for one employee, one component, and one product. Notice that the Assembly class (box) is connected to the Assembly association (diamond) by a dashed line.

entities (Employee, Product, and Component) are actually related to each other through an Assembly association. When more than two classes are related, the relationship is called an **n-ary association** and is drawn as a diamond. This association (actually any association) can be described by its own class data. In this example an entry in the assembly list would contain an EmployeeID, a ComponentID, and a ProductID. In total many employees can work on many products, and many components can be installed in many products. Each individual event is captured by the Assembly association class. The Assembly association solves the many-to-many problem, because a given row in the Assembly class holds data for one employee, one component, and one product. In real life you would also include a Date/Time column to record when each event occurred.

According to the UML standard, multiplicity has little meaning in the n-ary context. The multiplicity number placed on a class represents the potential number of objects in the association when the other n-1 values are fixed. For example, if ComponentID and EmployeeID are fixed, how many products could there be? In other words, can an employee install the same component in more than one product? In most situations the answer will be yes, so the multiplicity will generally be a "many" asterisk.

Eventually, the many-to-many relationships must be converted to a set of one-to-many relationships by adding a new entity. Like the Assembly entity, this new entity usually represents an activity and often includes a date/time stamp.

Designers use class diagrams for different purposes. Sometimes you need to see the detail; other times you only care about the big picture. For large projects, it sometimes helps to create an overview diagram that displays the primary relationships between the main classes. On this diagram it is acceptable to use many-to-many relationships to hide some detail entities.

Association Details: Aggregation

Some special types of associations arise often enough that UML has defined special techniques for handling them. One category is known as an **aggregation** or a collection. For example, a Sale consists of a collection of Items being purchased. As shown in Figure 2.9, aggregation is indicated by a small diamond on the association line next to the class that is the aggregate. In the example, the diamond is next to the Sale class. Associations with a many side can be ordered or unordered. In this example the sequence in which the Items are stored does not matter. If order did

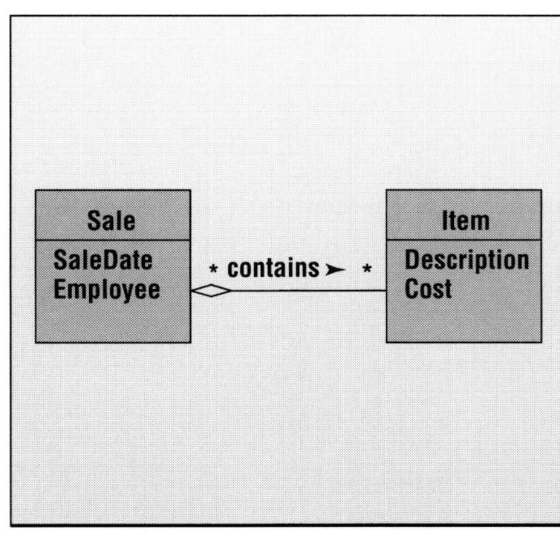

FIGURE 2.9 Association aggregation. A Sale contains a list of Items being purchased. A small diamond is placed on the association to remind us of this special relationship.

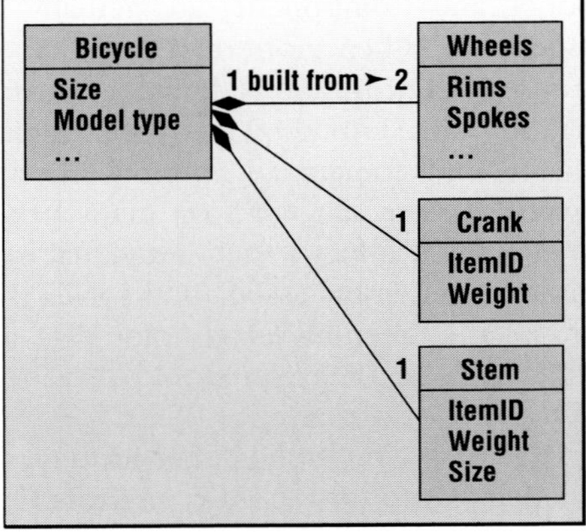

FIGURE 2.10 Association composition. A bicycle is built from several individual components. These components no longer exist separately; they become the bicycle.

matter, you would simply put the notation {ordered} underneath the association. Be sure to include the braces around the word.

Association Details: Composition

The simple aggregation indicator is not used much in business settings. However, **composition** is a stronger aggregate association that does arise more often. In a composition, the individual items become the new object. Consider a bicycle, which is built from a set of components (wheels, crank, stem, etc.). UML provides two methods to display composition. In Figure 2.10 the individual classes are separated and marked with a filled diamond. In Figure 2.11 the composition is indicated by drawing the component classes inside the main Bicycle class. It is easier to recognize the relationship in the embedded diagram, but it could get messy trying to show 20 different objects required to define a bicycle. Figure 2.11 also highlights the fact that the component items could just as easily be described as properties of the main Bicycle class.

The differences between aggregation and composition are subtle. The UML standard states that a composition can exist only for a one-to-many relationship. Any many-to-many association would have to use the simple aggregation indicator. Composition relationships are generally easier to recognize than aggregation relationships and are particularly common in manufacturing environments. Just remem-

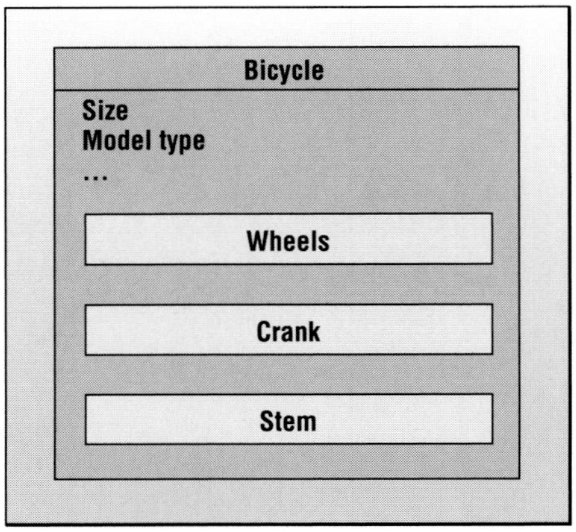

Bicycle
Size
Model type
...
Wheels
Crank
Stem

FIGURE 2.11 Association composition. It is easier to see the composition by embedding the component items within the main class.

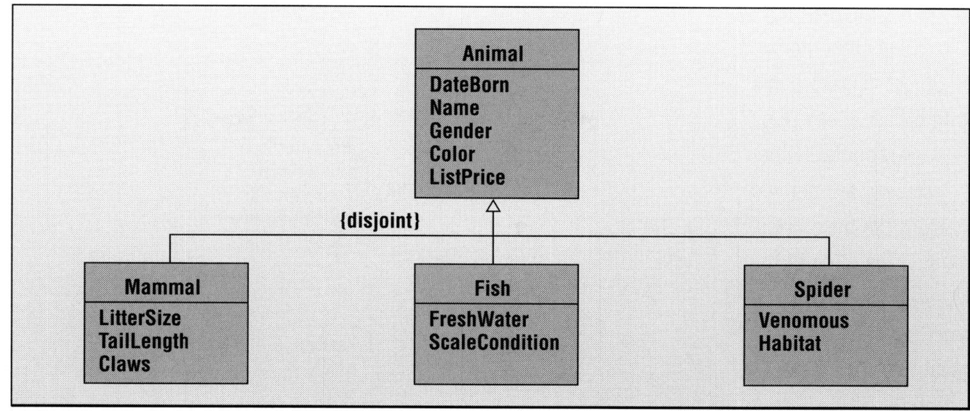

FIGURE 2.12 Association generalization. The generic Animal class holds data that applies to all animals. The derived subclasses contain data that is specific to each species.

ber that a composition exists only when the individual items become the new class. After the bicycle is built, we no longer refer to the individual components.

Association Details: Generalization

Another common association that arises in business settings is **generalization.** This situation generates a class hierarchy. The most general description is given at the top, and more specific classes are derived from it. Figure 2.12 presents a sample from Sally's Pet Store. Each Animal has certain generic properties (e.g., DateBorn, Name, Gender, ListPrice) contained in the generic Animal class. But specific types of animals require slightly different information. For example, for a mammal (perhaps a cat), buyers want to know the size of the litter and whether or not the animal has claws. On the other hand, fish do not have claws, and customers want different information, such as whether they are fresh- or saltwater fish and the condition of their scales. Similar animal-specific data can be collected for each species. There can be multiple levels of generalization. In the Pet Store example, the Mammal category could be further split into Cat, Dog, and Other.

A small, unfilled triangle is used to indicate a generalization relationship. You can connect all of the subclasses into one triangle, as in Figure 2.12, or you can draw each line separately. For the situation in this example, the collected approach is the best choice because the association represents a disjoint (mutually exclusive) set. An animal can fall into only one of the subclasses.

An important characteristic of generalization is that lower-level classes inherit the properties and methods of the classes above them. Classes often begin with fairly general descriptions. More detailed classes are **derived** from these base classes. Each lower-level class inherits the properties and functions from the higher classes. **Inheritance** means that objects in the derived classes have all of the properties from the higher classes—as well as those defined in their own class. Similarly, functions defined in the related classes are available to the new class.

Consider the example of a bank accounting system displayed in Figure 2.13. A designer would start with the basic description of a customer account. The bank is always going to need basic information about its accounts, such as AccountID, CustomerID, DateOpened, and CurrentBalance. Similarly, there will be common functions like opening and closing the account. All of these basic properties and actions will be defined in the base class for Accounts.

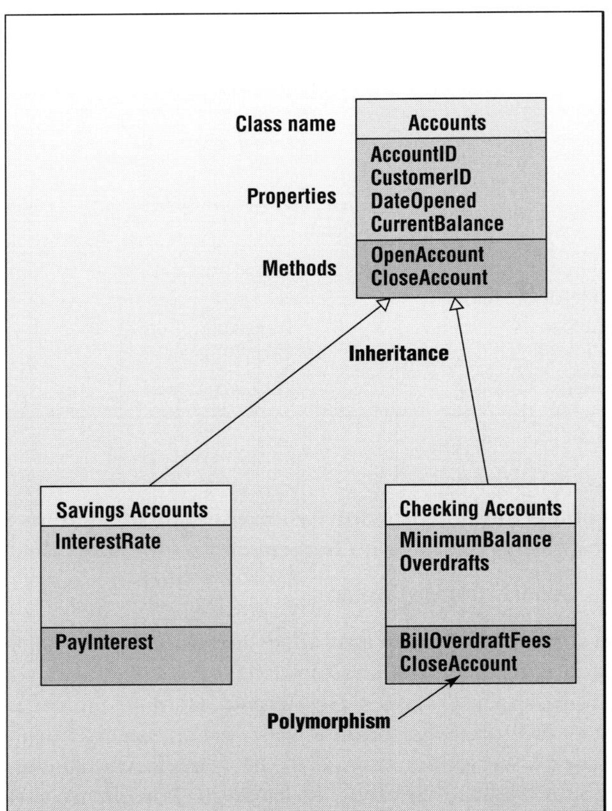

FIGURE 2.13 Class inheritance. Object classes begin with a base class (e.g., Accounts). Other classes are derived from the base class. They inherit the properties and methods and add new features. In a bank all accounts need to track basic customer data. Only checking accounts need to track overdraft fees.

New accounts can be derived from these accounts, and designers would only have to add the new features—saving time and reducing errors. For example, Checking Accounts have a MinimumBalance to avoid fees, and the bank must track the number of Overdrafts each month. The Checking Accounts class is derived from the base Accounts class, and the developer adds the new properties and functions. This new class automatically inherits all of the properties and functions from the Accounts class, so you do not have to redefine them. Similarly, the bank pays interest on savings accounts, so a Savings Accounts class is created that records the current InterestRate and includes a function to compute and credit the interest due each month.

Additional classes can be derived from the Savings Accounts and Checking Accounts classes. For instance, the bank probably has special checking accounts for seniors and for students. These new accounts might offer lower fees, different minimum balance requirements, or different interest rates. The design diagram is simply expanded by adding new classes below these initial definitions. These diagrams display the **class hierarchy,** which shows how classes are derived from each other and highlights which properties and functions are inherited. UML uses open diamond arrowheads to indicate that the higher-level class is the more general class. In the example, the Savings Accounts and Checking Accounts classes are derived from the generic Accounts class, so the association lines point to it.

Each class in Figure 2.13 can also perform individual functions. Defining properties and methods within a class is known as **encapsulation**. It has the advantage of placing all relevant definitions in one location. Encapsulation also provides some security and control features because properties and functions can be protected from other areas of the application.

Another interesting feature of encapsulation can be found by noting that the Accounts class has a function to close accounts. Look carefully, and you will see that the Checking Accounts class also has a function to close accounts (CloseAccount). When a derived class defines the same function as a parent class, it is known as **polymorphism.** When the system activates the function, it automatically identifies the object's class and executes the matching function. Designers can also specify that the derived function (CloseAccount in the Checking Accounts class) can call the related function in the base class. In the banking example, the checking Account's CloseAccount function would cancel outstanding checks, compute current charges, and update the main balance. Then it would call the Account's CloseAccount function, which would automatically archive the data and remove the object from the current records.

Polymorphism is a useful tool for application builders. It means that you can call one function regardless of the type of data. In the bank example you would simply call the CloseAccount function. Each different account could perform different actions in response to that call, but the application does not care. The complexity of the application has been moved to the design stage (where all of the classes are defined). The application builder does not have to worry about the details.

Note that in complex situations, a subclass can inherit properties and methods from more than one parent class. In Figure 2.14, a car is motorized, and it is designed for on-road use, so it inherits properties from both classes (and from the generic Vehicle class). The bicycle situation is slightly more complex because it could inherit features from the On-Road class or from the Off-Road class, depending on the type of bicycle. If you need to record data about hybrid bicycles, the Bicycle class might have to inherit data from both the On-Road and Off-Road classes.

Association Details: Reflexive Association

A reflexive relationship is another situation that arises in business that requires special handling. A **reflexive association** is a relationship from one class back to itself. The most common business situation is shown in Figure 2.15. Some employees are managers, and they manage other employees. Hence there is an association from Employee (the manager) back to Employee (the workers). Notice how UML enables you to label both ends of the relationship (manager and worker). Also, the "◀man-

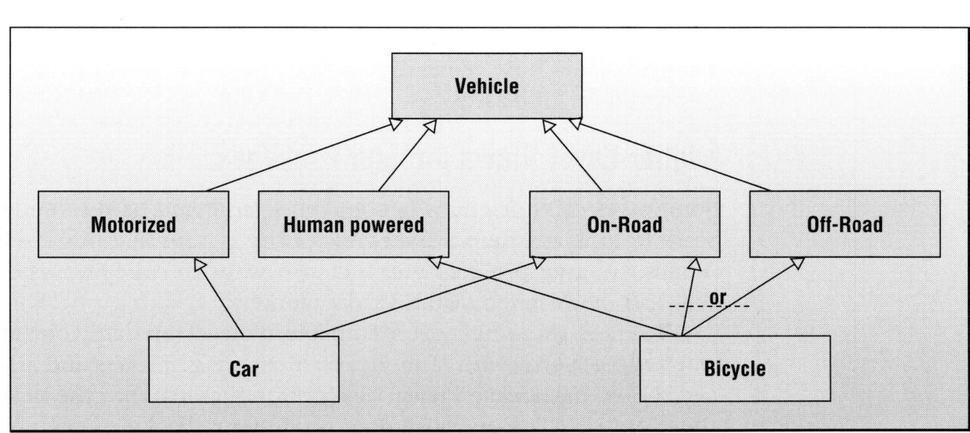

FIGURE 2.14 Multiple parent classes. Classes can inherit properties from several parent classes. The key is to draw the structure so that users can understand it and to make sure that it matches the business rules.

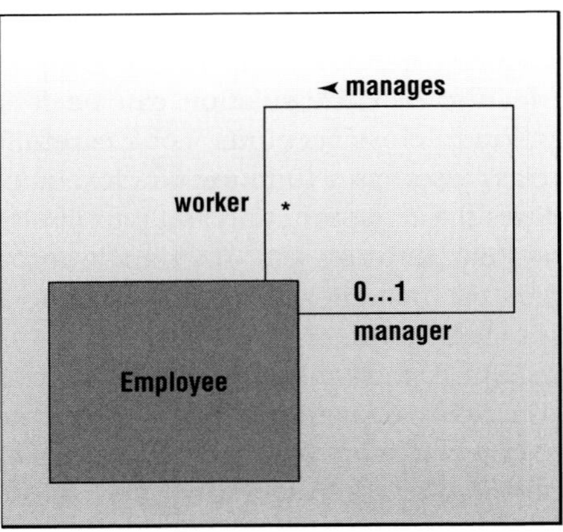

FIGURE 2.15 Reflexive relationship. A manager is an employee who manages other workers. Notice how the labels explain the purpose of the relationship.

ages" label indicates how the association should be read. The labels and the text clarify the purpose of the association. Some associations may not need to be labeled, but reflexive relationships should always be carefully explained.

Association Details: Summary

These last few sections represent more than minor changes to your class diagram. They represent common business situations. You need to recognize these situations because they will affect the way you design and build database applications. To create a class diagram, first identify the main classes, including their properties. Then note the associations among the classes, paying particular attention to the proper multiplicity. Be on the lookout for many-to-many relationships. When you see them, look for n-ary associations or new classes that will provide one-to-many relationships. Look for cases of composition or aggregation. Is one class made up of several smaller objects? If so, consider embedding the subclasses within the main class. Watch for examples of generalization. Are there classes that have similar purposes? If so, try to define a generic class and derive the detailed classes using inheritance. Watch for disjoint (or mutually exclusive) classes. Be sure to indicate them on the diagram. Finally, look for reflexive associations where objects in one class are related to other objects in the same class. You should always see this relationship in the Employee class, but it can show up in other classes as well. For instance, a company can produce products that are built from other products.

At this point, you do not have to be concerned with drawing a perfect class diagram. Just make sure that you have correctly identified all the business rules. Chapter 3 explains how to analyze the classes and associations and how to create an improved set of classes.

Higher-Level Views through Packages

Sometimes class diagrams become very large and hard to understand. You will often want to look at a higher-level view of the system that purposely ignores some of the details. In large projects, you will also want to split the system into smaller pieces that can be assigned to individual workers.

To meet these needs, UML enables you to separate your model into packages. A **package** is a grouping of model elements (e.g., classes and associations). Each package should have some logical description that matches the business needs. However, there are no rules or constraints on defining packages. Just remember the purpose of a package is to group elements together to simplify a design. Make sure that the grouping still reflects the true organization of the business.

It is often helpful to provide a top-level diagram that displays the primary relationships among packages and overarching classes. An example for Sally's Pet Store is shown in Figure 2.16. Each package will contain additional classes and will show the properties and associations in more detail. In Figure 2.16 the dashed lines between the packages are not true associations, but signify dependence. For example, the Sell Animals package needs information from the Customer, the Employee (sales clerk), and the Purchase Animals package.

Designing the final database requires more detailed class diagrams. In large projects these detail diagrams may be split onto several pages, where each page ties to a section of an initial overview diagram. The detailed class diagrams should avoid many-to-many relationships, and all relationships should be shown. Additionally, detailed class diagrams should contain the list of properties for each class.

SALLY'S PET STORE CLASS DIAGRAM

Remember that Sally, the owner of the Pet Store, wants to create the application in sections. The first section will track the basic transaction data of the store. Hence we need to identify the primary entities involved in operating a pet store.

The first step in designing the Pet Store database application is to talk with the owner (Sally), examine other stores, and identify the primary components that will be needed. After talking with Sally, it becomes clear that the Pet Store has some features that make it different from other retail stores. The most important difference is that the store must track two separate types of sales: animals are handled differently from products. For example, the store tracks more detailed information on each animal. Also, products can be sold in multiple units (e.g., six cans of dog food), but animals must be tracked individually. Figure 2.17 shows an initial class diagram for Sally's Pet Store that is based on these primary entities. An important design feature of the diagram is that the animals and merchandise are treated separately.

Because of Sally's philosophy of providing good homes for the pets, she also wants to collect detailed information about each customer. Sally also monitors sup-

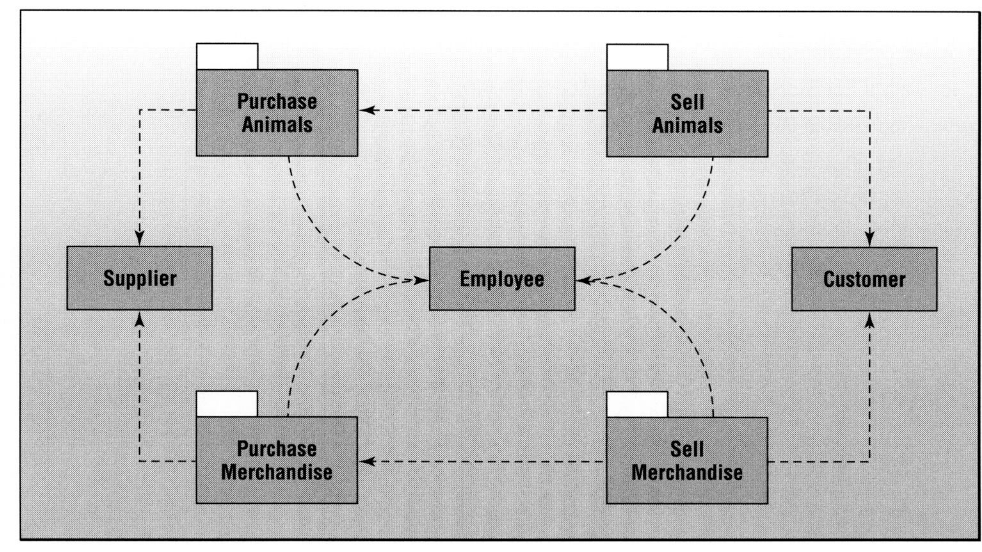

FIGURE 2.16
UML packages. Packages can be used to look at a higher-level view. Each package (e.g., Purchase Animals) contains more classes and shows the detailed associations.

pliers more carefully than most store owners. She is even thinking about hiring people to inspect various breeders. The inspectors would provide reports on a variety of features, such as cleanliness, number of animals boarded, number of trainers, type of food served at each meal, and quality of veterinary care.

While talking with Sally, a good designer will write down some of the basic items that will be involved in the database. This list consists of entities for which we need to collect data. For example, the Pet Store database will clearly need to collect data on customers, suppliers, animals, and products. Likewise, we will need to record each purchase and each sale. Right from the beginning, we will want to identify various attributes or characteristics of these entities. For instance, customers have names, addresses, and phone numbers. For each animal, we will want to know the type of animal (cat, dog, etc.), the breed, their date of birth, and so on.

The detailed class diagram will include the attributes for each of the entities. Notice that the initial diagram in Figure 2.17 includes several many-to-many relationships. All of these require the addition of an intermediate class. Consider the MerchandiseOrder class. Several items can be ordered at one time, so we will create a new entity (OrderItem) that contains a list of items placed on each MerchandiseOrder. The AnimalOrder and Sale entities will gain similar classes.

Figure 2.18 shows the more detailed class diagram for the Pet Store with these new intermediate classes. There are also new classes for City, Breed, and Category. Postal codes and cities raise issues in almost every business database. There is a relationship between cities and postal codes, but it is not one-to-one. One simple solution is to store the city, state, and postal code for every single customer and supplier. However, for local customers, it is highly repetitive to enter the name of the city and state for every sale. A solution is to store city and postal code data in a separate class. Commonly used values can be entered initially. An employee can select the desired city from the existing list without having to reenter the data.

The Breed and Category classes are used to ensure consistency in the data. One of the annoying problems of text data is that people rarely enter data consistently. For example, some clerks might abbreviate the dalmatian dog breed as *Dal*, others might use *Dalma*, and a few might enter the entire name. To solve this problem, we

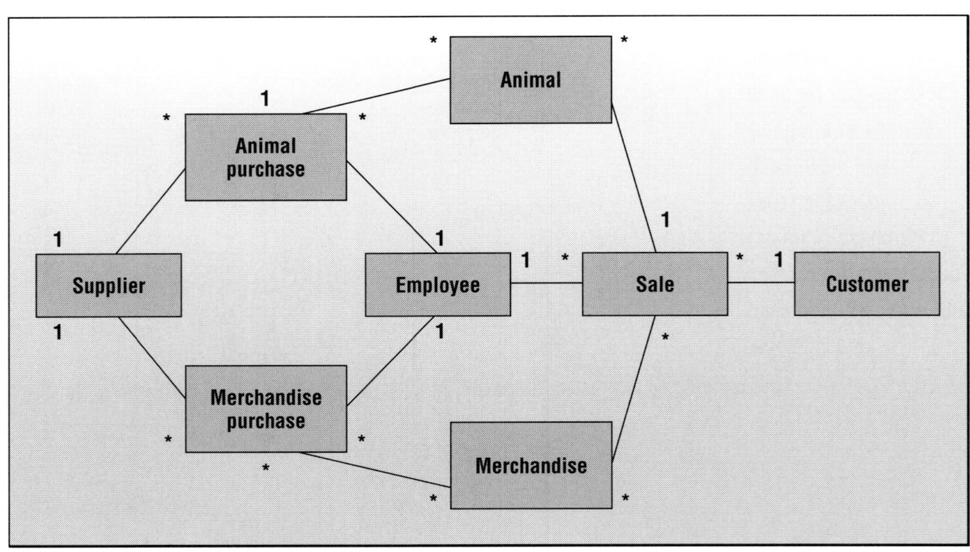

FIGURE 2.17
Initial class diagram for Sally's Pet Store. Animal purchases and sales are tracked separately from merchandise because the store needs to monitor different data for the two entities.

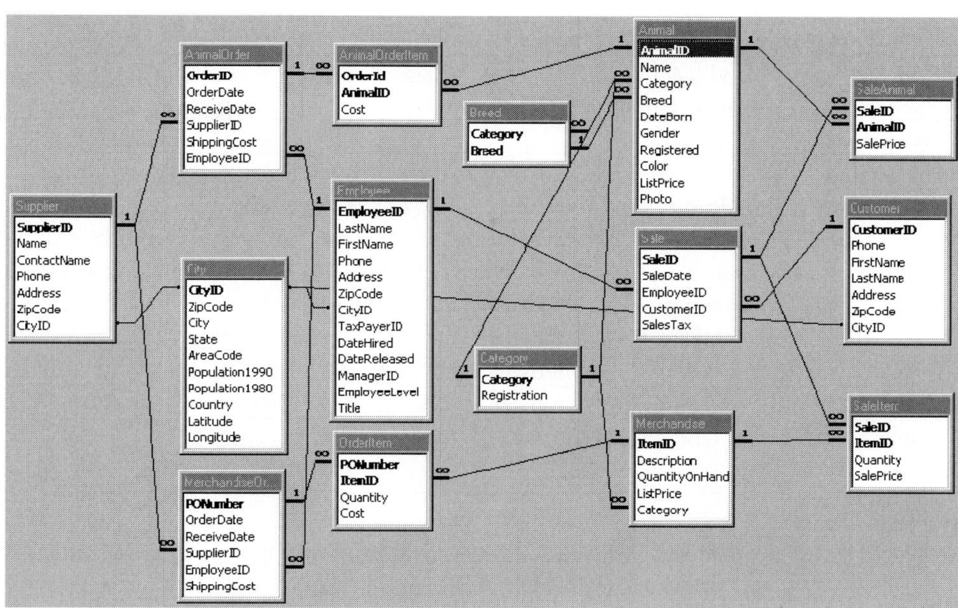

FIGURE 2.18
Detailed class diagram for Sally's Pet Store. Notice the tables added to solve many-to-many problems: OrderItem, AnimalOrderItem, SaleItem, and SaleAnimal. The City table was added to reduce data entry. The Breed and Category tables were added to ensure data consistency. Users select the category and breed from these tables, instead of entering text or abbreviations that might be different every time. Notice that Microsoft Access uses an infinity sign (∞) instead of an asterisk to denote the many side of the relationship.

want to store all of the category and breed names one time in separate classes. Then employees simply choose the category and breed from the list in these classes. Hence data is entered exactly the same way every time.

Both the overview and the detail class diagrams for the Pet Store can be used to communicate with users. Through the entities and relationships, the diagram displays the business rules of the firm. For instance, the separate treatment of animals and merchandise is important to the owner. Similarly, capturing only one customer per each sale is an important business rule. This rule should be confirmed by Sally. If a family purchases an animal, does she want to keep track of each member of the family? If so, you would need to add a Family class that lists the family members for each customer. The main point is that you can use the diagrams to display the new system, verify assumptions, and get new ideas.

DATA TYPES (DOMAINS)

As you list the properties within each class, you should think about the type of data they will hold. Each attribute holds a specific **data type** or data domain. For example, what is an EmployeeID? Is it numeric? At what value does it start? How should it be incremented? Does it contain letters or other alphanumeric characters? You must identify the domain of each attribute or column. Figure 2.19 identifies several common domains. The most common is text, which holds any characters.

Note that any of the domains can also hold missing data. Users do not always know the value of some item, so it may not be entered. Missing data is defined as a **null** value.

Text

Text columns are often limited to no more than 255 characters. Some database management systems ask you to distinguish between fixed-length and variable-length text. Fixed-length strings always take up the amount of space you allocate and are most useful to improve speed in handling short strings like identification numbers or two-

DATA TYPES	FORMAT	STORAGE SIZE	RANGE OF DATA
Text	Fixed length Variable length	1 to 64K bytes 1 to 2G bytes	
Memo/Note			
Numeric	Byte	1 byte	0 to 255
	Boolean	2 bytes	True or False
	Integer	2 bytes	−32,768 to 32,767 (no decimal point)
	Long	4 bytes	−2,147,483,648 to 2,147,483,647 (no decimal point)
	Floating	4 bytes	1.401298E-45 to 3.402823E38
	Double	8 bytes	4.94065645841247E-324 to 1.79769313486232E308
	Currency	8 bytes	−922,377,203,685,477.5808 to 922,377,203,685,477.5807
Date/Time		8 bytes	Jan 1, 100 to Dec 31, 9999
Objects	Any type of data supported by the machine Pictures, sound, video . . .		

FIGURE 2.19

Data types (domains). Common data types, with sizes and ranges as implemented by Microsoft Access.

letter state abbreviations. Variable-length strings are usually stored so they take only as much space as needed for each row of data.

Memo or note columns are also used to hold variable-length text data. The difference from variable-length text is that the database can allocate more space for memos. The exact limit depends on the DBMS and the computer used, but memos typically range up to 32K or 64K bytes in one database column. Memo columns are often used for long comments or even short reports. However, some systems limit the operations that you can perform with memo columns, such as not allowing you to sort the column data.

Numbers

Numeric data is also common, and computers recognize several variations of numeric data. The most important decision you have to make about numeric data columns is choosing between integer and floating-point numbers. Integers cannot hold fractions (values to the right of a decimal point). Integers are often used for counting and include values such as 1; 2; 100; and 5,000. Floating point numbers can include fractional values and include numbers like 3.14 and 2.718.

The first question raised with integers and floating-point numbers is, Why should you care? Why not store all numbers as floating point values? The answer lies in the way that computers store the two types of numbers. In particular, most machines store integers in 2 (or 4) bytes of storage for every value; but they store each floating-point number in 4 (or 8) bytes. Although a difference of 2 bytes might seem trivial, it can make a huge difference when multiplied by several million rows of data. Additionally, arithmetic performed on integers is substantially faster than computations with floating-point data. Something as simple as adding two numbers together can be 10 to 100 times faster with integers than with floating-point numbers. Although machines have become faster and storage costs keep declining, performance is still an important issue when you deal with huge databases and a large customer base. If you can store a number as an integer, do it—you will get a measurable gain in performance.

Most systems also support long integers and double-precision floating-point values. In both cases the storage space is doubled compared to single precision data. The main issue for designers involves the size of the numbers and precision that users need. For example, if you expect to have 100,000 customers, you cannot use an integer to identify and track customers (a key value). Note that only 65,536 values can be stored as integers. To count or measure larger values, you need to use a long integer, which can range between +/−2,000,000,000. Similarly, floating-point numbers can support about six significant digits. Although the magnitude (exponent) can be larger, no more than six or seven digits are maintained. If users need greater precision, use double-precision values, which maintain 14 significant digits.

Many business databases encounter a different problem. Monetary values often require a large number of digits, and users cannot tolerate round-off errors. Even if you use long integers, you would be restricted to values under 2,000,000,000 (20,000,000 if you need two decimal point values). Double-precision floating-point numbers would enable you to store numbers in the billions even with two decimal values. However, floating-point numbers are often stored with round-off errors, which might upset the accountants whose computations must be accurate to the penny. To compensate for these problems, many database systems offer a currency data type, which is stored and computed as integer values (with an imputed decimal point). The arithmetic is fast, large values in the trillions can be stored, and round-off error is minimized.

Dates and Times

All databases need a special data type for dates and times. Some systems combine the two into one domain; others provide two separate definitions. Many beginners try to store dates as string or numeric values. Avoid this temptation. Date types have important properties. Dates (and times) are actually stored as single numbers. Dates are typically stored as integers that count the number of days from some base date. This base date may vary between systems, but it is only used internally. The value of storing dates by a count is that the system can automatically perform date arithmetic. You can easily ask for the number of days between two dates, or you can ask the system to find the date that is 30 days from today. Even if that day is in a different month or a different year, the proper date is automatically computed. Although you probably need 8 bytes to store date/time columns, doing so removes the need to worry about the year 2000 problem. (Although, looking at the ranges in Figure 2.19, some people might be concerned about the year 10,000 problem.)

A second important reason to use internal date and time representations is that the database system can convert the internal format to and from any common format. For example, in European nations dates are generally displayed in day/month/year format, not the month/day/year format commonly used in the United States. With a common internal representation, users can choose their preferred method of entering or viewing dates. The DBMS automatically converts to the internal format, so internal dates are always consistent.

Binary Objects

A relatively new domain is a separate category for objects or **binary large objects (BLOB).** It enables you to store any type of object created by the computer. A good example is to use a BLOB to hold files from other software packages. For example, each row in the database could hold a different spreadsheet, picture, or graph. An engineering database might hold drawings and specifications for various components.

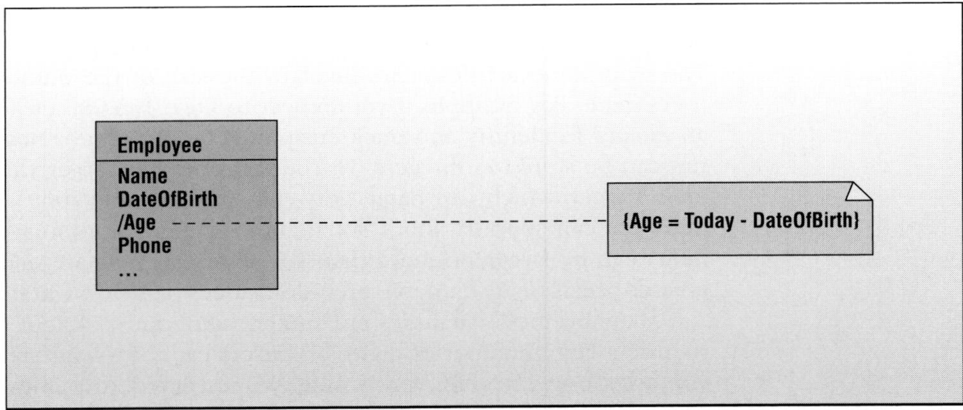

FIGURE 2.20 Derived values. The Age attribute does not have to be stored, since it can be computed from the date of birth. Hence it should be noted on the class diagram. Computed attribute names are preceded with a slash.

The advantage is that all of the data is stored together, making it easier for users to find the information they need and simplifying backups. Similarly, a database could hold several different revisions of a spreadsheet to show how it changed over time or to record changes by many different users.

Computed Values

Some business attributes can be computed. For instance, the total value of a sale can be calculated as the sum of the individual sale prices plus the sales tax. Or an employee's age can be computed as the difference between today's date and the DateOfBirth. At the design stage, you should indicate which data attributes could be computed. The UML notation is to precede the name with a slash (/) and then describe the computation in a note. For example, the computation for a person's age is shown in Figure 2.20. The note is displayed as a box with folded corner. It is connected to the appropriate property with a dashed line.

EVENTS

Events are another important component of modern database systems that you need to record. Three basic types of events occur in a database environment:

1. Business events that trigger some function, such as a sale triggering a reduction in inventory,
2. Data changes that signal some alert, such as an inventory that drops below a preset level, which triggers a new purchase order, and
3. User interface events that trigger some action, such as a user clicking on an icon to send a purchase order to a supplier.

Events are actions that are dependent on time. UML provides several diagrams to illustrate events. The collaboration diagram is probably the most useful for recording business processes and events. Complex user interface events can be displayed on sequence diagrams or statechart diagrams. These latter diagrams are beyond the scope of this book. You can consult an OO design text for more details on how to draw them.

Business events can be related so that one event can trigger a second one, and so on. For complex chains of events, you should probably draw a process diagram to show the desired sequence of the events. Figure 2.21 is a small collaboration diagram. It shows how three classes interact by exchanging messages and calling func-

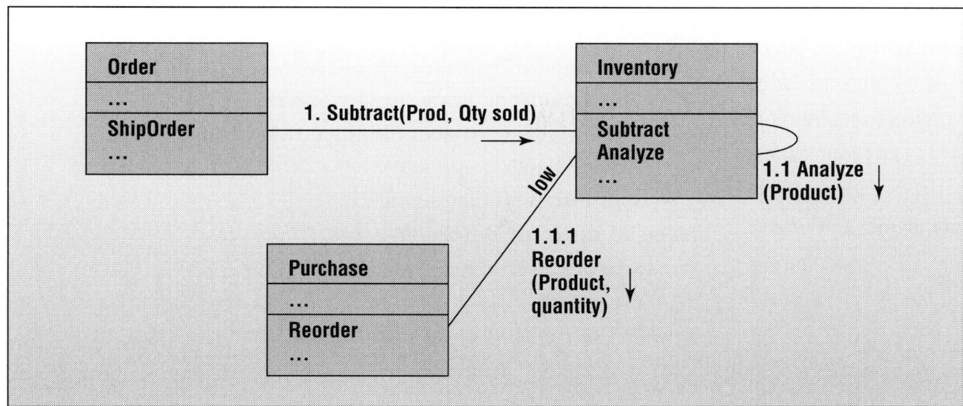

FIGURE 2.21 Combining models. Data objects are defined for easy storage. The business processes (ship order and analyze inventory) are events that trigger changes in the data objects. For example, shipping an order triggers an inventory change, which in turn triggers an analysis of the current level, which can trigger a new inventory order.

tions from the various classes. Note that because the order is important, the three major trigger activities are numbered sequentially. First, the Order class is called to ship an order, which triggers a message to the Inventory class to subtract the appropriate quantity. When an inventory quantity changes, an automatic trigger calls a routine to analyze the current inventory levels. If the appropriate criteria are met, a purchase order is generated and the product is reordered.

The example represents a linear chain of events, which is relatively easy to understand and to test. More complex chains can be built that loop back on themselves and involve more complex alternatives. The UML sequence diagram can be used to show more detail on how individual messages are handled in the proper order. UML statechart diagrams highlight how a class/object status varies over time. Events are important in building a system, but the complicated interactions and system design require a separate textbook to cover the details. For now you should be able to draw simple collaboration diagrams that indicate the primary message events.

In simpler situations you can keep a list of important events. You can write events as triggers, which describe the event cause and the corresponding action to be taken. For example, a business event based on inventory data could be written as shown in Figure 2.22. These triggers can be written in any basic format (e.g., pseudocode) at the design stage and later converted to database triggers or program code. UML also provides an Object Constraint Language (OCL) that you can use to write triggers and other code fragments. It is generic and will be useful if you are using a tool that can convert the OCL code into the database you are using.

LARGE PROJECTS

If you build a small database system for yourself or for a single user, you will probably not take the time to draw diagrams of the entire system. However, you really should provide some documentation so the next designer who has to modify your work will know what you did. On the other hand, if you are working on large projects involving many developers and users, everyone must follow a common design methodology. What is a large project and what is a small project? There are no fixed

FIGURE 2.22 Sample trigger. List the condition and the action.

```
ON (QuantityOnHand < 100)
THEN Notify Purchasing Manager
```

FIGURE 2.23
Development issues on large projects. Large projects require more communication, adherence to standards, and project monitoring.

Design is harder on large projects
- Communication with multiple users
- Communication between IS workers
- Need to divide project into pieces for teams
- Finding data/components
- Staff turnover—retraining

Need to monitor design process
- Scheduling
- Evaluation

Build systems that can be modified later

rules, but you start to encounter problems like those listed in Figure 2.23 when several developers and many users are involved in the project.

Methodologies for large projects begin with diagrams such as the class and collaboration diagrams described in this chapter. Then each company or team adds details. For example, standards are chosen to specify naming conventions, type of documentation required, and review procedures.

The challenge of large projects is to split the project into smaller pieces that can be handled by individual developers. Yet the pieces must fit together at the end. Project managers also need to plan the project in terms of timing and expenses. As the project develops, managers can evaluate team members in terms of the schedule.

Several types of tools can help you design database systems, and they are particularly useful for large projects. To assist in planning and scheduling, managers can use project-planning tools (e.g., Microsoft Project) that help create Gantt and PERT charts to break projects into smaller pieces and highlight the relationships among the components. Computer-assisted software engineering (CASE) tools (like Rational Rose) can help teams draw diagrams, enforce standards, and store all project documentation. Additionally, groupware tools (like Lotus Notes/Domino) help team members share their work on documents, designs, and programs. These tools annotate changes, record who made changes and their comments, and track versions.

As summarized in Figure 2.24, CASE tools perform several useful functions for developers. In addition to assisting with graphical design, one of the most important functions of CASE tools is to maintain the data repository for the project. Every element defined by a developer is stored in the data repository, where it is shared with other developers. In other words, the data repository is a specialized database that holds all of the information related to the project's design. Some CASE tools can gen-

FIGURE 2.24
CASE tool features. CASE tools help create and maintain diagrams. They also support teamwork and document control. Some can generate code from the designs. Others can examine applications and create the matching code through reverse engineering.

- Diagrams (linked)
- Data dictionary
- Teamwork
- Prototyping
  - Forms
  - Reports
  - Sample data
- Code generation
- Reverse engineering

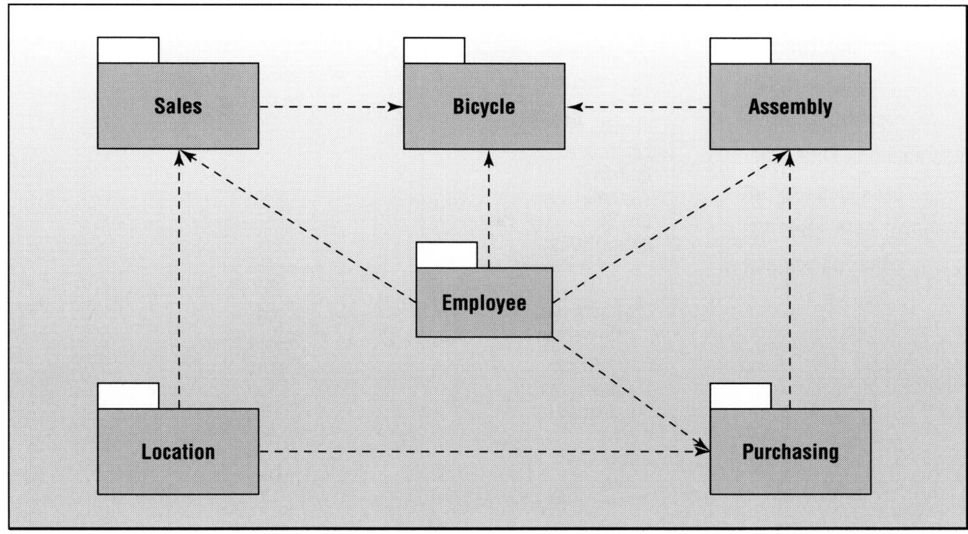

FIGURE 2.25
Rolling Thunder Bicycles—top-level view. The packages are loosely based on the activities of the firm. The goal is for each package to describe a self-contained collection of objects that interacts with the other packages.

erate databases and applications based on the information you enter into the CASE project. In addition, reverse-engineering tools can read files from existing applications and generate the matching design elements. CASE tools are available from many companies, including Rational Software, IBM, Oracle, and Sterling Software. CASE tools can speed the design and development process by improving communication among developers and through generating code. They offer the potential to reduce maintenance time by providing complete documentation of the system.

Good CASE tools have existed for several years, yet many firms do not use them, and some that have tried them have failed to realize the potential advantages. Two drawbacks to CASE tools are their complexity and their cost. The cost issue can be mitigated if the tools can reduce the number of developers needed on a given project. The complexity presents a larger hurdle. It can take a developer several months to learn to use a CASE tool effectively. Fortunately, some CASE vendors provide discounts to universities to help train students in using these tools. If you have access to a CASE tool, use it for as many assignments as possible.

ROLLING THUNDER BICYCLES

The Rolling Thunder Bicycle case illustrates some of the common associations that arise in business settings. Because the application was designed for classroom use, many of the business assumptions were deliberately simplified. The top-level view is shown in Figure 2.25. Loosely based on the activities of the firm, the elements are grouped into six packages: Sales, Bicycles, Assembly, Employees, Purchasing, and Location. The packages will not be equal in size—some contain far more detail than the others. In particular, the Location and Employee packages currently contain only one or two classes. They are treated as separate packages because they both interact with several classes in multiple packages. Because they deal with independent, self-contained issues, it made sense to separate them.

Each package contains a set of classes and associations. The Sales package is described in more detail in Figure 2.26. To minimize complexity, the associations with other packages are not displayed in this figure. For example, the Customer and RetailStore classes have an association with the Location::City class. These relationships will be shown in the Location package. Consequently, the Sales package is

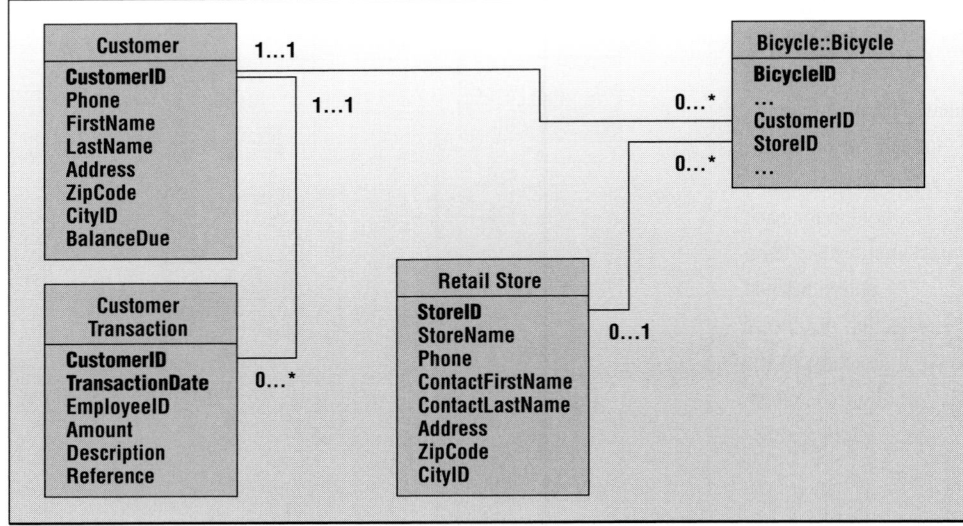

FIGURE 2.26 Rolling Thunder Bicycles—Sales package. Some associations with other packages are not shown here. (See the other packages.)

straightforward. Customers place orders for Bicycles. They might use a RetailStore to help them place the order, but they are not required to do so. Hence the association from the RetailStore has a (0 . . . 1) multiplicity.

The Bicycle package contains many of the details that make this company unique. To save space, only a few of the properties of the Bicycle class are shown in Figure 2.27. Notice that a bicycle is composed of a set of tubes and a set of components. Customers can choose the type of material used to create the bicycle (aluminum, steel, carbon fiber, etc.). They can also select the components (wheels, crank, pedals, etc.) that make up the bicycle. Both of these classes have a composition association with the Bicycle class. The Bicycle class is one of the most important classes for this firm. In conjunction with the BicycleTubeUsed and BikeParts classes, it completely defines each bicycle. It also contains information about which employees worked on the bicycle. This latter choice was a design simplification choice. Another

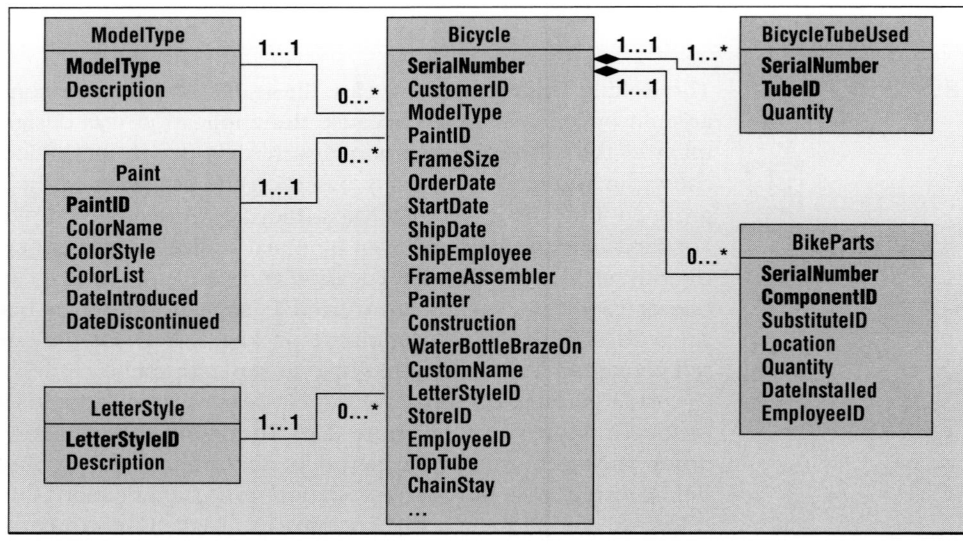

FIGURE 2.27 Rolling Thunder Bicycles—Bicycle package. Note the composition associations into the Bicycle class from the BikeTubes and BikeParts classes. To save space, only some of the Bicycle properties are displayed.

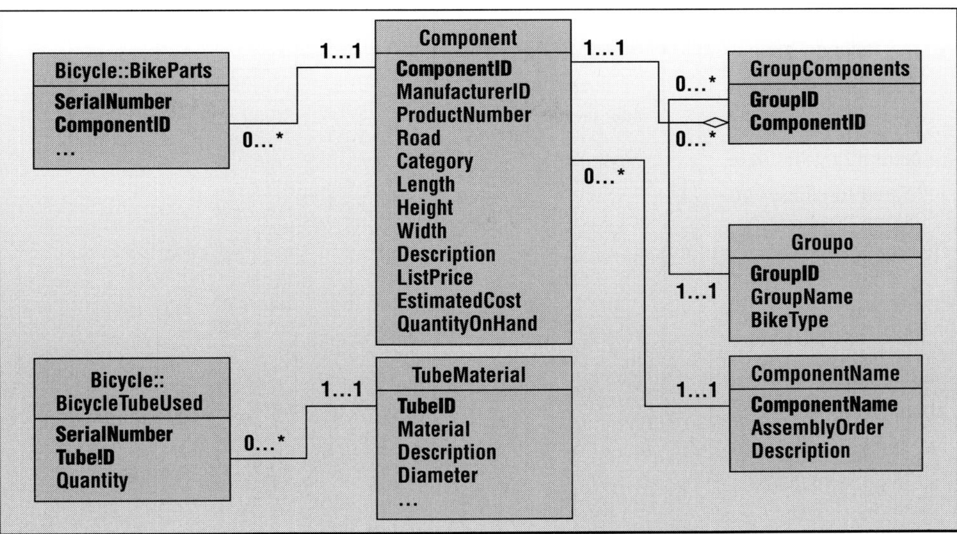

FIGURE 2.28 Rolling Thunder Bicycles—Assembly package. Several events occur during assembly, but they cannot be shown on this diagram. As the bicycle is assembled, additional data is entered into the Bicycle table within the Bicycle package.

alternative would be to move the ShipEmployee, FrameAssembler, and other employee properties to a new class within the Assembly package.

As shown in Figure 2.28, the Assembly package contains more information about the various components and tube materials that make up a bicycle. In practice, the Assembly package also contains several important events. As the bicycle is assembled, data is entered that specifies who did the work and when it was finished. This data is currently stored in the Bicycle class within the Bicycle package. A collaboration diagram or a sequence diagram would have to be created to show the details of the various events within the Assembly package. For now, the classes and associations are more important, so these other diagrams are not shown here.

All component parts are purchased from other manufacturers (suppliers). The Purchase package in Figure 2.29 is a fairly traditional representation of this activity.

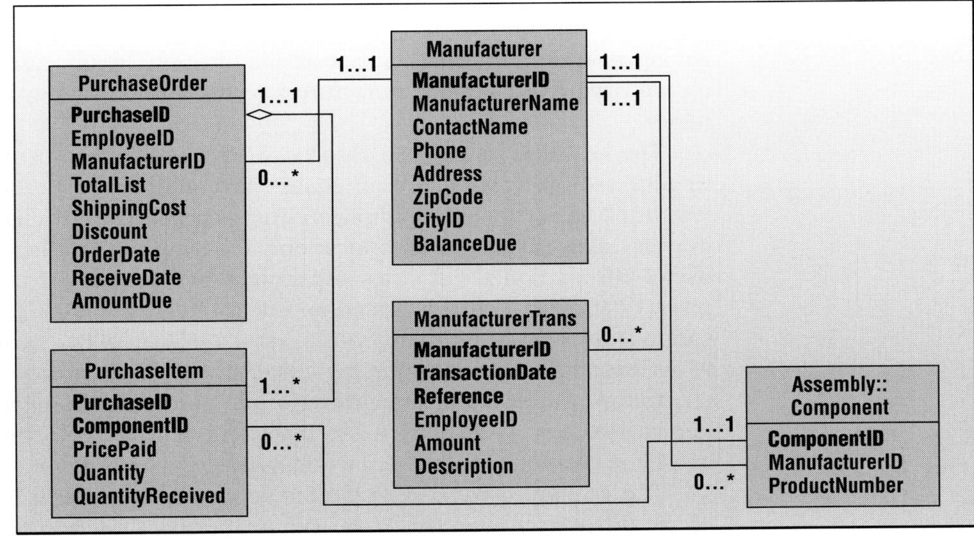

FIGURE 2.29 Rolling Thunder Bicycles—Purchasing package. Note the use of the Transaction class to store all related financial data for the manufacturers in one location.

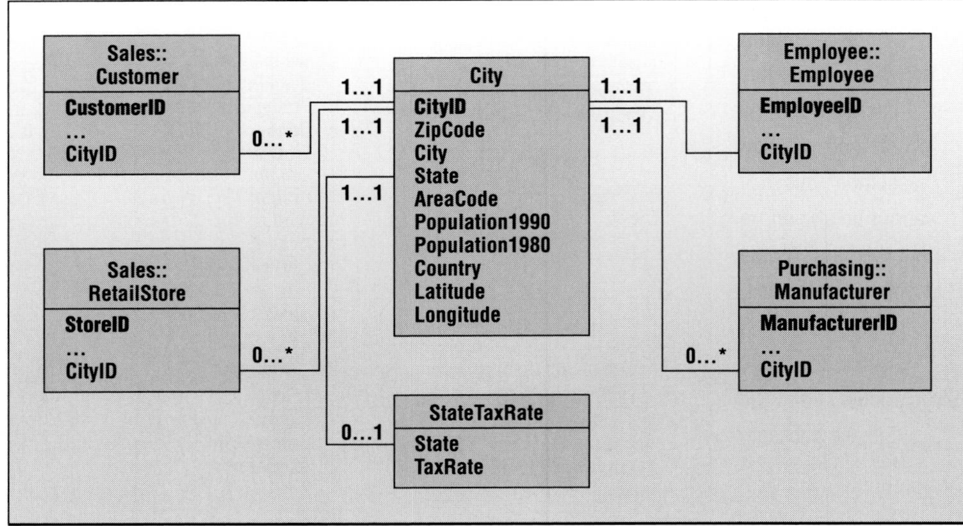

FIGURE 2.30 Rolling Thunder Bicycles—Location package. By centralizing the data related to cities, you speed clerical tasks and improve the quality of the data. You can also store additional information about the location that might be useful to managers.

Note that each purchase requires the use of two classes: PurchaseOrder and PurchaseItem. The PurchaseOrder is the main class that contains data about the order itself, including the date, the manufacturer, and the employee who placed the order. The PurchaseItem class contains the detail list of items that are being ordered. This class is specifically included to avoid a many-to-many association between the PurchaseOrder and Component classes.

Notice from the business rules that a Manufacturer ID must be included on the PurchaseOrder. It is dangerous to issue a purchase order without knowing the identity of the manufacturer. Chapter 10 explains how security controls can be imposed to provide even more safety for this crucial aspect of the business.

An additional class (ManufacturerTransactions) is used as a transaction log to record each purchase. It is also used to record payments to the manufacturers. On the purchase side, it represents a slight duplication of data (AmountDue is in both the PurchaseOrder and Transaction classes). However, it is a relatively common approach to building an accounting system. Traditional accounting methods rely on having all related transaction data in one location. In any case the class is needed to record payments to the manufacturers, so the amount of duplicated data is relatively minor.

The Location package in Figure 2.30 was created to centralize the data related to addresses and cities. Several classes have address properties. In older systems it was often easier to simply duplicate the data and store the city, state, and ZIP code in every class that referred to locations. Today, however, it is relatively easy to obtain useful information about cities and store it in a centralized table. This approach improves data entry, both in speed and data integrity. Clerks can simply choose a location from a list. Data is always entered consistently. For example, you do not have to worry about abbreviations for cities. If telephone area codes or ZIP codes are changed, you need to change them in only one table. You can also store additional information that will be useful to managers. For example, the population and geographical locations can be used to analyze sales data and direct marketing campaigns.

The Employee package is treated separately because it interacts with so many of the other packages. The Employee properties shown in Figure 2.31 are straight-

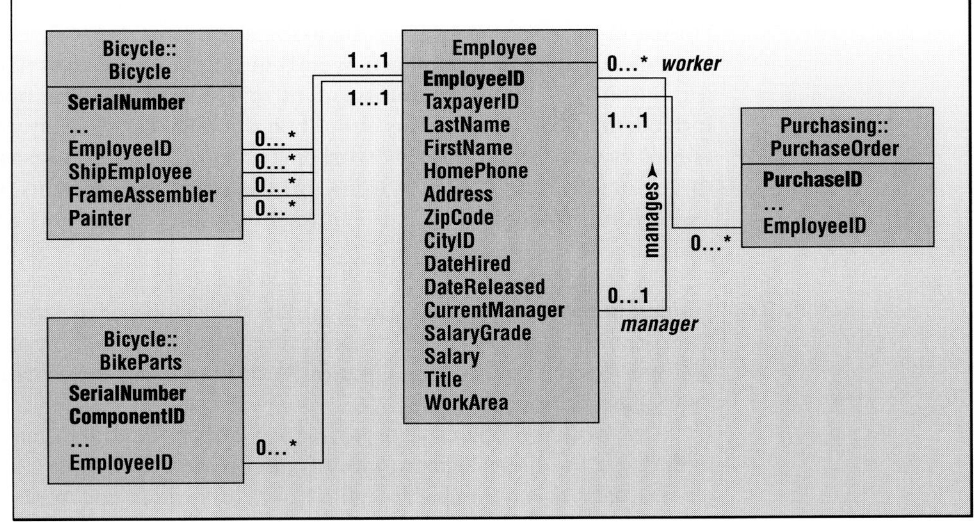

FIGURE 2.31 Rolling Thunder Bicycles—Employee package. Note the reflexive association to indicate managers.

forward. Notice the reflexive association that denotes the management relationship. For the moment there is only one class within the Employee package. In actual practice this is where you would place the typical human resources data and associations. For instance, you would want to track employee evaluations, assignments, and promotions over time. Additional classes would generally be related to benefits such as vacation time, personal days, and insurance choices.

A detailed, combined class diagram for Rolling Thunder Bicycles is shown in Figure 2.32. Some associations are not included—partly to save space. A more im-

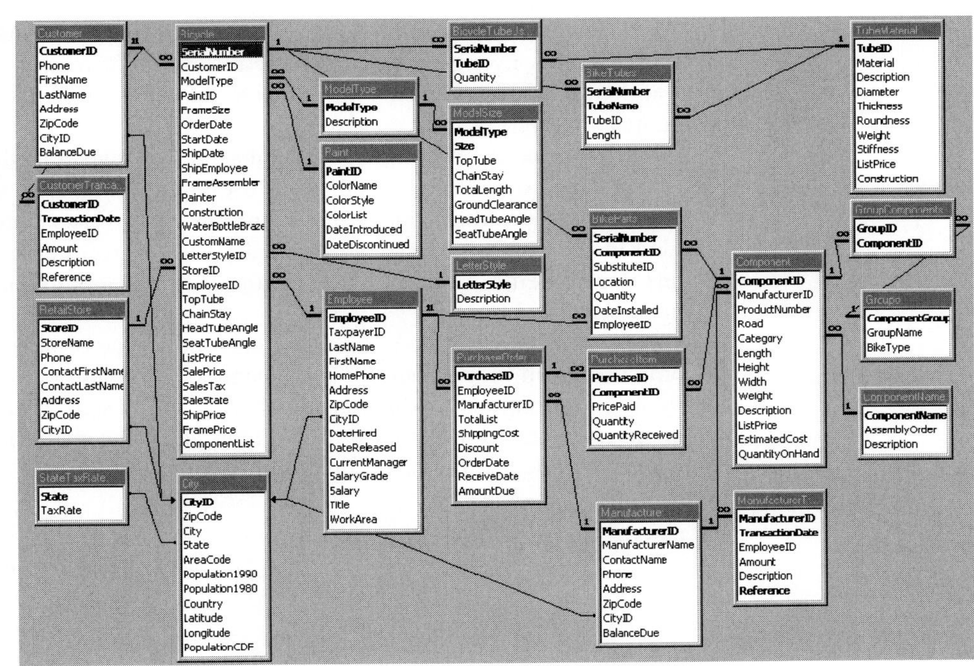

FIGURE 2.32 Rolling Thunder detailed class diagram. Microsoft Access varies slightly from UML. For example, Access uses an infinity sign (∞) instead of an asterisk (*) to indicate a many-relationship. The class diagram is a nice reference tool for understanding the organization, but for many organizations this diagram will be too large to display at this level of detail.

portant reason is that all of the drawn associations are enforced by Microsoft Access. For example, once you define the association from Employee to Bicycle, Access will only allow you to enter an EmployeeID into the Bicycle class that already exists within the Employee class. This enforcement makes sense for the person taking the order. Indeed, financial associations should be defined this strongly. On the other hand, the company may hire temporary workers for painting and frame assembly. In these cases the managers may not want to record the exact person who painted a frame, so the association from Employee to Painter in the Bicycle table is relaxed.

SUMMARY

Managing projects to build useful applications and control costs is an important task. The primary steps in project management are the feasibility study, systems analysis, systems design, and implementation. Although these steps can be compressed, they cannot be skipped.

The primary objective is to design an application that provides the benefits needed by the users. System models are created to illustrate the system. These models are used to communicate with users, communicate with other developers, and to help us remember the details of the system. Because defining data is a crucial step in developing a database application, the class diagram is a popular model.

The class diagram is created by identifying the primary entities in the system. Entities are defined by classes, which are identified by name and defined by the properties of each entity. Classes can also have functions that they can perform.

Associations among classes are important elements of the business design because they identify the business rules. Associations are displayed as connecting lines on the class diagram. You should document the associations by providing names where appropriate, and by identifying the multiplicity of the relationship. You should be careful to identify special associations, such as aggregation, composition, generalization, and reflexive relationships.

Designers also need to identify the primary events or triggers that the application will need. There are three types of events: business events, data change events, and user events. Events can be described in terms of triggers that contain a condition and an action. Complex event chains can be shown on sequence or statechart diagrams.

Designs generally go through several stages of revision, with each stage becoming more detailed and more accurate. A useful approach is to start with the big picture and make sure that your design identifies the primary components that will be needed in the system. Packages can be defined to group elements together to hide details. Detail items are then added in supporting diagrams for each package in the main system diagram.

Models and designs are particularly useful on large projects. The models provide a communication mechanism for the designers, programmers, and users. CASE tools are helpful in creating, modifying, and sharing the design models. In addition to the diagrams, the CASE repository will maintain all of the definitions, descriptions, and comments needed to build the final application.

A DEVELOPER'S VIEW

Like any developer, Miranda needs a method to write down the system goals and details. The feasibility study documents the goals and provides a rough estimate of the costs and benefits. The class diagram identifies the main entities and shows how they are related. The class diagram, along with notes in the data dictionary, records the business rules. For your class project, you should study the case. Then create a feasibility study and an initial class diagram.

KEY WORDS

aggregation, 37
association, 34
association role, 34
attribute, 33
binary large object (BLOB), 47
class, 33
class diagram, 31
class hierarchy, 40
collaboration diagram, 28
composition, 38
data type, 45
derived classes, 39
encapsulation, 40
entity, 33
event, 48
feasibility study, 29
generalization, 39
inheritance, 39
method, 33
multiplicity, 34
n-ary association, 37
null, 45
object, 33
object-oriented programming (OOP), 32
package, 42
polymorphism, 41
property, 33
rapid application development (RAD), 27
reflexive association, 41
relationship, 34
Unified Modeling Language (UML), 32

REVIEW QUESTIONS

1. What are the major categories of costs and benefits that can be expected with database application projects?
2. What is the purpose of a class diagram (or entity-relationship diagram)?
3. What are the primary data types used in business applications?
4. What is an object?
5. What is encapsulation and why is it important?
6. What is inheritance, and how can it help you design and build systems?
7. How is inheritance shown in an entity-relationship diagram?
8. How do events and triggers relate to objects or entities?
9. What problems arise with large projects?
10. How are CASE tools helpful in large projects?

EXERCISES

1. A company is considering a new system for tracking employee evaluations. On talking with users, you learn the potential benefits include less time spent to determine raises; a reduction of one full clerical position; elimination of printing 2,000 pages of reports four times a year; and better merit decisions, which should reduce the $500,000 per year EEO lawsuits. Costs include the initial development costs ($50,000); new hardware ($10,000); new software ($20,000); and annual maintenance costs estimated to be $5,000. There will also be some annual training costs of about $10,000. Prepare a feasibility study for this project. Examine the alternatives under different interest rates (5, 8, 10, and 15 percent) and different expected lifetimes of the project (1, 3, 5, and 10 years). Are there additional benefits and costs that should be considered?

2. You have been hired to design a system for a small health care organization. The clinic consists of several examining rooms and a few rooms for short-term critical-care patients. A core staff of seven physicians is supplemented by internists from a local teaching hospital. The clinic wants to computerize the patient records. All patient medical data is stored in a folder kept in a large central file cabinet. Arriving patients sign in at the front desk. A clerk checks the billing records, prints out a summary status sheet, and obtains the file number from the computerized system. The clerk then pulls the medical data folder and selects an examination room. After waiting for the physician, the clerk moves the data packet and the patient to the examination room. A nurse records basic medical data (weight, blood pressure, etc.). The physician makes additional notes to both the medical and billing data and generally writes a prescription order, which is given to the patient and recorded on the charts. When the patient leaves, the clerk enters the new billing data into the system, collects any payments, and prints a list of charges and a receipt. The new billing data is forwarded to the appropriate insurance company. The medical data is returned to the filing cabinet. When the patient gets a prescription filled, the pharmacist calls the clinic for verification. A clerk retrieves the medical data, identifies the prescription, and verifies or corrects the order. Draw an initial class diagram for this situation.

3. A friend of yours has just opened a photofinishing operation. She wants you to create a database system to help her run the business. The basic processing is straightforward: A customer drops or mails in one or more rolls of film. A clerk records the basic data on the customer and the film. The rolls are assigned a number, sorted, and run through the processor. Processing varies slightly depending on the type of film, film speed, and processing options. Your friend wants to keep track of which clerk performed the processing and match the names with any complaints that might arise. She also wants to offer a frequent-buyer program to reward the most active customers. It is also important to track the chemical usage for the processing—both to keep track of orders and expenses and to make sure the processors always have fresh chemicals. The clerks are also responsible for cleaning the processing equipment. Create an initial entity-relationship diagram for this company. Identify attributes where possible. (Hint: Obtain a film mailer that lists various options.)

4. You have been hired to design a new database for a large hardware store. The store carries many different types of products, including tools, lumber, plumbing items, and lawn-and-garden supplies. At first, you thought a simple sales system would work for this company. After all, each item has a cost, a description, and a list price. But after talking with the managers, you quickly learned that the items sold by this company have important differences. For example, the tools have warranties, but the garden plants and lumber do not. Some items, like the plumbing supplies, have special attributes and managers often want to search on those characteristics. For example, the plumbing department manager might want to know the inventory level of all 1/4-inch-interior-diameter pipes. Products are also grouped by category (plumb-

ing, garden, tools, etc). The categories have important differences; for example, all garden products have a temperature constraint—some plants have to be moved inside if the temperature drops below a certain level. A related problem you encountered is that clerks and managers often have to take different actions depending on which item is sold. For instance, when clerks ring up a sale for certain chemicals, they are supposed to get the Federal pesticide license number of the customer. On the other side, when the company orders certain electrical equipment, it must send license and authorization numbers to the supplier. The store also has several types of customers. Licensed contractors who have registered with the store obtain a lower price. Certain large contractors get additional discounts on some items like plumbing, electrical, and heating equipment. Discounts for these special contractors are negotiated individually. A similar problem exists with suppliers—each one grants the company a different level of discounts. Each one also asks for different types of authorization numbers, and some require the use of electronic data interchange (EDI) or touch-tone orders to get the best discounts. When managers order items, they must identify the supplier, find the best conditions, and follow the rules specified by that supplier. Create a class diagram to identify the primary objects and show the inheritance relationships.

5. Experience exercise: Talk to a manager (or a local store) and create a class diagram for the system.

6. Find a book on rapid application development and identify five steps that can be used to reduce the application development time. Identify five common problems that firms face when they try to reduce development time. Suggest ways to avoid these problems.

7. Identify the relationships between the following entities. Write down any assumptions or comments that affect your decision.
   a. Employee, Spouse
   b. Employee, Child
   c. Employee, Automobile
   d. Employee, Manager
   e. Employee, Specialty
   f. Radio Station, Disk Jockey
   g. Radio Station, Call Letters
   h. Radio Station, Songs
   i. Radio Station, Advertiser
   j. Radio Station, Vehicles
   k. U.S. citizen, Taxpayer Identification Number (SSN)
   l. U.S. citizen, State of Residence
   m. Class, Student
   n. Class, Instructor
   o. Class, Classroom
   p. Automobile, Owner
   q. Automobile, Insurance Company
   r. Automobile, Vehicle Identification Number (VIN)

8. For each of the entities in the following list (left side), identify whether each of the items on the right should be attributes of that entity or separate entities.

a. Employee	Manager, Date of Birth, Spouse, Specialty, Office, Phone Number
b. Automobile	Color, Owner, Engine Size, Insurance Policy, Repair Shop, Damage
c. Movie	Actor, Director, Length, Date Made, Cost, Theater
d. Ship	Captain, Crew, Passenger, Name, Country of Registry
e. Order	Customer, Date, Items, Order Number, Employee

9. You have been asked to develop a ride-sharing application for your school. Students will use the Internet to select a destination on a local map. Your system will then try to match riders with drivers. When a destination is selected, the following form is displayed:

Destination: *Milwaukee* Meet at (e.g., Union): Arrive at (e.g., Mall):	Message # Date posted Date removed
☐ Driver #Riders: ☐ Rider	Date leaving: Date returning:
Name: Phone: Best time to call: E-mail:	
Comments or questions	

10. You have been hired by an environmental consulting company (ECC) that specializes in creating environmental impact statements (EIS) for large projects. It needs a database to track the progress of each EIS. The company is particularly concerned about tracking public comments, questions from state and federal officials, and the responses to all of these comments. All comments are scanned and stored as digital files.

EIS Project #: Date initiated: Date ECC involved: Date ECC finished:	Client Principal contact Phone Contact address City, State, ZIP	Phone Billing address City, State, ZIP
Site location: latitude Site address: Site description	longitude City State ZIP	
Proposed development description	Proposed activities (standard list) Drain wetlands Fill Build roads Store waste	

Comments and Responses						
Date received	Category	Source	File	Response date	Person	Title

11. You have been appointed as project manager on a consulting project for a firm that manufactures basic apparel—particularly T-shirts. These shirts are often sold to active-wear companies that remarket them to small printing shops. Your team has been asked to design a Web site for the manufacturer that can be used by the print shops and the remarketers to place orders, determine production status, and track orders and shipment dates. The company currently has almost no Internet facilities or experience. An old AS/400-based internal information system produces printed reports of production schedules. For the new system to function correctly, your team has to collect internal sales and production data, store it in a database, and make the database available on the Internet. You will have to build the database, establish the Internet connections and any internal LAN extensions, create the Web site, identify security needs, publicize the site, and train internal staff and the remarketers. You will also have to perform extensive testing of all of the applications and the final system. Create a project plan that schedules all the steps. Identify potential problems. Determine an implementation and testing scheme. Option 1: Draw a Gantt chart for the activities. Option 2: Create the project schedule with project-scheduling software.

Sally's Pet Store

12. Do some initial research on retail sales and pet stores. Identify the primary benefits you expect to gain from a transaction processing system for Sally's Pet Store. Estimate the time and costs required to design and build the database application.

13. Extend the class diagram for Sally's Pet Store by including the details needed to track the genealogy of all of the animals.

14. Extend the class diagram for Sally's Pet Store by including the details needed to track the health and veterinary records for the animals.

Rolling Thunder Bicycles

15. Redesign the Rolling Thunder class diagram using an object-oriented approach. Identify all of the classes, properties, and methods.

16. Rolling Thunder Bicycles is thinking about opening a chain of bicycle stores. Explain how the database would have to be altered to accommodate this change. Add the proposed components to the class diagram.

WEB SITE REFERENCES

Site	Description
http://www.rational.com/uml	The primary site for UML documentation and examples
http://www.iconixsw.com/Spec Sheets/Uml2.html	UML documentation and comments

ADDITIONAL READING

Bahrami, A., *Object-Oriented Systems Development.* Burr Ridge, IL: Irwin/McGraw-Hill, 1999. [A good introduction to OO Design and UML.]

Codd, E. F. "A relational model of data for large shared data banks." *Communications of the ACM* 13 no. 6 (1970), pp. 377–387. [The paper that initially described the relational model.]

Constantine, L. "Under pressure." *Software Development,* October 1995, pp. 111–112. [The importance of design.]

Constantine, L. "Re: Architecture." *Software Development,* January 1996, pp. 87–88. [Update on a design competition.]

Gamma, E., R. Helm, R. Johnson, and J. Vlissides. *Design Patterns: Elements of Reusable Object-Oriented Software.* New York: Addison-Wesley, 1995. [Sample designs for object-oriented analysis.]

McConnell, S. *Rapid Development: Taming Wild Software Schedules.* Redmond: Microsoft Press, 1996. [An excellent introduction to building systems, with lots of details and examples.]

PC Week, January 16, 1995, p. 68. [Problems in building and canceling projects.]

Reingruber, M. and W. Gregory. *The Data Modeling Handbook.* New York: Wiley, 1994. [Many details and rules on higher-level modeling, with emphasis on entity relationship diagrams.]

Whitten, J. L., and L. Bentley. *Systems Analysis and Design Methods.* Burr Ridge, IL: Irwin/McGraw-Hill, 1998. [An introductory text on systems analysis and design.]

Data Normalization

CHAPTER 3

WHAT YOU WILL LEARN IN THIS CHAPTER

OVERVIEW

Miranda: *That was actually fun. I learned a lot about the company's procedures and rules. I think I have everything recorded properly on the class diagram; along with some notes in the data dictionary.*

Ariel: *Great! We should go to the concert tonight and celebrate.*

Miranda: *I could use a night off. Maybe giving my brain cells a rest will help me figure out what to do next.*

Ariel: *What do you mean? How much longer do you think the project will take?*

Miranda: *That's the problem. I put all this time in, and I don't really have a start on the application at all.*

Ariel: *Well, isn't the data the most important aspect to building a database application? I heard that database systems are touchy. You have to define the data correctly the first time; otherwise, you will have to start over.*

Miranda: *Maybe you're right. I'll take the night off; then I'll study these rules to see how I can turn the class diagram into a set of database tables.*

INTRODUCTION

A database is a powerful tool. It provides many advantages over traditional programming and hierarchical files. However, you get these advantages only if you design the database correctly. Recall that a database is a collection of tables. The goal of this chapter is to show you how to design the tables for your database.

The essence of data normalization is to split your data into several tables that will be connected to each other based on the data within them. Mechanically, this process is not very difficult. There are perhaps four rules that you need to learn. On the other hand, the tables have to be created specifically for the business or application that you are dealing with. Therefore, you must first understand the business, and your tables must match the rules of the business. So the challenge in designing a database is to first understand how the business operates and what its rules are. We saw some of these rules in Chapter 2 when we focused on relationships. Business relationships (one-to-one and one-to-many) form the foundation of data normalization. These relationships are crucial to determining how to set up your database. These relationships and rules vary from firm to firm and sometimes even depend on which person you talk to in the firm. So when you create your database, you have to build a picture of how the company works. You talk to many people to understand the relationships among the data. The goal of data normalization is to identify the business rules so that you can design good database tables.

The goal is to design database tables carefully. By doing so, we (1) save space, (2) minimize duplication, and (3) protect the data to ensure its consistency. One method for defining database tables is to use the graphical approach presented in Chapter 2 and build a class diagram. A related method is to collect the basic paperwork, starting with every form and every report you might use. Then take apart each collection of data and break it down into respective tables. Most people find that a combination of both approaches helps them find the answer. However, we will start by describing the two methods separately.

TABLES, CLASSES, AND KEYS

Chapter 2 described the creation of class diagrams. The point was to go through the business organization and identify anything that might be an object or entity, such as customers, orders, or products. The business analysis stage also identifies how classes are related to each other. This higher-level approach is useful because it provides a picture of the entire firm and shows how the pieces fit together. To turn the class diagram into a database, we need more information. We have to add properties to the classes and identify every relationship precisely: one-to-one, one-to-many, and many-to-many. Even then, the classes might need further refinement. Ultimately, the classes must be converted into a set of tables.

Relational databases operate on tables of data. These tables must be carefully defined to obtain the advantages of the database approach. The process of determining the proper tables for a database is called *normalization*. The process of normalization applies to class diagrams as well. The classes in the class diagram become tables in the database.

Normalization rules are useful even if you will be using a different type of database. For example, the newer object-oriented approach is both similar to and different from traditional database design. Yet most designers of OO systems still use data normalization to help define their primary classes. The advantages of minimizing duplication and avoiding hidden dependencies apply equally well to objects. The attributes (columns) from the relational tables become properties of the objects/classes. The OO designer then adds the relevant methods or functions to each class.

Definitions

The basic definitions are shown in Figure 3.1. Codd created formal mathematical definitions of these terms when he defined relational databases. However, for designing and building business applications, the definitions presented here are easier to understand. For example, no one uses the word *tuple* in conversation; everyone calls it a "row." You can always read Codd's papers or a computer science textbook to find the formal definitions, but you will probably never need them.

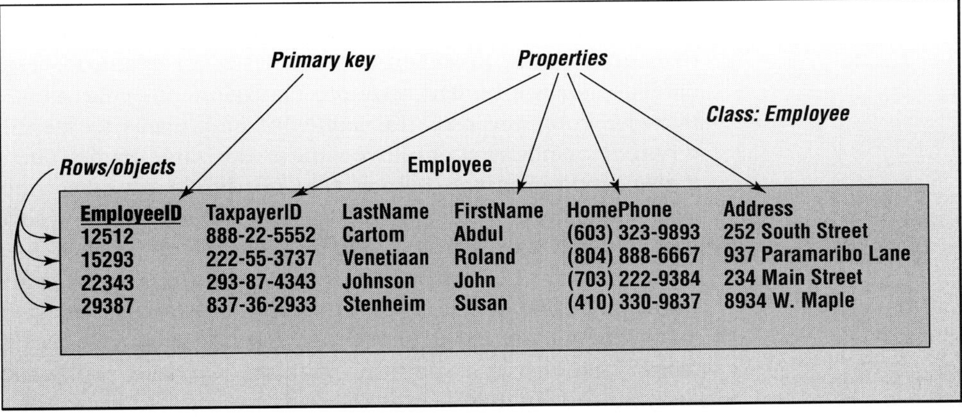

FIGURE 3.1 Basic database definitions. Codd has more formal terms and mathematical definitions, but these are easier to understand. One row in the data table represents a single object, a specific employee in this situation. Each column (attribute) contains one piece of data about that employee.

A **relational database** is a collection of tables. A **table** is a collection of columns (attributes) that describe an entity. Individual objects are stored as rows (tuples) within the table. For example, EmployeeID 12512 represents one instance of an employee and is stored as one row in the Employee table. An attribute (property) is a characteristic or descriptor of an entity. Two important aspects to a relational database are that (1) all data must be stored in tables and (2) all tables must be carefully defined to provide flexibility and minimize problems. **Data normalization** is the process of defining tables properly to provide flexibility, minimize redundancy, and ensure data integrity. The goal of database design and data normalization is to produce a list of nicely behaved tables. Each table describes a single type of object in the organization. These objects are described by various attributes that ultimately become columns in the table.

Primary Key

Every table must have a primary key. The **primary key** is a column or set of columns that we use to identify a particular row. For example, in the customer table we might use customer name to find a particular entry. But that column does not make a good key. What if eight customers are named "John Smith"? In most cases we will create our own keys to ensure they are unique. For example, we might create a customer identification number. The relationship between the primary key and the rest of the data is one-to-one. That is, each entry for a key points to exactly one customer row. To highlight the primary key, we will underline the name of the column (or columns) that make up the primary key.

In some cases we will have several choices to use as a primary key. In the customer example we might choose name or phone number, or we might create a unique CustomerID. If we have a choice, the primary key should be the smallest set of columns needed to form a unique identifier.

Some U.S. organizations might be tempted to use personal Social Security numbers (SSN) as the primary key. Even if you have a need to collect the SSN, you will be better off using a separate number as a key. One reason is that a primary key must always be unique, and with the SSN you run a risk that someone might present a forged document. Also, primary keys are used and displayed in many places within a database. If you use the SSN, too many employees will have access to your customers' private information. Because SSNs are used for many financial, governmental, and health records, you should protect customer privacy by limiting employee access to these numbers.

The most important issue with a primary key is that it can never point to more than one row or object in the database. For example, assume you are building a database for the human resource management department. The manager tells you that the company uses the names of employees to identify them. Then you ask whether or not two employees have the same name. The manager examines the list of employees and reports that no duplicates exist among the 30 employees. The manager also suggests that if you include the employee's middle initial, you should never have a problem identifying the employees. So far, it sounds like name might be a potential key. But wait! You really need to ask what the possible key values might be in the future. If you build a database with employee name as a primary key, you are explicitly stating that no two employees will ever have the same name. That absurd assumption will cause serious problems when you actually try to build the database.

Composite Keys

In many cases, as you design a database, you will have tables that will use more than one column as part of the primary key. These are called **composite keys** (or concatenated keys). You need composite keys when the table contains a one-to-many or many-to-many relationship.

As an example of composite keys, look at the OrderItems example in Figure 3.2. The Orders table is straightforward. It has one column as a primary key, where we created the OrderID. This table contains the basic information about an order, including the date and the customer. The OrderItems table has two columns as keys: OrderID and Item. The purpose of the OrderItems table is to show which products the customers chose to buy. In terms of keys the important point is that each order can contain many different items. In the example OrderID 8367 has three items. Because each order can have many different items, Item must be part of the key. Reading from left to right, we can say that each OrderID may have many Items. The "many" says that Item must be keyed. What about the other direction in the OrderItems table? Do we really need to key OrderID? The answer is yes because the firm can sell the same item to many different people (or to the same customer at different times). For example, Item 229 appears on OrderIDs 8367 and 8368. Because each item can appear on many different orders, the OrderID must be part of the primary key. For comparison, reconsider the Orders table in Figure 3.2. Each OrderID can have only one Customer, so Customer is not keyed.

To properly normalize the data and store the data as efficiently as possible, you must identify keys properly. Your choice of the key depends on the business relationships, the terminology in the organization, and the one-to-many and many-to-many relationships within the company.

Surrogate Keys

It can be difficult to ensure that any real-world data will always generate a unique key. Consequently, you will often ask the database system to generate its own key values. These surrogate keys are used only within the database and are often hidden so users do not even know they exist. For example, the database system could assign a unique key to each customer, but clerks would look up customers by conventional data such as name and address. Surrogate keys are especially useful when

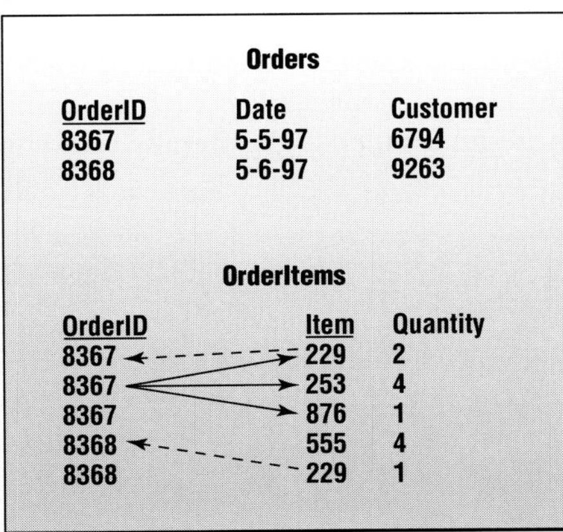

Orders

OrderID	Date	Customer
8367	5-5-97	6794
8368	5-6-97	9263

OrderItems

OrderID	Item	Quantity
8367	229	2
8367	253	4
8367	876	1
8368	555	4
8368	229	1

FIGURE 3.2 Concatenated keys. OrderItems uses a concatenated key (OrderID + Item) because there is a many-to-many relationship. Each order can contain many items (shown by the solid arrows). Each item can show up on many different orders (dotted arrows).

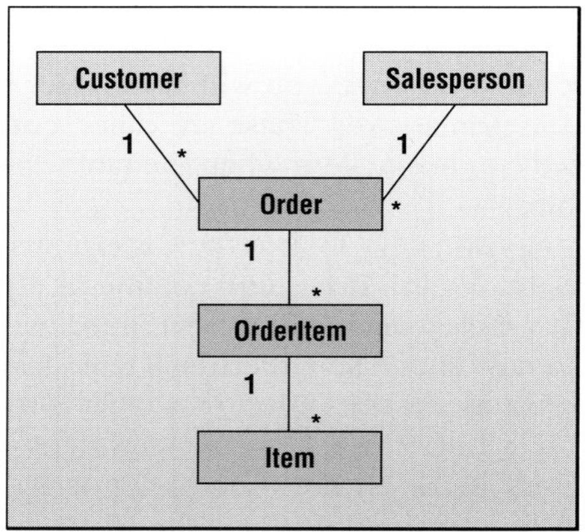

FIGURE 3.3
A small class diagram for a basic order system. The numbers indicate relationships. For instance, each customer can place many orders, but a given order can come from only one customer.

there is some uncertainty with the business key. Think about the problems that you would face if a company changed the format of its product numbers every 2 years? If you rely on business keys, you must trust that they will always be consistent and never be duplicated.

The use of surrogate keys can be tricky when the database becomes large. With many simultaneous users, creating unique numbers becomes more challenging. Additionally, there are several performance questions involving surrogate keys in large databases. For example, a common method of generating a surrogate key is to find the largest existing key value and increment it. But what happens if two users attempt to generate a new key at the same time? A good DBMS handles these problems automatically.

Notation

It is possible to describe each table on a detailed class diagram that includes all properties within each class and marked key columns. The advantage to using class diagrams is that they highlight the associations among the classes. Additionally, some people understand the system better with a visual representation. Figure 3.3 shows a simple class diagram, but it leaves out the properties.

The drawback to class diagrams is that they can become very large. By the time you get to 30 classes, it is hard to fit all the information on one page. Also, many of the association lines will cross, making the diagram hard to read. CASE tools help resolve some of these problems by enabling you to examine a smaller section of the diagram.

However, you can also use a shorter notation, as shown in Figure 3.4. The notation consists of a straight listing of the tables. Each column is listed with the table name. The primary keys are underlined and generally listed first. This notation is easy

FIGURE 3.4
Table notation. Column details are easier to see in a simple listing of the tables. This list is also useful when the tables are entered into the database.

Customer(<u>CustomerID</u>, Name, Address, City, Phone)
Salesperson(<u>EmployeeID</u>, Name, Commission, DateHired)
Order(<u>OrderID</u>, OrderDate, CustomerID, EmployeeID)
OrderItem(<u>OrderID</u>, <u>ItemID</u>, Quantity)
Item(<u>ItemID</u>, Description, ListPrice)

FIGURE 3.5
Client-billing example. Note the business rule that each client can be assigned many partners results in both PartnerID and ClientID being keys in the PartnerAssignment table.

Client(<u>ClientID</u>, Name, Address, BusinessType)

Partner(<u>PartnerID</u>, Name, Specialty, Office, Phone)

PartnerAssignment(<u>PartnerID</u>, <u>ClientID</u>, DateAcquired)

Billing(<u>ClientID</u>, <u>PartnerID</u>, <u>Date/Time</u>, Item, Description, Hours, AmountBilled)

to write by hand or to type, and it can display many tables in a compact space. However, it is hard to show the relationships between the tables. You can draw arrows between the tables, but your page can become messy.

Designers frequently create both the class diagram and the list of tables. The list identifies all of the columns and the keys. The class diagram shows the relationships between the tables. The class diagram can also contain additional details, such as existence constraints and minimum requirements.

Consider the example in Figure 3.5 of a small client-billing system. Basic data includes clients and partners. You probably have a relationship that shows which partners are assigned to each client. You also want to track the amount of work that partners perform for each client. The Client and Partner tables use specially created columns for the primary key. Hence we do not have to worry about uniqueness or possible duplication of names. Keep in mind that customers and partners do not have to know anything about their identification numbers. Techniques presented in Chapter 8 will show how to look up client data while hiding key values.

Notice that in the PartnerAssignment table, both PartnerID and ClientID are keyed. Just by writing the table in this form, we have identified an assumption about the way the firm operates. First, each partner performs work for many clients—a fairly common practice. Additionally, each client could be assigned many partners. This second assumption might not hold in some firms. Smaller firms might simply assign a primary partner to each client. If a different partner performs work for the client, the Partner could still be listed in the billing table. The choice of keys in the PartnerAssignment table depends on the way that the business operates.

Figure 3.6 illustrates what happens in a firm with a rule that each client is assigned to exactly one primary partner. In this case PartnerID is no longer a key in the PartnerAssignment table. Notice also that the Client and PartnerAssignment ta-

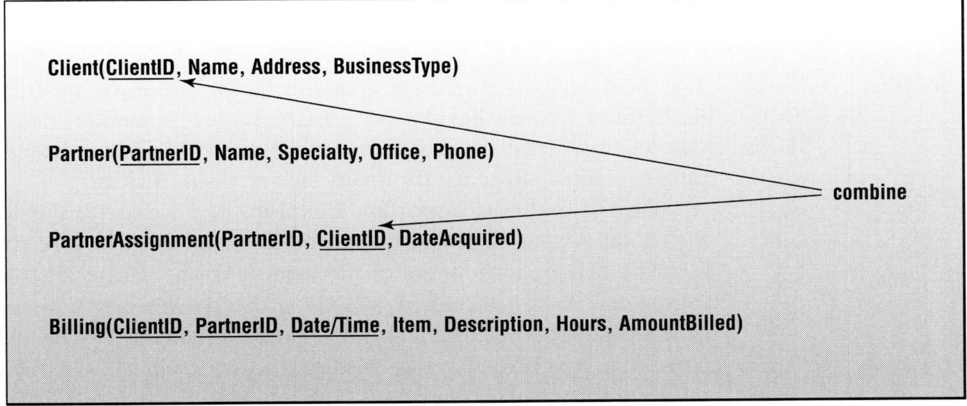

FIGURE 3.6
Simplified client billing. If each client is assigned exactly one primary partner, then the PartnerID cannot be keyed in the PartnerAssignment table. However, now the Client table and the PartnerAssignment table have the same key (ClientID). Hence the columns should be combined into one (Client) table.

FIGURE 3.7
Sample data for the Billing table. Note that Partner 967 can perform the same task for Client 115 several times—because Date/Time is part of the primary key.

Billing						
ClientID	PartnerID	Date/Time	Item	Description	Hours	AmountBilled
115	963	8-4-97 10:03	967	Stress analysis	2	500
295	967	8-5-97 11:15	754	New design	3	750
115	063	8-8-97 09:30	967	Stress analysis	2.5	650

bles have exactly the same keys (ClientID). If these keys are correct, the columns should be combined into one table (Client). There is no reason to have two tables with exactly the same key. Hence the data tables for the second firm will be different from those of the first firm—simply because of a difference in business procedures.

The Billing table in Figure 3.7 has three columns in the primary key: ClientID, PartnerID, and Date/Time. The keys indicate that for each client many partners can perform work. Conversely, each partner can work for many different clients. Similarly, each client can have work performed by each partner at many different times. Consider the implications if we did not key Date/Time. Then each client could be billed by many partners, but only one time for each partner. Although the clients might be happy with that constraint, it is not realistic from the perspective of the firm using the database. The problem with not keying Date/Time is that rows 1 and 3 would no longer be unique. To test your primary keys, enter sample data and cover up the other columns. Looking at the first two columns in the table, we see duplicate entries for rows 1 and 3. To solve the problem, we asked, How can a partner perform work for a client more than once? The answer is that the work must be performed at different times. Hence the Date/Time column is added and becomes part of the primary key.

Already you can see how the business rules affect the database design. The choice of the primary key depends heavily on the business relationships, and can be different for each organization. Be careful to double-check all of your keys. If you make a mistake in the keys, it will be difficult to get the rest of the database correct. In the case of simple entities (customer, employee, etc.) you will generally create a unique key. For more complex entities, you need to watch for one-to-many and many-to-many relationships. You test composite keys by looking at the first underline (ClientID) then ask, for all other underlined columns (in this case PartnerID), Are there many of these partners? If so, then the column should be keyed. If there is only one entry, then the column should not be a key. Be sure to check the reverse relationship as well (PartnerID to ClientID).

SAMPLE DATABASE FOR A VIDEO STORE

The best way to illustrate data normalization is to examine a sample problem. Remember that the results we get (the tables we create) depend heavily on the specific example and the assumptions we make. We have chosen an example that is familiar to most students: the main task at a video store.

One of the most important functions of a video store is to check out the videos for rental. A sample checkout screen is displayed in Figure 3.8.

The main components of the sample form are the customer and the videos being rented. When the form is built in the database, it will automatically keep track of the total amount due. It should also automatically assign a RentalID that is unique. Note that the form also has buttons and controls to help the user enter data with a minimum of effort. Forms and controls are discussed in Chapter 5. For now, as you talk with the manager, you should sketch the desired features of the form. Values that can be computed (e.g., subtotals) should be marked, and the appropriate equations provided if needed. For the most part you do not want to store computed values in the data tables.

Initial Objects

Begin by identifying the main objects that you will need. The obvious ones are customer and videos. In real life you would also have employees, VCRs to rent, and possibly other sale items, but you can ignore those for now. However, managers also need to keep track of who rented specific videos. For example, if a video is not returned on time, managers need to know who to call. Hence you need two additional objects. The first is a transaction that records the date and the customer. The second is a list of the videos rented by that customer at that time.

Examine the initial objects in Figure 3.9. We need a primary key for customers (and videos). Clearly, Name will not work, but you might consider using the Phone number. This approach would probably work, but it might cause some minor difficulties down the road. For example, if a customer gets a new phone number, you would have to change the corresponding phone number in every table that referred to it. As a primary key, it could appear in several different tables. A bigger problem would arise if a customer (Adams) moves, freeing up the phone number, which the phone company reassigns to another person (Brown) several months later. If Brown

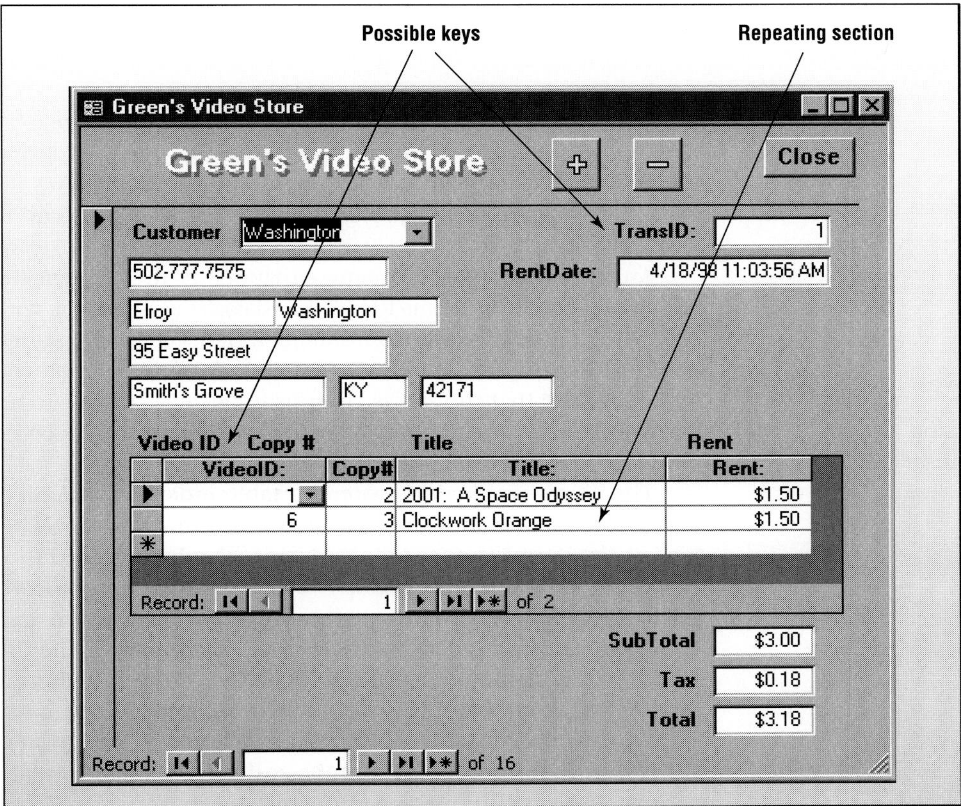

FIGURE 3.8
Sample video rental screen. First look for possible keys, keeping in mind that repeating sections (one-to-many relationships) will eventually need concatenated keys.

FIGURE 3.9 Initial objects for the video store. Note that the transaction has two parts, RentalTransaction and VideosRented because many videos can be rented at one time.

INITIAL OBJECTS	KEY	SAMPLE PROPERTIES	COMMENT
Customer	Assign CustomerID	Name Address Phone	
Video	Assign VideoID	Title RentalPrice Rating Description	
RentalTransaction	Assign TransactionID	CustomerID RentDate	Event/Relationship
VideosRented	TransactionID + VideoID	Copy#	Event/Repeating list

opens an account at your store, your database might mistakenly identify customer Brown as customer Adams. The safest approach is to have the database create a new number for every customer.

The Video object (which could include video games) also needs a key. In practice you might be able to use the product identifiers created by the publisher. For now, it is easiest to assign a separate number. Common properties would include Title, Rating, Description, and RentalPrice (Rent). More attributes can be added later if necessary.

Every transaction must be recorded. A *transaction* is an event that identifies which customer rented videos and when the rental occurred. This object refers to the base rental form and is also assigned a unique key value. Remember this approach. Almost all of the problems you encounter will end up with a table to hold data for the base form or report.

An important issue in many situations is the presence of a repeating section, which can cause problems for storing data (see "Problems with Repeating Sections"). Hence the section is split from the main transaction and stored in its own table. Keys here include the TransactionID (TransID) from the Rental Transaction table and the VideoID. Note that the key is composite because a many-to-many relationship exists. A customer can rent many videos at one time, and a video can be rented (at different times) by more than one customer.

The Copy# in the VideosRented table indicates which copy of the movie is being rented. (There can be multiple copies of each movie.) When the movie is returned, the copy number tells the manager who returned the video. Notice that you have a choice about making Copy# a key. If Copy# is not a key—the way it is drawn—the corresponding business assumption is that a given customer can rent many movies but only one copy of that movie. By designing the database this way, we are saying that a customer will never rent two copies of the same movie at the same time. Whether that is a reasonable assumption depends on the business. The catch is that if you build the database this way, a customer can never rent more than one copy of a given movie at a time. If a customer wanted to rent two copies, you would have to write two transactions.

Initial Form Evaluation

Without practice, it can be difficult to identify all four of the tables in Figure 3.9. Most people should be able to identify the Customer and Video tables. Some will recognize the need for a RentalTransaction table. However, the purpose of the VideosRented table is not as clear. Fortunately, there is a method to derive the individual tables by starting with the entire form and breaking it into pieces. This method is the data normalization approach, and it is a mechanical process that follows from the business assumptions.

Figure 3.10 shows the first step in the evaluation. As you learn normalization, you should be careful to write out this first step. As you gain experience, you might choose to skip this step. The procedure is to look through the form or report and write down everything that you want to store. The objective is to write it in a structured format.

Give the form a name and then list the items as column names. You can generally start at the top left of the form and write a column name for each data element. Try to list items together that fall into natural groupings—such as all customer data. The RentalForm begins with the TransID, which looks like it would make a good key. The RentDate and CustomerID are listed next, followed by the basic customer data. The next step is slightly more complicated because we have to signify that the section with the videos contains repeating data. That is, it has multiple lines of data, or the potential for several similar entries. Repeating data represents a one-to-many relationship that must be handled carefully. An easy way to signify the repeating section is to put it inside another set of parentheses. Some people also list it on a new line.

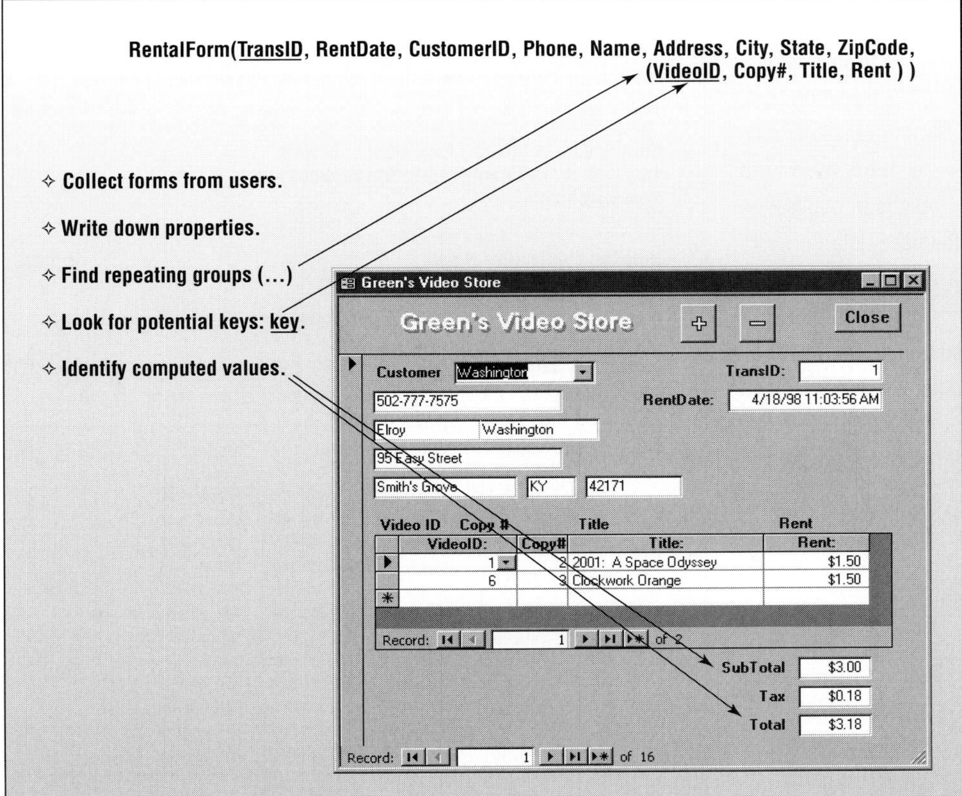

FIGURE 3.10
Initial form evaluation. Once you have collected basic user forms, you can convert them into a more compact notation. The notation makes the normalization steps easier by highlighting potential issues.

Observe that we did not include the computed data (subtotal, tax, and total), since they can be recalculated when they are needed. However, in some cases you might want to store computed data. Just be careful to list the columns with the overall form—not inside the repeating data section. Also, you should mark these items, or make a notation in the data dictionary so that you remember they are computed values.

While you are working on the first step, be sure to write down every item that you want to store in the database. In addition, make sure to identify every repeating section. Here you have to be careful. Sometimes repeating sections are obvious—they might be in a separate section, highlighted by a different color, or contain sample data so you can see the repetition. Other times, repeating sections are less obvious. For example, on large forms repeating sections might appear on separate pages. Other times, some entries might not seem to be repeating. Consider a phone number. In a business environment, some customers will have only one phone number, but others might have several phone numbers: office, work, cellular, pager, and so on. If you need to store multiple phone numbers, they become a repeating entry and should be marked. For instance, the phone numbers could be stored as (PhoneType, Number). You should also try to mark potential keys at this point, both to indicate repeating sections and to highlight columns that you know will contain unique data.

Problems with Repeating Sections

The reason we have to be so careful in identifying repeated sections or one-to-many relationships is that they can cause problems in the database. The situation in Figure 3.11

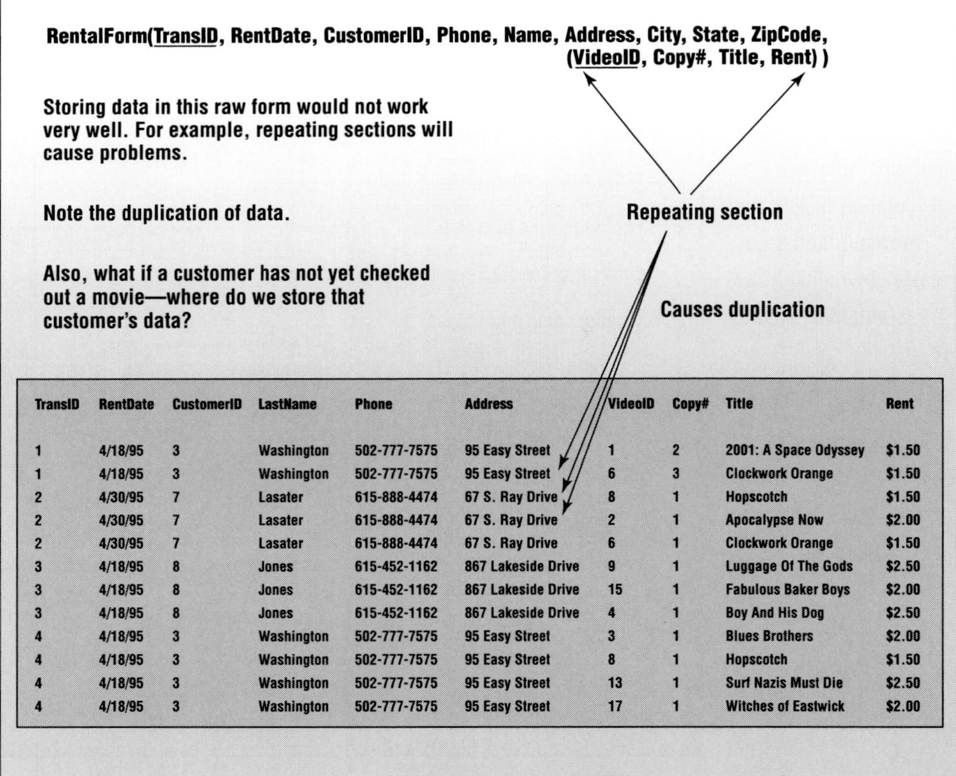

TransID	RentDate	CustomerID	LastName	Phone	Address	VideoID	Copy#	Title	Rent
1	4/18/95	3	Washington	502-777-7575	95 Easy Street	1	2	2001: A Space Odyssey	$1.50
1	4/18/95	3	Washington	502-777-7575	95 Easy Street	6	3	Clockwork Orange	$1.50
2	4/30/95	7	Lasater	615-888-4474	67 S. Ray Drive	8	1	Hopscotch	$1.50
2	4/30/95	7	Lasater	615-888-4474	67 S. Ray Drive	2	1	Apocalypse Now	$2.00
2	4/30/95	7	Lasater	615-888-4474	67 S. Ray Drive	6	1	Clockwork Orange	$1.50
3	4/18/95	8	Jones	615-452-1162	867 Lakeside Drive	9	1	Luggage Of The Gods	$2.50
3	4/18/95	8	Jones	615-452-1162	867 Lakeside Drive	15	1	Fabulous Baker Boys	$2.00
3	4/18/95	8	Jones	615-452-1162	867 Lakeside Drive	4	1	Boy And His Dog	$2.50
4	4/18/95	3	Washington	502-777-7575	95 Easy Street	3	1	Blues Brothers	$2.00
4	4/18/95	3	Washington	502-777-7575	95 Easy Street	8	1	Hopscotch	$1.50
4	4/18/95	3	Washington	502-777-7575	95 Easy Street	13	1	Surf Nazis Must Die	$2.50
4	4/18/95	3	Washington	502-777-7575	95 Easy Street	17	1	Witches of Eastwick	$2.00

FIGURE 3.11 Problems with repeating data. Storing repeating data with the main form results in duplicating the base data for every entry in the repeated section. In this case customer data must be entered for every video that is rented—even those rented at the same time.

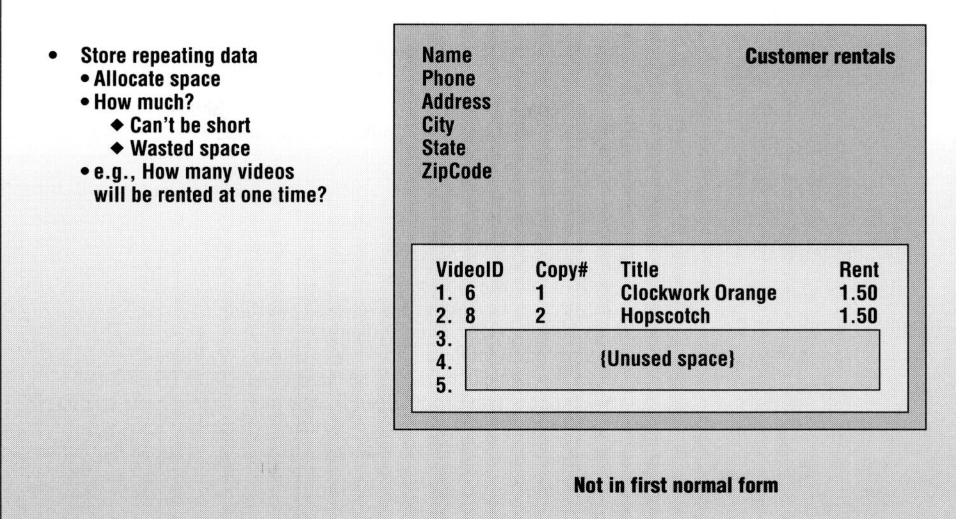

FIGURE 3.12 Allocation problems with repeating data. Storing repeating data in a hierarchical format generally forces designers to allocate a fixed amount of space for each repeating entry. There is no good way to determine how much space will be needed, so the database tends to have considerable unused space.

shows what happens when we try to store the data from the form exactly the way it is written now. The first problem with this raw format is that it contains duplicate data. For example, every time a customer rents a video, the clerk would have to reenter the address, phone, and so on because the repeating data is in the same table as the base data. Therefore every video that is rented requires a copy of all the base data. Computers may be fast and have lots of memory, but it is pointless to list the customer more than once.

A related problem occurs when someone wants to become a member at the video store. Because they have not rented any videos yet, you cannot store their personal information in the database. Conversely, what if you delete old data, such as all of last year's rentals? As you delete rentals, you also delete customer data. Suddenly, you notice that you deleted half of the customer base. Technically, these problems are known as an **insertion anomaly** and a **deletion anomaly,** that is, when the data is not stored in a proper format, we encounter difficulties as we try to add or delete data. These problems arise because we tried to store all the data in one table.

Another problem with using repeating sections, illustrated in Figure 3.12, resembles the problem that COBOL programmers used to encounter. In older, hierarchical files the database designer had to allocate a certain amount of space for each repeating section. In the video case the programmer would have to allocate space for a fixed number of videos rented on each form. The challenge was to estimate the maximum number of spaces that would be needed. The problem is that if one or two customers might rent many videos (say 10 or more), the program would always allocate 10 spaces for each rental. Yet this space would go unused and be wasted for most transactions. On the other hand, failure to set aside enough spaces might cause problems and upset the best customers. Think about the issue with phone numbers again. If you do not treat them as repeating, how many columns do you need to allocate for various phone numbers, and how can you be sure you have enough? By moving the repeating data to a separate table, each entry takes one row, and you do not have to guess how many rows might be necessary. The database simply allocates a new row as it is needed.

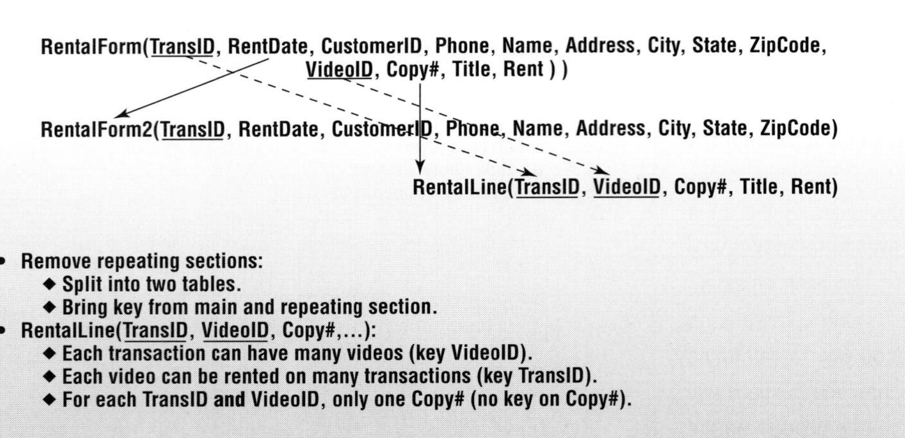

RentalForm(TransID, RentDate, CustomerID, Phone, Name, Address, City, State, ZipCode, VideoID, Copy#, Title, Rent))

RentalForm2(TransID, RentDate, CustomerID, Phone, Name, Address, City, State, ZipCode)

RentalLine(TransID, VideoID, Copy#, Title, Rent)

- Remove repeating sections:
  - Split into two tables.
  - Bring key from main and repeating section.
- RentalLine(TransID, VideoID, Copy#,...):
  - Each transaction can have many videos (key VideoID).
  - Each video can be rented on many transactions (key TransID).
  - For each TransID and VideoID, only one Copy# (no key on Copy#).

FIGURE 3.13 First normal form. All repeating groups must be split into new tables. Be sure that the new table includes a copy of the key from the original table. The table holding the repeating group must have a concatenated key so that the data can be recombined in queries.

FIRST NORMAL FORM

The answer to the problem with repeating sections is to put them into a separate table. When a table has no repeating groups, it is said to be in **first normal form (1NF).** That is, for each cell in a table (one row and one column), there can be only one value. This value should be *atomic* in the sense that it cannot be decomposed into smaller pieces.

Repeating Groups

As shown in some of the prior examples, some **repeating groups** are obvious. Others are more subtle, and deciding whether to split them into a separate table is more difficult. The first normalization rule is clear: If a group of items repeats, it should be split into a new table. The problem is that items that repeat in one case might not be an issue in another situation. Consider the phone number example. In many cases, you can easily include one or two columns for a phone number within a customer table (treated as nonrepeating). In a different situation with a huge number of customers and the potential to store a widely varying set of phone numbers, the best solution is to split the phone numbers into a new table.

Return to the video example, as shown in Figure 3.13, and notice the repeating section that is highlighted by the parentheses. To split this form, first separate everything that is not in the repeating group. These columns might need other changes later, but the section contains no repeating groups. Second, put all the columns from the repeating video rentals section into a new table. However, be careful. When you pull out a repeating section, you must bring down the key from the original table. The RentalForm table has TransID as a primary key. This key, along with the VideoID key, must become part of the new table RentalLine. We need the TransID key so that the data from the two tables can be recombined later. Note that the new table (RentalLine) will always have a composite key—signifying the many-to-many relationship between rentals and videos.

Splitting off the repeating groups solves several basic problems. First, it reduces the duplication: we no longer have to enter customer data for every video that is rented. In addition, we do not have to worry about allocating storage space: Each video rented will be allocated to a new row. By storing rental data for all customers in one table, we avoid the problem of allocating space for each customer.

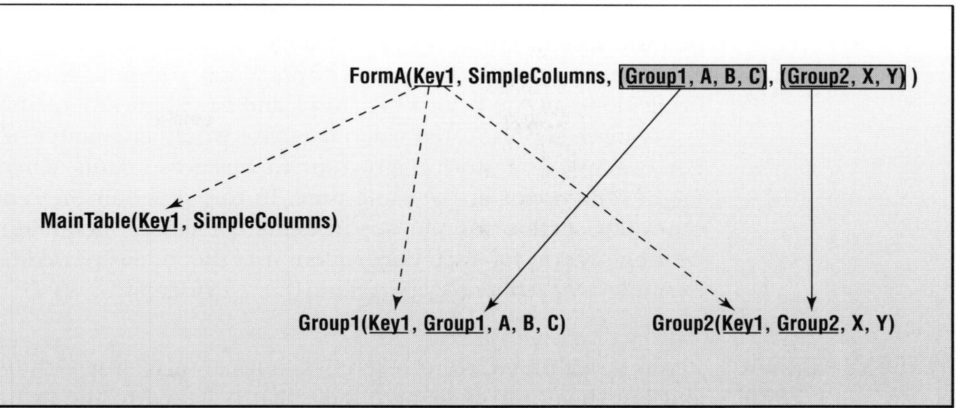

FIGURE 3.14 Independent groups. In this example two groups are repeating independently of each other. They are split separately into new tables. Remember to include the original key (Key1) in every new table.

Many forms will have several different groups that repeat. As shown in Figure 3.14, if they repeat independently of each other, the split is straightforward; each group becomes a new table. Just be careful to include the original key in every new table so the tables can be linked together later. Using the base notation, groups are independent if the parentheses do not overlap. For example, a more complex video store case would have the repeating group for the videos rented, and it might have a separate section that lists the family members related to a particular customer. The list of family members would be stored independently from the list of videos rented.

Nested Repeating Groups

More complicated situations arise when several different repeating groups occur within a table—particularly when one repeating group is nested inside another group. The greatest difficulty lies in identifying the nested nature of the groups. As illustrated in Figure 3.15, after you identify the relationships, splitting the tables is straightforward. Just go one step at a time, pulling the outermost groups first. Always

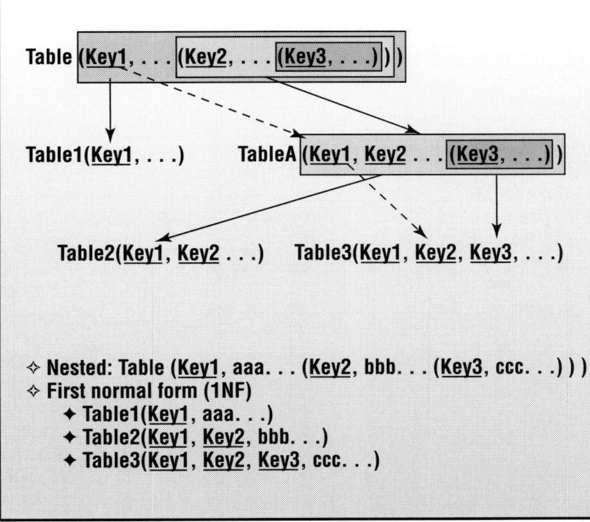

FIGURE 3.15 Nested repeating groups. Groups are nested when they repeat within another group (Key3 inside Key2 inside K1). Split them in steps: pull all of Group2 from Group1, then pull Group3 from Group2. Note that every table will contain the original key (Key1). With three levels, the final table (Table3) must contain three columns in the key.

remember to bring along the prior key each time you split the tables. So when you pull the second group (Key2. . . (Key3. . .)) from the first group (Key1. . .), the new TableA must include Key1 and Key2. When you pull Table3 from TableA, you must bring along all the prior keys (Key1 and Key2) and then add the third key (Key3).

A more sophisticated video database would encounter nested repeating groups. For example, the store might rent to business clients where several departments might rent videos at the same time. In this situation the rental form would have a repeating section for the departments (or family members). A second, nested repeating section for each department lists the videos rented by that department. For example, Department(<u>DepartmentID</u>, . . . (<u>VideoID</u>, . . .)).

SECOND NORMAL FORM

It was straightforward to reach first normal form: just identify the repeating groups and put them into their own table that is linked to the main table through the initial key. The next step is a little more complicated because you have to look at relationships between the key value and the other (non-key) columns in the table. Correct specification of the keys is crucial. At this point it would be wise to double-check all the keys to make sure they are unique and that they correctly identify many-to-many relationships.

Problems with First Normal Form

You can guess by the names of the tables in Figure 3.13 that first normal form might still have problems storing data efficiently. Consider the situation in Figure 3.16 that illustrates the current Video Rental table. Every time someone rents video 6, the database stores the title *Clockwork Orange*. The problem is that the movie title depends on only part of the key (VideoID). If we know the VideoID, we always know the corresponding title. The movie title does not change with every transaction. There is an additional problem, then, besides the waste of space: if a video has not yet been rented, what is its title? Because movies are only entered into the database with a transaction, this data will not be stored in the database. Similarly, if all the rows for video 8 are deleted, we will lose all the associated information about that movie.

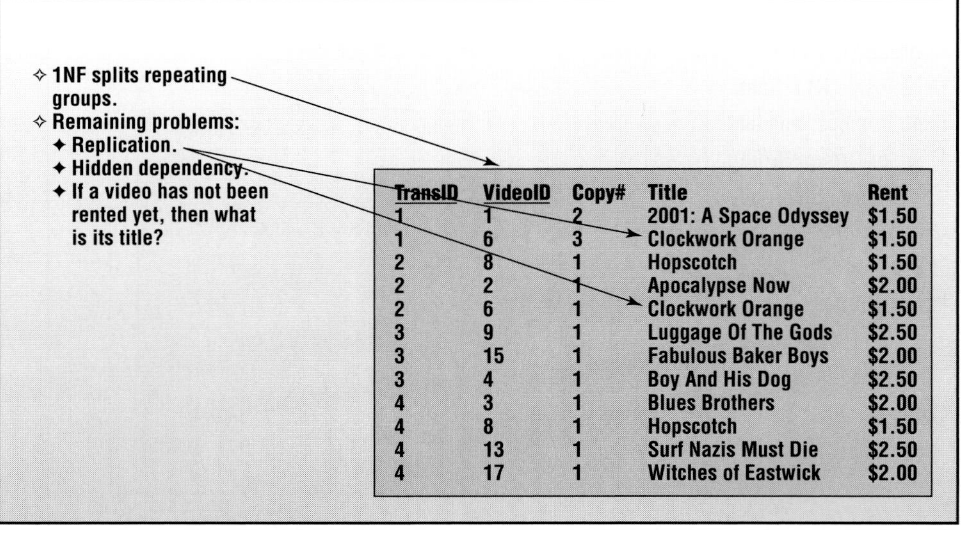

TransID	VideoID	Copy#	Title	Rent
1	1	2	2001: A Space Odyssey	$1.50
1	6	3	Clockwork Orange	$1.50
2	8	1	Hopscotch	$1.50
2	2	1	Apocalypse Now	$2.00
2	6	1	Clockwork Orange	$1.50
3	9	1	Luggage Of The Gods	$2.50
3	15	1	Fabulous Baker Boys	$2.00
3	4	1	Boy And His Dog	$2.50
4	3	1	Blues Brothers	$2.00
4	8	1	Hopscotch	$1.50
4	13	1	Surf Nazis Must Die	$2.50
4	17	1	Witches of Eastwick	$2.00

FIGURE 3.16
Problems with first normal form. There are no repeating groups, but the Video Rental table still contains duplicated data. Every time a video is rented, we have to reenter its title. Also, if a video has not yet been rented, what is its title? The problem is that the title depends only on the VideoID, not on the TransID.

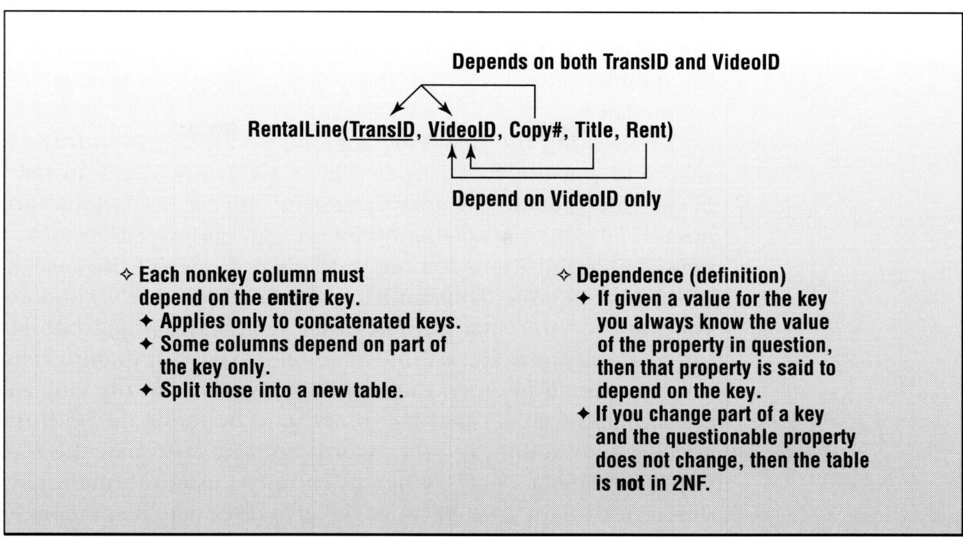

Depends on both TransID and VideoID
RentalLine(TransID, VideoID, Copy#, Title, Rent)
Depend on VideoID only
Each nonkey column must depend on the entire key.
Applies only to concatenated keys.
Some columns depend on part of the key only.
Split those into a new table.
Dependence (definition)
If given a value for the key you always know the value of the property in question, then that property is said to depend on the key.
If you change part of a key and the questionable property does not change, then the table is not in 2NF.

FIGURE 3.17 Second normal form definition. Each non-key column must depend on the entire key. It is only an issue with concatenated keys. The solution is to split off the parts that depend on only part of the key.

Second Normal Form Definition

The problem with the preceding example is that once you know the VideoID, you always know the movie title. A one-to-one relationship exists between the VideoID and the Title (perhaps many-to-one). As shown in Figure 3.17, the important point is that the transaction does not matter. If someone rents video 6 in June, the title is *Clockwork Orange*. If someone rents video 6 in December, the title is still *Clockwork Orange*. We say that the title depends on only part of the key (the VideoID and not the TransID). A table is in **second normal form (2NF)** if every non-key column depends on the entire key (not just part of it). Note that this issue arises only for composite keys (with multiple columns).

The solution is to split the table. Pull out the columns that depend on part of the key. Remember to include that part of the key in the new table. The new tables (VideosRented and Videos) are shown in Figure 3.18. Note that VideoID must be in

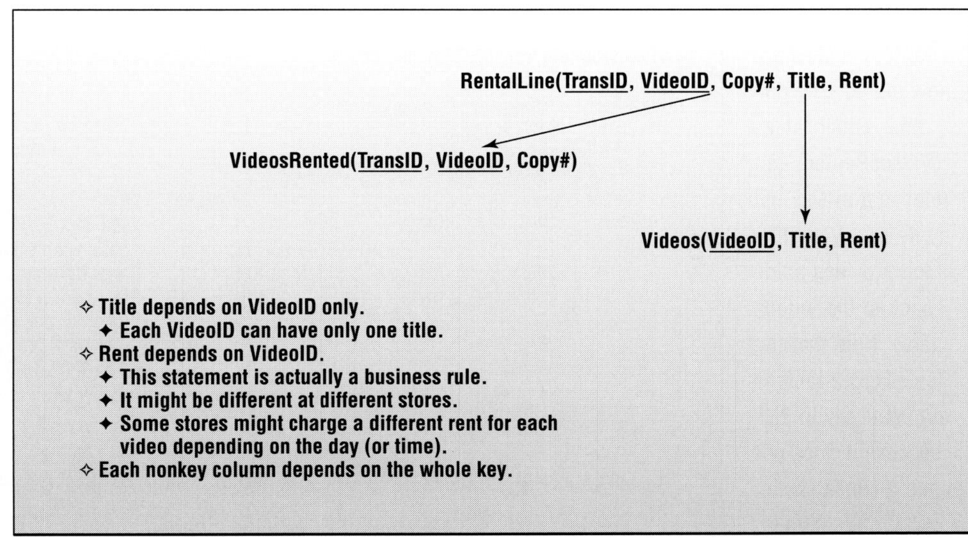

RentalLine(TransID, VideoID, Copy#, Title, Rent)
VideosRented(TransID, VideoID, Copy#)
Videos(VideoID, Title, Rent)
Title depends on VideoID only.
Each VideoID can have only one title.
Rent depends on VideoID.
This statement is actually a business rule.
It might be different at different stores.
Some stores might charge a different rent for each video depending on the day (or time).
Each nonkey column depends on the whole key.

FIGURE 3.18 Creating second normal form. Split the original table so that the items that depend on only part of the key are moved to a separate table. Note that both tables must contain the VideoID key.

both tables. It stays in the VideosRented table to indicate which movies have been rented by each person. It is the primary key in the Videos table because it is the unique identifier. Including the column in both tables enables us to link the data together later.

In creating the new Videos table, we are faced with the interesting question of where to put the rental price. There are two choices: in the VideosRented table or in the Videos table. The answer depends on the operations and rules used in the business. From a technical standpoint we can choose either table. However, from a business standpoint there is a big difference. Consider the case where the rental rate is in the Videos table. This model of the firm says that if you know the VideoID, you always know the rental rate. In other words, the rental rate is fixed for each movie. For example, new release movies might have a premium rental rate. Now consider the interpretation when the rental rate is stored in the VideosRented table. Here you are explicitly saying that the rental rate depends on both the VideoID and on the specific transaction. In other words, for one customer the rental rate for *Clockwork Orange* might be $2.00, whereas another customer might pay only $1.50. The price difference might arise because we give discounts if someone rents several movies or because the store charges different prices on different days. Most business database designers quickly encounter the problem of where to store prices. One solution is to store prices in both tables. That is, the price in the Videos (product) table would be the list price. The price in the VideosRented table would be the actual rental price paid that incorporates various discounts. The key point is that the final list of tables depends not just on these mechanical rules but is also determined by the operations of the business. The assumptions you make about how a particular business operates determine the tables you get. For now, we will stick with the simpler assumption that assigns a fixed rate to each video.

Figure 3.19 gives sample data for the new tables. Notice that 2NF resolves the problem of repeating the movie title each time it is rented. The base movie data is stored one time in the Videos table. It is referenced in the VideosRented table by the VideoID. Looking through the VideosRented table, we can easily get the corresponding title by finding the matching ID in the Videos table. Chapter 4 explains how the database query system handles this link automatically.

FIGURE 3.19
Second normal form data. Movie titles are now stored only one time. Other tables (VideosRented) can refer to a movie just by its key (VideoID), which provides a link back to the Videos table. Note that the RentalForm2 table is automatically in 2NF because it does not contain a concatenated key.

VideosRented(TransID, VideoID, Copy#)

TransID	VideoID	Copy#
1	1	2
1	6	3
2	2	1
2	6	1
2	8	1
3	4	1
3	9	1
3	15	1
4	3	1
4	8	1
4	13	1
4	17	1

Videos(VideoID, Title, Rent)

VideoID	Title	Rent
1	2001: A Space Odyssey	$1.50
2	Apocalypse Now	$2.00
3	Blues Brothers	$2.00
4	Boy And His Dog	$2.50
5	Brother From Another Planet	$2.00
6	Clockwork Orange	$1.50
7	Gods Must Be Crazy	$2.00
8	Hopscotch	$1.50

(Unchanged)

RentalForm2(TransID, RentDate, CustomerID, Phone, Name, Address, City, State, ZipCode)

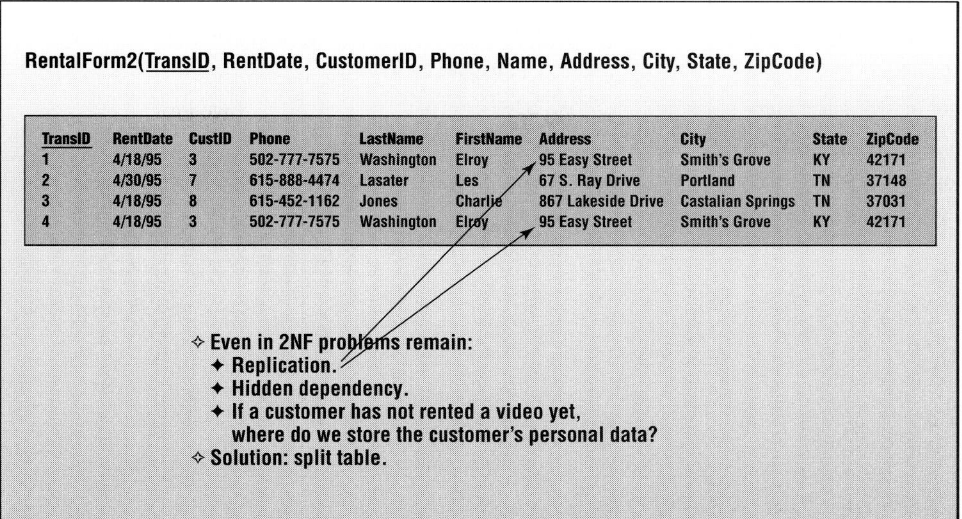

TransID	RentDate	CustID	Phone	LastName	FirstName	Address	City	State	ZipCode
1	4/18/95	3	502-777-7575	Washington	Elroy	95 Easy Street	Smith's Grove	KY	42171
2	4/30/95	7	615-888-4474	Lasater	Les	67 S. Ray Drive	Portland	TN	37148
3	4/18/95	8	615-452-1162	Jones	Charlie	867 Lakeside Drive	Castalian Springs	TN	37031
4	4/18/95	3	502-777-7575	Washington	Elroy	95 Easy Street	Smith's Grove	KY	42171

FIGURE 3.20 Problems with second normal form. The hidden dependency in the customer data leads to duplicating the customer address each time a customer rents videos from the store. Similarly, if old transaction rows are deleted, the firm might lose all of the data for some customers.

Dependence

The discussion of 2NF (and 3NF) uses the term *depends.* We say that attribute Y depends on X if and only if each value of X determines exactly one value of Y. In the video case, if you know the VideoID (6), there is only one corresponding movie title *Clockwork Orange.* Similarly, if you are given a CustomerID (3), there is only one LastName (Washington).

The issue arose in 2NF by noting that if the TransID was changed, the movie title remained the same. Hence we concluded that movie title did not depend on the TransID. This dependence (or lack of it) presents the greatest difficulty to most students. Once you know the relationships in the data, normalization is mechanical. The problem lies in determining those relationships in real life. **Dependence** is an issue of business assumptions and operations. When you write down the final list of normalized tables (3NF or beyond), you have explicitly stated those business relationships.

In practice, you can generally ask clients to clarify relationships between attributes. However, avoid using terms like *one-to-one* and *dependence.* Instead, ask questions like these: Can more than one entry occur for each item? or Can different customers be charged different prices? However, as a database designer, you will find that you rarely have time to ask clients all the questions you want to ask. Try to identify common relationships yourself and save the difficult questions for the clients. Many business problems have similar rules and assumptions. Experience saves you time, because you will not have to ask users to spell out every rule.

THIRD NORMAL FORM

The logic, analysis, and elements of designing for **third normal form (3NF)** are similar to those used in deriving 2NF. In particular, you still concentrate on the issue of dependence. With experience, most designers combine the derivation of 2NF and 3NF into a single step. Technically, a table in 3NF must also be in 2NF.

Problems with Second Normal Form

At this point, we need to examine the RentalForm2 table that we ignored in the earlier analysis. It is displayed in Figure 3.20. In particular, notice that TransID is the key.

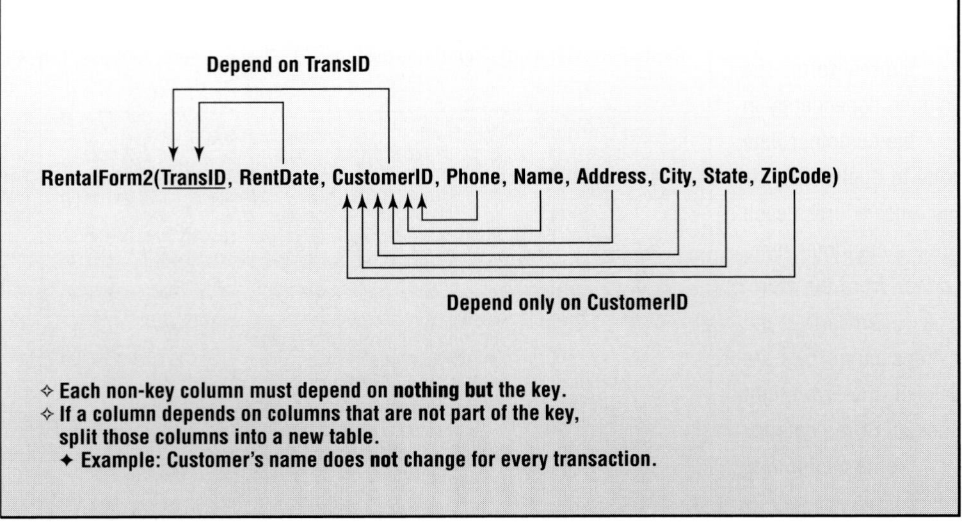

FIGURE 3.21 Third normal form definition. This table is not in 3NF, since some of the columns depend on CustomerID, which is not part of the key.

The problem can be seen in the sample data. Every time a customer rents a video, the database stores his or her name, address, and phone number again. This unnecessary duplication is a waste of space and probably a waste of the clerk's data entry time. Consider what happens when a customer moves. We would have to find the address and change it for every transaction the customer had with us.

If the customer has not yet rented any movies, we do not have a place to store the customer data. Similarly, if we delete old transactions from the database, we risk losing customer data. Once again, we have to deal with a hidden dependency.

Third Normal Form Definition

The problems in the previous section are fairly clear. The customer name, address, phone, and so on depend on the CustomerID. The catch is that CustomerID is not part of the key for the table. In other words, some non-key columns do not depend on the key. So why are they in this table? The question also provides the solution. If columns do not depend on the primary key, they should be placed in a separate table.

To be in 3NF a table must already be in 2NF, and every non-key column must depend on nothing but the key. In the video example in Figure 3.21, the problem is that basic customer data columns depend on the CustomerID, which is not part of the key.

At first glance, two solutions seem possible: (1) make CustomerID part of the key or (2) split the table. If the table is already in 2NF, splitting the table is the only choice that will work. The problem with the first option is that making CustomerID part of the key is equivalent to stating that each transaction can involve many customers. This assumption is not likely to be true. However, even if it is, your table would no longer be in 2NF, since the customer data would then depend on only part of the key (CustomerID and not TransID). Hence the correct solution is to split the table into two parts: the columns that depend on the whole key and the columns that depend on something else (CustomerID).

The solution in the video store example is to pull out the columns that are determined by the CustomerID. Remember to include the CustomerID column in both tables so they can be relinked later. The resulting tables are displayed in Figure 3.22. Notice that CustomerID is not a key in the Rentals table. Tables can be linked by columns even if they are not part of a key. Figure 3.22 also illustrates how splitting the tables resolves the problems from the hidden dependency.

The final collection of tables is presented in Figure 3.23. This list is in 3NF: There are no repeating groups within a table (1NF), and each non-key column depends on the whole key (2NF) and nothing but the key (3NF). The tables are displayed in notational form and in a class diagram format. The class diagram was created within the Microsoft Access database management system and shows how the tables are linked together through the columns they have in common.

The astute reader should raise a question about the address data. That is, City, State, and ZipCode have some type of dependent relationship. Perhaps the Customer table is not really in 3NF? In theory, yes, ZIP codes were created as a means to identify locations. The catch is that at a five-digit level, the relationship is relatively weak. A ZIP code identifies an individual post office. Each city can have many ZIP codes, and a ZIP code can be used for more than one city. At the moment, it is true that a ZIP code always identifies one state. However, can we be certain that this relationship will always hold—even in an international setting? Hence it is generally acceptable to include all three items in the same table. On the other hand, as pointed out in the Pet Store discussion in Chapter 2, there are some advantages to creating a separate City table. The most important advantage is that you can reduce data entry time and errors by selecting a city from a predefined list.

FIGURE 3.22
Third normal form. Putting customer data into a separate table eliminates the hidden dependency and resolves the problems with duplicate data. Note that CustomerID remains in both tables, but it is still not a key in the Rentals table.

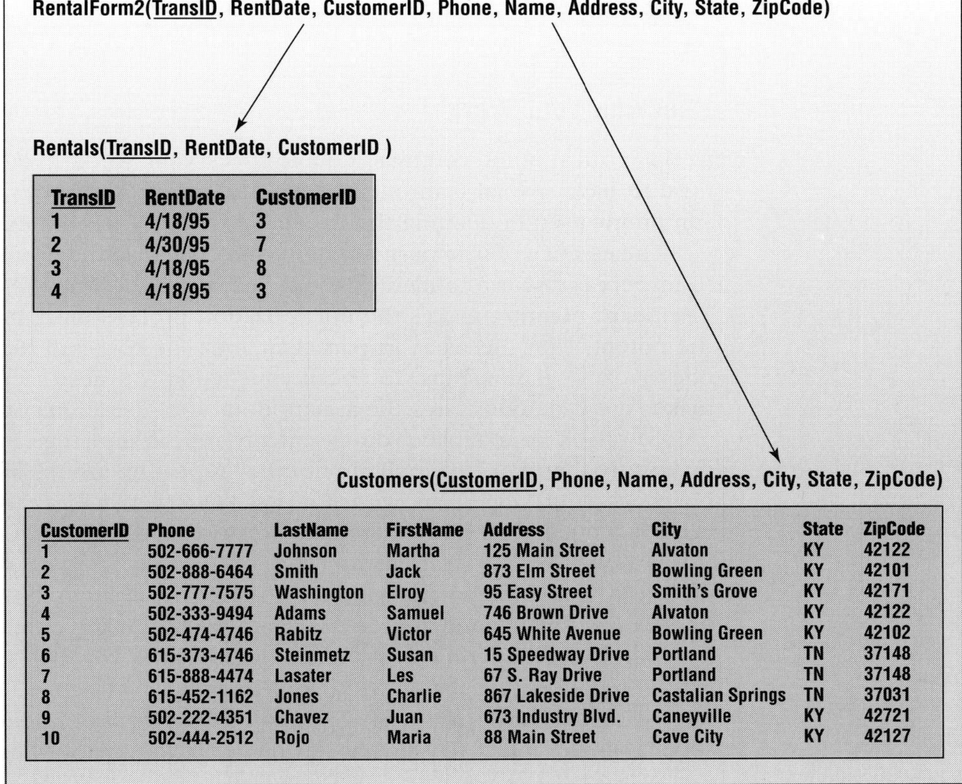

TransID	RentDate	CustomerID
1	4/18/95	3
2	4/30/95	7
3	4/18/95	8
4	4/18/95	3

CustomerID	Phone	LastName	FirstName	Address	City	State	ZipCode
1	502-666-7777	Johnson	Martha	125 Main Street	Alvaton	KY	42122
2	502-888-6464	Smith	Jack	873 Elm Street	Bowling Green	KY	42101
3	502-777-7575	Washington	Elroy	95 Easy Street	Smith's Grove	KY	42171
4	502-333-9494	Adams	Samuel	746 Brown Drive	Alvaton	KY	42122
5	502-474-4746	Rabitz	Victor	645 White Avenue	Bowling Green	KY	42102
6	615-373-4746	Steinmetz	Susan	15 Speedway Drive	Portland	TN	37148
7	615-888-4474	Lasater	Les	67 S. Ray Drive	Portland	TN	37148
8	615-452-1162	Jones	Charlie	867 Lakeside Drive	Castalian Springs	TN	37031
9	502-222-4351	Chavez	Juan	673 Industry Blvd.	Caneyville	KY	42721
10	502-444-2512	Rojo	Maria	88 Main Street	Cave City	KY	42127

FIGURE 3.23
Third normal form tables. There are no repeating groups within a table, and each non-key column depends on the whole key and nothing but the key.

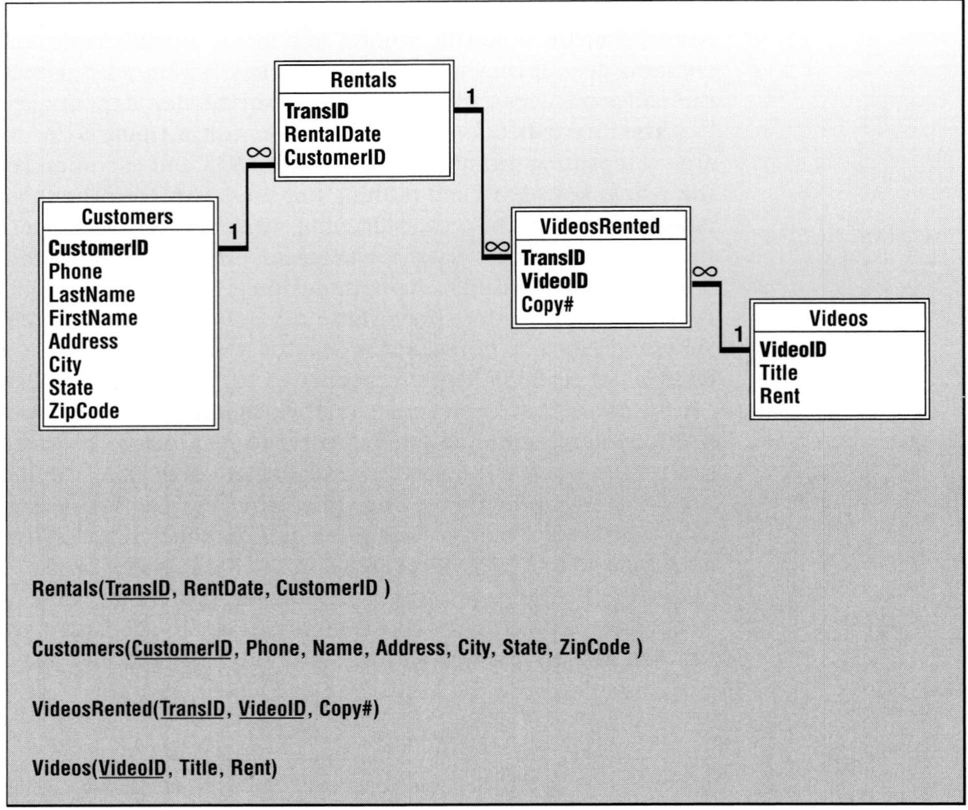

Checking Your Work

At this critical point, you must double-check your work. In large projects it is beneficial to have several team members participate in the review to make sure the assumptions used in defining the data tables match the business operations.

The essence of data normalization is to collect all the forms and reports and then to inspect each form to identify the data that will be stored. Writing the columns in a standard notation makes the normalization process more mechanical, minimizing the potential for mistakes. In particular, look for keys and highlight one-to-one and one-to-many relationships. To check your work, you need to examine each table to make sure it demonstrates the assumptions and operations of the firm.

To check your tables, you essentially repeat the steps in normalization. First, make sure that you have pulled out every repeating group. While you are at it, double-check your keys. Start with the first key column in a table and ask yourself if there is a one-to-one or a one-to-many relationship with each of the other columns. If it is a one-to-many relationship (or many-to-many), you need to underline the column title. If it is one-to-one (or many-to-one), the column in question should not be underlined. The second step is to look at each non-key column and ask yourself if it depends on the whole key and nothing but the key. Third, verify that the tables can be reconnected. Try drawing lines between each table. Tables that do not connect with the others are probably wrong. Fourth, ask yourself if each table represents a single object. Try giving it a name. If you cannot find a good single name for the table, it probably represents more than one object and needs to be split. Finally, enter sample data for each table and make sure that you are not entering duplicate rows. Some underlying problems may become obvious when you begin to enter data. It is best to enter test data during the design stage, instead of waiting until the final implementation.

BEYOND THIRD NORMAL FORM

In designing relational database theory, E. F. Codd first proposed the three normalization rules. On examining real-world situations, he and other writers realized that additional problems could occur in some situations. In particular, Codd's initial formal definition of 3NF was probably too narrow. Hence he and Boyce defined a new version, which is called **Boyce-Codd normal form (BCNF).**

Other writers eventually identified additional problems that could arise and created further "normal forms." Fortunately, these situations do not arise often in practice. If you are careful in designing your database—particularly in creating keys—you should not have too many problems with these issues. However, occasionally problems arise, so a good database designer will check for the problems described in the following sections. In particular, in large projects with many designers, one member of the team should check the final list of tables.

Boyce-Codd Normal Form

We have already seen how problems can arise when hidden dependencies occur within a table. A secondary relationship between columns within a table can cause problems with duplication and lost data. Consider the example in Figure 3.24, which contains data about employees. From the business rules, it is clear that the table is in 3NF. The keys are correct, and from rule (*c*) we know that the non-key column (Manager) depends on the entire key. That is, each employee can have a different manager for each specialty. The problem arises because of business rule (*d*): Each manager has only one specialty. The manager determines the specialty, but since Manager can never be a key for the entire table, we have a **hidden dependency**

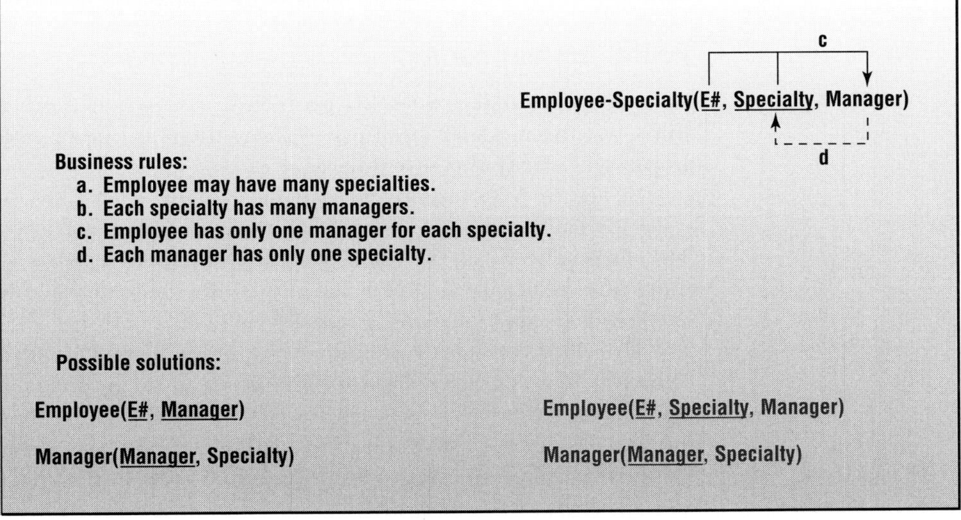

c
Employee-Specialty(E#, Specialty, Manager)
d
Business rules:
a. Employee may have many specialties.
b. Each specialty has many managers.
c. Employee has only one manager for each specialty.
d. Each manager has only one specialty.
Possible solutions:
Employee(E#, Manager)
Manager(Manager, Specialty)
Employee(E#, Specialty, Manager)
Manager(Manager, Specialty)

FIGURE 3.24 Boyce-Codd normal form. There is a hidden dependency (*d*) between manager and specialty. If we delete rows from the original table, we risk losing data about our managers. The solution is to add a table to make the dependency explicit. For flexibility, it might be wise to leave the original table—just in case the assumptions change.

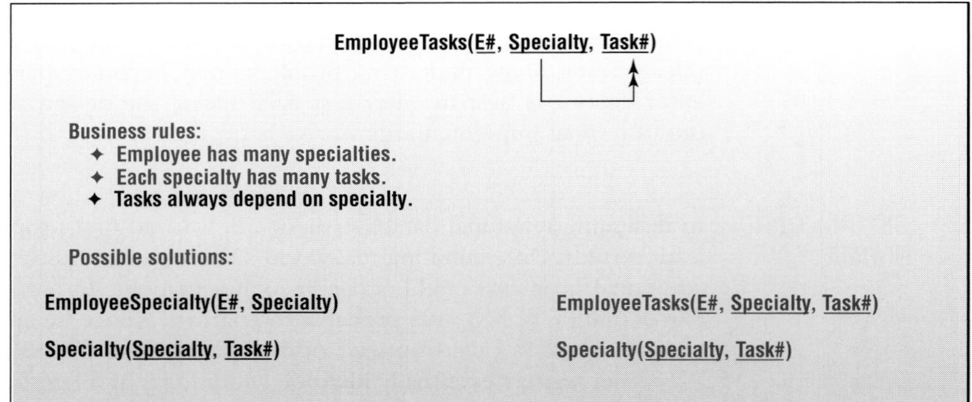

FIGURE 3.25 Fourth normal form. The original table is 3NF because there are no non-key columns. The keys are legitimate, but there is a hidden (multivalued) dependency in the third rule. The solution is to add the Specialty table to make the dependency explicit. If every employee performs every task within a specialty, we could then drop the Task# from the original table. However, for flexibility, it might be wise to leave it in and simply add the new table.

(Manager → Specialty) in the table. What if we delete old data rows and delete all references to one manager? Then we lose the data that revealed that manager's specialty. BCNF prevents this problem by stating that any dependency must be explicitly shown in the keys.

The solution is to add a table to make the dependency explicit. Because each specialty can have many managers, the best solution is to add the table Manager(Manager, Specialty). Note that technically, we can now remove the Specialty column from the original table (and key Manager). Because a manager can have only one specialty, as soon as we know the manager, we can use a link to obtain the specialty. However, the database is more flexible if we retain the three columns in the original table, even though it results in some duplication of data. The reason is that it takes some unusual assumptions to cause this particular problem. If these assumptions change, we would have to change the tables. In the example it is not very realistic to believe the firm will always have managers with only one specialty. It is better to leave the original table and add the new Manager table. Then if the assumptions change, we simply need to make Specialty a key in the Manager table. The main point is that we have explicitly recorded the hidden relationship—so we no longer need to worry about losing important relationships when we delete rows.

Fourth Normal Form

Fourth normal form (4NF) problems arise when there are two binary relationships, but the modeler attempts to show them as one combined relationship. An example will clarify the situation.

In Figure 3.25 employees can have many specialties, and they perform many tasks for each specialty. Because all three columns are keyed, the table must be in 3NF. From the business rules, we can see that the keys are legitimate. However, there are really two binary relationships instead of one ternary relationship: Employee → Specialty and Specialty → Task.

The third business rule indicates a hidden dependency in that tasks are predefined for each specialty. The problem is that if no employee is assigned to some specialty, then we have no task list for that specialty. Again, the solution is to make the hidden dependency explicit by creating a new table: Specialty(Specialty, Task#). Hence it would be better to split the initial table into two tables: EmployeeSpecialty and Specialty.

The catch with 4NF is that it generally requires very artificial assumptions to create the situation. These assumptions rarely hold in a business environment. Even if they are true today, they might not be true tomorrow. In this example, if every employee performs every task within a specialty, then Task# could be removed from the original EmployeeTasks table. However, for the sake of flexibility it would usually be better to leave the original table alone and simply add the new Specialty table. The question is, Will every employee always perform exactly those tasks within the described specialty? It is more realistic to believe this assumption will eventually be relaxed. That case would require two tables: one table to show which tasks are defined by each specialty and one to show which tasks are actually performed by a given employee. Just make sure that there are no hidden dependencies—even in the key columns.

Domain-Key Normal Form

In 1981 Fagin described a different approach to normalized tables when he proposed the **domain-key normal form (DKNF).** DKNF describes the ultimate goal in designing a database. If a table is in DKNF, Fagin proved that it must also be in 4NF, 3NF, and all of the other normal forms. The catch is that there is no defined method to get a table into DKNF. In fact, it is possible that some tables can never be converted to DKNF.

Despite these difficulties, DKNF is important for application developers because it is a goal to work toward when designing applications. Think of it as driving to the mall when you do not have exact directions. You can still get there as long as you know how to start (1NF, 2NF, and 3NF are well defined) and can recognize the mall when you arrive (DKNF).

The goal of DKNF is to have each table represent one topic, and for all business rules to be expressed in terms of domain constraints and key relationships. That is, all business rules are explicitly described by the table rules. Domain constraints are straightforward—they represent limitations placed on the data held in a column. For example, prices cannot be negative.

All other business rules must be expressed in terms of relationships with keys. In particular, there can be no hidden relationships. Consider the example in Figure 3.26, which shows a table for students and advisors. It could be in DKNF—we do not know until we examine the business rules. A typical university rule might be that a student can have multiple advisors, but only one for each major. Additionally, faculty members can only be advisors for students majoring in the instructor's discipline. With these two rules the two tables are clearly not in DKNF. First, the primary key SID would not be unique. Second, there must be an explicit rule concerning the major and discipline. Figure 3.27 shows that the three tables are in DKNF. Notice that all of the business rules are now explicitly stated—in terms of the primary key and foreign key relationships.

FIGURE 3.26
DKNF example. The tables are not in DKNF. Because a student can have more than one major, SID would not be a unique primary key. Also, Advisor is related to Major, which is a hidden relationship.

Student(<u>SID</u>, Name, Major, Advisor)
Advisor(<u>FID</u>, Name, Office, Discipline)

Business rules: *A student can have many advisors, but only one for each major*
Faculty members can be advisors only for their discipline.

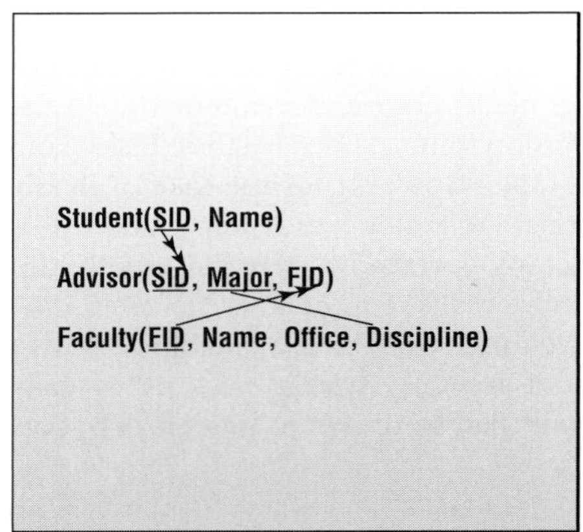

FIGURE 3.27 DKNF solution. Splitting the tables makes the primary keys unique. The previously hidden relationship between Major and Discipline is made explicit through a foreign key constraint.

To define a set of tables in DKNF, you can start by working through the 3NF rules. Then be sure that you have a complete list of the business rules. Next make sure that the business rules are all expressed in terms of domain constraints and key relationships. Check the primary keys to be sure they are unique—and that you have captured all of the many-to-many relationships. Be sure there are no hidden rules or dependencies. Set foreign key relationships to enforce existence rules and to match data in other tables.

DKNF returns to where we started in Chapter 2. Our goal in designing the database was to build a model of the organization. DKNF clarifies this goal by stating that the best database design is one that explicitly states all business rules as database rules.

In theory, there can be no normal forms beyond DKNF. That is a nice theory, but since there is no well-defined way to put a set of tables in DKNF, it is not always helpful. Several authors have identified other potential problems and devised additional versions of "normal forms," such as fifth normal form. For the most part these definitions are not very useful in practice; they will not be described here. You can consult Date's textbooks for details and examples of more theoretical concepts.

DATA RULES AND INTEGRITY

As you talk to users and managers to design reports and tables, you also need to think about what business rules need to be enforced. One of the goals of database designers is to ensure that the data remains accurate. In many cases there are straightforward business rules. For example, you typically want to make sure that price is greater than zero. Similarly, you may have a constraint that salaries should not exceed some number like $100,000 or that the date hired has to be greater than the date the company was founded. These **data integrity** constraints are easy to assign in most databases. Typically, you can go to the table definitions and add the simple constraints along with a message. The advantage of storing these constraints with the tables is that the DBMS enforces the conditions for every operation on the table, regardless of the source or method of data entry. No programming is necessary, and the constraint is stored in one location. If you need to change the condition, it is readily accessible (to authorized users).

A second type of constraint is to choose data from a set of predefined options. For example, gender may be listed as male, female, or unavailable. Providing a list helps clerks enter data, and it forces them to enter only the choices provided. For example, you do not have to worry whether someone might enter *f*, *F*, or *fem*. The data is more consistent.

A third type of data integrity is a bit more complicated but crucial in a relational database. The tables are nicely organized with properties that ensure efficient storage of the data. Yet we need to be able to reconnect the data in the tables to get the reports and forms the users need. Consider the video example when a clerk enters a customer number in the Rentals table. What happens if the clerk enters a customer number that does not exist in the Customer table? If the videotapes were not returned, we would have no way of finding the customer. Hence we need a constraint to ensure that when a customer number is entered into the Rentals table, that number must already exist in the Customer table. Technically, the CustomerID in the Rentals table is called a **foreign key,** which is a primary key in a different table (Customer). The constraint we need is known as referential integrity. **Referential integrity** exists when a value for a foreign key can be entered only if the corresponding value already exists in the originating table.

The way referential integrity is handled depends on the DBMS. Some have no provisions for it, some handle it internally, and others require the use of triggers or stored procedures. When data is entered into one table, a trigger executes a few lines of code to see whether the value exists in a second table. If not, the DBMS prevents the value from being entered and displays an error message.

As shown in Figure 3.28, Microsoft Access uses a more automatic procedure. You can define relationships between tables and specify that the DBMS maintain referential integrity automatically. These relationships are built and displayed using a version of a class diagram where the connecting line indicates the referential integrity constraint. Access also supports **cascading delete,** which uses the same concepts. If a user deletes a row in the Customer table, you also need to delete the related entries in the Rentals table. Then you need to delete the corresponding rows in the VideosRented table. If you build the relationships and specify cascade on delete, Access will automatically delete the related rows when a user deletes an entry in the Customer table. In other databases triggers and stored procedures are written to perform the same tasks. These actions maintain the consistency of the database by ensuring that links between the tables always refer to legitimate rows.

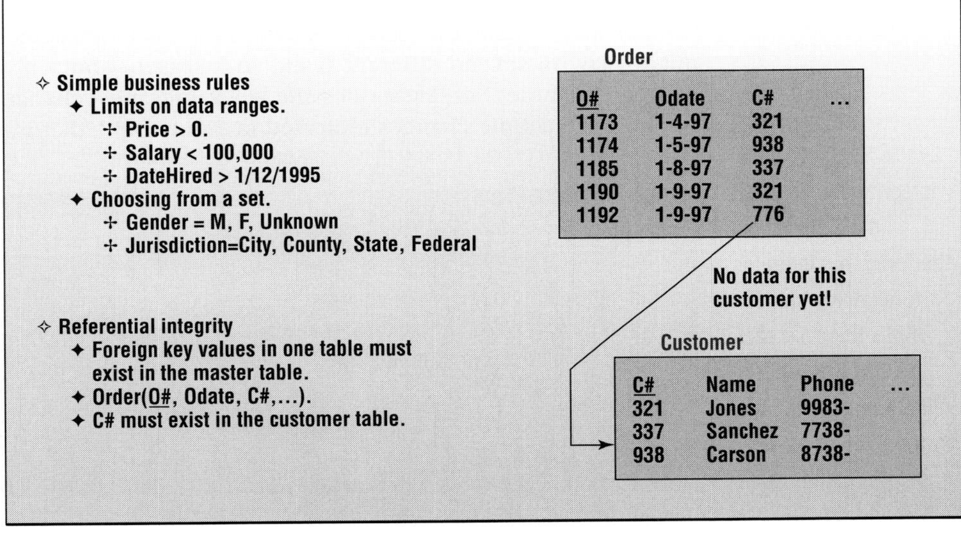

FIGURE 3.28
Data integrity. Integrity can be maintained by simple rules. Relational databases rely on referential integrity constraints to ensure that customer data exists before the customer number can be entered in the Order table.

Oracle supports referential integrity by declaring a foreign key when you create the VideosRented table. Figure 3.29 shows the command that could be used to create an Order table with three columns. The company wants to make sure that all orders are sent to legitimate customers, so the customer number (C#) in the Order table must exist in the Customer table. The foreign key constraint enforces this relationship. The constraint also specifies that the relationship should handle cascading deletes. Oracle uses the standard SQL language to create tables.

When you start to enter data into a DBMS, you will quickly see the role played by referential integrity. Consider two tables: Order(<u>OrderID</u>, Odate, CustomerID) and Customer(<u>CustomerID</u>, Name,Address, etc.). You have a referential integrity constraint that links the CustomerID column in the Order table to the CustomerID column in the Customer table. Now say you enter sample data in the two tables, but you begin with the Order table. The DBMS will not accept any data—because the corresponding CustomerID must already exist in the Customer table. That is, the referential integrity rules force you to enter data in a certain order. Clearly, these rules would present problems to users, so you cannot expect users to enter data directly into tables. Chapters 6, 7, and 8 explain how forms and applications will automatically ensure that the user enters data in the proper sequence.

THE EFFECTS OF BUSINESS RULES

It is important to understand how different business rules affect the database design and the normalization process. As a database designer, you must identify the basic rules and build the database to match them. However, be careful, because business rules can change. If you think a current business rule is too restrictive, you should design the database with a more flexible structure.

Consider the example shown in Figure 3.30. The local parks and recreation department runs a soccer league and collects basic statistics at the end of every match. You need to design the data tables for this problem.

To illustrate the effect of different rules, consider the two main rules and the resulting tables displayed in Figure 3.31. The first rule states that there can only be one referee per match. Hence the RefID can be placed in the Match table. Note that it is not part of the primary key. The second rule states that a player can play on only one team; therefore, the appropriate TeamID can be placed in the Player table.

Now consider what happens if these two rules are relaxed as shown in Figure 3.32. The department manager believes that some day there might be several referees per match. Also, the issue of substitute players presents a problem. A substitute might play on several different teams in a season—but only for one team during a match. To handle these new rules, the key values must change. You might be tempted to make the simple changes indicated in Figure 3.32; that is, make RefID part of the

FIGURE 3.29 Oracle/SQL referential integrity definition. In the Order table, declaring a column as a foreign key tells the DBMS to check each value in this table to find a matching value in the referenced (e.g., Customer) table.

```
CREATE TABLE ORDER
(O#     NUMBER(5) NOT NULL,
Odate   DATE,
C#      NUMBER(5)
        CONSTRAINT fk_Customer
          FOREIGN KEY (C#)
          REFERENCES Customer (C#)
          ON DELETE CASCADE
)
```

FIGURE 3.30
Database design for a soccer league. The design and normalized tables depend on the business rules.

<table>
<tr><td colspan="5">Location
Date Played</td><td colspan="5">Referee Name
Phone Number, Address</td></tr>
<tr><td colspan="2">Team 1
Name
Sponsor</td><td colspan="3">Score</td><td colspan="2">Team 2
Name
Sponsor</td><td colspan="3">Score</td></tr>
<tr><td>Player Name</td><td>Phone</td><td>Age</td><td>Points</td><td>Penalties</td><td>Player Name</td><td>Phone</td><td>Age</td><td>Points</td><td>Penalties</td></tr>
<tr><td></td><td></td><td></td><td></td><td></td><td></td><td></td><td></td><td></td><td></td></tr>
<tr><td></td><td></td><td></td><td></td><td></td><td></td><td></td><td></td><td></td><td></td></tr>
<tr><td></td><td></td><td></td><td></td><td></td><td></td><td></td><td></td><td></td><td></td></tr>
<tr><td></td><td></td><td></td><td></td><td></td><td></td><td></td><td></td><td></td><td></td></tr>
<tr><td></td><td></td><td></td><td></td><td></td><td></td><td></td><td></td><td></td><td></td></tr>
<tr><td></td><td></td><td></td><td></td><td></td><td></td><td></td><td></td><td></td><td></td></tr>
<tr><td></td><td></td><td></td><td></td><td></td><td></td><td></td><td></td><td></td><td></td></tr>
</table>

key in the Match table and make TeamID part of the primary key in the Player table. Now each Match can have many Referees, and each Player can play on many teams. The problem with this approach is that the Match and Player tables are no longer in 3NF. For example, DatePlayed does not depend on RefID. Likewise, Name in the Player table does not depend on TeamID. For example, Paul Ruiz does not change his name every time he plays on a different team.

The solution is displayed in Figure 3.33. A new table is added to handle the many-to-many relationship between referees and matches. Similarly, the player's TeamID is moved to the PlayerStats table, but it is not part of the primary key. In this solution each match has many players, and players can participate in many matches. Yet, for each match, each player plays for only one team. This new database design is different from the initial design. More important, it is less restrictive. As a designer, you must look ahead and build the database so that it can handle future needs of the department.

Which of these database designs is correct? The answer depends on the needs of the department. In practice, it would be wiser to choose the more flexible design that can assign several referees to a match and allows players to substitute for dif-

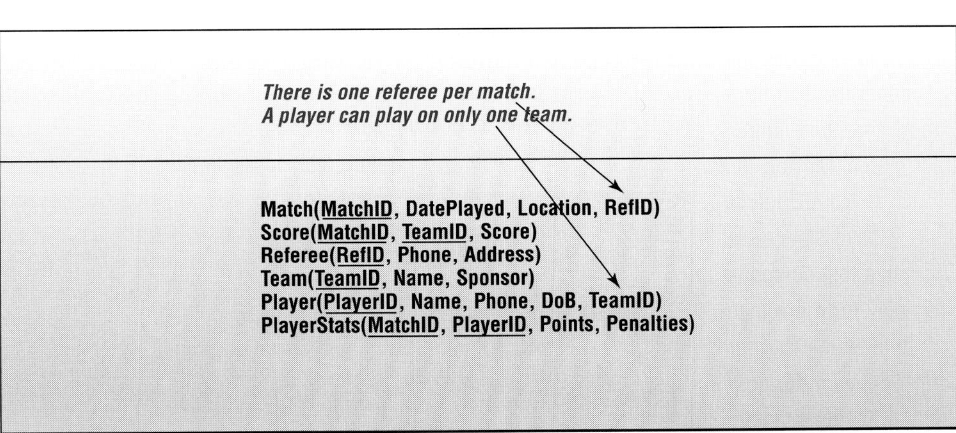
There is one referee per match.
A player can play on only one team.
Match(MatchID, DatePlayed, Location, RefID)
Score(MatchID, TeamID, Score)
Referee(RefID, Phone, Address)
Team(TeamID, Name, Sponsor)
Player(PlayerID, Name, Phone, DoB, TeamID)
PlayerStats(MatchID, PlayerID, Points, Penalties)

FIGURE 3.31
Restrictive rules. With only one referee per match, the referee key is added to the Match table. Similarly, the TeamID column is placed in the Player table.

FIGURE 3.32
Relaxing the rules to allow many-to-many relationships. You might try to make the RefID and TeamID columns part of the primary key, but the resulting tables are not in 3NF. Location does not depend on RefID, and Player Name does not depend on TeamID.

There can be several referees per match. A player can play on several teams (substitute), but on only one team per match.

Match(MatchID, DatePlayed, Location, RefID)
Score(MatchID, TeamID, Score)
Referee(RefID, Phone, Address)
Team(TeamID, Name, Sponsor)
Player(PlayerID, Name, Phone, DoB, TeamID)
PlayerStats(MatchID, PlayerID, Points, Penalties)

ferent teams throughout the season. However, in practice you should make one minor change to this database design. If no matches have been played, how do we know which players are on each team? As it stands, the database cannot answer this question. The solution is to add a BaseTeamID to the Player table. At the start of the season, each team will submit a roster that lists the initial team members. Players can be listed on only one initial team roster. If someone substitutes or changes teams, the data can be recorded in the PlayerStats table.

CONVERTING A CLASS DIAGRAM TO NORMALIZED TABLES

Each normalized table represents a business entity or class. Hence a class diagram can be converted into a list of normalized tables. Likewise, a list of normalized tables can be drawn as a class diagram. Technically, the entities in a class diagram do not have to be in 3NF (or higher). Some designers use a class diagram as an overview, or big picture, of the business, and they leave out some of the normalized details. In this situation you will have to convert the classes into a list of normalized tables. As noted in Chapter 2, some features commonly arise on a class diagram, so you should learn how to handle these basic conversions.

Figure 3.34 illustrates a typical class diagram for a purchase order with four basic types of relationships: (1) a one-to-many relationship between supplier and the purchase order, (2) a many-to-many relationship between the purchase order and the items, (3) a subtype relationship that contains different attributes, and (4) a recursive relationship within the Employee entity to indicate that some employees are managers of others.

One-to-Many Relationships

The most important rule in converting class diagrams to normalized tables is that relationships are handled by placing a common column in each of the related tables. This column is usually a key column in one of the tables. This process is easy to see with one-to-many relationships.

FIGURE 3.33
Relaxing the rules and normalizing the tables. The RefereeMatch table enables the department to have more than one referee per match. Moving the TeamID to the PlayerStats table indicates that someone can play for more than one team—but for only one team during a given match.

Match(MatchID, DatePlayed, Location)
RefereeMatch(MatchID, RefID)
Score(MatchID, TeamID, Score)
Referee(RefID, Phone, Address)
Team(TeamID, Name, Sponsor)
Player(PlayerID, Name, Phone, DoB)
PlayerStats(MatchID, PlayerID, TeamID, Points, Penalties)

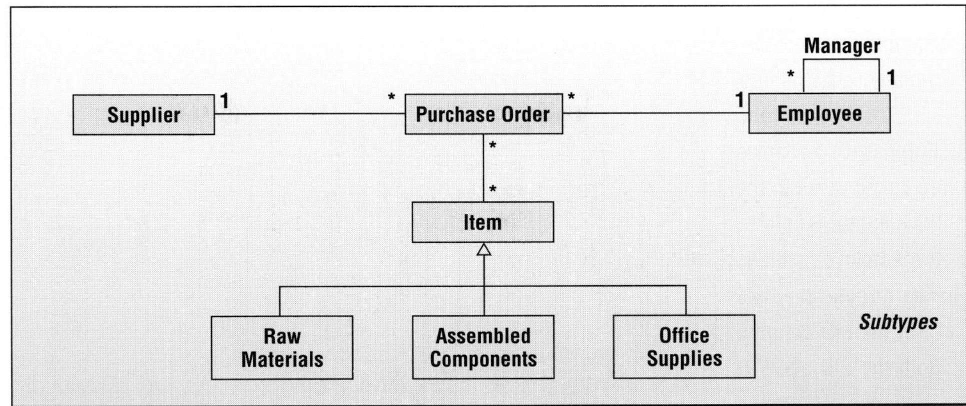

FIGURE 3.34
Converting a class diagram to normalized tables. Note the four types of relationships: (1) one-to-many, (2) many-to-many, (3) subtype, and (4) recursive.

The purchase order example has 2 one-to-many relationships. (1) Many different purchase orders can be sent to each supplier, but only one supplier appears on a purchase order. (2) Each purchase order is created by only one employee, but an employee can create many purchase orders. To create the normalized tables, first create a primary key for each entity (Supplier, Employee, and PurchaseOrder). As shown in Figure 3.35, the normalized tables can be linked by placing the Supplier key (SID) and Employee key (EID) into the PurchaseOrder table. Note carefully that all class diagram associations are expressed as relationships between keys.

Note also that SID and EID are not key columns in the PurchaseOrder table. You can verify which columns should be keyed. Start with the POID column. For each PurchaseOrder (POID), how many suppliers are there? The business rule says only one supplier for a purchase order; therefore, SID should not be keyed, so do not underline SID. Now start with SID and work in the other direction. For each supplier, how many purchase orders are there? The business rule says many purchase orders can be sent to a given supplier, so the PID column needs to be a key. The same process indicates that EID should not be a key; it belongs in the PurchaseOrder table, since each Employee can place many orders. Figure 3.36 uses sample data to show how the tables are linked through the key columns.

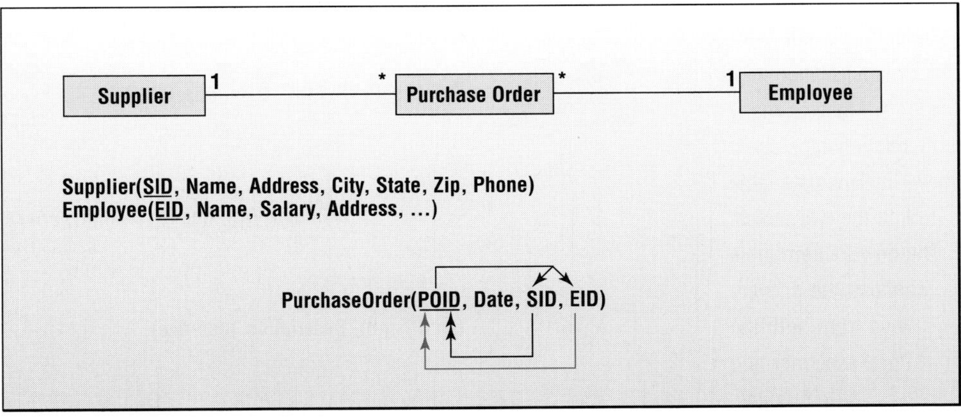

FIGURE 3.35
Converting one-to-many relationships. Add the primary key from the one-side into the many-side table. In the example SID and EID are added to the PurchaseOrder table. Note that they are not primary keys in the PurchaseOrder table.

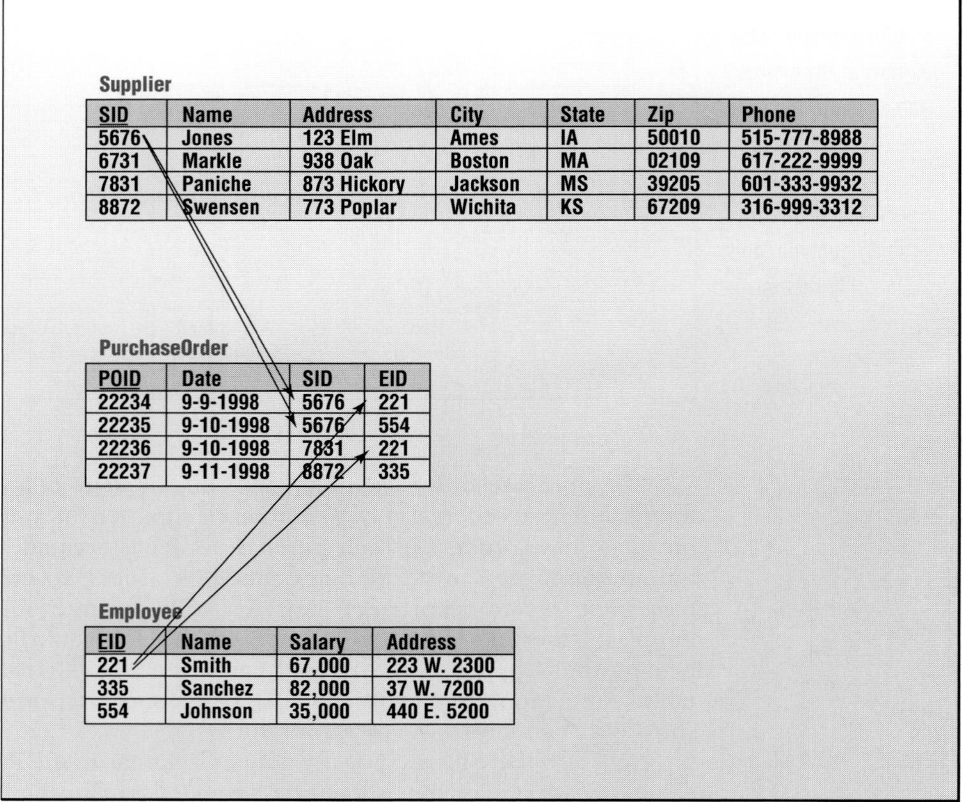

Supplier

SID	Name	Address	City	State	Zip	Phone
5676	Jones	123 Elm	Ames	IA	50010	515-777-8988
6731	Markle	938 Oak	Boston	MA	02109	617-222-9999
7831	Paniche	873 Hickory	Jackson	MS	39205	601-333-9932
8872	Swensen	773 Poplar	Wichita	KS	67209	316-999-3312

PurchaseOrder

POID	Date	SID	EID
22234	9-9-1998	5676	221
22235	9-10-1998	5676	554
22236	9-10-1998	7831	221
22237	9-11-1998	8872	335

Employee

EID	Name	Salary	Address
221	Smith	67,000	223 W. 2300
335	Sanchez	82,000	37 W. 7200
554	Johnson	35,000	440 E. 5200

FIGURE 3.36 Sample data for one-to-many relationships. The Supplier and PurchaseOrder tables are linked through the SID column. Similarly, the Employee table is linked through the data in the EID column. Both the SID and EID columns are foreign keys in the PurchaseOrder table, but they are not primary keys in that table.

Many-to-Many Relationships

Overview class diagrams often contain many-to-many relationships. However, in a relational database many-to-many relationships must be split into 2 one-to-many relationships to get to BCNF. Figure 3.37 illustrates the process with the PurchaseOrder and Item tables.

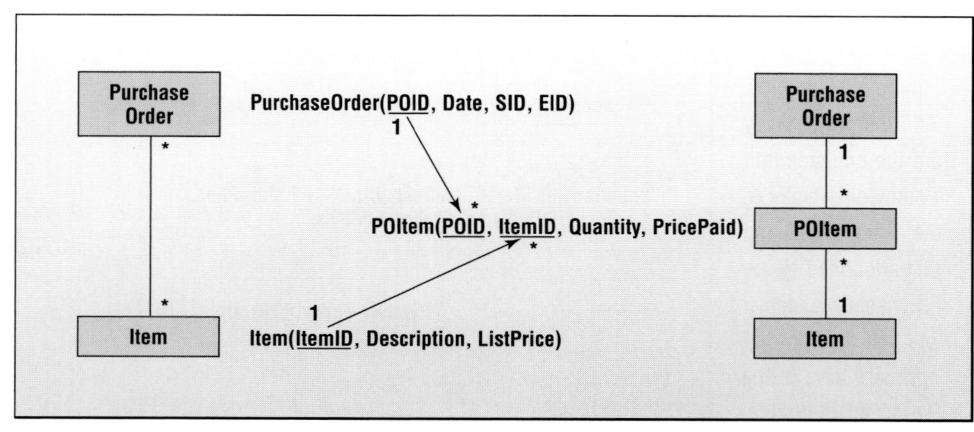

FIGURE 3.37 Converting a many-to-many relationship. Many-to-many relationships use a new, intermediate table to link the two tables. The new POItem table contains the primary keys from both the PurchaseOrder and Item tables.

FIGURE 3.38
Sample data for the many-to-many relationship. Note that the intermediate POItem table links the other two tables. Verify that the three tables are in 3NF, where each non-key column depends on the whole key and nothing but the key.

PurchaseOrder

POID	Date	SID	EID
22234	9-9-1998	5676	221
22235	9-10-1998	5676	554
22236	9-10-1998	7831	221
22237	9-11-1998	8872	335

POItem

POID	ItemID	Quantity	PricePaid
22234	444098	3	2.00
22234	444185	1	25.00
22235	444185	4	24.00
22236	555828	10	150.00
22236	555982	1	5800.00

Item

ItemID	Description	ListPrice
444098	Staples	2.00
444185	Paper	28.00
555828	Wire	158.00
555982	Sheet steel	5928.00
888371	Brake assembly	152.00

Each of the two initial entities becomes a table (PurchaseOrder and Item). The next step is to create a new table (POItem) that contains the primary keys from both of the other tables (POID and ItemID). This table represents the many-to-many relationship. Each purchase order (POID) can contain many items, so ItemID must be a key. Similarly, each item can be ordered on many purchase orders, so POID must be a key.

You must have a table that contains both POID and ItemID as keys. Can you create this relationship without creating a third table? In most cases the answer is no. Consider what happens if you try to put the ItemID column into the PurchaseOrder table and make it part of the primary key. The resulting entity would not be a 3NF table, because Date, SID, and EID do not depend on the ItemID. A similar problem arises if you try to place the POID key into the Item table. Hence the intermediate table is required. Figure 3.38 uses sample data to show how the three tables are linked through the keys.

N-ary Associations

As noted in Chapter 2, n-ary associations are denoted with a diamond. This diamond association also becomes a class. In a sense, an n-ary association is simply a set of several binary associations. As shown in Figure 3.39, the new association class holds the primary key from each of the other classes. As long as the binary associations are one-to-many, each column in the Assembly class will be part of the primary key. If for some reason a binary association is one-to-one, then the corresponding column would not be keyed.

Generalization or Subtypes

Some business entities are created as subtypes. Figure 3.40 illustrates this relationship with the Item entity. An item is a generic description of something that is purchased. Every item has a description and a list price. However, the company deals with three types of items: raw materials, assembled components, and office supplies. Each of these subtypes has some additional properties that we wish to track. For ex-

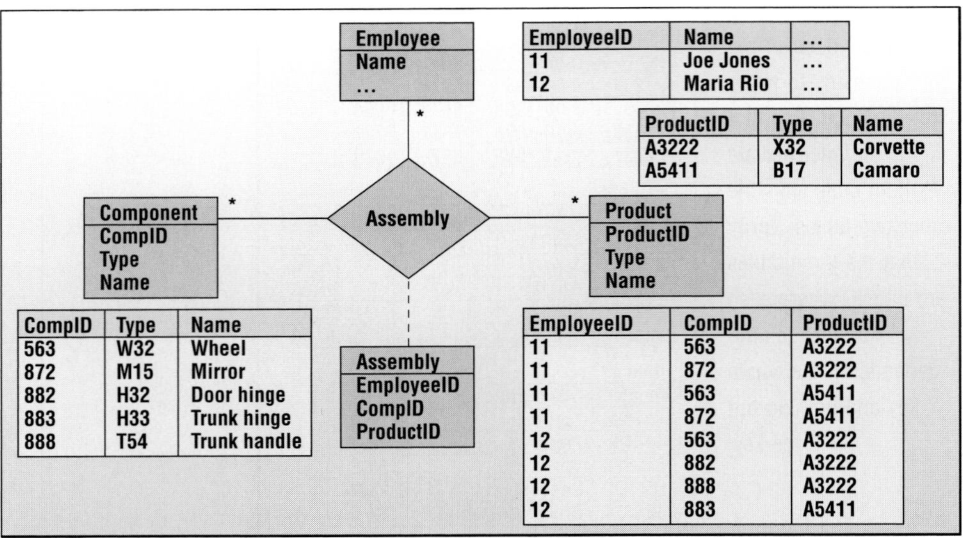

EmployeeID	Name	...
11	Joe Jones	...
12	Maria Rio	...

ProductID	Type	Name
A3222	X32	Corvette
A5411	B17	Camaro

CompID	Type	Name
563	W32	Wheel
872	M15	Mirror
882	H32	Door hinge
883	H33	Trunk hinge
888	T54	Trunk handle

EmployeeID	CompID	ProductID
11	563	A3222
11	872	A3222
11	563	A5411
11	872	A5411
12	563	A3222
12	882	A3222
12	888	A3222
12	883	A5411

FIGURE 3.39
N-ary association. The Assembly association is also a class. It can be modeled as a set of binary (one-to-many) associations. The primary key from each of the main classes is included in the new Assembly class.

ample, the company tracks the weight of raw materials, the dimension of assembled components, and quantity discounts for office supplies.

In converting this design to a relational database, there are two basic approaches. (1) If the subtypes are similar, you could ignore the subclasses and compress all the subclasses into the main class that would contain every property for all of the subclasses. In this case each item entry would have several null values. (2) In most cases a better approach is to create separate tables for each subclass. Each table will contain the primary key from the main Item class.

As shown in Figure 3.41, each item has an entry in the Item table. There is another entry in one of the three subtype tables—depending on the specific item. For example, item 444098 is described in the Item table and has additional data in the OfficeSupplies table.

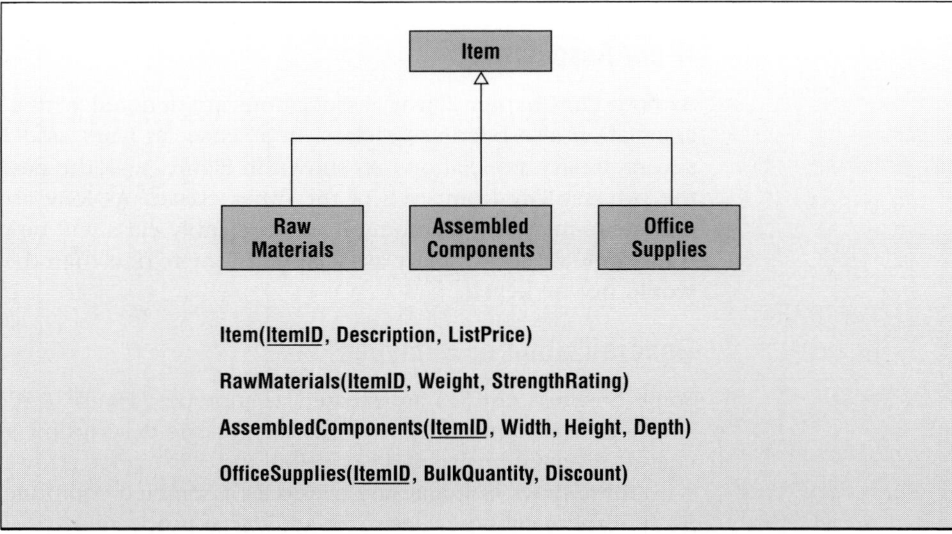

FIGURE 3.40
Converting subtypes. Every item purchased has basic attributes, which are recorded in the Item table. Each item can be placed in one of three categories, which have different attributes. To convert these relationships to 3NF, create new tables for each subtype. Use the same key in the new tables and in the generic table. Add attributes specific to each of the subtypes.

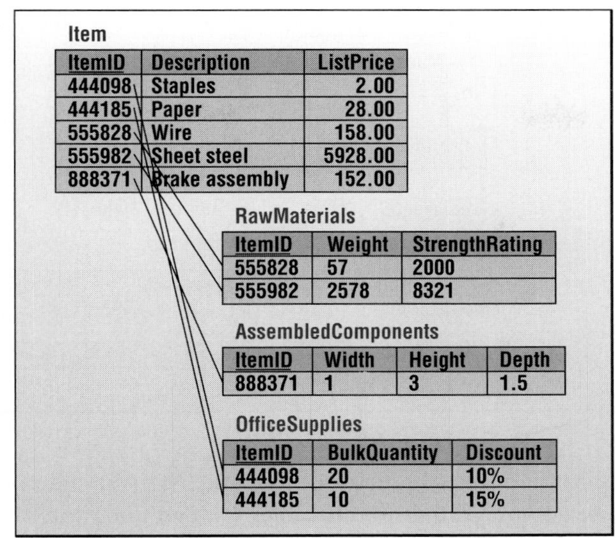

Item

ItemID	Description	ListPrice
444098	Staples	2.00
444185	Paper	28.00
555828	Wire	158.00
555982	Sheet steel	5928.00
888371	Brake assembly	152.00

RawMaterials

ItemID	Weight	StrengthRating
555828	57	2000
555982	2578	8321

AssembledComponents

ItemID	Width	Height	Depth
888371	1	3	1.5

OfficeSupplies

ItemID	BulkQuantity	Discount
444098	20	10%
444185	10	15%

FIGURE 3.41 Sample data for the subtype relationships. Notice how each Item has an entry in the Item table and a row in one of the three subtype tables.

If the subclass relationships are not mutually exclusive, then each main item can have a matching row in more than one of the subclass tables.

Composition

In some ways composition is a combination of an n-ary association and subtypes. Consider the bicycle example in Figure 3.42 in which a bicycle is built from various components. The first decision to make is how to handle the many components. It is a question of subtypes. In this situation the business keeps almost identical data for each component (ID number, description, weight, cost, list price, and so on). Hence a good solution is to compress each subtype into a generic Component class. However, it would also make sense to handle wheels separately because they are a more complex component.

We can solve the main composition problem by creating properties in the main Bicycle table for each of the component items (WheelID, CrankID, StemID, and so on). These columns are foreign keys in the Bicycle table (but not primary keys).

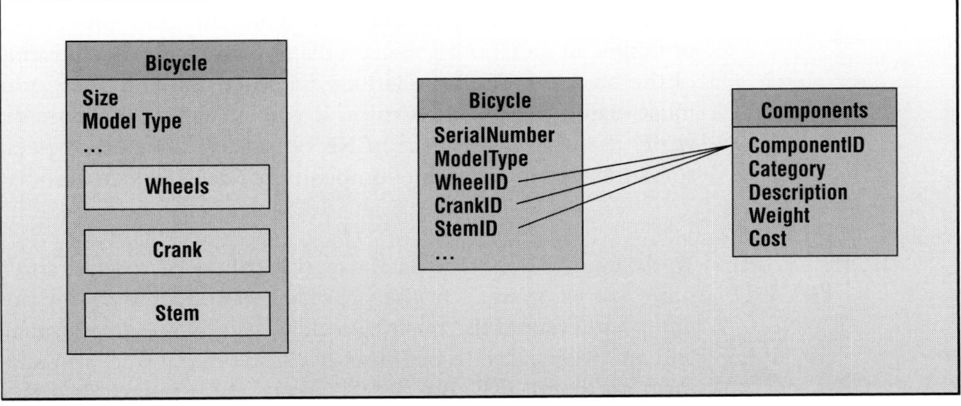

FIGURE 3.42 Normalizing a composition association. First decide how to handle the subclasses. In this case they are combined into one Components table. Then handle the composition by storing the appropriate Component key values into the main Bicycle table.

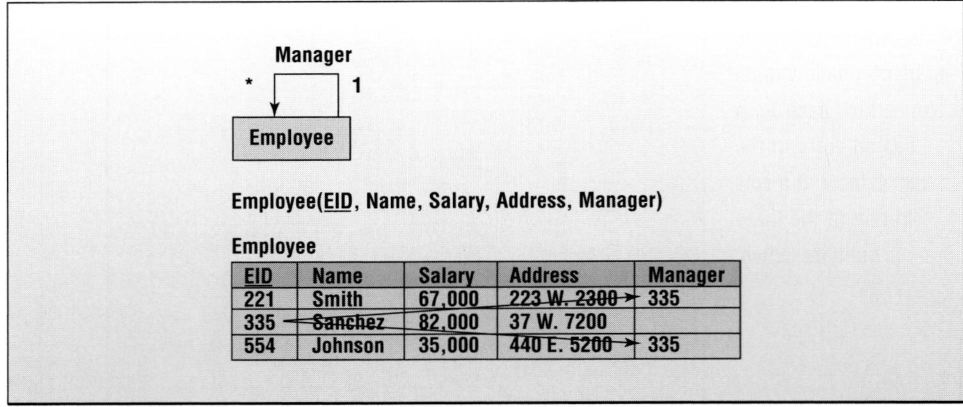

FIGURE 3.43 Converting recursive relationships. An employee can have only one manager, so add a Manager column to the Employee table which contains the EID to point to the manager. In the example, Smith reports to Manager 335 (Sanchez).

When a bicycle is built, the ID values for the installed components are stored in the appropriate column in the Bicycle table. You can find more details by examining the actual Rolling Thunder database.

Reflexive Associations

Occasionally, an entity may be linked to itself. A common example is shown in Figure 3.43, where employees have managers. Because managers are also employees, the entity is linked to itself. This relationship is easy to see when you create the corresponding table. Simply add a Manager column to the Employee table. The data in this column consists of an EID. For example, the first employee (Smith, EID 221) reports to manager 335 (Sanchez). Is the Manager column part of the primary key? No, because the business rule states that each employee can have only one manager.

How would you handle a situation in which an employee can have more than one manager? Key the Manager column? No, because then the Employee table would not be in BCNF (an employee's address would not depend on the manager). The solution is to create a new table that lists EmployeeID and ManagerID—both part of the primary key. The new table would probably have additional data to describe the relationship between the employee and the manager, such as a project or task.

Summary

Creating a detailed class diagram is really the same thing as creating a normalized list of tables. In fact, both the class diagram and the list of normalized tables are models of the business. The associations, whether drawn as lines or expressed through keys, must match the business rules. If you start with the class diagram, be sure that you verify that each class is in BCNF. Be sure to check the special situations of n-ary associations, generalization, composition, and reflexive associations.

THE PET STORE EXAMPLE

To design the Pet Store database, you talk to the owner and investigate the way that other stores operate. In the process you collect ideas for various forms, and you begin to understand the business rules. To expedite development and hold down costs, you and Sally agree to begin with a simplified model and add features later. The sales form sketched in Figure 3.44 contains the primary data that will be needed when sales are made.

Sally wants you to create separate purchase orders for animals and products. She has repeatedly emphasized the importance of collecting detailed animal data from the breeders and eventually wants to collect the genealogical data for the animals whenever possible. With registered animals like cats and dogs, this data is readily available. However, she said it is hard to get good records for fish. Sally would also like to get medical records for the animals she buys. Common data would include their shots, any illnesses, and any medications or treatments they have received. For now, she is relying on the breeders to keep this information. However, once the sales and basic financial applications have been created, she wants to add these features to the database.

For the moment the most important job is to collect the transaction data. Figure 3.45 shows the minimal financial data that must be collected when purchasing animals from suppliers. Note the importance of collecting information on the animals, suppliers/breeders, customers, and employees. Because of the anticipated changes, it is important to design the database for flexibility. The design should make it easy to add new attributes for all of the major entities. It should also be easy to add new tables (such as health records) without making major alterations to the initial structure.

Purchasing merchandise from suppliers represents a similar process. However, there are some slight differences. In particular, we need to collect different data on the individual items.

FIGURE 3.44 Pet Store sample sales form. Separate sections for selling animals and merchandise reflect a business rule to treat them differently.

Sales

Sales# Date

Customer	Employee ID
Name	Name
Address	
City, State, ZIP	

Animal Sale

ID	Name	Category	Breed	DoB	Gender	Reg.	Color	ListPrice	SalePrice

Animal SubTotal

Merchandise Sale

Item	Description	Category	ListPrice	SalePrice	Quantity	Extended

Merchandise SubTotal

Subtotal

Tax

Total

FIGURE 3.45 Pet Store sample purchase order for animals. More information will be collected later—particularly data on each animal's health and lineage.

Purchase Order for Animals

Order# | Date Ordered
Date Received

Supplier	Employee ID
Name	Name
Contact	Home Phone
Phone	Date Hired
Address	
City, State, ZIP	

Animal Descriptions

Name	Category	Breed	Gender	Registration	Price

Subtotal
Shipping Cost
Total

A sample form is shown in Figure 3.46. Again, remember that Sally wants to start with a small database. Later we will have to collect additional data. For example, what happens if an order arrives and some items are missing? The current form can only record the arrival of the entire shipment. Similarly, each supplier probably uses a unique set of Item numbers. For example, a case of cat food from one supplier might be ordered with ItemID 3325, but the same case from a different supplier

FIGURE 3.46 Pet Store sample purchase order for merchandise. Note the similarities and differences between the two types of orders. Keep in mind that additional data will have to be collected later.

Purchase Order for Merchandise

Order# | Date Ordered
Date Received

Supplier	Employee ID
Name	Name
Contact	Home Phone
Phone	
Address	
City, State, ZIP	

Items Ordered

ItemID	Description	Category	Price	Quantity	Ext.	QOH

Subtotal
Shipping Cost
Total

FIGURE 3.47
Pet Store normalized tables for the basic sales form. You should do the normalization first and see if your results match these tables.

Sale(SaleID, Date, CustomerID, EmployeeID)
SaleAnimal(SaleID, AnimalID, SalePrice)
SaleMerchandise(SaleID, ItemID, SalePrice, Quantity)
Customer(CustomerID, Name, Address, City, State, Zip)
Employee(EmployeeID, Name)
Animal(AnimalID, Name, Category, Breed, DateBorn, Gender, Registered, Color, ListPrice)
Merchandise(ItemID, Description, Category, ListPrice)

would be ordered with ItemID A9973. Eventually, Sally will probably want to track the numbers used by her major suppliers. That way, when invoices arrive bearing their numbers, matching the products to what she ordered will be easier.

The next step in designing the Pet Store database is to take each form and create a list of normalized tables that will be used to hold data for that form. Figure 3.47 shows the tables that were generated from the Sales form. Before examining the results in detail, you should attempt to normalize the data yourself. Then see whether you derived the same answer. You should also derive the normalized tables for the other two forms. Remember to double-check your work. First make sure the primary keys are correct and then check to see that each non-key column depends on the whole key and nothing but the key.

There is an interesting assumption in both the SaleAnimal and AnimalOrderItem tables (Figure 3.48). The SaleAnimal table uses both SaleID and AnimalID as the primary key. This approach means that each sale can consist of several animals. It also means that each animal can be sold many times. Is this latter situation possible? Can the same animal be sold more than once? If not, then SaleID should not be part of the primary key—and it can simply be inserted into the Animal table. Likewise, can the same animal be purchased more than once? If not, the OrderID can be placed into the Animal table—but not as part of the key. The rest of the data in the SaleAnimal and AnimalOrderItem tables can also be placed in the Animal table. Although this approach appears realistic, it is less flexible. Designing the database this way means that the Pet Store can *never* sell the same animal twice. Then how would you handle returns of an animal?

VIEW INTEGRATION

Up to this point, we have demonstrated database design and normalization using individual reports and forms, which is the basic step in designing a database. However, most projects involve many reports and forms. Some projects involve teams of designers, where each person collects forms and reports from different users and departments. Each designer creates the normalized list of tables for the individual forms, and you eventually get several collections of tables related to the same topic. At this point you need to integrate all these tables into one complete, consistent set of table definitions.

When you are finished with this stage, you will be able to enter the table definitions into the DBMS. Although you might end up with a large list of interrelated tables, this step is generally easier than the initial derivation of the 3NF tables. At this point you collect the tables, make sure everything is named consistently, and consolidate data from similar tables. The basic steps involved in consolidating the tables are as follows:

- Collect the multiple views (documents, forms, etc.).
- Create normalized tables for each document.
- Combine the views into one complete model.

The Pet Store Example

Figure 3.48 illustrates the view integration process for the Pet Store case. The tables generated from the three input forms are listed first. The integration occurs by looking at each table to see which ones contain similar data. A good starting point is to look at the primary keys. If two tables have exactly the same primary keys, the tables should usually be combined. However, be careful. Sometimes the keys are wrong, and sometimes the keys might have slightly different names.

Notice that the Employee table shows up three times in the example. By carefully checking the data in each listing, we can form one new table that contains all of the columns. Hence the Phone and DateHired columns are moved to one table, and the two others are deleted. A similar process can be used for the Supplier, Animal, and Merchandise tables. The goal is to create a complete list of normalized tables that will hold the data for all the forms and reports. Be sure to double-check your work and to verify that the final list of tables is in 3NF or BCNF. Also, make sure that the tables can be joined through related columns of data.

The finalized tables can also be displayed on a detailed class diagram. The class diagram for the Pet Store is shown in Figure 3.49. One strength of the diagram is the ability to show how the classes (tables) are connected through relationships. Double-check the normalization to make sure that the basic forms can be re-created. For example, the sales form will start with the Customer, Employee, and Sale tables. Sales of animals requires the SaleAnimal and Animal tables. Sales of products requires the SaleItem and Merchandise tables. All of these tables can be connected by relationships on their attributes.

Most of the relationships are one-to-many relationships, but pay attention to the direction. Access denotes the many side with an infinity (∞) sign. Of course, you first have to identify the proper relationships from the business rules. For instance, there can be many sales to each customer, but a given sale can list only one customer.

FIGURE 3.48 Pet Store view integration. Data columns from similar tables can be combined into one table. For example, we need only one Employee table. Look for tables that have the same keys. The goal is to have one set of normalized tables that can hold the data for all the forms and reports.

Sale(SaleID, Date, CustomerID, EmployeeID)
SaleAnimal(SaleID, AnimalID, SalePrice)
SaleItem(SaleID, ItemID, SalePrice, Quantity)
Customer(CustomerID, Name, Address, City, State, Zip)
Employee(EmployeeID, Name, Phone, DateHired)
Animal(AnimalID, Name, Category, Breed, DateBorn, Gender, Registered, Color, ListPrice, Cost)
Merchandise(ItemID, Description, Category, ListPrice, QuantityOnHand)

AnimalOrder(OrderID, OrderDate, ReceiveDate, SupplierID, EmpID, ShipCost)
AnimalOrderItem(OrderID, AnimalID, Cost)
Supplier(SupplierID, Name, Contact, Phone, Address, City, State, Zip)
~~Employee (EmployeeID, Name, Phone, DateHired)~~
~~Animal(AnimalID, Name, Category, Breed, Gender, Registration, Cost)~~

MerchandiseOrder(PONumber, OrderDate, ReceiveDate, SID, EmpID, ShipCost)
MerchandiseOrderItem(PONumber, ItemID, Quantity, Cost)
~~Supplier(SupplierID, Name, Contact, Phone, Address, City, State, Zip)~~
~~Employee(EmployeeID, Name, Phone)~~
~~Merchandise (ItemID, Description, Category, QuantityOnHand)~~

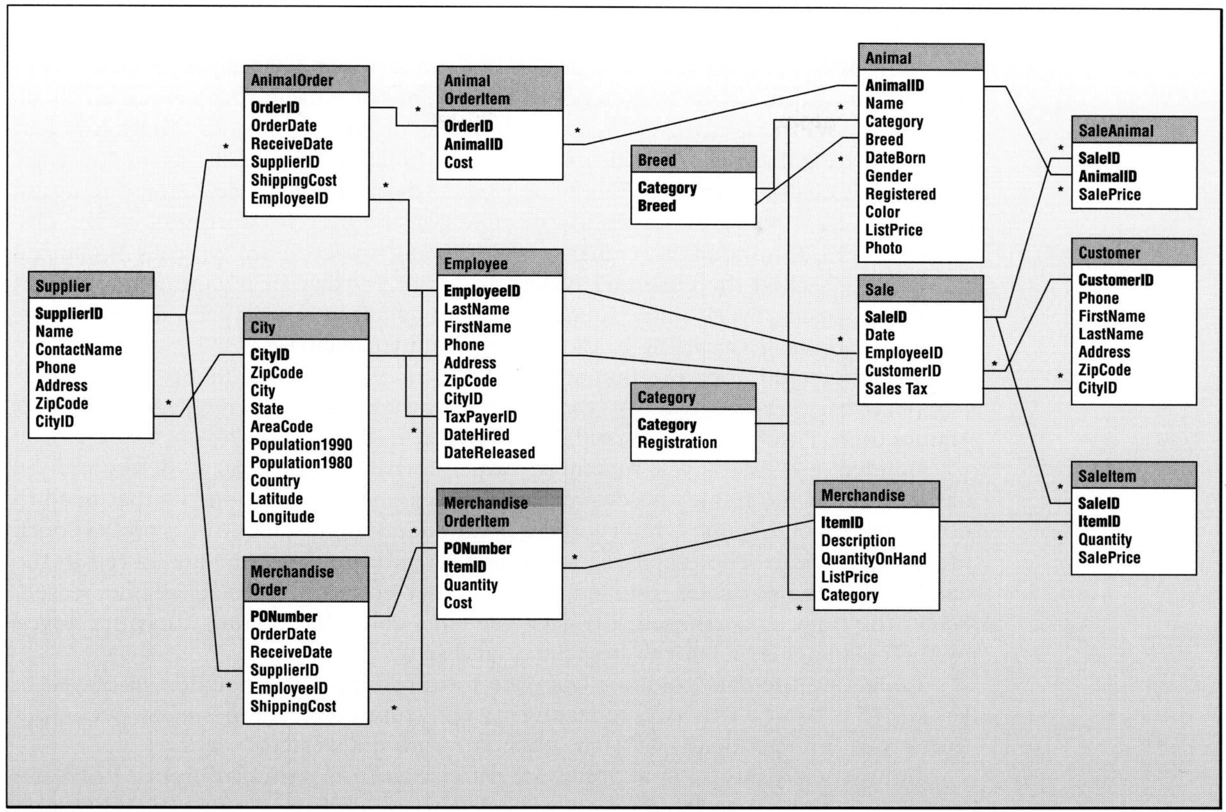

FIGURE 3.49

Pet Store class diagram. The tables become entities in the diagram. The relationships verify that the tables are interconnected through the data. Some new data has been added for the employees. Also, cities have been defined in a single table to simplify data entry. Likewise, the new Breed and Category tables ensure consistency of data.

The final list shown in the class diagram in Figure 3.49 has three new tables: City, Breed, and Category. These validation tables have been added to simplify data entry and to ensure consistency of data. Without these tables employees would have to repeatedly enter text data for city name, breed, and category. There are two problems with asking people to type in these values: (1) it takes time, and (2) people might enter different data each time. By placing standardized values in these tables, employees can select the proper value from a list. Because the standard value is always copied to the new table, the data will always be entered exactly the same way each time it is used.

Asking the DBMS to enforce the specified relationships raises an interesting issue. The relationships require that data be entered in a specific sequence. The foreign key relationship specifies that a value for the customer must exist in the Customer table before it can be placed in the Sale table. From a business standpoint the rule makes sense; we must first meet customers before we can sell them something. However, this rule may cause problems for clerks who are entering sales data. We need some mechanism to help them enter new Customer data before attempting to enter the Sales data. Chapters 6 and 7 explain one way to resolve this issue.

Rolling Thunder Sample Integration Problem

The only way to learn database design and understand normalization is to work through more problems. To practice the concepts of data normalization and to illustrate the methods involved in combining sets of tables, consider a new problem involving a database for a small manufacturer: Rolling Thunder Bicycles. The company builds custom bicycles. Frames are built and painted in-house. Components are purchased from manufacturers and assembled on the bicycles according to the customer orders. Components (cranks, pedals, derailleurs, etc.) are typically organized into groups so that the customer orders an entire package of components without having to specify every single item. Additional details about bicycles and the company operations are available in the Rolling Thunder database.

To understand normalization and the process of integrating tables from various perspectives, consider four of the input forms: Bicycle Assembly, Manufacturer Transactions, Purchase Orders, and Components.

Builders use the Bicycle Assembly form shown in Figure 3.50 to determine the basic layout of the frame, the desired paint styles, and the components that need to be installed. As the frame is built and the components are installed, the workers check off the operations. The employee identification and the date/time are stored in the database. As the parts are installed, the inventory count is automatically decreased. When the bicycle is shipped, a trigger executes code that records the price owed by the customer so a bill can be printed and sent.

Collecting the data columns from the form results in the notation displayed in Figure 3.51. Notice that two repeating groups (tubes and components) occur, but they repeat independently of each other. They are not nested.

Components and other supplies are purchased from manufacturers. Orders are placed as supplies run low and are recorded on a Purchase Order form. Shown in Figure 3.52, the Purchase Order form contains standard data on the manufacturer, along with a list of components (or other supplies) that are ordered.

The notation and the 4NF tables are derived in Figure 3.53. For practice you should work through the normalization on your own. Note that the computed

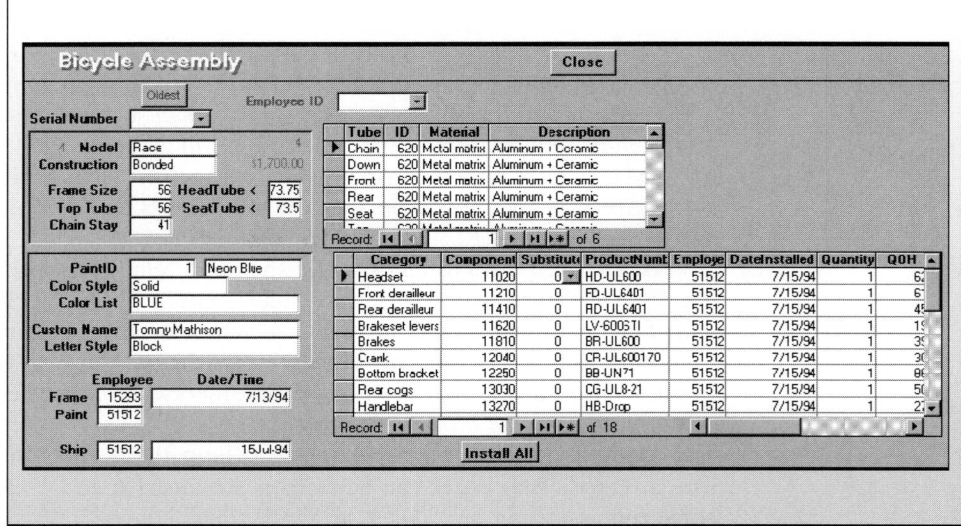

Tube	ID	Material	Description
Chain	620	Metal matrix	Aluminum + Ceramic
Down	620	Metal matrix	Aluminum + Ceramic
Front	620	Metal matrix	Aluminum + Ceramic
Rear	620	Metal matrix	Aluminum + Ceramic
Seat	620	Metal matrix	Aluminum + Ceramic

Category	Component	Substitute	ProductNumb	Employe	DateInstalled	Quantity	QOH
Headset	11020	0	HD-UL600	51512	7/15/94	1	6
Front derailleur	11210	0	FD-UL6401	51512	7/15/94	1	6
Rear derailleur	11410	0	RD-UL6401	51512	7/15/94	1	4
Brakeset levers	11620	0	LV-6006TI	51512	7/15/94	1	1
Brakes	11810	0	BR-UL600	51512	7/15/94	1	3
Crank	12040	0	CR-UL600170	51512	7/15/94	1	3
Bottom bracket	12250	0	BB-UN71	51512	7/15/94	1	8
Rear cogs	13030	0	CG-UL8-21	51512	7/15/94	1	5
Handlebar	13270	0	HB-Drop	51512	7/15/94	1	2

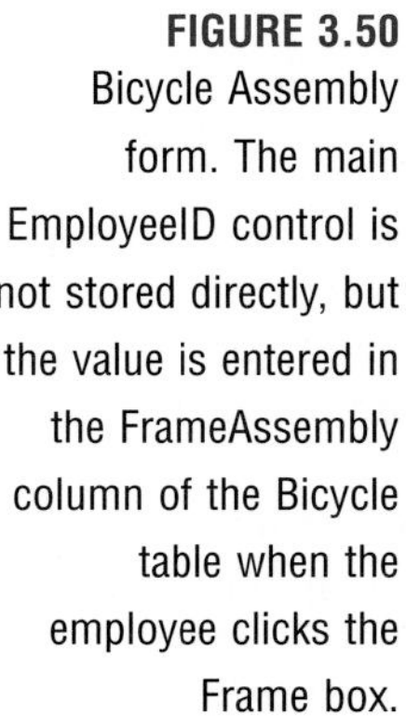

FIGURE 3.50
Bicycle Assembly form. The main EmployeeID control is not stored directly, but the value is entered in the FrameAssembly column of the Bicycle table when the employee clicks the Frame box.

FIGURE 3.51
Notation for the BicycleAssembly form. There are two repeating groups, but they are independent. The 4NF tables from this form are displayed, but you should try to derive the tables yourself.

BicycleAssembly(
SerialNumber, Model, Construction, FrameSize, TopTube, ChainStay, HeadTube, SeatTube, PaintID, PaintColor, ColorStyle, ColorList, CustomName, LetterStyle, EmpFrame, EmpPaint, BuildDate, ShipDate,
(TubeID, TubeType, TubeMaterial, TubeDescription),
(CompCategory, ComponentID, SubstID, ProdNumber, EmpInstalled, DateInstalled, Quantity, QOH))

Bicycle(SerialNumber, Model, Construction, FrameSize, TopTube, ChainStay, HeadTube, SeatTube, PaintID, ColorStyle, CustomName, LetterStyle, EmpFrame, EmpPaint, BuildDate, ShipDate)

Paint(PaintID, ColorList)

BikeTubes(SerialNumber, TubeID, Quantity)

TubeMaterial(TubeID, TubeType, TubeMaterial, TubeDescription)

BikeParts(SerialNumber, ComponentID, SubstID, Quantity, DateInstalled, EmpInstalled)

Component(ComponentID, ProdNumber, CompCategory, QOH)

columns do not need to be stored. However, be careful to store the shipping cost and discount, since those might be negotiated specifically on each order.

Payments to manufacturers are collected with a basic transaction form shown in Figure 3.54. Note that the initial balance and balance due are computed by code behind the form to display the effects of adding new transactions. Row entries for purchases are automatically generated by the Purchase Order form, so this form is generally used for payments or for corrections.

The 4NF tables resulting from the manufacturer transactions are shown in Figure 3.55. Again, work through the normalization yourself. Practice and experience are the best ways to learn normalization. Do not be misled: It is always tempting to read the "answers" in the book and say that normalization is easy. Normalization becomes

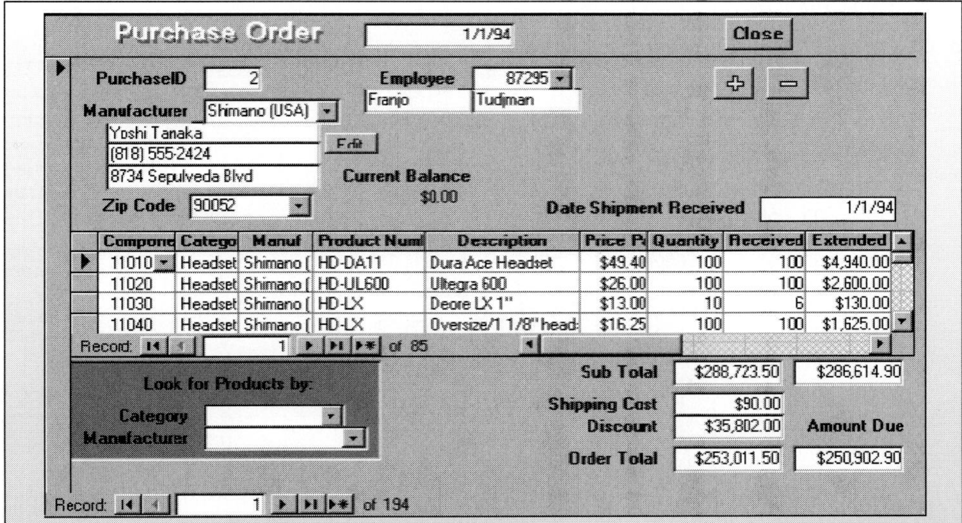

FIGURE 3.52
Purchase Order form. Only the items ordered is a repeating group. The Look for Products section is a convenience for users and does not store data. The Date Shipment Received box is initially blank; it is filled in when the product arrives at the loading dock.

FIGURE 3.53 Tables from the Purchase Order form. Note that the computed columns (extension is price * quantity) are not stored in the tables.

PurchaseOrder(PurchaseID, PODate, EmployeeID, FirstName, LastName, ManufacturerID, MfgName, Address, Phone, CityID, CurrentBalance, ShipReceiveDate, (ComponentID, CompCategory, ManufacturerID, ProductName, Description, PricePaid, Quantity, ReceivedQuantity, ExtendedValue, QOH, ExtendedReceived), ShippingCost, Discount)

PurchaseOrder(PurchaseID, PODate, EmployeeID, ManufacturerID, ShipReceiveDate, ShippingCost, Discount)
Employee(EmployeeID, FirstName, LastName)
Manufacturer(ManufacturerID, MfgName, Address, Phone, Address, CityID, CurrentBalance)
City(CityID, Name, ZipCode)
PurchaseItem(PurchaseID, ComponentID, Quantity, PricePaid, ReceivedQuantity)
Component(ComponentID, CompCategory, ManufacturerID, ProductName, Description, QOH)

much more complex when you face a blank page. Investigating and determining business rules is challenging when you begin.

The Component form in Figure 3.56 is used to add new components to the list and modify the descriptions of the components. It can also be used to make changes to the manufacturer data. Notice the use of two identification numbers: one is assigned by Rolling Thunder, and the other is assigned by the manufacturer. Assigning

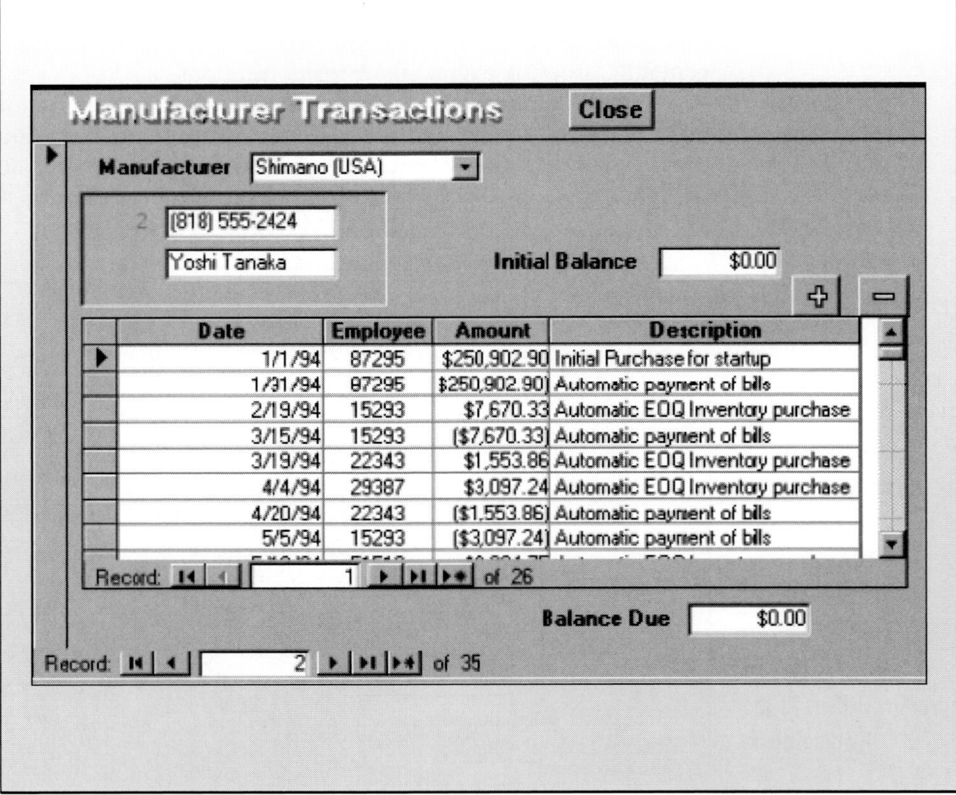

FIGURE 3.54 Manufacturer Transactions form. The balance due is stored in the database but only one time. The Initial Balance and Balance Due boxes are computed by the form to display the effect of transactions added by the user.

FIGURE 3.55 Tables for Manufacturer Transactions form. This normalization is straightforward. Note that the TransactionDate column also holds the time, so it is possible to have more than one transaction with a given manufacturer on the same day.

ManufacturerTransactions(ManufacturerID, MfgName, Phone, Contact, BalanceDue, (TransactionDate, EmployeeID, Amount, Description))

Manufacturer(ManufacturerID, MfgName, Phone, Contact, BalanceDue)

ManufacturerTransaction(ManufacturerID, TransactionDate, EmployeeID, Amount, Description)

our own number ensures consistency of the data format and guarantees a unique identifier. The manufacturer's product number is used to help place orders, since the manufacturer would have no use for our internal data.

The 4NF tables derived from the Component form are shown in Figure 3.57. For the most part they are straightforward. One interesting difference in Rolling Thunder is the treatment of addresses and cities. Many business tables for customers, employees, suppliers, and so on, contain columns for city, state, and ZIP code. Technically, there is a hidden dependency in this basic data because the three are related. Hence a database can save space and data entry time by maintaining a separate City table. Of course, a City table for the entire United States, much less the world, could become large. A more challenging problem is that there is not a one-to-one relationship between cities and ZIP code. Some cities have many ZIP codes, and some ZIP codes cover multiple

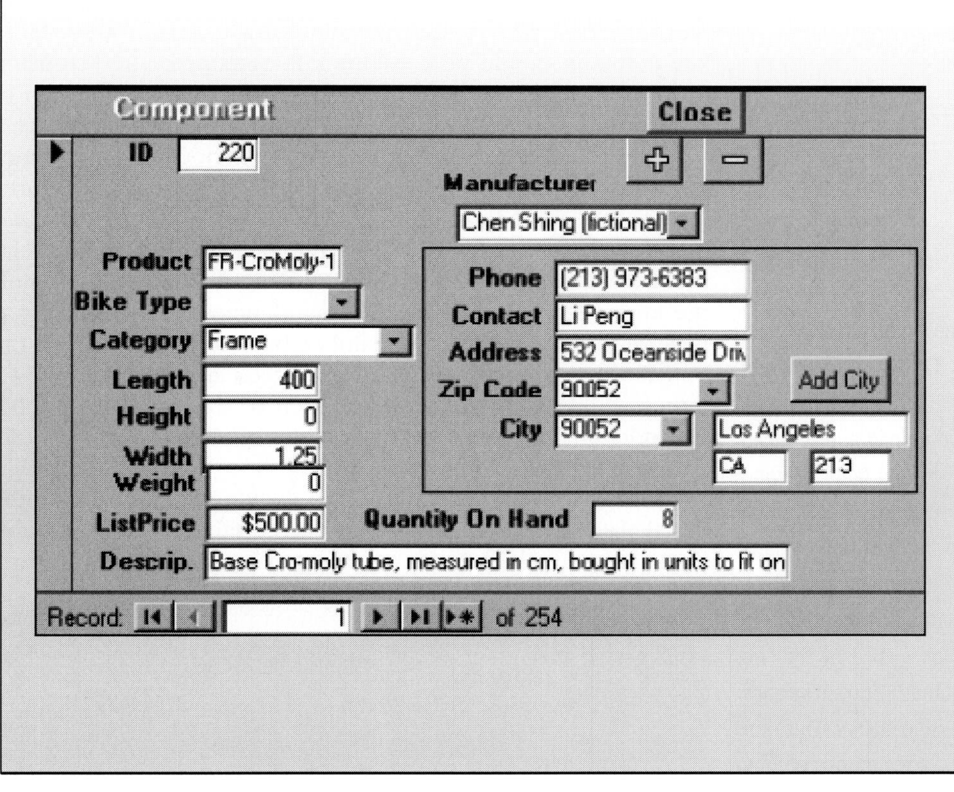

FIGURE 3.56 Component form. Note that components have an internal ID number that is assigned by Rolling Thunder employees. Products usually also have a Product number that is assigned by the manufacturer. It is difficult to rely on this number, since it might be duplicated across suppliers and the formats vary widely.

FIGURE 3.57 Tables derived from the Component form. The ZipCode in the Manufacturer table is specific to that company (probably a nine-digit code). The ZipCode in the City table is a base (five-digit) code that can be used for a reference point, but there are often many codes per city.

ComponentForm(ComponentID, ProdNumber, BikeType, CompCategory, Length, Height, Width, Weight, ListPrice, Description, QOH, ManufacturerID, MfgName, Phone, Contact, Address, ZipCode, CityID, City, State, AreaCode)

Component(<u>ComponentID</u>, ProdNumber, BikeType, CompCategory, Length, Height, Width, Weight, ListPrice, Description, QOH, ManufacturerID)

Manufacturer(<u>ManufacturerID</u>, MfgName, Phone, Contact, Address, ZipCode, CityID)

City(<u>CityID</u>, City, State, ZipCode, AreaCode)

cities. Rolling Thunder resolves these two issues by keeping a City table based on a unique CityID. If space is at a premium, the table can be reduced to contain only cities used in the database. As customers arrive from new cities, the basic city data is added. The ZIP code problem is handled by storing a base ZIP code for each city. The specific ZIP code related to each address is stored with the appropriate table (e.g., Manufacturer). This specific ZIP code could also be a nine-digit code that more closely identifies the location of the customer or manufacturer. Although it is possible to create a table of complete nine-digit codes, the size is enormous, and the data tends to change. Companies that rely heavily on nine-digit mailings usually purchase verification software that contains authenticated databases to check their addresses and codes.

Look at the tables from Figures 3.51, 3.53, 3.55, and 3.57 again. Notice that similar tables are listed in each figure. In particular, look for the Manufacturer tables. Notice that the overlapping tables often contain different data from each form. In practice, particularly when there is a team of designers, similar columns might have different names, so be careful. The objective of this step is to combine the similar tables. The best way to start is to look for common keys. Tables that have the same key columns should be combined. For example, the Manufacturer variations are reproduced in Figure 3.58. The version from the PO table can be extended by adding the Contact and ZipCode columns from the other variations.

After combining duplicate tables, you should have a single list of tables that contain all of the data from the forms. This list is shown in Figure 3.59. It is also a good idea at this point to double-check your work. In particular, verify that the keys are unique and that composite keys represent many-to-many relationships. Then verify the 3NF rules: Does each non-key column depend on the whole key and nothing but the key? Also look for hidden dependencies that you might need to make explicit. Be sure that the tables can be linked back together through the data in the columns. You should be able to draw lines between all the tables. Now is a good time to draw a more complete class diagram. Each of the normalized tables becomes an entity. The relationships show how the tables are linked together. (See the Rolling Thunder database for the complete example.)

Finally, examine each table and decide whether you might want to collect additional data. For example, the Employee table would undoubtedly need more data,

FIGURE 3.58 Multiple versions of the Manufacturer table. Tables with the same key should be combined and reduced to one table. Moving Contact and ZipCode to the first table means the other two tables can be deleted. Do not be misled by the two names (CurrentBalance and BalanceDue) for the same column.

PO	Manufacturer(<u>ManufacturerID</u>, MfgName, Address, Phone, CityID, CurrentBalance)
Mfg	Manufacturer(<u>ManufacturerID</u>, MfgName, Phone, **Contact,** BalanceDue)
Comp	Manufacturer(<u>ManufacturerID</u>, MfgName, Phone, Contact, Address, **ZipCode,** CityID)

FIGURE 3.59 Integrated tables. Duplicate tables have been combined, and normalization (4NF) has been verified. Also draw a class diagram to be sure the tables link together. Note the addition of the Reference column as an audit trail to hold the corresponding PurchaseID. Observe that some tables (e.g., Employee) will need additional data.

Bicycle(<u>SerialNumber</u>, Model, Construction, FrameSize, TopTube, ChainStay, HeadTube, SeatTube, PaintID, ColorStyle, CustomName, LetterStyle, EmpFrame, EmpPaint, BuildDate, ShipDate)
Paint(<u>PaintID</u>, ColorList)
BikeTubes(<u>SerialNumber</u>, <u>TubeID</u>, Quantity)
TubeMaterial(<u>TubeID</u>, TubeType, TubeMaterial, TubeDescription)
BikeParts(<u>SerialNumber</u>, <u>ComponentID</u>, SubstID, Quantity, DateInstalled, EmpInstalled)
Component(<u>ComponentID</u>, ProdNumber, BikeType, CompCategory, Length, Height, Width, Weight, ListPrice, Description, QOH, ManufacturerID)
PurchaseOrder(<u>PurchaseID</u>, PODate, EmployeeID, ManufacturerID, ShipReceiveDate, ShippingCost, Discount)
PurchaseItem(<u>PurchaseID</u>, <u>ComponentID</u>, Quantity, PricePaid, ReceivedQuantity)
Employee(<u>EmployeeID</u>, FirstName, LastName)
Manufacturer(<u>ManufacturerID</u>, MfgName, Contact, Address, Phone, CityID, ZipCode, CurrentBalance)
ManufacturerTransaction(<u>ManufacturerID</u>, <u>TransactionDate</u>, EmployeeID, Amount, Description, Reference)
City(<u>CityID</u>, City, State, ZipCode, AreaCode)

such as Address and DateHired. Similarly, we concluded that the ManufacturerTransaction table could use a Reference column that will contain the PurchaseID when a transaction is automatically generated by the Purchase Order form. This column functions as an audit trail and makes it easier to trace accounting transactions back to the source. Some people might use date/time for the same purpose, but round-off in seconds could cause problems.

DATA DICTIONARY In the process of collecting data and creating normalized tables, be sure to keep a data dictionary to record the data domains and various assumptions you make. A **data dictionary** or **data repository** consists of **metadata,** which is data that describes the data stored in the database. It typically lists all of the tables, columns, data domains, and assumptions. It is possible to store this data in a notebook, but it is easier to organize if it is stored on a computer. Some designers create a separate database to track the underlying project data. Specialized computer tools known as computer-aided software engineering (CASE) tools help with software design. One of their strengths is the ability to create, store, and search a comprehensive data dictionary.

DBMS Table Definition

When the logical tables are defined and you know the domains for all of the columns, you can enter the tables into a DBMS. Most systems have a graphical interface that makes it easier to enter the table definitions. In some cases, however, you might have to use the SQL data definition commands described in Chapter 4. In both cases, the process is similar. Define the table name, enter the column names, select the data type for the column, and then identify the keys. Sometimes keys are defined by creating a separate index. Some systems enable you to create a description for each column and table. This description might contain instructions to users or it might be an extension of your data dictionary to help designers make changes in the future.

A useful feature offered by some relational database systems is an **autonumber** or counter data type. Recall that many of the relational tables use an internally generated key that must be unique. If possible, the DBMS should generate this key value automatically; otherwise, users might have difficulty creating a unique value. An autonumber option will always generate a unique value, usually by adding 1 to the highest existing entry in the database. Some systems give you more control over the format and the increment, including the option to enter alphabetic characters. In systems without the autonumber option, you should write a short subroutine to automatically assign key values by locating the highest value in the table and adding an increment. Just be careful to think about multiple users updating the table at the same time.

You can also set **default values** for each column to speed up data entry. In the video store example, you might set a default value for the base rental rate. Default values can be particularly useful for dates. Most systems enable you to set a default value for dates that automatically enters the current date. At this point you should also set validation rules to enforce data integrity. As soon as the tables are defined, you can set relationships. With systems like Microsoft Access, the database system enforces referential integrity automatically. In other cases you will have to write your own triggers.

Data Volume and Usage

One more step is required when designing a database: estimating the size of the resulting database. The process is straightforward, but you have to ask a lot of questions of the users. When you design a database, it is important to estimate the overall size and usage of the database. These values enable you to estimate the hardware requirements and cost of the system. The first step is to estimate the size of the tables. Generally, you should investigate three situations: How big is the database now? How big will the database be in 2 or 3 years? and How big will the database be in 10 years?

Begin with the list of normalized tables. The process consists of estimating the average number of bytes in each row of the table and then estimating the number of rows in the table. Multiply the two numbers to get an estimate of the size of the table and then add the table sizes to estimate the total database size. This number represents the minimum size of the database. Many databases will be three to five times larger than this base estimate. Some systems have more complex rules and estimation procedures. For example, Oracle provides a utility to help you estimate the storage required for the database. You still begin with the data types for each column and the approximate number of rows. The utility then uses internal rules about Oracle's procedures to help estimate the total storage space needed.

An example of estimating **data volume** is presented in Figure 3.60. Consider the Customer table. The database system sets aside a certain amount of storage space for each column of data. The amount used depends on the particular system, so consult the documentation for exact values. In the abbreviated Customer table, the identification number takes 4 bytes as a long integer, and we estimate that Names take an average of 15 characters. Other averages are displayed in the table. Better estimates could be obtained from statistical analysis of sample data. In any case the estimated size of one row of Customer data is 76 bytes. Evaluating the business provides an estimate of approximately 1,000 customers; hence the Customer table would be approximately 76K bytes.

Estimating the size of the Order table follows a similar process, yielding an estimate of 16 bytes per row. Managers might know how many orders are placed in a given year. However, it might be easier to obtain the average number of orders

FIGURE 3.60
Estimating data volume. First estimate the size of each row and then estimate the number of rows in the table. If there is a concatenated key, you will usually multiply an average value times the number of rows in a prior table, as in the calculation for OrderItem.

Customer(<u>C#</u>, Name, Address, City, State, Zip)
Row: 4 + 15 + 25 + 20 + 2 + 10 = 76

Order(<u>O#</u>, C#, Odate)
Row: 4 + 4 + 8 = 16

OrderItem(<u>O#</u>,<u>P#</u>, Quantity, SalePrice)
Row: 4 + 4 + 4 + 8 = 20

$$Orders \text{ in } 3\ yrs = 1000\ Customers * \frac{10\ Orders}{Customer} * 3\ yrs = 30{,}000$$

$$OrderItem = 30{,}000\ Orders * \frac{5\ Lines}{Order} = 150{,}000$$

- Business rules
  - 3-year retention.
  - 1,000 customers.
  - Average 10 orders per customer per year.
  - Average five items per order.

Customer	76 * 1000	76,000
Order	16 * 30,000	480,000
OrderItem	20 * 150,000	3,000,000
Total		3,556,000

placed by a given customer in 1 year. If that number is 10, then we could expect 10,000 orders in a given year. Similarly, to get the number of rows in the OrderItem table, we need to know the average number of products ordered on one order form. If that number is 5, then we can expect to see 150,000 rows in the OrderItem table in 1 year.

The next step is to estimate the length of time data will be stored. Some companies plan to keep their data on-line for many years, whereas others follow a strict retention and removal policy. For legal purposes data must be maintained for a certain number of years, depending on its nature. Keep in mind that agencies like the IRS also require that retrieval software (e.g., the DBMS) be available to reproduce the data.

In addition to the basic data storage, your database will also reserve space for indexes, log files, forms, programs, and backup data. Experience with a particular database system will provide a more specific estimate, but the final total will probably be three to five times the size of the base estimate.

The final number will give you some idea of the hardware needed to support the database. Although performance and prices continue to change, only small databases can be run effectively on personal computers. Larger databases can be moved to a file server on a local area network (LAN). The LAN provides access to the data by multiple users, but performance depends heavily on the size of the database, the characteristics of the DBMS, and the speed of the network. As the database size increases (hundreds or thousands of megabytes), it becomes necessary to move to a dedicated computer to handle the data. Very large databases (terabytes) need multiple computers and specialized disk drives to minimize capacity and performance bottlenecks. The data estimates do not have to be perfect, but they provide basic information that you can give to the planning committee to help allocate funds for development, hardware, software, and personnel.

While you are talking with the users about each table, you should ask them to identify some basic security information. You will eventually need to assign security access rights to each table. Chapter 10 presents the details, but for now you should find out which people use the tables and which people should be denied some privileges. For example, clerks who order merchandise should not be allowed to acknowledge receipt of that merchandise. Otherwise, an unethical clerk could order merchandise, record it as being received, and then steal it. Four basic operations can be granted to data: read it, change it, delete it, or add new data. You should keep a list of who may or may not access each table.

SUMMARY

Database design relies on normalization, or the process of splitting data into tables. Ultimately, each table refers to a single entity or concept. Each table must have a primary key that uniquely identifies each row of data. To create the tables, you begin with a collection of data—generally derived from a user form or report. You reach 1NF by finding the repeating groups of data and putting them in a separate table. Next, you go through each of the intermediate tables and identify primary keys. You reach 2NF by checking each non-key column and asking whether it depends on the whole key. If not, put the column into a new table along with the portion of the key that it does depend on. To reach 3NF, you check whether the non-key column depends on anything that is not in the key. If so, pull out the column and the dependent column and put them into a new table. BCNF and 4NF apply to similar problems within the primary key. In particular, you want to look for hidden dependencies within the keys. If you find one, create an additional table that makes that dependency explicit.

Each form, report, or description that you collect from a user must be analyzed and a set of 4NF tables defined. For large projects several analysts may be given different forms, resulting in several lists of normalized tables. These tables must then be integrated into one standardized set of normalized data tables. Along the way you must specify the domain, or type of data, for each column. This final list of tables, with any comments, will be entered into the DBMS to start the database construction.

You should also collect estimates of data volume in terms of number of rows for each table. These numbers will enable you to estimate the average and maximum size of the database so that you can choose the proper hardware and software. You should also collect information on security conditions: Who owns the data? Who can have read access? Who can have write access? All of these conditions can be entered into the DBMS when you create the tables.

At this point, after you review your work, you can enter sample data to test your tables. When you are certain that the design is complete and accurate, you can begin building the application by constructing queries and creating forms and reports.

A DEVELOPER'S VIEW

Miranda learned that the class diagram is converted into a set of normalized tables. These tables are the foundation of the database application. Database design is crucial to developing your application. Engrave the basic normalization rule onto the back of your eyelids: Each non-key column depends on the whole key and nothing but the key. Since the design depends on the business rules, make certain that you understand the rules. Listen carefully to the users. When in doubt, opt for flexibility. For your class projects, you should now be able to create the list of normalized tables. You should also be able to estimate the size of the database.

KEY WORDS

autonumber, 109
Boyce-Codd normal form (BCNF), 85
cascading delete, 89
composite key, 67
data dictionary/repository, 109
data integrity, 88
data normalization, 66
data volume, 110
default values, 110
deletion anomaly, 75
dependence, 81
domain-key normal form (DKNF), 87
first normal form (1NF), 76
foreign key, 89
fourth normal form (4NF), 86
hidden dependency, 85
insertion anomaly, 75
metadata, 109
primary key, 66
referential integrity, 89
relational database, 66
repeating groups, 76
second normal form (2NF), 79
table, 66
third normal form (3NF), 81

REVIEW QUESTIONS

1. What is a primary key and why is it needed?
2. What is a composite key?
3. What are the main rules for normalization?
4. What problems do you encounter if data is not stored in normalized tables?
5. Explain the phrase *a column is dependent on another column.*
6. How are BCNF and 4NF different from 3NF?
7. What are the primary types of data that can be stored in a table?
8. Give examples of rules you would store as integrity constraints.
9. What elements do you look for when integrating views?
10. How do you estimate the potential size of a database?
11. Why is referential integrity important?
12. What complications are caused by setting referential integrity rules?

EXERCISES

1. Create the normalized tables needed for Exercise 9 in Chapter 2 (ride sharing).
2. Create the normalized tables needed for Exercise 10 in Chapter 2 (environmental consulting company).

3. The local historical society wants to track donations and print receipts. Create the normalized tables needed for this project.

DONATION	
Donor Name Member: ☐ Yes ☐ No Phone Address City, State, ZIP	Date Location

		Items		
Description	Est. Age	Est. Price	Quantity	Est. Value
			Total Value	

4. A local electronics/appliance store wants a system to track its inventory. Note that the store collects slightly different data for each type of product. Create the normalized tables needed for this project.

INVENTORY **DATE**

Televisions

Manufacturer	**Model**	**SVHS**	**Year**	**Size**	**Cost**	**ListPrice**	**Quantity**
Toshiba	TX330	yes	1998	27″	157	450	18
Sony	TR909	yes	1999	32″	332	750	8
Magnavox	MX98	no	1998	27″	132	400	19

Stereos

Manufacturer	**Model**	**Year**	**Cost**	**ListPrice**	**Quantity**	**AV**	**DVD**	**Special**
Sony	AV300	1998	200	450	14	yes	yes	Dolby
Pioneer	DH905	1999	350	700	8	yes	yes	THX
Technics	Z200	1998	150	320	16	no	no	

Appliances

Category	**Manuf.**	**Warranty**	**Cost**	**ListPrice**	**EnergyCost**	**Quantity**
Refrigerator	Amana	3 years	657	1300	56	7
Refrigerator	GE	2 years	418	1100	89	12
Microwave	GE	3 years	157	389	72	13
Dishwasher	Whirlpool	2 years	228	500	45	5
Dishwasher	GE	1 year	178	475	82	11

5. A small law firm wants to track the time its staff spends on each client. Using the current form, create the list of normalized tables needed to build the database. Create the normalized tables needed for this project.

Name Office Phone		**Time and Billing**				
Date	Time	Client	Contact	Phone		Fax
		Task	Description	Task Category	Cost Category	Length
					Total Charge	Total Time
		Client	Contact	Phone		Fax

6. A local marina wants to track slip reservations on an Internet Web site. Create the list of normalized tables needed to support the initial form. Create the normalized tables needed for this project.

Marina Reservations					Week of:	
Slip #	Size	Water Depth	Hookups	Available	Used	Base Charge
Boat Name Registration State License ID			Electric Water Waste Phone Cable TV	☐ ☐ ☐ ☐ ☐	☐ ☐ ☐ ☐ ☐	
Owner						
Phone Address City State, Zip						
Billing						
Phone Address City State, Zip						

Daily Charge	Days to Reserve	Payment Method
Hookups Total	Days Used	Credit Card Number
Total Est. Charges	Total Actual Charges	Expiration

7. The local volunteer fire department wants a small database to track the basic property under its jurisdiction and to record the number of incidents. Eventually, the department wants to build a geographic information system (GIS) to illustrate geographical relationships. Create the list of normalized tables needed to support the initial form.

VFD Incident Report					
Location			Owner		
Address GPS Latitude GPS Longitude Date Updated			Name Phone Business Phone Time Contacted		
Date/Time Start		Date/Time Return			
Truck ID		Description/Type			
Crew ID	Name	Phone	Specialty	Personal Vehicle	Injuries

8. A local machine shop needs a small database to record orders and track sales. Create the list of normalized tables needed to support the initial form.

Order #		**Machine Shop Orders**							
Salesperson		Customer							
Phone Office Commission		Type of Business Address City, State Zip			Contact Title Phone Fax Credit Rating		Payment Notes Amount Due Date Due		
Package Requirements									
Estimated Production Time		Estimated Delivery Date							
Items									
Item	Description	Size	Qty	Price	Extended	Prod.Date	Plant#	Run#	Ship Date

Date/Time

9. You have been hired to develop a small database for a company that wants to offer products for sale on the Internet. Create the list of normalized tables needed to support the initial form.

<table>
<tr><td>Date/Time</td><td colspan="8">Order Form</td></tr>
<tr><td colspan="3">Customer</td><td colspan="3">Credit Card</td><td colspan="3">Internet</td></tr>
<tr><td rowspan="3">Name
Phone</td><td colspan="2" rowspan="3">Shipping Address
City, State Zip</td><td colspan="3">Card #</td><td colspan="3">E-mail</td></tr>
<tr><td colspan="3">Expiration Date</td><td colspan="3">IP Address</td></tr>
<tr><td colspan="3">Bank</td><td colspan="3">Referred From</td></tr>
<tr><td colspan="9">Items</td></tr>
<tr><td>Item#</td><td>Name</td><td>Description</td><td>Quantity</td><td>List Price</td><td>Sale Price</td><td>Quantity Shipped</td><td>Back Order</td><td>Extended</td></tr>
<tr><td></td><td></td><td></td><td></td><td></td><td></td><td></td><td></td><td></td></tr>
<tr><td></td><td></td><td></td><td></td><td></td><td></td><td></td><td></td><td></td></tr>
<tr><td></td><td></td><td></td><td></td><td></td><td></td><td></td><td></td><td></td></tr>
<tr><td colspan="6"></td><td colspan="2">Item Total
Shipping
Tax
Total Due</td><td></td></tr>
</table>

10. You want to build a small database to keep track of your new and growing DVD collection. You could let the Microsoft Access Wizard build the application for you, but you really want to impress that "significant other" with your talents. Create the list of normalized tables needed to support the initial form. To make it easier, assume that a DVD can only hold one type of data.

DVD Collection								
Title Category	Label Company	Catalog #	Date Released	Date Purchased	Price Paid	List Price	Length	☐ Audio ☐ Video ☐ Computer
Audio								
Band Name	Date Formed	Background Information						
Personnel	Name	Instrument		Gender	Age/Birthdate			
Songs	Title	Track#	Length	Comment				
Video: Title								
Performer	Name	Character/Job	Gender	Age/Birthdate				
Computer								
File	Name	Size	Category	Date Created	Data Type	Comments		

11. You have been asked to develop a database for a lawn care service company. Two sample forms (initial order and a service receipt) have been provided, along with some notes that you took regarding the standard bill. Create the list of normalized tables needed to support a database for this company. Bill(Bill#, Date, Customer, Location, AmountPastDue, CustomerWorkPhone, NewAmountDue, Total, (Job#, Description, Date, Time, Comment/Suggestions, CrewChief))

Lawn Care Service	**Initial Contract and Order**		Start Date	End Date
Date/Time	SalesPerson	Commission	Estimated Monthly Cost	
Customer	Location		Signature	
Bank/Credit ID Name Phone Billing Address City, State Zip	Address City, State Zip			

Desired Tasks				
Task	Size Est.	Time Est.	Cost Est.	Frequency/How Often?

Lawn Care Service				**Service Receipt**				
Job#	Location	Address	Subdivision	Difficulty Rating	Date	Start Time	End Time	Contact

Task	Description			Category	
	Equipment	Description	Time Used	Cleaned (Y/N)	Fuel Used

Crew				
Name	Specialty	Hourly Rate	Date Hired	Amount Due Payment Method Payment Amount

12. A shipping company has asked you to create an initial design for a database. You have three forms and some notes on delivery tracking that you can use to design the database. Create the list of normalized tables needed to support a database for this company. Delivery(Date, Time, PackageID, Driver, CustomerSignature, Location/Address, Route#)

Shipping Company		**Order Form**				**Date**	
Customer		Pickup Location					
Name Address City, State Zip		Zone Office ID Address					
Items							
Destination Zone Name Address City, State Zip	Item	Description	Value	COD	Weight	Cost	Package ID Bar Code

Shipping Company			**Plane Loading**			Zone	Manager Fax
Date	Time	Plane#	Type	Cargo Size	Max Container	Cargo Weight	
	Size	Weight	Destination Zone			Load Time	
Box ID/Code	Package ID	Cubic Feet	Comments				
	Size	Weight	Destination Zone			Load Time	
Box ID/Code	Package ID	Cubic Feet	Comments				

Shipping Company		**Employee Records**	
Employee ID		Last Name	First Name
Date Hired Date Released		Equipment Assigned Equipment ID Description Date Purchased	
Manager	Cell Phone	Office	
Positions			
Date	Position	Salary	Location

Sally's Pet Store

13. Define the tables needed to extend the Pet Store database to handle genealogy records for the animals.

14. Define the tables needed to extend the Pet Store database to handle health and veterinary records for the animals.

Rolling Thunder Bicycles

15. Using the class diagram, identify five business rules that are described by the table definitions and table relationships (similar to the RentPrice rules described by the Video store).

16. The company wishes to add more data for human resources, such as tax withholding, benefits selected, and benefit payments by the employees and by the company. Research common methods of handling this type of data and define the required tables.

WEB SITE REFERENCES

Site	Description
http://www.dbpd.com/	*Database Programming & Design* magazine.
http://www.for.gov.bc.ca/isb/datadmin/	Canadian Ministry of Forests data administration site, with useful information on data administration and design. Start with the development standards.
http://www.sybase.com/products/ white papers/pkey_wpaper.html	A paper on the relative merits and costs of surrogate keys, especially within Sybase database systems.

ADDITIONAL READING

Date, C. J. *An Introduction to Database Systems. 6th ed.* Reading: Addison-Wesley, 1995. [A classic higher-level textbook that covers many details of normalization and databases.]

Diederich, J., and J. Milton. "New methods and fast algorithms for database normalization." *ACM Transactions on Database Systems* 13 no. 3 (September 1988), 339–65. [One of many attempts to automate the normalization process.]

Fagin, R. "Multivalued dependencies and a new normal form for relational databases." *ACM Transactions on Database Systems* 2 no. 3 (September 1977), pp. 262–78. [A classic paper in the development of normal forms.]

Fagin, R. "A normal form for relational databases that is based on domains and keys." *ACM Transactions on Database Systems* 6 no. 3 (September 1981), pp. 387–415. [The paper that initially described domain-key normal form.]

Kent, W. "A simple guide to five normal forms in relational database theory." *Communications of the ACM* 26 no. 2 (February 1983), 120–25. [A nice presentation of normalization, with examples.]

P A R T 2

Queries

An important step in building applications is creating queries to retrieve exactly the data that you want. Queries are used to answer business questions and serve as the foundation for forms and reports.

Chapter 4 shows you how to use two basic query systems: SQL and QBE. SQL has the advantage of being a standard that is supported by many database management systems. Once you learn it, you will be able to work with many different systems.

Chapter 5 shows some of the powerful aspects of SQL queries. In particular, it examines the use of subqueries to answer difficult business questions. It also shows that SQL is a complete database language that can be used to define new databases and tables. SQL is also a powerful tool to manipulate data.

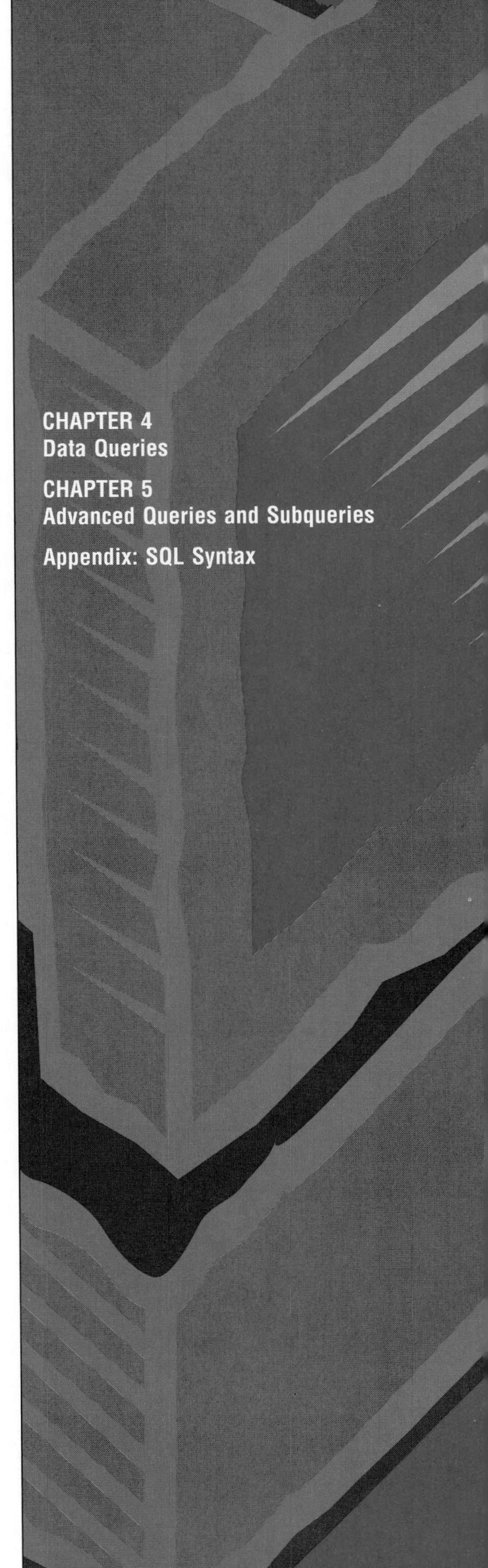

CHAPTER 4

Data Queries

WHAT YOU WILL LEARN IN THIS CHAPTER

OVERVIEW

Miranda: *Wow that was hard work! I sure hope normalization gets easier the next time.*

Ariel: *At least now you have a good database. What's next? Are you ready to start building the application?*

Miranda: *Not quite yet. I told my uncle that I had some sample data. He already started asking me business questions: Which products were backordered most often? and Which employees sold the most items last month? I think I need to know how to answer some of those questions before I try to build an application.*

Ariel: *Can't you just look through the data and find the answer?*

Miranda: *Maybe, but that would take forever. Instead, I'll use a query system that will do most of the work for me. I just have to figure out how to phrase the business questions as a correct query.*

INTRODUCTION

Why do we need a query language? Why not just ask your question in a natural language like English? Natural language processors have improved, and several companies have attempted to connect them to databases. Similarly, speech recognition is improving. Eventually, computers may be able to answer ad hoc questions using a natural language. However, even if we had an excellent natural language processor, we would still use a specialized query language. The main reason is communication. If you ask a question of a database, a computer, or even another person, you can get an answer. The catch is, did the computer give you the answer to the question you asked? In other words, you have to know that the machine (or other person) interpreted the question in exactly the way you wanted. The problem with any natural language is that it can be ambiguous. If there is any doubt in the interpretation, you run the risk of receiving an answer that might appear reasonable but is not the answer to the question you meant to ask.

We need a query system that is more structured than a natural language so there is less room for misinterpretation. We also need a standardized system, which works the same way on different hardware and database systems from different vendors so that users and developers can learn one query method that works on most systems. The two basic approaches to query systems are **query by example (QBE)** and **SQL.**

QBE is a fill-in-the-form approach to designing queries. You select tables and columns from a list and fill in blanks for conditions and sorting. It is relatively easy to use, requires minimal typing skills, generally comes with a Help system, and is useful for beginners.

SQL is more standardized and is supported by most database vendors, although there are variations in syntax and features. Compared to QBE, SQL is a written language, so you have to know the table and column names, and type in the SQL statement. On the other hand, in addition to handling ad hoc queries, SQL can be used from within programming code or passed efficiently across networks. In some ways SQL queries are easier to read than QBE, so you can check your queries to make sure they ask the question you intended.

This chapter covers both methods of queries. The key point to recognize is that the two methods—in fact, all query systems—are similar. Every relational query system must address four basic questions. Once you understand those four questions, the rest is pure syntax or organization.

As you work on queries, you should also think about the overall database design. Chapter 3 shows how normalization is used to split data into tables that can be stored efficiently. Queries are the other side of that problem—they are used to put the tables back together to answer ad hoc questions and produce reports.

FOUR QUESTIONS TO CREATE A QUERY

Every query or attempt to retrieve data from a relational DBMS requires answering the four basic questions shown in Figure 4.1. The difference among query systems is how you fill in those answers. You need to remember these four questions, but do not worry about the specific order. When you first learn to create queries, you should write down these four questions each time you construct a query. With easy problems, you can almost automatically fill in answers to these questions. With more complex problems, you might fill in partial answers and switch between questions until you completely understand the query.

Notice that in some easy situations you will not have to answer all four questions. Many easy questions involve only one table, so you will not have to worry about joining tables (question 3). As another example, you might want the total sales for the entire company, as opposed to the total sales for a particular employee, so there may not be any constraints (question 2).

What Output Do You Want to See?

You generally answer this question by selecting columns of data from the various tables stored in the database. Of course, you need to know the names of all of the columns to answer this question. Generally, the hardest part in answering this question is to wade through the list of tables and identify the columns you really want to see. The problem is more difficult when the database has hundreds of tables and thousands of columns.

You can also ask the computer to make aggregate computations, such as totals and averages. Similarly, the computer can perform basic arithmetic operations (add, subtract, multiply, and divide) on numeric data.

What Do You Already Know?

In most situations you want to restrict your search based on various criteria. For instance, you might be interested in sales on a particular date or sales from only one department. The search conditions must be converted into a standard Boolean notation (phrases connected with AND or OR). The most important part of this step is to write down all the conditions to help you understand the purpose of the query.

What Tables Are Involved?

With only a few tables, this question is easy. With hundreds of tables, it could take a while to determine exactly which ones you need. A good data dictionary with synonyms and comments will make it easier for you (and users) to determine exactly which tables you need for the query. It is also critical that tables be given names that accurately reflect their content and purpose.

FIGURE 4.1
Four questions to create a query. Every query is built by asking these four questions.

- What output do you want to see?
- What do you already know (or what constraints are given)?
- What tables are involved?
- How are the tables joined?

One hint in choosing tables is to start with the tables containing the columns listed in the first two questions (output and criteria). Next decide whether other tables might be needed to serve as intermediaries to connect these tables.

How Are the Tables Joined?

This question relates to the issues in data normalization and is the heart of a relational database. Tables are connected by data in similar columns. For instance, an Order table has a CustomerID column. Corresponding data is stored in the Customer table, which also has a CustomerID column. In many cases matching columns in the tables will have the same name (e.g., CustomerID), and this question is easy to answer. However, the columns are not required to have the same name, so you sometimes have to think a little more carefully. For example, an Order table might have a column for SalesPerson, which is designed to match the EmployeeID key in an Employee table.

SALLY'S PET STORE

The initial Pet Store database has been built, and some basic historical data has been transferred from Sally's old files. When you showed your work to Sally, she became very excited. She immediately started asking questions about her business. She wants to see how the database can answer them.

The examples in this chapter are derived from the Pet Store database. The tables and relationships for this case are shown in Figure 4.2. After reading each section,

AnimalOrder: **OrderID**, OrderDate, ReceiveDate, SupplierID, ShippingCost, EmployeeID

Animal OrderItem: **OrderID**, **AnimalID**, Cost

Breed: **Category**, **Breed**

Animal: **AnimalID**, Name, Category, Breed, DateBorn, Gender, Registered, Color, ListPrice, Photo

SaleAnimal: **SaleID**, **AnimalID**, SalePrice

Supplier: **SupplierID**, Name, ContactName, Phone, Address, ZipCode, CityID

City: **CityID**, ZipCode, City, State, AreaCode, Population1990, Population1980, Country, Latitude, Longitude

Employee: **EmployeeID**, LastName, FirstName, Phone, Address, ZipCode, CityID, TaxPayerID, DateHired, DateReleased

Sale: **SaleID**, Date, EmployeeID, CustomerID, Sales Tax

Customer: **CustomerID**, Phone, FirstName, LastName, Address, ZipCode, CityID

Category: **Category**, Registration

Merchandise OrderItem: **PONumber**, **ItemID**, Quantity, Cost

Merchandise: **ItemID**, Description, QuantityOnHand, ListPrice, Category

SaleItem: **SaleID**, **ItemID**, Quantity, SalePrice

Merchandise Order: **PONumber**, OrderDate, ReceiveDate, SupplierID, EmployeeID, ShippingCost

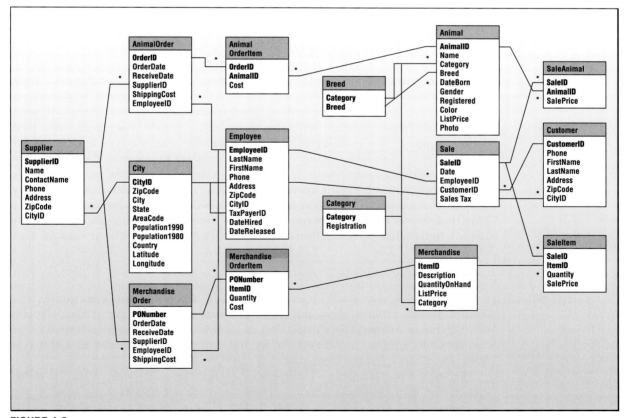

FIGURE 4.2
Tables for the Pet Store database. Notice that animals and merchandise are similar, but they are treated separately.

FIGURE 4.3
Sample questions for the Pet Store. Most of these are relatively easy since they involve only one table. They represent typical questions that a manager or customer might ask.

- List all animals with yellow in their color.
- List all dogs with yellow in their color born after 6/1/98.
- List all merchandise for cats with a list price greater than $10.
- List all dogs who are male and registered, or who were born before 6/1/98 and have white in their color.
- What is the average sale price of all animals?
- What is the total cost we paid for all animals?
- List the top 10 customers and total amount they spent.
- How many cats are in the animal list?
- Count the number of animals in each category.
- List the CustomerID of everyone who bought something between 4/1/98 and 4/30/98.
- List the first name and phone of every customer who bought something between 4/1/98 and 4/30/98.
- List the last name and phone of anyone who bought a registered white cat between 6/1/98 and 8/31/98.
- Which employee sold the most items?

you should work through the queries on your own. You should also solve the exercises at the end of the chapter. Queries always look easy when the answers are printed in the book. To learn to write queries, you must sit down and struggle through the process of answering the four basic questions.

Chapter 3 notes that data normalization results in a business model of the organization. The list of tables gives a picture of how the firm operates. Notice that the Pet Store treats merchandise a little differently than it treats animals. For example, each animal is listed separately on a sale, but customers can purchase multiple copies of merchandise item (e.g., bags of cat food). The reason for the split is that we need to keep additional information about the animals that does not apply to general merchandise.

When you begin to work with an existing database, the first thing you need to do is familiarize yourself with the tables and columns. You should also look through some of the main tables to become familiar with the type and amount of data stored in each table. Make sure you understand the terminology and examine the underlying assumptions. For example, in the Pet Store case, an animal might be registered with a breeding agency, but it can be registered with only one agency. If it is not registered, the Registered column is **NULL** (or missing) for that animal. This first step is easier when you work for a specific company, since you should already be familiar with the firm's operations and the terms that it uses for various objects.

QUERY BASICS

It is best to begin with relatively easy queries. This chapter first presents queries that involve a single table to show the basics of creating a query. Then it covers details on constraints, followed by a discussion on computations and aggregations. Groups and subtotals are then explained. Finally, the chapter discusses how to select data from several tables at the same time.

Figure 4.3 presents several business questions that might arise at the Pet Store. Notice that many business queries do not end with a question mark. Most of the questions are relatively easy to answer. In fact, if there are not too many rows in the Animal table, you could probably find the answers by hand-searching the table.

Actually, you might want to work some of the initial questions by hand to help you understand what the query system is doing.

The foundation of queries is that you want to see only some of the columns from a table and that you want to restrict the output to a set of rows that match some criteria. For example, in the first query (animals with yellow color), you might want to see the AnimalID, Category, Breed, and their Color. Instead of listing every animal in the table, you want to restrict the list to just those with a yellow color.

Single Tables

The first query we want to consider is, List all animals with yellow in their color. Note that an animal could have many colors. The designer of this database has chosen to store all the colors in one column of the database. So an animal's colors could be described as "yellow, white, brown." Presumably, the primary color is listed first, but there is no mechanism to force the data to be entered that way.

First consider answering this question with a QBE system, as shown in Figure 4.4. The QBE system asks you to choose the tables involved. This situation involves only one table: Animal. Note that all the output columns are in the Animal table. Similarly, the Color column in the criteria is also in the Animal table. With the table displayed, you can now choose which columns you want to see in the output. The business question is a little vague, so we selected AnimalID, Category, Breed, and the Color. Another option would have been to choose all the columns (*), but that ap-

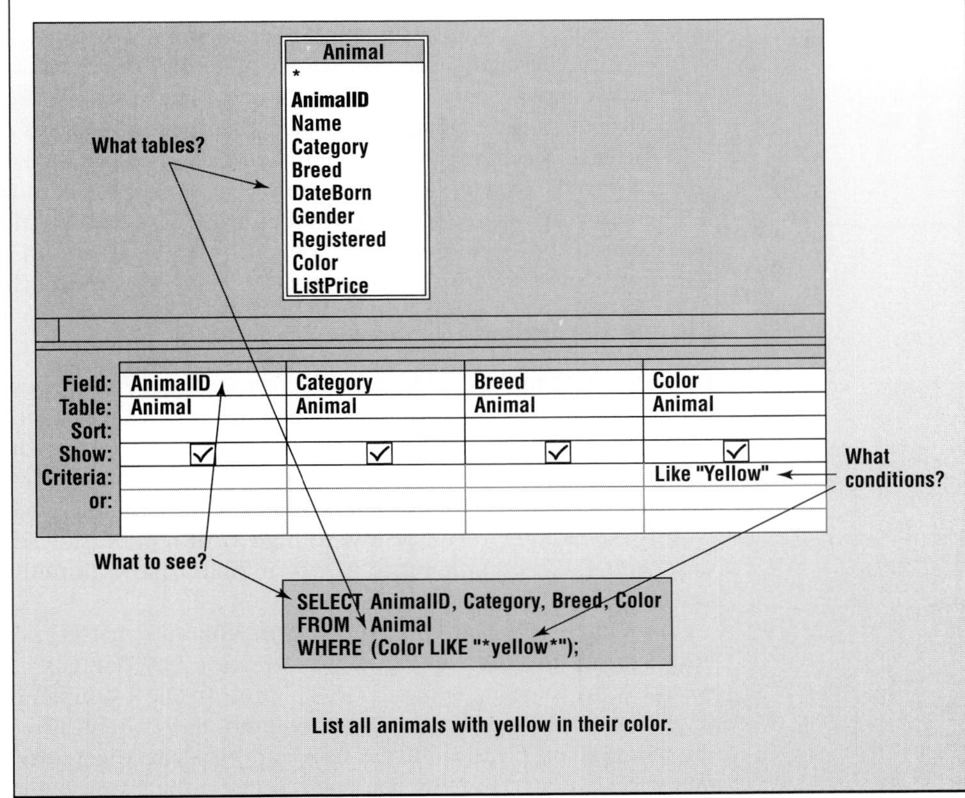

FIGURE 4.4 Sample query shown in QBE and SQL. Since there is only one table, only three questions need to be answered: What tables? What conditions? What do you want to see?

SELECT	columns	What do you want to see?
FROM	tables	What tables are involved?
JOIN	conditions	How are the tables joined?
WHERE	criteria	What are the constraints?

FIGURE 4.5
The basic SQL SELECT command matches the four questions you need to create a query. The uppercase letters are used in this text to highlight the SQL keywords. They can also be typed in lowercase.

proach often results in more columns than we need. To select the columns in QBE, you can drag the column name down from the table listing or select the column from the combo box on the Field line of the grid.

The next step is to enter the criteria that we already know. In this example we are looking for animals with "yellow" in their color. On the QBE screen enter the condition "yellow" under the Color column. However, there is one catch: The Color column generally contains more than one word. For some animals, *yellow* might show up as the second or third color in the list. To match the animal regardless of where the word *yellow* is located, you need to use the LIKE pattern-matching function. By entering the condition LIKE "*yellow*", you are asking the query system to match the word *yellow* anywhere in the list (with any number of characters before or after the word). It is a good idea to run the query now. Check the Color column to make sure the word *yellow* appears somewhere in the list.

Introduction to SQL

SQL is a powerful query language. However, unlike QBE, you generally have to type in the entire statement. Some systems like Microsoft Access enable you to switch back and forth between QBE and SQL, which saves some typing. Perhaps the greatest strength of SQL is that it is a standard that most vendors of DBMS software support. Hence once you learn the base language, you will be able to create queries on all of the major systems in use today. Some people pronounce SQL as "sequel," arguing that it descended from a vendor's early DBMS called quel. Also, "Sequel" is easier to say than "ess-cue-el."

The most commonly used command in SQL is the SELECT statement, which is used to retrieve data from tables. A simple version of the command is shown in Figure 4.5, which contains the four basic parts: **SELECT, FROM, JOIN,** and **WHERE.** These parts match the basic questions needed by every query. In the example in Figure 4.4, notice the similarity between the QBE and SQL approaches.

Sorting the Output

Database systems treat tables as collections of data. For efficiency purposes the DBMS is free to store the table data in any manner or any order that it chooses. Yet in most cases you will want to display the results of a query in a particular order. The SQL **ORDER BY** clause is an easy and fast means to display the output in any order you choose. As shown in Figure 4.6, simply list the columns you want to sort. The default is ascending (A to Z or low to high with numbers). Add the phrase **DESC** (for descending) after a column to sort from high to low. In QBE you select the sort order on the QBE grid.

In some cases you will want to sort columns that do not contain unique data. For example, the rows in Figure 4.6 are sorted by Category. In these situations you would want to add a second sort column. In the example, rows for each category (e.g., Bird) are sorted on the Breed column. The column listed first is sorted first. In the example all birds are listed first, and birds are then sorted by Breed. To change this sort sequence in QBE, you have to move the entire column on the QBE grid so that Category is to the left of Breed.

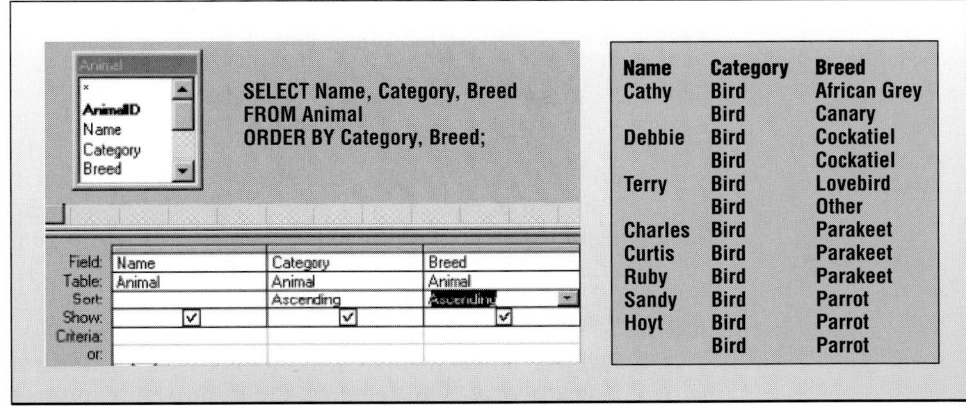

FIGURE 4.6
The ORDER BY clause sorts the output rows. The default is to sort in ascending order; adding the keyword DESC after a column name results in a descending sort. When columns such as Category contain duplicate data, use a second column (e.g., Breed) to sort the rows within each category.

Distinct

The SELECT statement has an option that is useful in some queries. The **DISTINCT** keyword tells the DBMS to display only rows that are unique. For example, the query in Figure 4.7 (*SELECT Category FROM Animal*) would return a long list of animal types (Bird, Cat, Dog, etc.). In fact, it would return the category for every animal in the table—obviously, there are many cats and dogs. To prevent the duplicates from being displayed, use the SELECT DISTINCT phrase.

Note that the DISTINCT keyword applies to the entire row. If there are any differences in a row, it will be displayed. For example, the query *SELECT DISTINCT Category, Breed FROM Animal* will return more than the seven rows shown in Figure 4.7 because each category can have many breeds. That is, each category/breed combination will be listed only once, such as Dog/Retriever.

Microsoft Access supports the DISTINCT keyword, but you have to enter it in the SQL statement. Also note that Microsoft created a proprietary keyword DISTINCTROW that Access uses in almost every query. Be careful; this keyword is

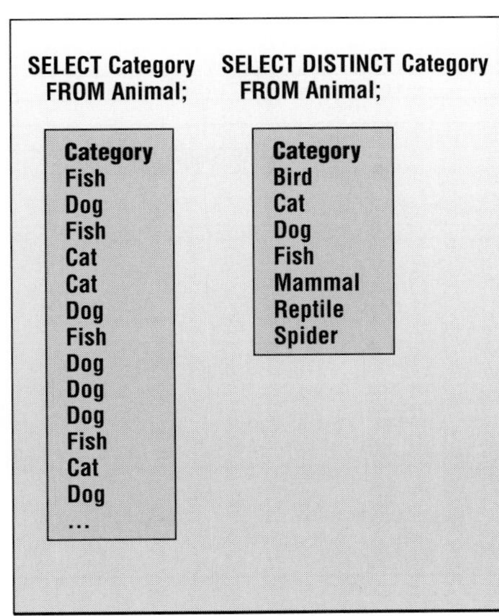

FIGURE 4.7
The DISTINCT keyword eliminates duplicate rows of the output. Without it the animal category is listed for every animal in the database.

different from the SQL standard DISTINCT. In fact, the DISTINCTROW statement is meaningless in most well-formed queries.

Criteria

In most questions identifying the output columns and the tables is straightforward. If there are hundreds of tables, it might take a while to decide exactly which tables and columns you want, but it is just an issue of perseverance. On the other hand, identifying constraints and specifying them correctly can be more challenging. More important, if you make a mistake on a constraint, you will still get an "answer." The problem is that it will not be the answer to the question you asked—and it is often difficult to see that you made a mistake.

The primary concept of constraints is based on **Boolean algebra,** which you learned in mathematics. In practice, the term simply means that various conditions are connected with AND and OR clauses. Sometimes you will also use a **NOT** statement, which negates or reverses the truth of the statement that follows it. For example, NOT (Category = "Dog") means you are interested in all animals except dogs.

Consider the example in Figure 4.8. The first step is to note that the business question defines three conditions: dog, yellow, and date of birth. The second step is to recognize that all three of these conditions need to be true at the same time, so they are connected by AND. As the database system examines each row, it evaluates all three clauses. If any one clause is false, the row is skipped.

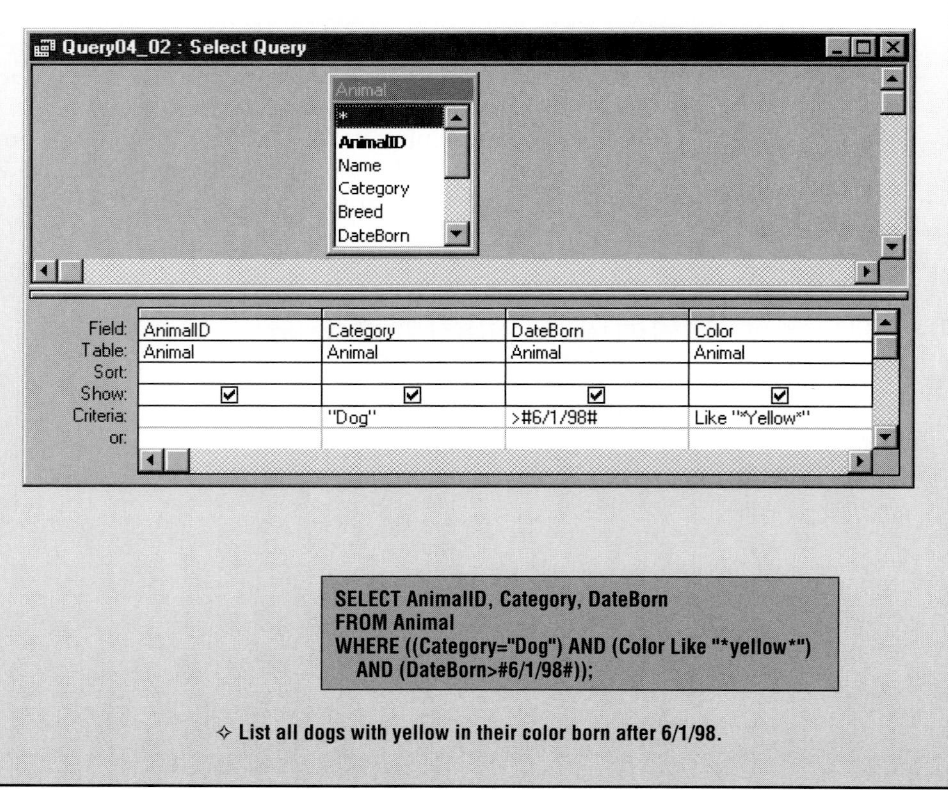

FIGURE 4.8
Boolean algebra. An example of three conditions connected by AND. The # signs surrounding the date are a convention used by Microsoft Access to help it recognize a date. They are particularly useful if you want to enter a text date (e.g., June 1, 1998).

FIGURE 4.9
A truth table shows the difference between AND and OR. Both clauses must be true when connected by AND. Only one clause needs to be true when clauses are connected by OR.

A	B	A AND B	A OR B
T	T	T	T
T	F	F	T
F	T	F	T
F	F	F	F

Notice that the SQL statement is straightforward—just write the criteria. The QBE is a little trickier. With QBE every condition listed on the same criteria row is connected with an AND clause Conditions on different criteria rows are joined with an OR clause. You have to be careful creating (and reading) QBE statements—particularly when there are many different criteria rows.

Boolean Algebra

One of the most important aspects of a query is the choice of rows that you want to see. Most tables contain a huge number of rows, and you want to see only the few that meet a business condition. Some conditions are straightforward. For example, you might want to examine only dogs. Other criteria are complex and involve several conditions. For instance, a customer might want a list of all yellow dogs born after June 1, 1998, or registered black labs. Conditions are evaluated according to Boolean algebra—which is a standard set of rules for evaluating conditions. You are probably already familiar with the rules from basic algebra courses. However, it pays to be careful.

The DBMS uses Boolean algebra to evaluate conditions that consist of multiple clauses. The clauses are connected by these operators: AND, OR, NOT. Each individual clause is evaluated as true or false, and then the operators are applied to evaluate the truth value of the overall criterion. Figure 4.9 shows how the primary operators (AND, OR) work. The DBMS examines each row of data and evaluates the Boolean condition. The row is displayed only if the condition is true.

A condition consisting of two clauses connected by AND can be true only if both of the clauses (a and b) are true. A statement that consists of two clauses connected by OR is true as long as at least one of the two conditions is true. Consider the examples shown in Figure 4.10. The first condition is false because it asks for both

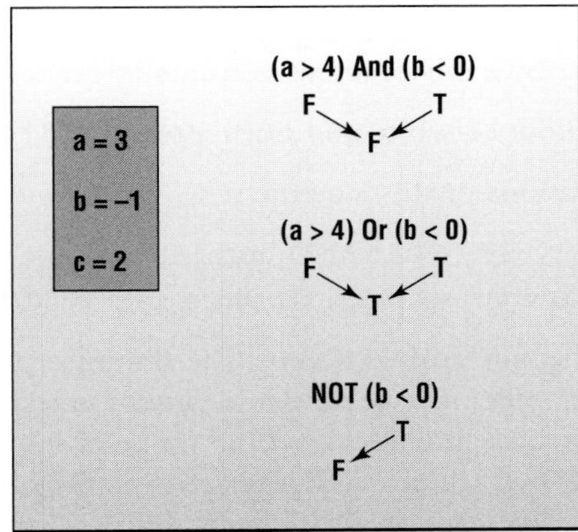

FIGURE 4.10
Boolean algebra examples. Evaluate each clause separately. Then evaluate the connector. The NOT operator reverses the truth value.

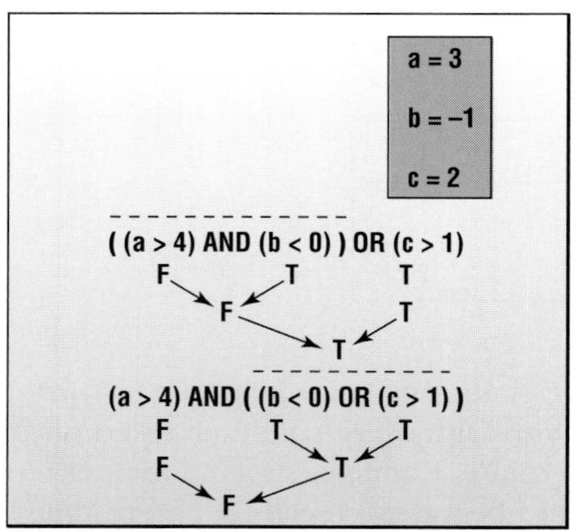

FIGURE 4.11 Boolean algebra mixing AND and OR operators. The result changes depending on which operator is applied first. You must set the order of evaluation with parentheses. Innermost clauses are evaluated first.

clauses to be true, and the first one is false. The second example is true because it requires that only one of the two clauses be true. Consider an example from the Pet Store. If a customer asks to see a list of yellow dogs, he or she wants a list of animals where the category is Dog AND the color is yellow.

As shown in Figure 4.11, conditions that are more complex can be created by adding additional clauses. A complication arises when the overall condition contains both AND connectors and OR connectors. In this situation the resulting truth value depends on the order in which the clauses are evaluated. You should always use parentheses to specify the desired order. Innermost parentheses are evaluated first. In the example at the top of Figure 4.11, the AND operation is performed before the OR operation giving a result of true. In the bottom example, the OR connector is evaluated first, leading to an evaluation of false.

If you do not use parentheses, the operators are evaluated from left-to-right. This result may not be what you intended. Yet the DBMS will still provide a response. To be safe, you should build complex conditions one clause at a time. Check the resulting selection each time to be sure you get what you wanted. To find the data matching the conditions in Figure 4.11, you would first enter the (a > 4) clause and display all of the values. Then you would add the (b < 0) clause and display the results. Finally, you would add the parentheses and then the (c > 1) clause.

No matter how careful you are with Boolean algebra, there is always room for error. The problem is that natural languages like English are ambiguous. For example, consider the request by a customer who wants to see a list of

All dogs that are yellow or white and born after June 1.

There are two interpretations of this statement:

1. (dogs AND yellow) OR (white AND born after June 1).
2. (dogs) AND (yellow OR white) AND (born after June 1).

These two requests are significantly different. The first interpretation returns all yellow dogs, even if they are older. The second interpretation requests only young dogs, and they must be yellow or white. Most people do not use parentheses when they speak—although pauses help indicate the desired interpretation. A good designer (or salesperson) will ask the customer for clarification.

DeMorgan's Law

Designing queries is an exercise in logic. A useful technique for simplifying complex queries was created by a logician named DeMorgan. Consider the Pet Store example displayed in Figure 4.12. A customer might come in and say, "I want to look at a cat, but I don't want any cats that are registered or that have red in their color." Even in SQL, the condition for this query is a little confusing: (Category = "cat") AND NOT ((Registered is NOT NULL) OR (Color LIKE "*red*")). The negation (NOT) operator makes it harder to understand the condition. It is even more difficult to create the QBE version of the statement.

The solution lies with **DeMorgan's law,** which explains how to negate conditions when two clauses are connected with an AND or an OR. DeMorgan's law states that to negate a condition with an AND or an OR connector, you negate each of the two clauses and switch the connector. An AND becomes an OR, and vice versa. Figure 4.13 shows how to handle the negative condition for the Pet Store customer. Each condition is negated (NOT NULL becomes NULL, and red becomes NOT red). Then the connector is changed from OR to AND. Figure 4.13 shows that the final truth value stays the same when the statement is evaluated both ways.

The advantage of the new version of the condition is that it is a little easier to understand and much easier to use in QBE. In QBE you enter the individual clauses for Registration and Color. Placing them on the same line connects them with AND.

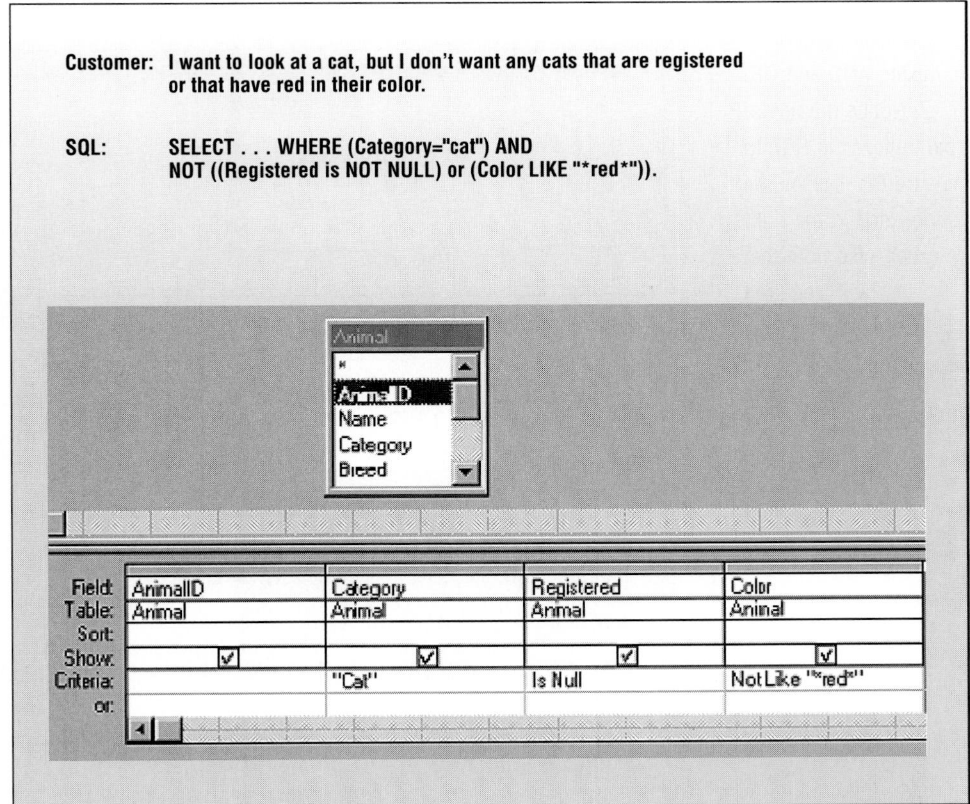

FIGURE 4.12
Sample problem with negation. Customer knows what he or she does not want. SQL can use NOT, but you should use DeMorgan's law to negate the Registered and Color statements.

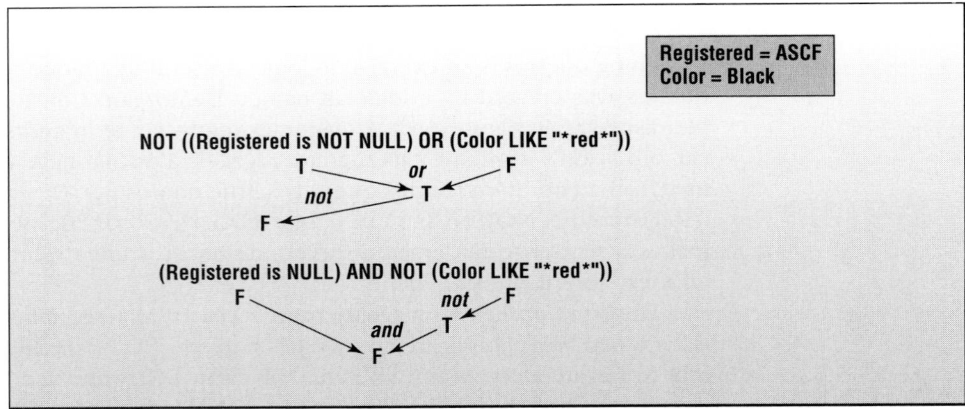

FIGURE 4.13 DeMorgan's law. Compound statements are negated by reversing each item and swapping the connector (AND for OR). Use truth tables to evaluate the examples.

In natural language the new version is expressed as follows: A cat that is not registered and is not red.

In practice DeMorgan's law is useful to simplify complex statements. However, you should always test your work by using sample data to evaluate the truth tables.

Criteria can become more complex when you mix clauses with AND and OR in the same query. Consider the question in Figure 4.14 to list all dogs who are male and registered or who were born before 6/1/98 and have white in their color.

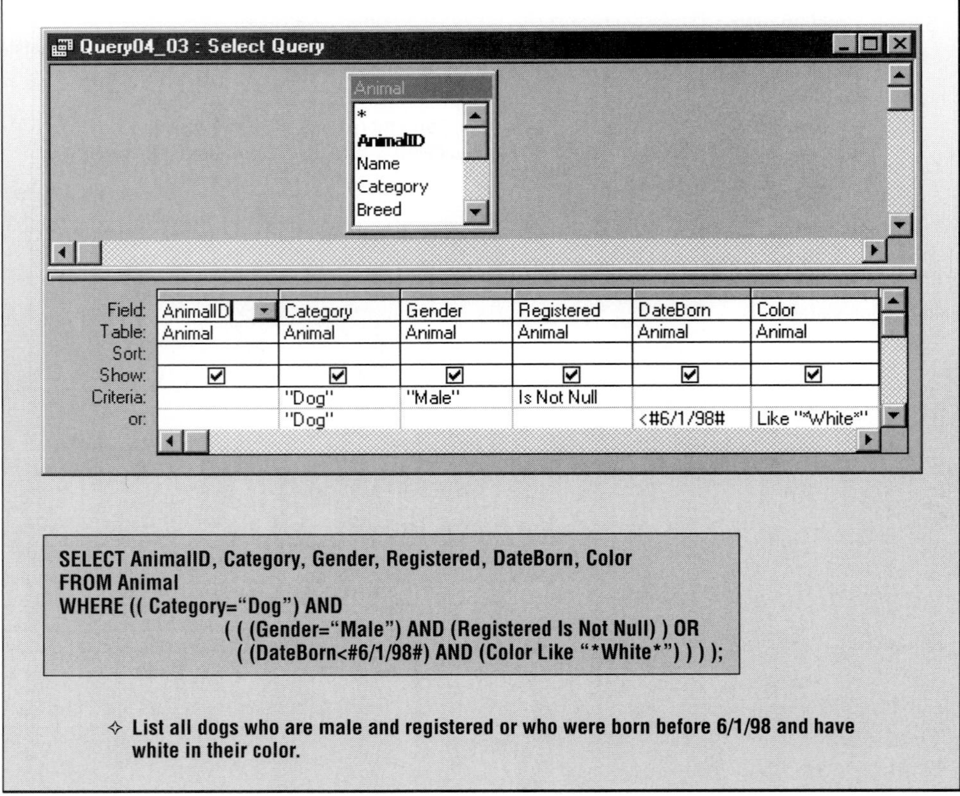

FIGURE 4.14 Boolean criteria—mixing AND and OR. Notice the use of parentheses in SQL to ensure the clauses are interpreted in the right order. Also note that QBE required duplicating the condition for "Dog" in both rows.

FIGURE 4.15
Ambiguity in natural languages means the sentence could be interpreted either way. However, version (1) is the most common interpretation.

List all dogs who are male and registered or who were born before 6/1/98 and have white in their color.
1. (male and registered) or (born after 6/1/98 and white)
2. (male) and (registered or born after 6/1/98) and (white)

First, note that there is some ambiguity in the English statement about how to group the two clauses. Figure 4.15 shows the two possibilities. The use of the second *who* helps to clarify the split, but the only way to be absolutely certain is to use either parentheses or more words.

The SQL version of the query is straightforward—just be sure to use parentheses to indicate the priority for evaluating each phrase. Innermost clauses are always evaluated first. A useful trick in proofreading queries is to use a sample row and mark T or F above each condition. Next combine the marks based on the parentheses and connectors (AND, OR). Then read the statement in English and see whether you arrive at the same result.

With QBE you list clauses joined by AND on the same row, which is equivalent to putting them inside one set of parentheses. Separate clauses connected by OR are placed on a new row. To interpret the query, look at each criteria row separately. If all of the conditions on one line are true, then the row is determined to be a match. A data row needs to match only one of the separate criteria lines (not all of them).

A second hint for building complex queries is to test just part of the criteria at one time—particularly with QBE. In this example you would first write and test a query for male and registered. Then add the other conditions and check the results at each step. Although this process takes longer than just leaping to the final query, it helps to ensure that you get the correct answer. For complex queries it is always wise to examine the SQL WHERE clause to make sure the parentheses are correct.

Useful WHERE Clauses

Most database systems provide the comparison operators displayed in Figure 4.16. Standard numeric data can be compared with equality and inequality operators. Text comparisons are usually made with the **LIKE** operator for pattern matching. The SQL standard uses the percent sign (%) to match any number of characters and the underscore (_) to match exactly one character. Microsoft Access uses an asterisk (*) and a question mark (?) instead. The single-character match (?) is particularly useful for searches

FIGURE 4.16
Common comparisons used in the WHERE clause. The BETWEEN clause is useful for dates but can be used for any type of data.

COMPARISONS	EXAMPLES
Operators	<, =, >, <>, BETWEEN
Numbers	AccountBalance > 200
Text	
Common	Name > "Jones"
Match all	Name LIKE "J*"
Match one	Name LIKE "?m*"
Dates	SDate BETWEEN #8/15/99# AND #8/31/99#
Missing Data	City IS NULL
Negation	Name IS NOT NULL

involving defined text strings like product numbers. For example, product numbers might be defined as DDDCCC9999 where the first three characters represent the department, the next three the product category, and the last four digits are a unique number. Then to find all products that refer to the Dog category you could use the WHERE condition: ProductID LIKE "???dog????". Most systems also provide an option that controls whether text comparisons are sensitive to upper- and lower-case. Many people prefer to ignore case, since it is easier to type words without worrying about case.

The **BETWEEN** clause is not required, but it saves some typing and makes some conditions a little clearer. The clause (SDate BETWEEN #8/15/99# AND #8/31/99#) is equivalent to (SDate >= #8/15/99# AND SDate <= #8/31/99#). Note that Microsoft introduced the pound sign (#) to indicate date data. It is not standard in SQL. Dates within pound signs can be entered with any common format.

Another useful condition is to test for missing data with the NULL comparison. Two common forms are IS NULL and IS NOT NULL. Be careful—the statement (City = NULL) will not work with most systems, because NULL is not really a value. You must use (City IS NULL) instead.

COMPUTATIONS

For the most part you would use a spreadsheet or write separate programs for serious computations. However, queries can be used for two types of computations: aggregations and simple arithmetic on a row-by-row basis. Sometimes the two types of calculations are combined. Consider the row-by-row computations first.

Basic Arithmetic Operators

SQL and QBE can both be used to perform basic computations on each row of data. This technique can be used to automate basic tasks and to reduce the amount of data storage. Consider a common order or sales form. As Figure 4.17 shows, the basic tables would include a list of items purchased: OrderItem(<u>OrderID</u>, <u>ItemID</u>, Price, Quantity). In most situations we would need to multiply Price by Quantity to get the total value for each item ordered. Because this computation is well defined (without any unusual conditions), there is no point in storing the result—it can be recomputed whenever it is needed. Simply build a query and add one more column. The new column uses elementary algebra and lists a name: Price*Quantity AS Extended. Remember that the computations are performed for each row in the query.

Some systems provide additional mathematical functions. For example, basic mathematical functions like absolute value, logarithms, and trigonometric functions

FIGURE 4.17 Computations. Basic computations (+ − * /) can be performed on numeric data in a query. The new display column should be given a meaningful name.

OrderItem(<u>OrderID</u>, <u>ItemID</u>, Price, Quantity)

```
Select OrderID, ItemID, Price, Quantity,
Price*Quantity As Extended
From OrderItem;
```

OrderID	ItemID	Price	Quantity	Extended
151	9764	19.50	2	39.00
151	7653	8.35	3	25.05
151	8673	6.89	2	13.78

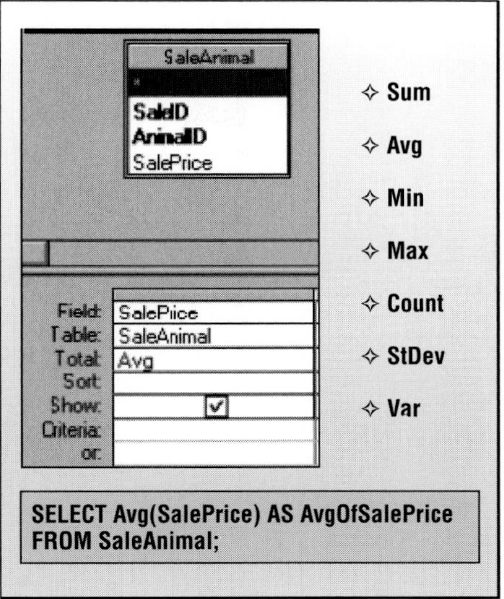

FIGURE 4.18 Aggregation functions. Sample query in QBE and SQL to answer: What is the average sale price for all animals? Note that with Microsoft Access you have to click the summation button on the toolbar (Σ) to display the Total line on the QBE grid.

might be available. Although these functions provide extended capabilities, always remember that they can operate only on data stored in one row of a table or query.

Aggregation

Databases for business often require the computation of totals and subtotals. Hence query systems provide functions for **aggregation** of data. The common functions listed in Figure 4.18 can operate across several rows of data and return one value. The most commonly used functions are Sum and Avg, which are similar to those available in spreadsheets.

With SQL the functions are simply added as part of the SELECT statement. With QBE the functions are generally listed on a separate Total line. With Microsoft Access, you first have to click the summation (Σ) button on the toolbar to add the Total line to the QBE grid. In both SQL and QBE, you should provide a meaningful name for the new column.

The Count function is useful in many situations, but make sure you understand the difference between Sum and Count. Sum totals the values in a numeric column. Count simply counts the number of rows. You can supply an argument to the Count function, but it rarely makes a difference—generally you just use Count(*). The difficulty with the Count function lies in knowing when to use it. You must first understand the English question. For example, the question How many employees do we have? would use the Count function: SELECT Count(*) From Employee. The question How many units of Item 9764 have been sold? requires the Sum function: SELECT Sum(Quantity) FROM OrderItem. The difference is that there can be only one employee per row in the Employee table, whereas a customer can buy multiple quantities of an item at one time. Also keep in mind that Sum can be used only on a column of numeric data (e.g., Quantity).

In many cases you will want to combine the **row-by-row calculations** with an aggregate function. The example in Figure 4.19 asks for the total value of a particular order. To get total value, the database must first calculate Price * Quantity for each row and then get the total of that column. The example also shows that it is common to specify a condition (WHERE) to limit the rows used for the total. In this example we want the total for just one order.

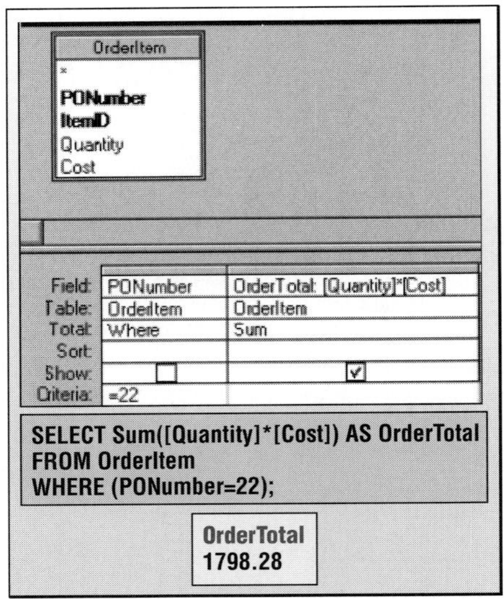

FIGURE 4.19 Computations. Row-by-row computations (Quantity*Cost) can be performed within an aggregation function (Sum), but only the final total will be displayed in the result.

There is one important restriction to remember with aggregation. You cannot display detail lines (row by row) at the same time you display totals. In the order example you can see either the detail computations (Figure 4.17) or the total value (Figure 4.19). In most cases, it is simple enough to run two queries. However, if you want to see the detail and the totals at the same time, you need to create a report as described in Chapter 6.

Note that you can compute several aggregate functions at the same time. For example, you can display the Sum, Average, and Count at the same time: SELECT Sum(Quantity),Avg(Quantity), Count(Quantity) From OrderItem. In fact, if you need all three values, you should compute them at one time. Consider what happens if you have a table with a million rows of data. If you write three separate queries, the DBMS has to make three passes through the data. By combining the computations in one query, you cut the total query time to one-third. With huge tables or complex systems, these minor changes in a query can make the difference between a successful application and one that takes days to run.

Sometimes when using the Count function, you will also want to include the DISTINCT operator. For example, *SELECT COUNT (DISTINCT Category) FROM Animal* will count the number of different categories and ignore duplicates. Although the command is part of the SQL standard, note that as of version 97, Microsoft Access does not support this version of the Count statement. To obtain the same results in Access, you would first build the query with the DISTINCT clause shown in Figure 4.7. Save the query and then create a new query that computes the Count on the saved query.

SUBTOTALS AND GROUP BY

To look at totals for only a few categories, you can use the Sum function with a WHERE clause. For example, you might ask, How many cats are in the animal list? The query is straightforward: SELECT Count (AnimalID) FROM Animal Where (Category = "Cat"). This technique will work, and you will get the correct answer. You could then go back and edit the query to get the count for dogs or any other category of animal. However, eventually you will get tired of changing the query. Also, what if you do not know all the categories?

Consider the more general query: Count the number of animals in each category. As shown in Figure 4.20, this type of query is best solved with the GROUP BY clause. This technique is available in both QBE and SQL. The SQL syntax is straightforward: just add the clause GROUP BY Category. The **GROUP BY** statement can be used only with one of the aggregate functions (Sum, Avg, Count, and so on). With the GROUP BY statement, the DBMS looks at all the data, finds the unique items in the group, and then performs the aggregate function for each item in the group.

By default, the output will generally be sorted by the group items. However, for business questions, it is common to sort (ORDER BY) based on the computation. The Pet Store example is sorted by the Count—listing the animals with the highest count first.

Be careful about adding multiple columns to the GROUP BY clause. The subtotals will be computed for each distinct item in the entire GROUP BY clause. So if you include additional columns (e.g., Category and Breed), you might end up with a more detailed breakdown than you wanted.

Microsoft added a useful feature that can be used in conjunction with the ORDER BY statement. Sometimes a query will return thousands of lines of output. Although the rows are sorted, you might want to examine only the first few rows. For example, you might want to list your 10 best salespeople or the top 10 percent of your customers. When you have sorted the results, you can easily limit the output displayed by including the **TOP** statement; for example, SELECT TOP 10 SalesPerson, SUM(Sales) FROM Sales GROUP BY SalesPerson ORDER BY SUM(Sales) DESC. This

FIGURE 4.20
GROUP BY computes subtotals and counts for each type of animal. This approach is much more efficient than trying to create a WHERE clause for each type of animal. To convert business questions to SQL, watch for phrases such as *by* or *for each,* which usually signify the use of the GROUP BY clause.

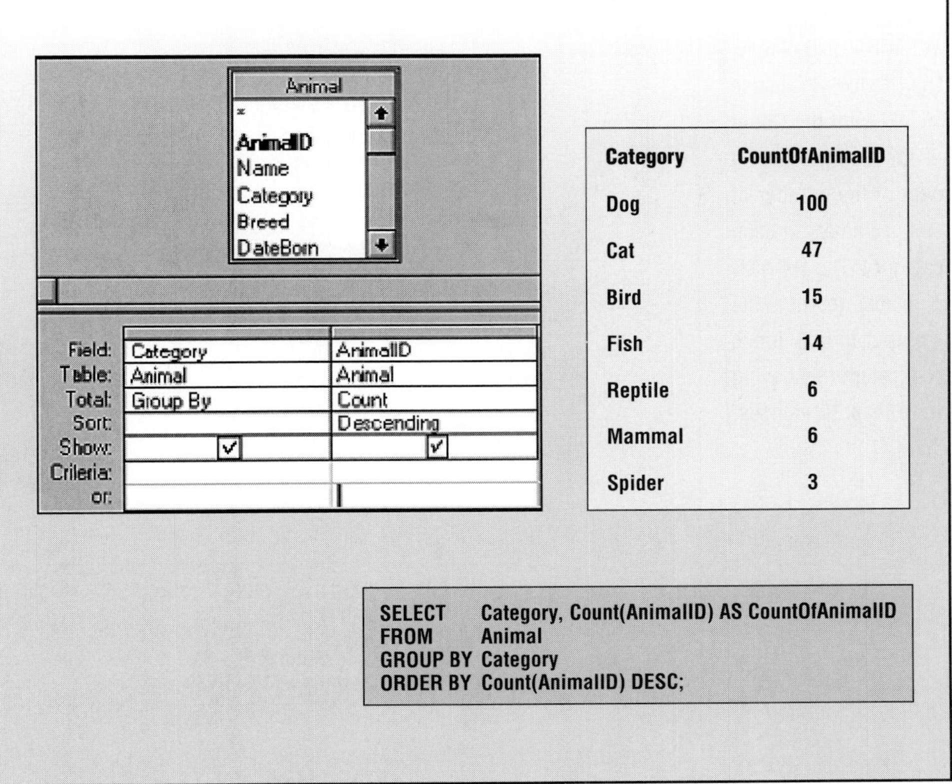

query will compute total sales for each SalesPerson and display a list sorted in descending order. However, only the first 10 rows of the output will be displayed. Of course, you could choose any value instead of 10. You can also enter a percentage value (e.g., TOP 5 PERCENT), which will cut the list off after 5 percent of the rows have been displayed. These commands are useful when a manager wants to see the "best" of something and skip the rest of the rows.

Conditions on Totals (HAVING)

The GROUP BY clause is powerful and provides useful information for making decisions. In cases involving many groups, you might want to restrict the output list, particularly when some of the groups are relatively minor. The Pet Store has categories for reptiles and spiders, but they are usually special-order items. In analyzing sales the managers might prefer to focus on the top-selling categories.

One way to reduce the amount of data displayed is to add the **HAVING** clause. The HAVING clause is a condition that applies to the GROUP BY output. In the example presented in Figure 4.21, the managers want to skip any animal category that has fewer than 10 animals. Notice that the SQL statement simply adds one line. The same condition can be added to the criteria grid in the QBE query. The HAVING clause is powerful and works much like a WHERE statement. Just be sure that the conditions you impose apply to the computations indicated by the GROUP BY clause.

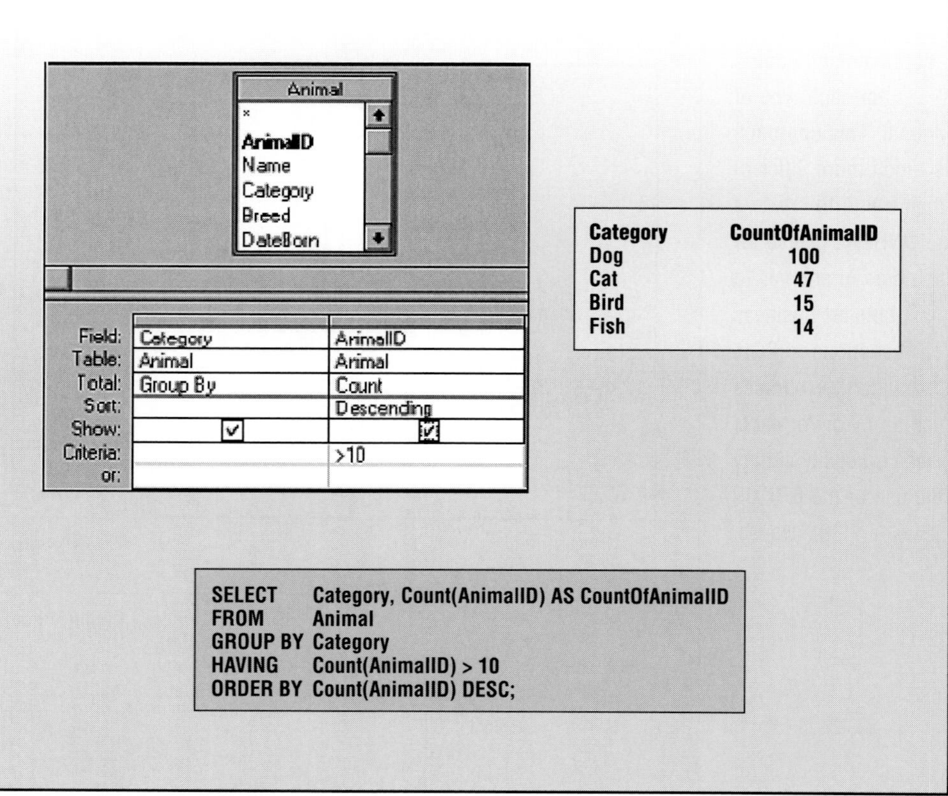


```
SELECT    Category, Count(AnimalID) AS CountOfAnimalID
FROM      Animal
GROUP BY  Category
HAVING    Count(AnimalID) > 10
ORDER BY  Count(AnimalID) DESC;
```

FIGURE 4.21 Limiting the output with a HAVING clause. The GROUP BY clause with the Count function provides a count of the number of animals in each category. The HAVING clause restricts the output to only those categories having more than 10 animals.

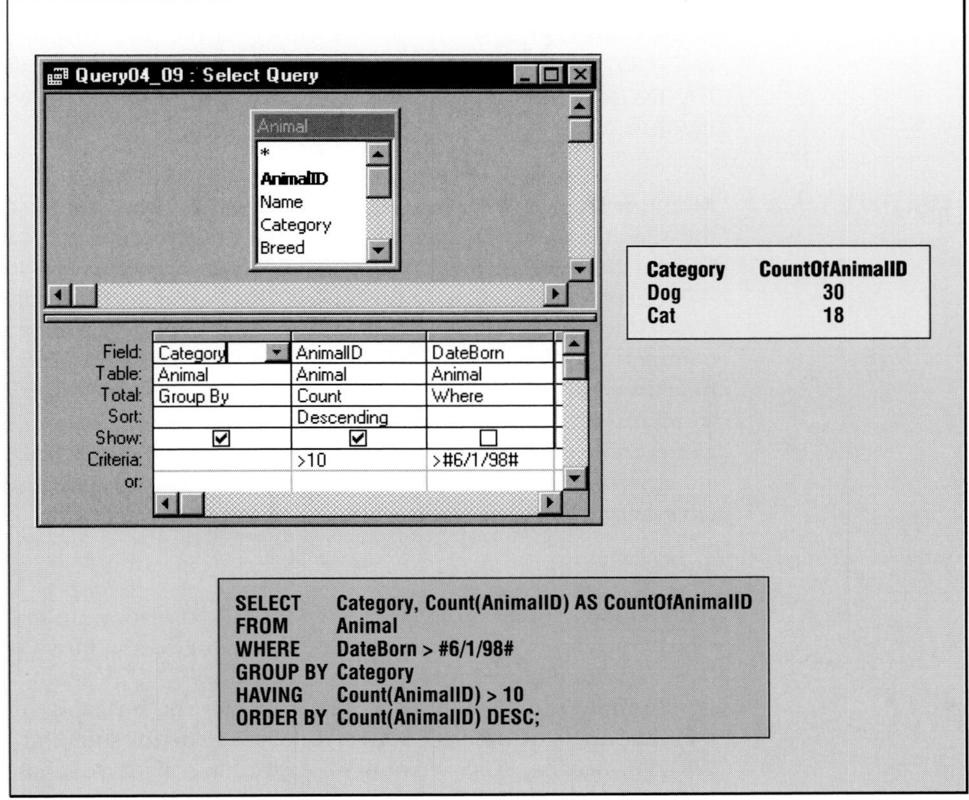

FIGURE 4.22 WHERE versus HAVING. Count the animals born after June 1, 1998, in each category, but list the category only if it has more than 10 of these animals. The WHERE clause first determines whether each row will be used in the computation. The GROUP BY clause produces the total count for each category. The HAVING clause restricts the output to only those categories with more than 10 animals.

WHERE versus HAVING

When you first learn QBE and SQL, WHERE and HAVING look very similar, and choosing the proper clause can be confusing. Yet it is crucial that you understand the difference. If you make a mistake, the DBMS will give you an answer, but it will not be the answer to the question you want.

The key is that the WHERE statement applies to every single row in the original table. The HAVING statement applies only to the subtotal output from a GROUP BY query. To add to the confusion, you can even combine WHERE and HAVING clauses in a single query—because you might want to look at only some rows of data and then limit the display on the subtotals.

Consider the question in Figure 4.22 that counts the animals born after June 1, 1998, in each Category, but lists the Category only if there are more than 10 of these animals. The structure of the query is similar to the example in Figure 4.21. The difference in the SQL statement is the addition of the WHERE clause (DateBorn > #6/1/98#). This clause is applied to every row of the original data to decide whether it should be included in the computation. Compare the count for dogs in Figure 4.22 (30) with the count in Figure 4.21 (100). Only 30 dogs were born after June 1, 1998. The HAVING clause then limits the display to only those categories with more than 10 animals.

The query is processed by first examining each row to decide whether it meets the WHERE condition. If so, the Category is examined and the Count is increased for that category. After processing each row in the table, the totals are examined to see whether they meet the HAVING condition. Only the acceptable rows are displayed.

The same query in QBE is a bit more confusing. Both of the conditions are listed in the criteria grid. However, look closely at the Total row, and you will see a Where entry for the DateBorn column. This entry is required to differentiate between a HAVING and a WHERE condition. To be safe, you should always look at the SQL statement to make sure your query was interpreted correctly.

MULTIPLE TABLES

All the examples so far have used a single table—to keep the discussion centered on the specific topics. In practice you often need to combine data from several tables. In fact, the strength of a DBMS is its ability to combine data from multiple tables.

Chapter 3 shows how business forms and reports are dissected into related tables. Although the normalization process makes data storage more efficient and avoids common problems, ultimately, to answer the business question, we need to recombine the data from the tables. For example, the Sale table contains just the CustomerID to identify the specific customer. Most people would prefer to see the customer name and other attributes. This additional data is stored in the Customer table—along with the CustomerID. The objective is to take the CustomerID from the Sale table and look up the matching data in the Customer table.

Joining Tables

With modern query languages, combining data from multiple tables is straightforward. You simply specify which tables are involved and how the tables are connected. QBE is particularly easy to use for this process.

To understand the process, first consider the business question posed in Figure 4.23: List the CustomerID of everyone who bought something between 4/1/98 and 5/31/98. Because some customers might have made purchases on several days, the DISTINCT clause can be used to delete the duplicate listings.

Most managers would prefer to see the customer name instead of CustomerID. However, the name is stored in the Customer table because it would be a waste of space to copy all of the attributes to every table that referred to customers. If you only had these tables as printed reports, you would have to take the CustomerID from the sale report and find the matching row in the Customer table to get the cus-

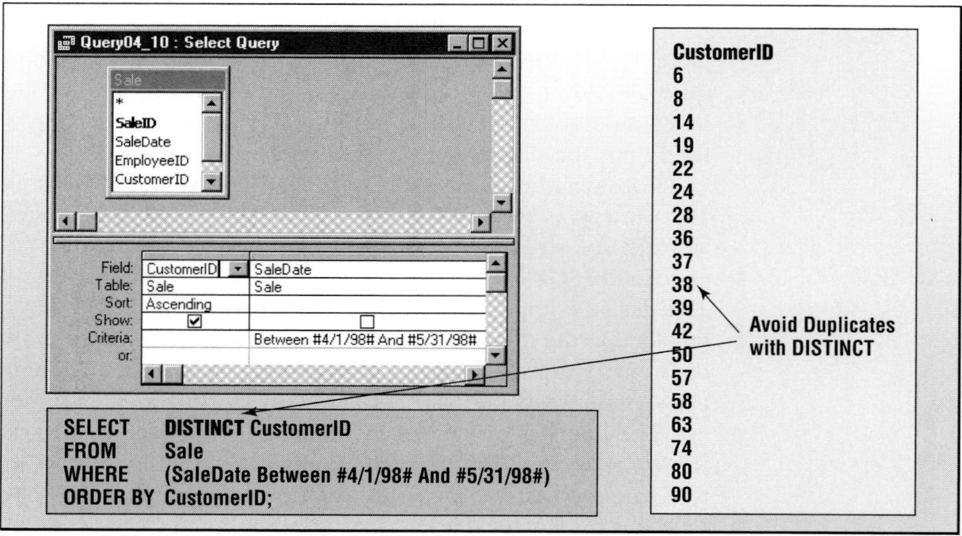

FIGURE 4.23
List the CustomerID of everyone who bought something between 4/1/98 and 5/31/98. Most people would prefer to see the name and address of the customer—those attributes are in the Customer table.

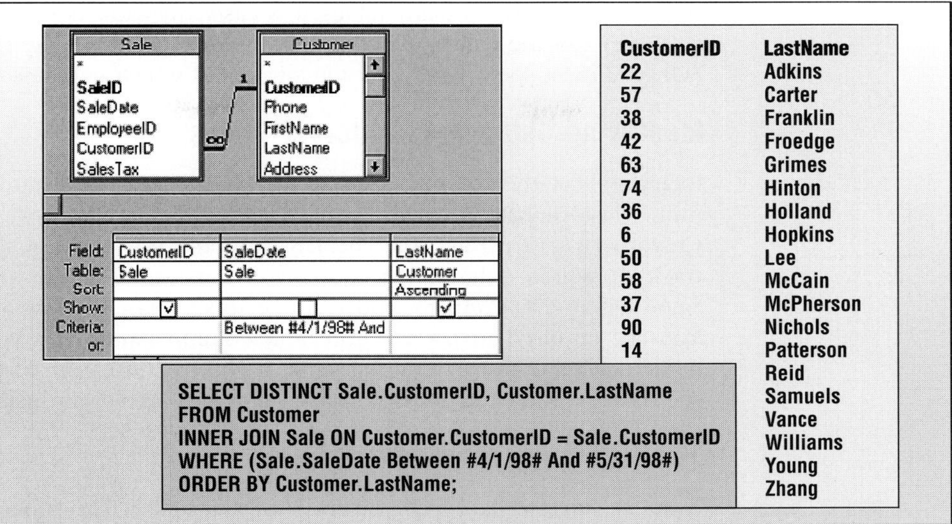

Sale
*
SaleID
SaleDate
EmployeeID
CustomerID
SalesTax
Customer
*
CustomerID
Phone
FirstName
LastName
Address
Field: CustomerID | SaleDate | LastName
Table: Sale | Sale | Customer
Sort: Ascending
Show:
Criteria: Between #4/1/98# And
or:
SELECT DISTINCT Sale.CustomerID, Customer.LastName
FROM Customer
INNER JOIN Sale ON Customer.CustomerID = Sale.CustomerID
WHERE (Sale.SaleDate Between #4/1/98# And #5/31/98#)
ORDER BY Customer.LastName;
CustomerID LastName
22 Adkins
57 Carter
38 Franklin
42 Froedge
63 Grimes
74 Hinton
36 Holland
6 Hopkins
50 Lee
58 McCain
37 McPherson
90 Nichols
14 Patterson
Reid
Samuels
Vance
Williams
Young
Zhang

FIGURE 4.24 Joining tables causes the rows to be matched based on the columns in the JOIN statement. You can then use data from either table. The business question is, List the last name of customers who bought something between 4/1/98 and 5/31/98.

tomer name. Of course, it would be time-consuming to do the matching by hand. The query system can do it easily.

As illustrated in Figure 4.24, the QBE approach is somewhat easier than the SQL syntax. However, the concept is the same. First, identify the two tables involved (Sale and Customer). In QBE you select the tables from a list, and they are displayed at the top of the form. In SQL you enter the table names on the FROM line. Second, you tell the DBMS which columns are matched in each table. In this case we match CustomerID in the Sale table to the CustomerID in the Customer table. Most of the time the column names will be the same, but they could be different.

In Microsoft Access QBE you join the columns by dragging the column from one table and dropping it onto the matching column in the second table. In SQL tables are connected with the JOIN statement. This statement was changed with the introduction of SQL 92—however, some systems still use the older SQL 89 syntax. With SQL 89 the JOIN condition is part of the WHERE clause. Most vendors are converting to the SQL 92 syntax, so this text will rely on that format.

The syntax for a JOIN is displayed in Figure 4.25. An informal syntax similar to SQL 89 is also shown. The DBMS will not accept statements using the informal syntax, but

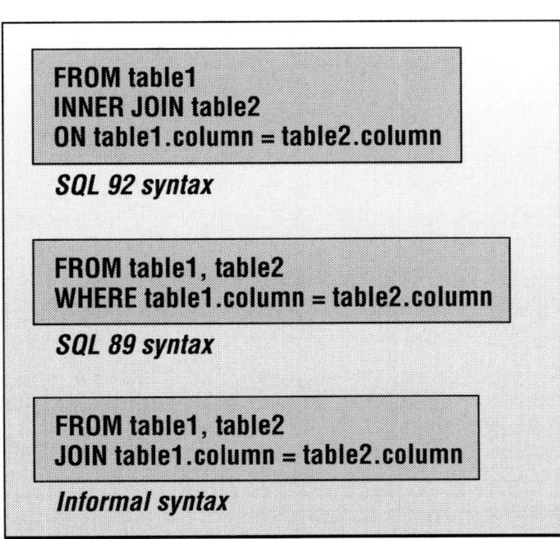

FROM table1
INNER JOIN table2
ON table1.column = table2.column
SQL 92 syntax
FROM table1, table2
WHERE table1.column = table2.column
SQL 89 syntax
FROM table1, table2
JOIN table1.column = table2.column
Informal syntax

FIGURE 4.25 SQL 92 and SQL 89 syntax to join tables. The informal syntax cannot be used with a DBMS, but it is easier to read when you need to combine many tables.

when the query uses many tables, it is easier to write down the informal syntax first and then add the details needed for the proper syntax. Note that with both QBE and SQL, you must specify the tables involved and which columns contain matching data.

Identifying Columns in Different Tables

Examine how the columns are specified in the SQL JOIN statement. Because the column CustomerID is used in both tables, it would not make sense to write CustomerID = CustomerID. The DBMS would not know what you meant. To keep track of which column you want, you must also specify the name of the table: Sale.CustomerID. Actually, you can use this syntax anytime you refer to a column. You are required to use the full table.column name only when the same column name is used in more than one table. If you use QBE with Microsoft Access, you will see that it always includes the table name—to avoid confusion as tables are added.

Joining Many Tables

A query can use data from several different tables. The process is similar regardless of the number of tables. Each table you want to add must be joined to one other table through a data column. If you cannot find a common column, either the normalization is wrong, or you need to find a third table that contains links to both tables.

Consider the example in Figure 4.26: List the name and phone number of anyone who bought a registered white cat between two given dates. An important step

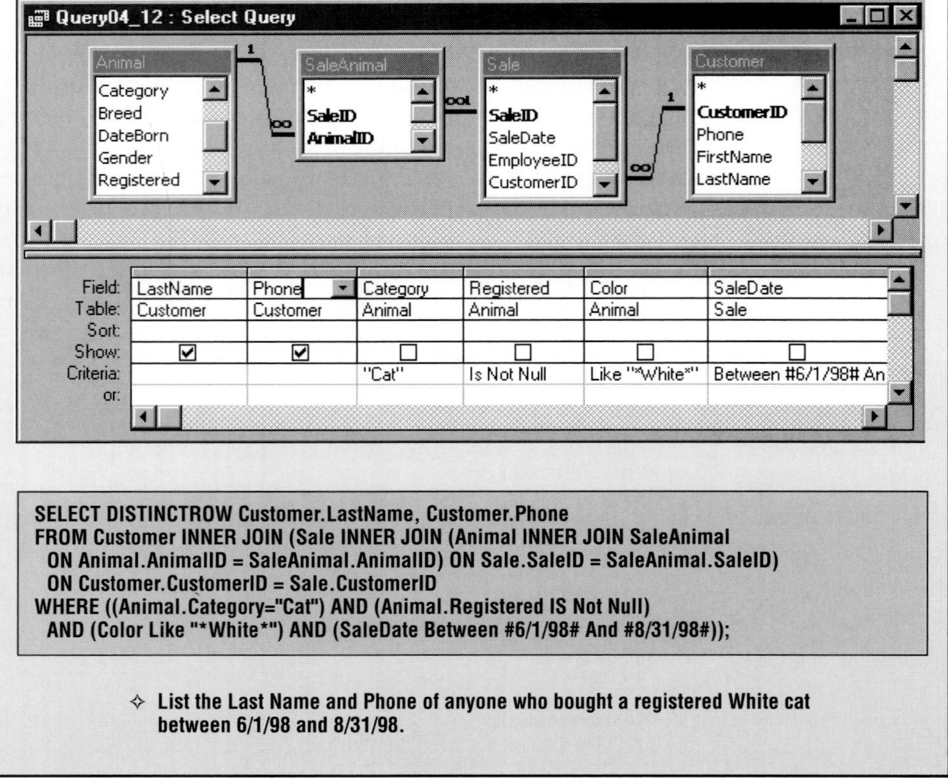

FIGURE 4.26
Joining multiple tables. QBE makes joining multiple tables relatively easy—just connect the tables with a line. With SQL, just start with two tables and expand outward, for example, start with (Animal INNER JOIN SaleAnimal ON Animal.AnimalID = SaleAnimal.AnimalID) and then add a third table (Sale) with its JOIN.

FIGURE 4.27
Joining multiple tables. With SQL 92 syntax, first JOIN two tables within parentheses and then add a table and its JOIN condition. When you want to focus on the tables being joined, use the easier notation—just remember that it must be converted to SQL 92 syntax for the computer to understand it.

SQL 92 syntax to join three tables:

```
FROM Table1
  INNER JOIN (Table2 INNER JOIN Table3 ON Table2.ColA = Table3.ColA)
  ON Table1.ColB = Table2.ColB
```

Easier notation, but not correct syntax:

```
FROM   Table1, Table2, Table3
JOIN   Table1.ColB = Table2.ColB
       Table2.ColA = Table3.ColA
```

is to identify the tables needed. For large problems involving several tables, it is best to first list the columns you want to see as output and the ones involved in the constraints. In the example the name and phone number we want to see are in the Customer table. The Registration status, Color, and Category (cat) are all in the Animal table. The SaleDate is in the Sale table. However, when you try to join these three tables, you quickly realize that the Animal table cannot be connected to the other two. Remember that customers might purchase more than one animal at a time, so this repeating list is stored in a separate table: SaleAnimal, which includes columns for SaleID and AnimalID. Hence the query uses four tables.

When the database contains a large number of tables, complex queries can be challenging to build. You need to be familiar with the tables to determine which tables contain the columns you want to see. For large databases, an entity-relationship (ERD) or a class diagram can show how the tables are connected. If the database is built in Access, be sure that you predefine relationships when you create the tables. Chapter 3 explains how Access sets referential integrity for foreign key relationships. Access uses the relationships to automatically add the JOINs to QBE when you choose a table. You can also use the ERD to help users build queries.

When you first see it, the SQL 92 syntax for joining more than two tables can look confusing. In practice, it is best not to memorize the syntax. When you are first learning SQL, understanding the concept of the JOIN is far more important than worrying about syntax. Figure 4.27 shows the syntax needed to JOIN three tables. To read it or to create a similar statement, start with the innermost JOIN (in the parentheses). Then add a table with the corresponding ON condition. If you need additional tables, continue adding parentheses and ON statements, working out from the center. Just be sure that the new table can be joined to one of the tables inside the parentheses. Figure 4.27 also shows an easier syntax that is faster to write when you are first developing a query or when you are in a hurry—perhaps on a midterm exam. It is similar to the older SQL 89 syntax (but not exactly correct) where you list all the tables in the FROM clause and then join them in the WHERE statement.

Hints on Joining Tables

Joining tables is closely related to data normalization. Normalization splits data into tables that can be stored and searched more efficiently. Queries and SQL are the reverse operation: joins are used to recombine the data from the tables. If the normalization is incorrect, it might not be possible to join the tables. As you build queries, double-check your normalization to make sure it is correct. Students often have trouble with joins, so this section provides some hints to help you understand the potential problems.

Remember that any time you use multiple tables, you must join them together. Surprisingly, many database query systems will accept a query even if the tables are not joined. They will even give you a result. Unfortunately, the result is usually meaningless. The joined tables also create a huge query. Without any constraints most query systems will produce a **Cross join,** where every row in one table is paired with every row in the other table. In algebra a cross join is known as a Cartesian product of two sets. If the tables have m and n rows each, the resulting query will have $m*n$ rows!

Where possible, you should double-check the answer to a complex query. Use sample data and individual test cases in which you can compute the answer by hand. You should also build a complex query in stages. Start with one or two tables and check the intermediate results to see if they make sense. Then add new tables and additional constraints. Add the summary calculations last (e.g., Sum, Avg). It's hard to look at one number (total) and decide whether it is correct. Instead, look at an intermediate listing and make sure it includes all of the rows you want; then add the computations.

Columns used in a JOIN are often key columns—but you can join tables on any column. Similarly, joined columns may have different names. For example, you might join an Employee.EmployeeID column to a Sale.SalesPerson column. The only technical constraint is that the columns must contain the same type of data (domain). In some cases you can minimize this limitation by using a function to convert the data. For example, you might use Left(ZipCode,5) = ZipCode5 to reduce a nine-digit ZipCode string to five digits. Just make sure that it makes sense to match the data in the two columns. For instance, joining tables on Animal.AnimalID = Employee.EmployeeID would be meaningless. The DBMS would actually accept the join (if both ID values are integers), but the join does not make any sense because an Employee can never be an Animal (except in science fiction movies).

Avoid multiple ties between tables. This problem often arises in Access when you have predefined relationships between tables. Access QBE automatically uses those relationships to join tables in a query. If you select the four tables shown in Figure 4.28 and leave all four JOINs, you will not get the answer you want. The four

FIGURE 4.28 A query with these four tables with four JOINS would return only rows where the Employee had the same CityID as the Supplier. If you need only the supplier city, just delete the JOIN between Employee and CityID. If you want both cities, add a second copy of the City table as a fifth table.

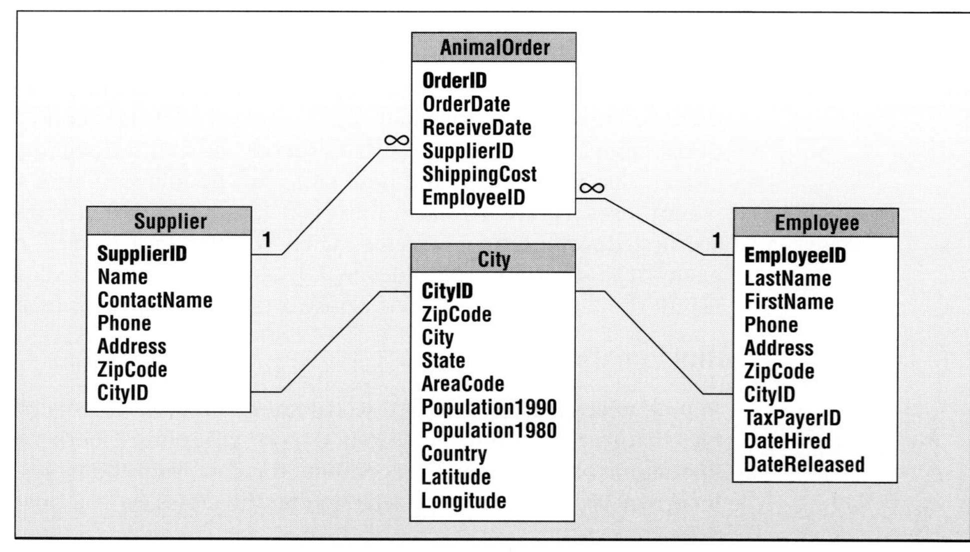

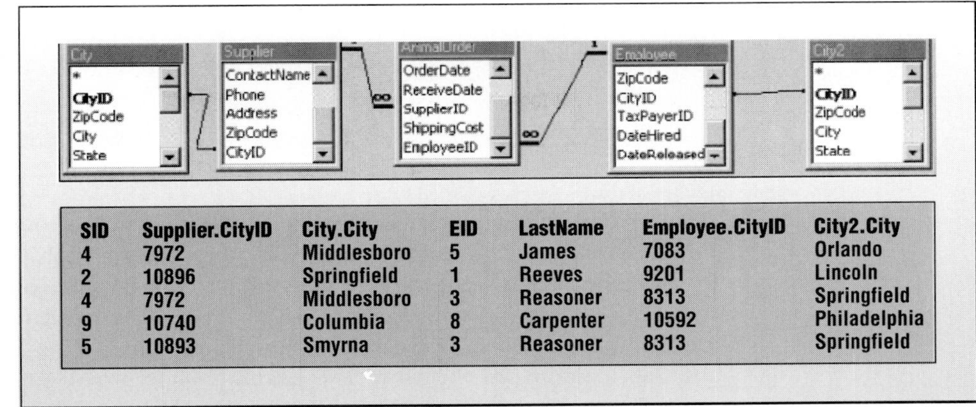

SID	Supplier.CityID	City.City	EID	LastName	Employee.CityID	City2.City
4	7972	Middlesboro	5	James	7083	Orlando
2	10896	Springfield	1	Reeves	9201	Lincoln
4	7972	Middlesboro	3	Reasoner	8313	Springfield
9	10740	Columbia	8	Carpenter	10592	Philadelphia
5	10893	Smyrna	3	Reasoner	8313	Springfield

FIGURE 4.29 Table alias. The City table is used twice. The second time, it is given the alias City2 and treated as a separate table. Hence, different cities can be retrieved for Supplier and for Employee.

JOINs will return AnimalOrders only where the Employee placing the order has the same CityID as the Supplier! If you only need the City for the Supplier, the solution is to delete the JOIN between Employee and City. In general, if your query uses four tables, you should have three JOINs (one less than the number of tables).

Table Alias

Consider the preceding example in more detail. What if you really want to display the City for the Supplier and the City for the Employee? Of course, we want to allow the cities to be different. The answer involves a little-known trick in SQL: just add the City table twice. The second "copy" will have a different name (e.g., City2). You give a table a new name **(alias)** within the FROM clause: FROM City AS City2. As shown in Figure 4.29, the City table is joined to the Supplier. The City2 table is joined to the Employee table. Now the query will perform two separate JOINS to the same table—simply because it has a different name.

Create View

Any query that you build can be saved as a **view.** Microsoft simply refers to them as saved queries, but SQL calls them Views. In either case the DBMS analyzes and stores the SQL statement so that it can be run later. If a query needs to be run many times, you should save it as a view so that the DBMS has to analyze it only once. Figure 4.30 shows the basic SQL syntax for creating a view. You start with any SELECT statement and add the line (CREATE VIEW . . .).

The most powerful feature of a view is that it can be used within another query. Views are useful for queries that you have to run many times. You can also create views to handle complex questions. Users can then create new, simpler queries based on the views. In the example in Figure 4.30, you would create a view (Kittens) that

FIGURE 4.30 Views. Views are saved queries that can be run at any time. They improve performance because they have to be entered only once and the DBMS has to analyze them only once.

```
CREATE VIEW Kittens AS
SELECT*
FROM Animal
WHERE (Category = 'cat') AND (Today – DateBorn < 180);
```

FIGURE 4.31 Queries based on views. Views can be used within other queries.

```
SELECT Avg(ListPrice)
FROM Kittens
WHERE (Color LIKE "*Black*");
```

displays data for Cats born within the last 180 days. As shown in Figure 4.31, users could search the Kittens view based on other criteria such as color.

As long as you want to use a view only to display data, the technique is straightforward. However, if you want to use a view to change data, you must be careful. Depending on how you create the view, you might not be able to update some of the data columns in the view. The example shown in Figure 4.32 is an updatable view. The purpose is to add new data for ordering items. The user enters the OrderID and the ItemID. The corresponding description of that Item is automatically retrieved from the Item table.

Figure 4.33 illustrates the problem that can arise if you are hasty in choosing the columns in a view. Here the OrderLine view uses the ItemID value from the Item table (instead of from the OrderItem table). Now you will not be able to add new data to the OrderLine view. To understand why, consider what happens when you try to change the ItemID from 57 to 32. If it works at all, the new value is stored in the Item table, which simply changes the ItemID of cat food from 57 to 32.

To ensure that a view can be updated, the view should be designed to change data in only one table. The rest of the data is included simply for display—such as verifying that the user entered the correct ItemID. You should never include primary key columns from more than one table. Also, to remain updatable, a view cannot use the DISTINCT keyword or contain a GROUP BY or HAVING clause.

Views have many uses in a database. They are particularly useful in helping business managers work with the database. A database administrator (DBA) or IS worker can create views for the business managers, who only see the section of the database expressed in the views. Hence you can hide the view's complexity and size. Most important, you can hide the joins needed to build the view, so managers can work with simple constraints. By keeping the view updatable, managers never need to use the underlying raw tables.

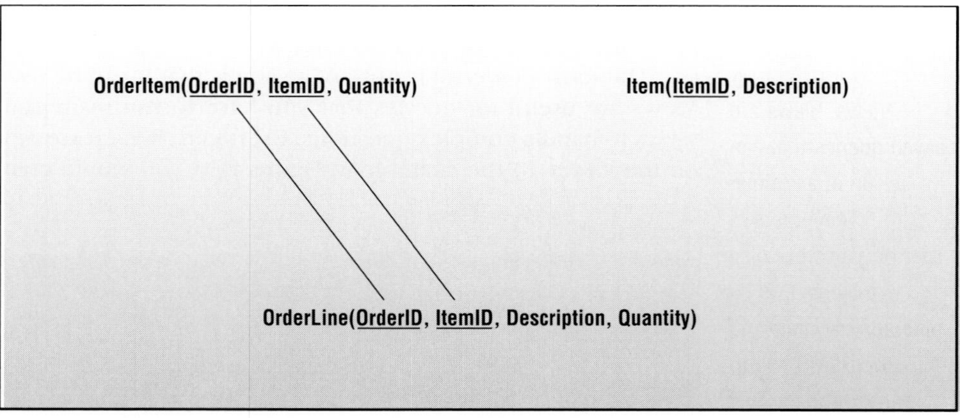

FIGURE 4.32 Updatable view. The OrderLine view is designed to change data in only one table (OrderItem). The Description from the Item table is used for display to help the user verify that the ItemID was entered correctly.

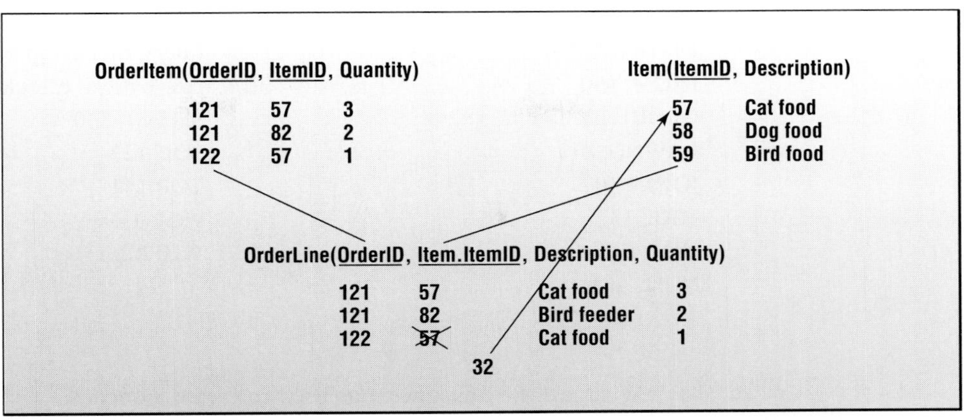

FIGURE 4.33 Nonupdatable view. Do not mix primary keys from different tables. If this view works at all, it will not do what you want. If you try to change the ItemID from 57 to 32, you will only change the ItemID of cat food. You will not be able to enter new data into the OrderItem table.

SUMMARY

The key to creating a query is to answer four questions: (1) What output do you want to see? (2) What constraints do you know? (3) What tables are involved? (4) How are the tables joined? The essence of creating a query is to use these four questions to get the logic correct. The WHERE clause is a common source of errors. Be sure that you understand the objectives of the query. Be careful when combining OR and AND statements and use DeMorgan's law to simplify the conditions.

Always test your queries. The best method to build complex queries is to start with a simpler query and add tables. Then add conditions one at a time and check the output to see whether it is correct. Finally, enter the computations and GROUP BY clauses. When performing computations, be sure that you understand the difference between Sum and Count. Remember that Count simply counts the number of rows. Sum produces the total of the values in the specified column.

Joining tables is straightforward. Generally the best approach is to use QBE to specify the columns that link the tables and then check the syntax of the SQL command. Remember that join columns can have different names. Also remember that you need to add a third (or fourth) table to link two tables with no columns in common. Keep the class diagram handy to help you determine which tables to use and how they are linked to each other.

A DEVELOPER'S VIEW

As Miranda noted, SQL and QBE are much easier than writing programs to retrieve data. However, you must still be careful. The most dangerous aspect of queries is that you may get a result that is not really the answer to the business question. To minimize this risk, build queries in pieces and check the results at each step. Be particularly careful to do aggregation and GROUP BY clauses last, so that you can see whether the WHERE clause was entered correctly. If you name your columns carefully, it is easier to see how tables should be joined. However, columns do not need the same names to be joined. For your class project, you should identify some common business questions and write queries for them.

KEY WORDS

aggregation, 139
alias, 149
BETWEEN, 138
Boolean algebra, 132
Cross join, 148
DeMorgan's law, 135

REVIEW QUESTIONS

1. What are the four questions used to create a query?
2. What is the basic structure of the SQL SELECT command?
3. What is the purpose of the DISTINCT operator?
4. What is DeMorgan's law, and how does it simplify conditions?
5. What is the difference between the ORDER BY and GROUP BY commands?
6. How do the basic SQL arithmetic operators (+, −, etc.) differ from the aggregation (SUM, etc.) commands?
7. What basic aggregation functions are available in the SELECT command?
8. What is the difference between Count and Sum? Give an example of how each would be used.
9. What is the difference between the WHERE and HAVING clauses? Give an example of how each would be used.
10. What is the SQL syntax for joining two tables?

EXERCISES

Write the SQL statements that will answer questions 1 through 20 based on the following tables for a small hardware store. A useful option is to create the tables in a DBMS, add some data, and test your queries.

Customer (<u>CID</u>, Name, Address, City, State, Zip, Category)
Inventory (<u>ItemID</u>, Description, ListPrice, Cost, QuantityOnHand, Category)
Item Category (<u>Category</u>, Description, StoreLocation, Season)
Order (<u>OrderID</u>, OrderDate, CID)
OrderItem (<u>OrderID</u>, <u>ItemID</u>, Quantity, SalePrice)

1. List all government (Category) customers.
2. What were the total orders on July 15?
3. Compute total orders by month.

4. What is the largest discount (ListPrice − SalePrice) given? The largest discount by percentage of ListPrice?

5. Which customers have placed the most orders? Compute once for dollar value and once for total number of orders.

6. Which product category had the highest orders in December?

7. List the spring (Season) products ordered by florist (Category) customers with a ListPrice over $200.

8. List the QuantityOnHand of all the hammers (Description).

9. List all Items that sold for less than Cost in the last month.

10. Which products for dogs (Category) have the most orders in June from walk-in customers (Category)?

11. Which Category has more sales: cat products, dog products, or garden products? Compute the answer first by value and then by number of products sold.

12. List the customers who ordered more than 10 bags of dog food (Item Description) in January.

13. Which items are stored in location 351 for the Summer season?

14. Which Category of customers placed the most orders in February?

15. What is the average quantity sold for ItemID 8776 by month?

16. On average, do customers in Boston get a better discount than customers in Springfield?

17. What are average sales (value and quantity) by Item Category?

18. What is the total value and total discount given on Order 12948?

19. What is the current value of our inventory, based on Cost and based on ListPrice?

20. List all items sold in March by Category that were ordered from Customers in Boston.

21. Who were the top five customers from Massachusetts that bought the most summer season merchandise (in value)?

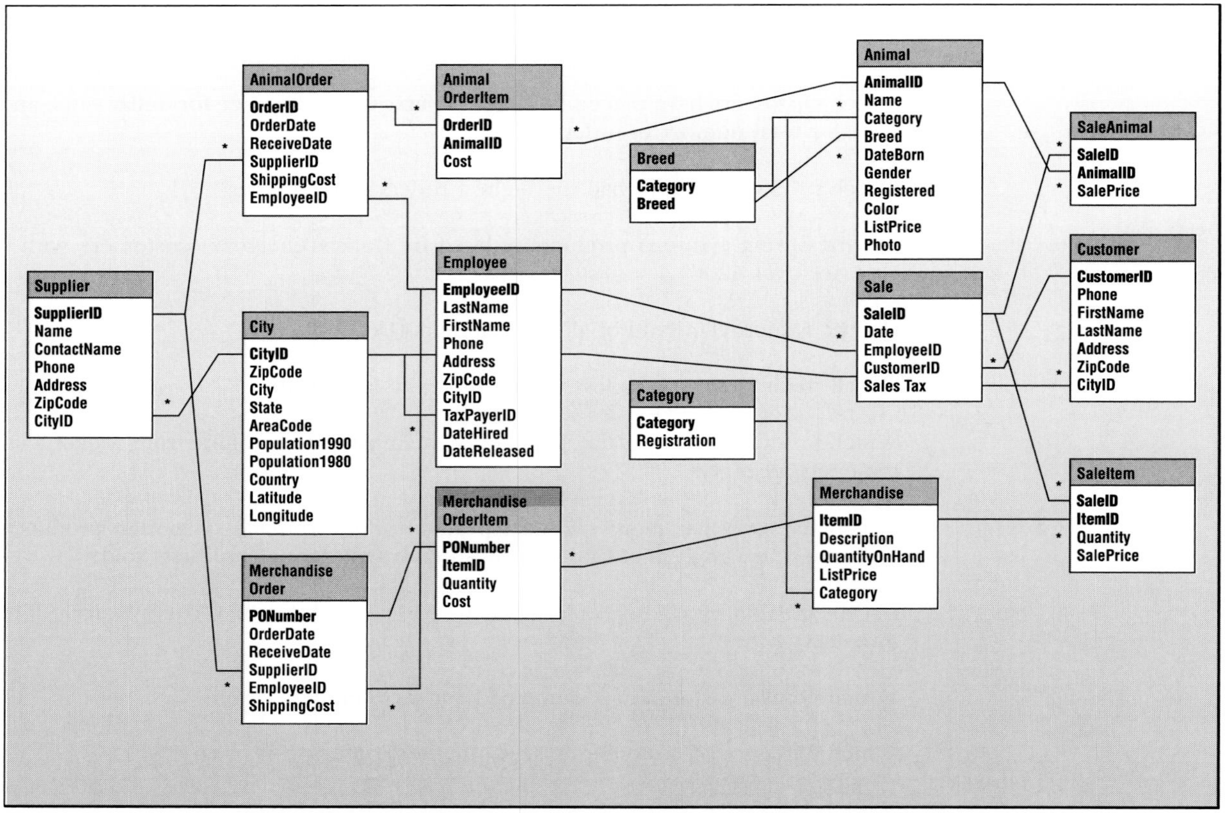

AnimalOrder
OrderID
OrderDate
ReceiveDate
SupplierID
ShippingCost
EmployeeID

Animal OrderItem
OrderID
AnimalID
Cost

Animal
AnimalID
Name
Category
Breed
DateBorn
Gender
Registered
Color
ListPrice
Photo

Breed
Category
Breed

SaleAnimal
SaleID
AnimalID
SalePrice

Supplier
SupplierID
Name
ContactName
Phone
Address
ZipCode
CityID

City
CityID
ZipCode
City
State
AreaCode
Population1990
Population1980
Country
Latitude
Longitude

Employee
EmployeeID
LastName
FirstName
Phone
Address
ZipCode
CityID
TaxPayerID
DateHired
DateReleased

Sale
SaleID
Date
EmployeeID
CustomerID
Sales Tax

Customer
CustomerID
Phone
FirstName
LastName
Address
ZipCode
CityID

Category
Category
Registration

Merchandise OrderItem
PONumber
ItemID
Quantity
Cost

Merchandise
ItemID
Description
QuantityOnHand
ListPrice
Category

SaleItem
SaleID
ItemID
Quantity
SalePrice

Merchandise Order
PONumber
OrderDate
ReceiveDate
SupplierID
EmployeeID
ShippingCost

Sally's Pet Store

Write the SQL statements that will answer questions 22 through 37 based on the tables in the Pet Store database. Build your queries in Access.

22. How many animals have we ordered from suppliers in Kentucky?
23. What is the average SalePrice of Manx (Breed) cats born before May 1, 1998?
24. Who were the best (and worst) employees in terms of sales of Animals in November?
25. What is the difference in the average SalePrice of registered cats versus cats that are not registered?
26. How many animal sales did we make to customers from New Jersey in October?
27. Did the employee who had the highest sales of animals in July also have the highest sales of merchandise in July?
28. What is the age and identity of the oldest animal we have sold?
29. What is the longest time an animal has been kept in the store (and the Category, AnimalID, and Name of the animal)?
30. Which breed of dog is the best seller? (Calculate for both quantity and revenue.)

31. What is the largest value of a PurchaseOrder that we have placed?
32. Which supplier received the most merchandise orders from our company? (Measure in both cost and number of orders.)
33. How much sales tax do we owe to each state for sales in the month of August?
34. Which category of animal provides the most profit (ignore shipping)?
35. Do we make higher profits on male dogs (or on female dogs)?
36. What is the average length of time to receive each category of animal?
37. Which of our customers have received the best total discounts? (Compute first for animals and then for merchandise.)

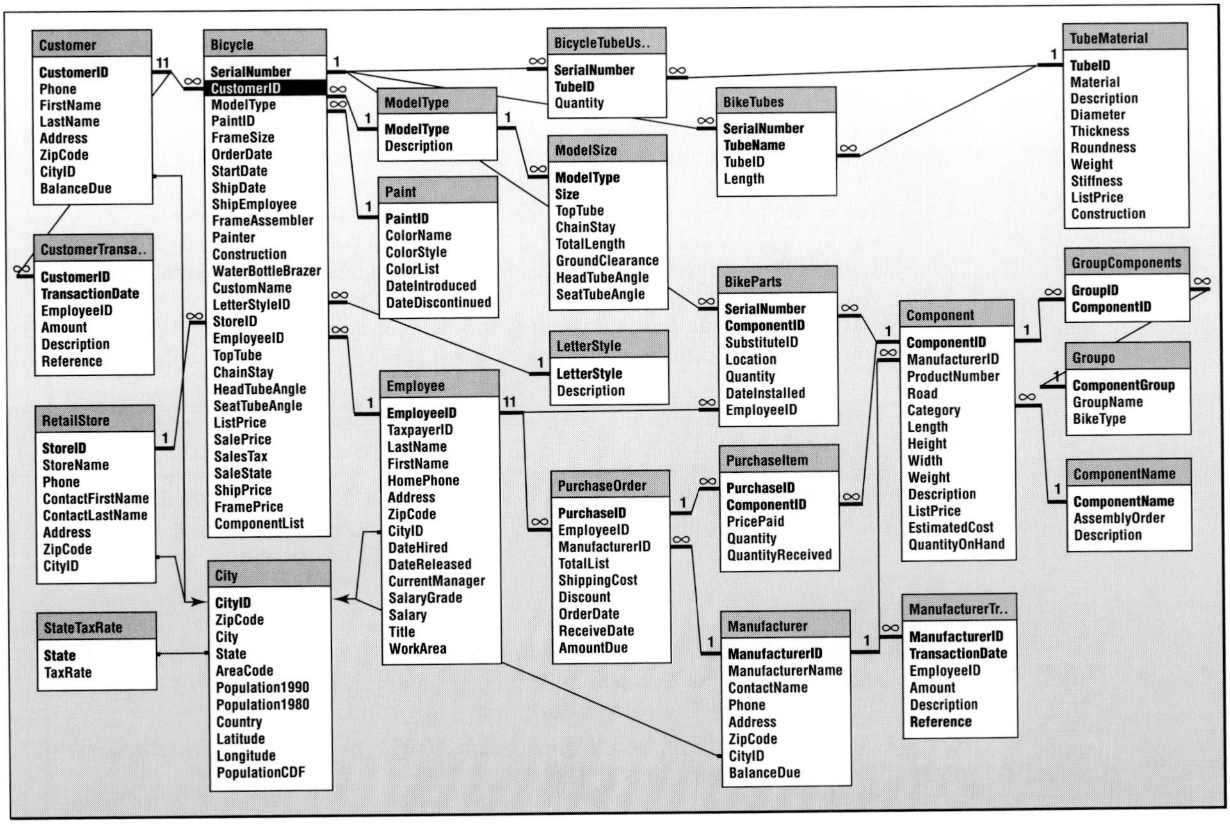

Customer: CustomerID, Phone, FirstName, LastName, Address, ZipCode, CityID, BalanceDue

CustomerTransa..: CustomerID, TransactionDate, EmployeeID, Amount, Description, Reference

RetailStore: StoreID, StoreName, Phone, ContactFirstName, ContactLastName, Address, ZipCode, CityID

StateTaxRate: State, TaxRate

Bicycle: SerialNumber, CustomerID, ModelType, PaintID, FrameSize, OrderDate, StartDate, ShipDate, ShipEmployee, FrameAssembler, Painter, Construction, WaterBottleBrazer, CustomName, LetterStyleID, StoreID, EmployeeID, TopTube, ChainStay, HeadTubeAngle, SeatTubeAngle, ListPrice, SalePrice, SalesTax, SaleState, ShipPrice, FramePrice, ComponentList

City: CityID, ZipCode, City, State, AreaCode, Population1990, Population1980, Country, Latitude, Longitude, PopulationCDF

ModelType: ModelType, Description

Paint: PaintID, ColorName, ColorStyle, ColorList, DateIntroduced, DateDiscontinued

Employee: EmployeeID, TaxpayerID, LastName, FirstName, HomePhone, Address, ZipCode, CityID, DateHired, DateReleased, CurrentManager, SalaryGrade, Salary, Title, WorkArea

BicycleTubeUs..: SerialNumber, TubeID, Quantity

ModelSize: ModelType, Size, TopTube, ChainStay, TotalLength, GroundClearance, HeadTubeAngle, SeatTubeAngle

LetterStyle: LetterStyle, Description

PurchaseOrder: PurchaseID, EmployeeID, ManufacturerID, TotalList, ShippingCost, Discount, OrderDate, ReceiveDate, AmountDue

BikeTubes: SerialNumber, TubeName, TubeID, Length

BikeParts: SerialNumber, ComponentID, SubstituteID, Location, Quantity, DateInstalled, EmployeeID

PurchaseItem: PurchaseID, ComponentID, PricePaid, Quantity, QuantityReceived

Manufacturer: ManufacturerID, ManufacturerName, ContactName, Phone, Address, ZipCode, CityID, BalanceDue

TubeMaterial: TubeID, Material, Description, Diameter, Thickness, Roundness, Weight, Stiffness, ListPrice, Construction

GroupComponents: GroupID, ComponentID

Component: ComponentID, ManufacturerID, ProductNumber, Road, Category, Length, Height, Width, Weight, Description, ListPrice, EstimatedCost, QuantityOnHand

Groupo: ComponentGroup, GroupName, BikeType

ComponentName: ComponentName, AssemblyOrder, Description

ManufacturerTr..: ManufacturerID, TransactionDate, EmployeeID, Amount, Description, Reference

Rolling Thunder Bicycles

Write the SQL statements that will answer questions 38 through 51 based on the tables in the Rolling Thunder database. Build your queries in Access.

38. What is the total value of orders for each type of bicycle (model)?

39. List all of the employees who installed parts on bicycles shipped to Customer Shatika Embry (who just sent us a letter praising the quality).

40. What is the total cost of all components (not tubes) installed on July 19, 1994?

41. What five retail stores are the best at helping us sell bicycles? (Check both revenue and quantity.)

42. Which (if any) bicycles have been ordered using paint colors that were discontinued before the order was placed?

43. What is the most popular color scheme for racing bikes?

44. How many mountain bikes were sold that did not have a Shimano (Manufacturer) rear derailleur?

45. What is the total weight of the components installed on bicycle 566?

46. What is the total value of all purchase orders placed by employee Schuba?

47. How many customers used more than five payments to purchase their bicycle?

48. What is the average length of time Rolling Thunder takes to pay suppliers (break it down by each supplier)?

49. What is the greatest number of headsets ever installed in one day?

50. What are the average head-tube and seat-tube angles for each model type?

51. What is the average percentage of shipping cost compared to total purchase order value for each supplier?

WEB SITE REFERENCES

Site	Description
http://www.opengroup.org/index.htm	Standards group including SQL.
http://thebestweb.com/db/sqlrefs.htm	Consulting group with SQL hints and lots of links to other sites.

ADDITIONAL READING

Melton, J., and A. R. Simon. *Understanding the New SQL: A Complete Guide.* San Mateo: Morgan Kaufmann Publishers, 1993. [An in-depth presentation of SQL-92, by those who played a leading role in developing the standard.]

Groff, J. R., and P. Weinberg, *LAN Times Guide to SQL.* Berkeley: Osborne/McGraw-Hill, 1994. [Complete coverage of SQL topics.]

CHAPTER 5

Advanced Queries and Subqueries

WHAT YOU WILL LEARN IN THIS CHAPTER

OVERVIEW

Ariel: *Hi Miranda. You look happy.*

Miranda: *I am. This query system is great. I can see how it will help the managers. Once I get the application done, they can get answers to any questions they have. They won't have to call me for answers every day. Plus, I can really see how the query system relates to data normalization. With normalization I split the tables so the database could store them properly. Now the query system helps me rejoin them to answer my questions.*

Ariel: *Does that mean you're finally ready to create the application?*

Miranda: *Close, but I'm not quite ready. Yesterday my uncle asked me a question that I don't know how to answer.*

Ariel: *Really, I thought you could do anything with SQL. What was the question?*

Miranda: *Something about customers who did not order anything last month. I tried several times to get it to work, but the answers I get just aren't right.*

Ariel: *It doesn't sound like a hard question.*

Miranda: *I know. I can get a list of customers and orders that were placed any time except last month. But every time I join the Customer table to the Order table, all I get are the customers who did place orders. I don't know how to find something that's not there.*

INTRODUCTION

Now that you understand the basics of the SQL SELECT statement as described in Chapter 4, we can study more complex questions. One of the most powerful features of the SQL SELECT command is known as a **subquery** or **nested query.** This feature enables you to ask complex questions that entail retrieving different types of data or data from different sources. SQL is also more than a query language. It can be used to create the entire database (data definition language). SQL also has powerful commands to alter the data (data manipulation language).

Two key points will help you learn how to use subqueries: (1) SQL was designed to work with sets of data—avoid thinking in terms of individual rows, and (2) you can split nested queries into their separate parts and deal with the parts individually.

The features of SQL covered in Chapter 4 are already quite powerful. Why do we need more features? Consider this common business question for the Pet Store: Which animals have not been sold? Think about how you might answer that question using the SQL you know to this point. The first step might be to choose the tables: SaleAnimal and Animal appear to be likely choices. Second, select the columns as output: AnimalID and Name. Third, specify a condition. Fourth, join the tables. These last two steps cause the most problems in this example. How do you specify that an animal has not been sold? You cannot refer to any data in the SaleAnimal table. Because the animal has not been sold, the SaleAnimal table will not contain any entries for it.

Actually, the fourth step (joining the tables) causes you even more problems. Say you wrote a query like this: SELECT AnimalID, Name FROM Animal INNER JOIN

- How many cats are in stock on 10/1/98?
- Which cats sold for more than the average price?
- Which animals sold for more than the average price of animals in their category?
- Which animals have **not** been sold?
- Which customers (who bought something at least once) did **not** buy anything between 11/1/98 and 12/31/98?
- Which customers who bought dogs also bought products for cats (at any time)?

FIGURE 5.1 Harder questions. Even though there are few constraints on the problems, these questions are more complex. To answer many of them, we need to use subqueries or outer joins.

SaleAnimal ON (Animal.AnimalID = SaleAnimal.AnimalID). As soon as you write that join condition, you eliminate al! the animals you want to see. The join clause restricts the output—just like a WHERE clause would. In this example you told the DBMS to return only those animals that are listed in both the Animal and SaleAnimal tables. But only animals that have been sold are listed in the SaleAnimal table, so this query can never tell you anything about animals that have not been sold.

The following sections describe two solutions to this problem: either fix the join statement so that it is not as restrictive or use a subquery.

SALLY'S PET STORE

Figure 5.1 shows some more business questions that Sally needs to answer to manage her business. Again, think about how you might answer these questions using the basic SQL of Chapter 4. At first glance they do not seem too difficult. However, even the easier question to identify cats that sold for more than the average price is harder than it first appears. In all of these questions, we need an additional tool: the subquery.

SUBQUERIES

Calculations or Simple Look Up

Perhaps the easiest way to see the value of a subquery is to consider the relatively simple question: Which cats sold for more than the average price of cats? If we already know the average sale price of cats (say, $170), the query is easy, as shown in the top half of Figure 5.2.

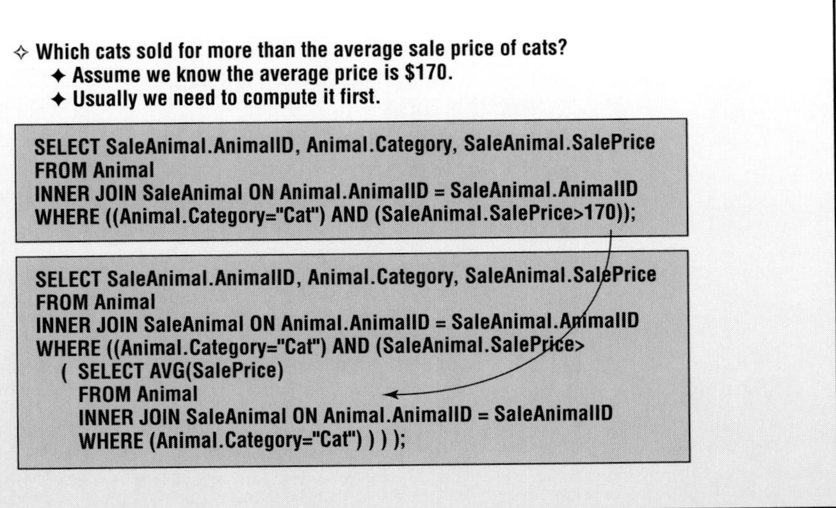

Which cats sold for more than the average sale price of cats?
Assume we know the average price is $170.
Usually we need to compute it first.
SELECT SaleAnimal.AnimalID, Animal.Category, SaleAnimal.SalePrice
FROM Animal
INNER JOIN SaleAnimal ON Animal.AnimalID = SaleAnimal.AnimalID
WHERE ((Animal.Category="Cat") AND (SaleAnimal.SalePrice>170));
SELECT SaleAnimal.AnimalID, Animal.Category, SaleAnimal.SalePrice
FROM Animal
INNER JOIN SaleAnimal ON Animal.AnimalID = SaleAnimal.AnimalID
WHERE ((Animal.Category="Cat") AND (SaleAnimal.SalePrice>
(SELECT AVG(SalePrice)
FROM Animal
INNER JOIN SaleAnimal ON Animal.AnimalID = SaleAnimalID
WHERE (Animal.Category="Cat"))));

FIGURE 5.2 Subqueries for calculation. If we do not know the average SalePrice of cats, we can use a query to look up the value. With a subquery we can put the result of that calculation directly into the original query (the subquery in parentheses replaces the 170 in the original query).

If we do not know the average SalePrice of cats, we could look it up with a basic query. We could write the result down on paper and then run the original query. However, with a subquery, we can go one step further: The result (average) from the query can be transferred directly to the original query. Simply replace the value (170) with the complete SELECT AVG query as shown in the lower half of Figure 5.2. In fact, any time you want to insert a value or comparison, you can use a subquery instead. You can even go to several levels, so a subquery can contain another subquery and so on. The DBMS generally evaluates the innermost query first and passes the results back to the higher level.

Two useful practices you should follow when building subqueries are to indent the subquery to make it stand out so humans can read it and to test the subquery before inserting it into the main query. Fortunately, most modern database systems make it easy to create a subquery and then cut and paste the SQL into the main query. Similarly, if you have problems getting a complex query to work, cut out the inner subqueries and test them separately.

Subqueries and Sets of Data

Some special SQL operators **(IN, ALL, ANY, EXISTS)** are often used with subqueries. They are a little easier to understand if we begin with simple numbers instead of a subquery. Consider the relatively easy query illustrated in Figure 5.3: List all customers who purchased one of the following items: 1, 2, 30, 32, 33.

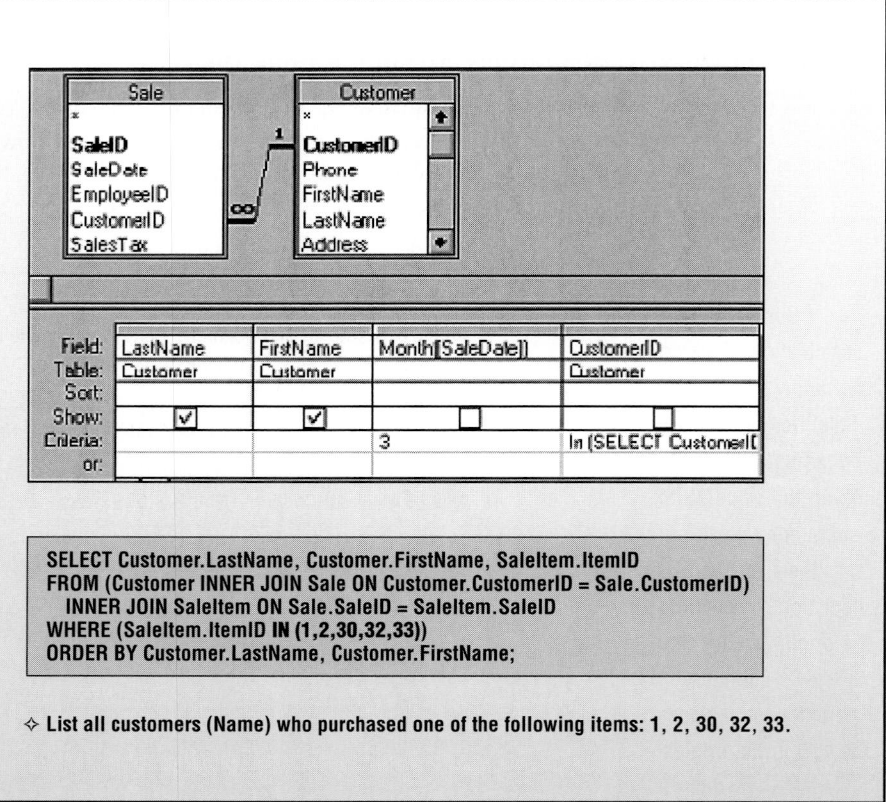

FIGURE 5.3
Queries with sets (IN). Could use OR statements, but the IN operator is easier. The WHERE condition is true if the ItemID matches any of the ID values in the accompanying list.

FIGURE 5.4
Using IN with a subquery. The subquery generates a list of ItemIDs designated as cat products. The main query then matches if the ItemID being purchased is in that subquery list.

```
List all customers who bought items for cats.

SELECT Customer.LastName, Customer.FirstName, SaleItem.ItemID
FROM (Customer
   INNER JOIN Sale ON Customer.CustomerID = Sale.CustomerID)
   INNER JOIN SaleItem ON Sale.SaleID = SaleItem.SaleID
WHERE (SaleItem.ItemID IN
   (SELECT ItemID FROM Merchandise WHERE Category = "Cat"));
```

You might consider writing a basic SQL statement to answer this question. Just use lots of OR connectors in the WHERE statement. You might start: ItemID=1 OR ItemID=2 OR ItemID=30. This approach would work for this simple example, although it would entail some extra typing. A better approach is to treat the list as a set of data and use the IN operator: WHERE ItemID IN (1,2,30,32,33). This condition is true if ItemID matches any of the values in the set of numbers.

Although the IN operator saved us some typing in this example, it actually has considerably more power. The power comes by noting that the list of numbers can be generated from a subquery. For example, the manager might want a list of customers who bought products for cats. Although you could look up all ItemID values for cat products, it is easier to let the DBMS do it. Simply change the WHERE clause to ItemID IN (SELECT ItemID FROM Merchandise WHERE Category="Cat").

Notice one crucial feature with the IN operator: The values in the list must be of the same data type (domain) as the variable being tested. The example in Figure 5.4 compares SaleItem.ItemID to SELECT ItemID. Like a join statement, the IN operator compares only similar types of data. For example, mixing ItemID with EmployeeID would lead to a nonsensical result. In fact, the IN operator can be used as a substitute for a join statement—although a join query is usually performed faster.

Subquery with ANY and ALL

The ANY and ALL operators combine comparison of numbers with subsets. In the preceding section, the IN operator compared a value to a list of items in a set—however, the comparison was based on equality. The test item had to exactly match an entry in the list. The ANY and ALL operators work with a less than (<) or greater than (>) operator and compare the test value to a list of values.

Figure 5.5 illustrates the use of the ANY query. It is hard to find a solid business example that needs the ANY operator. In the example it would be just as easy to

FIGURE 5.5
Subquery with ANY and ALL. The example computes 80 percent of the list price of each cat sold. Then it identifies any animal that sold for more than any of those amounts. In other words, it lists animals that sold for prices close to the list price of cats.

```
SELECT DISTINCTROW Animal.AnimalID, Name, SalePrice, ListPrice
FROM Animal
INNER JOIN SaleAnimal ON Animal.AnimalID = SaleAnimal.AnimalID
WHERE (((SalePrice) > ANY

   (SELECT 0.80*ListPrice
   FROM Animal
   INNER JOIN SaleAnimal ON Animal.AnimalID = SaleAnimal.AnimalID
   WHERE Category = "Cat"))

AND ((Category) = "Cat"));
```

first find the minimum value in the list and then do the comparison. However, it is sometimes clearer to use the ANY operator. The word SOME can be used in place of the word ANY, but they work exactly the same way.

The ALL operator behaves similarly, but the test value must be greater than all of the values in the list. In other words, the test value must exceed the largest value in the list. Hence the ALL operator is much more restrictive. The ALL operator can be a powerful tool—particularly when used with an equals (=) comparison. For instance, you might want to test whether one salesperson made all of the sales on a particular day, so the WHERE clause would contain this statement: WHERE EmployeeID = ALL (SELECT EmployeeID FROM Sale WHERE SaleDate = Date()).

SUBTRACTION: NOT IN

One question that commonly arises in business settings is illustrated in Figure 5.6 with the question: Which animals have not been sold? This question is deceptive. At first glance it looks like you could just join the Animal table to the SaleAnimal table. But then what? The standard join statement will display only those animals that appear in both the Animal and the SaleAnimal tables. As soon as you enter the join statement, you automatically restrict your list to only those animals that have been sold. One way to solve this problem is to change the behavior of the join command—which is explored in the next section.

Another useful approach is to think about the problem in terms of sets of data. Think about how you would solve this problem if you had only paper lists: one list

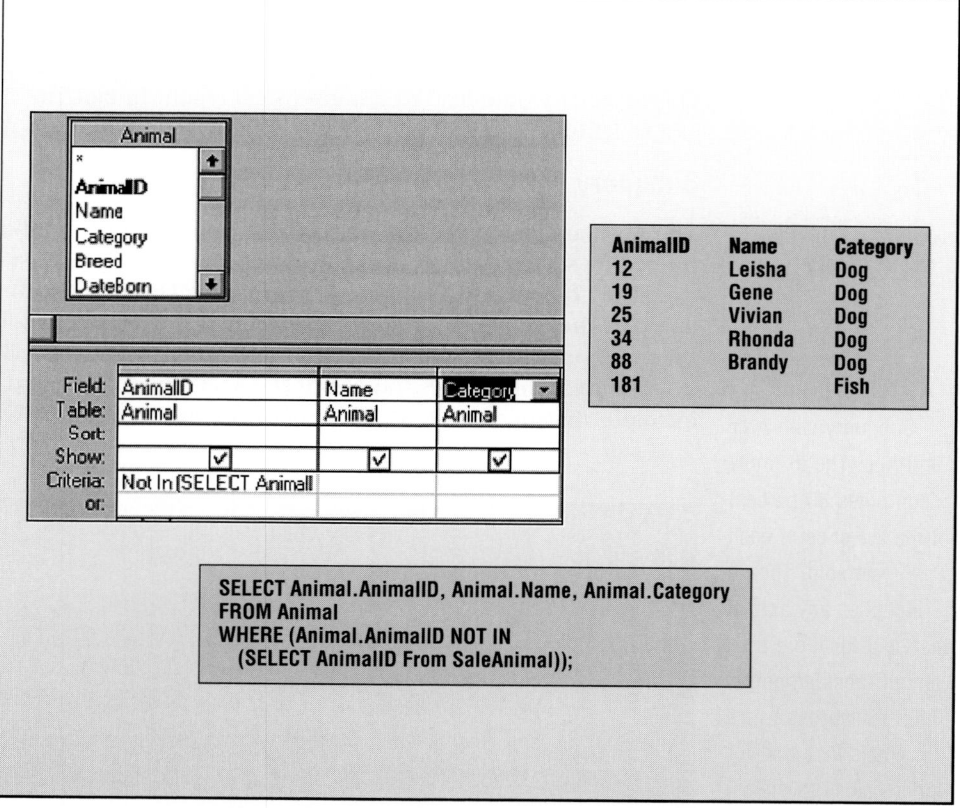

FIGURE 5.6 Subquery for NOT IN. Which animals have not been sold? Start with a list of all the animals and then subtract the list of those that were sold.

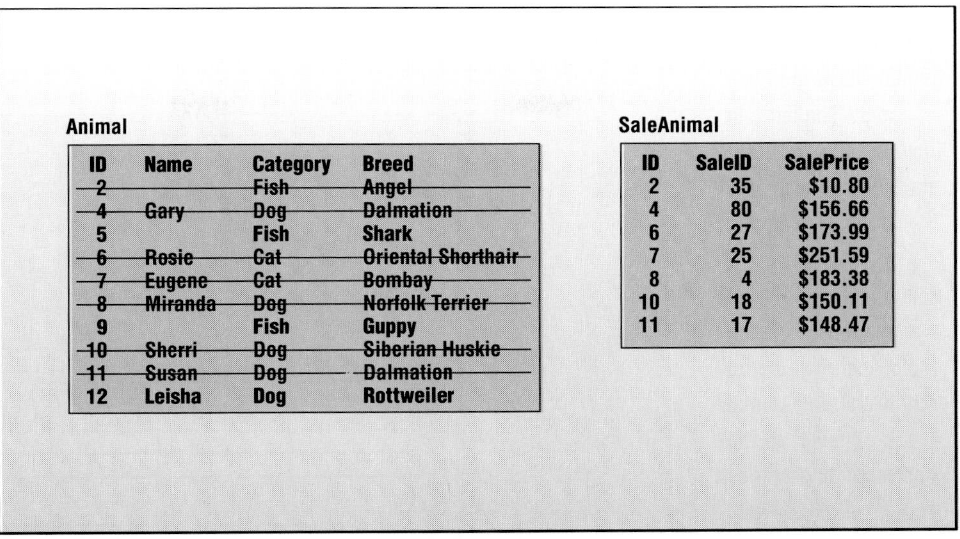

Animal

ID	Name	Category	Breed
~~2~~		~~Fish~~	~~Angel~~
~~4~~	~~Gary~~	~~Dog~~	~~Dalmation~~
5		Fish	Shark
~~6~~	~~Rosie~~	~~Cat~~	~~Oriental Shorthair~~
~~7~~	~~Eugene~~	~~Cat~~	~~Bombay~~
~~8~~	~~Miranda~~	~~Dog~~	~~Norfolk Terrier~~
9		Fish	Guppy
~~10~~	~~Sherri~~	~~Dog~~	~~Siberian Huskie~~
~~11~~	~~Susan~~	~~Dog~~	~~Dalmation~~
12	Leisha	Dog	Rottweiler

SaleAnimal

ID	SaleID	SalePrice
2	35	$10.80
4	80	$156.66
6	27	$173.99
7	25	$251.59
8	4	$183.38
10	18	$150.11
11	17	$148.47

FIGURE 5.7 Sample data for subtraction subquery. The NOT IN statement removes animals that have been sold, leaving only those that were not sold.

of all the animals the store has purchased and one list of all the animals that have been sold. As illustrated in Figure 5.7, to answer the question you would go through the main Animal list and cross off all the animals that have been sold (which appear on the SaleAnimal list). The ones remaining on the animal list are the animals that have not been sold.

SQL can accomplish the same task in a similar fashion using a subquery. The first step is to list all the animals—as shown in the main part of the query in Figure 5.6. But only list the animals that do not appear in the SaleAnimal table (the subquery).

The SQL NOT IN command is a useful tool. It is particularly useful for complex queries that involve several constraints. By moving the relevant constraints to the subquery, the main query becomes easier to understand.

OUTER JOINS

Up to this point, the examples and discussions have focused on the INNER JOIN (or **equi-join**) when multiple tables were involved. This type of join is the most common, and you should use it for most of your queries. However, you need to understand its limitations and the use of a different type of join known as an **outer join.**

To illustrate an outer join, consider the question from the previous section: Which animals have not been sold? Note that if you use an inner join between the Animal and SaleAnimal tables, the result will be a list of only those animals that appear in both tables. The INNER JOIN command instructs the DBMS to match every entry in the SaleAnimal table with a corresponding AnimalID in the Animal table. If it cannot make the match for any reason, the data in question will not be displayed.

Outer joins change the way the data is matched from the two tables. In particular, the outer join describes what should happen when values in one table do not exist in the second table.

In joining two tables, you have to consider two basic situations: (1) A value might exist in the left table with no matching value in the right table, or (2) a value might exist in the right table with no matching value in the left table. Of course, it really does not matter which table is on the left or right. However, you have to be careful

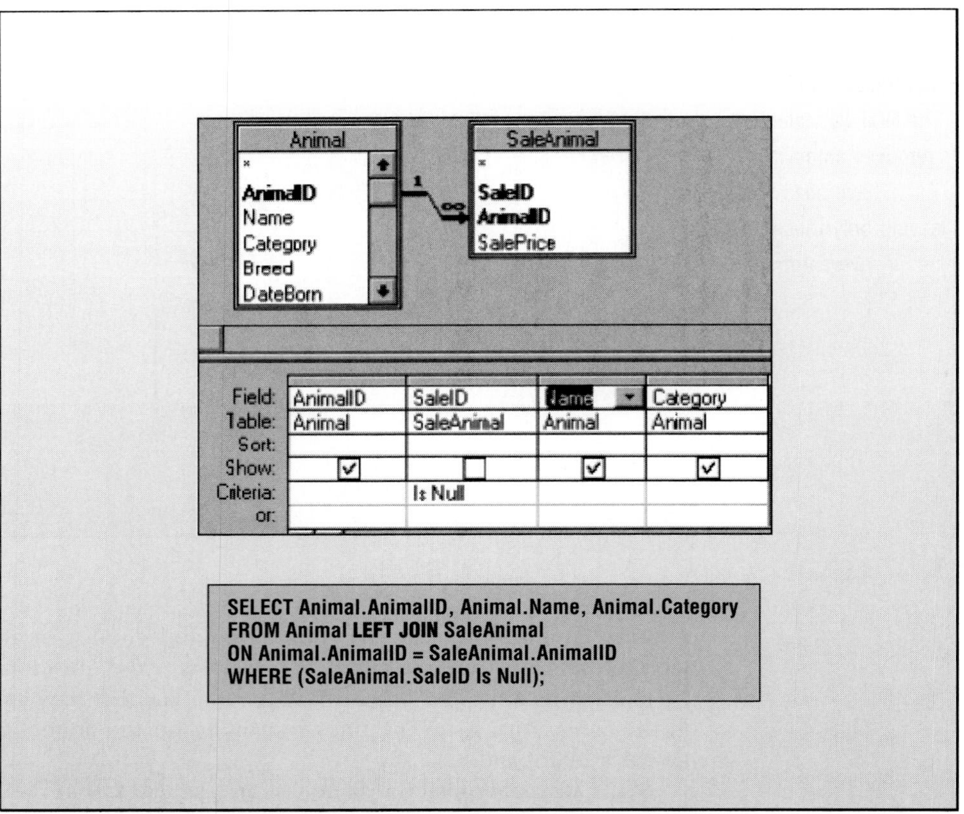


```
SELECT Animal.AnimalID, Animal.Name, Animal.Category
FROM Animal LEFT JOIN SaleAnimal
ON Animal.AnimalID = SaleAnimal.AnimalID
WHERE (SaleAnimal.SaleID Is Null);
```

FIGURE 5.8 Left outer join. Which animals have not been sold? The left join includes all rows from the Animal (left) table and any matching rows from the SaleAnimal table. If an animal has not been sold, there will be no entry in the SaleAnimal table, so the corresponding entries will be Null.

about not mixing them up after you list the tables. In QBE the tables are physically displayed in the order mentioned. With SQL the left table is listed first.

The query in Figure 5.8 illustrates a typical left outer join (or just **LEFT JOIN**). With a LEFT JOIN, all rows in the table on the left will be displayed in the results. If there is no matching value from the table on the right, Null values will be inserted into the output. Note how the LEFT JOIN resolves the problem of identifying animals that have not been sold. Because the query will now list all animals, the rows where the SaleID is Null represent animals that are not in the Sale table and have not been sold. Sample output from the query is displayed in Figure 5.9.

The **RIGHT JOIN** behaves similarly to the LEFT JOIN. The only difference is the order of the tables. If you want to use all the rows from the table on the right side, use a RIGHT JOIN. Why not just have a LEFT JOIN and simply rearrange the tables? Most of the time that is exactly what you will do. However, if you have a query that joins several tables, it is sometimes easier to use a RIGHT JOIN instead of trying to rearrange the tables.

Another is join the full outer join (**FULL JOIN**) that combines every row from the left table and every row from the right table. Where the rows do not match (from the ON condition), the join inserts Null values into the appropriate columns.

Warning: Be careful with outer joins—particularly full joins. With two large tables that do not have much data in common, you end up with a very large result that is not very useful. Also be careful when using outer joins on more than two tables in one query. You get different results depending on the order in which you join the tables.

FIGURE 5.9
Results from the left outer join. Note the missing (Null) values for animals that have not been sold.

ID	Name	Category	Breed	ID	SaleID	SalePrice
2		Fish	Angel	2	35	$10.80
4	Gary	Dog	Dalmation	4	80	$156.66
5		Fish	Shark	Null	Null	Null
6	Rosie	Cat	Oriental Shorthair	6	27	$173.99
7	Eugene	Cat	Bombay	7	25	$251.59
8	Miranda	Dog	Norfolk Terrier	8	4	$183.38
9		Fish	Guppy	Null	Null	Null
10	Sherri	Dog	Siberian Huskie	10	18	$150.11
11	Susan	Dog	Dalmation	11	17	$148.47
12	Leisha	Dog	Rottweiler	Null	Null	Null

Finally, note that we have been relying on the SQL 92 syntax, which is fairly easy to read and understand. Some database systems do not yet support that syntax. A common older technique to specify outer joins is to use an asterisk in conjunction with an equals sign; for example, (*=) indicates a left outer join, since the asterisk is to the left of the equals sign. The animal query for SQL Server is displayed in Figure 5.10. Although the syntax is different from SQL 92, the effect is the same. Be on the lookout for this syntax when you read queries developed for older systems—that little asterisk can be hard to spot, but it radically alters the query results.

Oracle uses yet another syntax to signify an outer join. The WHERE statement in Figure 5.10 would become Animal.AnimalID = (+) SaleAnimal.AnimalID. The plus sign in parentheses indicates an outer join, but be careful. The plus is to the right of the equal sign. In other words, if you want a left outer join, you place the plus sign to the right of the equals sign. It is opposite from what you might expect and opposite from the asterisk notation.

CORRELATED SUBQUERIES ARE DANGEROUS

Recall the example in Figure 5.2 that asked, Which cats sold for more than the average price of cats? This example used a subquery to first find the average sale price of cats and then examined all sales of cats to display the ones that had higher prices. It is a reasonable business question to extend this idea to other categories of animals. Managers would like to identify all animals that were sold for a price greater than the average price of other animals within their respective categories (dogs greater than the average price of dogs, fish compared to fish, etc.).

Although this business question is perfectly reasonable, it can lead to serious problems as a query. To start with, it is not immediately obvious how to build this query. One approach might be to take the query in Figure 5.2 and substitute the

FIGURE 5.10
Older syntax for left join. Which animals have not been sold? Note the asterisk-equals operator (*=), which is used for a left join. The reverse (=*) would be used for a right join.

```
SELECT ALL
FROM Animal, SaleAnimal
WHERE Animal.AnimalID *= SaleAnimal.AnimalID
And SaleAnimal.SaleID Is Null;
```

```
SELECT AnimalID, Name, Category, SalePrice
FROM Animal INNER JOIN SaleAnimal ON Animal.AnimalID = SaleAnimal.AnimalID
WHERE (SaleAnimal.SalePrice >
   (SELECT Avg(SaleAnimal.SalePrice)
   FROM Animal INNER JOIN SaleAnimal ON Animal.AnimalID = SaleAnimal.AnimalID
   WHERE (Animal.Category = Animal.Category)) )
ORDER BY SaleAnimal.SalePrice DESC;
```

FIGURE 5.11 Correlated subquery creation. List the animals that have sold for more than the average price of other animals in their category. The subquery needs to compute the average sale price for the category of animal shown in the main query. But both tables are called 'Animal,' so this query will not work yet.

category "Dog" for "Cat" in both the main and the subquery. This approach will work, but you will first have to find all of the categories and then edit the query for each category.

Instead of having you enter each category by hand, perhaps the subquery can get the category from the main query and then compute the average sale price for that category. Figure 5.11 shows a first attempt to create this query. The difficulty is that the main query refers to the Animal table and the subquery also uses the Animal table. Consequently, the WHERE constraint does not make sense. It needs to specify that one of the Animal tables is in the main query and the other is in the subquery. To do that, we need to rename (alias) the tables, as shown in Figure 5.12.

The query in Figure 5.12 will run. However, it is extremely inefficient. Even on a fast computer, queries of this type have been known to run for several days without finishing! This type of query is called a **correlated subquery** because the subquery refers to data rows in the main query. The calculation in the subquery must be recomputed for each entry in the main table. The problem is illustrated in Figure 5.13. Essentially, the DBMS starts at the top row of the main Animal table. When it sees the category is Fish, it computes the average sale price of fish ($37.78). Then it moves to the next row and computes the average sale price for dogs. When the DBMS encounters the third row and sees Fish again, it must recompute the average for fish (still $37.78). Recomputing the average sale price for every single row in the main query is time-consuming. To compute an average, the DBMS must go through every row in the table that has the same category of animal. Consider a relatively small query of 100,000 rows and five categories of animals. On average there are 20,000 rows per category. To recompute the average each time, the DBMS will have to retrieve 100,000 * 20,000 or 2,000,000,000 rows!

Unfortunately, you cannot just tell the manager that it is impossible to answer this important business question. Is there an efficient way to answer this question? The answer illustrates the power of SQL and highlights the importance of thinking about the problem before you try to write a query. The problem with the correlated

```
SELECT A1.AnimalID, A1.Name, A1.Category, SaleAnimal.SalePrice
FROM Animal As A1 INNER JOIN SaleAnimal ON A1.AnimalID = SaleAnimal.AnimalID
WHERE (SaleAnimal.SalePrice >
   (SELECT Avg(SaleAnimal.SalePrice)
   FROM Animal As A2 INNER JOIN SaleAnimal ON A2.AnimalID =
      SaleAnimal.AnimalID
   WHERE (A2.Category = A1.Category)) )
ORDER BY SaleAnimal.SalePrice DESC;
```

FIGURE 5.12 Correlated subquery that will run. Note the use of aliases to distinguish the two tables. However, never use this approach—it is incredibly inefficient!

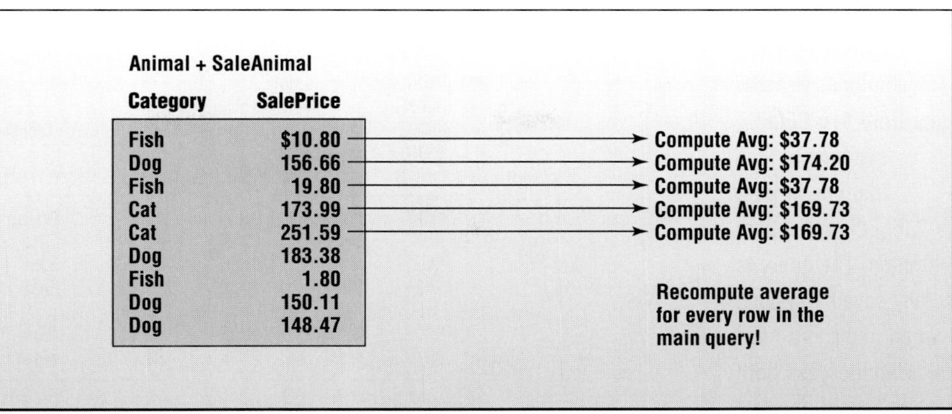

FIGURE 5.13 Problem with correlated subquery. The average is recomputed for every row in the main query. Every time the DBMS sees a fish, it computes the average to be $37.78. It is inefficient (and very slow) to force the machine to recalculate the average each time.

subquery lies in the fact that it has to continually recompute the average for each category. Think about how you might solve this problem by hand. You would first make a table that listed the average for each category and then simply look up the appropriate value when you needed it. As shown in Figure 5.14, the same approach can be used with SQL. Just create the query for the averages using GROUP BY and save it. Then join it to the Animal and SaleAnimal tables to do the comparison. Although this approach requires two complete passes through the query rows, or reading 200,000 rows in our small example, it is 10,000 times more efficient than the correlated subquery! If this new query takes 1 minute to run, the correlated subquery could take 7 days to finish!

MORE FEATURES AND TRICKS WITH SQL SELECT

As you may have noticed, the SQL SELECT command is powerful and has plenty of options. There are even more features and tricks that you should know about. Business questions can be difficult to answer. It helps to study different examples to gain a wider perspective on the problems and solutions you will encounter.

UNION, INTERSECT, EXCEPT

Up to this point the tables we have encountered have contained unique columns of data. The join command links tables together so that a query can display and com-

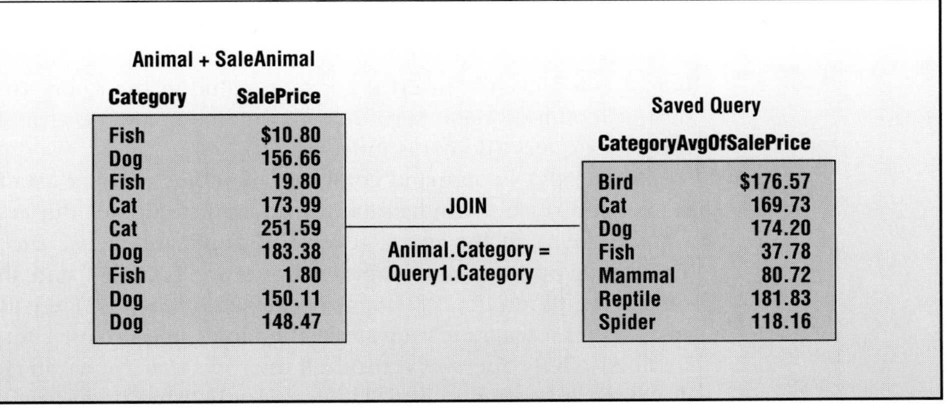

FIGURE 5.14 More efficient solution. Create and save a query to compute the averages using GROUP BY Category. Then join the query to the Animal and SaleAnimal tables to do the comparison.

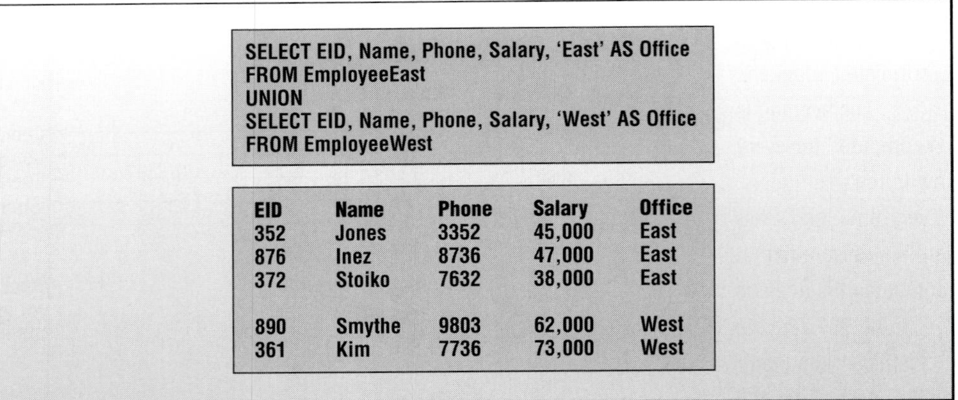

```
SELECT EID, Name, Phone, Salary, 'East' AS Office
FROM EmployeeEast
UNION
SELECT EID, Name, Phone, Salary, 'West' AS Office
FROM EmployeeWest
```

EID	Name	Phone	Salary	Office
352	Jones	3352	45,000	East
876	Inez	8736	47,000	East
372	Stoiko	7632	38,000	East
890	Smythe	9803	62,000	West
361	Kim	7736	73,000	West

FIGURE 5.15 The UNION operator combines rows of data from two SELECT statements. The columns in both SELECT lines must match. The query is usually saved and used when managers need to search across both tables. Note the use of a new, constant column (Office) to track the source of the data.

pare different columns of data from tables. Occasionally you will encounter a different type of problem where you need to combine rows of data from similar tables. The **UNION** operator is designed to accomplish this task.

As an example, assume you work for a company that has offices in Los Angeles and New York. Each office maintains its own database. Each office has an Employee file that contains standard data about its employees. The offices are linked by a network, so you have access to both tables (call them EmployeeEast and EmployeeWest). But the corporate managers often want to search the entire Employee file—for example, to determine total employee salaries of the marketing department. One solution might be to run their basic query twice (once on each table) and then combine the results by hand.

As shown in Figure 5.15, the easier solution is to use the UNION operator to create a new query that combines the data from the two tables. All searches and operations performed on this new query will treat the two tables as one large table. By combining the tables with a view, each office can make changes to the original data on its system. Whenever managers need to search across the entire company, they use the saved query, which automatically examines the data from current versions of both tables.

The most important concept to remember when creating a UNION is that the data from both tables must match (e.g., EID to EID, Name to Name). Another useful trick is to insert a constant value in the SELECT statement. In this example the constant keeps track of which table held the original data. This value can also be used to balance out a SELECT statement if one of the queries will produce a column that is not available in the other query. To make sure both queries return the same number of columns, just insert a constant value in the query that does not contain the desired column. Make sure that it contains the same type of data that is stored in the other query (domains must match).

The UNION command combines matching rows of data from two tables. The basic version of the command automatically eliminates duplicate rows of data. If you want to keep all the rows—even the duplications, use the command UNION ALL. Two other options for combining rows are: **EXCEPT** and **INTERSECT.** Figure 5.16 shows the difference between the three commands. They all apply to sets of rows, and the Venn diagram shows that the tables might have some data in common (area B). The UNION operator returns all the rows that appear in either one of the tables—but rows appearing in both tables are only listed once. The INTERSECT operator re-

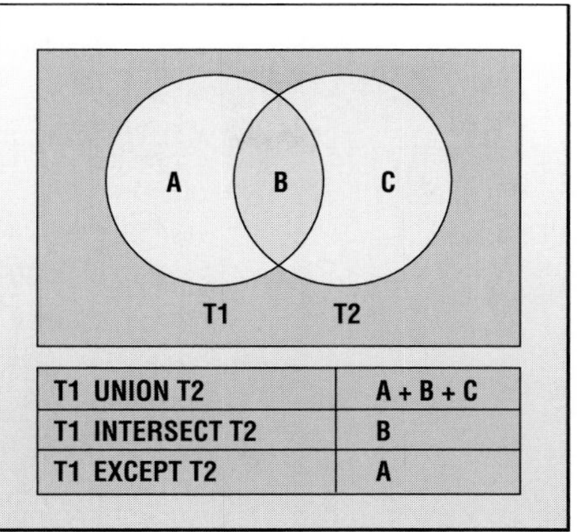

FIGURE 5.16 Operators for combining rows from two tables. UNION selects all rows. INTERSECT retrieves only the rows that are in both tables. EXCEPT retrieves rows that exist in only one table.

turns the rows that appear in both tables (area B). The EXCEPT operator returns only rows that appear in the first table (area A). Notice that the result of the EXCEPT operator depends on which table is listed first.

Multiple Join Columns

Sometimes you will need to join tables based on data in more than one column. In the Pet Store example, each animal belongs to some category (Cat, Dog, Fish, etc.). Each category of animal has different breeds. For example, a Cat might be a Manx, Maine Coon, or Persian; a Dog might be a Retriever, Labrador, or St. Bernard. A portion of the class diagram is reproduced in Figure 5.17. Notice the two lines connecting the Breed and Animal tables. This relationship ensures that only breeds listed in the Breed table can be entered for each type of Animal. A real store might want to include additional features in the Breed table (such as registration organization, breed description, or breed characteristics). The key point is that the tables must be connected by both the Category and the Breed.

In Microsoft Access QBE, the join can be created by marking both columns and simultaneously dragging the two columns to the Animal table. The syntax for the SQL join command is given in Figure 5.17. Simply expand the ON statement by listing both column connections. In this case we want both sets of columns to be equal at the same time, so the statements are connected with an AND.

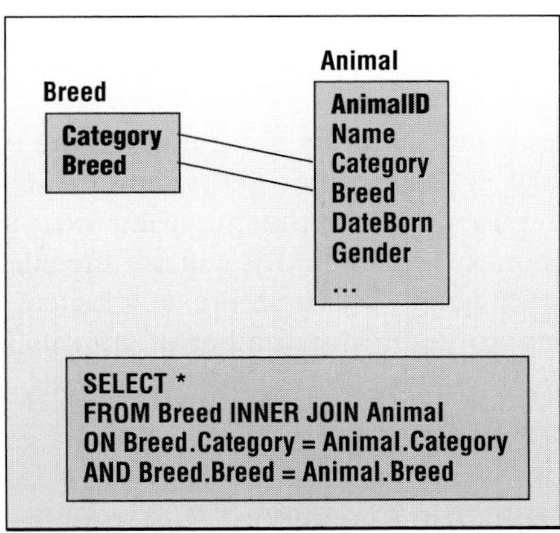

FIGURE 5.17 Multiple join columns. The values in the tables are connected only when both the category and the breed match.

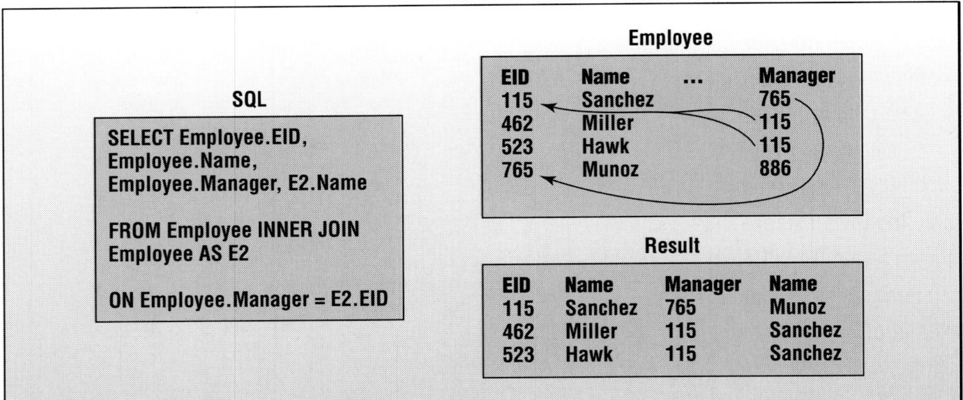

FIGURE 5.18 Reflexive join to connect Employee table with itself. A manager is also an employee. Use a second copy of the Employee table (renamed to E2) to get the manager's name.

Reflexive Join

A **reflexive join** or **self-join** simply means that a table is joined to itself. One column in the table is used to match values in a second column in the same table. A common business example arises with an Employee table as illustrated in Figure 5.18. Employees typically have one manager. Hence the manager's ID can be stored in the row corresponding to each employee. The table would be Employee(<u>EID</u>, Name, Phone, . . . , Manager). The interesting feature is that a manager is also an employee, so the Manager column actually contains a value for EID. To get the corresponding name of the manager, we need to join the Employee table to itself.

The only trick with this operation is that you have to be careful with the ON condition. For instance, the following condition does not make sense: ON Employee.Manager = Employee.EID. The query would try to return employees who were their own managers, which is not likely to be what you wanted. Instead, you must use two instances of the Employee table and use an alias (say, E2) to rename the second copy. Then the correct ON condition becomes ON Employee.Manager = E2.EID. The key to self-joins is to make sure that the columns contain the same type of data and to create an alias for the second copy of the table.

CASE Function

SQL 92 added the **CASE** function to simplify certain types of queries. However, many database systems have not yet implemented all the features of SQL 92. Hence Microsoft Access 97 does not support it, whereas Microsoft SQL Server version 6.5 does provide this function.

Perhaps the managers want to classify the animals in the Pet Store based on their age. Figure 5.19 shows the SQL statement that would create four categories based on different ages. Note the use of date arithmetic using today's date—(Date()—) and DateBorn. Whenever this query is executed, it will use the current day to assign each animal to the appropriate category. Of course, the next logical step is to run a GROUP BY query against this view to count the number of animals falling within each age category.

Inequality Joins

A join statement is actually just a condition. Most problems are straightforward and use a simple equality condition. For example, the following statement joins

FIGURE 5.19
CASE function to convert DateBorn into age categories. Note the use of date arithmetic to generate descriptions that are always current.

```
Select AnimalID,
  CASE
    WHEN Date()-DateBorn <90 Then "Baby"
    WHEN Date()-DateBorn >=90
     AND Date()-DateBorn <270 Then "Young"
    WHEN Date()-DateBorn >=270
     AND Date()-DateBorn <365 Then "Grown"
    ELSE "Experienced"
  END
FROM Animal;
```

the Customer and Order tables: FROM Customer INNER JOIN Order ON (Customer.CustomerID = Order.CustomerID).

SQL supports complex conditions including **inequality joins,** where the comparison is made with inequality operators (less than, greater than) instead of an equals sign. The generic name for any inequality or equality join is a theta join.

There are a few situations where this type of join can be useful. For example, consider a common business problem. You have a table for AccountsReceivable(<u>TransactionID</u>, CustomerID, Amount, DateDue). Managers would like to categorize the customer accounts and determine how many transactions are past due by 30, 90, and 120 or more days. There are a couple of ways to build this query. For instance, you could write three separate queries. However, what happens if managers decide to change the business rules or add a new category? Then someone has to find your three queries and modify them. A more useful trick is to create a new table to hold the business rules or categories. For example, as shown in Figure 5.20, create the table LateCategory(<u>Category</u>, MinDays, MaxDays, Charge, etc.). This table defines the late categories based on the number of days past due. Now use inequality conditions to join the two tables. First, compute the number of days late using the current date (Date() − AR.DateDue). Finally, compare the number of days late to minimum and maximum values specified in the LateCategory table.

The ultimate value of this approach is that the business rules are now stored in a simple table (LateCategory). If managers want to change the conditions or add new criteria, they simply alter the data in the table. You can even build a form that makes it easy for managers to see the rules and quickly make the needed changes (see Chapter 6). With any other approach, a programmer would have to rewrite the code for the queries.

FIGURE 5.20
Inequality join. Managers want to classify the AccountsReceivable (AR) data into three categories of overdue payments. First, store the business rules/categories in a new table. Then join the table to the AR data through inequality joins.

AR(<u>TransactionID</u>, CustomerID, Amount, DateDue)

LateCategory(<u>Category</u>, MinDays, MaxDays, Charge, . . .)

Month	30	90	3%
Quarter	90	120	5
Overdue	120	9999	10

```
SELECT*
FROM AR INNER JOIN LateCategory
ON ((Date() – AR.DateDue) >= Category.MinDays)
AND ((Date() – AR.DateDue) < Category.MaxDays
```

Cross Tabulation

Crosstab capabilities are useful in many business databases. Although the crosstab function is not part of SQL 92, it is supported within Microsoft Access. Cross tabulation is essentially a GROUP BY operation that works with two groups instead of one. The results are displayed as a table, with one group across the top as columns and the other down the side as rows.

It is easiest to understand cross tabulation with an example. Figure 5.21 shows the result of the query that describes total sales by month by each category of animal. Note the two uses of the word *by* in that query. This example also highlights why cross tabulation has so many business applications. There are many situations in which managers want to see totals displayed by a time period (e.g., month), as well as by an internal category. Related examples include sales by employee per week and expenses by department by quarter. Cross tabulation would also be useful for computing sales by product line by region.

In Access, crosstab queries can be written with a TRANSFORM command. However, it is generally easier to use the QBE grid to create the query. Simply pick the tables and join them as usual. Then use the Query option on the menu to select a crosstab query. Each crosstab query requires three entries or columns: a group for the rows; a group for the columns; and the computation (Sum, Count, etc.) to be performed. With QBE you choose the role of the three columns on the QBE grid. With TRANSFORM a GROUP BY statement, specifies the rows and a PIVOT statement specifies the columns. Both the QBE and TRANSFORM definitions are shown in Figure 5.22.

Because this type of query is so useful in business, examine the query to see how the months were generated. Typically, the database will store transaction dates. You will have to convert these days into more meaningful groups. The Month function extracts the month (by number) from a given date. If you want to add month names, you have several choices: write your own month function, use the CASE function, or store the month names in a separate table and join it to the results. In all of these situations, be careful with the results; you probably want to sort the output by sequence of the months, not by the name of the month.

FIGURE 5.21 Crosstab example for total sales by month by animal category. Note there is limited sample data. In certain months the company did not sell some animals (e.g., no fish were sold in January).

Month	Bird	Cat	Dog	Fish	Mammal	Reptile	Spider
1		$217.51	$1,655.01				
2	$324.87	597.74	1,281.81	$39.60		$127.78	
3	364.18	198.85	650.17			378.25	$40.50
4		334.50	1,221.10			172.88	
5	396.84	335.48	1,192.56	126.20			
6	119.71	459.91	1,607.46	5.40	$19.80		
7		573.60	1,644.73	319.07	19.80	182.31	
8	578.35	1,444.75	1,859.71	27.90	320.52		
9	538.07	792.46	1,219.03				
10	173.50	942.89	1,429.27	10.80	11.70	229.73	313.97
11	153.07	1,308.97	1,784.06		112.50		
12		770.87	1,178.47				

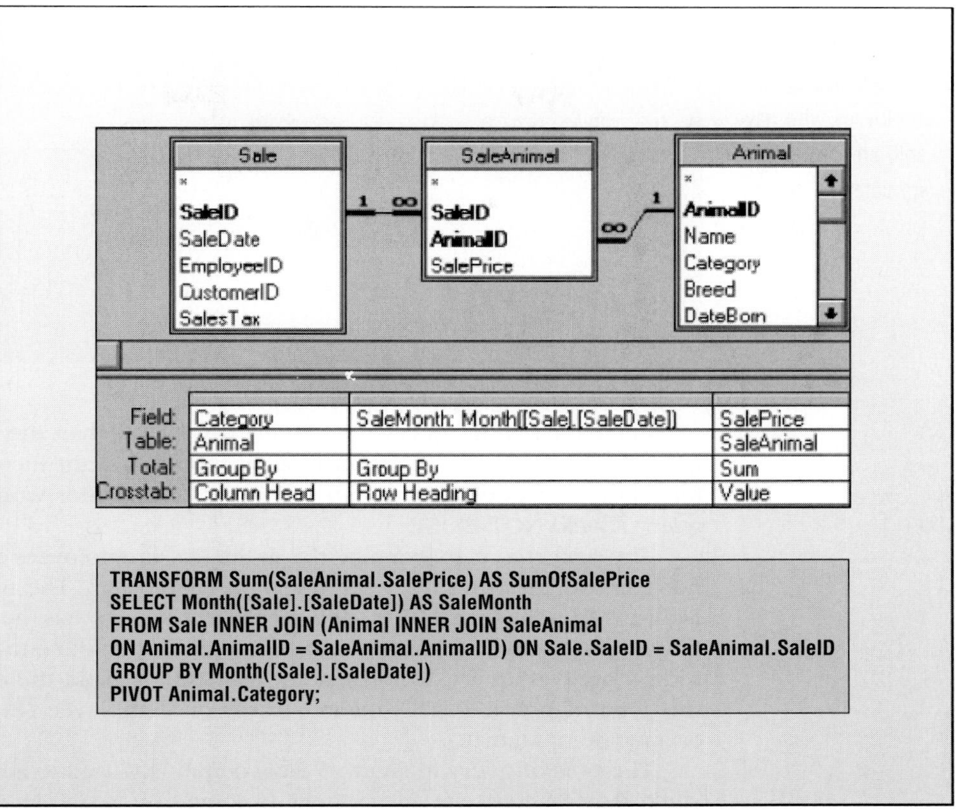

FIGURE 5.22 Crosstab definition in Microsoft Access. First select and join the tables needed; then use QBE by setting the Crosstab option in the Query menu. Choose a column to group the output columns, a column to group the rows, and an aggregation function for the values.

Questions with "Every" Need the EXISTS Clause

Some queries need the EXISTS condition. Consider the business question: Which employees have sold an animal in every category? The word *every* is the key here. Think about how you would answer that question if you did not have a computer. For each employee you would make a list of animal categories (Bird, Cat, Dog, etc.). Then you would go through the list of AnimalSales and cross off each animal category sold by the employee. When finished, you would look at the employee list to see which people have every animal crossed off (or an empty list). We will do the same thing using queries.

First, we need a query that lists all the animal categories that have not been sold by an employee. Consider the list for EmployeeID 5, with the query shown in Figure 5.23. Notice that it uses the basic NOT IN query. You could also use an outer join, but with three tables, it is easier to use NOT IN.

FIGURE 5.23 List the animal categories that have not been sold by EmployeeID 5. Use a basic NOT IN query.

```
SELECT Category
FROM Category
  WHERE (Category <> "Other") And Category NOT IN
    (SELECT Animal.Category
    FROM Animal INNER JOIN (Sale INNER JOIN SaleAnimal
      ON Sale.SaleID = SaleAnimal.SaleID)
      ON Animal.AnimalID = SaleAnimal.AnimalID
    WHERE Sale.EmployeeID = 5)
```

```
SELECT Employee.EmployeeID, Employee.LastName
FROM Employee
WHERE Not Exists
(SELECT Category
  FROM Category
  WHERE (Category <> "Other") And Category NOT IN
    (SELECT Animal.Category
    FROM Animal INNER JOIN (Sale INNER JOIN SaleAnimal
      ON Sale.SaleID = SaleAnimal.SaleID)
      ON Animal.AnimalID = SaleAnimal.AnimalID
    WHERE Sale.EmployeeID = Employee.EmployeeID));
```

FIGURE 5.24 Example of NOT EXISTS clause. List the employees who have sold an animal from every category (except "Other").

Remember, if this query returns any rows at all, then the selected employee has not sold every one of the animals. What we really want then is a list of employees for whom this query returns no rows of data. In other words, the rows from this query should NOT EXIST.

The next step is to examine the entire list of employees and see which ones do not retrieve any rows from the query in Figure 5.23. The final query is shown in Figure 5.24. Note that the specific EmployeeID 5 has been replaced with the EmployeeID matching the value in the outer loop. Notice that this action results in a correlated subquery. Unfortunately, you cannot avoid the correlated subquery in this type of problem. This query returns one employee (Reasoner) who has sold every type of animal.

The type of query in Figure 5.24 is commonly used to answer questions that include some reference to "every" item. In some cases a simpler solution is to just count the number of categories for each employee. One catch to this approach is that the DBMS must support the Count(DISTINCT) format. Microsoft Access does not allow this syntax, so you would have to form a separate query to list the distinct categories sold for each employee.

Another approach in Access, which has more promise, is to use a Crosstab query that counts the number of each type of animal sold for each employee. Figure 5.25

EID	LastName	Bird	Cat	Dog	Fish	Mammal	Reptile	Spider
1	Reeves			7				
2	Gibson	2	6	12	2	1		2
3	Reasoner	3	6	14	2	1	1	1
4	Hopkins	2	4	14			1	
5	James	3	8	7	5	1	2	
6	Eaton	1	5	6		1		
7	Farris	1	6	16			2	
8	Carpenter	2	6	10	2	1		
9	O'Connor		6	8	3	1		
10	Shields	1		2				

FIGURE 5.25 A Crosstab approach in Access to find the employees who have sold every category of animal. If there are a large number of employees or categories, this approach may not be feasible.

FIGURE 5.26
SQL SELECT options. Remember that WHERE statements can have subqueries.

```
SELECT DISTINCT Table.Column {AS alias}, . . .
FROM Table/Query
INNER JOIN Table/Query ON T1.ColA = T2.ColB
WHERE (condition)
GROUP BY Column
HAVING (group condition)
ORDER BY Table.Column
{Union second select}

TRANSFORM aggfunction                      {Crosstab values}
   SELECT . . . FROM . . . GROUP BY        {Crosstab rows}
   PIVOT pivotfield                        {Crosstab columns}
```

shows the result of this query. Scanning each row for blank columns shows that only Reasoner has sold animals from every category.

This approach provides more information than the prior (NOT EXISTS) query. However, if there are a large number of employees or categories, the crosstab technique can provide too much data and might cause mistakes because a person has to read each row carefully.

SQL SELECT Summary

The SQL SELECT command is powerful and has many options. To help you remember the various options, they are presented in Figure 5.26. This list is relatively generic except for the TRANSFORM (crosstab) options that are provided by Microsoft Access. Each DBMS has a similar listing for the SELECT command, and you should consult the relevant Help system for details. Remember that the WHERE clause can have subqueries.

Most database systems are picky about the sequence of the various components of the SELECT statement. For example, the WHERE statement should come before the GROUP BY statement. Sometimes these errors can be hard to spot, so if you receive an enigmatic error message, verify that the segments are in the proper order. Figure 5.27 presents a mnemonic that may help you remember the proper sequence. Also, you should always build a query in pieces, so you can test each piece. For example, if you use a GROUP BY statement, first check the results without it to be sure that the proper rows are being selected.

SQL DATA DEFINITION COMMANDS

So far we have focused on only one aspect of a database: retrieving data. Clearly, we need to perform many more operations with a database. SQL was designed to handle all common operations. One set of commands is described in this section: **data**

FIGURE 5.27
Mnemonic to help remember the proper sequence of the SELECT operators.

Someone	SELECT
From	FROM
Ireland	INNER JOIN
Will	WHERE
Grow	GROUP BY
Horseradish and	HAVING
Onions	ORDER BY

```
Create Schema Authorization dbName password
Create Table TableName (Column Type, . . . )
Alter Table Table {Add, Column, Constraint, Drop}
Drop {Table Table|Index Index On table}
Create Index IndexName ON Table (Column {ASC|DESC})
```

FIGURE 5.28 Primary SQL data definition commands. In most cases you will avoid these commands and use a visual or menu-driven system to define and modify tables.

definition commands to create and modify the database and its tables. Note that the SQL commands can be cumbersome for these tasks. Hence most modern database systems provide a visual or menu-driven system to assist with these tasks. The SQL commands are generally used when you need to automate some of these tasks and set up or make changes to a database from within a separate program.

The five most common data definition commands are listed in Figure 5.28. In building a new database, the first step is to **CREATE** a **SCHEMA.** A **schema** is a collection of tables. In some systems the command is equivalent to creating a new database. In other systems it simply defines a logical area where each user can store tables, which might or might not be in one physical database. The Authorization component describes the user and sets a password for security.

CREATE TABLE is one of the main SQL data definition commands. It is used to define a completely new table. The basic command lists the name of the table along with the names and data types for all of the columns. Figure 5.29 shows the format for the data definition commands. Additional options include the ability to assign default values with the DEFAULT command.

SQL 92 provides several standard data types, but system vendors do not yet implement all of them. SQL 92 also enables you to create your own data types with the **CREATE DOMAIN** command. For example, to ensure consistency you could create a domain called DomAddress that consists of CHAR (35). Then any table that used an address column would refer to the DomAddress.

With SQL 92 you identify the primary key and foreign key relationships with constraints. SQL **constraints** are rules that are enforced by the database system. Figure 5.30 illustrates the syntax for defining both a primary key and a foreign key for an Order table. First, notice that each constraint is given a name (e.g., pkorder). You can choose any name, but you should pick one that you will recognize later if problems arise. The primary key constraint simply lists the column or columns that

```
CREATE TABLE Customer
   (CustomerID INTEGER NOT NULL,
   LastName CHAR (10),
   more columns);

ALTER TABLE Customer
   DROP COLUMN ZipCode;

ALTER TABLE Customer
   ADD COLUMN CellPhone CHAR(15);
```

FIGURE 5.29 The CREATE TABLE command defines a new table and all of the columns that it will contain. The NOT NULL command typically is used to identify the key column(s) for the table. The ALTER TABLE command enables you to add and delete entire columns from an existing table.

FIGURE 5.30
Identifying primary and foreign keys in SQL. Keys are defined as constraints that are enforced by the DBMS. The primary key constraint lists the columns that make up the primary key. The foreign key lists the column (CustomerID) in the current table (Order) that is linked to a column (CustomerID) in a second table (Customer).

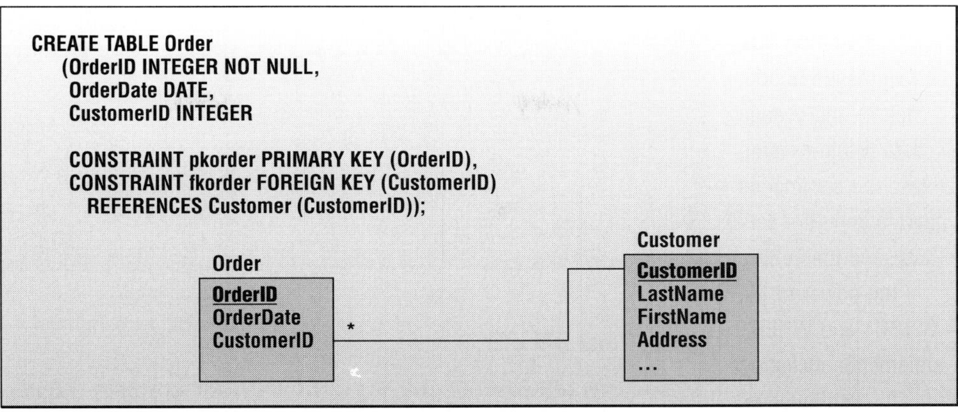
CREATE TABLE Order
(OrderID INTEGER NOT NULL,
OrderDate DATE,
CustomerID INTEGER
CONSTRAINT pkorder PRIMARY KEY (OrderID),
CONSTRAINT fkorder FOREIGN KEY (CustomerID)
REFERENCES Customer (CustomerID));
Order
OrderID
OrderDate
CustomerID
*
Customer
CustomerID
LastName
FirstName
Address
…

make up the primary key. Note that each column in the primary key should also be marked as NOT NULL.

The foreign key constraint is easier to understand if you examine the relevant class diagram. Here we want to place orders only to customers who have data in the Customer table. That is, the CustomerID in the Order table must already exist in the Customer table. Hence the constraint lists the column in the original Order table and then specifies a REFERENCE to the Customer table and the CustomerID.

The **ALTER TABLE** and **DROP TABLE** commands enable you to modify the structure of an existing table. Be careful with the DROP command, as it will remove the entire table from the database, including its data and structural definition. The ALTER TABLE command is less drastic. It can be used to ADD or DELETE columns from a table. Obviously, when you drop an entire column, all the data stored in that column will be deleted. Similarly, when you add a new column, it will contain Null values for any existing rows.

You can use the CREATE INDEX and DROP INDEX commands to improve the performance of the database. Chapter 9 describes the strengths and weaknesses of using indexes. In general, these commands are issued once for a table, so it is usually easier to set them using a menu-driven interface.

Finally, as described in Chapter 4, the **CREATE VIEW** command creates and saves a new query. The basic syntax is straightforward: CREATE VIEW myview AS SELECT . . . . The command simply gives a name and saves any SELECT statement. Again, these commands are almost always easier to create and execute from a menu-driven interface. However, someday you might have to create SQL data definition statements by hand, so it is nice to know they exist.

SQL DATA MANIPULATION COMMANDS

A third set of SQL commands demonstrates the true power of SQL. The SELECT command retrieves data, whereas **data manipulation** commands are used to change the data within the tables. The basic commands and their syntax are displayed in Figure 5.31. These commands are used to insert data, delete rows, and update (change) the values of specific cells. Remember two points when using these commands: (1) They operate on sets of data at one time—avoid thinking in terms of individual rows, and (2) they utilize the power of the SELECT and WHERE statements you already know.

FIGURE 5.31 Common SQL commands to add, delete, and change data within existing tables. The commands operate on entire sets of data, and they utilize the power of the SELECT and WHERE statements, including subqueries.

```
INSERT INTO target (column1, column2, . . . )
   VALUES (value1, value2, . . . )
INSERT INTO target (column1, column2, . . . )
   SELECT . . . FROM . . .
DELETE FROM table WHERE condition
UPDATE table
   SET Col1=Value1, Col2=Value2, . . . )
   WHERE condition
```

INSERT and DELETE

As you can tell from Figure 5.31, the **INSERT** command has two variations. The first version (VALUES) is used to insert one row of data at a time. Except for some programming implementations, it is not very useful. Most database systems provide a visual or tabular data entry system that makes it easy to enter or edit single rows of data. As discussed in Chapter 6, you will also build forms to make it easier for users to enter and edit single rows of data.

The second version of the INSERT command is particularly useful at copying data from one table into a second (target) table. Note that it accepts any SELECT statement, including one with subqueries, so it is far more powerful than it looks. For example, in the Pet Store database, you might decide to move older Animal files to a different computer. To move records for all animals ordered before January 1, 1998, you would issue the INSERT command displayed in Figure 5.32. Notice that the subquery selects the animals based on the date they were ordered. The INSERT command then copies the associated rows in the Animal table into an existing OldAnimals table.

The query in Figure 5.32 just copies the specified rows to a new table. The next step is to delete them from the main Animals table to save space and improve performance. The **DELETE** command performs this function easily. Figure 5.33 illustrates that you simply replace the first two rows of the query (INSERT and SELECT) with DELETE. Be careful not to alter the subquery. You can use the cut-and-paste feature to delete only rows that have already been copied to the backup table. Be sure you recognize the difference between the DROP and DELETE commands. The DROP command removes an entire table. The DELETE command deletes rows within a table.

UPDATE

The syntax of the **UPDATE** command is similar to the INSERT and DELETE commands. It too makes full use of the WHERE clause, including subqueries. The key to

FIGURE 5.32 INSERT command to copy older data rows. Note the use of the subquery to identify the rows to be copied.

```
INSERT INTO OldAnimals
SELECT *
FROM Animals
WHERE AnimalID IN
   (SELECT AnimalOrderItem.AnimalID
   FROM AnimalOrder INNER JOIN AnimalOrderItem
   ON AnimalOrder.OrderID = AnimalOrderItem.OrderID
   WHERE (AnimalOrder.OrderDate < #1/1/98#) );
```

FIGURE 5.33
DELETE command to remove the older data. Use cut and paste to make sure the subquery is exactly the same as the previous query.

```
DELETE
FROM Animals
WHERE AnimalID IN
   (SELECT AnimalOrderItem.AnimalID
   FROM AnimalOrder INNER JOIN AnimalOrderItem
   ON AnimalOrder.OrderID = AnimalOrderItem.OrderID
   WHERE (AnimalOrder.OrderDate < #1/1/98#) );
```

the UPDATE command is to remember that it acts on an entire collection of rows at one time. You use the WHERE clause to specify which set of rows need to be changed.

In the example in Figure 5.34, managers wish to increase the ListPrice of the cats and dogs. The price for cats should increase by 10 percent and the price for dogs by 20 percent. Because these are two different sets of animals, you will often use two separate UPDATE statements. However, this operation provides a good use for the CASE function. You can reduce the operation to one UPDATE statement by replacing the 1.10 and 1.20 values with a CASE statement that selects 1.10 for Cats and 1.20 for Dogs.

There are some additional features of the UPDATE statement. For example, you can change several columns at the same time. Just separate the calculations with a comma. You can also build calculations from any row within the table or query. For example, an animal's list price could take into consideration the animal's age with the command SET ListPrice = ListPrice*(1 − 0.001*(Date()-DateBorn)). This command takes 1/10 of 1 percent off the list price for each day since the animal was born.

Notice the use of the internal Date() function to provide today's date in the last example. Most database systems provide several internal functions that can be used within any calculation. These functions are not standardized, but you can generally get a list (and the syntax chart) from the system's Help commands. In Microsoft Access you can get a complete list by searching Help for Functions, Reference. The Date, String, and Format functions are particularly useful.

When using the UPDATE command, remember that all the data in the calculation must exist on one row within the query. There is no way to refer to a previous or next row within the table.

QUALITY: TESTING QUERIES

The greatest challenge with complex queries is that even if you make a mistake, you usually get "results." The problem is that the results are not the answer to the question you wanted to ask. The only way to ensure the results are correct is to thoroughly understand SQL, build your queries carefully, and test your queries.

FIGURE 5.34
Sample UPDATE command. If the CASE function is not available, use two separate statements to increase the list price by 10 percent for cats and 20 percent for dogs.

```
UPDATE Animal
SET ListPrice = ListPrice * 1.10
WHERE Category = "Cat";
```

```
UPDATE Animal
SET ListPrice = ListPrice * 1.20
WHERE Category = "Dog";
```

FIGURE 5.35
Steps to building quality queries. Be sure you have recent backups of the database before you execute UPDATE or DELETE queries.

- **Break questions into smaller pieces.**
- **Test each query.**
  - Check the SQL.
  - Look at the data.
  - Check computations.
- **Combine into subqueries.**
  - Use cut-and-paste techniques to avoid errors.
  - Check for correlated subqueries.
- **Test sample data.**
  - Identify different cases.
  - Check final query and subqueries.
  - Verify calculations.
- **Test SELECT queries before executing UPDATE queries.**

Figure 5.35 outlines the basic steps for dealing with complex queries. The first step is to break complex queries into smaller pieces—particularly when the query involves subqueries. You need to examine and test each subquery separately. You can do the same thing with complex Boolean conditions. Start with a simple condition, check the results, and then add new conditions. When the subqueries are correct, use cut-and-paste techniques to combine them into one main query. Be sure to avoid correlated subqueries. If necessary, save the initial queries as views and use a completely new query to combine the results from the views. The third step is to create sample data to test the queries. Find or create data that represents the different possible cases.

Consider the example in Figure 5.36: List customers who bought dogs and also bought cat products. There are four situations: (1) Customers bought dogs and cat products on the same sale. (2) Customers bought dogs and then cat products at a different time. (3) Customers bought dogs and never bought cat products. (4) Customers bought cat products and never bought dogs. Because there are only four cases, you should create data and test each one. If there are thousands of possible cases, you might have to limit your tests to the major possibilities.

FIGURE 5.36
Sample query: Which customers who bought dogs also bought cat products (at any time)? Build each query separately. Then paste them together in SQL and add the connecting link. Use sample data to test the results.

```
SELECT DISTINCT Animal.Category, Sale.CustomerID
FROM Sale INNER JOIN (Animal INNER JOIN SaleAnimal
ON Animal.AnimalID = SaleAnimal.AnimalID)
ON Sale.SaleID = SaleAnimal.SaleID
WHERE (((Animal.Category) = "Dog"))
AND Sale.CustomerID IN
   (SELECT DISTINCT Sale.CustomerID
   FROM Sale INNER JOIN (Merchandise INNER JOIN SaleItem
   ON Merchandise.ItemID = SaleItem.ItemID)
   ON Sale.SaleID = SaleItem.SaleID
   WHERE (((Merchandise.Category) = "Cat")));
```

The final step in building queries involves data manipulation queries (such as UPDATE). You should first create a SELECT query that retrieves the rows you plan to change. Examine and test the rows to make sure they are the ones you want to alter. When you are satisfied that the query is correct, make sure you have a recent backup of the database—or at least a recent copy of the tables you want to change. Now you can convert the SELECT query to an UPDATE or DELETE statement and execute it.

SUMMARY

Always remember that SQL operates on sets of data. The SELECT command returns a set of data that matches some criteria. The UPDATE command changes values of data, and the DELETE command deletes rows of data that are in a specified set. Sets can be defined in terms of a simple WHERE clause. They can also be defined by complex conditions involving subqueries and multiple tables. The key to understanding SQL is to think of the WHERE clause as defining a set of data.

Subqueries are powerful, but be careful to avoid correlated subqueries, where the inner loop has to be repeated for each value in the outer query loop. In these cases create a view first and store the intermediate results in a separate query. Also, test your subquery separately before placing it in the final query.

In some everyday situations data can exist in one table but not another. For example, you might need a list of customers who have not placed orders recently. The problem can also arise if the DBMS does not maintain referential integrity—and you need to find which orders have customers with no matching data in the customer table. Outer joins (or the NOT IN subquery) are useful in these situations.

Each database system has several internal functions that can be used in SQL statements. Unfortunately, these functions are not standardized, so each DBMS uses a different syntax. Nonetheless, some standard functions are commonly available and useful for business queries. Some important functions deal with dates and times. For example, the Month function will extract the month from a generic date column, enabling queries to compute totals by month.

The most important thing to remember when building queries is that if you make a mistake, most likely the query will still execute. Unfortunately, it will not give you the results you wanted. That means you have to build your queries carefully and always check your work. Begin with a smaller query and then add elements until you get the query you want. To build an UPDATE or DELETE query, always start with a SELECT statement and check the results. Then change it to UPDATE or DELETE.

A DEVELOPER'S VIEW

Miranda saw that some business questions are more complex than others. SQL subqueries and outer joins are often used to answer these questions. Practice the SQL subqueries until you thoroughly understand them. They will save you hundreds of hours of work. Think about how long it would take to write code to answer some of the questions in this chapter! For your class project, you should create several queries to test your skills, including subqueries, outer joins, and crosstab. You should build and test some SQL UPDATE queries to change sets of data. You should be able to use SQL to create and modify tables.

KEY WORDS

ALL, 160
ALTER TABLE, 177
ANY, 160
CASE, 170
constraint, 176
correlated subquery, 166
CREATE DOMAIN, 176
CREATE SCHEMA, 176
CREATE TABLE, 176
CREATE VIEW, 177
crosstab, 172
data definition, 175
data manipulation, 177
DELETE, 178
DROP TABLE, 177
equi-join, 163
EXCEPT, 168
EXISTS, 160
FULL JOIN, 164
IN, 160
inequality join, 171
INSERT, 178
INTERSECT, 168
LEFT JOIN, 164
nested query, 158
outer join, 163
reflexive join, 170
RIGHT JOIN, 164
schema, 176
self-join, 170
subquery, 158
UNION, 168
UPDATE, 178

REVIEW QUESTIONS

1. What is a subquery and in what situations is it useful?
2. What is a correlated subquery and why does it present problems?
3. How do you find items that are not in a list—such as customers who have not placed orders recently?
4. What are the three general categories of SQL commands?
5. How do you join tables when the join column for one table contains data that is not in the related column of the second table?
6. How do you join tables when two or more columns need to be matched?
7. What are inequality joins and when are they useful?
8. What is the SQL UNION command and when is it useful?
9. What is a reflexive join? Give an example of when it might be used.
10. What is the purpose of the SQL CASE function?
11. How is the cross tabulation command related to the GROUP BY command?
12. What are the basic SQL data definition commands?
13. What are the basic SQL data manipulation commands?
14. How are UPDATE and DELETE commands similar to the SELECT statement?

EXERCISES

Write the SQL statements that will answer questions 1 through 10 based on the following tables for a small hardware store. A useful option is to create the tables in a DBMS, add some data, and test your queries.

> Customer(CID, Name, Address, City, State, Zip, Category)
> Inventory(ItemID, Description, ListPrice, Cost, QuantityOnHand, Category)
> ItemCategory(Category, Description, StoreLocation, Season, ManagerID)
> Order(OrderID, OrderDate, CID, EID)
> Employee(EID, Name, Address, Phone, Specialty, ManagerID)
> OrderItem(OrderID, ItemID, Quantity, SalePrice)

1. In looking for space conflicts, which items are stored in the same store location at the same season?
2. Which products have a QuantityOnHand that is less than 10 percent of the average monthly sales for that product?
3. Which items have not had any orders for the last 3 months?
4. Which manager (Name and Category) had the best total sales by employees who work for him or her?
5. Write the SQL command to increase the ListPrice by 10 percent on all products that have sold more than 200 units in the last month.
6. Which employees did not sell any items in the Garden shop (Category) during June and July?
7. Of the top five best customers in June, July, and August, which ones were also in the top 10 percent of order value for December?
8. Which individual items sold for a higher profit than the average profit for items in their category?
9. List all employees who live in Boston, along with all customers who live in Boston.
10. Find the largest order that made the least profit.

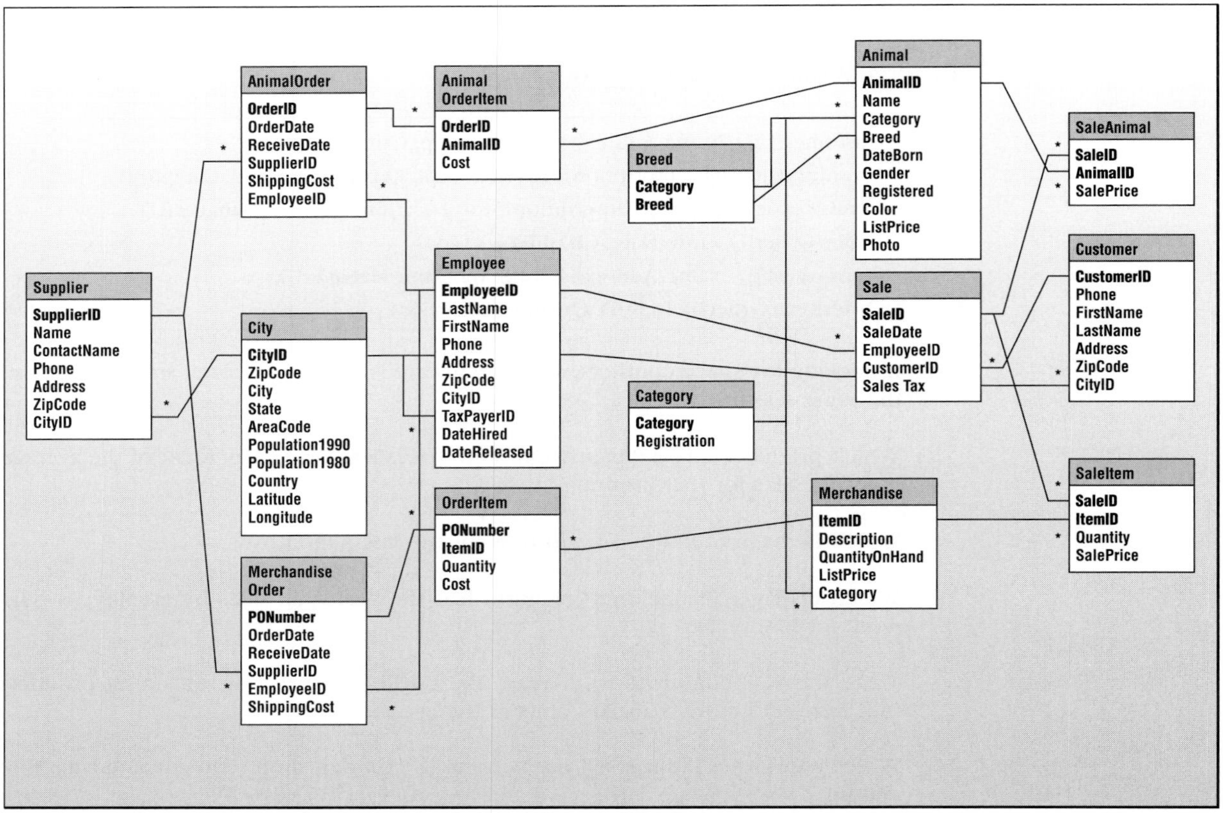

AnimalOrder
OrderID
OrderDate
ReceiveDate
SupplierID
ShippingCost
EmployeeID

Animal OrderItem
OrderID
AnimalID
Cost

Animal
AnimalID
Name
Category
Breed
DateBorn
Gender
Registered
Color
ListPrice
Photo

Breed
Category
Breed

SaleAnimal
SaleID
AnimalID
SalePrice

Supplier
SupplierID
Name
ContactName
Phone
Address
ZipCode
CityID

City
CityID
ZipCode
City
State
AreaCode
Population1990
Population1980
Country
Latitude
Longitude

Employee
EmployeeID
LastName
FirstName
Phone
Address
ZipCode
CityID
TaxPayerID
DateHired
DateReleased

Sale
SaleID
SaleDate
EmployeeID
CustomerID
Sales Tax

Customer
CustomerID
Phone
FirstName
LastName
Address
ZipCode
CityID

Category
Category
Registration

SaleItem
SaleID
ItemID
Quantity
SalePrice

Merchandise
ItemID
Description
QuantityOnHand
ListPrice
Category

OrderItem
PONumber
ItemID
Quantity
Cost

Merchandise Order
PONumber
OrderDate
ReceiveDate
SupplierID
EmployeeID
ShippingCost

Sally's Pet Store

Write the SQL statements that will answer questions 11 through 26 based on the tables in the Pet Store database. Build your queries in Access.

11. Which suppliers provided both Animals and Merchandise last year?
12. Which customers purchased both cats and dogs?
13. Which customers who bought cats also bought dog merchandise on the same day?
14. Which supplier is located farthest away? (Hint: Do some research in how to compute distance based on latitude and longitude. Assume the Pet Store is located in the same city as your university.)
15. Which animals are currently in the store (have not been sold)?
16. What is the average merchandise sale for people who purchased dogs? (Hint: You first need total per order.)
17. Which employee had the highest combined sales of animals and merchandise?
18. Which employees sold animals that they were also responsible for purchasing from suppliers?

19. Do customers who buy registered animals spend more money on merchandise (at any time, i.e., not necessarily on the same order)?

20. Graph total sales for each month by category of animal.

21. Are some suppliers faster at providing certain categories of animals (or products) than others? Compare suppliers by category.

22. Which customers bought both male and female animals of the same breed?

23. Do any employees live in the same city as any suppliers? (Which ones?)

24. Which category of animal brings the most merchandise sales on the same order?

25. Which category of items is the worst seller—in terms of taking the longest time to sell (average and maximum)?

26. Create one query that lists the total animal sales and total merchandise sales for each sale.

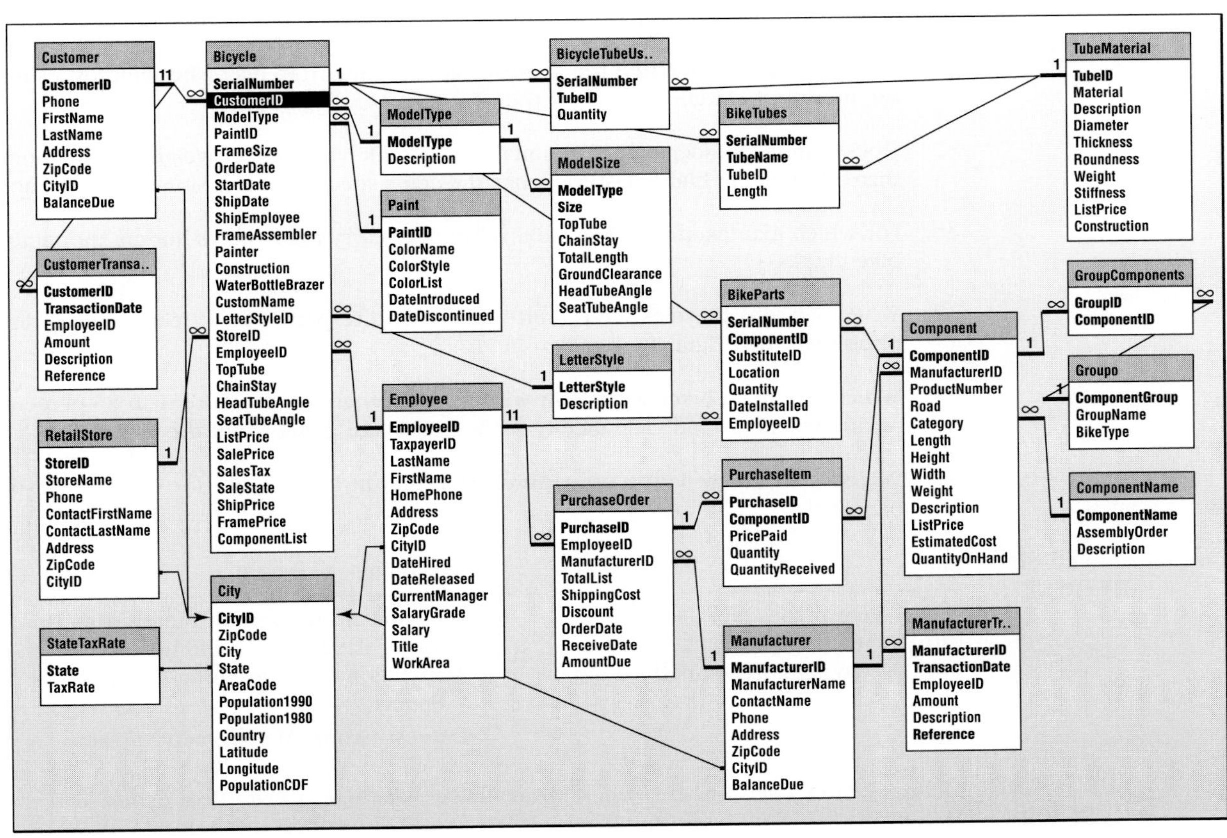

Rolling Thunder Bicycles

Write the SQL statements that will answer questions 27 through 41 based on the tables in the Rolling Thunder database. Build your queries in Access.

27. On how many days was the number of bikes produced (shipped) less than the number of bikes ordered?
28. How many bikes took longer than average to produce? By ModelType?
29. List all customers who bought mountain bikes and installed components that were not part of a major component group.
30. How many bicycles were made with carbon fiber top tubes and aluminum chain stays?
31. What is the difference in average profit between mountain bikes and road bikes? Assume that the cost for frames is about 50 percent of the frame price.
32. What percentage of sales is made through selling directly to customers—without the support of retail stores?
33. How many mountain bikers purchased tires for the rear that were different from the tires installed on the front?
34. List the number of bicycles sold in each state by model type; then list the total number of bicycles sold in each state (total across all model types).
35. What is the average weight of all components installed on racing bikes?
36. Which manager generated the highest sales revenue from his or her employees for the month of March?
37. Does Rolling Thunder carry a mountain bike crank with a lower weight and no more than a 33 percent higher ListPrice than the crank specified in the Shimano XT group?
38. For which manufacturers does Rolling Thunder carry road cranks but not mountain bike cranks?
39. Which (if any) bicycles were built with substitute parts that carried a lower list price than the originally specified item?
40. Which mountain bikes were built with a crank length that is more than 85 percent of the typical ground clearance (i.e., the pedals are going to hit the ground)?
41. Which component is the most purchased item in its category for each model of bicycle?

WEB SITE REFERENCES

Site	Description
http://www.metis.com/	SQL consulting firm with interesting tips.
http://www.jcc.com/	Another database consulting firm.
http://www.acm.org/sigmod/	Association for Computing Machinery—Special. Interest Group: Management of Data.

ADDITIONAL READING

Melton, J., and A. R. Simon. *Understanding the New SQL: A Complete Guide.* San Mateo: Morgan Kaufmann Publishers, 1993. [An in-depth presentation of SQL 92 with examples.]

APPENDIX

SQL Syntax

ALTER TABLE

```
ALTER TABLE table
   ADD COLUMN column datatype (size)
   DROP COLUMN column
```

COMMIT WORK

```
COMMIT WORK
```

CREATE INDEX

```
CREATE [UNIQUE] INDEX index
ON table (column1, column2, . . . )
WITH {PRIMARY | DISALLOW NULL | IGNORE NULL}
```

CREATE TABLE

```
CREATE TABLE table
   (column1   datatype (size) [NOT NULL] [index1],
    column2   datatype (size) [NOT NULL] [index2],
    . . . ,
   CONSTRAINT pkname PRIMARY KEY (column, . . . ),
   CONSTRAINT fkname FOREIGN KEY (column)
      REFERENCES existing_table (key_column),)
```

CREATE VIEW

```
CREATE VIEW viewname AS
SELECT . . .
```

DELETE

```
DELETE
FROM table
WHERE condition
```

DROP

```
DROP INDEX index ON table

DROP TABLE

DROP VIEW
```

INSERT

```
INSERT INTO table (column1, column2, . . . )
VALUES (value1, value2, . . . )

INSERT INTO newtable (column1, column2, . . . )
SELECT . . .
```

GRANT

```
GRANT privilege          privileges
ON object              ALL, ALTER, DELETE, INDEX,
TO user | PUBLIC       INSERT, SELECT, UPDATE
```

REVOKE

```
REVOKE privilege          privileges
ON object                ALL, ALTER, DELETE, INDEX,
FROM user | PUBLIC       INSERT, SELECT, UPDATE
```

ROLLBACK

```
SAVEPOINT savepoint    {optional}

ROLLBACK WORK
TO savepoint
```

SELECT

```
SELECT DISTINCT table.column {AS alias}, . . .
FROM table/query
INNER JOIN table/query ON T1.ColA = T2.ColB
WHERE (condition)
GROUP BY column
HAVING (group condition)
ORDER BY table.column
{UNION, INTERSECT, EXCEPT . . . }

TRANSFORM aggfunction                    {Crosstab values}
   SELECT . . . FROM . . . GROUP BY      {Crosstab rows}
   PIVOT pivot column                    {Crosstab columns}
```

SELECT INTO

```
SELECT column1, column2, . . .
INTO newtable
FROM tables
WHERE condition
```

UPDATE

```
UPDATE TABLE table
   SET column1 = value1, column2 = value2, . . .
   WHERE condition
```

PART 3

Applications

Building business applications in a database environment begins with creating forms and reports. Most database management systems have tools to help you construct the basic forms and reports. However, Chapter 6 shows you that you have to design and modify forms and reports to make them useful and user-friendly.

Chapter 7 introduces the use of the Visual Basic for Applications programming language to manipulate data. For some calculations, and to improve your applications, you sometimes have to write a few lines of custom code.

Chapter 8 illustrates some situations that typically arise in business applications. The cases presented show you how to use forms and programming to improve the usability of your applications. The chapter also discusses how to complete your application so that it is polished. You will learn how to add the menus, toolbars, and custom help features that users require from a modern application.

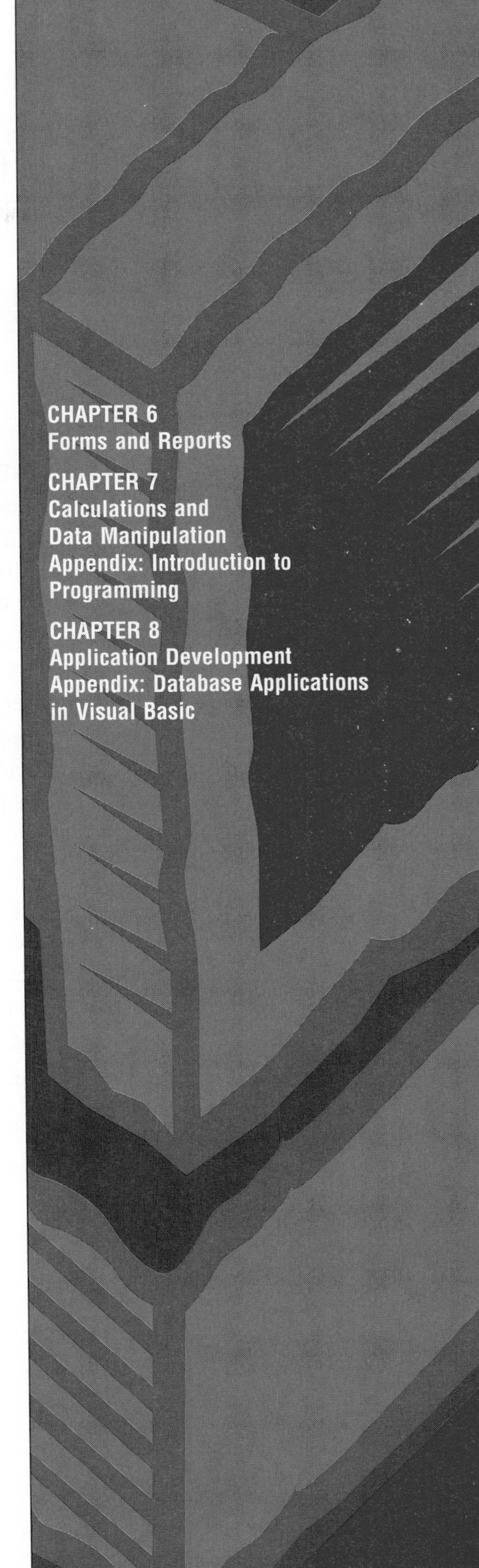

CHAPTER 6

Forms and Reports

WHAT YOU WILL LEARN IN THIS CHAPTER

- Why do we need input forms? Why not just enter data into tables? 192
- What colors should you put on your forms? 194
- What are the main types of controls you can use on forms? 205
- What is the purpose of direct manipulation of objects on forms? 215
- What are the primary components of reports? 219

OVERVIEW

Ariel: *Why the concerned look?*

Miranda: *Well, I finally figured out how to answer those hard questions. But I'm a little worried. Lots of times I got answers, but they were wrong. I have to be really careful with SQL.*

Ariel: *Oh, I'm sure you'll do fine. You're always careful about testing your work.*

Miranda: *I suppose it'll get easier.*

Ariel: *That's the spirit. Now, are you finally ready to start building the application?*

Miranda: *I sure am. I looked at some of the information about forms and reports. This is going to be easy.*

Ariel: *Really?*

Miranda: *Sure. And you know the best part? All the forms and reports are based on SQL. To get the initial forms and reports, all I have to do is build queries to get the data I want. There are even wizards that will help create the basic forms and reports.*

Ariel: *I knew that people would someday call on spirits again.*

INTRODUCTION

Forms and reports are an important part of the database application. Designers use them to create an integrated application, making it easier for users to perform their tasks. Decision makers and clerical workers use forms and reports on a daily basis. Years ago forms were used primarily as input devices, and reports were used to display results. However, as managers gained greater access to on-line databases, forms became increasingly important. Reports are still used for output that will be distributed or stored in paper form. However, forms can be distributed electronically, and can display a variety of outputs. The Internet, and specifically the World Wide Web, is becoming an increasingly popular means of distributing data as electronic forms. The same design principles used for database forms also apply to the Web. Specific issues in creating Web forms are discussed in Chapter 11.

As summarized in Figure 6.1, forms are used to collect data, display results of queries, display analysis, and perform computations. They are also used as switch-

FIGURE 6.1
Basic uses of database forms. It is important to understand the use of a form, since forms designed for data collection will be different from those designed to analyze data.

- Collect data
- Display query results
- Display analysis and computations
- Switchboard for other forms and reports
- Direct manipulation of objects
    - Graphics
    - Drag-and-drop

boards, or connectors, to other forms and reports. In sophisticated, Windows-based applications, a form can be used for direct manipulation of objects. A graphical interface enables users to drag-and-drop objects to indicate changes. With this type of form, users interact visually with a model of the firm.

Reports are typically printed on paper, but they are increasingly being created for direct display on the screen. Reports are used to format the data and present results from complex analysis. Reports can be detailed and cover several pages—an example would be a detailed inventory report. Alternatively, reports can present summary data, incorporating graphs and totals. A common business example would be a weekly sales report comparing sales by division for the past few weeks. The report would generally be presented graphically and would occupy one page.

Forms and reports have several common features. The basic elements are presented in this chapter, along with hints on how to create effective forms and reports. As usual, the key is to understand the needs of the users.

EFFECTIVE DESIGN OF REPORTS AND FORMS

The most important concept to remember when designing forms and reports is to understand that they are the primary contact with the users. Each form and report must be tailored to specific situations and business uses. For example, some forms will be used for **heads-down data entry**—where touch typists concentrate on entering data without looking at the screen. Other forms present exploratory analyses, and the decision maker will want to examine various scenarios. The features, layout, and capabilities of these two types of forms are radically different. If you choose the wrong design for the user, the form (or report) will be virtually useless.

The key to effective design is to determine the needs of the user. The catch is that users often do not know what they need (or want). In particular, they may not be aware of the capabilities and limitations of a modern DBMS. As a designer, you talk with the users to learn what they want to accomplish. Then you use your experience to provide features that make the form more useful. Just be careful to find the fine line between helping users and trying to sell an application they do not need.

Researchers in human factors have developed several guidelines to help you design forms. To begin, all forms and reports within an application (or even within an organization) should be as consistent as possible. Keystrokes, commands, and icons should be used for the same purposes throughout the application. Color, layout, and structure, should be coordinated so users can understand the data and context on any form or report. Developers can get help from software manufacturers. For example, Apple has defined standards for software applications running on the Macintosh to provide a common look and feel. Microsoft has provided similar standards for the Windows interface to encourage developers to build standardized programs. The guidelines are available on the Microsoft Web site listed at the end of the chapter. Basing applications on a set of common tasks reduces the time it takes for users to learn new applications. Research into **human factors design** has also led to several hints and guidelines that designers should follow when building forms and reports.

Human Factors Design

Figure 6.2 summarizes some human factors design elements that system designers should incorporate in their applications. With current operating systems, the primary factor is that the users—not the programmer and not the application—should always have control. For example, do not expect (or force) users to enter data in a particular sequence. Instead, set up the base forms and let users choose the data en-

FIGURE 6.2
Basic human factors design elements. All designs should be evaluated in terms of these basic features.

Human Factors	Examples
User Control	Match user tasks Respond to user control and events User customization
Consistency	Layout, design, and colors Actions
Clarity	Organization Purpose Terminology
Aesthetics	Art to enhance Graphics Sound

Feedback	Methods
	  Visual
	  Text
	  Audio
	Uses
	  Acceptance of input
	  Changes to data
	  Completion of tasks
	  Events/Activation

Forgiveness	Anticipation and correction of errors Confirmation on delete and updates Backup and recovery

try order that is easiest for them. In this approach the users' choices trigger various events. Your application responds to these events or triggers by performing calculations, retrieving or storing data, and offering new choices.

Also, whenever possible, provide options for user customization. Many users want to change display features such as color, typeface, or size. Similarly, users have their own preferences in terms of sorting results and the data to be included.

Both the layout (design and color) and the required actions should be consistent across an application. In terms of user actions, be careful to ensure consistency in basic features, such as whether the user must press the Enter key at the end of an input, which function key invokes the Help system, how the arrow keys are used, and the role of each icon. These actions should be consistent across the entire application. This concept seems obvious, but it can be challenging to implement—particularly when many designers and programmers are creating the application. Two practices help ensure **consistency:** (1) At the start establish a design standard and basic templates for all designers to use, and (2) toward the end of the application development always go back and check for consistency.

Always strive for **clarity.** In many cases *clarity* means keeping the application simple and well organized. If the application has multiple forms and reports, organize them according to user tasks. Avoid using a menu that points to Forms and Reports. It helps to have a clear purpose for an application and to make sure the design enhances that purpose. Use precise terminology, avoid jargon, and stick with terms that are used within the organization. If a company refers to its employees as "Associates," use that term, instead of "Employees."

Aesthetics also play an important role in the user interface. The goal is to use color and design (and sometimes sound) to enhance the forms and reports. Avoid the beginner's mistake of using different colors for every form or placing 10 different fonts on a page. Although design and art are highly subjective, bad designs are immediately obvious to others. If you have minimal experience in design aesthetics, consider taking a course or two in art or design. If nothing else, study work done by others to gain ideas, to train your artistic sensibility, and to stay abreast of current trends. Remember that graphics and art are important, and they provide an attractive and familiar environment for users.

Feedback is crucial to most human-computer interactions. People want to know that when they press a key, choose an option, or select an icon the computer recognized their action and is responding. Typical uses of feedback include accepting input, acknowledging changes of data, highlighting completion of a task, or signifying the start or completion of some event. Several options can be used to provide feedback. Visually, the cursor can be changed, text can be highlighted, a button can be "pushed in," or a box may change color. More direct forms of feedback, such as displaying messages on the screen, can be used in more complicated cases. Some systems use audio feedback, playing a musical theme or sound when the user selects a task or when the computer finishes an operation. If you decide to use audio feedback, be sure that you give users a choice—some people do not like "noisy" computers. On the other hand, do not be hasty to discard the use of audio feedback—it is particularly effective for people with low vision. Similarly, audio responses are useful when users need to focus their vision on an external task and cannot look at the computer screen.

Humans occasionally make mistakes or change their minds. As a designer, you need to understand these possibilities and provide for them within your application. In particular, your application should anticipate and provide for correction of errors. You should always confirm on deletions and major updates—giving users a chance to verify the changes. Finally, your overall application should include mechanisms for backup and recovery of data—both in case of natural disasters and in case of accidental deletions or loss of data.

Windows Interface Standards

Software development in the 1990s can be characterized by the increasing standardization across applications. This standardization has resulted largely from the design standards for Windows-based software. For instance, most applications need to copy, delete, or move individual items. The commands for performing these functions should be the same regardless of who created the application. To aid in this standardization, Microsoft created an **application design guide.**

As shown in Figure 6.3, the Microsoft guidelines specify keystrokes, mouse commands, menu layout, and icons that are used for performing basic navigation and selection functions. Most development tools now provide automatic support for these standard functions. For example, forms in Access automatically handle most mouse and keyboard actions. However, you must be careful in your definition of keystrokes (e.g., shortcut keys).

Microsoft also recommends useful feedback indicators, including the use of progress indicators, gauges, and tooltips. Tooltips are short text descriptions that pop up when the user's mouse is over an icon or other object. The status bar displays a one-line entry at the bottom of the screen that you can use for basic descriptions, comments, or short feedback messages. Three-dimensional controls provide visual feedback on activation and status—the controls can be "pressed" to show activation.

FIGURE 6.3
Windows interface design standards. The fundamental operations of your application should follow established design standards. Some components are automatically provided by the development tools (e.g., Access), but you have to maintain others yourself.

HUMAN FACTORS	STANDARD METHODS
Navigation and choices	Mouse, icons Keyboard shortcuts Menus
Selections from a list	Single Contiguous multiple Disjoint multiple
Focus	Outline box Cursor
Manipulation	Activation Drag and drop
Feedback	Progress indicators and status gauges Flashing Tooltips Status bar 3-D controls Message boxes

Source: *The Windows Interface: An Application Design Guide,* Microsoft.

Pop-up message boxes are used to display longer and more important messages. They can be used to interrupt the user in any task.

Window Controls

Designing applications that run under Windows requires a solid understanding of the Windows interface—in part because you want to provide the standard controls and operations that Windows offers, but also because the Windows functionality enables you to easily provide additional, powerful features within your application.

A basic window is displayed in Figure 6.4. The components of the window consist of the frame, the title bar, a Control menu box, and various standard buttons. The

FIGURE 6.4
Windows interface. A window consists of several common components. The DBMS performs the main tasks required to maintain the window. However, you can often add features or commands to these operations.

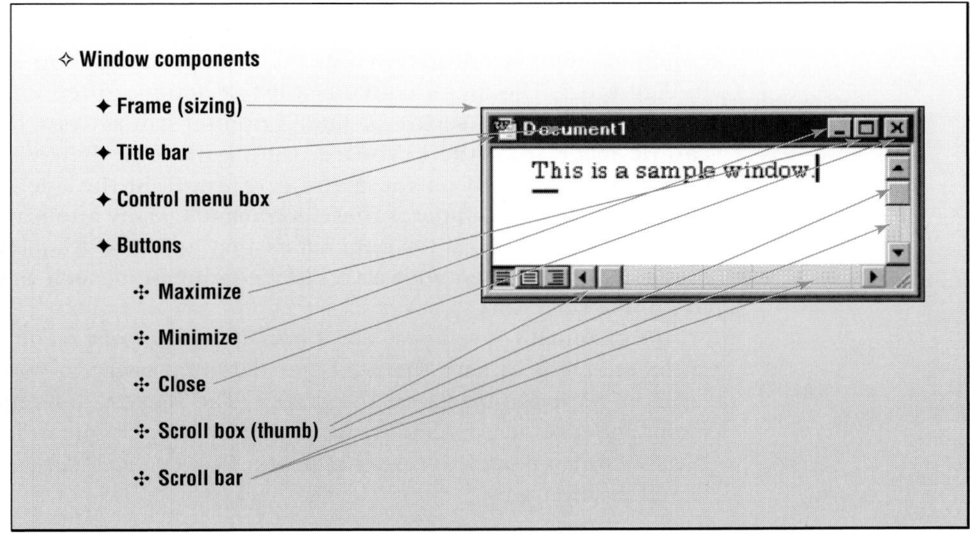

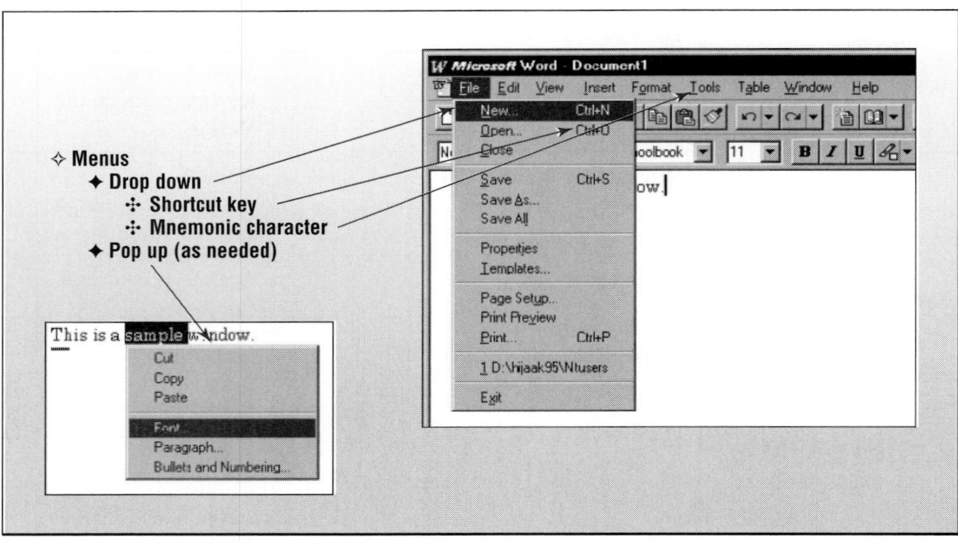

FIGURE 6.5 Windows menus. A standard menu is displayed at the top of the screen; a pop-up menu tends to be context sensitive and changes depending on the selected object.

frame can be resized by the user or the programmer can set it to a fixed size. Be sure to provide a short, but descriptive, title for each form. The Control menu box provides standard commands to move, resize, and close the form. Common window buttons include Maximize (full screen), Minimize (push to bottom of screen), and Close. **Scroll bars** enable the user to scroll the form horizontally and vertically. Your application or the DBMS typically handles these actions automatically. As you create a form, you have the ability to remove these standard controls, but avoid that temptation. More important, you can often override the standard actions and provide additional features. For instance, you might want to perform some cleanup operations when the user closes a form. Common cleanup operations include recomputing totals, storing changed data, triggering matching changes in other tables, or synchronizing the scrolling of one form as changes are made in a second form.

Menus are an important feature of any application. Most users (rightly) expect to have a menu that accesses the primary functions for each task. The most common menu is a drop-down menu displayed at the top of the screen, as shown in Figure 6.5. The menu contains a list of actions, often grouped by related commands, divided by a separator line. A pointer can activate the menu, or selections can be made from the keyboard using mnemonic letters. Mnemonic letters are generally underlined on the menu (e.g., the F in the File command). On a standard PC the Alt key initiates these commands. Many applications also define shortcut keys—particularly for commands that are used frequently. These commands are generally initiated with a Ctrl key combination, such as the Ctrl+C command to copy a selection.

Occasionally developers use a pop-up or shortcut menu. An increasingly popular technique is to have the right-mouse button trigger a pop-up menu to set properties of various objects on the screen. The biggest difference between a pop-up menu and a standard, fixed menu is that the pop-up menu is usually context sensitive. A **context-sensitive menu** is one that changes depending on the object selected by the user.

A useful feature within many forms and applications is a pop-up message box. As shown in Figure 6.6, a message box is a simple form with few controls. It is used to display short, one-line messages and obtain simple (usually yes/no) responses from the user. In general, it is best to avoid the use of message boxes—because they remove control from the user. In extreme cases a **modal form** takes priority on the screen and forces the user to deal with it before continuing. This type of message box is commonly used to handle errors or to set up a printer—situations that require an interruption. You can make any form modal by setting its modal property to Yes. However, this advice is worth repeating: Avoid modal forms—they take away control from the user.

User Interface—Web Notes

If all of your users have up-to-date browsers, the Web environment is similar to the standard Windows environment. You have control over layout, color, and data entry. One of the useful features of Web pages and forms is that they can be standardized so they are displayed the same way on almost any type of client computer or browser. However, you should select a set of features that is supported by the dominant Web browsers.

Style sheets can be powerful tools for designing consistent forms on the Web. They enable you to define a standard layout and color scheme that will be used by all of your pages.

Be careful with Web pages. It is tempting to insert animated GIFs and other graphical elements. Graphical elements are larger and take longer to download than text. While graphical elements may add interest to a form or display, make sure they do not detract from the overall purpose of the page. Be careful to avoid the pinball-machine look.

User Interface—Accessibility Issues

One of the greatest strengths of the Windows interface is its graphical orientation—which makes it easy for people to perform complex operations with a few moves of the mouse or selections on the screen. One of the drawbacks to this type of interface is that it is more difficult to make a system that is **accessible** to users facing some physical challenges. As a designer you can make your applications accessible to a wider base of users. To begin, your application should accept multiple

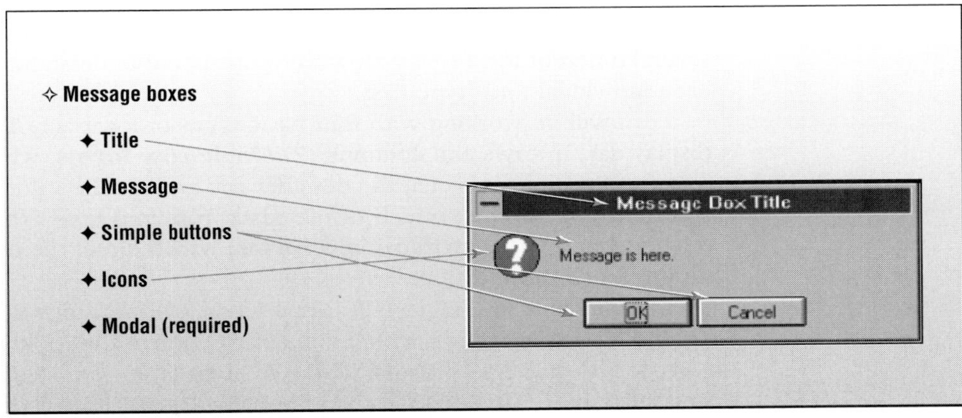

FIGURE 6.6 Message box. A message box is a simple form with a few buttons. This device should be used sparingly, since it interrupts the user's task. It is generally used to warn the user of problems or to offer immediate choices.

sources of inputs. Do not rely on just a mouse or a pointer but also use the keyboard, and increasingly, the user's voice. Similarly, it is helpful if your application can provide multiple types of output. Increasingly, you should consider how to integrate sound and voice output. The user must also be able to set the color and size of the output.

Microsoft guidelines provide some suggestions for making your applications accessible to more users. Detailed ideas and current developments can be found on its Web site. Human factors experience with other applications has generated some specific suggestions. For example, do not use red-green color combinations. Approximately 10 percent of the U.S. male population experiences some difficulty distinguishing between red and green. Try to pick high-contrast colors that most people can distinguish (e.g., yellow, blue, red and black). When in doubt, (1) ask people to test your color combinations or (2) let users select their own colors.

Second, avoid requiring rapid user responses. Do not put time limits on input. Although it might be fun in a game, many users have slower data entry skills. Some designers include pop-up messages to check on user progress after a delay in data entry. These messages are usually pointless and can be annoying. With modern screen-saver security systems, users can set their own delay controls and messages.

Third, avoid controls that flash rapidly on the screen. They tend to annoy most users. Worse, certain flash rates have been known to trigger epileptic seizures in some people. An interesting situation arose in Japan at the end of 1997 when a sequence of flashing graphics on an animated television show (*Pokemon*) sent about 700 children to the hospital.

Fourth, as much as possible enable users to customize their screen. Let them choose typefaces, font sizes, and screen colors. That way, users can adjust the screen to compensate for any vision problems they may have. And if you use sound, let people control the volume (even pitch if possible). In many cases the Windows environment provides much of this functionality, so the key point is to avoid overriding that functionality. Also, you should test your applications on various computers. Some video systems may distort your choice of colors or will be incapable of displaying your forms at the desired resolution.

FORM LAYOUT

Individual forms or windows are your primary means of communicating with people who use your application. Forms are used to collect data, display results, and organize the overall system. Several standard layouts are provided by the DBMS to simplify the development of many common forms. As you begin working with these basic layouts, keep in mind that you can create complex forms that use features from several different form types. However, you should understand the layout and uses of each individual form type first.

You will be working with four basic types of forms: (1) **Tabular forms,** which display data in rows and columns, (2) **single-row forms,** which show data for one row at a time and in which the designer can arrange the values in any format on the screen; (3) **subforms,** which display data from two tables that have a one-to-many relationship; and (4) **switchboard forms,** which direct the user to other forms and reports in the application.

As indicated in Figure 6.7, forms have several things in common. They have several basic properties, which you set to control the look and style of the form. Also, forms contain controls, which include labels and text boxes that are used to display basic text and data. Additionally, several events can occur with a form.

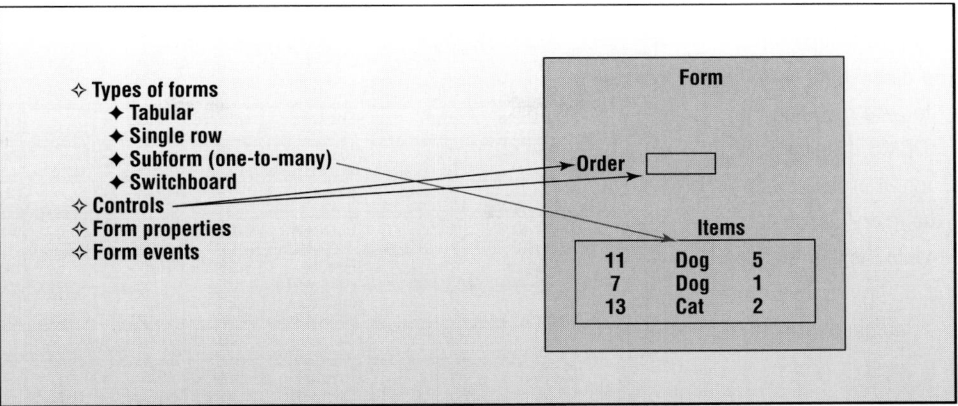

FIGURE 6.7
Form layout. Controls are placed on a form to display or collect data. A form's style is defined by its property settings. Form behavior is controlled by creating actions in response to form events.

For example, opening and closing a form are basic events for every form. You can control how the form operates by creating actions that are taken when each event occurs.

One of the most important properties of a form is its RecordSource. The RecordSource specifies the table or query that contains the data to be displayed or altered. Each form tends to be associated with one primary table.

Tabular Forms

One of the simplest forms is the tabular form, which displays the columns and rows from a table or query. It can be used as a subform and is rarely used as a stand-alone form. Note that Microsoft Access provides an even simpler version of a form called a **datasheet.** There are few differences between the tabular and datasheet forms. However, the tabular form provides a little more control over the display—such as three-dimensional controls and individual color settings. As a subform, the datasheet view takes up less space than the tabular form and looks like a spreadsheet.

One useful feature of the tabular form is that you can control the data entry sequence—if you need to help users enter data in a particular order. When there are multiple controls on a form and a user types on the keyboard, where will the keystrokes be placed? The answer is that the control that has the **focus** will receive the keystrokes. This control is often highlighted with an outline or a different color. The same situation exists when a screen contains multiple forms. Only one form can have the focus at a time. The user can change the focus by clicking on a particular form or control. The focus also moves when a user enters data into a form and presses the Enter key. The database system automatically moves the focus to the next control in the list. By changing the order of this list, the developer can make it easier to enter data in a particular order.

To set the data entry sequence, you change the tab order property of each control. The tab order is a number that begins at zero. As data is entered, the DBMS moves the focus to the control with the next higher tab order number. You can tell the DBMS to skip over a control by setting the tab stop property to No. For the example in Figure 6.8, you would want to skip the AnimalID column, since the DBMS automatically assigns that value and the user has no reason to change it.

The tabular form is useful when managers need a detailed listing of several rows of data. It is also useful for heads-down data entry where visual display is less im-

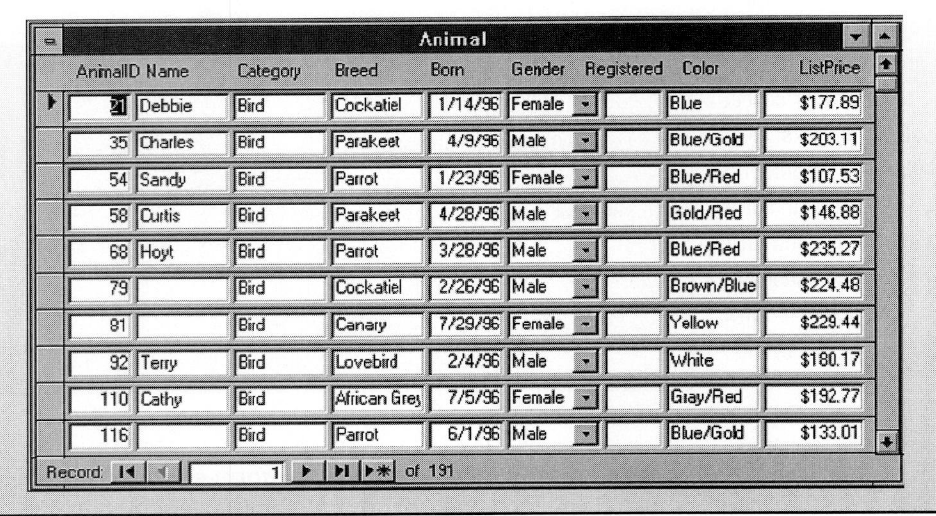

AnimalID	Name	Category	Breed	Born	Gender	Registered	Color	ListPrice
21	Debbie	Bird	Cockatiel	1/14/96	Female		Blue	$177.89
35	Charles	Bird	Parakeet	4/9/96	Male		Blue/Gold	$203.11
54	Sandy	Bird	Parrot	1/23/96	Female		Blue/Red	$107.53
58	Curtis	Bird	Parakeet	4/28/96	Male		Gold/Red	$146.88
68	Hoyt	Bird	Parrot	3/28/96	Male		Blue/Red	$235.27
79		Bird	Cockatiel	2/26/96	Male		Brown/Blue	$224.48
81		Bird	Canary	7/29/96	Female		Yellow	$229.44
92	Terry	Bird	Lovebird	2/4/96	Male		White	$180.17
110	Cathy	Bird	African Grey	7/5/96	Female		Gray/Red	$192.77
116		Bird	Parrot	6/1/96	Male		Blue/Gold	$133.01

FIGURE 6.8 Sample tabular form. You define the controls for one row, and the DBMS displays data for all of the rows in the query. Scroll bars enable the user to see more rows (or columns of data).

portant. However, the tabular approach is less useful when users need to see many columns of data at one time—because only a limited number of columns will fit on the screen.

Single-Row or Columnar Forms

A single-row form displays data for one row at a time. The goal is to display every column. Its greatest feature is that the designer can display the data at any location on the form. It is useful for designing a form that looks like a traditional paper form. The designer can also use color, graphics, and command buttons to make the form easier to use. As illustrated in Figure 6.9, this form design requires navigation controls that enable the user to scroll backward and forward through the rows of data.

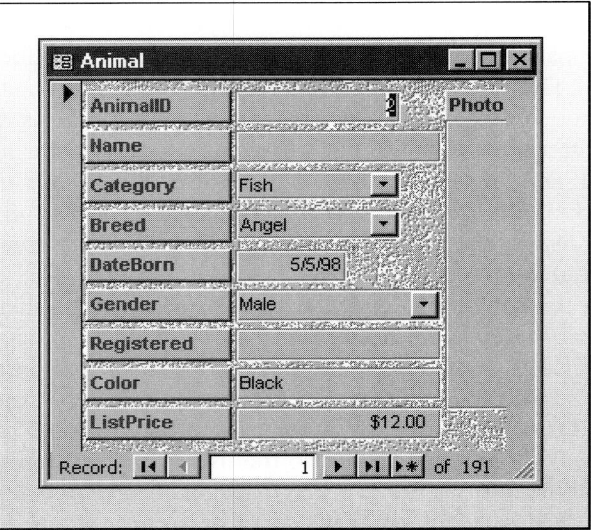

FIGURE 6.9 A simple single-row form. This form displays data for one row at a time. You have substantial control over layout through color, graphics, and command buttons. The navigation buttons on the bottom enable the user to display different rows.

Common navigation controls also include buttons to go to the first and last rows and to go to a particular row of data.

In general, you will want to include a Find command that enables the user to locate a particular row of data—based on the values in some row. For example, a form displaying customer data should have a search option based on customer name. Similarly, the user will often want to sort the rows in different orders. Both of these features are built into Microsoft Access; however, you might want to add buttons to make the commands easier to use.

The single-row form is generally the most-used form layout. With careful design you can use it to display substantial amounts of data. By including subforms, you can highlight relationships among various pieces of data and make it easy for users to enter data. You can also include charts to help users make decisions.

Subform Forms

A subform is usually a datasheet (or tabular form) embedded on the main form. A subform generally shows a one-to-many relationship. In the example in Figure 6.10, a sale could include many animals, so we need a subform to display this repeating list. The main form must be a single-row form, and the subform should be a tabular or datasheet view.

If you look at the underlying tables, you will see that SaleID links the main form (based on Sale) and subform (based on SaleAnimal) to each other. You will rarely dis-

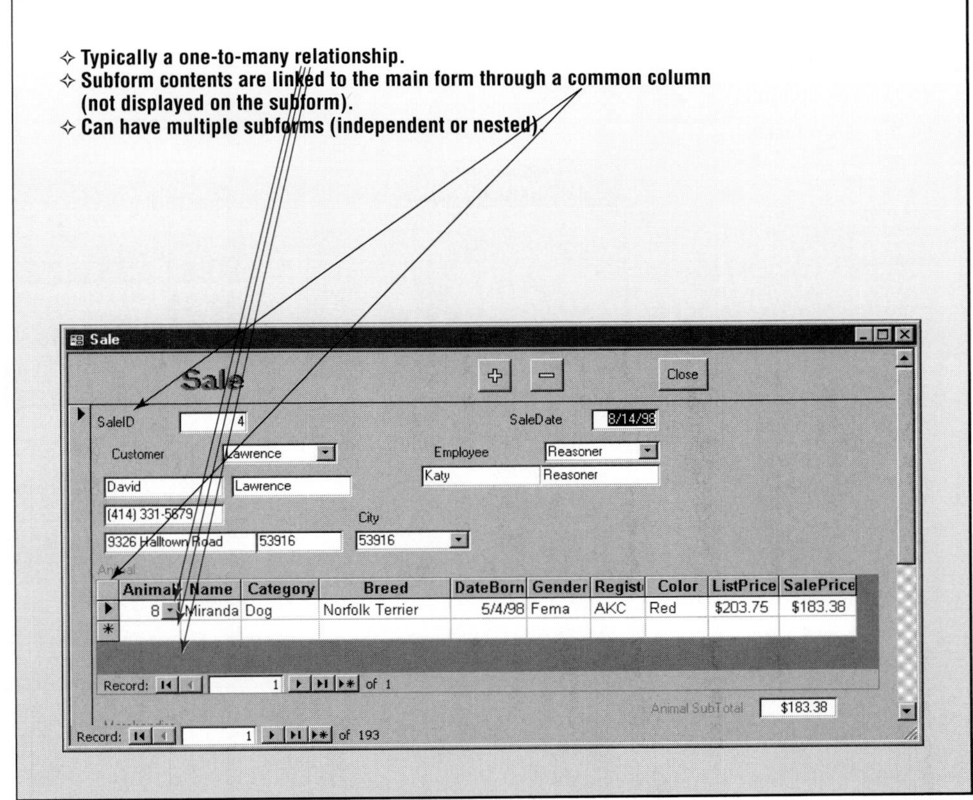

FIGURE 6.10
Subform example. The main form is based on the Sale table, which has a one-to-many relationship with the SaleAnimal table used on the subform. The datasheet view is used on the subform to display multiple rows at one time.

play the linking column on the subform. In general, doing so would be pointless, since the linking column would always display the same value as the related column on the main form. Think about what that means for a minute. The Sale table has a SaleID (that is generated by the DBMS when a new sale is created). The SaleAnimal table also has a SaleID column, and every animal sold must contain the same SaleID value from the main form. Yet it would be painful for the clerk to reenter the SaleID on the subform for each animal that is sold. By using the subform and specifying the SaleID as the link (Master and Child property), the DBMS automatically enters the main SaledID into the table for the subform.

Most database systems enable you to create forms that have multiple subforms. The subforms can be either independent—as separate boxes on the main form—or nested—where each subform lies inside another. In the case of nested forms, all but the innermost level must be single-row forms.

Switchboard Forms

Switchboard forms provide the overall structure to an application. They are straightforward to create—although you may want the assistance of a graphics designer. The switchboard form often contains images, and the design reflects the style of the company.

You begin with a blank form and remove the scroll bars and navigation controls. Pictures can be inserted as background images or as individual controls that can be used as buttons to open another form. As shown in Figure 6.11, command buttons are the most important feature of the switchboard form. When the user selects a but-

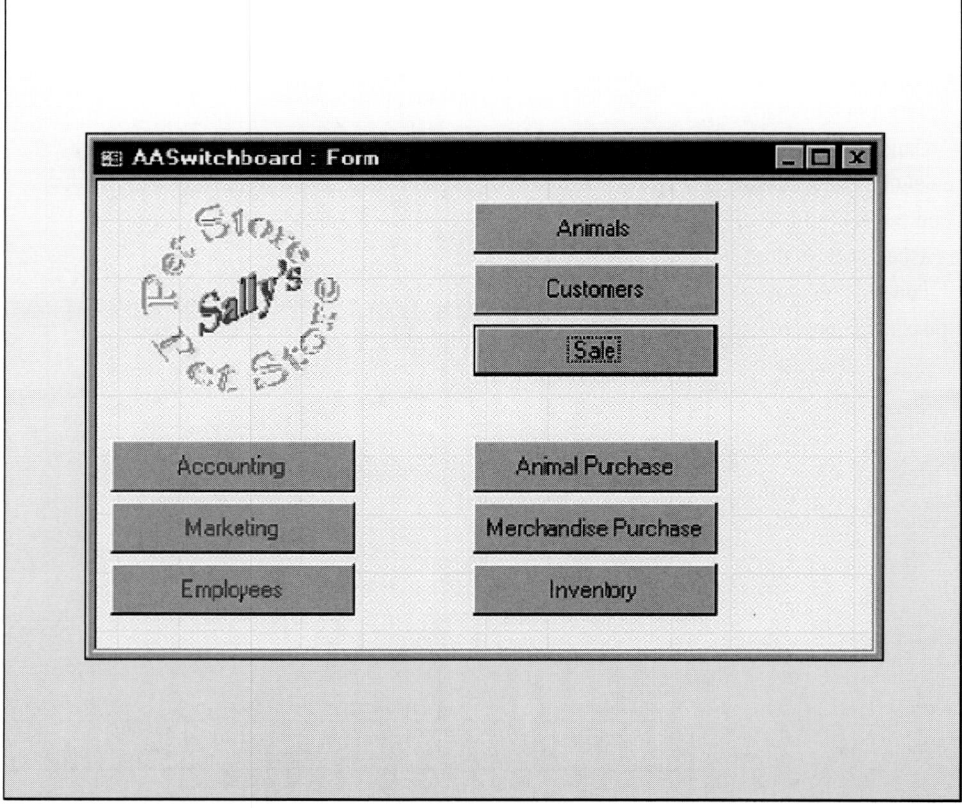

FIGURE 6.11 Sample switchboard form. The buttons match the user's tasks.

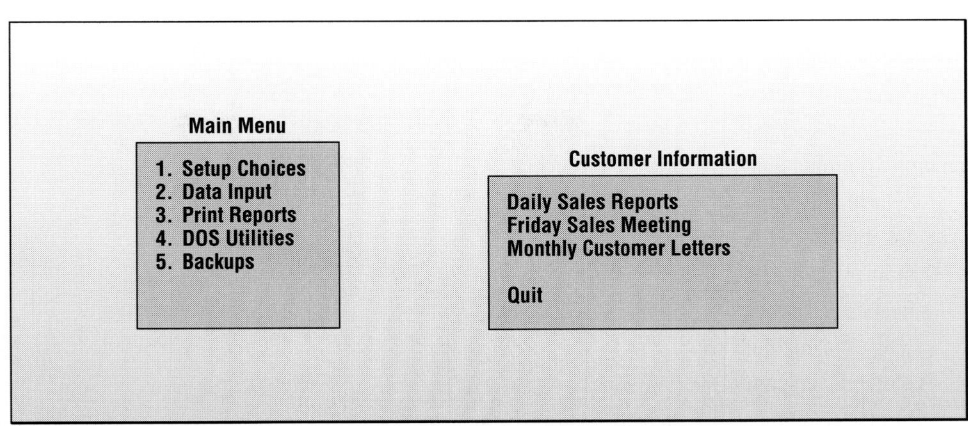

FIGURE 6.12 Designing menus for users. Which menu is easier for a secretary to understand? When designing applications, you should organize the application to match the processes users perform.

ton, a corresponding form or report is opened. The main switchboard form will be used quite often, so you should pay careful attention to its design.

The key to a successful application begins with the switchboard form—not just its design but also its content. The forms should match the user's tasks. One approach is to first identify the user and then provide a selection of buttons that match his or her tasks.

Consider a simple example. A manager needs to print a daily sales report of best-selling items. Every week the DBMS must print out a list of total sales by employee. The firm also sends letters to the best customers every month offering them additional discounts. A secretary will be in charge of printing these reports, so you create a simple menu that lists each report. The secretary chooses the desired report from the list. Some reports might ask questions, such as which week to use. The secretary enters the answers, and the report is printed.

The first step in creating an application is to think about the people who will use it. How do they do their jobs? How do the database inputs and reports fit into their job? The goal is to devise a menu system that reflects the way they work. Two examples of a first menu are shown in Figure 6.12. Which menu is easier for a clerk to understand? The one that best relates to the job. Once you understand the basic tasks, write down a set of related menus. Some menu options call up other menus, some print reports, and others activate the input screens you created.

Current versions of Access include a wizard that will generate switchboard forms. Unfortunately, these forms are difficult to modify, and you have little control over the layout and design. In many cases you will be better off creating your own switchboard form from scratch. Just start with a blank, unbound form. Then add images, text, and buttons to activate other forms.

CREATING FORMS

The actual process of creating a form depends on the DBMS. Most systems follow a similar design philosophy—although the commands and properties may have different names. The details described here reflect the object-oriented (OO) approach used by Microsoft. Most other OO approaches have a similar design. In learning a new DBMS, one of the first things you notice is the need to learn the overall structure and the detailed names of the various properties and events. The process of creating a form follows a defined framework, and you define properties and actions that respond to events. If your application and design match the framework of the DBMS, it will be easy to build the application. If you do not understand the underlying frame-

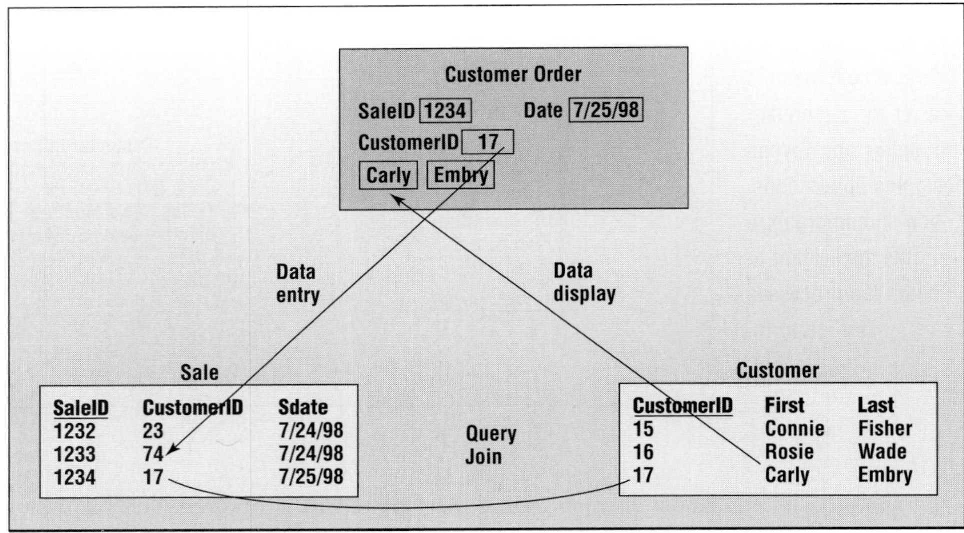

FIGURE 6.13 Basing the Order form on a query. The query contains all the columns from the Sale table and some columns from the Customer table. The query must never include the CustomerID column from the Customer table, which is the column used to join the two tables.

work, or need to do something not directly supported by the framework, your job will be more difficult. In fact, one of the key reasons for choosing a particular DBMS for generating forms is that the DBMS matches the needs of your form.

Queries

Most forms are based on queries rather than on individual tables. Through normalization, many tables contain key values or foreign keys. Yet the people using the form would much rather see the names or other information about the object. For example, the Sales table contains CustomerID. The corresponding customer Name, Address, and Phone are stored in the Customer table. Technically, you could build the Sales form with just the data in the Sales table, but a CustomerID of 17 is meaningless to the user. It would be more useful to display the customer name. The solution is to create a query that joins the Customer table to the Sale table—then you can display all the customer data.

Be careful when using queries on a form. Each form is designed to add new data to only one table at a time. Subforms are a new form and can store data into a different table. For example, you would create a Sale form to add a new row to the Sale table. You would not expect to simultaneously add a new Customer to the Customer table on that same form. The purpose of basing a form on a query is to be able to look up and display matching data from another table. It is not designed to make major changes to data in the new table. Stop. This limitation can be tricky, so read this paragraph again. Each form is designed to store data into one table.

The essence of this limitation is highlighted by the following rule: When creating a query for a form, include the key columns from only one table and never include more than one column that is created by AutoNumber. The Sale form example is illustrated in Figure 6.13. To record a sale, you need all the columns from the Sale table. To look up the corresponding customer name, you add the Customer.LastName and Customer.FirstName to the new query. The primary purpose of the form is to add new data to the Sale table—which is why it is important to include all of its columns. The form cannot be used to add new customers. However, users could change the data displayed from the Customer table. For example, a customer might have a new phone number. Any change made on this form is directly (and immediately) stored in the corresponding table. Hint: If you want to prevent people from changing a value, set the control's Enabled property to No and set the Locked property to Yes.

Look at Figure 6.13 again and think about the control holding the CustomerID column. This CustomerID column is in the Sale table. You must not, under any circumstance, add or use the CustomerID column from the Customer table. Storing the CustomerID in the Sale table means that CustomerID 17 is the one who bought the items. If you try to store the value 17 in the CustomerID column of the Customer table, it would try to change the ID value of the customer. For instance, it might change the ID of Carly Embry from 17 to 8, in the Customer table. Even if this change worked, it would be meaningless.

The basic rule to follow is that each form should be designed to add data to only one table. You can use a query to display additional data on the form, but that data (e.g., Customer Name) is secondary. When users need to alter data in more than one table, you have two choices: (1) You can provide a subform, or (2) you can provide a separate form opened with a button. In the example you could include an Edit button, which the user would click to add a new Customer. Conversely, you would include a subform from SaleAnimal to collect data on which animals were sold on each order.

Properties and Controls

Most modern software packages are built using an OO approach. With an OO design, each object has properties that describe it and methods or functions that it can perform. Objects are also closely tied to an event-driven system, where user actions and changes can trigger various events. Most database forms follow this methodology. However, you will generally use objects that have already been defined by the DBMS. Your job is to assign properties and write short programs to respond to various events to make the application easier for users.

As highlighted by the list of properties in Figure 6.14, form and control properties can be grouped into categories. Technically, Access divides the properties into

FIGURE 6.14 Basic properties for forms. At a minimum, you must set the data source and basic format properties. Additional properties are used to ensure consistency, protect data, and make the form easier to use. With Microsoft products, properties can usually be set using the right mouse button.

Category	Properties
Data	Base Table/Query Filters Sort
Integrity	Edits Additions, Deletions Locks
Format	Caption Scroll Bars Record Selectors Navigation Buttons Size and Centering Background/Pictures Colors Tab Order
Other	Pop-up menus Menu Bar Help

three categories: format, data, and other. However, the data category is large, so the list here splits out the properties related to data integrity.

The first category (data) relates to the source of the data, where you set the base table or query. You can set filters to display only the data rows that meet a specific condition. You can also specify the sort order directly on the form, but using a WHERE clause and ORDER BY statement on the query is usually more efficient. However, these properties can be useful, since you can create a program that changes them in response to user actions.

A second set of properties refers to data integrity to help you control the type of editing and changes allowed on the form. For example, you might set the properties for individual users so that some users cannot add or delete data using a particular form. However, keep in mind that it is generally safer to set these conditions in SQL so that they apply throughout the database, and not just on one form. For example, sales clerks should probably be prevented from adding new suppliers.

A third level of properties controls the display of the form. Everything from the caption to scroll bars, form size, and background are set by display properties. Again, remember that consistency is a virtue. Before beginning a project, choose a design template and standards; then set all form and control properties to meet that standard.

Controls on Forms

Forms are built with controls. **Controls** consist of any object placed on a form. Common controls include simple text labels, text boxes for data entry, option buttons, pictures, and list boxes. More complex controls can be purchased from commercial software developers. The standard set of controls for Microsoft Access is illustrated in Figure 6.15.

One property shared by all controls is the name. Every control must have a name. Be careful with this name; once you have set it, it is hard to change. The name is used by other controls and program code (much like a variable name) to retrieve and store data on the form. You need to pick a meaningful name when you first create the control. If you try to change it later, you will have to find every control or program that refers to that control—which can be a time-consuming and error-prone

FIGURE 6.15
Controls on forms. These are the standard controls for Microsoft Access. The most common controls are the label, text box, command button, and combo box.

Pointer	Wizard
Label	Text box
Option group	Toggle button
Option button	Check box
Combo box	List box
Command button	Image
Unbound object	Bound object
Page break	Subform/report
Line	Box

task. Some people name controls based on the type of control. For example, the name of a label control would start with lbl, such as lblAddress. This naming convention is helpful to other programmers who read your code later.

Label Controls and Text Boxes

The most basic controls are the label, the text box, and the command button. The label is plain text that does not change. The text box is used to display data from the database and to enter new values. A control that retrieves and stores data in a table is called a **bound control**—because any data that is changed is automatically stored in the table. Data can be entered into an unbound control, but the values will not be stored in the database, and they will not change as the user scrolls through the table rows. Common properties of label and text box controls are color, typeface, and size. The difference between a bound and unbound box is that a bound box has a control source (column in a table). With an unbound box, this property is empty.

Command Buttons

Command buttons typically have only one function: When the user clicks one (On_Click event), some action will be performed. You have several choices for that action, including opening another form, printing a report, or running a custom program. Command buttons are the main component of switchboard forms, where they are used to open related forms.

Toggle Buttons, Check Boxes, and Option Buttons

These controls enable users to select from a choice of options. For example, clerks may indicate an animal's gender by picking one of three choices (male, female, and unknown). Notice that there are several ways to let users make a selection. Technically, there is no difference in the three methods. However, according to the Windows standard, they do have slightly different uses.

There are essentially two methods of making choices: mutually exclusive and multiple selections. Consider the example of an animal's gender. The three choices are mutually exclusive. An animal can be born as either male, or female, or we may not know the true status. (Neutering is a separate consideration that does not affect the genetic determination of gender.) The **option button** group (round) was designed for mutually exclusive choices. Users know that when they see a group of option buttons, they can pick only one of the options. On the other hand, a customer might place an order for a dog with certain features: registered, brown or black in color, even temperament, and short hair. You should use a form with a group of **check boxes** (square) for this situation, because several of these items can be checked. The selection of one option does not affect any of the others.

Toggle buttons are three-dimensional and are relatively new. Hence they have been used in both exclusive and nonexclusive situations.

Graphics Features

Occasionally you will want to add graphics features to your form. There are controls to add pictures, as well as simple lines and boxes. Lines and boxes are often used to create a three-dimensional effect for other controls by adding shading or highlighting.

Pictures must be created in a separate graphics package. Images can be stored as data in a table, used as a background image or texture, and used as a highlight that might or might not respond to user clicks.

Employee
Name: Che Zhang
ID: 3354
Phone: 222-111-1524
...
Photo:

FIGURE 6.16
Image bound to a data column. Employee photo is scanned and stored in the database column.

To display an image from a table as shown in Figure 6.16, you must first define an Object column within that table. Then the bound object frame is used like a text box to position and display the image on the form.

To use an image or texture as a background, first use a graphics package to make sure the image is light enough to not interfere with the readability of the other boxes. Then set the Picture property of the form to the name of the image file. In most cases you want to embed the image on the form so the picture is included directly with the database.

To display a picture on part of the form without storing it in a table, use the unbound object frame. This image can be decorative, or you can attach code to the On_Click event so that when users click on the image, a predefined action is taken.

Combo and List Boxes

Figure 6.17 displays the basic controls on a form. The **list box** and **combo box** are useful controls in most database applications. The purpose of these two controls is to display a list of items from which the user can choose one value. There are two primary differences between the combo box and list box. The combo box displays only one of the available choices—until the user clicks on the down arrow. Second, a user can directly type in a value with the combo box. (The name for the combo box indicates that it is a combination of a list box and a text box.) Most designers rely on the combo box—largely because it takes up less space then the list box.

A combo box has two basic uses. The first is to insert a value into a table. The second is to search for a particular row of data. If you decide to use both types of combo boxes in your application, you should use color or some other attribute to make the purpose clear to the user.

When you look through the normalized tables, you can see why the combo box is so useful in a relational database. Many of the tables are joined together by internally generated ID numbers. For example, the Sale table uses the CustomerID to identify a customer. In Figure 6.13 a clerk would have to enter the value 17 to indicate which customer made the purchase. But how does the clerk know that value? We certainly cannot expect employees to memorize thousands of customer numbers.

Similarly, we cannot ask customers to memorize their ID numbers. In some situations (e.g., a video rental store) we might ask customers to carry an ID card that contains the number. You might think about using some common ID number like a taxpayer ID or phone number. But it is hard to ensure that these numbers are unique and harder to convince customers to give them to you.

A better solution is to let the database use the internally generated ID and then have the clerk pick the customer from a list of names. Hence the use of the combo box. The combo box displays a list of all the entries in the Customer table (sorted by name or phone number). Entering the first few letters of a customer's name forces the combo box to scroll to the matching entries. When the clerk selects the appropriate customer, the corresponding ID is entered into the Sale table.

Figure 6.18 shows the basic properties for the CustomerID combo box on the Sale form. The most important feature of the combo box is that it is driven by an SQL query. You can use any SQL SELECT statement. Just be careful when choosing the column from the query that will be stored in the database table. In this case the CustomerID from the query (Customer table) will be stored in the CustomerID column of the Sale table (ControlSource). In many cases you can set the width of the ID column to zero—the users never need to know that the ID number exists.

In a few situations with a fixed and limited number of choices, you might not have a table of values to choose from. In these cases a short list can be entered directly into the RowSource property, which defines exactly the items that will be displayed in the list. For the most part you want to avoid this use of the combo box,

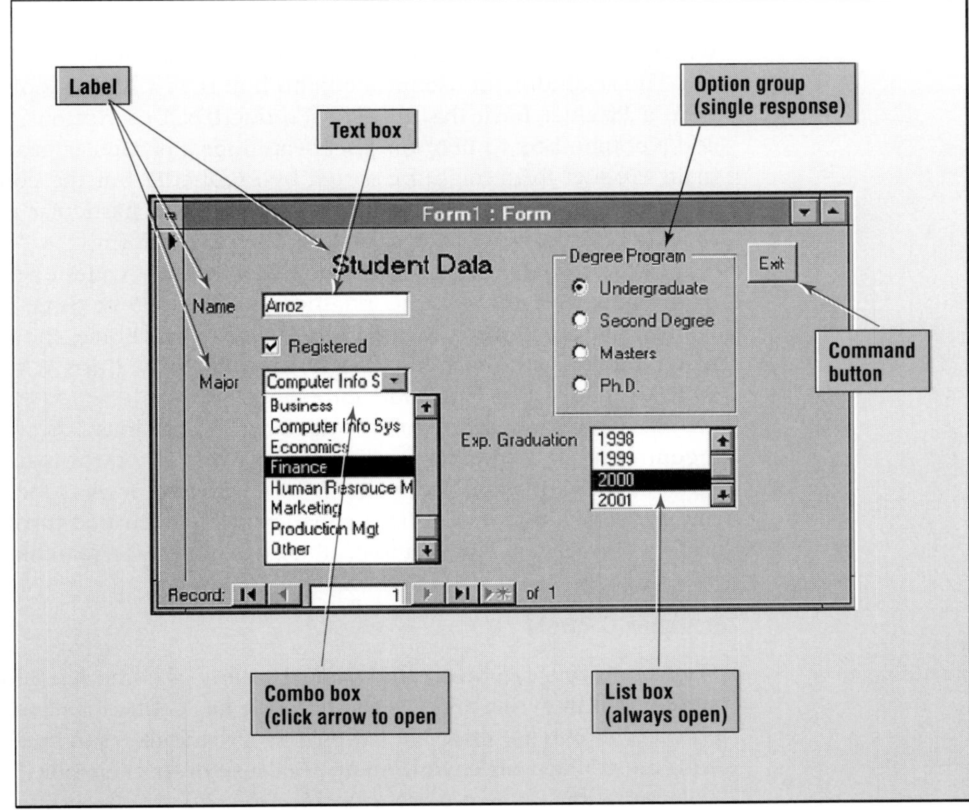

FIGURE 6.17
Sample controls. Notice the difference between a combo box and a list box. The combo box fills one line until the user clicks the arrow. Then it displays the list box so the user can choose an entry.

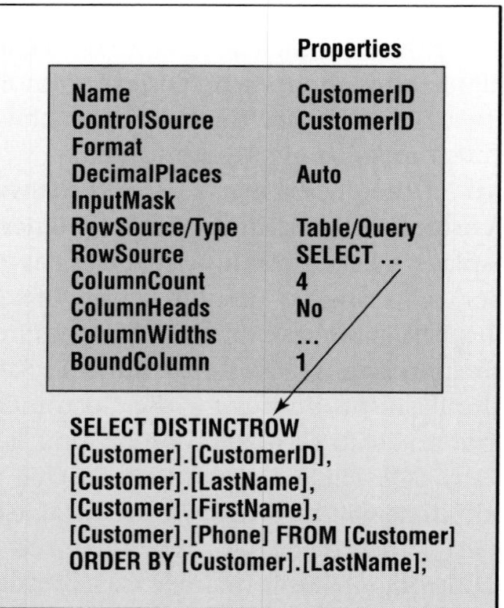

Properties
Name CustomerID
ControlSource CustomerID
Format
DecimalPlaces Auto
InputMask
RowSource/Type Table/Query
RowSource SELECT ...
ColumnCount 4
ColumnHeads No
ColumnWidths ...
BoundColumn 1
SELECT DISTINCTROW
[Customer].[CustomerID],
[Customer].[LastName],
[Customer].[FirstName],
[Customer].[Phone] FROM [Customer]
ORDER BY [Customer].[LastName];

FIGURE 6.18 Combo box properties. The standard SQL SELECT statement generates the data to be displayed. The ControlSource sets the column in the Sale table that will hold the choice. The BoundColumn identifies which of the four displayed columns will be stored.

since lists are rarely fixed. If necessary, create a separate table with one column and have the query retrieve that column. Later, when you have to change the database, adding a row of data to a table is much easier than finding and modifying a combo box.

Because the combo and list boxes are based on a query, one interesting trick described in Chapter 7 is to alter the query in response to some other event. In other words, while the application is running, you can have a program change the query, which alters the choices that are presented to the user.

The second main use for a combo box is as a search tool. For example, say you have a Product form that displays ProductIDs, Descriptions, and Prices. You could add a combo box to help the user search for a particular product. For example, the main Product form might be sorted by ProductID, but the combo box could be organized by Description. When the user selects a particular description, the DBMS quickly brings up the corresponding row on the form.

The key to this use of the combo box is that it cannot be bound to any column in the underlying tables. Second, there will be two or three lines of program code behind the combo box. After the user makes a choice, the code searches for the matching row and then shifts the form to that row. Current versions of Access have a wizard that writes this code automatically.

Be careful when designing your forms. Users must always be able to tell when a control is used to enter new data and when a control is used to search for data. In some cases it might be wiser to have separate forms: one for entering data and one for searching for data. This situation can be clarified through good use of color or font properties. For example, all controls used for searching can be marked in a special color.

Complex Controls

Control objects can be created using a variety of computer languages, although they are commonly written in C++. Microsoft has defined a standard format for control objects (known as Active X) that enables programmers to create new objects for use with most Microsoft environments. Because of this flexibility, many varieties of controls are available. Some are available from Microsoft; thousands of additional controls can be purchased from other companies. You can also create your own controls for specialized applications within an organization.

A few additional controls are shown in Figure 6.19. The Tab and Calendar controls are particularly useful in business applications. There is also a Grid control that enables you to display data in a spreadsheet layout. These types of controls are not as easy to use as the standard bound controls. The developer has to write short programs to load data into the control and to respond to the control's events.

Charts

Database applications used for making decisions often contain charts or graphs. Charts are another type of control that can be placed on a form (or report). The first step in creating a useful chart is to discuss with the user exactly what type of data and what type of chart will be needed. Then you usually build a new SQL query that will collect the data to be displayed on the chart. The chart control places the chart on the form and specifies the individual attributes (like type of chart, axis scale, and colors).

Two basic types of charts are used on database forms and reports: (1) graphs that show detail from the currently displayed row and (2) graphs that display summary data across all (or several) of the rows. The difference between the two approaches lies in the level of data displayed. Detail graphs change with each row of data displayed. Summary graphs are usually generated from totals or averages.

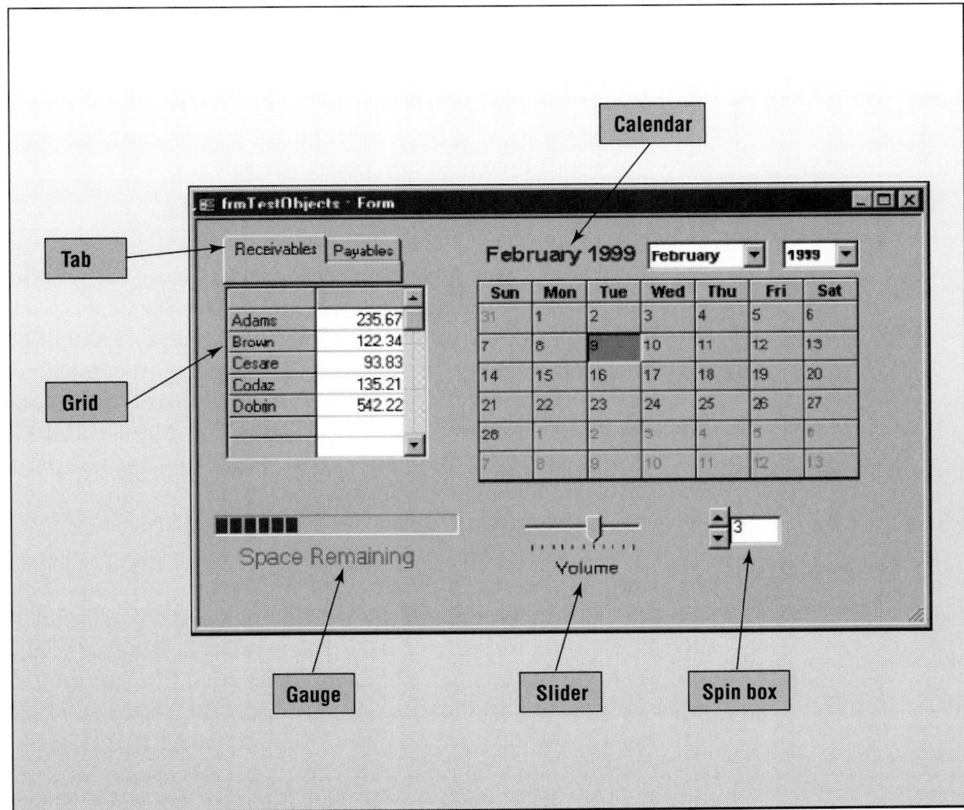

FIGURE 6.19
Additional controls. Thousands of controls are available to improve the user interface or perform specialized tasks. Common controls include tabs, grid, calendar, gauges, sliders, and the spin box. You can also create custom controls.

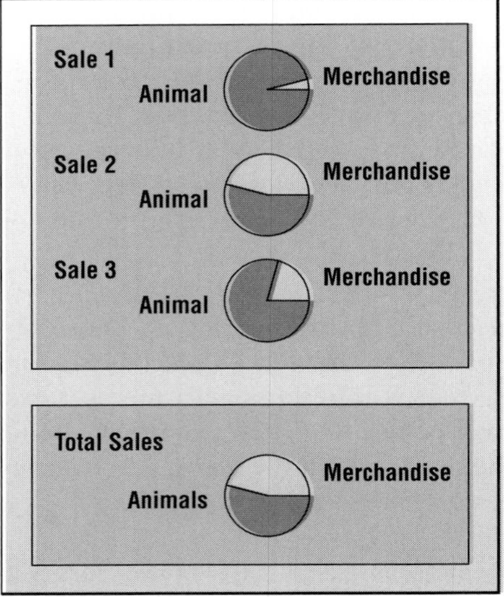

FIGURE 6.20 Charts on forms or reports. The top charts show the split in sales for each individual sale and will change with each row of data. The bottom graph shows the sales split for all sales and is not bound to an individual row.

Figure 6.20 illustrates the two types of graphs as they might be used in the Pet Store database. Each chart shows the amount of money spent on animals versus the amount spent on merchandise. However, the top set of charts shows the split for each individual sale, so the graphs vary with each row in the Sale query. The bottom chart shows the overall total for the store—even if it is placed on a Sales form that shows each row of data, it will not change (except over time). To create the two types of charts, the main difference is in the query. The query for the detail charts contains a column (SaleID) that is linked to the row of data being displayed on the form (based on its SaleID). The summary graph computes the totals across all of the sales and is not linked to any particular sale.

Multiple Forms

As you can guess, an application will quickly spawn many different forms. Of course, the forms should be linked to each other so users can quickly move between the forms by clicking a button, data value, or image. Switchboard forms play an important role in tying forms together. However, you can also connect forms directly. The most common example is the use of subforms placed on a main form. In this situation the forms are linked by setting the Master and Child properties of the subform. Then Access keeps the data synchronized so that when the user selects a new row in the main form, the matching rows in the subform are located and displayed automatically.

It is easy to open a new form when a user clicks on some item. In Access simply insert the DoCmd.OpenForm command for the On_Click event of the control. When the forms contain related data, you sometimes want to open the new form and display only the row of data that is related. For example, if the Order form contains customer data, when the user clicks an Edit button (or double-clicks on the customer name), the application should open the Customer form. As shown in Figure 6.21, the Customer form should display the data that corresponds to the customer on the Order form. The OpenForm command uses a LinkCriteria parameter to accomplish this task. The criteria limit the data displayed in the new form. In this example the LinkCriteria would be defined as "CustomerID=" & [CustomerID]. This

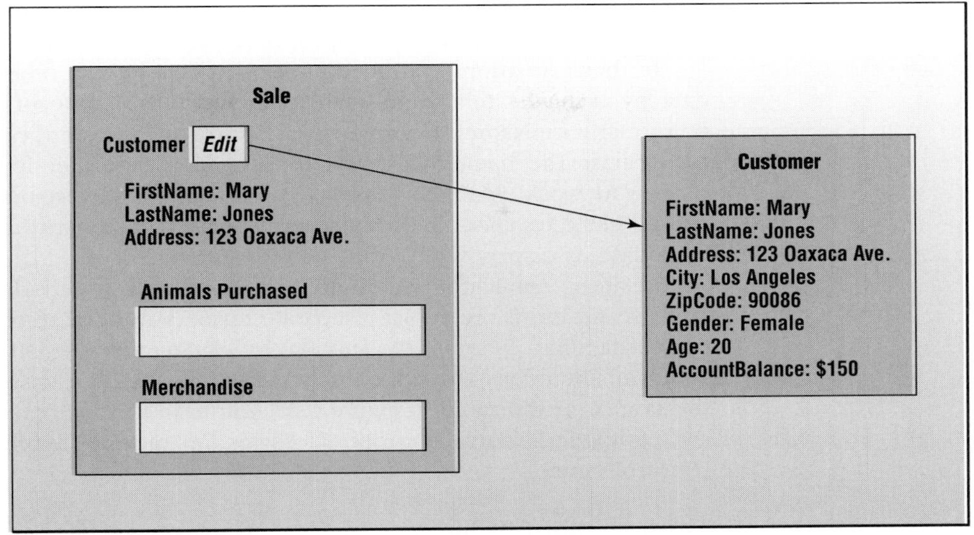

FIGURE 6.21 Connect forms with matching data. The Customer form is opened to display the data corresponding to the customer already entered in the Sale form.

command takes the current value of the CustomerID on the Sale form and passes it to the new (Customer) form.

In most cases the user would close the Customer form and return to the main Sale form. But what if users commonly keep both forms open at the same time? Then they would expect the data between the two forms to be synchronized so that when a new row is displayed on the Sale form, the matching data would be displayed on the Customer form. This situation is similar to the preceding example, but you need an additional command. When a new row is selected on the Sale form (On_Current event), you set the Filter property in the Customer form and then you call the Requery method of the Customer form to force it to update its display.

A third, related situation is shown in Figure 6.22. Perhaps while looking at animal data, the customer decides to buy that animal. A Purchase button on the Animal

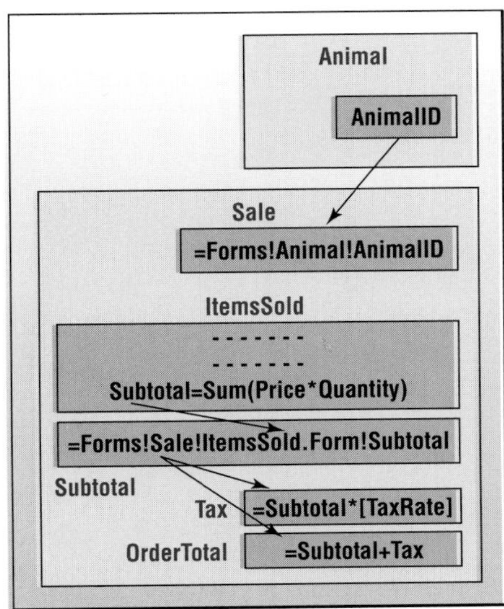

FIGURE 6.22 Copying data from a different form. The default AnimalID is copied into the Sale form from the Animal table. Likewise, the subtotal is first computed on the subform and then copied to the main form.

form could quickly bring up the Sale form. It would be convenient if the button then copied the AnimalID into the appropriate space on the Sale form.

In these situations you need to refer to data held in other forms. You reference data by using its full name—which includes the name of the form. The syntax is Forms![FormName]![ControlName]. Note the use of the exclamation point (!) to separate the names. Similarly, to keep the Customer form linked to the Sale form, you would issue the following command: Forms![Customer].Filter = "CustomerID= Forms![Sale]![CustomerID]". Then whenever the Sale data changes, the Customer form is told to update its display with Forms![Customer].Requery.

Business applications commonly need to compute subtotals from subforms. Because subforms are actually separate forms, you need to use a similar process to copy data. First, compute the subtotal by placing a new control on the footer of the subform. Then copy the value into a new control on the main form. Be careful with the syntax. As indicated in Figure 6.22, you have to specify that it is a subform with the following Form property: Forms![MainformName]![SubformName].**Form**![ControlName].

International Attributes

When designing forms and reports, you increasingly need to consider the use of the application in an international setting. An obvious complication is the need to translate the data to a different language. Some application development systems facilitate language translation by enabling developers to store all written comments (e.g., screen names, labels, and error messages) in one location. You can do the same thing with a DBMS by creating a separate language table that holds the phrases that would need to be translated. Then build your form by looking up the appropriate phrase based on a code value. This separate table is then changed by the translators—without requiring any changes to your forms or code. The one drawback is that without a compiler, every form will take longer to load, since each phrase will have to be retrieved separately from the table.

As noted in Figure 6.23, another problem related to language is that most languages use special character sets. For example, Latin-based languages often include accents and other diacritical marks. Oriental languages are even more difficult, since

FIGURE 6.23
International attributes. When creating forms and reports for international use, be careful to consider different formats for characters and data. Also, be sure to abide by all national laws—particularly in terms of data privacy.

- Language
- Character sets and punctuation marks
- Sorting
- Data formats
  - Date
  - Time
  - Metric v. English
  - Currency symbol and format
  - Separators (decimal, . . .)
  - Phone numbers
    - Separators
    - International code prefix
  - Postal codes
  - National ID numbers

they require thousands of different pictographs instead of a few characters. The computer must be capable of displaying the particular character set for each nation. Currently, the leading solution to this problem is based on a system known as **Unicode,** which is an international standard to store and display characters from virtually any language. Several operating systems support Unicode. For instance, Windows 95, Windows NT, NetWare, and some varieties of UNIX can handle the 2-byte character codes. Some modern applications and development tools support Unicode; if your application truly needs international support, be sure to choose tools that provide that support. The issue of language and characters also affects the sorting of data. Hence databases typically enable you to set the sort order based on the character set being used.

Data formats for date, time, telephone numbers, postal codes, and currency all vary by region or nation. Most can be set within the Windows environment (Control Panel). However, be careful when converting data from one country to another. Dates and times will translate fine, since they are stored as a difference from a base date or time. But currencies will not convert correctly. Say you build a database application in the United States with a currency column and enter prices denoted in dollars (e.g., $18.20). What happens when you copy the database to a machine in London that has currency settings in pounds? The answer is that the currency sign will be changed, but not the data. In the example, the user would see £18.20, which is not the correct value (e.g., £11.44). You have two choices: (1) avoid the currency data type and leave the prices denominated in dollars or (2) write a query to convert all currency data to the new currency. It is possible in the first case to use the currency format and avoid conversion of the currency sign by defining your own currency type. The second method is probably the best for many applications and is easy to do with a query that multiplies the original value by a conversion factor. Of course, the conversion factor changes over time, so you have to be careful to track the conversion date.

A more difficult problem arises with respect to phone numbers and postal codes. When defining data and creating forms, be sure to allocate enough spaces to hold the country codes and longer phone numbers. Also note that postal codes in some countries contain letters as well as numbers. Programmers used to think that they could reduce data entry errors by restricting data entry of ZIP codes to five digits. In an international setting, you cannot make this assumption. One way to reduce data entry errors is to rely on combo boxes that pull data from a (huge) table of postal codes. A more reliable approach is to purchase software that automatically checks and updates postal codes in your database based on addresses.

Finally, be careful to abide by all national laws with respect to security and access to the data. For example, many European nations have strong privacy statutes—particularly with respect to customer data and national ID numbers. In some cases it may be illegal to transfer data collected in Europe to the United States.

DIRECT MANIPULATION OF GRAPHICAL OBJECTS

In the last few years, the user interface to applications has been changing. The heavy use of graphics has led to an emphasis on **direct manipulation of objects.** Instead of typing in commands, the user can drag an item from one location on the screen to another to indicate a change. Most people have seen this approach used with basic operating system commands. For example, in the day of DOS, you had to type a command like COPY MYFILE.DOC A:MYFILE.DOC to copy a file. Today you click on the file icon and drag it to a disk drive icon.

Sally's Pet Store Example

A graphical approach can make your applications easier to use. However, it requires changing the way you think about applications, and a good dose of creativity. Consider the Pet Store example. The forms designed earlier in this chapter were easy to create, and they will perform adequately. However, we could change the entire approach to the application.

Figure 6.24 shows a partial screen for the Pet Store example. Compare this form to the traditional data entry form shown in Figure 6.10. The traditional approach requires users to enter text into a box. With the graphical approach the user sees photos of the individual animals and drags them to the customer to indicate a sale. Double-clicking on an item provides more pictures or additional details. A similar approach would be used to special order animals, using drag-and-drop techniques to define an animal (breed, color, etc.), and to place the order.

Note that you cannot entirely eliminate data entry. At some point you need to collect basic data on customers (name, address, phone number, etc.). This data could be entered on a traditional form that is activated when the clerk double-clicks the customer icon or photo. That is, the form in Figure 6.24 replaces the traditional sales form but does not replace the basic customer form. Of course, once the customer data is on file, it can be dragged back to this main form whenever the customer returns.

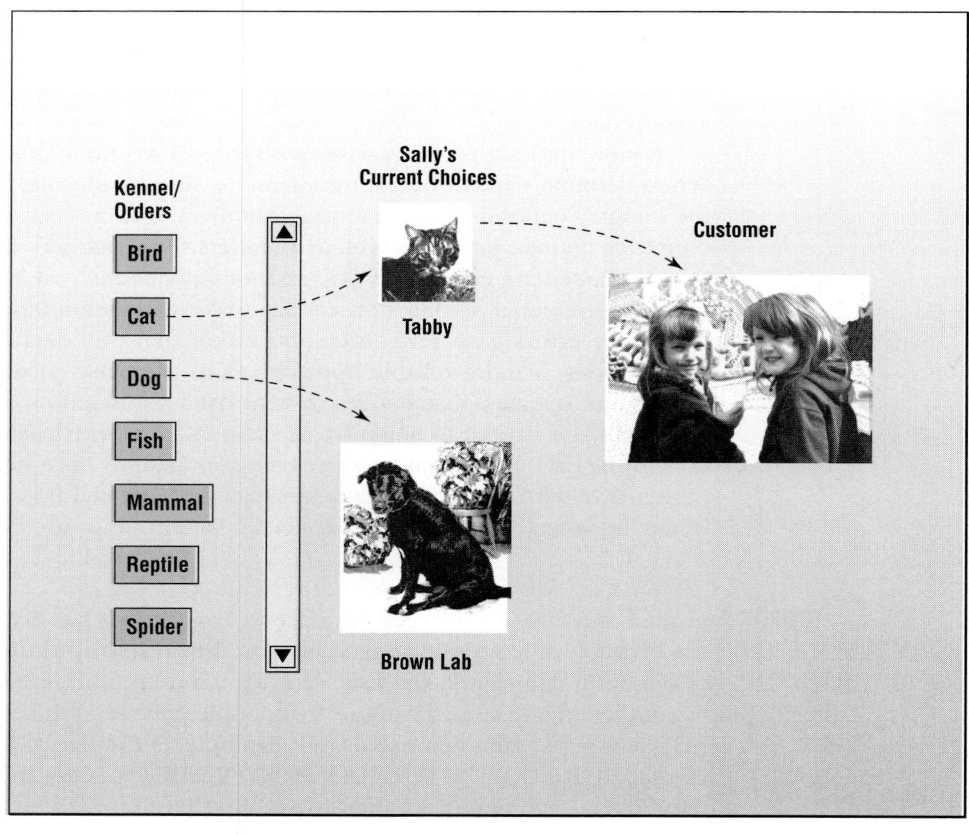

FIGURE 6.24
Direct manipulation of graphical objects at the Pet Store. Instead of entering an AnimalID into a box, you drag the picture of the animal to the customer to indicate a sale. Double-clicking on an item brings up more detail or related graphics screens.

FIGURE 6.25
Basic steps in creating a graphical approach. Note the extra demands on hardware. The method also requires custom programming and creativity in design.

- Get the hardware
  - Images: scanners
  - Sound: microphone and sound card
  - Video: camera and capture card
  - Lots of disk space
  - High-speed processors
- Add an object column to your table definition
- Design the screens
  - Be creative
  - Get user input
  - Make the user's job easier
  - Avoid using graphics just for show
  - Double-click
  - Drag-and-drop
- Programming!

Creating a Graphical Approach

This graphical approach to applications requires considerably more effort, software, and hardware than a traditional text-based approach. The basic steps are outlined in Figure 6.25. To start, you need to be able to capture photos (and sometimes sound and video). The costs of this basic hardware have declined, but it is an expense that must be budgeted. Scanners are used to convert photographs into high-resolution digital pictures. Digital cameras can be used to save a picture directly to the computer—without the need for a scanner. However, be sure you get a camera that can create good resolution images. Microphones and sound cards are used to convert sound into digital format. Video cameras and video-capture cards similarly convert video clips to digital format. Also, be sure that you install sufficient storage capacity. Photos, sound, and video clips can take up huge amounts of storage space. If in doubt, test a few images to get an average size and then multiply by the number of rows. Similarly, be sure to install high-speed processors and communication links.

Most modern database systems can save digital images, sound, and video clips within a row in a table. For example, the Animal table would have a column called Photo. The type of data for this column would be an object. For each animal you would bring up the appropriate row on the Animal form and scan the photo. The image would then be stored with this row of data. Later, as you scroll through the animals, the individual photos will be displayed.

After defining the tables, the next step is to design the main screens. This step requires creativity—particularly because there are few examples to analyze. This process also requires extensive discussions with users. The objective is to make the process easy and intuitive. Avoid using graphics just for show. Some ideas may look interesting, but could be ineffective if they take too long to use. The two main commands you will use are double-click and drag-and-drop. Double-click is used to reveal detail information. **Drag-and-drop** is used to transfer an object to another location. This user interface is still evolving. Look at Windows-based software for additional ideas that can be applied to a business setting.

The next step is to create the code that will make the forms work. Do not be misled. Even with advanced tools, this approach requires considerable skill in programming. Database environments have typically focused on text and numbers. Recent advances have added more capabilities with respect to storing objects. However, direct manipulation of user objects typically requires custom programming. Languages like Visual Basic have the fundamental components to do the job. However, you might have to rely on more powerful languages like C++ or Java for improved control and better performance. Some basic issues in programming are explored in Chapter 7.

The Internet

The emphasis on graphics and a direct manipulation of objects can be particularly valuable for forms used with the Internet. For starters, most users will have little experience with databases and only limited knowledge of your company. Creating a graphical model of the company and its processes achieves two important objectives: (1) It makes the site easier to use because it matches the physical purchase methods users already know, and (2) it limits the actions of the users to those that you have defined.

One of the goals of the graphical approach is to hide the use of the database. Yes, all basic product information, figures, and sales data are stored in the database. The database system provides search capabilities and stores user selections. It also provides reports and data analysis for managers. However, users never need to know about the database itself. Users simply see an image of a store and its products. They manipulate the objects to learn more or to place orders.

The Internet can also simplify some aspects of data collection. As the Internet evolves and standards improve, certain base data can be obtained automatically. Common data about customers is already available in many places on the Internet. For example, the www.switchboard.com site provides names, addresses, and phone numbers for millions of people. With a little additional programming, your application could collect that data instead of asking users to enter it. Chapter 11 discusses the concepts of distributed databases in more detail.

Complications and Limitations of a Graphical Approach

There are several potential drawbacks to basing a form on the direct manipulation of graphical objects. The most important is that it can be an inefficient way to enter data. For example, you would not expect workers at a receiving dock to use a drag-and-drop form to record the receipt of several hundred boxes. A bar-code scanner would be considerably more efficient. Likewise, a quality control technician would prefer a simple keystroke (or voice) system so he or she could enter data without looking away from the task.

Even the Pet Store sales form is a debatable use of the drag-and-drop approach. Think about the operations at a typical large pet store. Consider what would happen when dozens of customers bring shopping carts full of merchandise to the checkout counter. If a clerk has to use a drag-and-drop screen, the checkout process would take forever. Again, bar-code scanners would speed up the process. On the other hand, perhaps the operations of the store could be improved by eliminating the checkout clerk. Think about how the store would function if shoppers used the store's drag-and-drop Web site to select products, which were then delivered, or bagged and stacked for drive-through pickup. The difference in the value of the approach depends on the operations of the business and on who will be using the application.

A second difficulty with the graphics approach is that each application requires a considerable amount of custom programming. The traditional approach is relatively straightforward. Common tools exist for entering data with forms made up of text boxes, combo boxes, and subforms. These tools can be used for virtually any database application. On the other hand, direct manipulation of objects requires that individual business objects be drawn on the screen and associated with data. Then each user action (double-click and drag-and-drop) has to be defined specifically for that application. In the future tools may be created to assist in this programming. However, today a graphical approach requires considerably more programming effort than other approaches.

Building graphical database applications across the Internet carries similar problems. There are two primary limitations: transmission speed and limitations of software tools. However, a huge amount of money and effort is being directed toward the Web. Many firms in several industries are working on solutions to both limitations.

REPORTS

When you understand forms, reports are straightforward. Increasingly, the main difference between forms and reports is that reports are designed to be printed, whereas forms are displayed on the screen. There are two additional differences: (1) Forms can be used to collect data, and (2) reports are generally used to present summarized data. Consequently, reports cannot have controls that collect data. But, why, if you can print forms, would you need reports? The two main strengths of a report are that (1) it can easily handle multiple pages of output (with consistent page headers and page numbering) and (2) it can combine both detailed and summary data. Chapter 5 illustrates how SQL queries can produce relatively complex results with the GROUP BY clause. However, a single SQL query can be used to display either detail rows of data or the summaries—not both. A good DBMS report writer also provides additional control over the output, such as printing negative values in red.

Report Design

As summarized in Figure 6.26, several issues are involved in designing reports. As in the development of forms, you and the users need to determine the content and layout. You must also identify the typical size of the report (number of pages and num-

FIGURE 6.26
Fundamentals of report design. Determine content and layout with users. Estimate size and printing times. Identify security controls. Check typefaces and sizing for user readability.

- Report usage/user needs
- Report layout choices
  - Tabular
  - Columns/subgroups
  - Charts/graphs
- Paper sizes
- Printer constraints
- How often is it generated
- Events that trigger report
- How large is the report
- Number of copies
- Colors
- Security controls
  - Distribution list
  - Unique numbering
  - Concealed/nonprinted data
  - Secured printers
  - Transmission limits
  - Print queue controls
- Output concerns
  - Typefaces
    - Readability
    - Size
    - User disabilities
  - OCR needs

ber of copies), along with noting how often it must be printed. Because of the physical steps involved, printing reports can be a time-consuming process. A report of a few dozen pages is no problem. However, when a report blooms into hundreds of pages with thousands of copies, you have to plan more carefully. First, you need a fast, heavy-duty printer. Then you need machines and people to assemble and distribute the report copies. You generally have to schedule time to use the printer for large reports.

Paper reports also present a different challenge to security. Chapter 10 examines some of the basic issues in security and presents controls that can be applied to data handled by the DBMS. Paper reports require the use of more traditional security controls, such as written distribution lists, numbered copies, and control data. If security is an important issue in an organization, then these controls should be established when the report is designed.

Several physical and artistic aspects are involved in designing reports. The size of the page, typeface used, and overall design of the page all must be determined. Fewer DBMS report writers are relatively flexible, which is good and bad. The good part is that designers have greater control over the report. The bad part is that designers need to understand more about design—including the terminology.

Artistic design and a thorough treatment of design issues are beyond the scope of this book. If you are serious about design (for paper reports, forms, or Web pages), you should consider taking a course in graphic design. Nonetheless, it helps if you learn a few basic terms.

Terminology

Many of the basic terms come from typesetting and graphics design. The terms shown in Figure 6.27 will help you understand report writers and produce better reports. The first step is to choose the page layout, in terms of paper size; orientation (portrait versus landscape); and margins. The type of binding system will affect the margins, and you might have to leave an extra gutter margin for binding.

FIGURE 6.27 Basic publishing terminology. Understanding the basic design terms helps you design better reports and communicate with publishers and typesetters.

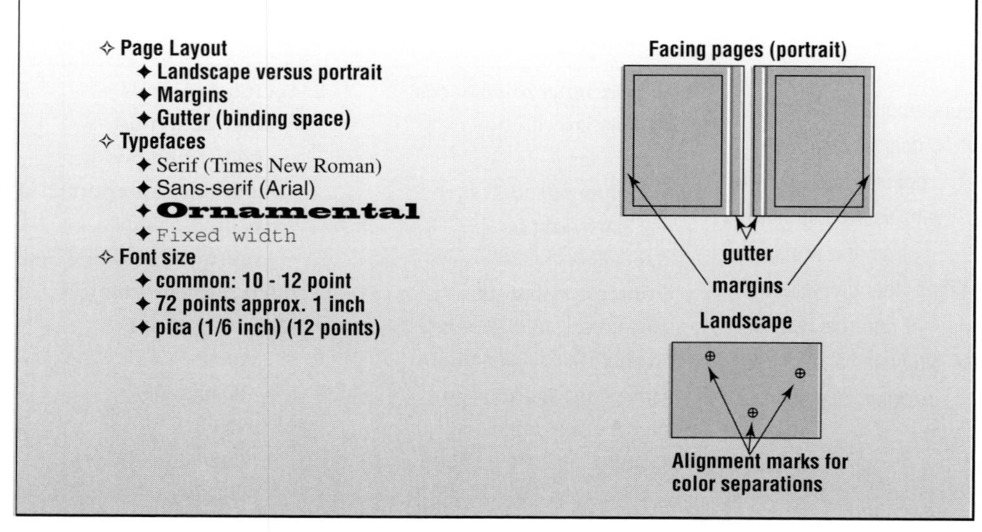

The next step is to choose the typeface and font size. In general, serif typefaces are easier to read, but sans serif faces have more white space, making them easier to read at larger and smaller sizes. Avoid ornamental typefaces except for covers and some headings. Columns of numbers are generally printed at a fixed width to keep columns aligned. Special fixed-width typefaces (e.g., Courier), in which all of the characters use exactly the same width, are especially appropriate if you need to align columns of nonnumeric data without the use of tab stops.

Font size is generally specified in terms of points. Most common printed material ranges from 10- to 12-point fonts. A useful rule of thumb is that a capitalized letter in a 72-point font is approximately 1 inch tall. Some report systems measure sizes and distance in picas. A pica is 1/6 of an inch, or the same height as a 12-point font.

If your reports include graphs and images, the terminology becomes more complex. Be aware that the quality of bitmap images depends on the resolution of the original image and the resolution of the output device. Common laser printers have a 600-dots-per-inch (dpi) resolution. Typesetters typically achieve about 2,400-dpi resolution. An image that looks good on a 600-dpi laser may be too small or too jagged on a 2,400-dpi typesetter.

If your reports are in color, you quickly encounter additional problems. In particular, colors on your screen may not be the same on the printer. Similarly, a sample report printed on a color ink jet might look completely different when submitted to a typesetter. The Pantone® color standard is designed to minimize these problems by providing numbers for many standard colors. The related issue you will encounter in color printing is the need to create color separations for all of your reports. For full-color submissions to print shops, each report page will need four separate color sheets. Denoted CMYK for each of the three primary colors—cyan (blue), magenta (red), and yellow—and the key color (black). In this case each page will need high-resolution alignment marks so the colors can be reassembled properly.

One of the first elements of design that you must learn is to keep your reports simple and elegant. For instance, stick to one typeface and one or two font sizes on a page. Use plenty of white space to highlight columns and features. Most important, since design style continually changes, examine newspaper and magazine layouts regularly for new ideas and patterns.

Basic Report Types

From the perspective of data layout, there are essentially three types of report designs: tabular, groups or subtotals, and labels. The choice you make depends on the type of data and use of the report.

Tabular and Label Reports

The tabular layout, shown in Figure 6.28, is the simplest report design. It basically means printing columns of data—much like the output of a query. The advantage over a simple query is that the tabular report can print page headings and page numbers on every page. You also have a little more control over font size and column width. Tabular reports are generally used for detail item listings, such as inventory reports. Note that the sort order becomes crucial, since these reports will be used to search for specific items.

As shown in Figure 6.29, labels are also straightforward. The essence of a label report is that all of output for one row of data is printed in one "column" on the page. Then the next row is printed in the following column. The name *label report*

FIGURE 6.28
Tabular report layout. Tabular reports have few options but are good for detailed data listings. They are used for itemized listings of data.

Customer

CustomerID	Phone	FirstName	LastName	Address	ZipCode
1		Walkin	Walkin		
2	(808) 801-9830	Brent	Cummings	9197 Hatchet Dri	96815
3	(617) 843-6488	Dwight	Logan	1760 Clearview	02109
4	(502) 007-0907	Shatika	Gilbert	4407 Green Stre	40342
5	(701) 384-5623	Charlotte	Anderson	4333 Highland C	58102
6	(606) 740-3304	Searoba	Hopkins	3183 Highland C	40330
7	(408) 104-9807	Anita	Robinson	8177 Horse Park	95035
8	(606) 688-8141	Cora	Reid	8351 Locust Str	41073
9	(702) 533-3419	Elwood	Henson	4042 West Ridg	89125
10	(302) 701-7398	Kaye	Maynard	5095 Sugar Gro	19901

comes from the use of preprinted or precut pages used for labels. These reports are sometimes named based on the number of physical columns. The example in Figure 6.29 has three labels across a page, so it is a three-up report. Before report orders printing a label report was quite challenging, since the printer could only work from the top of the page. Hence, you had to write a program that printed the top line for three different rows of data, then return and print the second line, and so on. Today's printers are more flexible, and report writers make the job easy. Keep in mind that label reports can be useful for other tasks—whenever you want to group data for one row into separate locations on a page. For instance, by inserting blank rows and changing the label size, you might create a tic-tac-toe pattern of data. It could be an interesting effect for a cover page or advertising sheet, but avoid using such patterns for hundreds of pages of data.

Groups or Subtotals

The most common type of report is based on groups and computes subtotals. It also provides the most flexibility over the layout of items on the report. Common ex-

FIGURE 6.29
Label report layout. This three-up report is commonly used to print on label paper. It can be used for small sets of data that need to be printed across a page.

Dwight Perrish 9904 Plum Springs Road Worcester, MA 01613	Dwight Logan 1760 Clearview Street Boston, MA 02109	David Sims 6623 Glenview Drive Boston, MA 02116
Hershel Keen 8124 Industrial Drive Nashua, NH 03060	Reva Kidd 5594 Halltown Road Bangor, ME 04401	Dan Kennedy 3108 Troon Court Burlington, VT 05401
Sharon Sexton 2551 Elementary Drive Barre, VT 05641	Kelly Moore 6116 Clearview Street Middlebury, VT 05753	Casey Tuck 7977 Fairways Drive Clifton, NJ 07015

FIGURE 6.30
Group or subtotal report. Note that several orders are being printed. Each order has a detailed repeating section of items being ordered. The report can compute subtotals for each order and a total for the entire report.

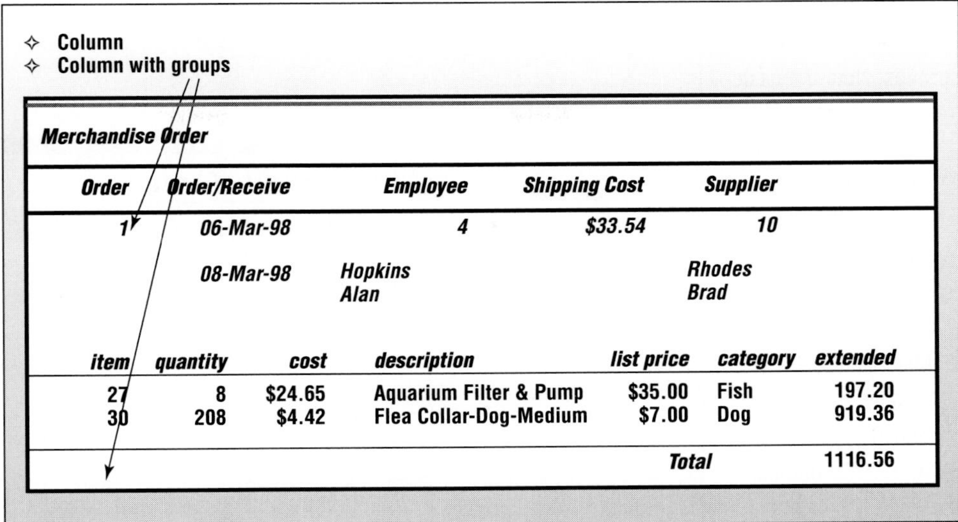

amples would include printing a receipt or a bill. Many times the report will print several rows of data—like the order form shown in Figure 6.30. Each order for the month is printed in one report, but the items are grouped together to show the individual order subtotals. Many people refer to these reports as control break reports.

The key to the subtotal report is to note that it includes both detail item listings (item ordered, quantity, cost, etc.), and group or total data (order date, customer, and order total). To create this report, you first build a query that contains the data that will be displayed. The example would probably include the Order, OrderItem, Merchandise, Customer, Employee, and Supplier tables. Be careful: If you want to see the detail, do not include a GROUP BY statement in the query. If you examine the data from this huge query, you will see a large number of rows and columns—many with repeating data. That is fine at this point, but not exactly what the user wants to see. The objective of the report is to clean up the display of the data.

To create a grouped report, examine the report design shown in Figure 6.31. This layout page shows the **group breaks** in the data and specifies the layout of each element on the page. Again, layout is set by the individual controls. The controls have properties that can be changed to alter the appearance of the data displayed by that control. For example, you can set basic typeface and font attributes.

The basic elements of a report are headers, footers, group breaks and detail areas. The **report header** contains data that is displayed only when the report is first printed, such as a cover page. Similarly, the **report footer** is used to display data at the end of the report—for example, summary statistics or graphs. The **page header** and **page footer** are displayed on every page that is printed—except for the report header and footer pages. Page headers and footers can be used to display column headings, page numbers, corporate logos, or security identifiers.

The report features that define this type of report are the groups. Microsoft Access has a grouping and sorting button that enables you to specify which items specify the group. The example shown in Figure 6.31 has one group defined: MerchandiseOrder.PONumber. The report will break, or create a new group of data, for each PONumber in the query. Notice that each Order can contain many items ordered. The report design specifies that these rows will be sorted by the ItemID

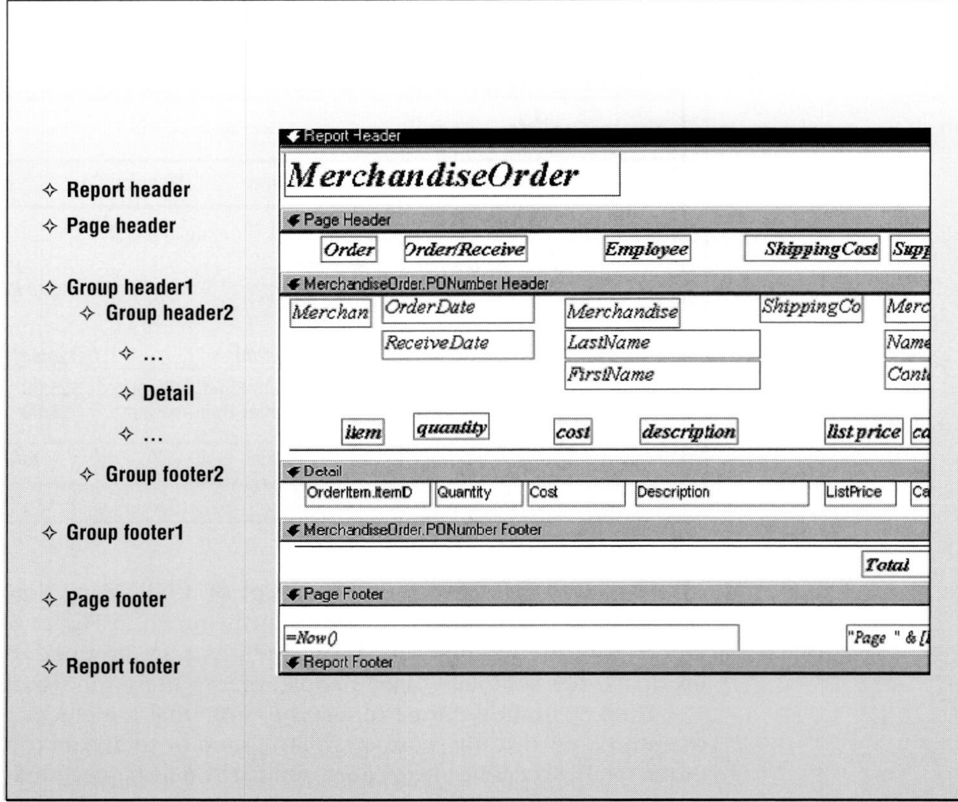

FIGURE 6.31 Report layout for groups. Note the basic report elements (report header, etc.). Also notice that the page layout is set by the position and properties of the data controls. In the sample report for Merchandise Orders, only one group is defined (on the Order number).

number (within each order). Each grouping can have a group header and a group footer. The group header displays data that applies to the entire order (e.g., Date, Customer, Employee, and Supplier). It also holds the column labels for the detail (repeating) section. The group footer displays the subtotal for each group.

The common uses of each report element are summarized in Figure 6.32. Note that all of the elements (except detail) can work in pairs—headers and footers. You

FIGURE 6.32 Common uses for report layout elements. Most elements are available in pairs, but you are free to delete any components you do not need.

Report Section	Usage
Report header	Title pages that are printed one time for entire report.
Page header	Title lines or page notes that are printed at the top of every page.
Group header	Data for a group (e.g., Order) and headings for the detail section.
Detail	Innermost data.
Group footer	Subtotals for the group.
Page footer	Printed at the bottom of every page—page totals or page numbers and notes.
Report footer	Printed one time at the end of the report. Summary notes, overall totals, and graphs for entire data set.

are not required to use both. For instance, you might choose to display page numbers in a page header and delete the page footer to provide additional space on the page.

Note that groups represent one-to-many relationships. For example, each order can have many items in the detail section. If there are several one-to-many (or many-to-many) relationships in the data, you might want to use multiple levels of groups. As illustrated in Figure 6.33, each group is nested inside another group, with the detail at the innermost level.

To create this report, you must build a query that contains every item that will be displayed. Begin by focusing on the detail level and then join additional tables until you have all the columns you need. You can use computed columns for minor computations like Price*Quantity. Be careful to avoid aggregate functions (e.g., Sum) and avoid the use of GROUP BY statements. The only time you might include these two features is if your "detail" row is actually a subtotal (or average) itself.

Group reports are generally used for computations—particularly subtotals. In general, computations on one row of data should be performed with the query. On the other hand, aggregations (Sum, Average, etc.) are handled by the report writer. Report writers have different methods of defining the scope of the operation—that is, what data should be included in the total. For example, in Access the formula Sum(Quantity) can produce different results depending on where it is placed. If the control holding the formula is located in the group footer, then the formula will produce the total of Quantity for all data rows displayed within that group. If the same formula is placed in the report footer, it will compute the total quantity for all orders displayed on the report. This graphical approach is intuitive, but you have to be careful to test the results to be sure you placed the formula where the user wants it. The method can also be challenging to debug. If you try to modify a report written by someone else, in addition to checking the formula, you have to verify that it is placed in the proper location.

As shown in Figure 6.33, the situation for the Pet Store sales report is a little more challenging. In this case every sale could have two sets of (unrelated) repeating items: purchases of animals and purchases of merchandise. In addition, the repeating sections cannot be nested. Microsoft Access handles this problem by pro-

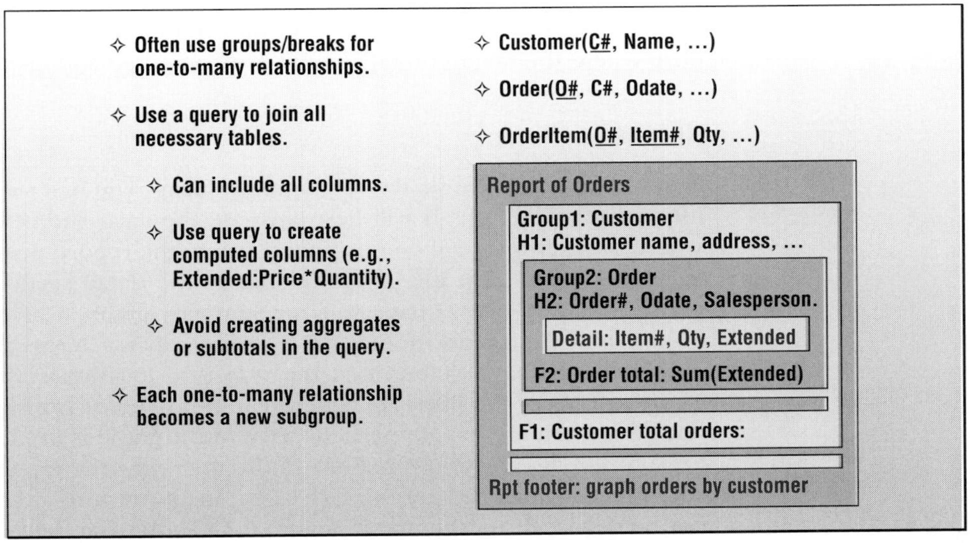

FIGURE 6.33
Nested groups. For example, each customer can place many orders, and each order has many detail lines. Two groups are used: (1) to show the total orders for each customer and (2) to show the total value of each order.

- Often use groups/breaks for one-to-many relationships.
- Use a query to join all necessary tables.
  - Can include all columns.
  - Use query to create computed columns (e.g., Extended:Price*Quantity).
  - Avoid creating aggregates or subtotals in the query.
- Each one-to-many relationship becomes a new subgroup.

- Customer(<u>C#</u>, Name, ...)
- Order(<u>O#</u>, C#, Odate, ...)
- OrderItem(<u>O#</u>, <u>Item#</u>, Qty, ...)

Report of Orders
Group1: Customer
H1: Customer name, address, ...
Group2: Order
H2: Order#, Odate, Salesperson.
Detail: Item#, Qty, Extended
F2: Order total: Sum(Extended)
F1: Customer total orders:
Rpt footer: graph orders by customer

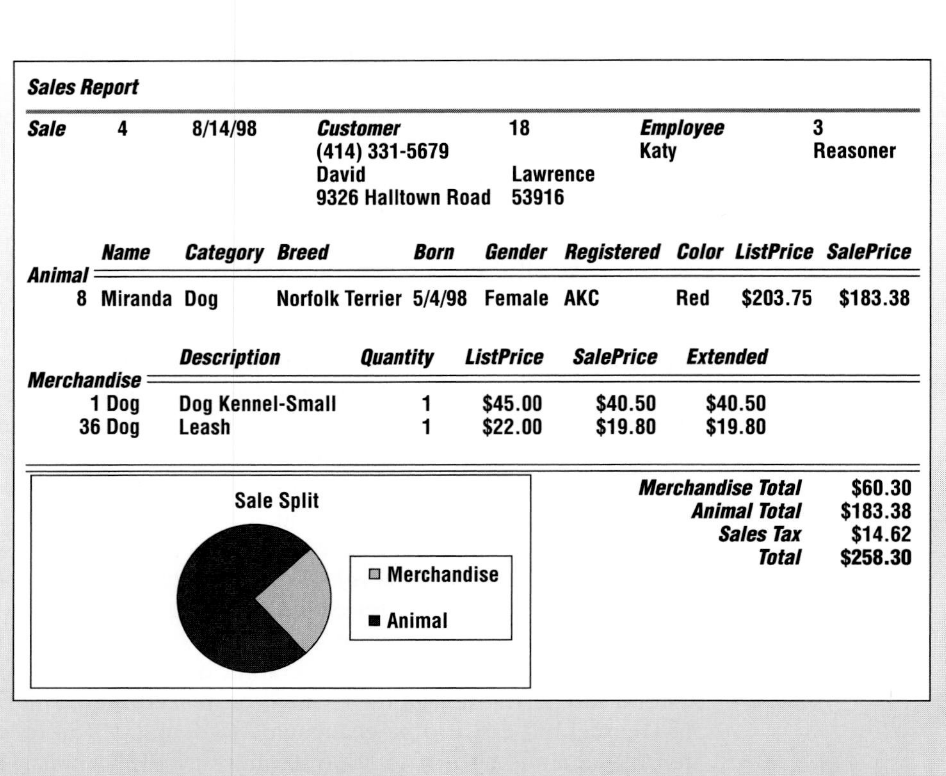

FIGURE 6.34 Sample graph on the sales report. It illustrates the portion of the sale spent on animals versus merchandise. Note that the graph appears on the same level as the Sale table—not on the Animal or Merchandise detail level and not on the report footer.

viding a separate subreport. Like a subform, a subreport is built separately and then embedded on the main form (Sales). Each subform (Animal and Merchandise) prints the detail lines for its category. The detail level on the main form stops at the level of the Sale table—the query does not include the SaleAnimal or SaleMerchandise tables. The subtotals are computed on the subreports and copied onto the main report, where the tax and total amount are computed and displayed.

Graphs

Graphs on reports are similar to graphs on forms. The first step is to decide with the user what type of graph will best illustrate the data. The next step is to determine where the graph should be positioned within the report elements. If you are graphing detail items, then the graph belongs in the detail section, where it will be redrawn for every row of data. If it is a summary graph, it belongs in a group footer, or perhaps in the report footer if it summarizes data across the entire report.

Once you have determined the type and location of the graph, you build a query to collect the data. This query can be different from the query used to produce the overall report. In particular, when the graph is in a group footer, you might need to use aggregation functions in the query for the graph. Be sure to include a column that links the graph to the data in the report—even if that column will not be displayed on the graph. Figure 6.34 shows one sale on the Sales report for the Pet Store. The totals for the graph are computed by a separate query. The dual detail sections (Animal and Merchandise) make this query particularly interesting (see exercise 17).

SUMMARY

Forms must be designed to match the user's tasks and make your application easy to use. To meet this goal, you need to pay attention to design principles, operating system guidelines, and human limitations. Where possible, you should build the form to use direct manipulation of objects, such as dragging items from one location to another to signify shipment.

Forms are based on tables or queries. Each form has a single purpose and can store data in one table. More complex forms can be created by placing subforms onto the main form. Controls on the form are used to enter data into the tables, perform lookup functions, and manipulate data. Several standard controls are available for a Windows environment (e.g., text boxes, combo boxes, and option buttons). Additional controls can be purchased to handle more complex tasks, such as calendars for scheduling, and three-dimensional imaging.

Reports are generally printed and differ from forms because reports are designed only to present data, not to collect it. There are several types of forms, but many business forms rely on subtotals or groupings to display different levels of data. For example, a sales report might be grouped by sales division or salesperson or both. You use a query to combine all data items needed for a report. There are two benefits to using a report writer: (1) It is a straightforward way to set data formats and alignment, and (2) the report can include detail listings as well as subtotals and totals.

A DEVELOPER'S VIEW

As Miranda noted, the database wizards can create basic forms for you. However, before you crank up the form wizard and generate hundreds of small forms, think about the tasks of the users and the overall design. Try to put the most important information on one central form with a few secondary forms to help. Strive for a clean, well-organized screen and use colors and graphics sparingly to enhance the appearance. You should also develop a design standard and layout for the application to ensure consistency. Just be sure to leave room for creativity. For your class project, you should begin creating the basic forms and reports.

KEY WORDS

accessibility, 197
aesthetics, 194
application design guide, 194
bound control, 207
check box, 207
clarity, 193
combo box, 208
command button, 207
consistency, 193
context-sensitive menu, 196
controls, 206
datasheet, 199
direct manipulation of objects, 215
drag-and-drop, 217
feedback, 194
focus, 199
group break, 223
heads-down data entry, 192
human factors design, 192
list box, 208
menu, 196
modal form, 197
option button, 207
page footer, 223
page header, 223
report footer, 223
report header, 223
scroll bars, 196
single-row form, 198
subform, 198
switchboard form, 198
tabular form, 198
toggle button, 207
Unicode, 215

REVIEW QUESTIONS

1. Which human factors are important to consider when designing forms?
2. What are the basic design standards of the Windows interface?
3. How can you make your applications accessible to a wider group of workers?
4. Which artistic rules should you follow when designing forms?
5. What are the main controls you can use on forms?
6. Explain the differences between a check box and an option button.
7. What are the primary types of forms?
8. What is the purpose of subforms?
9. Which international issues affect the design of forms?
10. What is direct manipulation of objects, and why is it a good user interface?
11. What are the primary sections of reports?
12. How is designing a form for a Web page different from designing a typical database form?
13. What are the first steps you take when building a report?

EXERCISES

Create the tables and build the initial forms for the databases described by the exercises in Chapter 3.

1. Parks and Recreation Department soccer matches.
2. Law firm time and billing.
3. Local marina reservation of slips.
4. Volunteer fire department.
5. Machine shop orders and sales.
6. Basic sales form.
7. Personal digital video disk collection.
8. Lawn care service firm.
9. Shipping company.

Sally's Pet Store

10. Create a form that potential customers can use to enter data about the type of animal they would like to purchase.
11. Create a form to record orders of animals from suppliers.
12. Create forms to record orders and receipt of merchandise from suppliers.

13. Create a form to be used when hiring new employees. You should add columns to the Employee table.

14. Create a report to list and total the sales for a specified day.

15. Create a report that details information on the animals currently in the store. Group them by type of animal.

16. Create a report that lists the purchases (animals and merchandise) by the top customers.

17. Create a report that displays sales for a given month. Include graphs that (1) compare sales of animals and merchandise and (2) compare sales of merchandise by category.

Rolling Thunder Bicycles

18. Draw a diagram to show how the forms in Rolling Thunder are interconnected.

19. Create a report to list daily sales totals for each manager and the employees who work for them.

20. Create a report to list sales by each type of bike for a given week. Include a graph to show the total sales value and count of sales by category.

21. Create a report to display all sales to a particular customer. List basic customer data, each bicycle, the components on that bicycle, and the total sales to that customer.

22. Create a report to show the production for each day by a given employee. List the bicycles by type of production (frame, painting, parts installation, and shipping).

23. Create a report that lists the purchase orders generated on a given day. Group them by the authorizing employee and list the top three items in value on each order.

24. Create a report on the paint choices that shows which colors were used on each day. For each day list the color and the number of times the color was used that day. Also list the total number of times each color was used.

25. Create a report that lists the basic size values (TopTube, ChainStay) for each type of bicycle produced. List the size values based on the FrameType and the FrameSize. Then list the average values for each type of bicycle.

WEB SITE REFERENCES

Site	Description
http://www.microsoft.com/win32dev/uiguide	Windows interface guidelines.
http://www.microsoft.com/enable	Accessibility guidelines.
http://www.unicode.org	Primary site for Unicode information.
http://www.acm.org/sigchi/	Association for Computing Machinery—Special Interest Group: Computer and Human Interaction.
http://www.acm.org/sigcaph/	Association for Computing Machinery—Special Interest Group. Computers and the Physically Handicapped.

ADDITIONAL READING

Cooper, A. *About Face: The Essentials of User Interface Design.* Foster City, CA: IDG Books, 1997. [A good discussion of various design issues.]

Microsoft Corporation. *The Windows Interface: An Application Design Guide.* Redmond: Microsoft Press, 1992. [An important set of definitions and standards that designers should follow.]

CHAPTER 7

Calculations and Data Manipulation

WHAT YOU WILL LEARN IN THIS CHAPTER

- Why would you need to use procedural code when SQL is so powerful? 232
- How does the graphical Windows environment affect programming? 234
- How do you access data on a form with programming code? 236
- How do you access data in the data tables with programming code? 239
- How do you handle unexpected errors? 250
- What are the basic logic elements of programming? 267

OVERVIEW

Ariel: *Well, is the application finished?*

Miranda: *No. The basic forms and reports are done, but I showed them to some of the workers.*

Ariel: *That's a good idea. What did they think?*

Miranda: *Well, I thought the forms made perfect sense, but the users kept having problems. I need to find some way to make the forms easier to use.*

Ariel: *I guess even wizards can't do everything.*

Miranda: *That's right. But to customize the way the forms work, I need to learn how to write some short programs. I also need to perform some computations on the data. I think I can use SQL to retrieve the data I need, but I really need some small programs to handle the calculations.*

INTRODUCTION

The SQL language is powerful and can be used to solve complex problems. However, it cannot solve every problem. There are times when you need to use a procedural language. For example, some computations may require several steps. In particular, decisions involving complex conditions can be easier to evaluate with a procedural language than with SQL. Similarly, complex transactions might require updating several tables, so you use a procedural language to sequence the changes in the proper order. You will often have to create modules to interact with users or to respond to user requests. Likewise, communicating with external devices (e.g., a cash register terminal) often requires a short programming module. You can also use procedures to create new functions or computations that can be used to expand the power of SQL. Essentially, any time you need to perform a set of operations in a sequence, evaluate complex conditions, or repeat a set of steps, you will need to use procedural code.

There are few standards in the use of procedural languages within a database environment. Each DBMS vendor has a unique procedural language. Even the basic approach to the language varies enormously. Fortunately, all procedural languages have some common features. Once you learn the logic of programming, you should be able to adapt and learn a specific procedural language. The objective of this chapter is to focus on the programming logic and show you how to begin creating modules within the database environment. The primary environment is Microsoft Access Visual Basic for Applications (VBA), which has some powerful (and complex) capabilities for user interaction in the Windows environment.

Programming can be a challenging, but interesting, profession. The material in this chapter will be easier to understand if you have completed at least one programming course. The appendix presents a review of the basic elements of VBA. You should first review the appendix. If you are still uncertain about the concepts, you might want to review a standard programming book.

Programming is a combination of logic, syntax, and creativity. In many ways programming is an art, but you can learn the logic components, and you can memorize the required syntax. Creating useful programs requires that you understand the business application needs and know how to solve various problems.

One common approach to learn (or teach) art forms is to study the work of other artists (programmers) to learn how they handle fundamental concepts. Hence the primary objective of this chapter (and the next) is to show you how to solve common problems that arise in the database environment.

This chapter presents the basic concepts of the Windows and database environments. You need to understand how programs control the environment. You also need to start learning about the various objects that are manipulated to perform most tasks. In a database environment, for example, forms and controls on the forms are the most common objects that your programs control. This chapter also outlines the basic procedures for using code to retrieve and store data in a database table. The final section focuses on trapping and responding to errors that might arise within your programs.

PROCEDURAL LANGUAGES

Procedural language is the generic term for a traditional programming language such as BASIC, COBOL, C++, or Java that evaluates commands in sequential order and contains certain basic logic elements. To write programs, you need to learn the basic operations listed in Figure 7.1. The key to programming is to understand the logic and purpose of these key elements. Every procedural language contains these basic commands. The appendix to this chapter presents a brief review of these common programming elements. You should read the appendix and decide whether you need a refresher course or some additional reading in a dedicated programming book.

In many cases the difference between languages is an issue of syntax. **Syntax** represents the specific commands and features in a programming language. For example, to send a statement to the printer, one language might use a Print command, whereas another uses a Write statement. The key to programming logic is to understand when you want to use an output command (and what to say). In many ways the programming syntax (print versus write) is easy—if nothing else, the computer will tell you when the syntax is wrong. It will not tell you when the logic is wrong.

This chapter focuses on the logic of programming, but it is impossible to demonstrate actual code without some reference to the environment and the syntax. The examples given here are based on the programming language available in Microsoft Access, VBA. The language is loosely based on the original BASIC programming language developed in the 1960s, but the current incarnation bears little resemblance to that early language.

Most current languages (including Visual Basic) have incorporated elements of object-oriented programming (OOP), which extends procedural languages by combining data properties and methods into defined objects. An object or class can be predefined, or you can create your own objects. In the database environment you use

FIGURE 7.1
Common logic elements of procedural languages. Every procedural language needs these basic commands. To be a programmer, you must understand each of these commands.

- Variables
- Computations
- Standard functions
- Debug
- Output
- Input
- Conditions
- Loops
- Arrays

predefined objects to control the user interface and to interact with the database. For example, a form is a defined object: You can set its properties (e.g., background color) to alter its appearance, you can use its methods (e.g., Close) to perform basic actions. The key to an object-oriented environment is to learn which objects are available and to understand their properties and methods.

PROGRAMMING ENVIRONMENT

Even beyond basic structure and syntax, DBMS vendors have several choices about how to create a programming language. Perhaps the biggest choice is exactly where the language will be used. There are three common choices: (1) within the database forms and reports, (2) within the query system as an extension to SQL, and (3) hosted within separate programs outside the DBMS (embedded SQL). Vendors sometimes support all three methods. The three approaches are illustrated in Figure 7.2. Microsoft Access predominantly relies on code written within the forms or reports. Oracle extends the SQL language with PL/SQL additions within individual queries. Both vendors also provide additional tools that enable external programs to host embedded SQL commands.

The location, or environment, of the language affects what it can do, how it is used, and what you will have to learn. For example, to embed SQL within an external program, if you already know the host language (e.g., C++ or COBOL), you only have to learn how to transfer data between SQL and the host language. On the other hand, languages inside the DBMS have their own logic and syntax, so you have to learn an entirely new system.

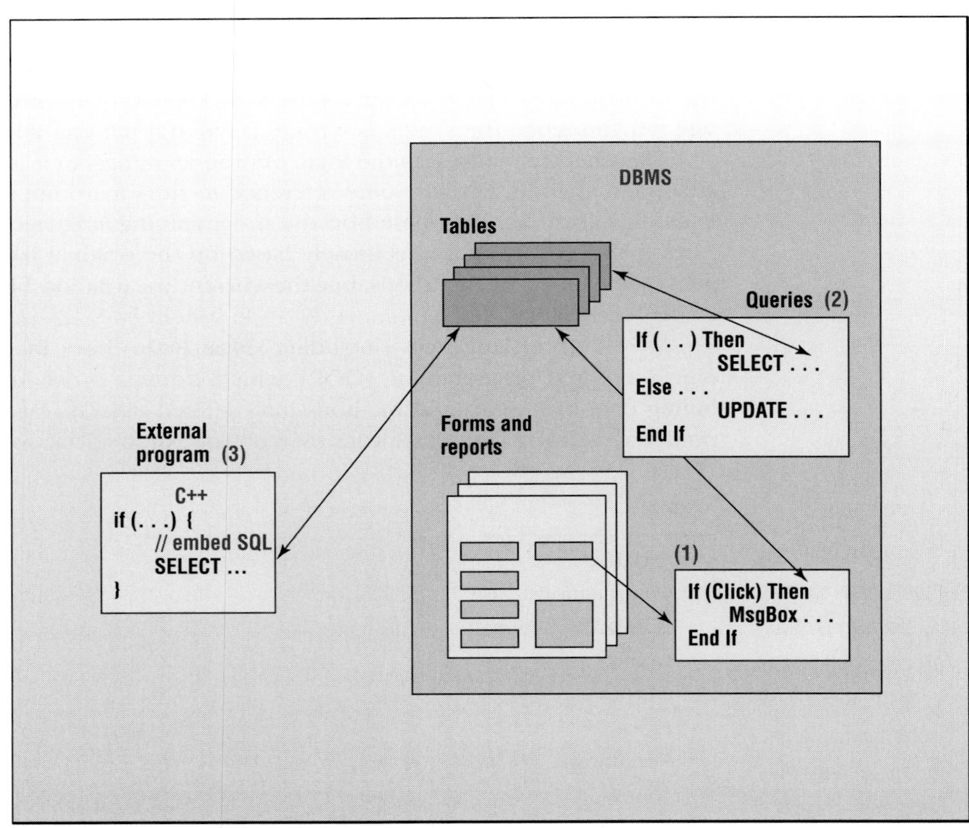

FIGURE 7.2 Three common methods to use code with a DBMS. (1) Within forms and reports. (2) Within queries as an extension to SQL. (3) Embedded within an external program.

FIGURE 7.3 Older programs were written in one large (monolithic) piece and were in complete control. Notice the need to wait for user input.

External languages provide the most flexibility, since your host program can perform any task. On the other hand, you have to write the entire code. Internal DBMS languages may have a limited number of features, but they are more tightly integrated with the DBMS. For example, you could use a form generator to create a form and then add a few lines of code to improve the way the form works for the user. To create the same form with an external language, you would have to write all of the code to display the form and respond to user choices.

WINDOWS ENVIRONMENT

The Windows interface has significantly changed the way programs operate. In the "old days," each program had its own style. The programmer had to design every aspect of the user interface. Consequently, users had to learn different commands to use each program. Also, the program was in control from the start of the session to the end. As illustrated in Figure 7.3, each **monolithic program** was in complete control, was separate from other programs, and rarely shared data. A common feature of these programs was waiting for the user to enter data, displaying a new prompt, waiting again. This approach causes two basic problems: (1) It forces users to deal with the program in exactly one way, and (2) it results in wasted time while waiting for user input.

Today the user and the operating system (Windows) have control of the computer. As a developer, you write **procedures** that are called by the user or the operating system to perform a specific task. When the task is accomplished, control is returned to the operating system. As illustrated in Figure 7.4, most procedures

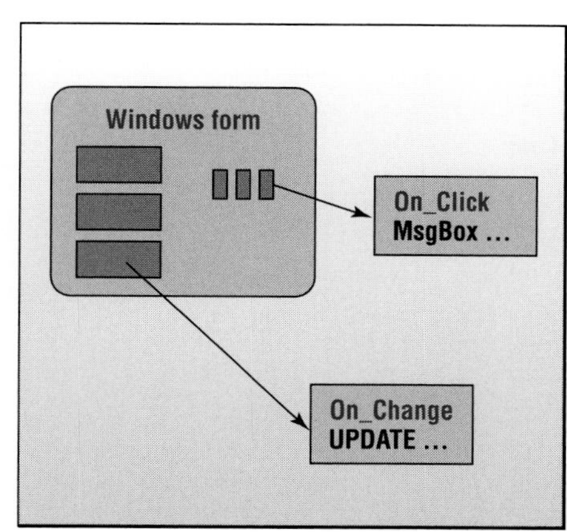

FIGURE 7.4 Event-driven Windows programming. Your code is written in small modules that are called when the user triggers some event.

run independently of the others. As the user performs some task, the event triggers your code to run. A key aspect of developing systems is to identify which of the many events should **trigger** your code. From the programmer's perspective, this approach has two important aspects. First, you have to decide where to put your code (i.e., which events need special handling). Second, you must avoid interrupting the user—keep your code short and let the user choose which sequence to follow.

In many database management systems—especially Oracle—triggers can also be defined directly on the data tables. Your code can be triggered to run whenever a piece of data is changed, added, or deleted.

The details about how events interact and how to use events to build an application are covered in Chapter 8. The important lesson for now is that you need to know where to write your code. Within Microsoft Access the answer is to create a form and store the code "behind" a control on the form. For example, you might put a command button on a form. When the user clicks the button, your code will be executed. Use the right mouse button and select Build Event to bring up the program code window.

DATA ON FORMS

When you need a user to enter data, you will create a form. Forms are also used to display data and results of computations. Each control on the form represents a type of data associated with that form. In Chapter 6 these controls are used to store data into the data tables—the control data is **bound** to a table. You can also create unbound controls that will hold and display data on a form temporarily. When the form is closed, the unbound data disappears. You can use unbound controls when you want users to enter raw data. Then your procedure performs computations on the data and stores it in the database.

Data Controls

Procedures treat data controls on forms much like any other data variable. As shown in Figure 7.5, to calculate and display the tax due on a sale, use a line similar to [ctlTax] = taxRate*Total. Note that the brackets are optional, and the line could have been written as Tax = taxRate*Total. However, this second version should raise several warning flags. Read that program line by itself. The objective is clear: Compute the tax owed. The problem lies in what the variables mean. What is "Tax"? If you

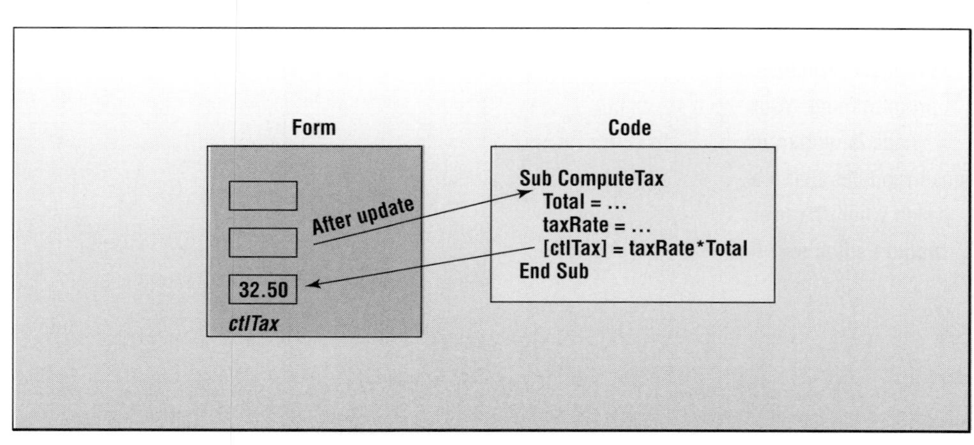

FIGURE 7.5
Data variables and controls. Controls on a form are treated like any other variable. When data is transferred to a text box, it is automatically displayed. But be careful in naming the controls so you know they are different from a program variable.

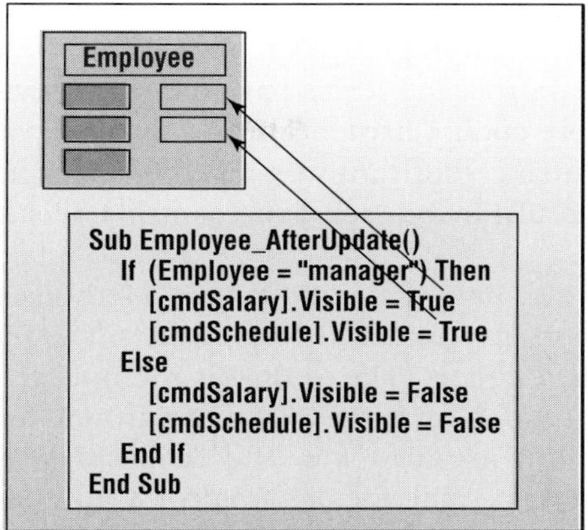

Employee
Sub Employee_AfterUpdate()
If (Employee = "manager") Then
[cmdSalary].Visible = True
[cmdSchedule].Visible = True
Else
[cmdSalary].Visible = False
[cmdSchedule].Visible = False
End If
End Sub

FIGURE 7.6
Code to set properties. With a few lines of code, employees can see forms tailored to their needs.

read this line in a procedure written by someone else, how do you know that the result is displayed on the form?

One solution to making your programs easier to read is to use a naming convention to name your variables and your controls. **Naming conventions** provide guidelines on how to name each object in the database so that other programmers can recognize the purpose and use of the object. For example, the text box that displays the tax owed could be named ctlTax or txtTax. Then other programmers would know that it is a control or a text box, and the result will be displayed automatically on the form.

The full name of a control describes its location, for example, Forms!TaxForm!ctlTax. The full name is useful when you want a procedure to change a value on a different form. You can set or retrieve data from a control on any open form or subform. However, be careful. If you change the name of the form, you will have to manually change all the code that refers to that form. In Microsoft Access the syntax is slightly different for subforms. For example, an OrderItem subform might be embedded on an Order form. To access the data in the SubTotal control on the subform, use the following command: Forms!Order!OrderItem.Form!SubTotal.

Data stored in controls is treated as a Variant data type. Hence you will often use the IsNull and VarType functions to check whether a user has entered a value and to verify the type of data. Remember, you do not want to control the order in which the user enters data. Consequently, users might click a button to execute your code before they have completed the data entry. Hence your code should check the data and display a warning message if any problems occur. Actually, your code should first try to resolve any problems, perhaps by using default values.

Control Properties

Another exciting use of code on a form is the ability to set the properties of the controls and the form itself. The goal is to help the user deal with your form by altering properties in response to some event. Consider the example illustrated in Figure 7.6, which is an entry form for employees. Employees click the buttons to bring up data entry forms and print reports. Most employees see only the three buttons on the left. The two on the right are invisible. However, if a manager uses the form, your code makes the two additional buttons visible. Of course, some additional security issues need to be resolved. The point of the example is that with a few lines of code, you can tailor a form for different groups of workers.

Keep in mind that controls and forms have many properties. Almost all of them can be set from procedure code. Chapter 8 provides some examples of how you can use these properties to make your forms easier to use. For now, you should review the properties that are available for each basic control and start thinking about how you might use them.

Controls and forms also have defined methods. Methods are functions that your procedure can call to perform predefined operations. The most common methods are SetFocus, Undo, and Requery. The SetFocus method gives the specified form (or control) the focus—which brings it to the foreground and sends keystrokes to the active control. You can use it to alter the default data entry order. For example, if a user enters a certain value for one control, your code can direct the focus to a new control; perhaps customers from California have to fill out an order form in a special way. Then AfterUpdate code could make the optional controls visible and set the focus to the first of those controls (e.g., [ctlLicense].SetFocus). The Requery method is another useful function—it forces a form or control to get updated data. In most situations the form retrieves data when it is first loaded. If you manually change an element of data, you often have to tell the form to requery the database to find matching values. This function is often used for subforms and combo boxes.

Internal Forms Commands

Some operations you will want to perform cannot be accomplished with data control properties and methods. For example, you might need to open a new form, print a report, or run some other application such as Microsoft Excel. To perform these operations, Microsoft Access provides the DoCmd object. This object also provides control over the form in terms of which data is currently displayed. For example, there are Find commands and GoToRecord commands. Additionally, this object can be used to initiate virtually any command that is listed on a menu.

The DoCmd object provides a few subcommands that you will find useful in a variety of situations. For example, when an operation will take a while to finish, you can force the cursor to become an hourglass to indicate to the user that the computer is busy. There are also commands to transfer data from the database into a different application format, such as a spreadsheet. Details of these commands are available in the Microsoft Access Help system. If you search for DoCmd, you can get a list of all the corresponding methods and sample code to show how they are used.

USING PROGRAMS TO RETRIEVE AND SAVE DATA IN THE DATABASE

Procedural code is often used to provide more flexibility and to handle situations that are too complex or too hard to do in standard SQL. Consequently, code is often used to update or alter data stored in the database. In most cases SQL is combined with, or embedded in, a procedural language. The goal is to keep all of the power of the SQL commands and to add flexibility.

There are two basic approaches to embedding SQL into a procedural language. The first approach uses code and variables to build an SQL statement, which is then executed independently. The second approach uses code to examine an SQL query one row at a time. Some systems, such as Microsoft Access, support both techniques for integrating SQL with a procedural language.

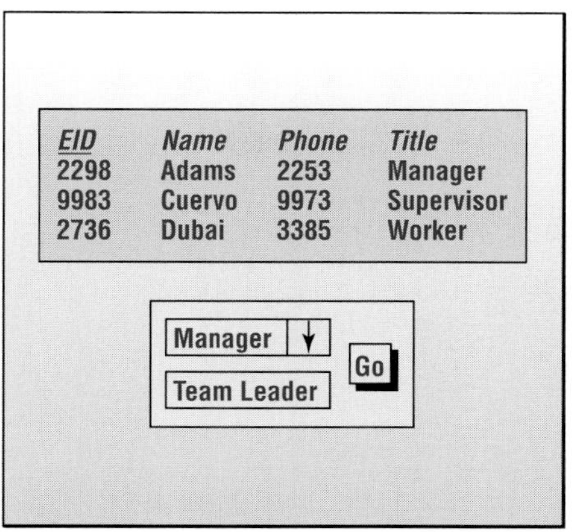

FIGURE 7.7 Embedded SQL example. Users want to change job titles. Use code to build an UPDATE statement that picks up the values from the form controls.

Building SQL Statements with Code

As described in Chapters 4 and 5, SQL is a powerful language that operates on an entire set of data with one command. In almost all cases, using an SQL command to change data is better than trying to write your own procedural code. Three common situations arise where you need to build custom SQL code: changing data, inserting or copying data, and deleting data.

Update

Sometimes it is not possible to build a query ahead of time. For example, you might need to collect basic information from the user and then update a table based on that information. Perhaps a company decides to change job titles, so that everyone who was a "manager" will be called a "team leader," and so on. As a database developer, it would be easy for you to write the SQL Update query to make this change. But what if there are hundreds of changes, or what if you want to enable users to make the changes themselves? As shown in Figure 7.7, one solution is to create a form that has two controls and a command button. The user selects a current title (Manager) with a combo box and then types in a new title (Team Leader) in a text box. Clicking the button runs your code, which builds and executes a query to replace all occurrences of the old title with the new one.

The biggest question here is choosing the event that should trigger the code. Consider what happens if you put just the two text-based controls on the form. You could put the code on the AfterUpdate event for the NewTitle. Whenever the user finishes entering the NewTitle, your code will run an Update query and immediately change the data. The drawback to this approach is that it assumes people will always enter the OldTitle first and then the NewTitle. A better solution is to let users enter data in any order and then click on the command button when they are ready to update the database. The code to perform the update is outlined in Figure 7.8. The basic objective is to build the SQL UPDATE command as a string. As shown in Figure 7.9, the values entered into the form controls will be substituted into the UPDATE command.

The value of the strSQL string is also shown in Figure 7.9. Notice that the command will not run yet. It must have quotation marks around the two titles, because they are text values. The quotation marks can be appended just like any other character; however, you have to be careful with quotation marks—the computer might

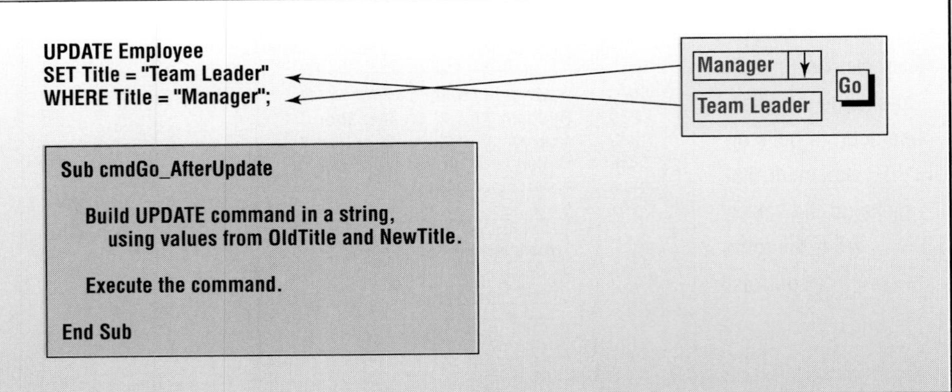

FIGURE 7.8
SQL UPDATE command to change the data. Code is triggered when the user clicks the Go button. The code builds the SQL statement as a string, then the SQL command is executed.

misinterpret them as marking the end of text. Figure 7.10 shows one way around the problem: you can define a variable as the quotation mark.

After the string is created, you use the **DoCmd.RunSQL** statement to execute it. The one remaining catch is that an UPDATE or DELETE command will cause a message box to be displayed to the user—asking for verification of the operation. Most of the time you will want to run the SQL statement without notifying the user. As shown in Figure 7.10, to prevent the message box from appearing, you turn off the warnings. Be sure to turn them back on after the SQL statement runs.

When you write code to build SQL statements, you will quickly find that the SQL syntax is fussy and difficult to correct in code. Rarely will your SQL statement run correctly the first time. There is a way to find errors and create the proper SQL statement. Create the SQL statement the best you can and then set a break point on the first statement in the subroutine. Now run your code. When the code stops, display the strSQL statement in the Debug window. You can use the debugger to step through the code line by line. As shown in Figure 7.11, at each line you can examine the strSQL statement and watch it being built.

Developers often make two types of errors when building SQL strings: (1) They leave out spaces, or (2) they get the quotation marks wrong. Before your string is executed, check it carefully. Another useful trick is to copy the entire SQL statement and paste it into a new SQL query window. Let the Query system build, and test your query for syntax errors. When the query is correct, make the appropriate changes to your code. While testing, you should also comment out the SetWarnings lines so that you can see any messages generated by the system. For example, you will probably want to cancel a command that says it is about to delete several hundred rows of your data.

```
Sub cmdGo_AfterUpdate
   Dim strSQL As String

   strSQL = "UPDATE Employee SET Title = " & txtNewTitle _
              & "WHERE Title = " & cboOldTitle

End Sub

   str SQL:

   UPDATE Employee SET Title = Team Leader
   WHERE Title = Manager
```

FIGURE 7.9
Building the SQL UPDATE command. The command is built by concatenating strings. Start with the fixed text (UPDATE . . .) and then append the titles that were entered on the form. The problem with the current strSQL command is that it needs quotation marks around the titles.

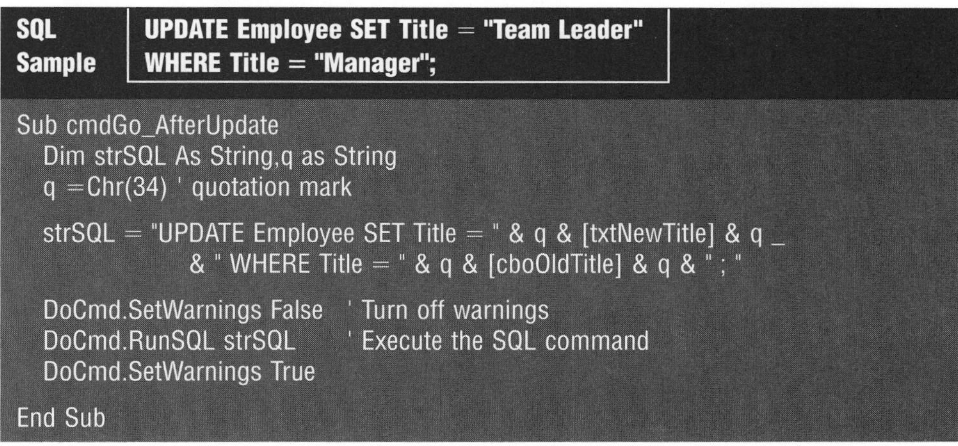

SQL Sample
UPDATE Employee SET Title = "Team Leader"
WHERE Title = "Manager";
Sub cmdGo_AfterUpdate
Dim strSQL As String,q as String
q =Chr(34) ' quotation mark
strSQL = "UPDATE Employee SET Title = " & q & [txtNewTitle] & q _
& " WHERE Title = " & q & [cboOldTitle] & q & " ; "
DoCmd.SetWarnings False ' Turn off warnings
DoCmd.RunSQL strSQL ' Execute the SQL command
DoCmd.SetWarnings True
End Sub

FIGURE 7.10 Adding quotation marks to SQL strings. It is safer to define a new variable (q) than to try to put the quotation marks in by themselves. By themselves, they can be misinterpreted as ending a piece of text. The variable is also easier for people to read.

INSERT Into (Values)

The basic purpose of the SQL INSERT command is to insert a row of data into an existing table. For the most part automatically this operation handles the form. However, there are times when a user will type some basic data into one form, and you will want to store the data into a table that is not serviced by that form.

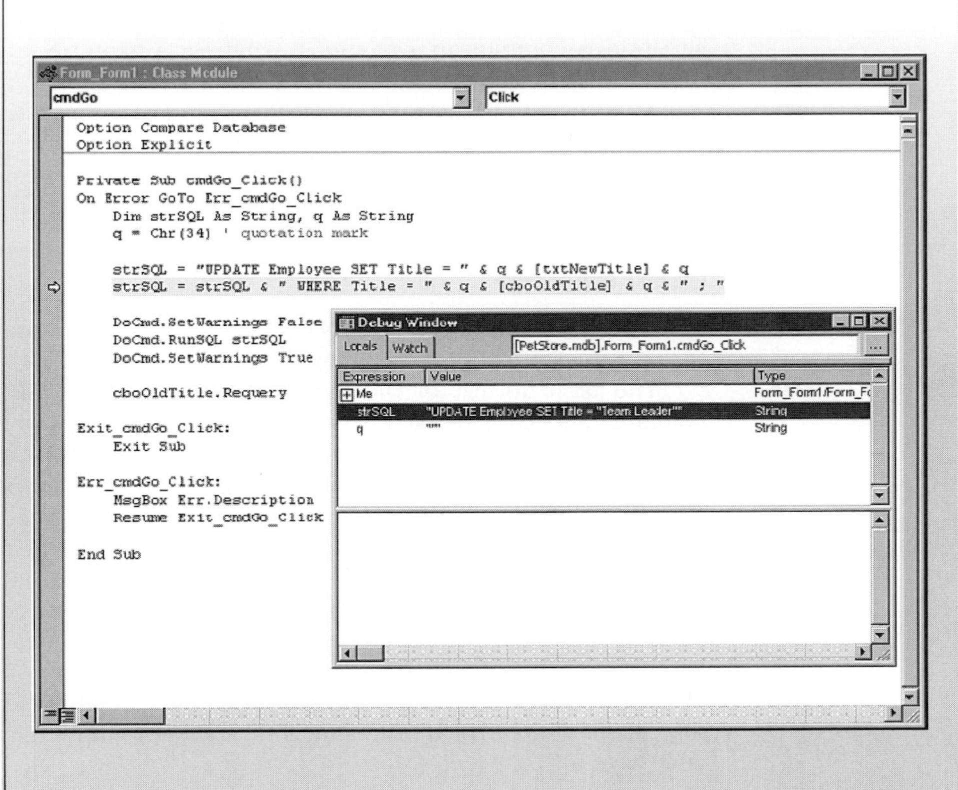

FIGURE 7.11 Microsoft Access debugging. By stepping through each line, you can watch the strSQL statement being built.

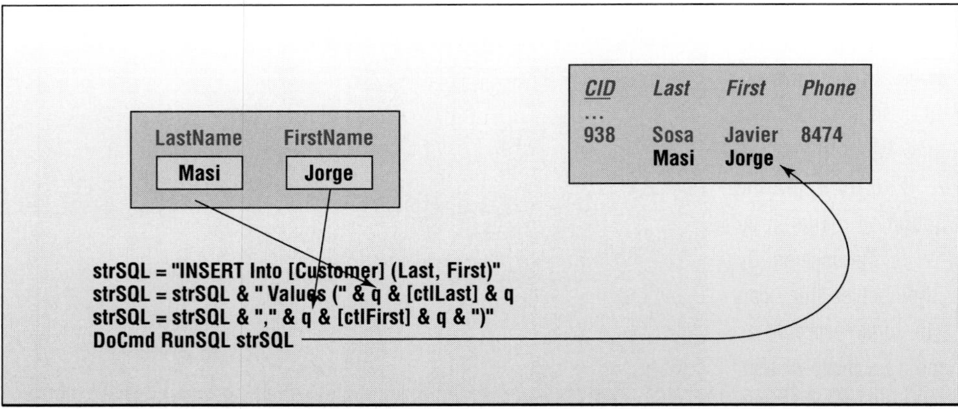

FIGURE 7.12 Insert new data into a table. A clerk enters a new customer on the Order form. The SQL code creates a new entry in the Customer table and inserts those new values. Remember that string data must be surrounded by quotation marks.

For example, an order form might ask a clerk to enter the customer's name. After the name is entered, your code could check to see whether the customer already exists. If the customer does not exist, the code would add a new row in the Customer table. One way to accomplish this task is to use the SQL INSERT command. As illustrated in Figure 7.12, the code is straightforward. Build the SQL statement as a string and append the values from the form controls.

A useful option with the INSERT command enables you to enter data for just the columns that have data. You do not need to have entries for every column. Simply list the columns you want, along with the corresponding values. After you create the new row, you might want to bring up a customer form with that data, so the clerk/user can enter additional information about the new customer. This situation is common in a relational database. Chapter 8 explores the problem in more detail.

As you might guess, the SQL INSERT command is a somewhat painful means to enter data into a table. It is generally used for inserting only one or two rows at a time. However, for some applications you might have to create an entire form based on INSERT commands. In particular, it is heavily used when SQL is embedded into an external host language.

INSERT Into (Copy)

A second variation of the SQL INSERT command is more powerful. It can be used to copy rows of data from one table into a new table.

The basic format of the INSERT command is INSERT Into {new table and columns} SELECT {any data from any query}. Again, if your users fully understand SQL, they could create this SQL statement themselves. However, most of the time, it is wise to have them enter some basic data on a form and then use code to build the SQL command for them.

There are also times when you want to automate a SQL process. A common situation is when you need to archive data. In the example in Figure 7.13, you want to remove old customer files from your database. If customers have not placed an order within a certain number of months, there is no point in keeping their data. Users can choose the time frame by entering the number of days since the last order into a form. Note the use of the NOT IN phrase, which first identifies those customers who have placed orders recently and then selects the opposite group (those who have not).

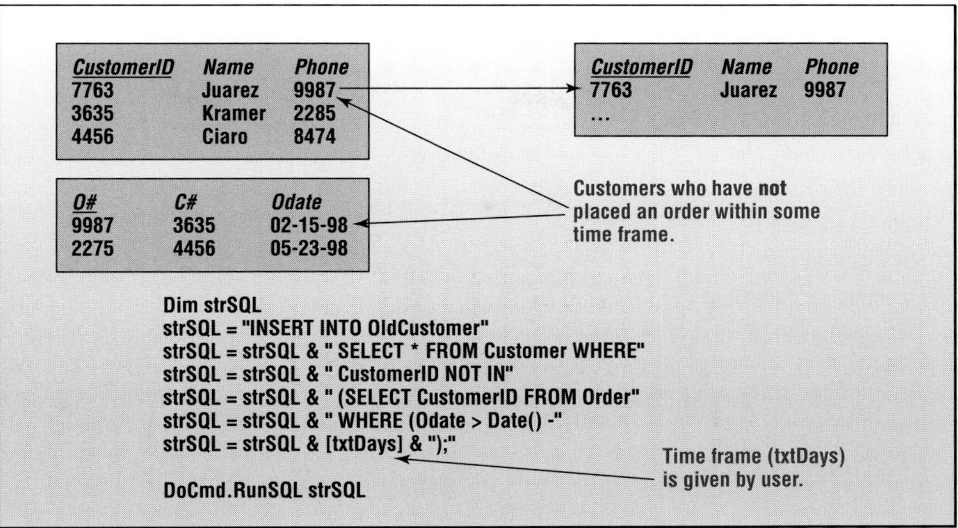

FIGURE 7.13 Code example for Insert. Copy all customer data for customers who have not placed orders recently. "Recently" is set by the number of days set by the user on a form.

Delete

To automate archival procedures, you often need to write programs. A DBMS typically has provisions to backup and restore the entire database—which requires no programming. However, many times you will want to archive or move a portion of the database. For example, you might want to move data for all customers who have not placed orders recently. You can use the INSERT Into command in the preceding section to copy the customer data to a backup table. Then you need to delete the data from the current database.

The syntax for the SQL DELETE command is described in Chapter 6. As shown in Figure 7.14, the key for this example is that the INSERT and DELETE commands can use the same WHERE condition. You must always be careful when deleting data. By building the WHERE condition separately and then using it for both statements, you ensure that your program will delete only the customer data that was copied.

Remember that deleting data in one table usually triggers cascade deletes in other tables. In this example deleting rows in the Customer table also deletes all entries for those customers in the table. If you want to keep the order data, your program will first have to copy the data from the Order table—and any other table that might be affected.

FIGURE 7.14 SQL program to backup and delete older data. Note the safety in building one WHERE statement that is used in both commands. Also note that you should backup data in related tables, such as Orders, before issuing the DELETE command.

```
strWhere = "CustomerID NOT IN (SELECT CustomerID FROM Order"
strWhere = strWhere & " WHERE (Odate > Date () - " & [txtDays] & ");"

strSQL = "INSERT INTO OldCustomer"
strSQL = strSQL & " SELECT * FROM Customer WHERE " & strWhere
DoCmd.RunSQL strSQL                    'Copy old customer data

To Do: Backup the data in related tables

strSQL = "DELETE FROM Customer WHERE" & strWhere
DoCmd.RunSQL strSQL                    'Delete from main table & cascade
```

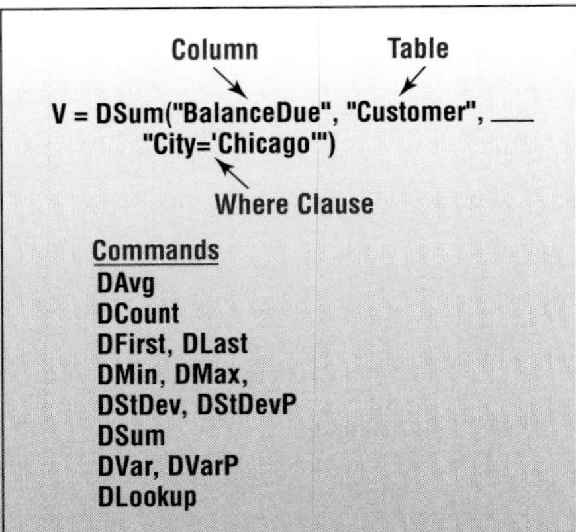

FIGURE 7.15 Data aggregation commands. These commands compute aggregate values and return the result to a program variable (v). This variable can be used for additional computations.

Data Aggregation and Computation

The SQL SELECT command provides several useful statistics (sum, average, count, and so on). However, the SELECT command is generally used to display the results. What if you need to use these values in calculations? For example, you might use the average and standard deviation to test statistical hypotheses. In this case you need to store the average and standard deviation in a programming variable so they can be used for the additional computations. There are three basic ways to compute aggregate values and use them in additional calculations.

First, if the computations are not too complex, you can use a query to generate the aggregate values. Then you build a second query, which joins the results from the first query to a new table to perform the additional computations. In most cases this method is preferred, since it requires no "programming" and usually runs fastest. However, it works only if the calculations are not very complex.

Second, as illustrated in Figure 7.15, several data commands can perform a single aggregate computation and return the result to a programming variable. The biggest drawback to these commands is that they are inefficient. It is acceptable to use one or two of these data commands in a program, but avoid putting them inside a loop or calling more than few of the functions within a program. For example, consider the OrderItem table in the Pet Store database. This table has two columns of interest: Quantity (quantity ordered) and Cost (price paid per item). Consider what happens if you use DAvg to first compute the average quantity ordered and then to compute the average item cost—each command requires a complete pass through the data table. Now examine the following SQL statement: SELECT Avg(Quantity), Avg(Cost) FROM OrderItem. Both values can be computed in one pass through the table. The SQL approach cuts your computation time in half. With a large table, the time saved can be measured in minutes or even hours.

Although the SQL approach is faster than the data commands, what if you need to use the averages for additional computations within your program? If the DBMS supports dynamic SQL statements, you could use the EXECUTE . . . INTO . . . command to move the SQL results into a programming variable. However, the Microsoft Access programming language does not support this command.

The third solution to this problem is to build a SQL query to perform the computations. Then write a program that looks at the individual rows of the result and retrieves the data for use in other computations. This general procedure is described in the next section.

Data Access Object (DAO) Programming and Cursors

SQL is a powerful language. By using programming strings to build SQL statements, you can accomplish many tasks with a few lines of code. However, remember that SQL always operates on sets or multiple rows of data. What if you need to examine one row of data at a time?

A related question is, Why would you need to examine one row of data at a time? The basic answer is that it is sometimes faster to avoid SQL, and it is sometimes easier to think of a solution that looks at one row of data at a time. As shown in the preceding section, if you need to perform several aggregate computations on a table, it is best to use SQL to make one pass through the table and compute the values at one time. In other cases you might need computations that are too complex to write in SQL. For instance, you might have complex conditions to test while computing a value. Another common situation arises when you want to compare data from one row with values in a previous row. For instance, consider the example in Figure 7.16, which was created from a SQL query that computed total sales for the last 5 years. Each year is stored in a new row. Now you need to compute the percent change in sales from the prior year. It is possible to perform this computation with SQL, but it is challenging. Most people find it easier to write the six or seven lines of code to solve this problem.

Purpose

As illustrated in Figure 7.16, the purpose of **Data Access Object (DAO)** programming is to track through one row at a time. The basic process is to define the table or query. Then a **cursor** or pointer highlights one row at a time. Some commands move the cursor to the next row or to the prior row; additional commands test whether the cursor is at the beginning or end of the query. You can examine or change data on the currently active row.

The key to understanding cursor programming is to recognize that only one row is active at a time. While that row is active, you can retrieve or change the values corresponding to any column. Generally, you start at the top of the query and use a MoveNext command to get the next row. This process is repeated in a loop until the program reaches the end of the query.

Some systems like Microsoft Access, can track upwards, or backwards, through the file from the end to the beginning. Sometimes you need this capability. However, you should try to avoid it, since it tends to slow the program operations.

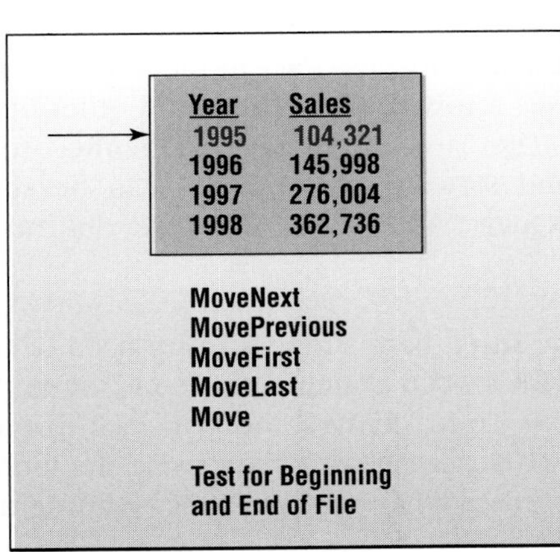

FIGURE 7.16
DAO or SQL cursors. One row is active at a time. You can retrieve or change any value on the active row. Move commands make another row active. Other commands test for the beginning or end of the query.

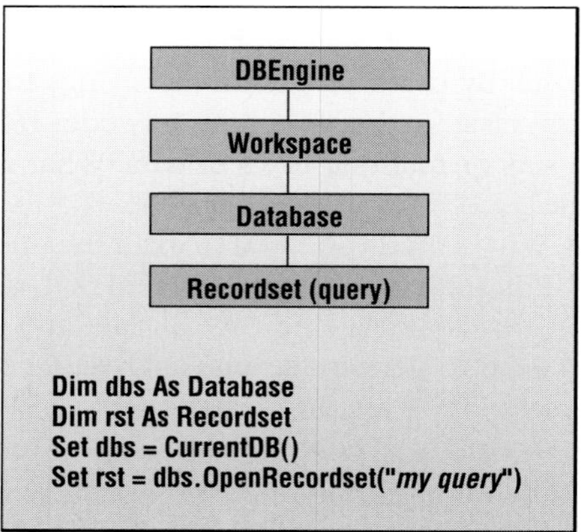

FIGURE 7.17
Data access objects. The Recordset object has most of the methods needed to track through the rows in a query.

Overview of the Process

Each DBMS uses a slightly different approach to handle cursors. Microsoft Access uses data access objects. These objects have properties and methods that are used to define the query and the operations you can perform on that query. The primary objects are shown in Figure 7.17. The top-level objects (**DBEngine,** Workspace, and Database) have only a few properties. The properties are not important to basic cursor operations. Instead, most of the common commands are defined within the **Recordset** object. The Recordset is opened using the OpenRecordset method of the Database object.

The data for the Recordset can be defined in terms of a table or a saved query. However, a powerful feature of Access is the ability to use a SQL command that you create within the program. Any SQL SELECT statement can be opened as a Recordset. You can even build that SQL statement as a string variable within the preceding program code.

The OpenRecordset function has some options that can improve the performance of your program. You need to be particularly careful with large Recordsets, databases with many users, or remote databases on a LAN. One useful option to improve performance is to open a Recordset as read only if you know that the program will not have to change the data. When the DBMS knows that no one will alter the data, it can skip some steps to improve access to the data. Another useful option is to set the cursor movement as forward only if you know that the program will never have to move back to a previous row of data. When the DBMS knows it only has to move forward, it holds less data in memory and performs fewer operations each time it retrieves a row of data. These and other options are explained in the Access Help system. They are set within the OpenRecordset command. For example, the read only and forward only options can be set with the command dbs.OpenRecordset("myQuery", dbOpenForwardOnly, dbReadOnly).

Program Structure

Figure 7.18 illustrates the three basic steps that are used to track through a query. First, define the query with an SQL statement. Second, open the Recordset—which makes the first row active. Third, define a loop to track through each row. Be sure the loop includes a MoveNext command—otherwise the loop will not end. Finally, be sure to close the Recordset when you are done—to free up internal memory.

FIGURE 7.18
Program structure to examine rows in a table. (1) Select the table or query. (2) Open the Recordset. (3) Build the loop. (4) Write the code to examine or change data on each row.

```
Set dbs = CurrentDB()                       Choose the database
strSQL = "SELECT . . . "                    Define the query
Set rst =dbs.OpenRecordset (strSQL)         Open the query to the first row

Do Until (rst.EOF)                          Loop through the query

   Read or Write data                          Read data
   in the current row                          or make changes

   rst.MoveNext                                Go to the next row

Loop                                        Repeat
rst.Close                                   Close the query
```

When you type in a program segment like this one, you should enter all of these outline statements first. For example, whenever you type a Do statement, you should automatically type the MoveNext and Loop statements. Do not try to write the code in the middle until the overall structure is in place. This practice reduces programming errors.

Moving the Cursor

Several commands will move the cursor to a new row. The most common are MoveNext and MovePrevious. Occasionally, you will need the MoveFirst or MoveLast commands to jump to the start or end of the Recordset. If you want to skip over a predefined (or random) number of rows, you can use the Move command.

One essential feature that you must remember about your database is that many people can use it at the same time. This fact could affect the results of your programs. When we think of a Recordset, we often picture it as being a fixed collection of data. But if there are many users, someone could insert a new row into a table your program is examining. Many times this change will not seriously affect your results. For example, if your program computes a total, it can only be accurate up to a certain point in time. If a new row is inserted behind your cursor movements, then the total will not include that new value. This result is not a problem as long as users understand the time dependence of the computations.

On the other hand, if your program uses more complicated cursor controls, the entire logic of the program could be wrong. For example, consider Figure 7.19. Start at the top row (Alice) and move to the next row (Carl). Now you decide to go back to the previous row (Alice). If the rows are fixed, there is no problem. However, what happens if someone inserts a new row of data (Neal) between these two, right before the program executes the MovePrevious command? Instead of moving to the first row (Alice), the cursor would move to the new row (Neal).

Any time you move a cursor in two directions, you run the risk of not returning to the row you wanted. Figure 7.20 illustrates a solution to this problem that uses bookmarks. A *bookmark* saves your location in the Recordset. In the example you set a bookmark for the first row and then move to a new row. When you want to return to the earlier row, simply restore the bookmark. Do not use a Move command.

Searching for Data

Sometimes you will need to find a specific row of data. You could use a loop and simply ignore every row that does not match your condition. However, this type of

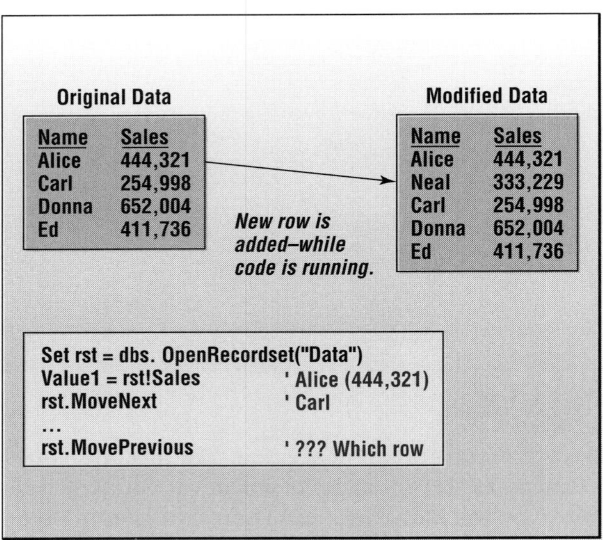

FIGURE 7.19 Multiuser problems. A new row of data might be inserted into a table while your code is running. This code reads the Alice row and moves to the Carl row. Then a row is inserted for Neal. The MovePrevious command will no longer return to the Alice row.

search is incredibly slow. Microsoft Access provides two related techniques that are more efficient: the Find and Seek commands. The Find commands can match data based on any condition—much like the SQL WHERE clause. There are four variations of the command: FindFirst, FindLast, FindNext, and FindPrevious. For example, you might use a command to locate a customer with a California address: rst.FindFirst "State = 'CA' ". The FindNext command could be used to repeat the search to locate the next row that matches the condition. The Find commands are easy to use but dangerous. They use a sequential search technique that examines every row of data in the Recordset, which can be very slow.

The Seek command is a more powerful search method. It can only be used on a Recordset that is indexed. As illustrated in Figure 7.21, you first choose the index, since a Recordset can have more than one index. In table design use the View Indexes option to see the names of the indexes available for a given table. To find a particular row, you use the Seek method and specify the comparison (equals, greater than, etc.), along with the value to be found. This key value could be specified by the user

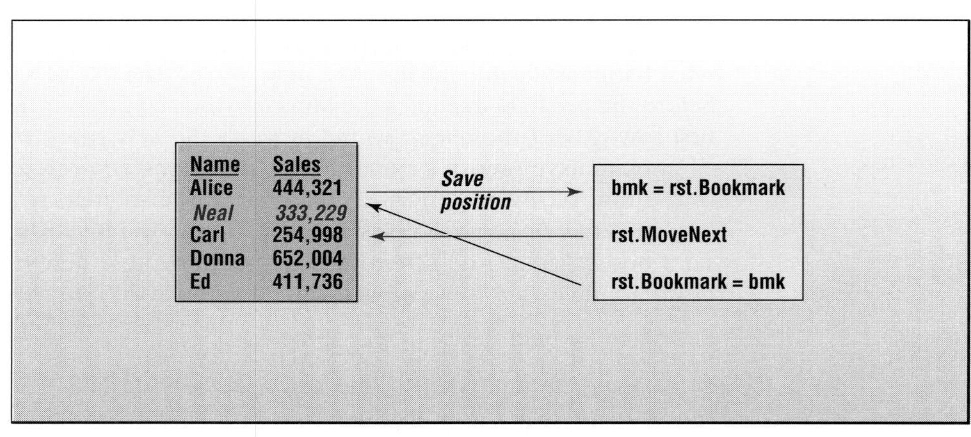

FIGURE 7.20 Bookmarks. Because users might insert a new row, it is safer to set a bookmark if you want to return to a specific row. Using Move commands would cause problems if another user inserts a new row while the program is running.

```
rst.Index = "PrimaryKey"
rst.Seek "=", keyvalue
If (rst.NoMatch = False) Then
   ' Make changes
End If
```

FIGURE 7.21 Finding data with the Seek command. The Recordset must have an index. Use the NoMatch property to verify that the row was found.

in a text box on the form, or it could be found in another table or program variable. If the value exists in the Recordset, the row cursor leaps immediately to that row.

Whichever search method you use, be certain that you test to see whether the program found the appropriate row. As shown in Figure 7.21, the NoMatch property will be set to False if the data is found.

Although the Seek method is preferred to the Find commands, it is still somewhat inefficient. In most applications the best solution is to use SQL to select only the data you want to work with. When you are tempted to use the Find command, write out a better SQL statement that uses a WHERE condition to select only the rows you want to see. Then you will not need to use any search commands. Likewise, when you are tempted to use the Seek command, try to use a SQL WHERE condition or perhaps JOIN another table. SQL is usually faster than the corresponding program code. As a bonus, SQL is also easier to write and less likely to cause errors.

Retrieving and Saving Data

Once you understand the basic operation of cursors, it is straightforward to retrieve or change the data. Just remember that you change data on one row at a time. In Microsoft Access you essentially treat the columns as variables. For example, to obtain the value in the BalanceDue column of the current row, you would use rst!BalanceDue. Figure 7.22 shows a simple program to compute the total amount owed by all customers. Of course, for a problem this simple, you would normally use an SQL command. The advantages of programming arise when the calculations are more complex. In particular, the code within the loop might have several conditions (If/Then/Else) and use data that was entered on the form.

As shown in Figure 7.23, altering data in a table is similar, but slightly more complicated than retrieving data. Again, you refer to the data with the rst!BalanceDue syntax, but this time you are assigning a new value, so the Recordset value ap-

```
Dim dblSum As Double
Dim dbs As Database
Dim rst As Recordset
Set dbs =CurrentDB()
Set rst = dbs.OpenRecordset("Customer")
dblSum = 0.0
Do Until (rst.EOF)
   dblSum = dblSum + rst!BalanceDue
   rst.MoveNext
Loop
rst.Close
MsgBox "Total Due = " & dblSum
```

FIGURE 7.22 Sample code to retrieve data. The rst!Column syntax refers to data in a specific column for the current row. Note that you would normally use SQL for this simple problem.

FIGURE 7.23
Altering data with cursor programming. Data on each row can be changed by assigning a new value to the desired column. The Edit and Update commands control the multiuser locks to prevent two users from changing the same data at the same time.

```
Dim dbs As Database
Dim rst As Recordset
Do Until (rst.EOF)
   rst.Edit
   rst!BalanceDue = rst!BalanceDue*(1 + [PctIncrease])
   rst.Update
   rst.MoveNext
Loop
rst.Close
```

pears on the left side. There is another crucial difference. Whenever you change rows of data, you must first issue a rst.**Edit** command, and after the data change, you must call the rst.**Update** method. These commands inform the DBMS that you plan to alter the data and indicate when you are finished with the changes to that row. If you want to insert a new row of data, replace the rst.Edit command with rst.**AddNew**. Then any values that you assign will be placed in a new row in the table.

The Edit and Update commands monitor and control the multiuser locking mechanism. When you issue the Edit command, the DBMS attempts to lock the current row so other users cannot alter or read the data while you are making changes. The Update command causes the DBMS to save the changes and release the locks. Be aware that whenever you alter data, there is a chance that the Edit or Update command may not be executed. For example, another user might be trying to change the same data, so the row will already be locked and the Edit command will fail. In Microsoft Access, the easiest way to deal with this problem is to use the error-handling techniques described in the next section.

HANDLING ERRORS

It would be nice if programs always ran perfectly and never experienced errors. Yet there are many sources of errors: mistakes in the code, faulty data entered by users, hardware or network failures, operating system glitches, and so on. You need to create your programs so that they can deal with errors. If you do not, the program might crash and the user will be left with a blank screen and lost data.

There are two primary philosophies for handling errors: (1) check whether every major operation is performed correctly or (2) write a special error-handling routine that is called only when any error arises. Microsoft Visual Basic relies heavily on the second method; however, you can include elements of the first approach within your code.

Error Events

Ideally, errors should never occur. More precisely, the application design and the programmer should do as much as possible to prevent errors. Where possible, the program should anticipate problems and compensate automatically—without bothering the user. However, it is generally not possible to anticipate all possible errors. If an error does arise that you have not controlled, your entire application could crash and the user will have no idea what to do. To prevent these problems, your code should always have a section to handle unexpected problems.

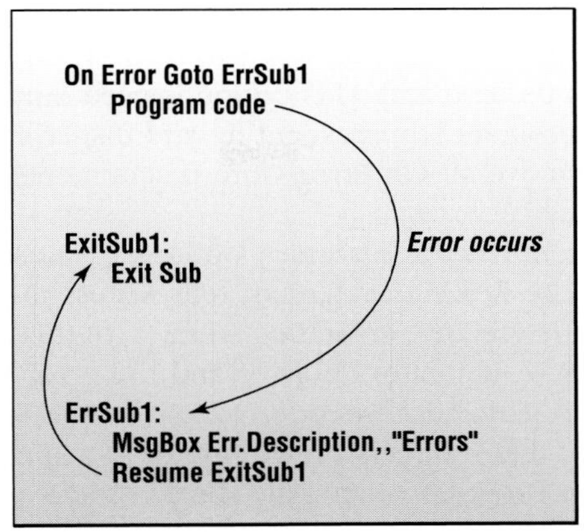
On Error Goto ErrSub1
Program code
ExitSub1:
Exit Sub
Error occurs
ErrSub1:
MsgBox Err.Description,,"Errors"
Resume ExitSub1

FIGURE 7.24
Separate error-handling code. The program normally runs straight through and exits. If an error occurs, the error subroutine is called to display a message and then exit.

In Microsoft Access an error is an *event.* For each subroutine you set up a special section that is called only when an error arises. Figure 7.24 illustrates a common situation. Usually, the program runs fine and exits without ever needing the error-handling code. However, if an error arises, the program is automatically routed to the error-handling section. In the simplest case the code uses the message box function to display the error message and then exit the subroutine. This minimalist code can catch all errors, but it does not provide the user with any options.

Remember that every subroutine (and function) in your code should have a separate error-handling section. One useful programming trick is to put a unique code number in the title of the message box to identify the subroutine. That way, when your program generates an error, you will always know which subroutine generated the message—making it easier to find the source of the error.

As you might guess, error-handling routines can become quite sophisticated. You can control error handling with two primary functions: (1) the **On Error** statement and (2) the **Resume** statement. The Err object provides information about the error and where it occurred.

The On Error statement tells Access where to go if an error occurs. The most common version is the On Error Goto label statement that directs Access to a specific error-handling routine. If you prefer to ignore errors or to test them after each primary operation, you can use the On Error Resume Next command. Figure 7.25 il-

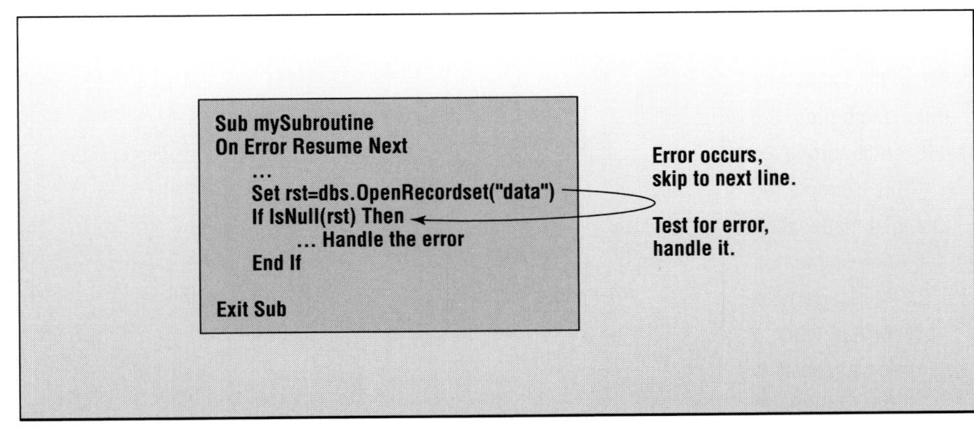
Sub mySubroutine
On Error Resume Next
...
Set rst=dbs.OpenRecordset("data")
If IsNull(rst) Then
... Handle the error
End If
Exit Sub
Error occurs,
skip to next line.
Test for error,
handle it.

FIGURE 7.25
Alternative error-handling code. You can test for common errors after each major operation. If an error arises that is not tested, the offending line is skipped and the error is ignored.

lustrates how the program skips the offending line and attempts to execute the next line of code if an error arises. A third option is to turn off error handling completely with the On Error Goto 0 command. This option is used only for testing your code; if an error occurs, the program stops executing and displays the line where the error arose. Be sure to remove all On Error Goto 0 statements before you release an application to the user.

The Resume statement has three primary options: (1) Resume, (2) Resume label, and (3) Resume Next. The Resume statement tells Access to go back and try to re-execute the line that generated the error. Be careful with this option. You could start an infinite loop: A bad line generates an error, and the error routine jumps back to try the line again, which generates a new error, and so on. The Resume label variation is a jump command that redirects the computer to a specific location. It is generally used to direct the program to an exit. The Resume Next command instructs the computer to skip to the line immediately following the one that generated the error.

Multiple Users and Concurrent Access

One of the most important features of a database is the ability to share data with many users or different processes. This concept is crucial in any modern business application—many people need to use the application at the same time. However, it does create a potential problem: What happens when two people try to change the same data at the same time? This situation is known as **concurrent access.** Consider the example of a mail-order system shown in Figure 7.26. The company records basic customer data and tracks charges and receipts from customers. Customers can have an outstanding balance—which is money they currently owe. In the example, Jones owes the company $800. When Jones makes a payment, a clerk receives the payment and checks the current balance ($800). The clerk enters the amount paid ($200), and the computer subtracts to find the new balance due ($600). This new value is written to the customer table, replacing the old value. So far, no problem. A similar process occurs if Jones makes a new purchase. As long as these two events take place at different times, there is no problem.

However, what happens if the two transactions do occur together? Consider the following intermingling: (1) The payments clerk receives the payment, and the computer retrieves the current amount owed by Jones ($800). (2) The clerk enters the

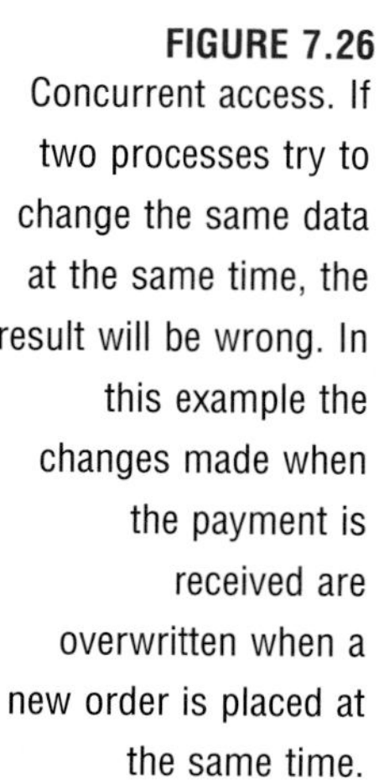

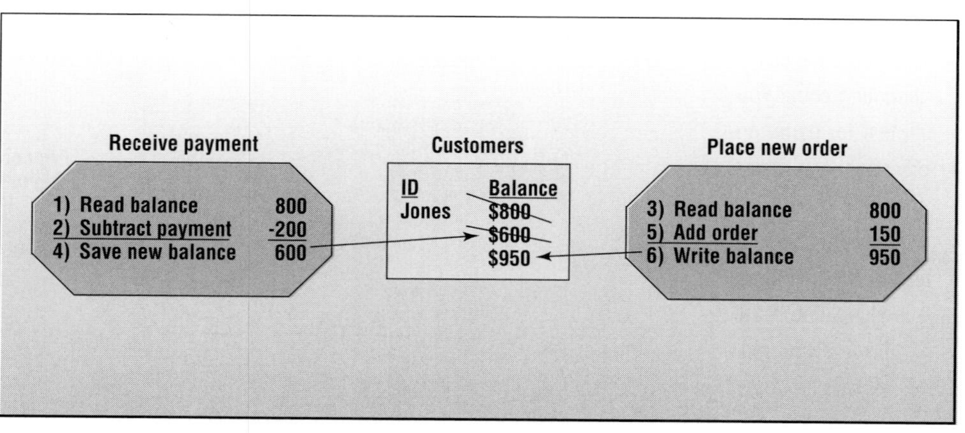

FIGURE 7.26
Concurrent access. If two processes try to change the same data at the same time, the result will be wrong. In this example the changes made when the payment is received are overwritten when a new order is placed at the same time.

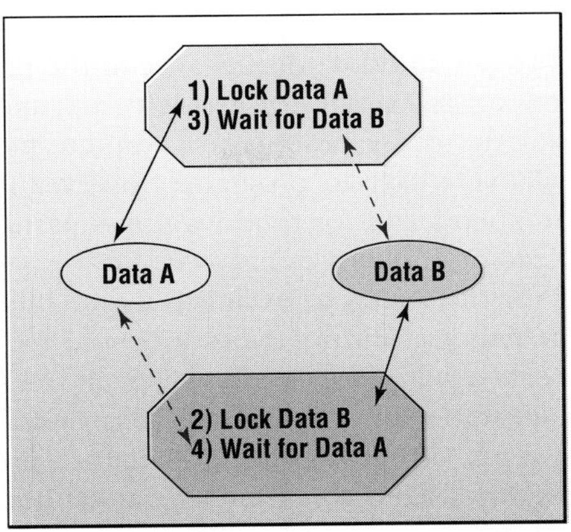

FIGURE 7.27
Deadlock. Process 1 has locked Data A and is waiting for Data B. Process 2 has locked Data B and is waiting for Data A. To solve the problem, one of the processes has to back down and release its lock.

$200 payment. Before the transaction can be completed, Jones is on the phone with a different clerk to place an order for $150 of new merchandise. (3) This clerk's computer also reads the current balance owed ($800) and adds the new purchases. Now, before this transaction can be completed, the first one finishes. (4) The payments clerk's computer determines that Jones now owes $600 and saves the balance due. (5) Finally, the order clerk's computer adds the new purchases to the balance due. (6) The order computer saves the new amount due ($950). Customer Jones is going to be justifiably upset when the next bill is sent. What happened to the $200 payment? The answer is that it was overwritten (and lost) when the new order change was mixed in with the receipt of the payment.

Multiuser Databases: Concurrent Access and Deadlock

Concurrent access is a problem that arises when two processes attempt to alter the same data at the same time. When the two processes intermingle, generally one of the transactions is lost and the data becomes incorrect. For most database operations the DBMS handles the problem automatically. For example, if two users open forms and try to modify the same data, the DBMS will provide appropriate warnings and prevent the second user from making changes until the first one is finished. Similarly, two SQL operations (e.g., UPDATE) will not be allowed to change the same data at the same time.

Even if you write program code, the DBMS will not allow two processes to change the same data at the same time. However, your code has to understand that sometimes a change to the data will not be allowed. This condition is often handled as an error.

The solution to the concurrency problem is to force changes to each piece of data to occur one at a time. If two processes attempt to make a change, the second one is stopped and must wait until the first process finishes. The catch is that this forced delay can cause a second problem: deadlock. **Deadlock** arises when two (or more) processes have placed locks on data and are waiting for the other's data. An example is presented in Figure 7.27. Process 1 has locked data item A. Process 2 has locked item B. Unfortunately, Process 1 is waiting for B to become free, and Process 2 is waiting for A to be released. Unless something changes, it could be a long wait.

There are two common solutions to the deadlock problem. First, when a process receives a message that it must wait for a resource, the process should wait for a random length of time, try again, release all existing locks, and start over if it still cannot obtain the resource. This method works because of the random wait. Of the two deadlocked processes, one of them will try first, give up, and release all locks. The release clears the way for the other process to complete its tasks. This solution is popular because it is relatively easy to program. However, it has the drawback of causing the computer to spend a lot of time waiting—particularly when there are many active processes, leading to many collisions.

A better solution is for the DBMS to establish a global lock manager as shown in Figure 7.28. A lock manager monitors every lock and request for a lock (wait). If the lock manager detects a potential deadlock, it will tell some of the processes to release their locks, allow the other processes to proceed, and then restart the other processes. It is a more efficient solution, because processes do not spend any time waiting. On the other hand, this solution can be implemented only within the DBMS itself. The lock manager must be able to monitor every process and its locks.

For typical database operations with forms and queries, the DBMS handles concurrent access and deadlock resolution automatically. When you write code to change data, the DBMS still tries to handle the situation automatically. However, the DBMS may rely on you to back out your transaction. Systems like Microsoft Access simply generate an error when your code tries to update a data row that is already locked. It then becomes your responsibility to handle the problem. The simple solution is to cancel the change, but in many cases, you or the user might prefer to wait and retry the operation.

Errors and Data Locks

Simple database errors can often be handled by canceling the operation and exiting the subroutine. If users want to retry the operation, they can start over and repeat the steps that brought them to the problem. If the problem is with your code, the error will repeat and you can fix it. If it was a temporary glitch in hardware, software, or a network, the operation should work fine the second time. However, some errors should not be ignored.

Figure 7.29 shows an error arising from a collision of user changes in a multiuser environment. The DBMS cannot allow two people to change the same data at the same time (concurrent access), because some of the changes will be lost. A com-

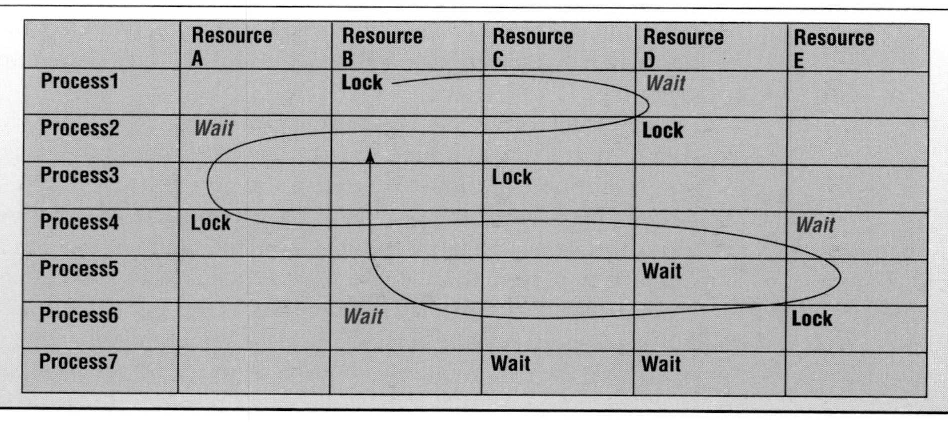

	Resource A	Resource B	Resource C	Resource D	Resource E
Process1		Lock		*Wait*	
Process2	*Wait*			Lock	
Process3			Lock		
Process4	Lock				*Wait*
Process5				Wait	
Process6		*Wait*			Lock
Process7			Wait	Wait	

FIGURE 7.28
Lock manager. A global lock manager tracks all locked resources and associated processes. If it detects a cycle, then a deadlock exists, and the lock manager instructs processes to release locks until the problem is solved.

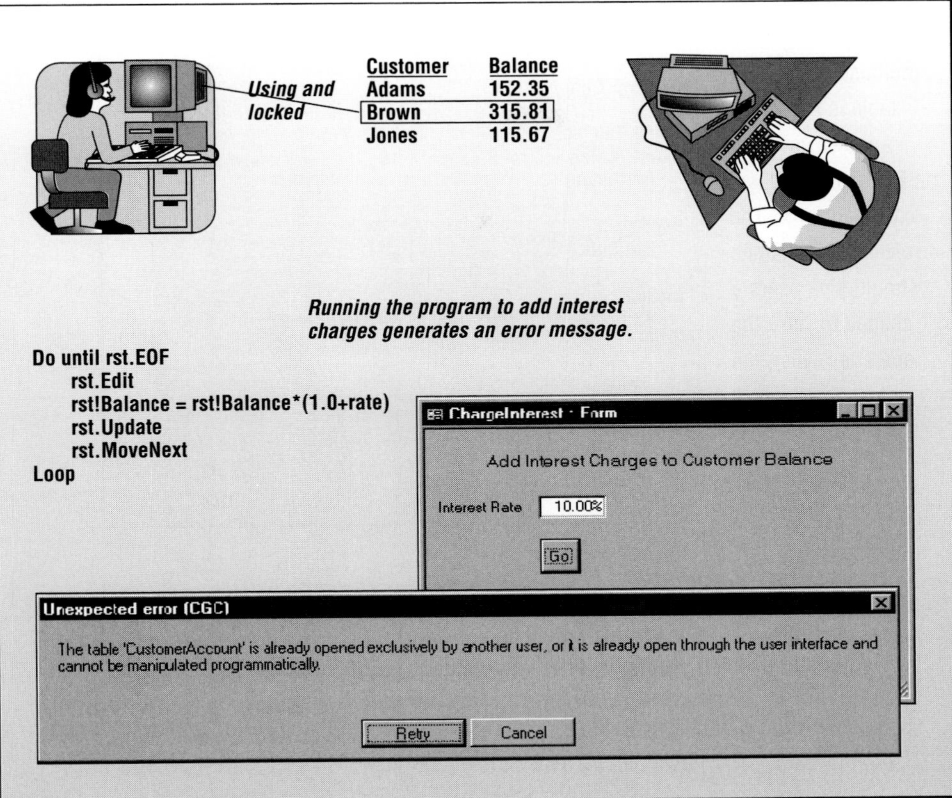

FIGURE 7.29 Concurrent access and error messages. If one user is changing a table, the second user will receive an error message. Your error-handling code should give the second user the option to cancel the attempt or to wait and retry when the first user is finished.

mon solution is to lock a portion of the data until the changes are completed. For example, the DBMS might lock a portion of a table for user A. When user B attempts to run a program that uses the same data, the DBMS generates an error and calls your error-handling routine. If you exit the routine, the necessary changes will not be made and the user may have to reenter the new data.

In any routine that alters data, your error routine should give users a chance to wait for other users and then retry the changes. Figure 7.30 illustrates the basic code. The key is to use the Retry and Cancel buttons on the message box. If the user clicks the Retry button, the code tells the computer to retry the original operation (Resume). If the other user is finished with the changes, then your program will continue as if nothing had happened. On the other hand, your user can always choose to cancel the changes (Resume ExitSub).

The one drawback to the approach in Figure 7.30 is that your code cannot run unattended. If an error occurs, someone has to retry the changes. It is possible to automate the retry attempt, but you have to be careful. The easiest method is to replace the MsgBox command with a random delay and then issue the Resume command. The catch is that you need to count the number of times the program retries the operation. At some point, the program should give up and cancel the operation. So you need to add a counter to the subroutine and increment it right before the Resume statement. Then test the counter to see whether it exceeds some value. For example: If (iRetry < 10) Then Resume.

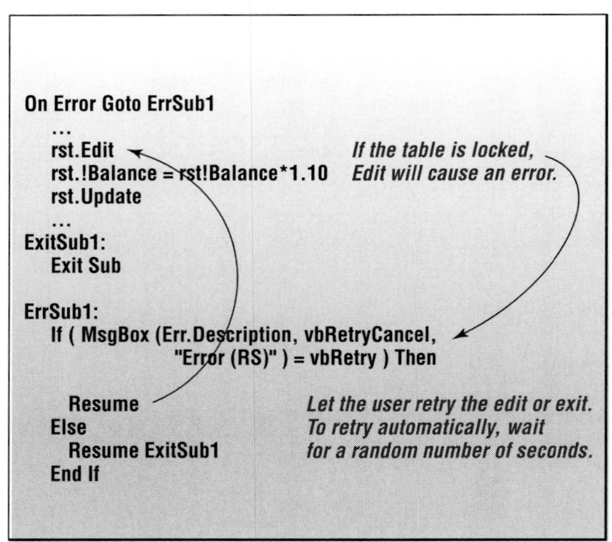
```
On Error Goto ErrSub1
   ...
   rst.Edit
   rst.!Balance = rst!Balance*1.10
   rst.Update
   ...
ExitSub1:
   Exit Sub

ErrSub1:
   If ( MsgBox (Err.Description, vbRetryCancel,
                "Error (RS)" ) = vbRetry ) Then

     Resume
   Else
     Resume ExitSub1
   End If
```


FIGURE 7.30 Handling errors with multiuser locks. If a table is locked by another user, the rst.Edit command will cause an error. The error-handling routine should give users a chance to retry the operation when the lock is released.

SALLY'S PET STORE EXAMPLE

After showing the initial forms to Sally and some of her employees you quickly realize that the system is still too cumbersome. Sally has little time (or money) to train employees to use the computer system. The sales employees are always busy and do not want to read through cluttered screens. One step you can take to simplify the screens is to make the main switchboard screen interactive. Most of the clerks need only to use the Sales, Animals, and Customer forms.

As shown in Figure 7.31, the employees can now enter their EmployeeID and the screen will show only the options that they need. The buttons are grouped into three categories: sales, purchases, and management tasks. Employees are classified into groups according to their employee level or rating. Higher-level employees need access to the higher-level tasks. The screen is considerably simplified for sales clerks who need access to only three tasks.

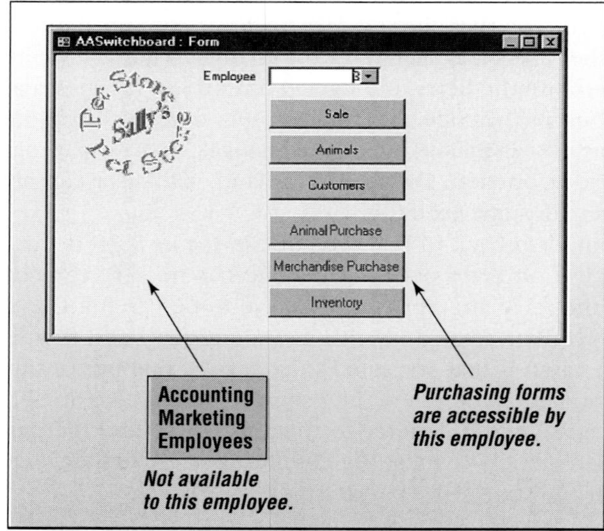

FIGURE 7.31 A simplified switchboard form. Options are displayed only for employees who need them.

FIGURE 7.32
Code to set buttons based on management level. Note the IsNull tests to avoid errors if entries are not found.

```
Private Sub EmployeeID_AfterUpdate()
On Error GoTo ErrEIDAU
  Dim varLevel, varMGTLEVEL1, varMGTLEVEL2
  If Not IsNull(EmployeeID) Then
    varLevel = DLookup("EmployeeLevel","Employee", _
                                    "EmployeeID=" & [EmployeeID])
  If Not IsNull(varLevel) Then
      varMGTLEVEL1 = DLookup("Value", "Preferences", _
                                    "KeyID=" & """" & "MGTLEVEL1" & """")
      varMGTLEVEL2 = DLookup("Value", "Preferences", _
                                    "KeyID=" & """" & "MGTLEVEL2" & """")
    End If
  End If
  cmdAnimalPurchase.Visible = False
  cmdMerchandisePurchase.Visible = False
  cmdInventory.Visible = False
  cmdAccounting.Visible = False
  cmdMarketing.Visible = False
  cmdEmployees.Visible = False
If (varLevel > Val(varMGTLEVEL1)) Then
    cmdAnimalPurchase.Visible = True
    cmdMerchandisePurchase.Visible = True
    cmdInventory.Visible = True
    If (varLevel > Val(varMGTLEVEL2)) Then
      cmdAccounting.Visible = True
      cmdMarketing.Visible = True
      cmdEmployees.Visible = True
    End If
  End If
ExitEIDAU:
  Exit Sub
ErrEIDAU:
  MsgBox Err.Description, , "Unexpected Error (EIDAU)"
  Resume ExitEIDAU
End Sub
```

This feature is provided by the code shown in Figure 7.32. The logic is straightforward. The code is activated when an employee enters a new EmployeeID. If the system used a security login for each user, the code could be activated when the form is loaded—but each employee would have to log out to change the settings for the next employee. The essential steps are as follows: (1) Make the purchasing and management section buttons invisible; (2) Look up the assigned Employee Level for the employee; (3) Look up the desired levels for access to the two sections; (4) If the employee is a first-level manager or above, make the purchasing options visible; (5) If the employee is a second-level manager or above, make the management buttons visible.

Several other improvements can make data entry easier and faster. Consider the two changes shown in the Employee form in Figure 7.33. First, to ensure consistency of data, employees should choose city names from a table. Otherwise, a city name

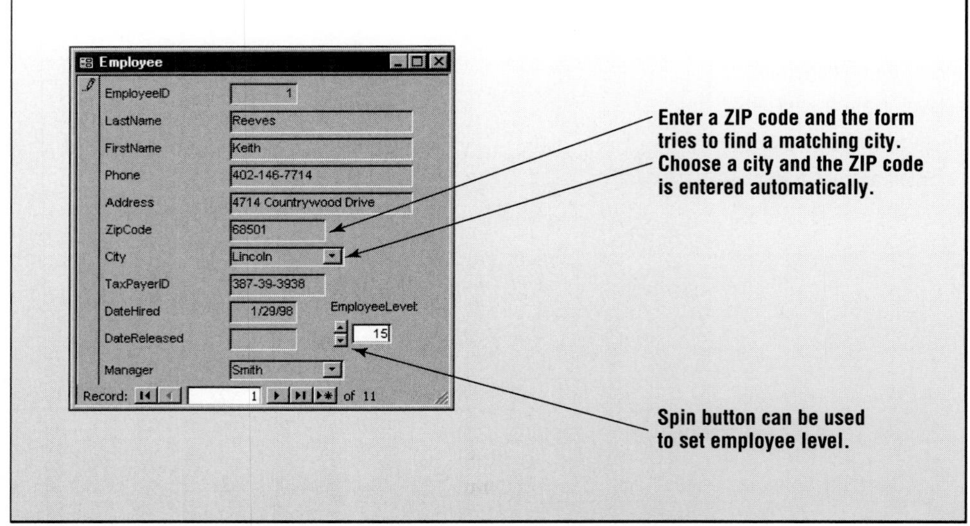

FIGURE 7.33 Improving data entry with automated look up and spin buttons. Maintaining a list of cities speeds data entry and ensures consistency in city names.

might be abbreviated or spelled differently each time. Also, choosing a city from a list is generally faster than retyping the name each time it is needed. Likewise, city and ZIP code are often related. Hence the form is designed so that when one value is entered, the DBMS automatically searches for the other value. For example, choosing a city enters a base ZIP code for that city. If you use this approach, be careful to allow users to enter nine-digit and nonnumeric postal codes.

The form in Figure 7.33 also uses a spin button to enter numeric data. Clicking an arrow increments or decrements the value by 1. Spin buttons are Active X objects that require a few lines of straightforward code. Just be sure to set minimum and maximum values on the data.

All the codes for the Employee form are in the sample database. The code to handle the ZIP codes is shown in Figure 7.34. Notice that you need a separate function

FIGURE 7.34 Procedure to handle ZIP codes and cities. A separate function converts nine-digit codes to the five-digit or text codes stored in the City table.

```
Private Sub Zipcode_AfterUpdate()
On Error GoTo ErrZCAU
   Dim strZipShort As Variant, newCityID As Variant
   strZipShort = Get5DigitZipCode(ZipCode)
   newCityID = DLookup("CityID", "City", _
                        "ZipCode=" & """" & strZipShort & """")
   If Not IsNull(newCityID) Then
      [CityID] = newCityID
   End If         'City table only uses 5 digit codes.
ExitZCAU:
   Exit Sub       ' But we need to store 9 digits in ZipCode.
ErrZCAU:
   MsgBox Err.Description, , "Unexpected Error (ZCAU)"
   Resume ExitZCAU
End Sub
```

FIGURE 7.35
Post's Picky Programming Hints for writing better code.

- Use a naming convention.
- Use proper indentation.
- Comment your work.
- Avoid spaces in variable names.
- Use Option Explicit.
- Recompile constantly.
- Use as many parentheses as possible.
- Split complex conditions.
- Make it easy for the user.
- Use the status bar and tooltips.
- All code must be subject to error trapping.
- Use Retry with rst.Edit sections.
- Use subroutines and functions to simplify.
- Keep backup copies.
- Never use a raw number—use Const.
- Remember that databases can be moved.
- Test applications on different hardware.
- Test all calculations by hand.

to convert nine-digit codes to the five-digit codes stored in the City table. It might be nice to use all nine-digit ZIP codes, but the table is very large; and cities usually can be identified with five-digit codes. Note that this technique for handling cities and ZIP codes can be used in many other forms.

PICKY PROGRAMMING HINTS

The programs you write must work correctly. They should also be easy to read and easy to modify. Useful applications will be created and modified by many programmers over time. By writing your code carefully, and by including appropriate comments, your code will be much easier to understand and to change later. Figure 7.35 lists some basic points you should try to follow when you write code. They are not absolute rules, but they will help you create better code.

Some companies have strict naming conventions—so that everyone understands the purpose and data type of each variable. A common method is to name each variable in terms of its data type. For example, intCustomers is an integer that counts the number of Customers, and dblSum is a double that computes a sum.

Indentation of code is crucial to writing code that other programmers can understand. For example, code within loops or conditions should be indented. The indentation visually separates the statements, makes the code easier to read, and helps the reader to spot problems.

Any experienced programmer will tell you that it is crucial to include comments in your code. Even if a section of code seems "perfectly obvious," its purpose may not be clear to other programmers. There is an art to writing good comments. A useful approach is to explain the purpose of each section. That is, explain the purpose of the code and why you chose to write it a certain way. Figure 7.36 illustrates two versions of comments for the same code. The comments in the first example simply describe each line. Because the lines of code are straightforward, the comments do not provide additional information. The comments in the second example are much

FIGURE 7.36
Sample comments. Useful comments explain the purpose of each section and explain why you chose to write the code a certain way. You can also provide hints on anticipated changes.

Weak comments

```
dblSum = 0#                              ' Initialize the accumulator
Do While Not rst.EOF                     ' Loop through the table
   dblSum = dblSum + rst!Balance         ' Accumulate the balance
   rst.MoveNext                          ' Move to the next row
Loop                                     ' End the loop
```

Useful comments

```
' Need to compute total balance from sales
' Will use a loop instead of SQL
' Because some conditions will be added later
dblSum = 0#
Do While Not rst.EOF
   ' Add condition when user provides it, for example
   ' If this customer has more than three sales past due,
   ' only count the three most recent (write off the older ones)
   dblSum = dblSum + rst!Balance
   rst.MoveNext
Loop
```

better because they explain the purpose of the section. The comments also explain why the programmer used a loop instead of SQL.

SUMMARY

You often need to write programs to perform computations, analyze data, or to make forms and reports easier to use. To create these programs, you need to understand the Windows and database environments. Programs in a Windows environment are tied to events. When the event occurs, your code is triggered. One of the most important steps is to determine which event should trigger your code.

Programming logic and the foundations of VBA are described in the following appendix. Your programs are built from several common features: loops, conditions, input, output, and subroutines. Most of the programs will consist of short subroutines. The key is to focus on the programming logic. Several features of VBA help you with the syntax—including the Help system and the automated completion system in the code editor.

Forms are the foundation for most of the coding within Access. Your programs can access data on the forms and alter the properties of the controls in response to events or data changes.

You can also retrieve and store data in any of the data tables. The best method is to use your code to build a new SQL statement based on data from the form. When you execute the statement, the data is inserted, updated, or deleted, based on the SQL statement. Another approach is to build an SQL query and then use code cursors to track through the result and examine or change each row of data.

Your programs must be able to handle a variety of errors. Microsoft Access and Visual Basic use a general On Error statement that traps all unexpected errors. With other systems you must be sure to test for errors whenever various functions are called.

A DEVELOPER'S VIEW

Miranda learned that even a good DBMS often needs some programming. You need programming to perform complex calculations, and you can use it to make the application easier to use. Just remember to let SQL do most of the work. Also, remember that there are three types of data: (1) data in tables, (2) data as variables in your program, and (3) data in controls on the forms. For your class project, you should now write any code needed to perform calculations (e.g., taxes and totals). Remember to anticipate and handle errors.

KEY WORDS

AddNew, 250
bound, 236
concatenate, 270
concurrent access, 252
cursor, 245
Data Access Objects (DAO), 245
data type, 267
DBEngine, 246
deadlock, 253
DoCmd.RunSQL, 240
Edit, 250
InputBox, 272
iteration, 273
lifetime, 268
local variable, 268
loops, 273
module, 269
monolithic program, 235
MsgBox, 272
naming conventions, 237
nested conditions, 273
On Error, 251
parameter, 275
pass-by-reference, 275
pass-by-value, 275
procedural language, 233
procedure, 235
Recordset, 246
Resume, 251
scope, 268
subroutine, 275
syntax, 233
trigger, 236
Update, 250
variable, 267

REVIEW QUESTIONS

1. Why would you need a procedural language when SQL is available?
2. Where do you put programming code in a Windows event-driven environment?
3. What are the differences between local and global variables?
4. What are the basic data types available for programs?
5. How do you transfer data from your code to a form?
6. What basic properties of controls can be set with programming statements?
7. Why is it better to build SQL statements to alter data than to use cursor (DAO) programming?
8. What is the basic structure of a program that uses cursors (DAO) to examine data from a query?
9. Why is it important to handle unexpected errors?
10. How do you trap unexpected errors?

EXERCISES

1. Write a program that adds up the numbers 1 through 20 and displays the total in a message box.

2. Create a form with three text boxes (StartingValue, EndingValue, and Result) and a command button. When the user clicks the button, add all the numbers between the starting and ending values. Display the total in the Result box.

3. Add option boxes to the form in exercise 2 so the user can choose to display the total in the Result box on the form or to place the result in a message box. Adjust the program to display the result as requested. Also, when the user selects the message box option, you should immediately hide the Result box on the form.

4. Write a short program to display a message box with an exclamation icon and the Abort, Retry, and Cancel buttons; make the Retry button the default. After the user selects a button, display the value of the selected choice in a text box on the form.

5. Write a program to define the variables and perform the calculations in the following table. Use the debug command to step through the program, and write down the results of the computations.

VARIABLES	RESULT/COMMENT
Integer: I, J Float: X, Y	
I = 3 X = 3.0	
J = 1 / I * 3	
Y = 1 / X * 3.0	
J = 72 / 50	
J = 72 \ 50	
J = (I<3) And (X>4) Or (Y>0)	
J = (I<3) And ((X>4) Or (Y>0))	
J = 2 ^ 17	

6. Write a program to define the string variables str1 and str2 and perform the computations shown in the following table. Use the debug command to step through the program, and write down the results of the computations.

COMPUTATION	RESULT/COMMENT
str1 = "abcdefghijklmnopqrstuvwxyz"	
str2 = Left$(str1, 5)	
str2 = Right$(str1, 5)	
str2 = Mid$(str1, 10, 5)	
str2 = "Robert" & "Goddard"	
Mid$(str1,21) = "AAA"	
str1 = Left$(str1,20) & "uvwxyz"	
str2 = "Goddard"	
str1 = "[LastName]="	
str1 = str1 & """" & str2 & """"	
str1 = "[LastName] =" & Chr(34) & str2 & Chr(34)	
i = Len(str1)	
c = 1.39	
str1 = "[Price] > " & c	
str2 = "[Price] > " & Format$(CStr(c), "$#,##0.00")	
str2 = "123.45"	
x = Val(str2) + 5	

7. Briefly describe five properties of controls on a form that you can control from within a program. Give an example of how you might use that property.

8. Create a form with a date text box (ctlDate) and a button. When the user clicks the button, test whether the date on the form is within 14 days of the current date. If it is, display a message box.

9. Create a form with text box and a button. When the user clicks the button, create a message box that gives two choices (OK and Cancel). If a user clicks the OK button, switch the background color of the text box between red and blue. Redisplay the message box until the user selects the Cancel button.

10. Create two forms. Form1 has a command button and a text box. Form2 has a text box. When the user clicks the button on Form1, copy the value in the text box to the text box on Form2. Move the focus to the second form.

11. Create a small database with a table of customers that includes a home and a work phone number. Write a program (DAO) to count the number of customers whose home area code is different from their work area code.

Sally's Pet Store

12. Create a purchase order form to order merchandise. You need a main form that lists the supplier data and a subform that lists the merchandise being ordered. Put a text control on the subform to compute the subtotal value of the order. Put a similar box on the main form to copy the value from the subform.

13. Create a form that has a text box for the user to enter an animal category and a percentage price increase. When the user clicks a button, update the list price of all the animals in the given category by the indicated percentage.

14. The user wants to remove all inactive customers from the current database. Inactive customers are customers who have not placed orders since a given date. Create a form that contains a text box to hold a cut-off date and a button. When the user clicks the button, copy the data for the customers who do not meet the cut-off date into a backup table. Then delete the customers from the active data table. You do not need to store the customer orders, just the basic customer data. Be sure that a legitimate date was entered before making changes to the database.

15. The user wants to see the number of animals sold during a given time period. Create a form with text boxes to accept a starting date and an ending date. Set default values to indicate the prior week (Sunday through Saturday). Include a combo box to select the category of animal. Put text boxes on the form to hold the output (count, average sale price, minimum sale price, and maximum sale price). Hint: Use the D data commands in Figure 7.15.

16. Modify exercise 14 so that the computations are performed with an SQL query and the results are displayed in a new form. Use a stop watch to compare the performance (time between button click and final results) of the two methods. You might want to test the methods with a few hundred sales.

17. Using the appropriate query, write a program that will compute the change in sales revenue by month for each category of animal. For example, the user wants to know the percentage change in sales from January to February for cats. Write a program that will compute the changes and store the results in a new (temporary) table when the user clicks a button. Then display a graph of the results.

18. Add a column called AvgOrderDays to the Supplier table. Then go through the MerchandiseOrder table and compute the average number of days between orders placed to each supplier. For example, if orders were placed with supplier 10 on 3/6/96, 8/18/96, and 9/30/96, the average is (165 + 43)/2=104.

19. Create a short form that lets the user change the name of a breed. Select the existing breed with a combo box. Use a text box to get the new name. After the user enters the new name, have your program update the breed name for the matching animals. Be sure to include the appropriate error handling. If you have a LAN, test your error code by having one computer open the table entry for the Shark breed. Then on a different computer using the same database, run your program to change the Shark breed to MiniShark.

Rolling Thunder Bicycles

20. Explain how the Rolling Thunder order form functions. In particular, why is code needed for the component choices? Outline the logic of the code used to handle the components. (Do not simply copy the code—describe each major section in a few sentences.)

21. Describe how the Rolling Thunder system estimates common dimensions (top tube length, chain stays, etc.) for bicycles that are not a standard size (e.g., 18.5-inch mountain bike).

22. The Rolling Thunder managers are not very good at developing queries, yet they need a query to examine sales by state by model type. Create a form that helps them to select a state, model type, starting date, and ending date. Then when they click a button, display the number of sales and dollar value of sales for that model in that state for the given time period. Optional: Compute the percentage of sales for the given state compared to all model types sold in that state during that time frame.

23. Add a column to the Customer table called CreditRating to hold a value from 1 to 10 (10 is the best credit rating). Write a program that generates a CreditRating for each customer based on the following rules: If the customer has never placed an order, the rating is 5. For customers who have placed orders, compute the total of their payments compared to the amount they owe. If the percentage paid is over 80 percent of what they owe, give them a credit rating of 5; otherwise, if it is less than 50 percent, give then a credit rating of 3. Next, compute the average number of payments they have made on a given bicycle. If it is four or more, subtract 1 from their credit rating. If it is under four, add 1 to their rating. If the average is less than 1.5, add two more points to their rating.

24. Write a program to update the estimated cost of components. For each component find the most recent purchase of that item and estimate the average cost. Start with the price paid (per unit) and then subtract the weighted discount applied to the order. To illustrate the weighted discount, consider an order for three items and the total value (list price * quantity received) of each item (A: 3,000, B: 4,000, C: 7,000). First compute the percentage contribution of each item to the total order (A: 21 percent, B: 29 percent, C: 50 percent). Multiply this value times the total discount for the order (A: 0.21*2000=420). Divide this result by the number of items received (A: 420/60=7). Subtract this discount from the list price for the item (A: 50 − 7 = 43). Store this new EstimatedCost in the Component table.

25. Create a form that summarizes basic financial data for the firm. The form should contain boxes to select a starting and ending date. When a button is clicked, the form should display the total sales revenue during that period. You should also estimate the cost of each bicycle sold based on estimated component costs and a cost factor of 50 percent of the frame price. Also include an estimate of the labor costs for that time period—based on the proportion of each worker's salary. Last, display the initial profit (revenue minus component, frame, and labor costs).

WEB SITE REFERENCES

Site	Description
http://www.microsoft.com/vbscript/us/vbstutor/vbsCodingConventions.htm	Microsoft Hungarian notation variable naming convention
http://www.acm.org/sigplan/	Association for Computing Machinery—Special Interest Group on Programming Languages (advanced).

ADDITIONAL READING

Bradley, J. C., and A. C. Millspaugh. *Programming in Visual Basic Version 5.0.* Burr Ridge, IL: Irwin/Mcgraw-Hill, 1997. [One of many introductory programming books. Spend some time at your local (or electronic) bookstore and choose your favorite.]

Burrows, W. E., and J. D. Langford. *Programming Business Applications with Visual BASIC.* Burr Ridge, IL: Irwin/McGraw-Hill, 1996. [One of many introductory programming books.]

McFedries, P. *Visual Basic for Applications Unleashed.* Indianapolis, IN: Sams, 1997. [One of many introductory programming books.]

Rahmel, D. *Visual Basic Programmer's Reference.* Berkeley: Osborne, 1997. [One of many introductory programming books.]

APPENDIX

Introduction to Programming

Many books will help you learn to write computer programs. The purpose of this appendix is to review the highlights of programming and to point out some of the features that are important to programming within a DBMS. If you are new to programming, you should consider reading several other books to explain the details and logic behind programming.

Variables and Data

One of the most important consequences of programming in a database environment is that there can be three categories of data: (1) data stored in a table, (2) data held in a control on a form or report, and (3) traditional data variables that are used to hold temporary results. Chapter 3 focuses on storing data within tables. Chapter 6 describes how to create forms and the role of data controls. Chapter 8 provides more details of how the three types of variables interact when building applications. For now, there are details to learn about basic programming variables.

Any procedure can create variables to hold data. A program **variable** is like a small box—it can hold values that will be used or transferred later. Variables have unique names. More important, variables can hold a certain **data type.** Common types of variables are displayed in Figure 7.1A. They can generally be classified into three categories: integers (1, 2, −10, . . .); reals (1.55, 3.14, . . .); and strings ("123 Main Street","Jose Rojas", etc.).

FIGURE 7.1A Program variable types. Sizes are given for Microsoft Access. Note that currency variables help prevent round-off errors

- Integer
  - 2 bytes
  - −32,768 to 32,767
- Long
  - 4 bytes
  - +/− 2,147,483,648
- Single
  - 4 bytes
  - +/− 3.402823 E 38
  - +/− 1.401298 E-45
- Global, Const, Static
- Double
  - 8 bytes
  - +/− 1.79769313486232 E 308
  - +/− 4.94065645841247 E-324
- Currency
  - 8 bytes
  - +/− 922,337,203,685,477.5808
- String and String*n
- Variant
  - Any data type
  - Null

Each type of variable takes up a defined amount of storage space. This space affects the size of the data that the variable can hold. The exact size depends on the particular DBMS and the operating system. For example, a simple integer typically takes 2 bytes of storage, which is 16 bits. Hence it can hold 2^{16} values or numbers between −32,768 and 32,767. Real numbers can have fractional values. There are usually two sizes: single and double precision. If you do not need many variables, it is often wise to choose the larger variables (long integers and double-precision reals). Although double-precision variables require more space and take longer to process, they provide room for expansion. If you choose too small of a variable, a user might crash your application or get invalid results. For example, it would be a mistake to use a 2-byte integer to count the number of customers—since a firm could generally anticipate having more than 65,000 customers. Along the same lines, use the Currency data type for monetary values. In addition to handling large numbers, it avoids round-off errors that are common to floating-point numbers.

Microsoft Access provides the Variant data type, which is useful when transferring data from a database table or from an input form. The Variant data type has two unique properties: (1) it can hold any type of data (including dates), and (2) it can identify missing data. If you think of a variable as a box that can hold values, you can see how it would be useful to know when the box is empty. Standard programming variables do not have a means to test for this condition. Access provides the IsNull function that will tell you whether a Variant data variable has not yet been assigned a value.

Variable Scope

The scope and lifetime of a variable are crucial elements of programming—particularly in an event-driven environment. Variable **scope** refers to where the variable is accessible, that is, which procedures or code can access the data in that variable. The **lifetime** identifies when the variable is created and when it is destroyed. The two properties are related and generally automatic. However, you can override the standard procedures by changing the way you declare the variable.

All data variables should be explicitly declared—they should be identified before they are used. The most common method is to use a Dim statement, for example, Dim i1 As Integer. In the default case the lifetime and scope of the variable depend on where the variable is created. Most commonly, the variable is created within the event procedure and is a **local variable**. When the procedure starts, the local variable is created. Any code within that procedure can use the variable. Code in other procedures cannot see the variable. When the procedure ends, the (local) variable and its data are destroyed.

Figure 7.2A shows two buttons on a form. Each button responds to a Click event, so two procedures are defined. Each procedure can have a variable called i1, but these two variables are completely separate. In fact, the variables are not created until the button is clicked. Think of the procedures as two different rooms. When you are in one room, you can see the data for that room only. When you leave the room, the data is destroyed.

However, what if you do not want the data to be destroyed when the code ends, or you want to access the variable from other procedures? You have two choices: (1) change the lifetime of the variable by declaring it static, or (2) change the scope of the variable by declaring it in a different location. You should avoid declaring a static variable unless it is absolutely necessary (which is rare). If the variable is sta-

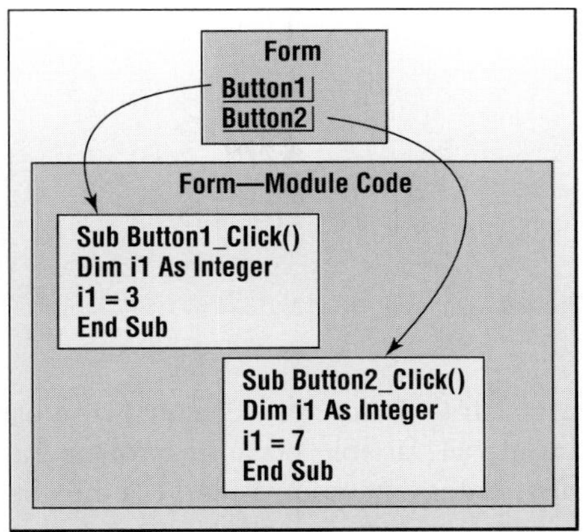

FIGURE 7.2A Variable scope and lifetime. Each event has its own procedure with independent variables that are created and destroyed each time the button is clicked.

tic, it keeps its value from the previous time the procedure was called. In the example, each time the button is clicked, the value for *i3* will remain from the prior click. You might use this trick if you need to count the number of times the button is clicked.

A more useful technique is to change where the variable is defined. Figure 7.3A shows that event procedures are defined within a form or a **module,** which is a collection of related procedures. The variable i2 is defined for the entire form or module (within the General section in Access). The lifetime of the variable is established by the form—that is, the variable is created and destroyed as the form is opened and closed. The scope of the variable is that all procedures in the form can see and change the value. On the other hand, procedures in other forms or modules do not know that this variable exists.

Procedures or functions also have a scope. Any procedure that you define on a form can be used by other procedures on that form. If you need to access a variable or a procedure from many different forms or reports, you should define it on a separate module and then declare it as global (or public).

Be careful with global or public variables. A programmer who tries to revise your code might not know that the variable is used in other procedures and might accidentally destroy an important value. On forms the main purpose of a global variable is to transfer a value from one event to another one. For example, you might need to keep

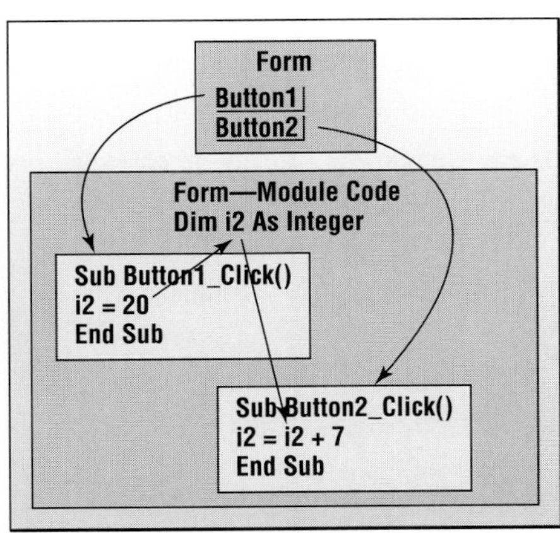

FIGURE 7.3A Global variables. Variables that are defined in the form's General section are accessible by any function on that form (or module).

FIGURE 7.4A
Common arithmetic operators. Add (+), subtract (-), multiply (*), and divide (/). Exponentiation and integer arithmetic are often used for special tasks. For example, integer arithmetic is useful for dividing objects into groups.

```
Arithmetic: + − * /
Exponentiation ^
  2^3=2*2*2=8
Integer divide \
  9\2=4
Modulus or remainder
  15 Mod 4=3, or 12+3=15
```

the original value of a text control—before it is changed by a user—and compare it to the new value. You need a global variable because two separate events examine the text control: (1) the user first enters the control, and (2) the user changes the data.

Computations

One of the main purposes of variables is to perform calculations. Keep in mind that these computations apply to individual variables—one piece of data at a time. If you need to manipulate data in an entire table, it is usually best to use the SQL commands described in Chapter 5. Nonetheless, there are times when you need more complex calculations.

Standard arithmetic operations (add, subtract, multiply, and divide) are shown in Figure 7.4A. These operators are common to most programming languages. Some nonstandard, but useful, operators include exponentiation (raise to a power, e.g., 2^3=2*2*2=8), and integer divide (9 \ 2 = 4), which always returns an integer value. The mod function returns the modulus or remainder of an integer division (e.g., 15 mod 4 = 3, since 15−12=3). These last two functions are useful when you need to know how many of some objects will fit into a fixed space. For example, if there are 50 possible lines on a page and you need to print a report with 185 lines, then 185 \ 50=3 pages, and 185 Mod 50 leaves 35 lines on the last page.

Most languages support string variables, which are used to hold basic text data, such as names, addresses, or short messages. A string is a collection (or array) of characters. Sometimes you will need to perform computations on string variables. How can you perform computations on text data? The most common technique is to **concatenate** (or add) two strings together. For example, if FirstName is "George" and LastName is "Jones", then FirstName & LastName is "GeorgeJones". Notice that if you want a space to appear between the names, you have to add one: FirstName & "" & LastName.

Figure 7.5A lists some of the common string functions. You can learn more about the functions and their syntax from the Help system within Access. Commonly used

FIGURE 7.5A
Common string functions to add strings, extract portions, examine characters, convert case, compare two strings, and format numerical data into a string variable.

```
& Concatenation
Left, Right, Mid
Trim, LTrim, RTrim
String
Chr, Asc
LCase, UCase
InStr
Len
StrComp
Format
```

```
"Frank" & Rose → "FrankRose"
Left("Jackson",5) → "Jacks"
Trim("     Maria     ") → "Maria"
Len("Ramanujan") → 9
String (5, "a") → "aaaaa"
InStr("8764 Main"," ") → 5
```

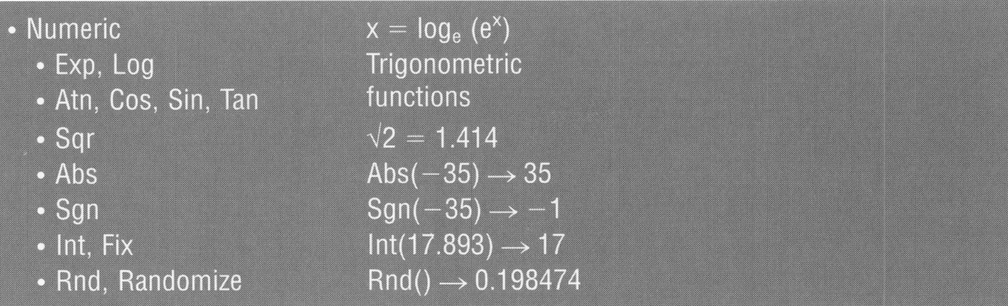

• Numeric
• Exp, Log
• Atn, Cos, Sin, Tan
• Sqr
• Abs
• Sgn
• Int, Fix
• Rnd, Randomize
x = log_e (e^x)
Trigonometric functions
√2 = 1.414
Abs(−35) → 35
Sgn(−35) → −1
Int(17.893) → 17
Rnd() → 0.198474

FIGURE 7.6A Standard mathematical functions. Even in business applications, you often need basic mathematical functions.

functions include the Left, Right, and Mid, which examine portions of the string. For example, you might only want to see the first five characters on the left side of a string.

Standard Internal Functions

As you may recall from courses in mathematics, several common functions are used in a variety of situations. As shown in Figure 7.6A, these functions include the standard trigonometric and logarithmic functions, which can be useful in mapping and procedures involving measurements. You also will need a function to compute the square root and absolute value of numbers. The Int (integer) function is useful for dropping the fractional portion of a number. Most languages also provide a random number generator, which will randomly create numbers between 0 and 1. If you need another range of numbers, you can get them with a simple conversion. For example, to generate numbers between 40 and 90, use the following function: $y = 40 + (90 - 40)*Rnd$.

In a database environment you will often need to evaluate and modify dates. It is also useful to have functions that provide the current date (Date) and time (Now). Two functions that are useful in business are the DateAdd and DateDiff functions. As illustrated in Figure 7.7A, the DateAdd function adds days to a given date to find some date in the future. The DateDiff function computes the difference between two dates. Usually, you will want to compute the number of days between various dates. However, the functions in VBA can compute number of months, weeks, and so on. You could even count the number of Fridays between two dates.

Recall that the Variant data type can contain any type of data—including dates, numbers, and strings. Sometimes you need to know exactly what type of data is

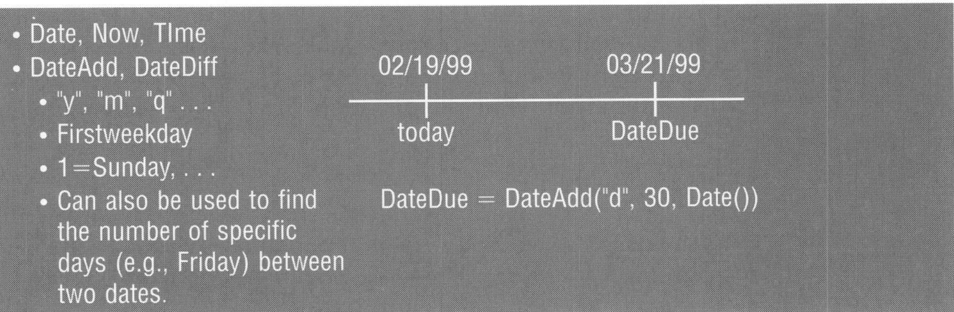

• Date, Now, TIme
• DateAdd, DateDiff
• "y", "m", "q" . . .
• Firstweekday
• 1=Sunday, . . .
• Can also be used to find the number of specific days (e.g., Friday) between two dates.
02/19/99
03/21/99
today
DateDue
DateDue = DateAdd("d", 30, Date())

FIGURE 7.7A Date and time functions. Business problems often require computing the number of days between two dates or adding days to a date to determine when payments are due.

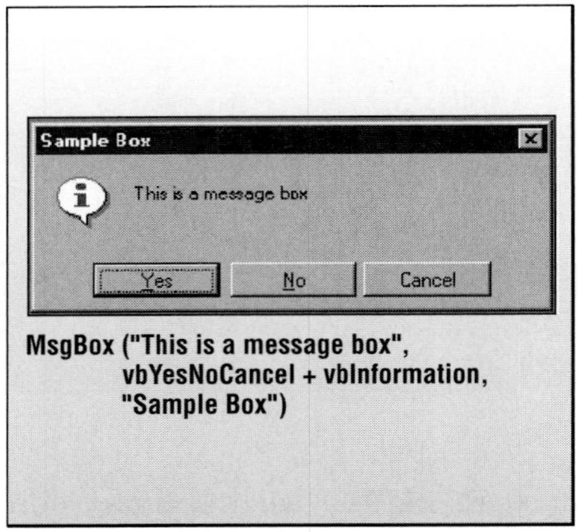

FIGURE 7.8A Sample message box. The message box interrupts the user and displays a few limited choices. It often handles errors or problems.

stored in the Variant before you try to perform an operation. Several functions, such as IsDate, IsNumeric, and VarType, provide this information. These functions enable you to determine whether a variable is the proper type before using it in an inappropriate situation.

Another useful feature of the Variant data type is the ability to test for missing data. Traditional programming variables do not support this feature. Microsoft Access provides two functions for this purpose: IsNull and IsEmpty. The IsNull function can test data table values and examine data entry controls to see whether the user entered a value.

Input and Output

Handling input and output were crucial topics in traditional programming. These topics are still important, but the DBMS now performs most data-handling routines, and the operating system handles most of the user interface. Common forms and reports (Chapter 6) are used for most input and output tasks.

Remember that an important feature of a Windows interface is that users control the flow of data entry; that is, the designer provides a form, and users work at their own pace without interruption. Occasionally, you might choose to interrupt the user—either to provide information or to get a specific piece of data. One common reason is to display error messages. Two basic functions serve this purpose (**MsgBox** and **InputBox**). As shown in Figure 7.8A, a message box can contain buttons. The buttons are often used to indicate how the user wants to respond to some problem or error.

An InputBox is a special form that can be used to enter very small amounts of text or a single number. Neither the user nor the developer has much control over the form. In most cases you would be better off creating your own blank form. Then you can have more than one text box, and you can specify and control the buttons. The InputBox is usually for temporary use when development time is extremely limited.

Conditions

The ability to test and respond to conditions is one of the most common reasons for writing your own procedures. The basic conditional statement (if . . . then . . . else)

FIGURE 7.9A
Conditions. Basic conditions are straightforward. Indenting conditions highlights the relationships.

```
If (Condition1) Then
   statements for true
Else
   statements for false
   If (Condition2) Then
      statements for true
   End If
End If
```

is relatively easy to understand. The structure is shown in Figure 7.9A. A condition is evaluated to be true or false. If it is true, then one set of statements is executed; otherwise, the second set is performed.

Conditions can be complex, particularly when the condition contains several AND and OR connectors. Some developers use a NOT statement to reverse the value of a condition. Be careful when writing conditions. Your goals are to make sure that the condition evaluates to the correct value and to make sure that other developers can understand the code.

You should always include parentheses to specify the order of evaluation and, for complex conditions, create sample data and test the conditions. Also, indent your code. Indenting is particularly important for **nested conditions,** in which the statements for one condition contain another conditional statement.

The Select Case statement is a special type of conditional statement. Many procedures will need to evaluate a set of related conditions. As a simple example, consider what happens if you use a message box with three buttons (Yes, No, and Cancel). You will have to test the user's choice for each option. Figure 7.10A shows how the code might look when you use nested conditions.

Figure 7.11A shows the same problem written with the Select Case statement. Note that this code is much easier to read. Now think about what will happen if you have 10 choices. The If-Then code gets much worse, but the Select Case code just adds new lines to the bottom of the list.

Loops

Iteration or **loops** are another common feature in procedures. Although you should use SQL statements (UPDATE, INSERT, etc.) as much as possible, sometimes you will need to loop through a table or query to examine each row individually.

FIGURE 7.10A
Nested conditions to test for a user response. The code becomes harder to read as more conditions are added.

```
response = MsgBox ( . . . )
If (response = vbYes) Then
   ' statements for Yes
Else
   If (response = vbNo) Then
      ' statements for No
   Else
      ' statements for Cancel
   End If
End If
```

FIGURE 7.11A The Select statement. The select statement tests the response variable against several conditions. If the response matches a case in the list, the corresponding code is executed.

Some of the basic loop formats are illustrated in Figure 7.12A. The For/Next loop is generally used only if you need a fixed number of iterations. The Do loop is more common. An important feature of loops is the ability to test the condition at the top or the bottom of the loop. Consider the example in which the condition says to execute the statements if ($x <= 10$). What happens when the starting value of x is 15? If you test the condition at the top of the loop, then the statements in the loop will never be executed. On the other hand, if you test the condition at the bottom, then the statements in the loop will be executed exactly one time—before the condition is tested.

Just as with conditions, it is good programming practice to indent the statements of the loop. Indents help others to read your code and understand the logic. If there are no problems within a loop, your eye can easily find the end of the loop.

Be careful with loops—if you make a mistake, the computer may execute the statements of your loop forever. (On most personal computers, Ctrl+Break will usually stop a runaway loop.) A common mistake occurs when you forget to change the conditional variable (x in the examples). In tracking through a data query, you might forget to get the next row of data—in which case your code will perform the same operations forever on one row of data. A good programming practice is to always write loops in four steps: (1) write the initial condition, (2) write the ending statement, (3) write a statement to update the conditional variable, and (4) write the interior code. The first three statements give you the structure. By writing and testing them first, you know that you will be using the correct data.

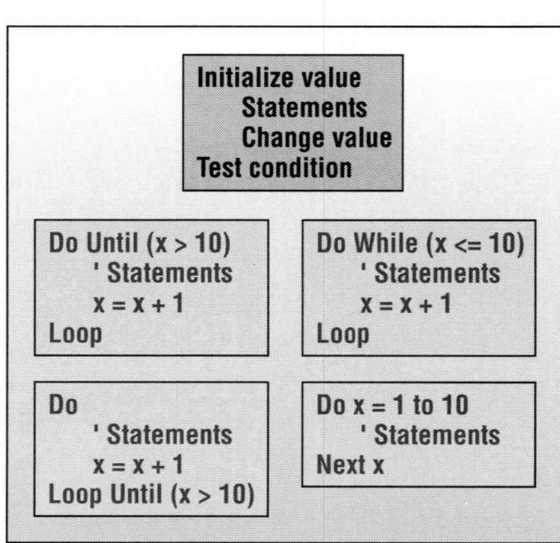

FIGURE 7.12A Iteration. All versions of loops follow a common format: initialize a counter value, perform statements, increment the counter, and test the exit condition. You can test the condition at the start or end of the loop.

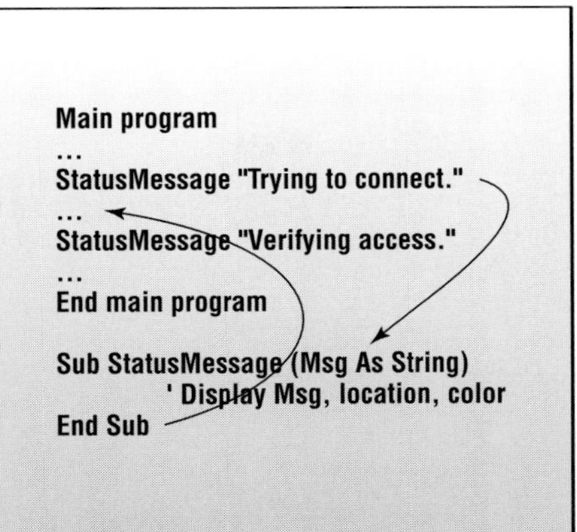

Main program
...
StatusMessage "Trying to connect."
...
StatusMessage "Verifying access."
...
End main program
Sub StatusMessage (Msg As String)
' Display Msg, location, color
End Sub

FIGURE 7.13A Subroutine. The StatusMessage subroutine can be called from any location. When the subroutine is finished, it returns to the calling program.

Subroutines

An important concept in programming is the ability to break the program into smaller pieces as subroutines or functions. A **subroutine** is a portion of code that can be called from other routines. When the subroutine is finished, control returns to the program code that called it. The goal of using subroutines is to break the program into smaller pieces that are relatively easy to understand, test, and modify.

A subroutine is essentially a self-contained program that can be used by many other parts of the program. For example, you might create a subroutine that displays a status message on the screen. As illustrated in Figure 7.13A, you would write the basic routine once. Then anytime you need to display a status message, your program calls this routine. By passing the message to the subroutine, the actual message can change each time. The advantage of using the subroutine is that you have to write it only once. In addition, your status messages can be standardized because the subroutine specifies the location, style, and color. To change the format, you simply modify the few lines of code in the one subroutine. Without the subroutine, you would have to find and modify code in every location that displayed a status message.

A data variable that is passed to a function or a subroutine is known as a **parameter.** There are two basic ways to pass a parameter: by reference and by value. The default method used by Microsoft Access is **pass-by-reference.** In this case, the variable in the subroutine is essentially the same variable as in the original program. Any changes made to the data in the subroutine will automatically be returned to the calling program. For example, consider the two examples in Figure 7.14A. Changes to the variable j2 in the subroutine will automatically be passed back to the calling program. However, when only the value is passed, a copy is made in the subroutine. Changes made to the data in the subroutine will not be returned to the calling program. Unless you are absolutely certain that you want to alter the original value in the calling program you should always **pass variables by value.** Subroutines that use pass-by-reference can cause errors in programs that are difficult to find. Some other programmer might not realize that your subroutine changed the value of a parameter.

Most languages also enable you to create new functions. There is a slight technical difference between functions and subroutines. Although subroutines and functions can receive or return data through pass-by-reference parameters, a function can return a result or a single value directly to the calling program. For instance, your

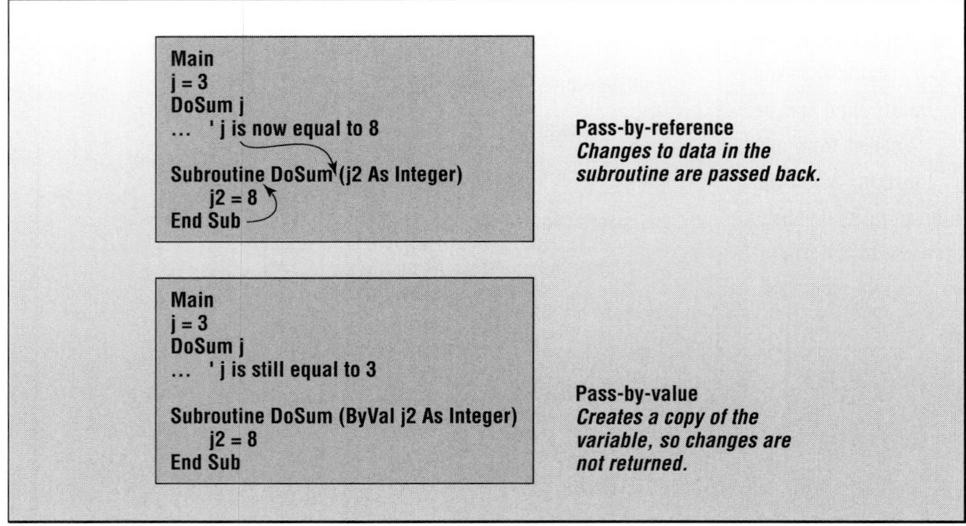

FIGURE 7.14A Two methods to pass data to a subroutine. Pass parameters by value as much as possible to avoid unwanted changes to data.

main program might have a statement like v1=Min(x, y). The function would choose the smaller of the two values and return it to the main program, where it is assigned to the variable v1.

Summary

The only one way to learn how to program is to write your own programs. Reading books, syntax documentation, and studying code written by others will help, but the only way to become a programmer is through experience.

As you write programs, remember that you (or someone else) might have to modify your code later. Choose descriptive variable names. Document your statements with comments that explain tricky sections and outline the purpose of each section of code. Write in small sections and subroutines. Test each section and keep the test data and results in the documentation. Keep revision notes so that you know when each section was changed and why you changed it.

Application Development

CHAPTER 8

WHAT YOU WILL LEARN IN THIS CHAPTER

OVERVIEW

Miranda: *Finally. I think I see the end of this project.*

Ariel: *That's terrific. What's left?*

Miranda: *Well, everyone is happy with the forms and reports. All I have to do now is tie them together into an application. I have a few details to add to make the forms a little easier to use. The salespeople complained about having to enter customer numbers twice, and they say the order lists are too long. They want to pick from a list of orders just for the given customer.*

Ariel: *That's it? Let's celebrate.*

Miranda: *Well, not quite yet. I also have to write some help files. Then I have to create a set of installation disks so they can install the system on all the computers.*

Ariel: *Sounds like a lot of details. Will it take long?*

Miranda: *I don't think so. But it will make the application more attractive and easier to use, so I really need to finish the details.*

INTRODUCTION

As a database developer, it is your responsibility to create systems that help users do their jobs. To help users, you develop applications. **Applications** are complete systems that perform specific tasks. The task is defined by the user. For example, you could develop an application to track the location and status of shipping containers. You build an application by defining the tables needed. Then you create the queries, forms, and reports. A complete application usually contains switchboard forms, menus, and toolbars. It should also contain customized help screens that provide information for every topic in the application—including definitions and hints on how to enter data in the forms.

The goal of an application is to provide information and help users make decisions. To achieve this goal, the application should be easy to use. As you create an application, think about the user's tasks and then use your creativity to build an application that meets that person's needs. Consider the example in Figure 8.1. The

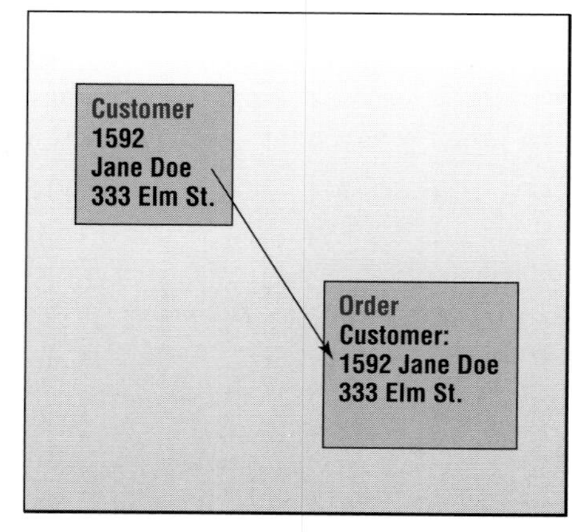

FIGURE 8.1 Application design choices. Example of bad design: enter data twice. Example of poor design: ask user to memorize ID on one form to enter on the second. Improved design: automatically transfer data across forms.

application has one form to collect customer data and a second form to enter new orders. A poorly designed application would force the user to enter data twice: once on the customer form and again on the order form. A slightly better design might ask users to memorize the ID number from the customer form and enter it into the order form. However, the best solution is to have the application automatically copy the data from the customer form into the order form.

THE POWER OF APPLICATIONS

Applications serve two primary functions: (1) They establish and control the user interface, and (2) they ensure data integrity. Additionally, applications can be used to build decision support systems and expert systems. Each application needs a different combination of these features. As a designer, you need to be aware of the choices and use them to improve your applications.

User Interface

One of the primary objectives in building an application interface is to help the users. Although this concept seems obvious, it is sometimes challenging to carry out in practice. What it means is that you will have many choices in designing the application. Some choices will make it easy for you to create the application. Other choices will make the user's job easier but will make more work for you as the developer. You should put forth the extra work to help the user. The one exception is that sometimes the user needs the application immediately and you might not have time to add all of the features. In this situation focus on the data integrity features and add user interface items later.

The basic concept of improving the user interface is that the application should reflect the way the user works. This statement is not as simple as it sounds. Designing a system that truly reflects the needs of the user requires careful thought, observation, and creativity. In many cases even the users will not know how the application should be designed. However, they will be able to tell you when the application causes problems. Listen carefully to these problems. You should also study other applications for clues on how to improve your own projects. In particular, pay attention to the current ideas and techniques in the leading commercial software applications.

A primary purpose of an application is to integrate the input forms and reports. Users should not have to go searching for input forms and reports. They should be available at the click of a mouse. For example, if users customarily print order forms when they are entered, the order-entry form should have a button to print the corresponding report.

Applications are also used to automate basic tasks. For example, the application might automatically create backup data at scheduled times. Similarly, once a year it could purge old customer data—for clients who have not placed orders in several years.

Ensure Data Integrity

A key purpose of applications is to ensure **data integrity.** Early computer systems suffered from several problems. For example, a user would complain that the computer says we have four of those items in stock, but I cannot find them. In other words, the data in the computer did not match the true situation. This problem might arise if some users avoid the computer. For example, a customer-service representative might replace an item for a customer without entering the data into the computer. Your job as an application developer is to provide features that encourage people to enter all data and to keep the data internally consistent.

The standard features to ensure data integrity are (1) data validation, (2) automatic computations, (3) verification of totals, (4) control of user access, (5) transaction integrity, and (6) backup and recovery.

Basic data validation occurs at the table level, where you enter conditions that will always be enforced by the DBMS. For example, you can set a condition that price must always be greater than 0. You might allow price to be equal to 0 if you plan on giving away items for promotions. These conditions are easy to create, and they provide strong controls on the basic data.

Applications should also be used to automatically perform all computations. For example, you could never expect users to compute sales tax. Likewise, an order application should always compute shipping charges and any other costs. These business rules are generally written as code within the forms.

Whenever you compute and store totals in a database, you need to write additional code that verifies and corrects the totals. For example, consider an application that tracks the quantity on hand (QOH) of the sales products. When an order is shipped, the quantity is automatically deducted from the inventory. When new items are purchased or built, the inventory is increased. But what if something goes wrong? You need to build an application section that rechecks the inventory total by examining all of the shipments and receipts. Similarly, when users perform a physical inventory count, you need to enable them to record any discrepancies to correct the database total.

Figure 8.2 illustrates how an application can automatically update inventory totals. When sales occur, the QOH is reduced. Similarly, purchases automatically increase the inventory. Again, remember that the database total could still become incorrect over time. A separate program can be used to compute the total sales and purchases for each item. A physical inventory count can identify any other discrepancies, which must then be inserted into the database.

APPLICATION STRUCTURE

The overall structure is an important feature of any application. The structure or layout defines how the user will deal with the application. Most database applications will use forms and reports as individual components. The first step in designing the structure or architecture of the application is to design each form. Basic design and layout of individual forms is discussed in Chapter 6.

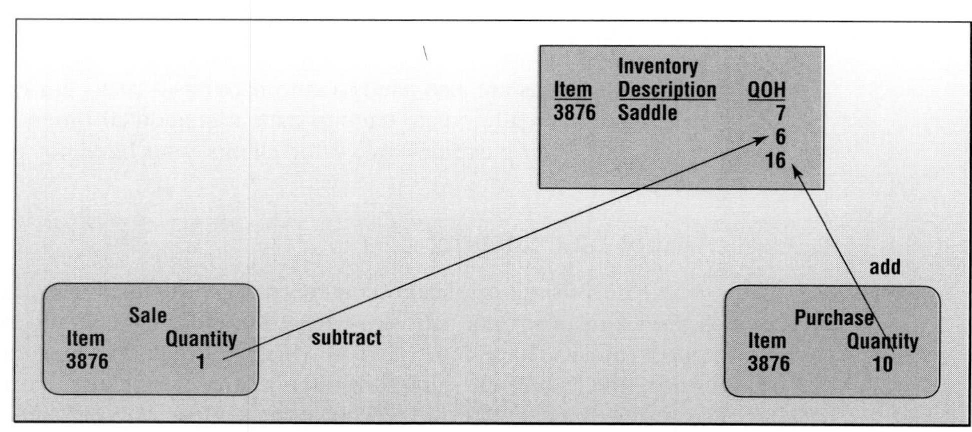

FIGURE 8.2
Automated inventory. Quantity on hand (QOH) is updated when an item is sold or purchased. A separate program is required to validate the current totals by examining all sales and purchases.

The objective of application structure is to organize all of the forms and reports to produce a complete application. In a few cases this purpose can be achieved with a central switchboard form, which contains buttons to direct users to the appropriate form. More commonly, you will also need to add interconnection buttons on individual forms. For example, a user entering data on an order form might want to look up additional information on the customer form.

Designing Applications

The first step in designing the overall application structure is to identify the various users and outline the tasks that will be performed with the application. The application must reflect the needs and working habits of the user. If several users have different needs, the application can be divided into sections for each group. A central switchboard form can be used to identify the user and direct him or her to the appropriate section.

This segmentation reduces complexity for the users and simplifies their tasks. However, there are two potential drawbacks. First, if the application has too many layers, users will have trouble finding the forms and reports they need. Second, poor organization confuses users and requires additional support and training. In other words, you must find an application structure that provides the functionality each user needs but is still easy to understand. The inherent conflict in these goals is what makes it so difficult to design a good application structure.

Even experienced programmers rarely design a "perfect" application the first time. In most cases you need to develop several ideas and test them. You can build **prototypes** by creating sample forms and including command buttons to tie them together. These prototypes can be given to users to test. You then incorporate user suggestions and modify the prototypes. By testing different structures, you can quickly learn which technique will work best.

In building a complex application structure, it is best to start with the core concepts. Once you have tested them with users, you can add additional features. Each revision constitutes a new application version. Keep track of the version number; record the date, the reason for the change, and the changes that were made. Most commercial software vendors follow this development process. No one tries to visualize a complete, massive application and create it up front. Instead, developers start with a basic concept and build a system that works and implements the fundamental concepts. Then they expand the capabilities by adding new features.

The two most important aspects in this type of development are (1) getting the overall structure correct up front and (2) using a flexible design that is easy to modify later. For example, your data tables must be normalized as described in Chapters 2 and 3. Normalized tables can be easily expanded later to provide new features.

The Switchboard Form

Designing an overall structure and appearance often requires artistic sensibility as well as logic and research. Each application is different and can require a unique approach. Yet, over time, designers have learned that some common elements can be used in many applications. The main menu or **switchboard form** is an element that many developers like to use. However, it is not really the ultimate answer to every problem. For example, popular applications like word processors or spreadsheets do not start with switchboard forms.

FIGURE 8.3
Uses of switchboard forms. As the initial form for an application, the main switchboard can be used to control tasks that apply to the complete session.

- Acts as a directory for the application
- Identifies users
- Contains startup and shutdown code
  - Can preload forms in background
    - Make them invisible
    - Speed up later usage
  - Can initiate transaction and security logs
  - Can establish network connections
- Contains copyright and usage notes

The main purposes of the switchboard form are shown in Figure 8.3. The switchboard form is generally the first form of the application. It provides a centralized directory to the rest of the application. It often contains an image or picture and usually consists entirely of command buttons. Clicking a button brings the user to another switchboard (menu) or to a specific form or report.

Because the switchboard form is the starting point for the application, it is a good place to identify the user. If possible, you should identify the user from the network login data. Otherwise, you will have to maintain a separate login for each user. The two primary reasons for identifying each user are (1) to maintain appropriate security controls and (2) to customize the application for each user group.

The switchboard can be customized through layout and the use of color. For example, options primarily intended for different managers (marketing, finance, etc.) can be displayed in different colors. If additional customization is needed, individual options can be made invisible and disabled so that users see only buttons that are designed for their use. This approach simplifies the screen layout and reduces confusion. However, it is less useful if managers need to share their tasks.

Sally's Pet Store: Application Organization

In many ways the switchboard form is a table of contents into the application. It presents the organization of the application. Before building the switchboard form, you must decide how the application will be organized. That is, you must learn which forms are most important to users, how they will switch between forms, and how often they use each form.

Although there are many useful ways to organize any application, consider two different approaches to the Pet Store application. The first approach is shown in Figure 8.4. At first glance this approach seems reasonable. Items are ordered, then received, and then sold to customers. Hence the store managers might want to start with orders and enter data by following each item from purchase through sale.

Although this approach might sound reasonable at first, it has several flaws. First, managers rarely want to track individual items. Perhaps they want to follow individual animals, but rarely merchandise. Second, when an order is placed, the item has not been received yet, so there is no point in linking an order to the receipt of the shipment. More important, there is no way to connect individual items to a sale. For example, we might know that a customer bought three cans of a particular dog food, but there is no way to tell exactly which cans. Hence managers rarely need a link from receipt of shipments to individual sales.

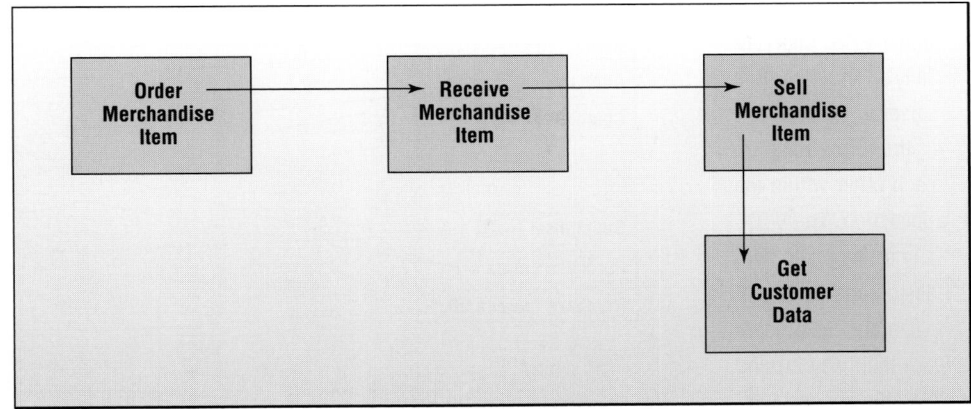

FIGURE 8.4
Poor organization of the Pet Store application. The links are at the wrong level (item instead of order). Managers rarely need to track individual items from order to receipt to sale. Application needs to get customer data before the item sales.

An improved approach appears in Figure 8.5. First, notice that it has more links—including bidirectional links. For example, when a shipment arrives, workers need to pull up the matching order to see whether the proper items were delivered. Hence an Orders button is placed on the Shipping Receipt form. Once in a while, a manager might want to check on the shipment of a particular order, so the link is bidirectional. Notice that Sales are connected to Orders and Receipts—but only through the Inventory items. Inventory QOH can be displayed directly on the Sale form. The Sale form also has a connection to Orders—to create special orders. If an item is out of stock, a salesperson might want to check on recent orders to see when the item might arrive. The designer should talk with users to determine how often this situation arises and how it should be handled on the form.

Eventually the Pet Store application will contain many forms and reports. Most of them are linked to a switchboard form. Many of them are linked to each other. Buttons or events on one form lead the user to a related form. Some of the forms are simple and affect one table, but most display data from several related tables. Each individual form represents specific business events and tasks. Figure 8.6 shows the volume table of contents chart for the Pet Store case. The **volume table of contents (VTOC)** chart shows how the various modules in the system are related. It displays the hierarchical relationships, beginning with the highest level (main switchboard) at the left and working down to modules or forms that are more detailed.

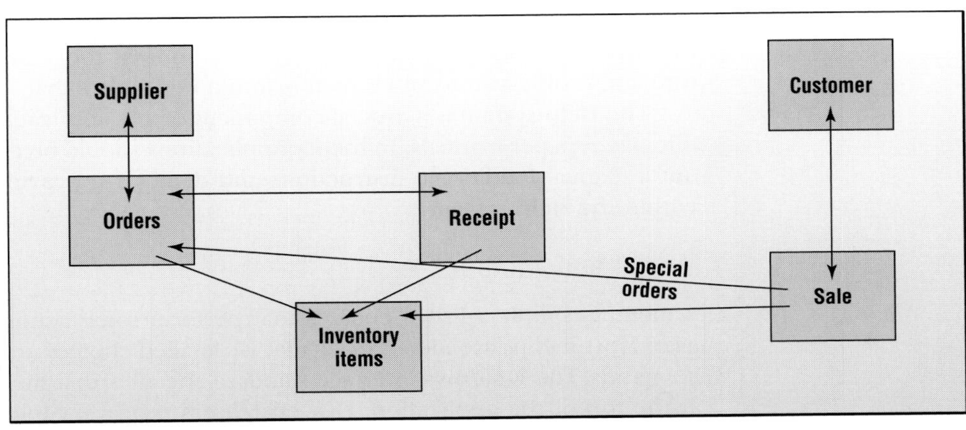

FIGURE 8.5
Improved organization for the Pet Store. The lines represent links from one form to a second form. The links are usually created through buttons placed on the form.

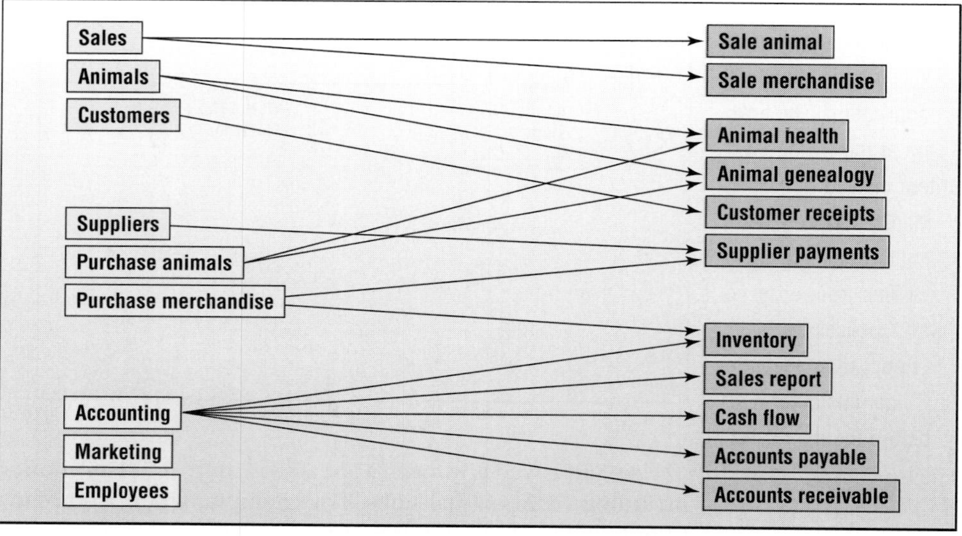

FIGURE 8.6 Initial VTOC chart for Sally's Pet Store. It is useful to show how the forms relate to each other within the application. The VTOC chart can help with design and testing. It can also help users learn their way around the new system.

The VTOC can help you and the users determine the best layout for the overall structure. It is also useful to make sure that all of your forms are easily reachable. Its biggest drawback is that it can be difficult to display for complex applications with many levels. In these situations you would have to display two or three levels on a page and use several pages to show the detailed lower levels.

USER INTERFACE FEATURES

Modern Windows-based applications have several **user interface** features that are designed to standardize the look and feel of applications and to make your applications relatively easy to use. Three features are particularly important: **menus, toolbars,** and the **Help system.**

The menu is a line of options displayed at the top of the application. The main menu is generally the same across the application. Hence the menu centralizes choices that can be activated at any time. Menus are also useful for visually challenged workers and those who prefer to use the keyboard instead of a pointing device (mouse), because choices can be activated with the keyboard.

Toolbars consist of a set of icons or buttons that perform common tasks. Some applications enable users to customize the toolbar with specific buttons; usually users can also reposition toolbars. Current development tools take advantage of this feature and enable you to place menus into a custom toolbar.

The Help system is a crucial component of any application. In most applications it replaces paper manuals. In theory, applications should be clear enough to use without a manual. Additional instructions and details are provided as text and pictures within the Help system.

Menus and Toolbars

A menu is simply a list of choices that perform some action when selected by the user. Most menus are hierarchical; that is, detailed choices are presented under a few keywords. The Windows interface standard specifies that menus should be displayed at the top of the application. However, users may want to move menus to a different location. Most applications use similar commands on their menus. For example, as illustrated in Figure 8.7, the main menu typically contains three common commands: File, Edit, and Help. The File command generally contains the New, Open, Save, and Close commands. As much as possible, your application should try to match these standards. By building applications with the same layout and the same words, users can understand your application with minimal training.

Purpose of the Menu

You might consider using the DBMS menu within your application. Then users will have full control over the database. In most cases, however, you will be better off building a custom menu for your application. A custom menu has several benefits. First, it can limit user actions. For example, if users do not need to delete data, the menu should not have delete commands. You still have to set the appropriate security conditions to prevent them from using other methods to delete data. Removing a command from the menu helps to restrict user choices. A second advantage of a custom menu is that it simplifies the user interface. If entry-level users need only four or five commands, just display those options on the menu. Then they can find them faster. Third, you can add special functions to a custom menu. For example, you might add a special Help command to send e-mail to your support desk. Fourth, menu choices can be activated by keystrokes. Hence touch typists and visually challenged workers can use your application without looking at the screen.

Toolbars

Toolbars are similar to menus. A toolbar generally contains a collection of buttons illustrated with icons. When the user clicks a toolbar button, a predefined operation is executed. Today most applications have combined the role of menus and toolbars. A toolbar can contain traditional buttons, and it can contain textual menus. Most toolbars are **dockable,** which means that users can drag them to any place on the application window.

The purpose of a toolbar is to provide single-click access to complex actions or to commands that are used frequently. For example, many toolbars have an icon to immediately save the current work. As shown in Figure 8.8, you can put virtually any icon and any command on a toolbar. You can set different toolbars and menus for each form. You can even have multiple toolbars. For example, one toolbar might contain commands that apply to the entire application. Then special toolbars can be added as each form is opened.

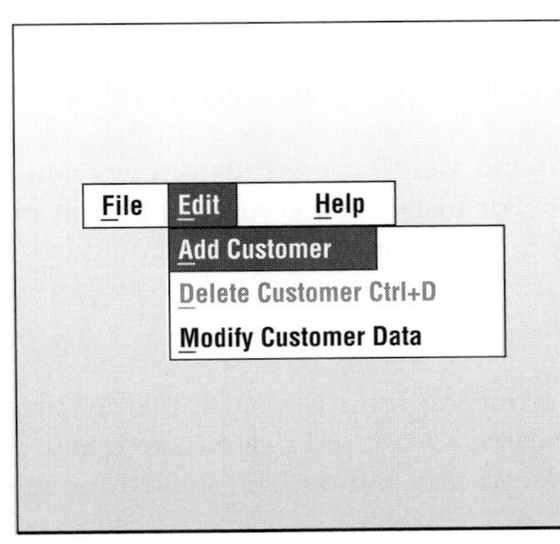

FIGURE 8.7
Sample menu. Note the hierarchical structure. The underlined letter represents the access key, which can be activated from the keyboard. You can also add shortcut keys (e.g., Ctrl+D) to activate a choice without going through the menu.

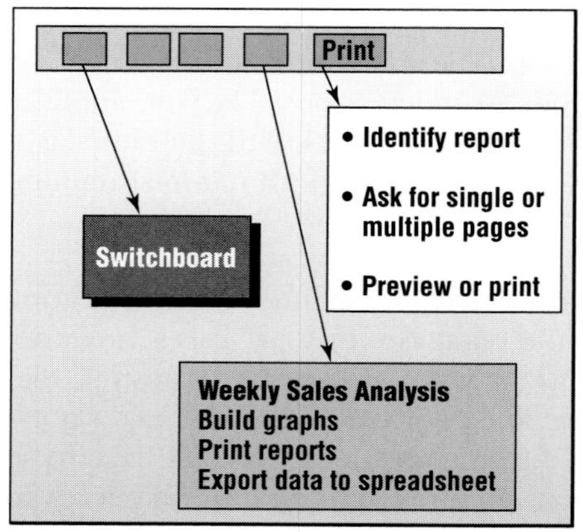

FIGURE 8.8 Sample toolbar. Toolbars can contain buttons and menus. Buttons generally display icons. When the pointer moves over them, a tooltip is displayed that briefly describes the button. When the button is clicked, an action is performed or a menu is displayed.

Creating Menus and Toolbars

To support standardization and to simplify creating menus, most application development environments have a menu-generation feature. Most personal computer–based systems utilize the standard Windows functions. Three basic steps are used to create a menu: (1) choose the layout or structure, (2) give each option a name and an access key, and (3) define the action to be taken when each option is selected.

The basic steps to creating toolbars are similar: (1) identify which tools you want to display for each form, (2) choose or create an icon to represent a command, and (3) define the action to be taken when the option is selected. A key feature in creating the toolbar is the choice of an icon. Never assume that users will recognize an icon or understand what it represents. Most current systems enable you to define a **tooltip** for each option. When the user moves the pointer over the icon, the tooltip, or short comment, is displayed. Every toolbar button must have a tooltip.

Creating toolbars and menus is straightforward with recent application development systems. You can customize an existing toolbar by adding or deleting options. Similarly, you can create a new toolbar. Button icons and menus can be dragged to the toolbar.

The main step is to set the properties of each item. Menu names should be short and descriptive. You should also try to follow the standard names used in commercial software. To specify the access key, precede the key letter with an ampersand. For example, the &File text will appear as *F*ile, and the Alt plus F keys will activate that option. Shortcut keys (e.g. Ctrl+D) can be specified in the property settings of the detail menu item or the button command.

As you create each toolbar button and menu option, you should define the actions to be taken. Several default actions are automatically associated with certain icons. For example, Exit and Help have standard icons and menu options. You can also define new actions. For instance, a command button might be used to display a certain form. Similarly, a button or menu option could call a detailed function that you programmed.

Icons

Toolbars often contain icons. An **icon** is a small picture that indicates the function to be performed. It is created and stored as a bitmap image, and you can edit or create new images to be placed on a button. The standard icon is square: 16 by 16 pix-

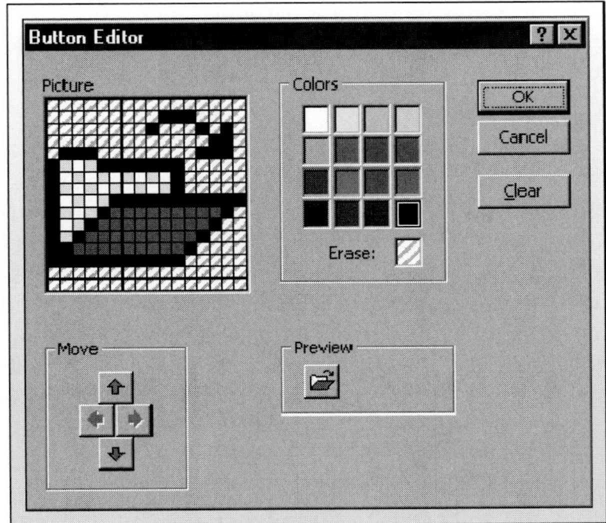

FIGURE 8.9
Icon editor. Icons are 16 by 16 pixels. You set the color of each individual pixel and use shading for three-dimensional effects. Outline the objects in black so that they stand out.

els. Each pixel can be displayed as one of 16 colors. The colors are chosen as pairs, so that there are eight bright colors and eight dimmed colors. These choices can be used as shading to create a three-dimensional effect. For any icon a useful rule to remember is that the objects in your icon should be outlined in black, which sharpens the image and makes it easier to see on a variety of backgrounds. Figure 8.9 shows a basic icon editor that you can use to create or modify icons. This button editor is built into Microsoft Access (View, Toolbars, Customize). If you do not want to create your own icons, you can purchase collections of icons created by artists that contain hundreds or thousands of specialized icons.

Controlling Toolbars and Menus

Many times you need to customize toolbars and menus. Different forms might need different choices. You might want to present different choices to each user. For some events you might want to remove or temporarily disable certain commands. In all of these cases, you need to alter the toolbars and menus based on events. By using events to trigger a procedure, you can write code to alter the menus.

Microsoft Access stores its toolbars in a collection. You can modify or create new toolbars by manipulating this collection through code. For example, if you already have a toolbar called Custom1, you can select it and make it visible with the code displayed in Figure 8.10. In the example you have already identified the user, and you

FIGURE 8.10
Setting menus for different users. In Microsoft Access the toolbars are referenced by the CommandBars collection. With the Visible and Enabled properties, you can control which menu is available to each user.

```
Set myBar = CommandBars("Custom1")
If user = "Clerk" Then
   myBar.Visible = True
Else
   CommandBars("Database").Reset
   myBar.Enabled = False
End If
```

want to provide a new menu for a particular group (e.g., Clerks). The CommandBars collection also has a Controls property. With this property you can enable or disable individual buttons or menu items on the toolbar.

Custom Help

On-line Help systems have grown to replace paper manuals. The goal is to provide the background information and the specific instructions that a user might need to effectively use the application system. Help files can contain text-based descriptions, figures, and hypertext links to related topics. As much as possible, the help messages should be **context sensitive.** The user should be presented with information that is designed to help with the specific task they are working on at the time. Yet the Help system must also have an extensive search engine so that users can find information on any topic. Figure 8.11 illustrates a sample page from a Help system. Do not be deceived by the simple layout. This figure represents only one page. A good Help system could have hundreds of pages of text and diagrams.

The Windows operating system contains a Help system that performs most of the functions you will need. As a developer, you can concentrate on creating the files that contain the basic information and the necessary links. Then the help compiler converts your data into a special file that the Windows Help system can display and search.

Creating a Help File

The first and most important step in creating a help file is to understand what information a user will need. Then you must write individual pages that explain the purpose of the system and how to use it. As with any communication project, you must first understand your audience. What types of people will use the application? What is their reading level? How much experience and training do they have with computers in general? Do they understand the business operations? The goal is to provide concise help information in a format that users can quickly understand.

Once you understand the needs of the users, you can write the individual Help pages. Seven basic components are used to create a Help system: (1) text messages and images written as pages, (2) hypertext links between topics, (3) sequential links that group pages together, (4) definitions of technical words and phrases, (5) keywords that describe each page, (6) title of the topic, and (7) a topic name and a number for each page.

The Windows 98 operating system changed the way that Help files are written and displayed. The basic concepts are the same in Windows 95 and Windows 98, but

FIGURE 8.11 Partial help screen. Screens can be linked sequentially. Underlined links display related topics. Individual terms can be defined in a glossary.

Sally's Pet Store—Contents
Copyright Notice
The Firm
  Introduction
  Processes
Entering Data
  Sales
  Animal Health

Breeds (and other terms)

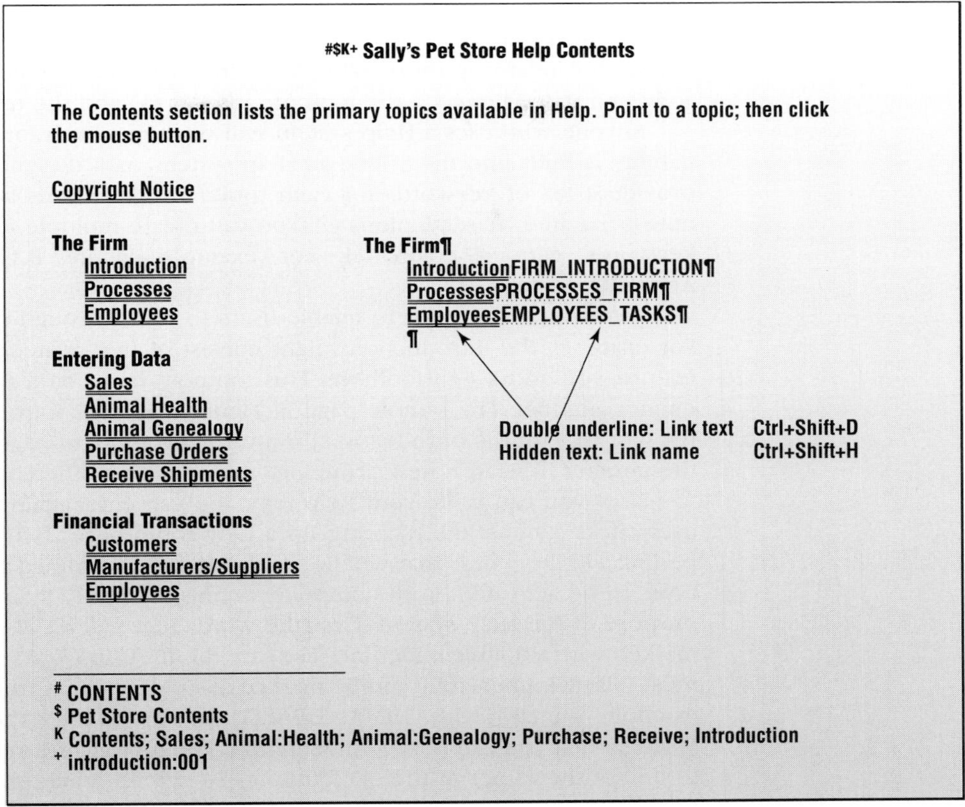

FIGURE 8.12 Sample help page. Each link is marked with a double underline and followed by a topic name in hidden text. The footnotes list the topic name (#), the title ($), the keywords (K), and a sequential reference (+).

the new system uses a Web-based hypertext system to display help content. The main advantage of this system is that many tools are available to help you create content. Second, more people are familiar with the way the system works—reducing training needs. Third, developers need to learn only one set of tools. The one catch to the new system is that it could take a couple of years for most companies to adopt Windows 98. Hence you may have to create help files in two versions: one for Windows 95 and one for Windows 98.

Windows 95 Help Files

Every topic is stored as a separate page in a word processor document. The pages can be in any order, but the document must be saved in rich text format. Users will be shown one page of material at a time. Try to keep topics short so they fit on one screen. Each help page will contain links to other topics. The rules for creating the help document are somewhat detailed. The easiest method is to copy and modify the sample help file.

As shown in Figure 8.12, each topic page should have a title line. This line contains several footnotes. You should fill in the appropriate entries for the footnotes before you try to write the text. To enable linking, each topic page must be given a unique name (e.g., ANIMAL_HEALTH). The name should be in all caps, and it cannot contain spaces. It is placed in the # footnote. You will also have to provide a unique number for each topic, so pick one now and write the topic name and the number in a different document.

Each topic should be given a title, which will be displayed in the help screen title bar. The $ footnote is used to mark the title. You can use any format for the title, but keep it relatively short. When entering or adding footnotes, you must leave exactly one space between the footnote marker ($) and the text you enter.

Anyone who uses a Help system will want to search for various topics. This capability is built into the Windows Help system. As a designer, all you have to do is provide a list of keywords for each topic. The keywords are listed in the K footnote, separated by semicolons (;). You can create multiple levels by separating two keywords with a colon (:). For example, Figure 8.12 uses Animal:Health; Animal:Genealogy.

Sometimes, you want to enable users to track through help pages sequentially. For example, the introduction might consist of five related topics. To activate this feature, you add a (+) footnote. This footnote contains a name, followed by a sequence number. The sample page in Figure 8.12 uses introduction:001 to indicate the first page of the introduction group. The subsequent pages would simply change the number. To start a new grouping, you provide a different group name.

Now you can write your help text. You can enter plain text or hyperlinks. The user clicks a hyperlink to bring up a new topic page. Two elements denote a hyperlink: (1) the words that will be displayed and underlined and (2) the name of the topic to be activated. Both components must be specially marked to indicate their purpose to the Help system. First, the words that will be displayed as links must be marked with a double underline (use Ctrl+Shift+D in Word). Second, the topic name must follow immediately and be marked as hidden text (Ctrl+Shift+H in Word). For example: Animal HealthANIMAL HEALTH. Be sure to click the Show/Hide button in Word so that you can see the hidden text. The topic name must match a name given to one of the topics in the (#) footnote. Be careful when marking the two types of text. There can be no spaces between them, and you must not overlap the markings.

You can also add graphics images to the help message. They should be created in a windows bitmap (bmp) or metafile (wmf) format. They are inserted using a special command, such as {bml plus2.bmp}. You should consult Microsoft's help documentation for options.

Once you have written the pages for the Help system, you use a help compiler to set various options and to convert the rich text format document into the desired help (hlp) file. Several commercial help compilers are available. Microsoft ships a version (HCW) with most of its development systems.

The help compiler stores the fundamental options in a project file. The project file has five major sections that are used in most projects. Additional sections and many different options can be used for special effects. The following description concentrates on the minimal components you need to create a usable help file. The five sections are (1) options, (2) files, (3) map, (4) windows, and (5) config. Figure 8.13 shows the main portions of a help project file.

The Options section sets some basic parameters for the project. You can accept the default values for most of the choices. However, you generally want to set the project title and include a copyright string in this section as well. When you have finished testing the help file and are ready to distribute the application, you should recompile the help file and set the compression to maximum to reduce space.

You use the Files section to specify which files will be included in the help project. This section is where you list all of the rich text format (rtf) files or graphics images that you created. The Windows section enables you to specify an initial size and position for the help window and for the glossary window (which is usually

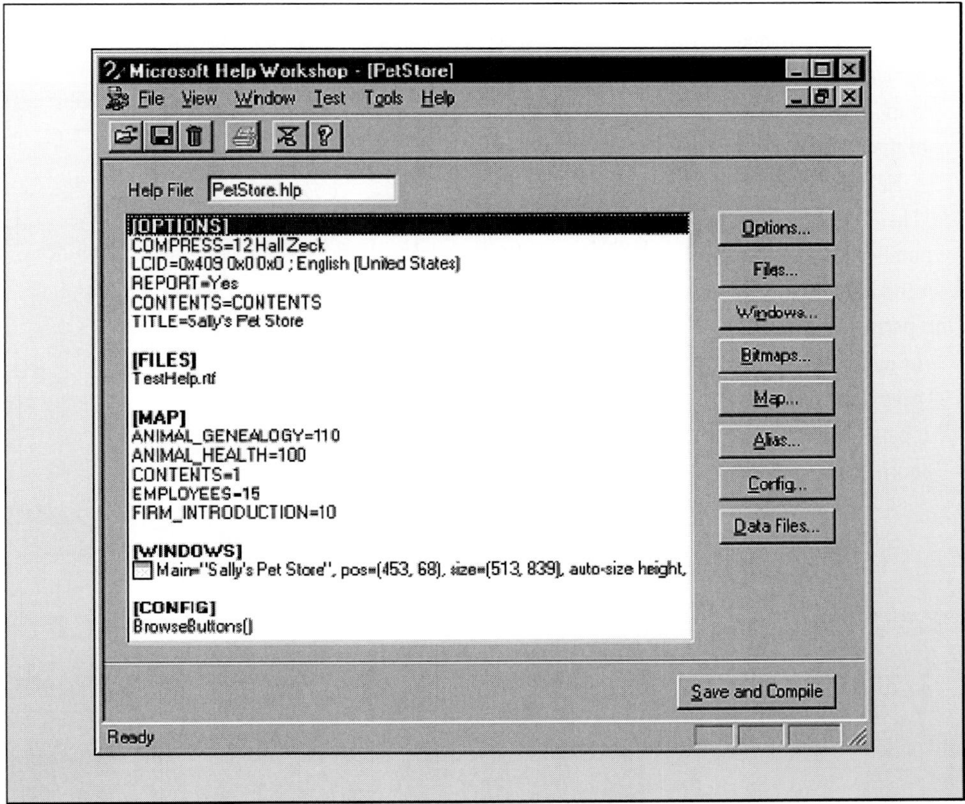

FIGURE 8.13
Sample help project file. The Map section is the most important, since it gives a number for every topic. The numbers are used in your application to select a context-sensitive topic.

smaller). The size is measured against a virtual screen that is 1,024 pixels wide and 1,024 pixels high. As much as possible, stick with the default values and allow the window to resize for the user's screen resolution.

The primary use of the Config section is to create buttons that appear at the top of the help screen. Many applications add a button for a Glossary section and BrowseButtons (←, →) for sequentially reading pages.

The Map section is the most vital. Remember that within the help file (rtf), you gave each topic a name. Unfortunately, your database application refers to topics by number—not by name. Hence you need to create a mapping that matches each name to a unique number. You can use long integers (up to 2,000,000,000), so space your numbers by groups. For instance, introductory topics might range from 10,000 to 11,000 and animal topics from 100,000 to 110,000. If you sequentially number the topics starting from 1, you are likely to make mistakes that will be hard to find later. In the Map section, you simply list the topic name, followed by the appropriate number.

You can now compile the text, graphics, and project files into one help (hlp) file. You can test the help file by opening it from Windows Explorer. Click on some hyperlinks and make sure the appropriate topic appears. If not, go back to your main document and change the topic name links.

The next step is to tell the database application that you have created a help file. In every form enter the help file name into the Help File property. If you start the database application now and press the F1 key, your help file should appear.

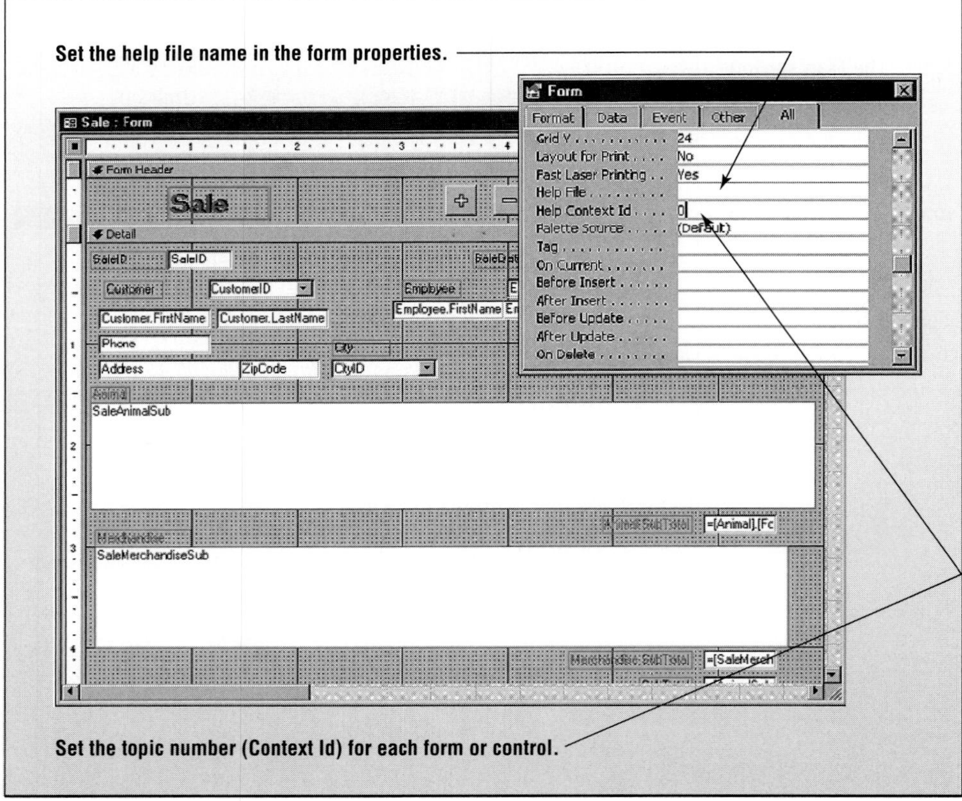

FIGURE 8.14 Setting context-sensitive help. In every form, enter the name of the help file in the Help File property. Then enter the topic number for that form in the Help Context Id property. Every control or subform can also have a different help topic—just enter the corresponding topic number.

You should also make the Help system context sensitive—so that the help message that appears depends on where the user is when he or she presses the F1 help key. As shown in Figure 8.14, to accomplish this task you need to go to each form (and probably each major control) and specify the help topic that you want to appear at that point. Note that each form could actually use a different help file. Also, note that every control could be assigned a different Help topic. In practice, it is usually easier to create one help file. Assign each form its own topic. Then you can consider adding special topics for some of the individual controls.

Windows 98 Help Files

As Windows 98 evolves and development tools change, the Help system will migrate toward traditional Web development tools. In many ways the Help system is already similar to Web documents. They both use hypertext links and graphics to help users navigate to a particular help topic. The additional tools and features available with Web pages will provide more sophisticated help features and a more familiar environment for users.

The fundamental concepts of building help files will remain the same: (1) know what the users need, (2) create text and images to explain a topic, and (3) use hypertext links and search commands to help users find related topics. The primary difference between the current Help system and a Web-based approach lies in how you create the text and the images. Web documents are created and stored in **hypertext markup language (HTML).** They use two types of images: joint photographic experts group (JPEG) and **graphics interchange file (GIF).** Most existing tools can create files in these formats. Standard tools will also enable you to easily create hypertext links.

Presumably, there will still be a need for a help compiler. Until Microsoft and other software developers change their applications (e.g., Access), you will still have to refer to help topic numbers to specify context-sensitive help pages. Hence a map file and compiler are needed to match the numeric value to the text name of the topic.

TRANSACTIONS

In building applications, it is tempting to believe that components will always work and that problems will never occur. Tempting, but wrong. Even if your code is correct, problems can develop. You might face power failure, a hardware crash, or perhaps someone accidentally unplugs a cable. You can minimize some of these problems by implementing backup and recovery procedures, storing duplicate data to different drives, and installing uninterruptible power supplies (UPS). Yet no matter how hard you try, failures happen.

An error that occurs at the wrong time can have serious consequences. In particular, many business operations require multiple changes to the database. A **transaction** is defined as a set of changes that must all be made together. Consider the example in Figure 8.15. You are working on a system for a bank. A customer goes to the ATM and instructs it to transfer $1,000 from savings to a checking account. This simple transaction requires two steps: (1) subtracting the money from the savings account balance and (2) adding the money to the checking account balance. The code to create this transaction will require two updates to the database. For example, there will be two SQL statements: one UPDATE command to decrease the balance in savings and a second UPDATE command to increase the balance in the checking account.

You have to consider what would happen if a machine crashed between these two operations. The money has already been subtracted from the savings account, but it will not be added to the checking account. It is lost. You might consider performing the addition to checking first, but then the customer ends up with extra money, and the bank loses. The point is that both changes must be made successfully.

How do you know that both operations are part of the same transaction? It is a business rule—or the definition of a transfer of funds. The problem is, How does the computer know that both operations must be completed together? As the application developer, you must tell the computer system which operations belong to a transaction. To do that you need to mark the start and the end of all transactions in-

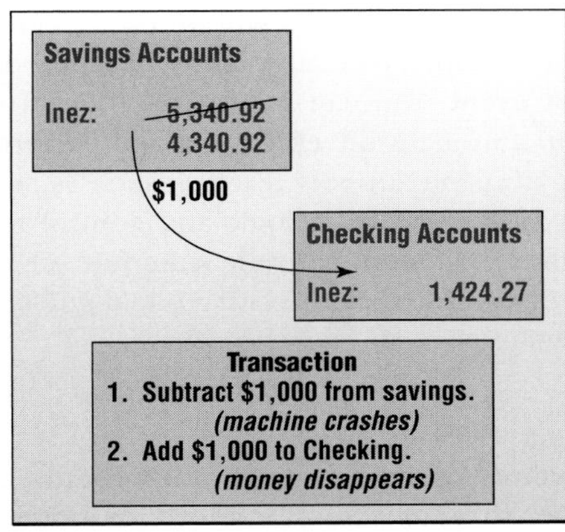

FIGURE 8.15
Transactions involve multiple changes to the database. All of the changes must be made, or the transaction will not be correct. To transfer money from a savings account to a checking account, for example, the system must subtract money from savings and add it to the checking balance. If the machine crashes after subtracting the money but before adding it to checking, the money will be lost.

```
Dim wsp As Workspace, dbs As Database, rst As Recordset
Set wsp = DBEngine.Workspaces(0)
Set dbs = CurrentDB()
Set rst = dbs.OpenRecordset( . . . )
wsp.BeginTrans
DoCmd.RunSQL "UPDATE Savings . . . "
DoCmd.RunSQL "UPDATE Checking . . . "
If (MsgBox("Save all changes?", vbQuestion + vbYesNo, "Save Changes") = vbYes)
Then
        wsp.CommitTrans
Else
        wsp.Rollback
End If
```

FIGURE 8.16 Transactions in Microsoft Access. Setting transactions is done within the Workspace. When all of the changes are made, issue a CommitTrans command. If there is a problem or the user wants to cancel the changes, use the Rollback method.

side your code. When the computer sees the starting mark, it first writes all the changes to a log file. When it reaches the end mark, it makes the actual changes to the data tables. If something goes wrong before the changes are complete, when the DBMS restarts, it examines the log file and completes any transactions that were incomplete. From a developer's perspective, the nice part is that the DBMS handles the problem automatically. All you have to do is mark the start and the end of the transaction. Figure 8.16 shows the basic code used to indicate transactions in Microsoft Access. Similar commands are available in other database systems. In particular, the Commit and Rollback commands are common. The Commit command tells the DBMS that the transaction is complete and to begin writing the changes. If an error occurred or if the user wants to cancel the changes, the Rollback command discards all of the changes back to the previous BeginTrans statement.

Some systems, such as SQL 92, do not use a BeginTrans statement. Instead, any Commit or Rollback command is taken as a breakpoint. The end of one transaction is automatically considered the start of a new transaction. So if you issue a Rollback command, all the updates since the last Commit statement will be dropped.

IMPROVING FORMS TO HELP USERS

You can do several things to make your forms easier to use. The key is to understand the business operations and how the forms will be used. Some basic ideas are presented in this section. For example, you can control combo boxes with the WHERE clause and the **NotInList** event. You can reduce user keystrokes by using mouse clicks and double-clicks to automatically enter data and perform advanced lookups. Additionally, you can add decision support features such as statistical analysis, optimization, and simulation. By adding more logic and control to your code, you can add expert system features that automatically compute or estimate key values. Similarly, your code or a sophisticated Help system could guide users through expert system questioning and analysis.

Form Events

To understand the possibilities for improvement, you must first understand the event model of forms. Remember that any event for a form or a control represents an op-

FIGURE 8.17
Form events. The variety of events provides you with precise control over the application. Each event provides an opportunity to execute your code to make the application "smarter" and easier to use.

Open, Close
Load, Unload
Activate, Deactivate, Got Focus, Lost Focus
Delete, Before Delete Confirm, After Delete Confirm
Before Update, After Update
Before Insert, After Insert
Current (Change row)
Click, Double Click
Mouse Down, Mouse Move, Mouse Up
Key Press, Key Down, Key Up
Timer

portunity for you to control the form. A partial list of events is given in Figure 8.17. You will never use all the events on one form or control at the same time. Nonetheless, you need to understand all of them so that you can decide which ones will best suit your needs.

The Open, Load, and Activate events are directly related to the form. Because a form is generally bound to a set of data, the Delete, Insert, Update, and Current events are related to the data on the form. The Current event arises when a new row of data is loaded into the form. The mouse and keyboard events provide detailed control over how the user activates and manipulates objects on the screen. However, be careful with these events because they can significantly affect system performance. The Timer event can be set to execute your code at preset intervals—much like an alarm clock. You never want to force a user to perform tasks based on time, but you can use this code to monitor activity and to initiate independent tasks such as making backup copies.

The sequence of events is important. The events that are triggered when a form is opened and closed are shown in Figure 8.18. Note that some of the events are very similar. In particular, when a user moves into a new text box control, the Enter event and then the GotFocus event will be triggered. In many cases you might not

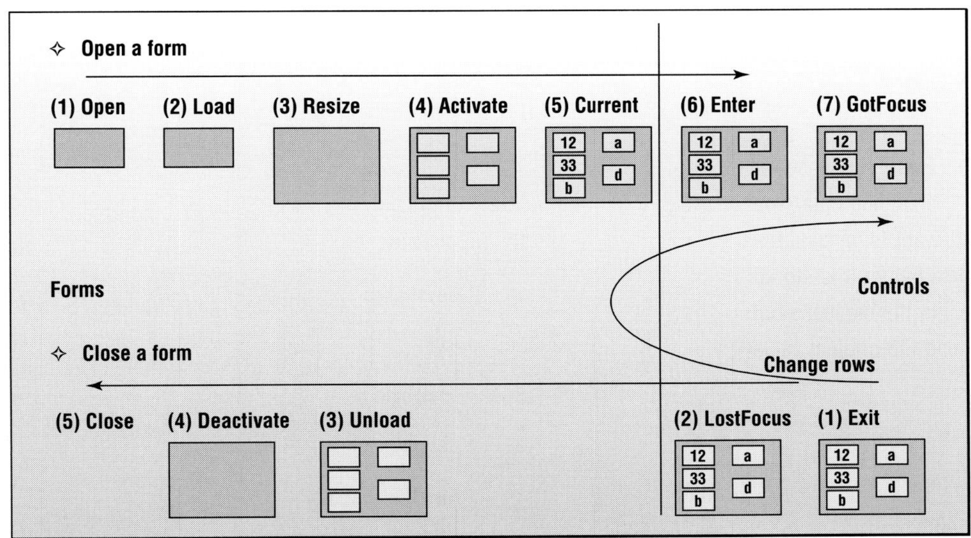

FIGURE 8.18
Event sequence for a form. Each event occurs at a slightly different point in opening and closing a form. Sometimes your triggering event is crucial; other times it may not matter. For example, there is only a small difference between the Enter and GotFocus events.

care which of the two events triggered your code. For example, if you want to display a simple message when the user enters a certain box, either event will work. However, if you want to intercept them before they attempt to make changes to the data in the box, you must assign your code to the Enter event. Once the GotFocus event occurs, keystrokes are routed to this control. Another difference between the two events arises when you examine what happens when a user has more than one form on the screen. If a user clicks to a second form, the control on the first form will experience a LostFocus event, but not an Exit event. Similarly, the active control on the new form will trigger a GotFocus event, but not an Enter event.

Notice that several events take place when a user moves to the next row of data in a table. First the old control triggers the Exit and LostFocus events. Then the form's Current event fires, then the leading control on the form experiences the Enter and GotFocus events. Keep in mind that the user will need the mouse or keyboard to cause this change, so mouse moves, clicks, and keystroke events will be triggered.

Examples

This section presents several examples of situations that are likely to arise in business applications. Portions of the programming code are presented for the examples, but you will have to add more code to use the examples in a real application. The objective is to highlight the capabilities and problems you are likely to encounter in an event-driven interface. The key to understanding the examples and their importance lies in the events. Many of the examples are utilized in the Rolling Thunder Bicycle database. You can find more detailed code within its forms.

Verify Changes

When a form is bound to a recordset, any changes made by the user are immediately stored in the corresponding database tables. You can use integrity constraints to place some limits on the data that can be accepted. However, what if you want to create a smarter application? When a user changes a value in one particular control, you have a set of logic conditions that evaluate the other data and determine if the new value is reasonable. If the value seems unreasonable, you want to warn the user and give him or her the chance to keep the original value. The basic code for this test is attached to the BeforeUpdate event. That is, you want to test the value before it is actually stored in the database. Then you give the user a chance to keep the original value. One catch is that you often need to know the original value. As shown in Figure 8.19, by the time

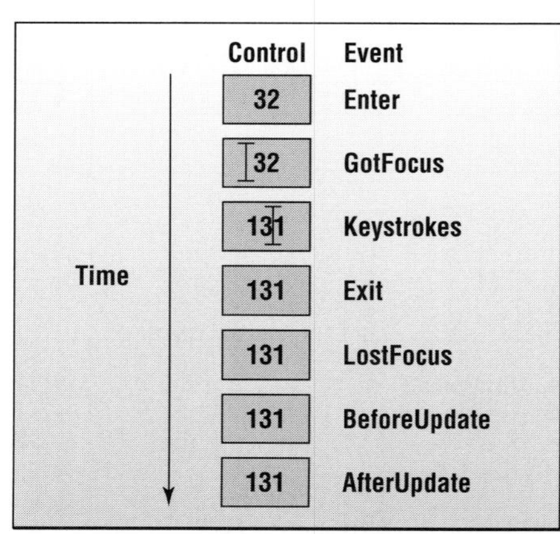

FIGURE 8.19 Event sequence for changing data. You want to validate the data before it is stored in the database but need the original value (32).

FIGURE 8.20
Code to save original value for later use. To make the variable accessible to both the Enter and BeforeUpdate subroutines, it must be created in the module declarations section.

```
General: Declarations
Dim varOld As Variant
Sub ctl_Enter
  varOld = ctl
End Sub
Sub ctl_Before Update
  If (MsgBox ("OK to change?" . . . ) = vbNo) Then
    [ctl] = varOld
  End If
EndSub
```

the BeforeUpdate event arises, the original value (32) is lost. Within the BeforeUpdate subroutine, you can examine only the current value (131).

The code fragments in Figure 8.20 show a way to solve this problem. You need to capture the original value as soon as the user enters the control. This value is moved to a temporary variable (varOld). The second catch is that any local variable created within the Enter subroutine exists only when the Enter subroutine is active. To share this value with other subroutines (e.g., BeforeUpdate), you need to create the variable in a location that is accessible to both the Enter and BeforeUpdate routines. Hence the variable is created in the declarations module for the form. Now the value that exists when the control is entered (32) is transferred to a safe location in memory (varOld in the module). When the data is changed and the DBMS attempts to move it to the database, the BeforeUpdate event is triggered and your code can retrieve the original value.

Updating Inventory

Although it is not obvious, a similar technique is used for updating inventory QOH. Many business applications involve inventory and sales data. The inventory table holds a list of items and the amount the company has on hand. When a customer places an order, the application should automatically change the corresponding QOH for that item. Hence when the salesperson (or clerk) fills out the computerized order form, the QOH should automatically be changed. The first issue you face is deciding which event should trigger this change to inventory: when the form is completed and the user closes the order form? when the user clicks a button that says all of the items have been shipped? when the user enters each item on the subform? The final choice depends on the business operations of the firm. However, the most direct method is to update the inventory as the item quantity is entered on the subform.

As shown in Figure 8.21, the first step in this process is to build the subform on a query that joins the ItemsSold table to the Item table. Then for each row on the subform, the corresponding QOH is immediately available. This join eliminates the need to look up the QOH value in a separate table. The query does it automatically.

The second step is to attach code to the AfterUpdate event of the QuantitySold (or shipped) control. That is, when a user enters a value, the quantity sold is stored in the database. Then you have to subtract this quantity from the QOH. The simplest code consists of one line: QOH = QOH − Quantity.

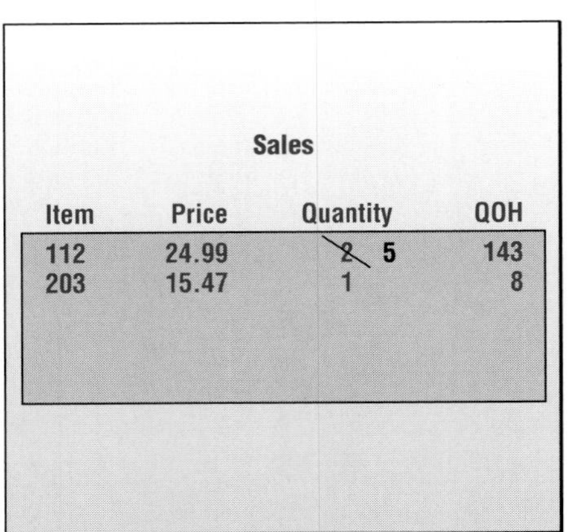

FIGURE 8.21 Updating inventory. Join the Item table to the ItemsSold table. Then use AfterUpdate in Quantity to change the QOH value. But what if the user goes back and changes the Quantity?

However, there is a problem with this code. What happens if the user goes back and changes the Quantity? To see the problem, examine the values step by step as shown in Figure 8.22. When the user enters a sale of two items, the code correctly subtracts two items from inventory QOH. But what happens when the user changes the two to a five? Then the five is correctly recorded as a sale, but the inventory code subtracts five more items from the QOH. The inventory QOH is incorrect, because the code subtracted a total of seven items from inventory instead of just five.

The problem is that the code assumes that there is no previous value in the Quantity control. The solution is to see whether there is already a value in the Quantity box and then modify the inventory update formula. Now you can see how this problem is similar to the previous section. You need to use the Enter event to capture any value that might already exist in the Quantity control. The skeleton code with the modified formula is shown in Figure 8.23. When the user enters the Quantity control, save the initial value in a safe location. In the process convert a missing value (Null) to zero. When the number has been changed (AfterUpdate), alter the QOH by the difference. In the example the QOH was originally decreased by the two units entered initially. When the user changes the two to a five, the code will decrease QOH by three more units (5 − 2).

There is an additional consideration with this type of code. Think about what happens in the following sequence of events. First, the user enters an item to be sold. Then a quantity of two units is entered. At this point the QOH is updated, and two units are removed from the QOH for that item. Now the user realizes that the wrong item was entered and goes back and changes the ItemID. What happens to the QOH for both the original and the new items? How can this problem be fixed?

FIGURE 8.22 Event sequence for simple update code. When the user changes the two to a five, the code deducts another five items from inventory. But that value is wrong.

	Inventory		Event
	Item	QOH QOH-Qty	
	112	145	Initial value.
Time ↓	112	143 = 145 − 2	User enters sale of 2 items.
	112	138 = 143 − 5	User changes value to a 5.

FIGURE 8.23
Correct code. Quantity on hand should be changed by the difference between the new (Quantity) and the original (varOld) values. That is, if the user changes a two to a five, then inventory should be decreased by three more.

```
Declarations
  Dim varOld As Variant

On Enter
  varOld = Quantity
  If IsNull(varOld) Then varOld = 0

AfterUpdate
  QOH = QOH - (Quantity - varOld)
```

Alternative Inventory Updates

Several techniques have been devised to handle inventory updates to a master inventory list. Each technique has different strengths and weaknesses. The method described in the preceding section always keeps the master inventory list accurate. Because this method records changes when items are ordered, there is less possibility of accidentally running out of stock. It is particularly valuable when many online sales occur at the same time. However, it is complex to program, which runs the risk of causing errors in the inventory database.

The reason for the complexity of the instantaneous update is that users might change the data. You need to anticipate the various changes. One solution to avoiding this complexity is to record the changes to the master inventory table only after all possible changes have been made.

The trick to deferring inventory updates is that you need to add a column to the transaction table that indicates whether or not the transaction has been updated. For example, in the Pet Store database, you would add a Posted column to the SaleItem table. The default value for this column would be Null (or No). At some point in time, a subroutine is run that subtracts the ordered quantity from the master inventory table. For example, when the order is shipped, no more changes are possible, so inventory updates can be safely recorded. The routine also sets the Posted column in the SaleItem table to True or to the date it was updated. A second routine can routinely check the SaleItem table for items that have not been posted. This approach is straightforward, relatively easy to program, and provides an audit trail for verifying changes.

Hierarchical Combo Box Data

Many business situations use hierarchical relationships. For example, a company may be divided into divisions, which are subdivided into departments. Similarly, individual products may be classified according to categories. It is likely that some of your application's forms will need to collect data on both of the related items. For example, consider the portion of the departmental evaluation form shown in Figure 8.24. The evaluator is asked to enter both the division and department. Obviously, it is best to use combo (or list) boxes for this purpose. That way, the user can simply choose the appropriate division and department. However, typical combo boxes for these values would be independent. That is, the first box would list all the divisions, and the second box would list all of the departments in the company. Yet after the user chooses the division, it makes sense to reduce the number of departments and display only the departments for the chosen division.

The basic trick in this technique is to understand that the combo box uses an SQL query to select the data to be displayed. In Access the query is stored in the RowSource property of the combo box. A traditional query simply selects all the

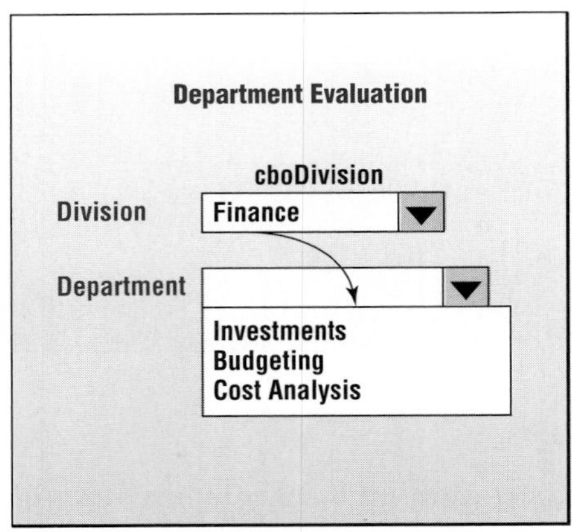

FIGURE 8.24
Related combo boxes. After the division is selected, all the choices in the department combo box should be from the chosen division.

rows from the department table. To limit the choices, simply add a WHERE clause to the SQL statement. The SQL query in the cboDepartment.RowSource becomes SELECT . . . FROM Department WHERE Department.Division = [cboDivision]. Now the department combo box will display only choices that match the division chosen in the other combo box.

There is one catch. In Access all combo box choices are generated when the form is loaded. When the user changes the entry in the division combo box, the choices in the department box have already been established and they will not be changed. To force them to update, you need to add one line to the division combo box in the AfterUpdate event: cboDepartment.Requery. That is, whenever the division combo box gets a new value, the department combo box list will be regenerated to include only those departments in the selected division.

Combo Box NotInList Event

Combo boxes are useful data entry tools. They also improve data integrity by requiring users to enter data from an existing list. They are particularly useful in relational databases. Chapters 2 and 3 show how normalization is used to improve the storage of data by splitting it into tables. These tables are connected by the key values. For example, an order form references the associated data in the customer table through a CustomerID. When users enter a new order, they need only enter the CustomerID. The problem is that you cannot expect users (or customers) to memorize their assigned CustomerID. The combo box offers a solution to this problem. Users select from the existing customer table, and the CustomerID is entered into the Order table.

However, this approach presents another problem. To ensure referential integrity, a CustomerID can be entered into the Order table only if the corresponding customer already exists in the Customer table. This method works fine for existing customers, but what happens if a new customer calls to place an order?

The basic answer is that the customer must first be entered into the Customer table. There are two common methods to accomplish this task. First, you could put a separate button on the form near the combo box. The user clicks this button to add a new customer, and the Customer form is displayed to collect the essential data. Of course, the new data should then be transferred back to the Order form combo box, so the user does not have to reselect the customer.

A second approach is to use the NotInList event of the combo box. To add a new customer, the user types a new name into the combo box. If the name is not in the existing list, the NotInList event is triggered. Your code in this event needs to

FIGURE 8.25
NotInList code to add a new customer. There are three basic steps: (1) be sure the user really wants to add a customer, (2) add a new row to the Customer table, and (3) open the Customer form at the new row.

```
Set dbs = CurrentDB()
Set rst = dbs.OpenRecordset("Customer")
Set ctl = Me!Customer
ctl.Undo
If (MsgBox("Do you wish to add a new Customer?", vbYesNo, _
   "Customer" & NewData & "is not in list yet.") = vbYes) Then
   rst.AddNew
   rst!CustomerName = NewData
   strMatch = "[CustomerID] = " & rst!CustomerID
   rst.UPDATE
   DoCmd.OpenForm "Customer", , , strMatch
   rst.Close
   Response = acDataErrAdded
Else
   Response = acDataErrContinue
End If
```

do three things: (1) ask the user whether they want to add a new customer, (2) add a new row to the customer table, and (3) bring up the Customer form so the user can fill in the details. Notice the similarity to using a separate button. The primary difference is that the combo box is more automatic. The drawback is that it does not work as well if two customers have the same name.

The basic code for this procedure is displayed in Figure 8.25. Note the use of the data access object (DAO) instead of SQL to add the new row to the Customer table. The reason is that you need the CustomerID that is generated from adding the new row. Using SQL would require at least two separate statements and would present additional problems if two customers happened to have the same name. Also, note the role played by the Response variable. If your code adds a new element to the combo box list, the combo box needs to be requeried to add the new element. The acDataErrAdded response tells Access to automatically requery the list.

Interactive Lookup List

The list box can be a useful tool when users need to see several items at the same time. Figure 8.26 illustrates a basic system to record receipt of purchases. The items

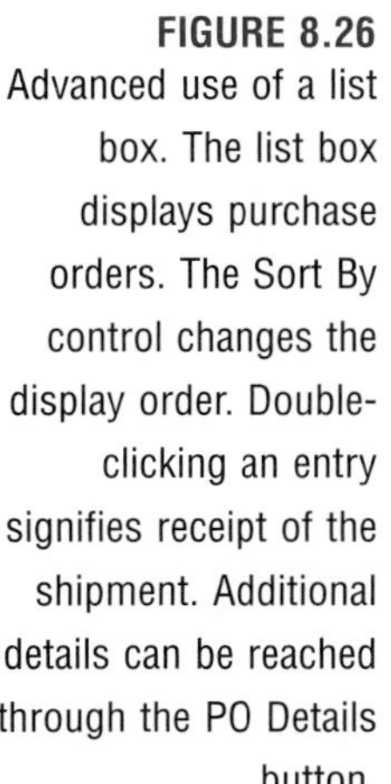

FIGURE 8.26
Advanced use of a list box. The list box displays purchase orders. The Sort By control changes the display order. Double-clicking an entry signifies receipt of the shipment. Additional details can be reached through the PO Details button.

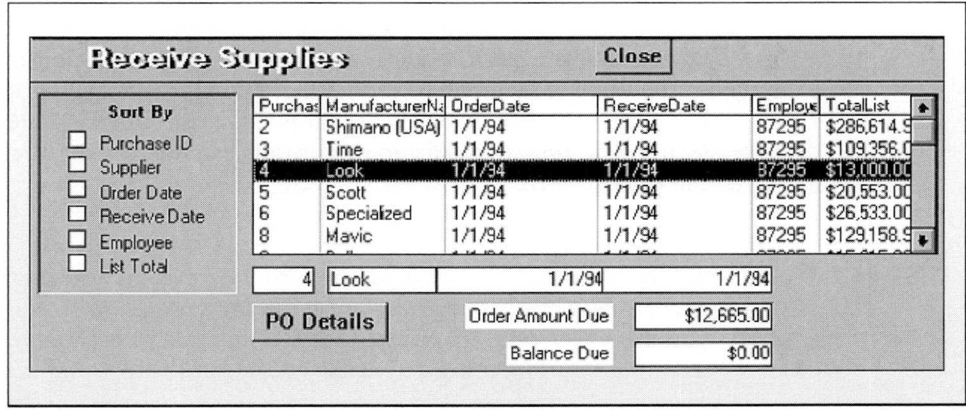

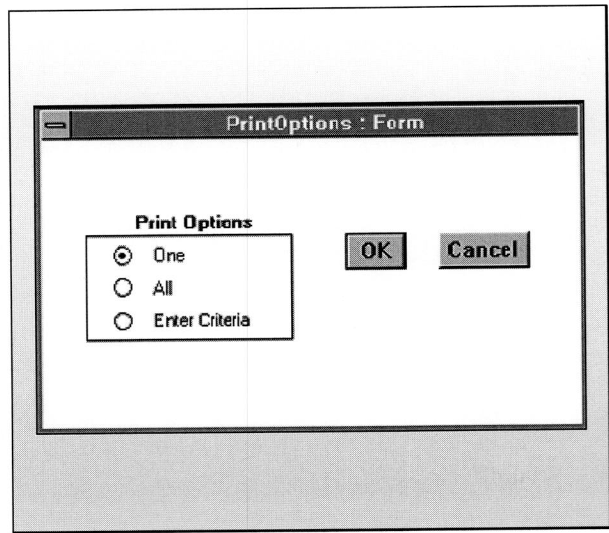

FIGURE 8.27 Print options form. This form can be called from other forms. Based on the response, your code opens the report with the appropriate data.

were already entered on a purchase order. As shipments arrive, users have to find the matching purchase order and mark the items as received. The list box displays the orders. Users can control the order of the display by checking the Sort By conditions. The corresponding purchase order can be retrieved by clicking the PO Details button. The form could be further improved by adding more extensive search capabilities.

Note that most common activities can be accomplished by point-and-click commands. For example, if an entire shipment is received, double-clicking the appropriate row records the date and time the shipment was received. All ordered items are recorded as received, and the inventory quantity is increased by the appropriate amount. If some items are not received, the user can go to the purchase order and set the received quantity on the appropriate items.

Print Options

Many people still like to keep paper copies of various forms and reports. Hence most forms will have a Print button. For example, an order form should have a Print button. Sometimes the user will want to print just the current order. Other times, a manager might want to print a range of orders based on a set of conditions. Because these options might apply to any form, it makes sense to write a general print option subroutine. A sample form is shown in Figure 8.27. This form can be called from any other form, but it requires code to interpret the responses. One possible version of the code is included in the Rolling Thunder Bicycles Order form. The basic idea is to open the report differently depending on which of the three options was selected. The only complication is passing parameters between your subroutine and the options form.

CUSTOM REPORTS

As discussed in Chapter 6, report writers are good at formatting data for common reports. Some report writers are powerful enough to handle complex reports. Yet you might encounter reports that are difficult to create with a report writer. For example, you might need specialized output controls, such as standard generalized markup language (SGML). Similarly, you might want conditional formatting, where the output changes based on the data. For example, if a particular value is large, you might be asked to create a new section to the report that provides additional detail.

As much as possible, you should use a report writer to display the final report. Creating reports with programming is time-consuming. Additionally, it is difficult to modify the code later. In some cases you can use custom programming to generate the data and then use the report writer for the layout and formatting. For instance, you might have a program that generates the final data. This data can be stored in a new table. Then you use the report writer to display the data.

If you have to create an entire report with programming, you face a challenging problem. In particular, you need to know the characteristics and capabilities of the output device (printer). Modern printers support multiple typefaces and various graphics capabilities. These features provide detailed control over the output but significantly increase the time it takes to program the report. Hence it is generally best to use programming for computations and to use the report writer to handle the layout and printing. If this option is not sufficient, you should consider generating the report in a standard document language like rich text format (rtf) or encapsulated postscript (eps). Then use a word processor to retrieve the report and provide touch-ups and layout controls.

The common report layout structure is shown in Figure 8.28. Grouping data and producing subtotals is known as a **control break** and is a common feature of business reports. As long as you understand the basic layout, it is not difficult to generate reports with a programming language. The first step is to create a query that provides the data on the report. It is best to use SQL to join all needed tables. Then you write a program that starts at the top of the query and examines each row. Your code must identify the breaks for each group. You should also keep track of the number of lines so that you can identify the end of the page. Your code becomes more complex if you want to keep all elements within a group on one page. Then you have to determine the size of the group before it is printed.

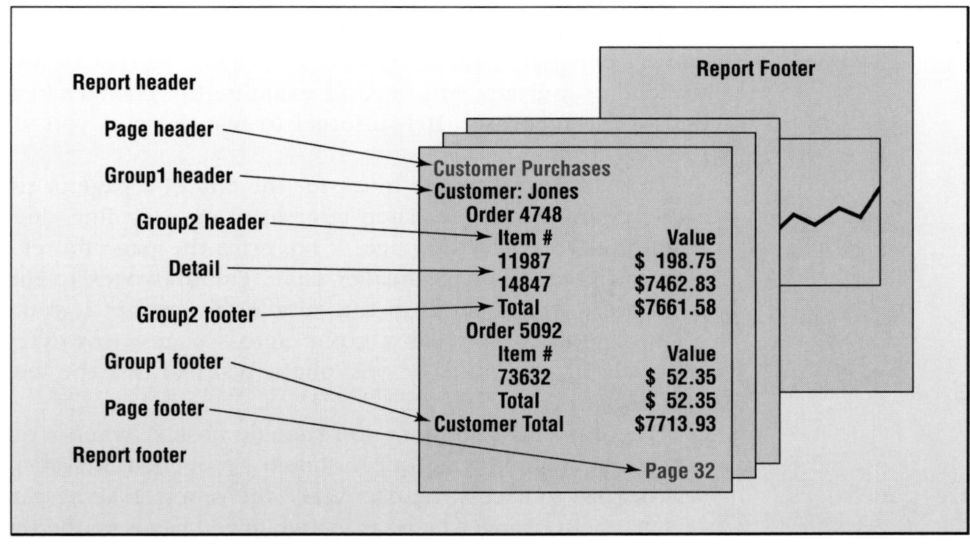

FIGURE 8.28 Common report layout. Each group break must be tracked within your program. Similarly, you will have to keep track of the number of lines on each page and the length of the page.

```
Report header
Loop
  Test for top of page
  Test for top of group 1
    Test for top of group 2 and so on
  Perform calculations and subtotals
  Print detail row
  Increment line and position counters
  Test for page break
    Print page footer
  Set all prior group values
  Read next row of data
  Test for end of groups
    Last to first
    Print group footers
End of main loop
Report footer
```

FIGURE 8.29
Logic to generate a standard report. You test for the end of a group by comparing the new key value to the key value in the preceding row. Hence you copy all of the preceding keys into variables before you read a new row.

The basic logic for a standard report is shown in Figure 8.29. Remember that your code examines one row of data at a time. You should keep a state indicator variable that keeps track of the current level. For example, is it time to print a group header? When you read a new row of data, you compare it to the preceding row to see whether you have reached the end of a group. In the example, you would look for a new order number to indicate the end of an order group. Similarly, a new CustomerID would signify the start of a new customer group. When you encounter a new group, you print the group footer for the preceding group and set a flag to print the group header for the new group.

Figure 8.30 illustrates the basic code to create a common report with one group break. The example monitors and prints the group header, the detail, and the group footer. Additional group breaks can be handled with additional variables and by expanding the conditional tests for the header and footer. In testing for the end of a group, you need to examine the changes in data and check for the end of the recordset. If you forget to test the end, you will not get a footer for the last group.

You also need to add a test for the end of a page. A simple method is to add a line counter variable. Then after printing each line, decide whether you have reached the end of the page. If so, print the page footer and set the state variable to trigger the page header code. The drawback to this approach is that the page break might occur in the middle of a group. If your groups are large, you might be forced to break a group across pages. However, if several groups will generally fit on one page, you might want to test the length of a group before you print it.

There is one final point you should consider when writing programs to create reports: Your underlying query should be opened in read-only mode. Then others will be able to access the data while the report is being generated. If you are concerned about changes being made while you generate the report, open the query as a snapshot, which makes a temporary copy of the data.

FIGURE 8.30
Partial code to create a report. Handling the group break is the important step. Be sure to test for the end of the data, as well as the change in key values.

```
Dim dbs As Database, rst As Recordset
Dim lngPriorKey1 As Long, bolTopGroup1 As Boolean
Dim dblSum1 As Double, dblSubTotal1 As Double

Set dbs = CurrentDB()
Set rst = dbs.OpenRecordset(" ")
rst.MoveFirst
bolTopGroup1 = True
dblSum1 = 0#
dblSubTotal1 = 0#
Do Until rst.EOF
   If (bolTopGroup1) Then
      ' Print group header
      bolTopGroup1 = False
   End If
   'Print detail line
   dblSubTotal1 = dblSubTotal1 + rst!Value1
   dblSum1 = dblSum1 + rst!Value1
   lngPriorKey1 = rst!Key1
   rst.MoveNext
   If (rst.EOF) Or (lngPriorKey1 <> rst!Key1) Then
      ' Print group footer
      dblSubTotal1 = 0#
      bolTopGroup1 = True
   End If
Loop
rst.Close
```

DISTRIBUTING APPLICATIONS WITH MICROSOFT ACCESS

Figure 8.31 summarizes the steps you follow to distribute your application. After you create the application, you need to package it so that users can easily install it. In those rare situations where you have only one user, you could install the application yourself and customize the installation. However, in most cases you will need to create a simple installation package so the user can click a few buttons and install the application.

The most important step is to make sure that the entire application will run from your forms—without the need to modify tables or entries using the Access tools. Your application should start as soon as the database is opened. You can use the Tools, Startup options to specify the initial form and control the menus. Or you can build a simple AutoExec macro that opens your main switchboard form. Just make sure that you test the entire application to be certain that you never need to use the main Access form (Tables, Queries, Forms, and Reports).

Depending on the needs of the users, you have two main choices in how to distribute an Access application. First, if users need access to all of the tables, forms, reports, and code, you can give them the full database you created as an mdb file. They will need a complete, licensed copy of Microsoft Access to run the application. Second, if you want to protect your tables, forms, and code, you can use the Tools, Database Utilities, Make MDE option to create an mde file. An mde file essentially encrypts the database application so that no one can examine or change the layout. Be careful to keep your original (mdb) database file—not even you will be able to modify the mde file. Unless the users need the ability to create new

- Make the application stand alone
  - Runs completely from your forms
  - Never needs to use the Access database menu (tables, queries, forms, reports)
  - Automatically starts when the database is opened
    - Tools | Database Utilities | Startup
    - AutoExec macro
- Application format
  - Standard mdb file
  - Encrypted mde file
- Run-time package (developer's edition)
- Security (Chapter 10)
- Installation package (developer's edition)

FIGURE 8.31 Distributing Access applications. For commercial applications, you should consider purchasing the developer's edition (or other software), which enables you to create a simple installation program.

tables, queries, and reports, the mde approach is the preferred format for distributing your database.

In some cases you may wish to take one more step. If you purchase the developer's edition of Access, you can distribute your application with a run-time module of Access. With this version, your users do not need to own a copy of Access. The developer's edition also includes a customizable installation package. With these two features, you can copy all the necessary files onto disks (or a CD-ROM). The user simply inserts the first disk and runs the Setup.exe file. The application is automatically installed on the user's computer. You can even include an icon that users can install on their desktop to start the application. With the run-time module, the Access application looks and behaves like any other Windows application.

One important catch with Access applications is that they are interpreted code, which runs slower than compiled code. If you want a truly stand-alone compiled application that uses multiple databases and takes advantage of in-depth Windows features, you can create the application in Visual Basic. The appendix shows how Visual Basic forms are similar to Access forms and discusses some of the details of creating database applications.

SUMMARY

An application is a collection of forms and reports designed to function as a system for a specific user task. Applications must be easy to use and designed to match the tasks of the users. Application design begins with the overall structure, which is often held together with switchboard forms. Menus and toolbars add structure to the application by providing commands that are common to the entire application. Toolbars can also be created for specific tasks and individual forms. A context-sensitive Help system with both general descriptions and detailed help notes is crucial to creating a useful application. Most applications also need to define individual transactions so that related changes will succeed or fail together.

Individual forms can be improved by utilizing the various events. For example, when data is changed, you could have a short program to analyze the effect and verify the change or make changes to other data. An expert system application might suggest other changes to the user. In a transaction processing application, several events are used to record changes to inventory as items are sold or purchased. Other useful features involving events include handling hierarchical data and NotInList event handling for new entries in combo boxes.

Sometimes you will have to write custom reports. Many of the same programming principles apply. First you define a query; then your code analyzes the data row by row and produces the output. Many times it is helpful to store the output in a new table and then create a report based on the output table. Other times you will have to send the output to a printer or to a word processor document. In either case you should be familiar with the fundamental concepts of control breaks and subtotals.

> **A DEVELOPER'S VIEW**
>
> Miranda is learning that applications are usefuly only if they make the user's job easier. A good application is more than just a collection of tables and forms. That means you have to organize the application by the tasks of the user. You also need to add help files and toolbars. Some problems occur repeatedly in business (e.g., inventory, adding new customers, hierarchical relationships, and customized reports). You should know how to handle these issues and incorporate them into your design. You must always remember that a key task is to protect the integrity of the data, so your application needs to identify and handle transactions properly. For your class project, you should create the overall application structure (switchboard forms, interlocking forms, toolbars, help files, and so on). You should also identify all transactions that involve multiple changes.

KEY WORDS

application, 278
context-sensitive Help, 288
control break, 303
data integrity, 279
dockable toolbars, 285
graphics interchange file (GIF), 292
Help system, 284
hypertext markup language (HTML), 292
icon, 286
menu, 284
NotInList, 294
prototype, 281
switchboard form, 281
toolbar, 284
tooltip, 286
transaction, 293
user interface, 284
volume table of contents (VTOC), 283

REVIEW QUESTIONS

1. What are the fundamental principles to follow when designing an application's structure?
2. How does the purpose of an application (transaction processing, decision support, or expert system) affect the design?
3. How are switchboard forms commonly used?
4. What are the potential problems with switchboard forms?
5. What is the purpose of menus and toolbars in an application?
6. What are the primary steps involved in creating a context-sensitive help file?
7. What are transactions and how do you define and control them in a database application?
8. What are the primary events that occur when opening a form in Microsoft Access?

9. Explain the complications that arise when a form automatically changes inventory levels as a product is sold.

10. What is the basic logic involved in creating a group control break for a report?

EXERCISES

1. Create a sales form with sale items linked to inventory. First, the user enters an item to be sold. Then a quantity of two units is entered. At this point the QOH is updated and two units are removed from the QOH for that item. Now the user realizes that the wrong item was entered and goes back and changes the ItemID. What happens to the QOH for both the original and the new items? Write the code to fix the problem.

2. Build two hierarchically related combo boxes with a WHERE clause in the lower-level box. What happens when there is no value in the top-level box? Should the lower-level box display all of the choices? Write the code to fix this problem.

3. Create a form and write the underlying code to compute the selling price of a custom-built wheel. Note that a wheel has a hub, a rim, and spokes. Front wheels and rear wheels use a different hub. The hub is drilled for a specified number of spokes (stored in the Height column). The rim is also drilled for a fixed number of spokes. The form should force users to select a rim and a hub with the same number of holes. The cost of the wheel consists of the component parts plus a labor charge that is 20 percent of the list price. You might want to add data to the component table to provide a more realistic test.

4. Create a small database with a Customer table that includes AmountOwed and a Transaction table that records payments by the customer. Create a form and write the transaction code to record a payment by the customer and decrease the AmountOwed.

5. Create a small database with Customer and Order tables. Build a form for adding new customers. Build a form for adding new orders. Use a combo box on the order form to select existing customers. Use the NotInList event to add new customers from the order form.

6. Create a small database with a table for a soccer game that lists two teams. Another table lists the teams. First, create a relationship that links the two tables. Now create a Game form that asks the user to enter the two teams. What happens if you enter a team that is not in the Team table? Next, delete the relationship. Write a short program to test the team data entered on the Game form. If the team is not in the Team table, display a message box. What are the advantages and drawbacks of the second method?

Sally's Pet Store

7. Design and create a completed switchboard menu system for the Pet Store database. Add sections that can be completed later.

8. Design and create a menu system and toolbars for the Pet Store database.

9. Create and write a set of help files for the Pet Store database.

10. Create a form for a potential customer to enter desired features of a new pet. Include two combo boxes: one to select the type of animal and one to select the breed for that type of animal. The second combo box should show breeds only for the animal type selected in the first combo box.

11. Create a print option form that is triggered from the Customer form. Allow users to print a report for one customer (the one displayed), all customers, or a range of customers specified by the user.

12. Create a form that enables users to look through the merchandise. Include the option to display a picture of the item. Include basic search buttons so the user can find products based on categories and types of animals. Provide the ability to drag and drop an item on an order icon (shopping cart) to place an order.

Rolling Thunder Bicycles

13. Examine the Rolling Thunder Bicycles application and outline the VTOC by checking the forms and reading the help file.

14. Examine the forms and identify the transaction processing components and decision support components provided by the Rolling Thunder Bicycles application.

15. Explain how the list box is used to handle receipt of merchandise from suppliers. Outline the process that is used to tie the receipt to the purchase order.

WEB SITE REFERENCES

Site	Description
http://www.microsoft.com/win32dev/uiguide/	Microsoft user interface guide.
http://www.microsoft.com/enable/	Microsoft site for accessibility issues.
http://www.ameritech.com/corporate/testtown/library/standard/std-guix.html	Ameritech user interface guide.
http://www.acm.org/sigapp/	Association for Computing Machinery: Special Interest Group on Applied Computing.

ADDITIONAL READING

Gray, J., and A. Reuter. *Transaction Processing: Concepts and Techniques.* San Mateo, CA: Morgan Kaufmann, 1993. [An in-depth treatment of transaction details.]

Melton, J., and A. R. Simon. *Understanding the New SQL: A Compete Guide.* San Mateo, CA: Morgan Kaufmann, 1993. [Particularly Chapter 14.]

Strijland, P. "Human interface standards: Can we do better?" *StandardView (ACM)* 1 no. 1 (September 1993), pp. 26–30. [One of many articles on the human-computer interface.]

APPENDIX

Database Applications in Visual Basic

Microsoft Visual Basic (VB) is a programming language that is designed to build standalone applications. These applications can connect to various databases—whether they are created in Access or another supported database. VB uses syntax similar to Visual Basic for Applications (VBA) that is used by Access. However, VB forms have fewer restrictions than forms created within Access. Additionally, VB applications can be compiled to executable programs, which run faster than Access forms do and are also easier to distribute to users. This last feature is a powerful advantage for creating applications. Your application runs like any other Windows application. It is fast and has access to and control over Windows resources. In addition, most people feel that VB is easier to program than C++, which is the traditional language used to create Windows applications.

On the other hand, VB is more complex, and applications require more programming than Access forms do. Version 5, the professional edition (and enterprise edition) of VB has database wizards that help you create forms that resemble the typical forms created in Access. However, many of the features and capabilities within VB are slightly different than their Access counterparts.

The purpose of this appendix is to show you how a database form can be created within VB. To demonstrate the concepts and to provide a working example, the main Sales form from the Pet Store has been created in a VB 5 project. Because of the length of the code, only portions are displayed here. The full project is on the instructor's CD-ROM and is available for download from the associated Web site.

Getting Started

Regardless of the programming environment, the first step in any database application is to identify the data needed and create the database tables. In most cases the easiest method is to create the tables within Access. VB enables you to use other database systems, but Access table definitions are easy to create and modify. You can always move the tables to a different DBMS later.

The second step is to design the application. Everything in VB is based on forms, so you need to draw all the forms that will be used. You should even consider building prototypes within Access. Because of the programming required, VB applications can be difficult to change. With Access, if you (or the users) do not like a form, deleting it and starting over is relatively easy.

The third step is to build skeleton forms within VB. The basic form design (layout, colors, etc.) is easy to create within VB. You can use drag-and-drop techniques

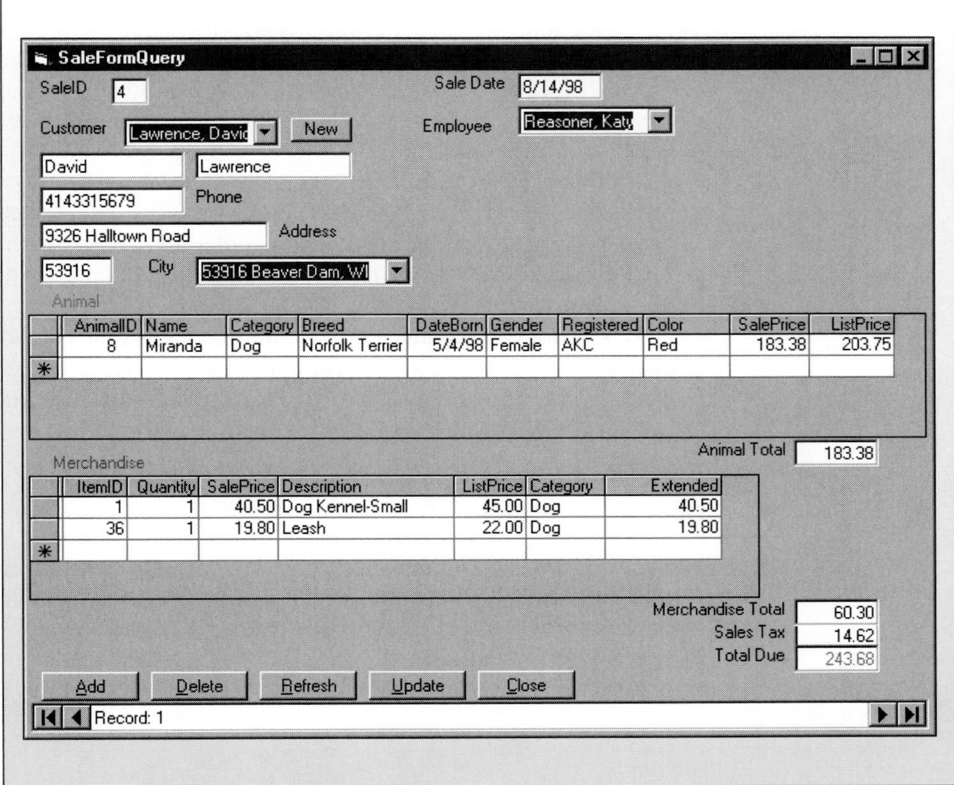

FIGURE 8.1A
Sales form in Visual Basic. Note the use of combo boxes, default values, and automatic computation of totals. Users can generally fill out the form by clicking the mouse a few times and by entering two or three basic items.

to place labels, text box controls, combo boxes, and so on. You can use the Application Wizard to create the structure and base forms for your database. However, you will have to make substantial modifications to all of the forms. The Data Form Wizard will help you construct forms that are more complex. In particular, it will help you build a common main/subform for one-to-many relationships. For example, a typical order form uses a subform grid to display the items being purchased. The wizard even creates the code that keeps the subform data synchronized with the main form. When the user selects a new order, only the items matching that order are displayed in the subform.

The fourth step is to add features that make your application easier to use. For example, users cannot memorize ID numbers, so combo boxes should be used to select items from a list. VB has two types of combo and list boxes: lists that are tied to a database and lists that have to be created with a programming loop. For most database applications, you will use the controls that can be tied to the database. As described in this chapter, you will want to include additional features, such as command buttons to link to other forms and automatic calculations.

Sally's Pet Store Sales

The VB Sales form is shown in Figure 8.1A. Notice the similarity with the original Sales form developed in Access. (An early version of that form is shown in Figure 6.10.) Notice the two subforms or grids, which are required because of the two one-to-many relationships. A given sale can contain many animals or many merchandise items. Also, note the use of combo boxes to select the sales employee and the customer. Some features can be seen only by using the form. You should obtain the executable application and the database and run the application to see how it works. Try entering new orders. Which values can you change? Which items cannot be changed from this form?

You begin to see the differences between VB and Access forms when you look at the design view of the VB form in Figure 8.2A. The Access design view is much simpler, since many of the details are handled in subforms. The data-bound subforms are not available in VB, so the animal and item details are handled with the data-bound grid control (dbGrid).

Combo boxes and dbGrids are common tools that you will use in your database applications. Each combo box and dbGrid is associated with a data control. The data control defines the database and the query that will be used by the combo box or the dbGrid. These data controls are usually made invisible on the final form (set the Visible property to False).

Overall Data-Bound Form

The initial step in building this form is to use the Data Wizard to create the initial form. The wizard does a poor job at layout and design; however, it does perform the most important task—it inserts the primary data control and the secondary data con-

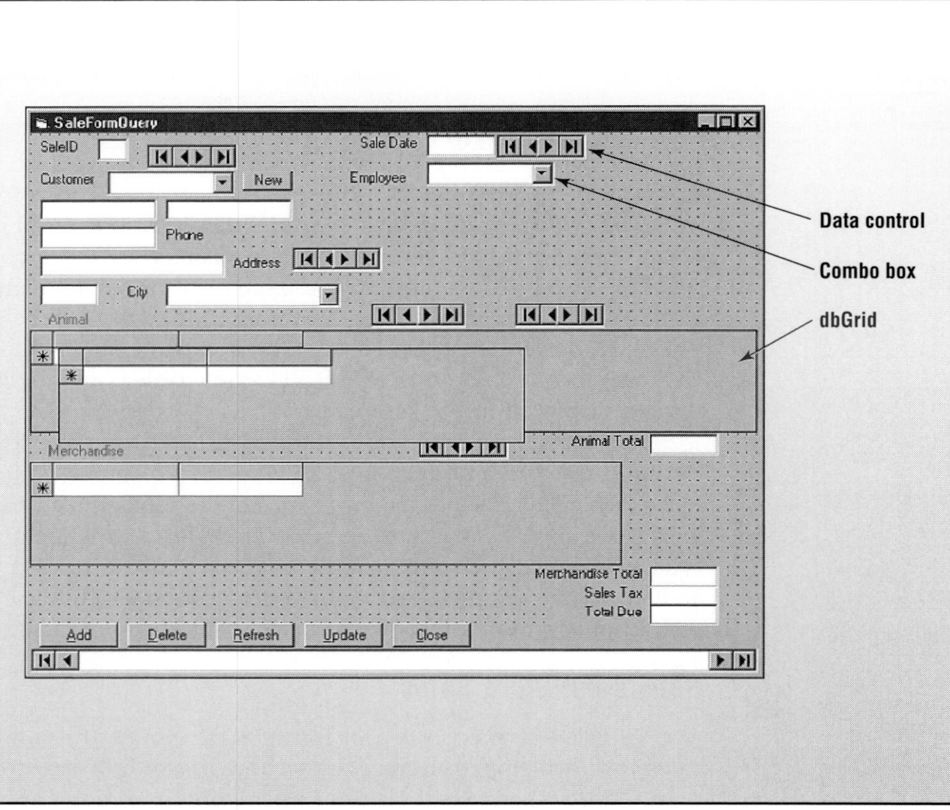

FIGURE 8.2A Design view of the Sales form in Visual Basic. For database applications, the data control, combo box, and dbGrid are commonly used tools. Note that each combo box and each dbGrid is tied to a data control. These data controls are usually set to invisible on the main form.

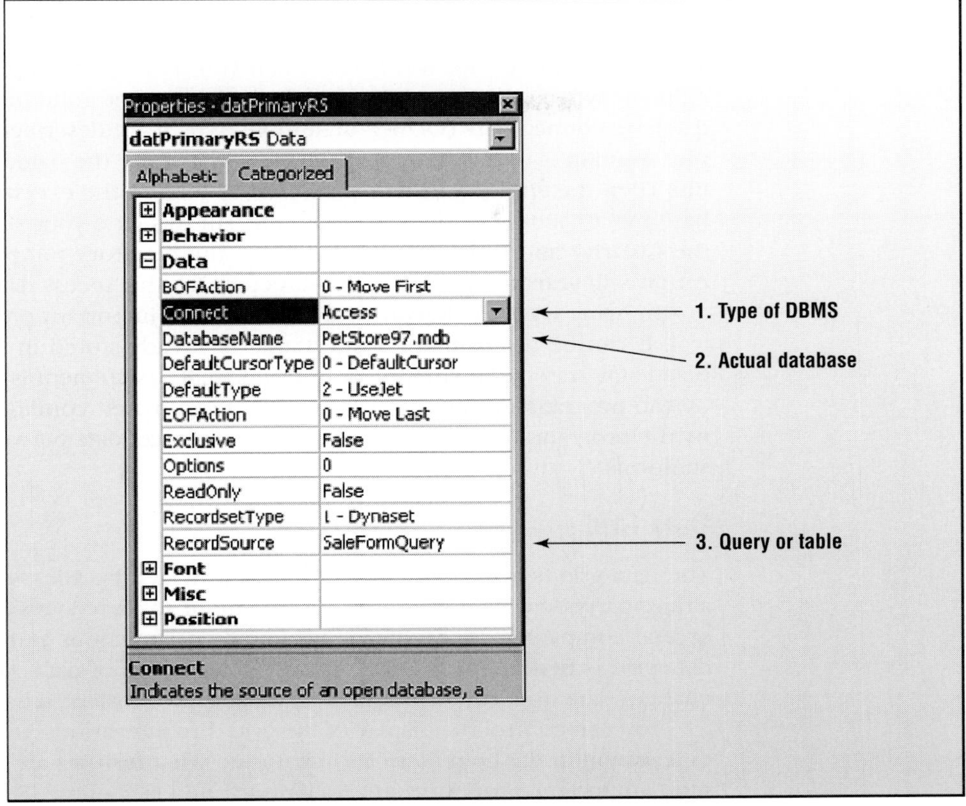

FIGURE 8.3A Data control properties. You must set these three properties, and they must be set in this order. You should also give the control a meaningful name.

trol for the Animal grid. The wizard also writes the code that links the two controls together so that the subform displays only animals purchased on the displayed sale.

Once the wizard builds the base form, you can rearrange the labels and controls to make the form more useful. You will also have to add a new data control and a new dbGrid for the Merchandise grid.

Data Control

The purpose of the data control is to handle the connection to the database. It locates rows of data, and it transfers data between the database and the form. Any time you want to look at or change data on the form, you must use the data control. You will almost never change the data directly on the form. Instead, you change the value in the data control, which transfers it to the database, and then refresh the screen so that it displays the current values.

The primary data control is visible to the user at the bottom of the Sales form. By clicking on the record selectors, the user can track through and display the various rows of sales data.

The most important properties of the data control are shown in Figure 8.3A. In addition to giving the control a meaningful name, you must set these three properties, and you have to set them in the order indicated.

The name of the database seems trivial, but it can present problems. VB likes to set the name using the full path name, which specifies the drive and the subdirectory containing the database. If you leave the full path name in the property setting, then your application can run only if the database is stored in that exact location. This situation does not work well when you transfer the application to a user's machine or when users rearrange their hard drives. One solution is to always use open database connectivity (ODBC) definitions, which are described in Chapter 11. A simpler solution is to delete the path name and just use the name of the actual database file. Then the application will work fine, as long as the executable file and the database file are stored in the same directory. In this case your startup form should use the ChDrive and ChDir commands to set the directory to App.Path; then the application will search the application directory for the Access database.

In many ways the RecordSource is the most important property of the data control. It can be the name of a query that is already stored in the database, or it can be an SQL statement. The power of using an SQL statement is that it can be changed by the program so that the data retrieved can match conditions set by the user or by the program. This feature is used to synchronize data between the main form and subforms.

Data Grid

The data grid is a separate control that is provided by Microsoft but was written by a third-party developer. You can purchase more advanced versions of the control from several companies. Each control has its unique functions and capabilities. The basic data grid is tied to a data control and displays rows of data. After the user enters or changes data on a row, the data is automatically transferred back to the database.

You can control the display of the grid through various properties. Read the documentation in the help files carefully to see what features are available. For now, the most important properties are DataMode and DataSource. Set DataMode to Bound and then enter the name of the data control in the DataSource property.

The method for synchronizing the data grid to the main form is outlined in Figure 8.4A. The key is to place the code in the Reposition event for the main data control. For example, when the user clicks to display a new sale, then the data in the grid

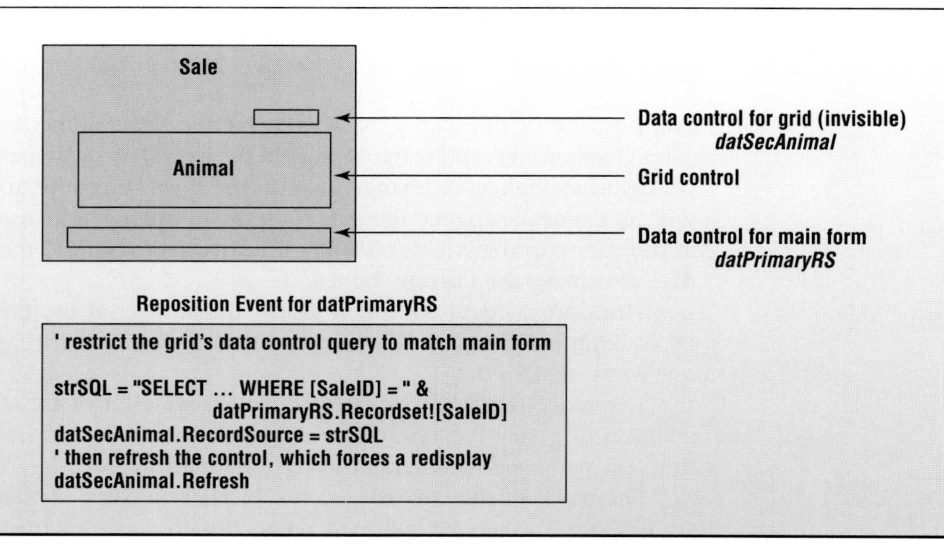

Sale
Animal
Data control for grid (invisible)
datSecAnimal
Grid control
Data control for main form
datPrimaryRS
Reposition Event for datPrimaryRS
' restrict the grid's data control query to match main form
strSQL = "SELECT ... WHERE [SaleID] = " &
datPrimaryRS.Recordset![SaleID]
datSecAnimal.RecordSource = strSQL
' then refresh the control, which forces a redisplay
datSecAnimal.Refresh

FIGURE 8.4A Synchronizing subform data controls with the main form. When the main form data changes (Reposition event), you have to restrict the data control source for the Animal grid and then call the Refresh method to refresh it to actually retrieve the data and redisplay the grid.

FIGURE 8.5A
Code to automatically assign key value in the subform data grid. The key value (SaleID) from the main form (datPrimaryRS) is placed into the key value (SaleID) for the subform (datSecAnimal).

```
Private Sub grdAnimal_BeforeUpdate(Cancel As Integer)
  If Not IsNull(grdAnimal.Columns(1).Value) Then
  datSecAnimal.Recordset.Fields("SaleID").Value _
       = datPrimaryRS.Recordset.Fields("SaleID").Value
  Else
     Cancel = True
  End If
End Sub
```

must be changed. In the Sale example, you want the secondary data control to retrieve just the items that are associated with the sale currently being displayed. You find them by altering the SQL statement to retrieve only those items where the SaleID matches the SaleID displayed on the main form. Hence the code sets the secondary data control's RecordSource and then calls its Refresh method.

Through data normalization one-to-many and many-to-many relationships are created using tables that are linked by ID numbers. For example, the Sales form uses tables for Sale(<u>SaleID</u>, SaleDate, EmployeeID, CustomerID, SalesTax) and SaleAnimal(<u>SaleID</u>, <u>AnimalID</u>, SalePrice). There is a similar SaleItem table. Whenever a clerk enters a new row to represent the sale of an animal, the key (SaleID) must also be entered into the SaleAnimal table. Your application should automatically insert the proper SaleID (from the Sale table).

The SaleID from the Sale table can be automatically copied to the SaleAnimal table with the code shown in Figure 8.5A. The SaleID is not even displayed on the grid. The code is triggered after the clerk enters the other data on the row. Immediately before the new data is written to the database, this code is executed. To avoid common errors, the code first checks to make sure an AnimalID value was entered. If not, there is no point in saving the data, so the update is canceled.

Combo Box

The data-bound combo box is similar to the combo boxes available in Microsoft Access, but there are some important differences. To start with, in Access, the SQL statement to retrieve the display choices is a property of the combo box. In VB, the SQL statement is handled by a separate data control.

The key to combo boxes lies in the five properties highlighted in Figure 8.6A. Again, you should enter the properties in the order shown. Notice that the combo box uses two different data controls. One of them is used to retrieve the values you want to display in the combo box. The second is used to store the particular item that the user chooses. In the Sales form example, the clerk needs to select the customer from the entire list of customers. The ID for the selected customer will then be stored in the Sale table. The list of all customers is retrieved by the datCustomer control and set in the RowSource. The users will see the CName column, but your program will see the corresponding CustomerID as specified in the BoundColumn. Once the user selects a customer, the chosen CustomerID will be stored in the CustomerID column (DataField) of the datPrimaryRS (DataSource).

A limitation of the VB combo box is that it can display only one column to the user. In the customer example, it looks like you are limited to displaying only the customer's last name. In practice, you would probably need to display the last name, first name, and phone number. You can overcome this limitation by creating a spe-

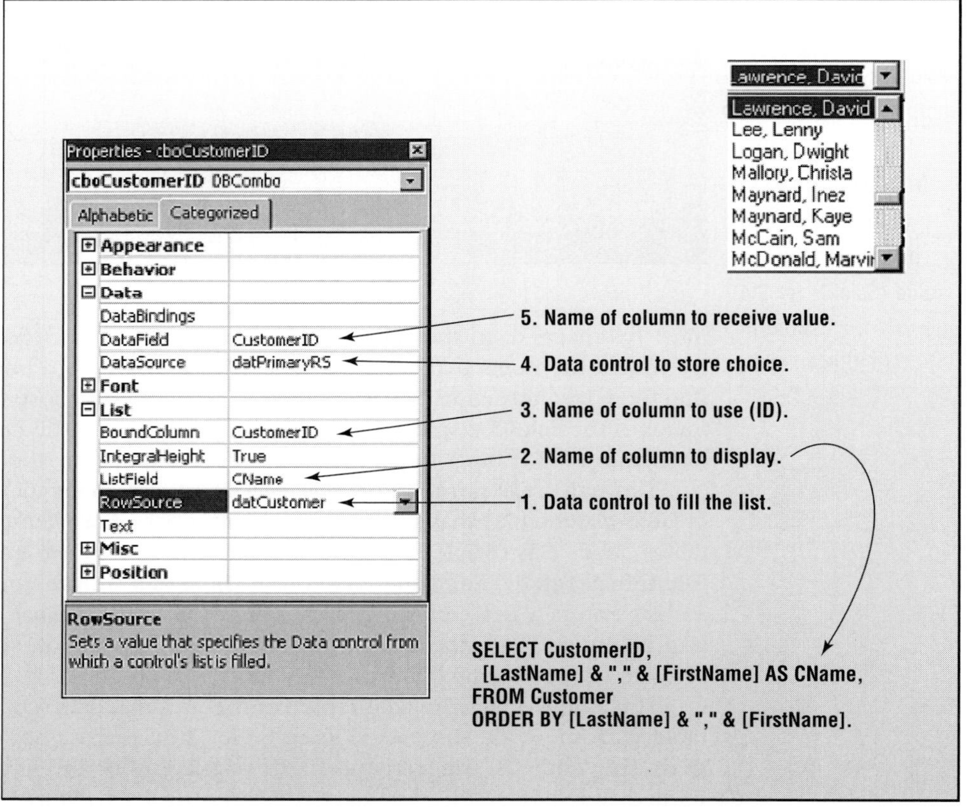

FIGURE 8.6A Visual Basic combo boxes. There are two main sets of properties to set. First, create the data control that displays the items you want to show. Enter the name of the data control, the column you want to display, and the column of data that you want to use. This third item is usually an ID value. That is, users will see the list shown in the ListField (CName), but when they select an item, your program will see the corresponding BoundColumn (CustomerID). The value they choose from this list will be stored in a different data table, set by the RowSource and the DataField.

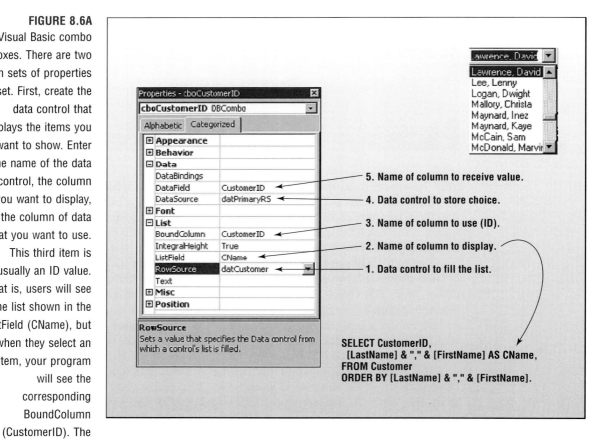

cial query in the database. Use SQL to combine all the items you want to see into one new column. For the Customer combo box, the query is SELECT CustomerID, [LastName] & "," & [FirstName] AS CName, FROM Customer ORDER BY [LastName] & "," & [FirstName]. Notice that the first name is appended to the last name and the combined result is treated as a new column (CName). Any number of columns can be combined using this technique. The only drawback is that it is difficult to align the columns in the final display.

Another difference between Access forms and the VB combo box is that it does not support the NotInList Event. In the Sales form example, how can a clerk add a new customer? The solution is to add a New button next to the combo box. When the clerk clicks this button, you need code to add a new row to the Customer table. Then place the automatically generated CustomerID into the primary data control for the Sales form. Finally, the clerk has to enter the corresponding name and address data for the customer. If all of the necessary data is displayed on the main form, users can enter it immediately. If additional data needs to be entered, your code should open a Customer form and display the appropriate row of data. The code to perform these tasks is shown in Figure 8.7A.

Because you already have a data control to display customer information, using the AddNew method to create a new customer is easy. Be sure to retrieve the new CustomerID. Then use the Edit method to assign that ID to the current Sales data (in the datPrimaryRS data control).

In most cases you will want to open an additional (Customer) form so that the clerk can enter more data about the customer. The key in this case is to use the FindNext method of the data control in the new form to locate the matching data.

Combo Box in Subform Data Grid

Combo boxes are useful tools in a relational database. They enable users to deal with data in a familiar format. For example, clerks can select animals based on name, breed, and category. In particular, users do not have to memorize ID numbers. Yet the database can utilize the underlying ID numbers to ensure that unique values are entered. Consequently, it would be nice to use a combo box lookup to identify the animal or merchandise being sold. That is, we need a combo box in the ID position on the subform grid. An Access database form can handle this situation easily. Because the grid is really a subform, you simply replace the ID textbox with a combo box and it will still function properly. VB requires a little more effort but can provide some additional features.

If you look closely at the design view of the Sale form (refer to Figure 8.2A), you will see that there are actually three data grids on the form: one for the animal sales, one for the merchandise sales, and one mysterious grid on top of the animal sales grid. (Actually, there should be four, but that one is saved for a student exercise.) If you check the properties or examine the run-time form, this mysterious third grid is normally invisible. The purpose of the grid is to hold the drop-down (or pop-up) values much like a combo box.

The primary steps to creating this combo box functionality are shown in Figure 8.8A. To create the functionality of a combo box in the data grid, you must first create a new data grid and make it invisible. Remember that to create a data grid, you must also add a data control that will perform the actual data transfer. In the Pet Store example, these controls are called grdAnimalID and datAnimal, respectively. The data control retrieves some basic data (name, category, breed, list price) about the animals. If it were visible, the data grid would simply display these values. To be safe,

FIGURE 8.7A
Code to add a new customer. First create a new row in the Customer table (datCustomer). Then place the CustomerID into the Sales table (datPrimaryRS). Then make it easy for the clerk to enter the rest of the customer data. On the same form, use SetFocus to move to the first entry point. In other cases you may want to open a separate Customer form.

```
Private Sub cmdNewCustomer_Click()
   Dim v As Variant
' Create new customer
   datCustomer.Recordset.AddNew
   v = datCustomer.Recordset.Fields("CustomerID")
   datCustomer.Recordset.Update
' get CustomerID, and stick it in the primary/sales recordset
   datPrimaryRS.Recordset.Edit
   datPrimaryRS.Recordset.Fields("CustomerID") = v
   datPrimaryRS.Recordset.Update

' Since all the necessary data is on this form, just fill it out
   txtFields(8).SetFocus

' If you need, you can open the Customer form, in case there is more data
   'frmCustomer.Show
   'frmCustomer.SetFocus
   'frmCustomer.datPrimaryRS.Recordset.FindNext "CustomerID=" & v
End Sub
```

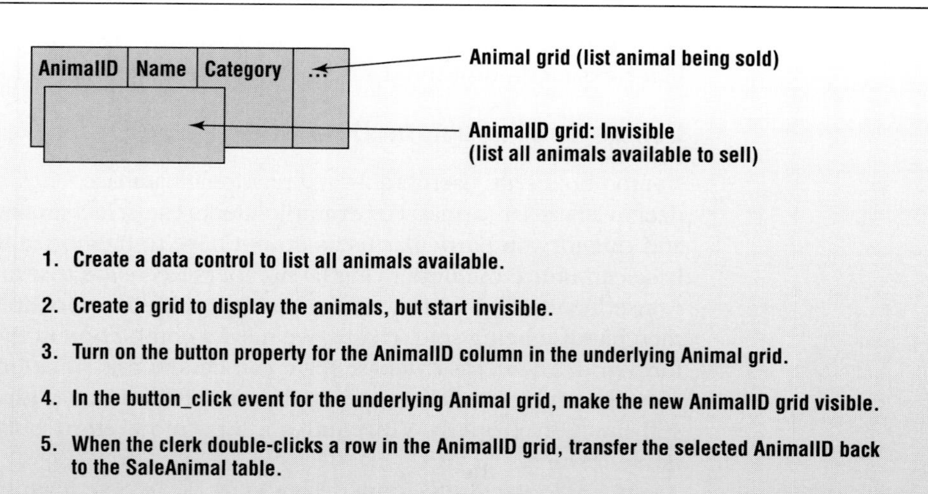

AnimalID
Name
Category
...
Animal grid (list animal being sold)
AnimalID grid: Invisible
(list all animals available to sell)
1. Create a data control to list all animals available.
2. Create a grid to display the animals, but start invisible.
3. Turn on the button property for the AnimalID column in the underlying Animal grid.
4. In the button_click event for the underlying Animal grid, make the new AnimalID grid visible.
5. When the clerk double-clicks a row in the AnimalID grid, transfer the selected AnimalID back to the SaleAnimal table.

FIGURE 8.8A Steps to create a combo box within a data grid. Create a new data control and data grid to list all the animals available (grdAnimalID). Make it invisible until the button is clicked in the AnimalID column. When the user selects an animal, transfer its AnimalID to the SaleAnimal table

you should set the AllowUpdate and AllowDelete properties to False so that users do not accidentally alter data. You can also set the ReadOnly property to True in the data control. Ideally, the data control should show only animals that are available to be sold (i.e., not including the animals that have been sold).

Now, you need some event to make the new data grid visible. The best solution is provided by the underlying animal grid. Each column has a Button property. If you set this property to true (grdAnimal.Columns"AnimalID".Button = True), then a small combo box arrow will be displayed in the cell when that column is selected. Now all you have to do is display the new grdAnimalID whenever that button is clicked. The basic code is straightforward. All you really need is grdAnimalID.Visible = True. However, as shown in Figure 8.9A, the user might have altered the display the last time it was activated. To be consistent, your code should reset the main properties to their default values.

The only remaining step is to transfer the selected value from the pop-up display into the underlying SaleAnimal table. The most common method for the user to select an item is to double-click the desired row. You could also use a single click,

FIGURE 8.9A Code to display the pop-up list of animals for sale. Only the Visible property is required. The others are used to set the default values in case they were changed by the user in an earlier display.

```
Private Sub grdAnimalButtonClick(ByVal ColIndex As Integer)
  If (ColIndex <> 1) Then Exit Sub
  datAnimal.RecordSource = "SELECT AnimalID, Category, Breed, . . . "
  datAnimal.Refresh
  grdAnimalID.Visible = True
  grdAnimalID.Columns("AnimalID").Width = 720 ' Reset to default values
  grdAnimalID.Columns("Category").Width = 945 ' in case user changed
  grdAnimalID.Columns("Breed").Width = 1545   ' them last time
  grdAnimalID.Columns("Name").Width = 1170
  grdAnimalID.Columns("ListPrice").Width = 870
  grdAnimalID.Columns("ListPrice").NumberFormat = "#,##0.00"
  grdAnimalID.SetFocus
End Sub
```

FIGURE 8.10A
Code to transfer the selected AnimalID to the SaleAnimal table. Note the additional subroutines to compute the total value of animals sold and the sales tax.

```
Private Sub grdAnimalID_DblClick()
   datSecAnimal.Recordset.Edit
   datSecAnimal.Recordset.Fields("AnimalID") _
        = datAnimal.Recordset.Fields("AnimalID")
   datSecAnimal.Recordset.Update
   varTotalAnimalSale
   Compute Tax
   datPrimaryRS.UpdateRecord
   grdAnimal.SetFocus     ' Just to be safe
   grdAnimalID.Visible = False
End Sub
```

but the user might want to use a single click just to highlight the row. In any case you should test the application with the users. You can always call the same code for a single click later. The code to perform the transfer is shown in Figure 8.10A.

The most important point to notice in Figure 8.10A is that the code changes the AnimalID in the underlying data control. It does not attempt to change the value in the grid itself. The datSecAnimal object refers to the data control that provides data to the animal sale grid. Also, notice that changing data in the database requires the familiar Edit and Update pair described in Chapter 7. The varTotalAnimalSale subroutine simply computes and displays the total value of animals being purchased on the form. Because the clerk has just changed the animal data, it is necessary to recalculate the total. Likewise, the ComputeTax subroutine uses the total to determine the new sales tax due. Calling datPrimaryRS.UpdateRecord quickly fills in the values in the animal grid that match the selected AnimalID. Finally, the code makes the pop-up grid invisible again.

These illustrations cover the code you need to create a pop-up combo box within a data grid. However, it is possible to make the pop-up grid more powerful. For example, if the clerk clicks on a column heading, the display will automatically sort the data by that column. Additionally, if the clerk presses a letter (or number), the grid will find the next row where the first letter matches the one pressed. For example, if the cursor is in the Category column and the clerk presses *d,* the display will leap to the next row containing a dog. These two features require additional programming. You can test them and examine the underlying code within the VB Pet Store application.

Summary

This appendix presented a quick overview of how to build an application within VB that interacts closely with a database. Part of the objective was to duplicate features available within a typical Access form. The most important items you will use are the data control, the data grid, and the database combo box. Remember that you will need a data control to set the SQL statement anytime you want to retrieve or store data in the database.

You should consult other books on VB programming to learn more details about the many controls. You should also read the VB help sections carefully—particularly the information about the dbGrid control. Finally, you can only learn programming by writing code. Remember that two subform grids appear on the Sale form. As an exercise you should add the ItemID pop-up combo box to the merchandise grid. Just copy and modify the code from the animal grid.

PART 4

Database Administration

Large applications require careful support. Most organizations hire a database administrator to monitor application performance, assess security, and ensure database integrity. Chapter 9 explains how application performance can be improved through physically controlling database storage. Chapter 10 highlights the tasks of the data administrator and the database administrator—with special emphasis on database security. Once again, SQL has a strong role in managing and protecting the database.

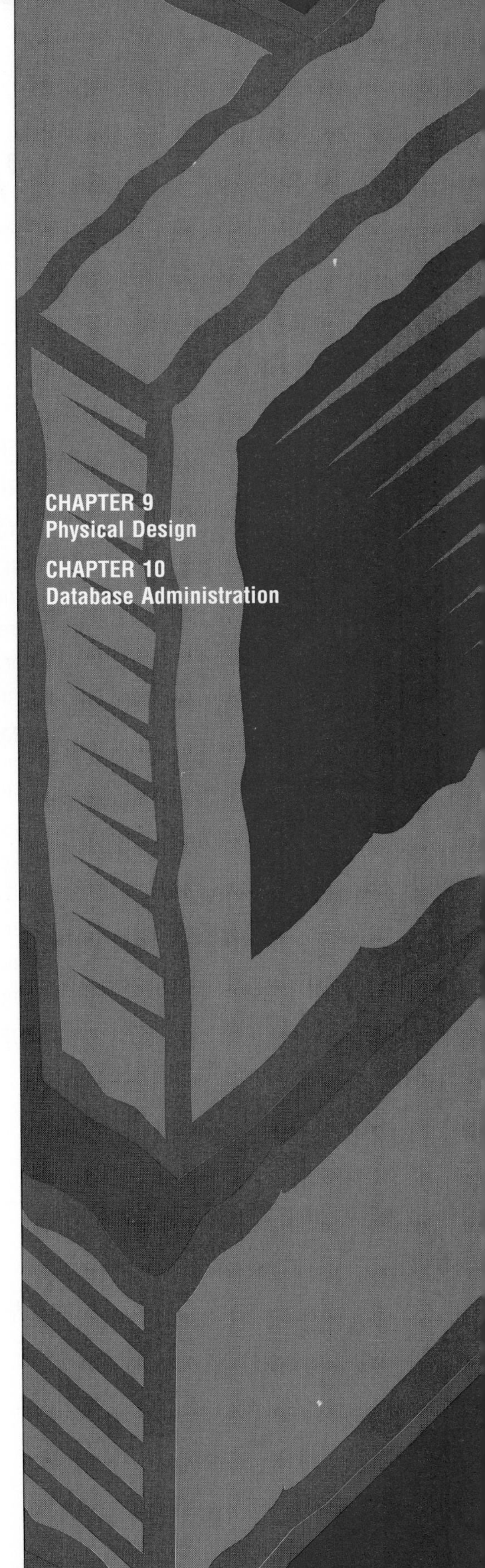

CHAPTER 9

Physical Design

WHAT YOU WILL LEARN IN THIS CHAPTER

- What happens when your application becomes large? 324
- How do database systems physically store data? 326
- How can you speed up your application? 328
- How do indexes improve performance? 331
- When do indexes degrade performance? 338
- When should tables be partitioned and stored in different locations? 342

OVERVIEW

Ariel: *Why do you look so tired?*

Miranda: *Well, I thought I was done with the application three weeks ago. Everyone loved it. Things were going great.*

Ariel: *So what's wrong with that?*

Miranda: *Nothing, but something strange happened.*

Ariel: *Those wizards didn't get loose did they?*

Miranda: *No, but I might need their help to solve this problem. My uncle said that all week long the application has been slowing down. Some of the combo boxes are taking a minute to display data, and one form takes 5 minutes to store new data.*

Ariel: *So? Why is that your problem? Can't they just buy faster computers?*

Miranda: *Maybe, but it sounds like something else is wrong. I think they just entered more data than I expected. I need to find some way to speed up the application.*

INTRODUCTION

Any database application is created through the basic steps described in Chapters 2 through 8. You get the user requirements, design the database through normalization, create the queries using SQL, build forms and reports, and then add the details to create a complete application. However, with large applications, one more step is critical to the success of your application. You must analyze its performance. Performance is largely controlled by telling the DBMS how to physically store and retrieve the data.

If computers were fast enough, how the DBMS physically stored the data for each table might not matter. Today, for small applications, this situation is probably true. The default storage method provides acceptable levels of performance, and you could skip this chapter. However, as databases and applications become larger or contain specialized types of data, physical storage becomes an important issue in the performance of your application. Large business applications routinely hold millions or even trillions of rows of data in tables. Proper configuration is essential—otherwise, even simple queries could take minutes or hours to run.

There are two basic questions to answer in storing data tables: (1) How should each row of data be stored and accessed? and (2) How should individual columns be stored? The first question is more difficult to answer and is determined largely by how the data is used. Hence we must first examine the possible uses of the database. The answer to the second question depends largely on the type of data being stored. For traditional business data (numbers and small text), the answers are straightforward. If your application stores more complex data objects, the second question becomes more critical.

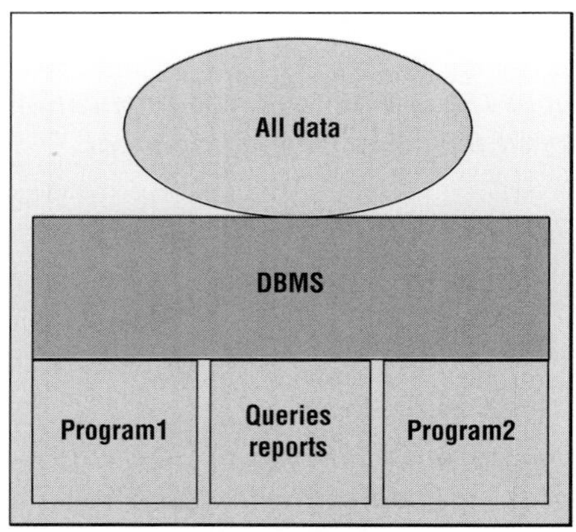

FIGURE 9.1
Data independence. The DBMS separates the programs from the data, which adds a layer to the processing—potentially delaying applications.

PHYSICAL DATA STORAGE

Early database systems—particularly relational databases—were criticized because of their sluggish performance. Recall the overall database approach shown in Figure 9.1. All access to the data is channeled through the DBMS. This extra layer means the processor must perform additional computations to store or retrieve any piece of data. Particularly with older, slower processors, this burden might result in slower application programs.

Look closely at the diagram and recall the purpose of the database approach described in Chapter 1. A key purpose was to separate the data from the programs. Achieving this goal means that the data is also separated from the programmer. The programmer no longer has control over how the individual data is stored or retrieved. Without the DBMS a good programmer could tailor the data storage to improve the application performance. The problem with this customization was that it made one application or one type of data retrieval very fast but made it slower for any other application or user to access the same data.

Recall the example of the hierarchical database described in Chapter 1, where customer data and their orders were stored in one file. As long as you want to retrieve data by customer starting from the top of the hierarchy, the system was very fast. However, it was painfully slow or impossible to find out which customers ordered a specific item.

The ability to share data and provide reasonable performance to answer any question is an important goal of the relational database. Yet application developers quickly learned that for large databases they needed some mechanisms to improve the performance. Some uses of the database might be more important than others. For example, a transaction processing application to sell products would need to rapidly look up product information and store sales data. To keep customers happy and improve the efficiency of the clerks, the system must not impose any delays. On the other hand, consider a store manager who wants to compare departmental sales from last week to this week. The manager would like to get the answer in a reasonable time, but a delay of a few minutes would probably be acceptable—especially if the report is only generated once a week. The point is that applications need different levels of performance. Hence developers need the ability to fine-tune the way that data is stored and retrieved. This tweaking can be accomplished by telling the DBMS how to physically store the data.

TABLE OPERATIONS

Database performance can be controlled by telling the DBMS how to store and retrieve data in each table. To understand the differences between storage methods, you must first understand how the DBMS will use the data. Then by evaluating how

FIGURE 9.2
Table operations. Every application must perform these operations. The key is to determine which operation is causing delays.

- Retrieve data
  - Read entire table
  - Read next row/sequential
  - Read arbitrary/random row
- Store data
  - Insert a row
  - Delete a row
  - Modify a row
- Reorganize/pack database
  - Remove deleted rows
  - Recover unused space

each storage method affects the various table operations, you can choose the best method for your particular application.

Three major categories of operations affect tables: (1) retrieving data, (2) storing data, and (3) reorganizing the database. Each category contains more detailed tasks that are described in the following sections. The operations are summarized in Figure 9.2.

Every application will perform all of the operations within the categories. As a developer you need to examine the application and identify the operations that are affecting performance.

Retrieve Data

Retrieving data constitutes some of the most common activities in a database application. These operations also present the best opportunity to improve performance. Applications commonly perform three types of data retrieval. They read the entire table, read the next row in a sequence, and find and retrieve an arbitrary row.

Reading the entire table, or large portions of it, might not seem like a common operation, but it does occur relatively often when printing reports. For the example in Figure 9.3, to print weekly paychecks, the application will have to read every row

FIGURE 9.3
Read a table sequentially. Sequential retrieval requires the data to be sorted; for example, this customer data is sorted alphabetically by LastName and FirstName. Fortunately, sort methods are so fast that they do not generally affect the application performance.

LastName	FirstName	Phone
Adams	Kimberly	(406) 987-9338
Adkins	Inga	(706) 977-4337
Allbright	Searoba	(619) 281-2485
Anderson	Charlotte	(701) 384-5623
Baez	Bessie	(606) 661-2765
Baez	Lou Ann	(502) 029-3909
Bailey	Gayle	(360) 649-9754
Bell	Luther	(717) 244-3484
Carter	Phillip	(219) 263-2040
Cartwright	Glen	(502) 595-1052
Carver	Bernice	(804) 020-5842
Craig	Melinda	(502) 691-7565

in the employee table. But what if hourly workers are paid weekly, but managers are paid monthly? In most companies the managers represent only a small percentage of the total workers, and retrieving 90 percent of a table is no different in performance than retrieving 100 percent.

Reading the next row in a sequence is related to retrieving all the data in a table. When an application needs to read an entire table, it is generally retrieved in some order or sequence. For example, paychecks might be printed in alphabetical order by employee name, department name, or postal code.

The more challenging retrieval operation is the ability to retrieve any arbitrary row. It is sometimes called random access because the database does not know which record might be requested. For example, any customer could place an order at random, and the database would have to retrieve the matching data for that customer.

This lookup process is one of the most critical elements to affect the performance of your application. It is easy to spot in situations like the customer example. The clerk enters a customer name or number, and the database has to retrieve the matching data. Clearly, you want to keep the lookup time as short as possible to avoid delays for the customer and the clerks.

Yet there is a more critical problem involving lookups. Any time you build a query, two types of random lookups come into play. First, joining two tables requires the database to match the values in one table with those in a second table. This matching requires the database to look up matching data in the second table. Second, any time you impose a condition with the WHERE statement, you are asking the DBMS to find rows that match that condition. So query performance is directly related to how fast the database can perform lookups and match the data requested. These lookups are critical because they are so numerous. Joining two tables could require thousands or millions of lookups—depending on the number of rows in the two tables. Remember that many tasks throughout the application use queries.

Store Data

A DBMS has to perform three basic operations involved with storing data: inserting a new row, deleting a row, or modifying the data in a row. Most systems implement a fast delete operation—they do not actually remove the deleted data. As shown in Figure 9.4, it is much faster to just mark the row as deleted. Then when the database

FIGURE 9.4
Delete a row. Deletion is fast because the DBMS just marks the row as deleted. It does not actually remove the data.

LastName	FirstName	Phone
Adams	Kimberly	(406) 987-9338
Adkins	Inga	(706) 977-4337
Allbright	Searoba	(619) 281-2485
Anderson	Charlotte	(701) 384-5623
Baez	Bessie	(606) 661-2765
xBaez	Lou Ann	(502) 029-3909
Bailey	Gayle	(360) 649-9754
Bell	Luther	(717) 244-3484
Carter	Phillip	(219) 263-2040
Cartwright	Glen	(502) 595-1052
Carver	Bernice	(804) 020-5842
Craig	Melinda	(502) 691-7565

wants to retrieve an item, the DBMS first checks to see whether the item has been deleted. If so, the DBMS ignores that row. Similarly, a good DBMS attempts to store data in fixed block lengths, so that if a row is modified, the DBMS can simply overwrite the data. With highly variable-length data, this operation is not always possible, so the DBMS must perform a delete and an insert operation.

In terms of performance, the biggest issue with delete operations involves storage space instead of speed. Although a row has been deleted, it still takes up physical space. Sometimes the DBMS can overwrite the old data, but after a while, there can be millions of bytes of unused fragments.

Inserting a new row of data is one of the more challenging aspects in a database management system. Next to random lookups, it is the source of the most performance problems. In fact, there is generally a trade-off between the two issues. If a system is good at random lookups, it is not as efficient at storing new data rows. That is, the techniques used to improve random lookups often require significantly more time to add data rows.

The performance issues of adding new data are somewhat technical and will be explained in more detail in the section on data storage methods. For now, examine your application to identify which tables will add new data on a regular basis and which tables might add data only occasionally. For example, a firm might add only a few new items a year to the Products table. However, thousands of new rows could be added to the Order table every day.

Reorganize the Database

Largely because of the deletion method, a database can become disorganized over time. Data that is flagged as deleted is still hiding in the table space. Empty holes of storage space are too small to hold new data, and data rows that are used together are no longer stored near each other.

These problems are particularly challenging with relational databases. In a relational database the system data is also stored in tables. For example, the form layout that you redesigned 20 times is stored as rows in a table. Each time you redesigned it, the database flagged the old version as deleted and saved the new version. Complex forms could take up several thousand bytes of storage.

Most systems have an administrative command to reorganize or **pack** the database. This command causes the DBMS to go through the data and rewrite each table—clearing up the storage space.

A major challenge to database administration is to determine how often to run this command. There are two complications. First, it can take several hours for this command to process large databases. Second, a few systems require that all users be logged off the DBMS before the administrator can run this command. You want to avoid database systems with the second requirement. It prevents you from providing 24-hour access to the database. However, even if other people can still use the system, database reorganization can affect the overall performance of the application, so the process generally needs to be performed during slow periods (e.g., at night).

On the flip side, if you forget to periodically reorganize the database, it can rapidly fill with wasted space. It is not uncommon for even a small Access database to grow from under 1 megabyte to 5 or 6 megabytes of storage space during development. Be sure to use the database utilities to compact the database. Doing so will make it much easier and faster to back up and copy the data files.

Identifying Problems

During the database design stage, you should be able to identify potential problems. You need to analyze the database usage and volume statistics collected in Chapter 3. In particular, look for large tables, heavily used tables, transaction tables requiring fast database responses, and queries with multiple joins, complex criteria, or detailed subqueries. You should also perform tests during the development of the applications. Generate large sample tables and test the performance of the queries, forms, and reports. Once the database application is operational, you can use the performance monitoring tools described in Chapter 10 to locate bottlenecks.

Once you identify the form, report, or query that is causing delays, you need to determine the cause of the problem: data retrieval, data storage, or data reorganization. You can use the programming debug feature to step through code that utilizes many different operations. By timing procedures and loops, you can determine which section is causing the longest delays. You can also use the Timer function to record the times of various operations.

Once you have identified the location of the delays, you can test various strategies for improving performance. If the delays involve your program, explore different ways to reorganize your code to improve performance. If delays are due to data retrieval or storage, think about ways to perform data operations in larger blocks. For example, your program might run faster if it writes individual changes to a temporary table and then uses SQL statements to transfer the changes to the primary tables in one large operation.

A second method to improve performance is to alter the way the data is stored. Each DBMS provides different controls over data storage. The following sections summarize the most common techniques.

DATA STORAGE METHODS

There are three primary methods of storing data tables—each with several variations. The simplest method is sequential storage—putting the data into tables in the order in which it is most commonly accessed. To provide faster access, particularly for random lookups, a second approach is to create indexes of the data. A third approach known as direct or hashed-key storage is radically different and is designed to optimize random lookup at all costs.

Sequential storage is relatively easy to understand, but probably the least useful. Hashed storage methods are also straightforward, but have their own limitations. Indexed tables are by far the most common means of storing and accessing data today. They are complex and have many variations. To choose the best storage method, you sometimes have to understand the differences between the variations.

Pointers and linked lists are key topics in understanding how indexes work. You might have heard computer science students discussing these topics. Do not panic. You do not need to know how to program routines using pointers and linked lists. To understand their strengths and weaknesses, you just need to be able to draw some basic diagrams.

Sequential Storage

Sequential files are the simplest method of storing data. Each row is stored in a predefined order as shown in Figure 9.5. As long as the data is retrieved in the order specified, access is fast and storage space is used efficiently. The real problems arise when data is added or when users need to retrieve data in several different sequences.

FIGURE 9.5
Sequential file. Each row is stored in some predefined order. Sequential storage is used primarily for backup or for transferring data to a different database.

ID	LastName	FirstName	DateHired
1	Reeves	Keith	1/29/96
2	Gibson	Bill	3/31/96
3	Reasoner	Katy	2/17/96
4	Hopkins	Alan	2/8/96
5	James	Leisha	1/6/96
6	Eaton	Anissa	8/23/96
7	Farris	Dustin	3/28/96
8	Carpenter	Carlos	12/29/96
9	O'Connor	Jessica	7/23/96
10	Shields	Howard	7/13/96

Uses

Sequential storage is useful when data is always retrieved in a fixed order. It is also useful when the file contains a lot of common data. For example, if most customers have the same ZIP code, you might as well leave the ZIP code data in simple sequential storage.

Another use of sequential files is for backup or transporting data to a different system. Each database system stores data in a proprietary internal format. To transfer data from one system to another generally requires exporting the data to a common format, moving the data, and importing it into the new database. A sequential ASCII file is a popular export/import format that most database systems support.

Drawbacks

To understand the drawbacks to sequential storage, consider the steps involved in performing the basic database operations listed in Figure 9.2. Reading the entire table and retrieving the next sequential row are easy. Finding an arbitrary row is much slower. If the rows can hold different lengths of data, the only way to find an item is to search from the start of the table until the desired row is found. With N rows of data, the expected number of retrievals required to find a random row is $(N + 1)/2$; a table with 1,000,000 rows would require 500,000 lookups on average to find a matching row. Obviously a bad idea.

Another major drawback can be seen by examining the data storage operations. As with every method, flagged deletion is fast and relatively efficient. The real problems arise when you want to insert a new row. Examine Figure 9.5 and decide how you would insert data for a new employee with the last name of Inez. The basic steps are shown in Figure 9.6. If you had to write a program to insert a row, the most efficient method is to follow four steps. First, read each row. Second, decide if this row comes before the new row. If so, store it in a new table. Third, when you reach the insertion point, save the new row of data. Fourth, append the rest of the data to the end of the new table. The main drawback to this approach is that any time you want to add a row of data, the database has to retrieve (and probably rewrite) every row in the table.

Pointers

The most common solution to the problems of sequential tables is to use indexes. To understand indexes, it helps to understand the use of pointers. When data is stored, it is stored at some location. This location can be in memory, but databases

FIGURE 9.6 Insert into a sequential table. Copy the top of the table to a new table. Store the new data row (Inez). Copy the rest of the data. The system must read every row in the table.

ID	LastName	FirstName	DateHired
8	Carpenter	Carlos	12/29/96
6	Eaton	Anissa	8/23/96
7	Farris	Dustin	3/28/96
2	Gibson	Bill	3/31/96
11	Inez	Maria	1/15/97
5	James	Leisha	1/6/96
9	O'Connor	Jessica	7/23/96
3	Reasoner	Katy	2/17/96
1	Reeves	Keith	1/29/96
10	Shields	Howard	7/13/96

are generally concerned with storage on disk drives. This location is identified by some type of address. A variable that points to this address is called a **pointer.**

The pointer or address can take many forms, depending on the operating system and the database you are using. It could be a physical location. As shown in Figure 9.7, a disk drive is physically divided into several pieces. An individual drive is a **volume.** Each drive consists of several **platters.** Each side of the platter is accessed by a **drive head.** Each side is divided into **tracks** of data. The tracks are further split into **sectors** or **cylinders.** Data is stored a certain number of bytes from the start of a sector, known as an **offset.**

Years ago, physical pointers were used to provide fast access to data. However, they have many problems, and they are no longer necessary. The main drawback to physical pointers is that your database is tied to a specific disk drive. If you want to restore a backup or move the database to a new drive, the data must be stored in exactly the same physical locations. A physical address makes it easier to understand the use of pointers. As illustrated in Figure 9.8, the data can be stored in one location and a key value can be stored in a different location. When the database retrieves the desired key value, it follows the pointer to retrieve the associated data. Pointers enable the database system to physically store the table in different locations. The pieces are linked through the pointers.

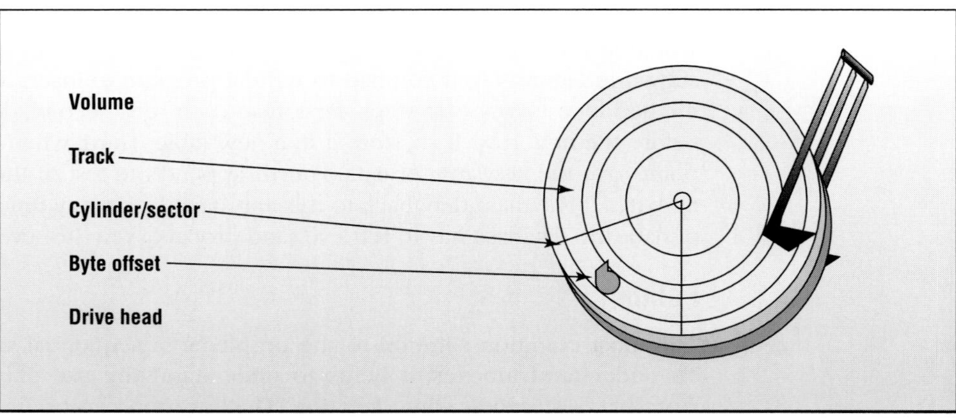

FIGURE 9.7 Physical disk addresses. Data can be found by specifying the volume (drive), track, sector, drive head (specifies the platter side), and a byte offset from the start of the sector.

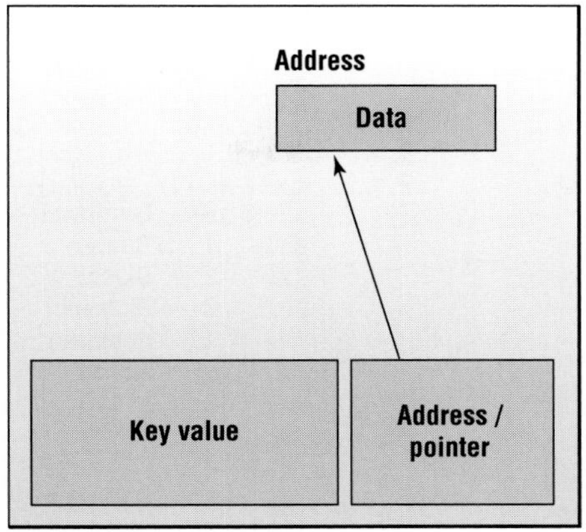

FIGURE 9.8
Use of pointers. The database searches the key values. When it finds the appropriate key, it follows the pointer to retrieve the associated data stored on the disk.

Today systems use **virtual addresses** instead of physical pointers. A virtual address could be based on an imaginary disk drive layout. The database refers to a base set of tracks and cylinders. The computer then translates or maps these values into actual storage locations. This arrangement is the basis of an approach known as the **virtual sequential access method (VSAM).** Another common approach is to define a location in terms of its distance from the start of a file. The operating system can move a file to any location, and the database can always find individual pieces of data just by specifying the relative distance or offset. Since modern processors are relatively fast, almost no database systems rely on physical addresses. Virtual or relative addresses are always better because of their portability.

Indexes

An **index** is the most common method used to provide faster access to data. An index sorts and stores the key values from the original table along with a pointer to the rest of the data in each row. Figure 9.9 illustrates the concept.

Notice that a table can have many indexes. Indexes can also be based on several columns of data. The ability to create multiple indexes in a table indicates their first strength. They enable relatively fast, sorted access to a table based on any criteria. Indexes generally provide a clear advantage over straight sequential files because they support high-speed access to any data columns.

Uses

Indexed tables are a common method of storing data. They provide fast random and sequential access to tables from any predetermined sort condition. Additional gains can be made if the indexes are small enough to fit into RAM. Then the database system can rapidly search the index and use the pointer to retrieve the desired data with almost no access to the disk drive. The gain arises because RAM access (nanoseconds) is almost a million times faster than access to data stored on a rotating disk drive (milliseconds).

Binary Search

Even if the index is too large to remain in RAM, by assigning fixed-length rows, it can be searched significantly faster than searching a sequential table. Consider the sorted data shown in Figure 9.10. If you search a file sequentially, on average you can ex-

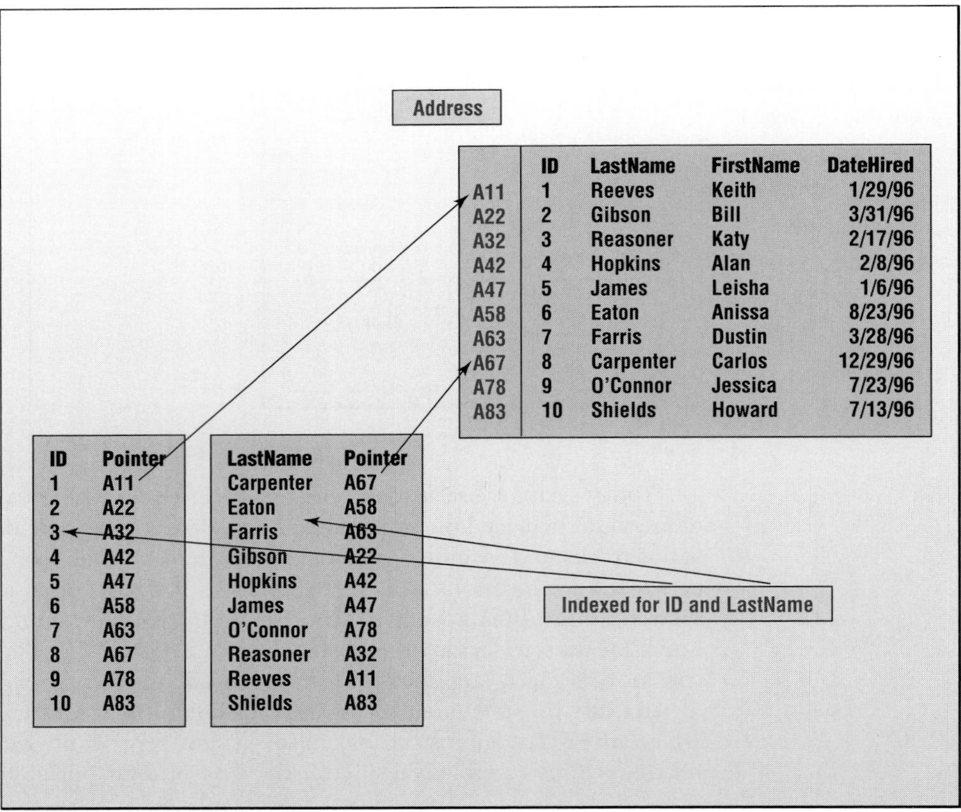

FIGURE 9.9 Indexes. An index sorts and stores a key value along with a pointer to the rest of the data. Indexes can be built for any column or combination of columns in the table.

pect to use $(N + 1)/2$ data lookups to find the desired row. The example requires 10 lookups to find the entry for Jones. But we can take advantage of the fact that the list (index) is sorted. For example, a **binary search** keeps splitting the data set in half until it finds the desired key.

Use the example again to find Jones. Start at the midpoint (14/2 = 7), and the seventh entry is Goetz. Since Jones comes after Goetz, you have just eliminated half of the entries in the table (everything that comes before Goetz). Now divide the remaining entries in half to find the new midpoint (7/2 = 3.5, which rounds up to 4).

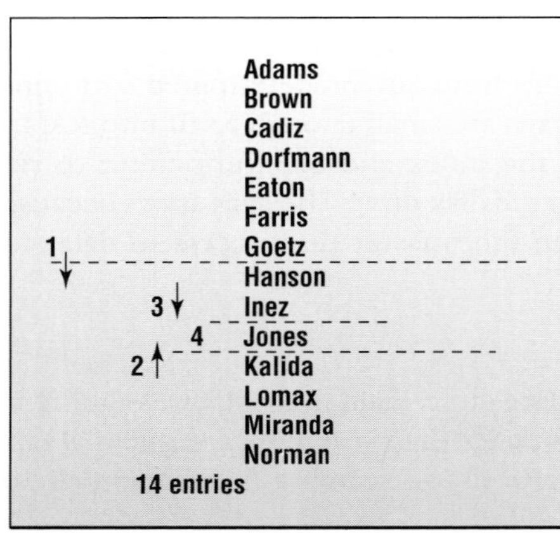

FIGURE 9.10 Binary search. A sorted index can be searched rapidly using a binary search. To find the entry for Jones, find the middle of the list (Goetz). Jones is past Goetz, so split the second half in half (Kalida). Keep splitting the remainder in half until you find the entry.

Jones comes before Kalida, so we have eliminated half of the remaining entries. Repeat this process until you find the desired value. This example requires four lookup steps to find the entry for Jones.

The true power of the binary search is revealed when you need to search large tables. A sequential search of a table with 1,000,000 rows would take 500,000 lookups on average. A binary search eliminates 500,000 entries on the first pass. How many tries does it take to find any row in a table with 1,000,000 rows? Rephrase the question: How many times can you divide 1,000,000 by 2. You could use your calculator and keep dividing by 2, but the answer is 20, since $2^{20} = 1{,}048{,}576$. In general, the maximum number of tries (t) needed to find an entry in a table of N rows is given by $t = \log_2(N)$. Twenty lookups is significantly less than the 500,000 average needed for a sequential search!

Drawbacks

There are two major drawbacks to the indexed approach. The first depends on how the index is actually stored. If the index is stored sequentially, then it faces the same difficulties with inserting a new row as the sequential approach. Granted, each row of the index is shorter than an entire row in the table. However, it is necessary to copy huge chunks of the index whenever a row is inserted into the table.

The second problem exists regardless of how the index is stored. Consider a table in which 10 indexes are defined. When a new row of data is added to the table, every index has to be modified. At a minimum the database has to insert a new row into each of the 10 indexes. In most cases it will also have to reorganize each index.

This issue is the heart of the problem in deciding how to improve the performance of your application. By creating an index, you substantially improve the ability to search a data table. But for every index you create, the application will slow down every time you add new data or modify indexed columns. So your big decision is, which columns to index.

The first step in the decision is to index only the columns that require random searches. The most important columns are the ones that are used to join tables in major queries. You could identify the queries that are commonly used in your application. Second, index the columns used in the JOIN condition. However, to be safe, you also need to identify the tables that experience rapid changes. Go to those tables and remove as many indexes as possible. The third step is to test your application with large amounts of sample data and heavy usage. Look for sections or forms that perform slowly. Then check to see whether you can speed up the access with an index. Then test the index and the overall application to see whether it interferes with other components. Use indexes only if they provide a clear and significant improvement in performance in a critical area of the application. The fourth, and probably most important step, is to get a performance analyzer tool for your DBMS. A good analyzer can monitor usage, identify bottlenecks, and suggest which columns should be indexed.

Linked Lists

Indexes are generally based on linked lists, instead of sequential lists. A linked list is a technique that splits data even further than a sequential index. With a linked list, any data element can be stored separately. A pointer is then used to link to the next data item. Figure 9.11 illustrates the basic concepts. In this example each row of data is stored separately. Then an index is created that is keyed on LastName. However,

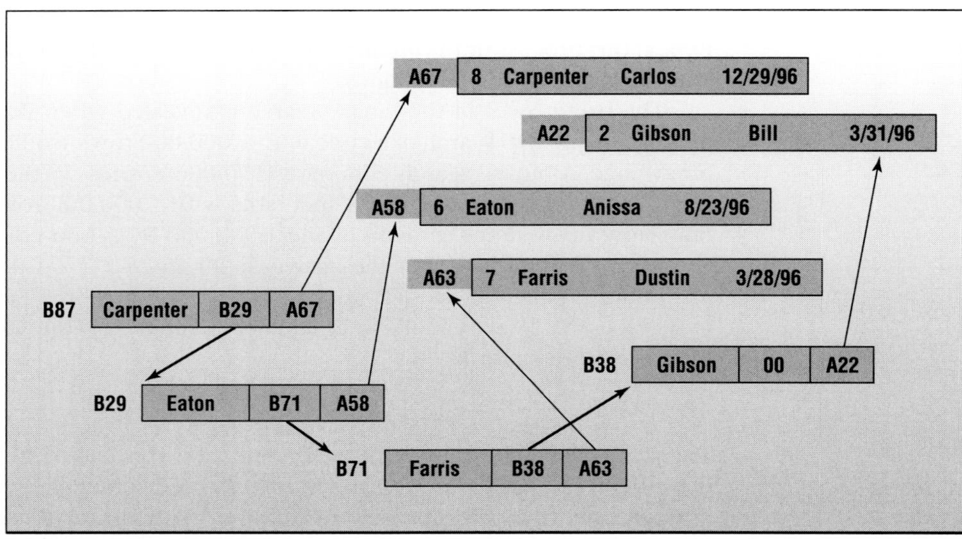

FIGURE 9.11 Linked list. The index is split into separate index elements. Each element contains a key value (LastName), a pointer to the next index element, and a pointer to the rest of the data for that row. To retrieve data sequentially, start at the first element (Carpenter) and follow the link (pointer) to the next element (Eaton).

each element of the index is stored separately. An index element consists of three parts: the key value, a pointer to the associated data element, and a pointer to the next index element.

To retrieve data sequentially, start at the first element for Carpenter. Follow the pointer to the next element (Eaton). Each element of the index is found by following the link (pointer) to the next element. The data pointer in each index element provides the entire data row for that key value.

The strength of a linked list lies in its ability to easily and rapidly insert and delete data. Remember the difficulty in inserting data with a sequential table. Even with a sequential index, inserting a new row generally results in copying half the index (or more). For large tables this approach is clearly inefficient.

On the other hand, as shown in Figure 9.12, inserting a new key row into a linked list requires three basic steps. First, store the data and store the index element—keeping the address of each. Second, find the point in the index to insert the new row using a binary search. In the example, Eccles comes between Eaton and Farris. Third, change the link pointers. The link in Eaton should point to Eccles, and the link

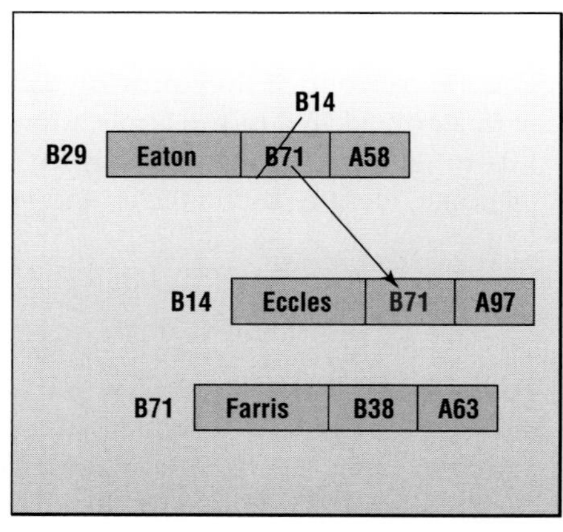

FIGURE 9.12 Insert into a linked list. To add the index element for Eccles: store the new data element, keep the address (B14); find the sort location—between Eaton and Farris; move the link pointer from Eaton into Eccles (B71); store the pointer for Eccles (B14) in Eaton.

in Eccles should point to Farris. Those are the only steps needed. No copying of data keys and no complicated code.

B^+-Tree

A linked list provides some powerful capabilities for building an index for a database. However, the basic linked list can be improved by changing the way we think about it. Figure 9.11 presented a simple linear list, where each element follows the next in a straight line. An even more powerful approach for database indexes is to link the elements into a tree. One version of a tree is shown in Figure 9.13. Only the key values are shown in this figure. In practice, each **node** or element on the tree would contain an index element much like those in Figure 9.11. That is, each element would contain the key value, a pointer to the rest of the data, and two link pointers. For the particular tree in Figure 9.13, each element has at most two links. One link (the line to the left) points to elements that have lower values. The other link (line to the right) points to elements that have a value greater than or equal to the value in the node. The **root** is the highest node on the tree. The bottom nodes are called **leaves** because they are at the end of the tree branches.

The power of the tree lies in its ability to find a data element. To find the data for Jones, start at the top of the tree (Hanson). Jones is alphabetically greater than Hanson, so go to the right side. Track down the tree depending on the key value until you reach the bottom element for Jones. Notice that every element requires at most four searches because there are only four levels in the tree. Wait a minute. That search was exactly the same as a binary search. The number of searches is given by the **depth** of the tree, which is the number of nodes between the root and the leaves. Notice that if you compress a B^+-tree down to one level, each element would be in one long key row. In other words, you would end up with indexed sequential access.

The power of a B^+-tree for searching is clear, but what if you want to retrieve the data sequentially? That is the purpose of the items on the bottom row. Each of these elements contains a new pointer linking it to the next. So you start at the left, follow the pointers to the right, and get a sequentially sorted list of the data.

B^+-Tree Definition

On examining Figure 9.13, it quickly becomes clear that there are many ways to organize a tree. For example, why is Brown listed beneath Cadiz instead of beneath

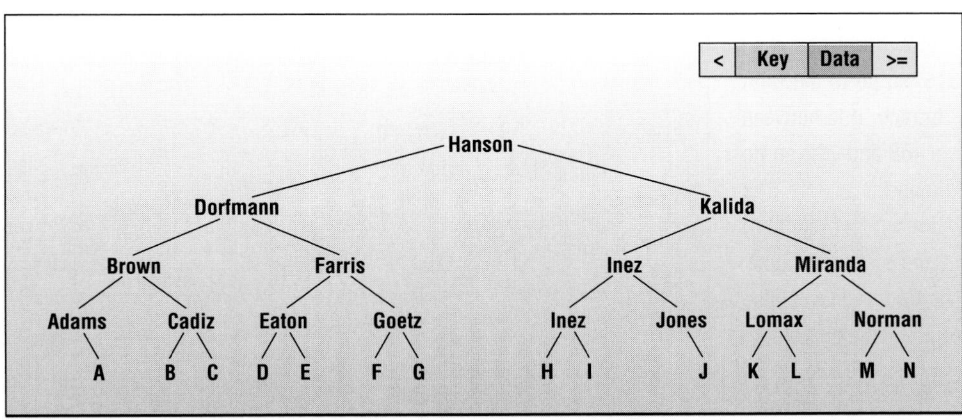

FIGURE 9.13
Simple tree. Each node element has a key value, a pointer to data for that key, and two link pointers. One pointer is for values less than the key. One is for values greater than or equal to the key.

FIGURE 9.14
B^+-tree rules. These rules will generate a tree structure that provides good database performance under a variety of conditions.

- Set the degree (m); $m >= 3$ and is usually an odd number.
- Every node (except the root) must have between $m/2$ and m children.
- All leaves are at the same level/depth.
- All key values are displayed on the bottom leaves.
- A nonleaf node with n children will contain $n - 1$ key values.
- Leaves are connected by pointers (sequential access).

Adams? There is no good answer to this first question. Minor positional choices like this one are arbitrary and do not affect the tree. But the question shows that there is some flexibility in the final tree. Bigger questions do affect the tree significantly, such as why is the tree approximately symmetrical—that is, why not let one side reach lower than the other side? Why does each node split into two branches—why not three or more?

Answers to each of these questions will affect the layout of the tree. As the layout changes, so does the performance. Computer scientists have studied these structures in detail. For database purposes, they have determined that the best overall performance is provided by a B^+-tree, which follows the six basic rules shown in Figure 9.14. The rules are not as complicated as they may first appear.

First, you have to choose the degree of the tree. The **degree** represents the maximum number of children that can fall below any node. Choosing the degree determines how fast the database can find any particular item. In Figure 9.13 the degree was 2, which produced a binary search. Higher degrees result in trees that are broader, requiring even fewer searches to find any item. Two rules that give the B^+-tree its power are that each node must have at least $m/2$ children (and no more than m children) and that all leaves must be at the same depth. In other words, the tree cannot be lopsided, but must be balanced so that data is distributed relatively evenly across the tree.

Figure 9.15 shows a small B^+-tree of degree 3. With a degree of 3, a node can point to three different children. If it does, the node must have two key values, such as (458, 792). To understand why, search the tree to find key value 692. Start at the top and note that 692 is greater than 315, so go to the right branch. Now 692 falls between 458 and 792, so branch to the middle child and then drop down to find the entry on the bottom leaf, which contains a pointer to the rest of the data. A node with three children must have two keys. Any value lower than the left-most key goes

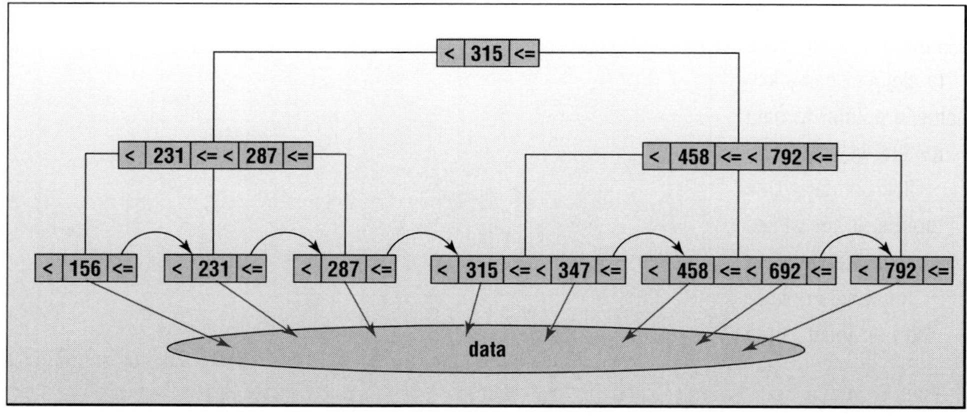

FIGURE 9.15
Sample B^+-tree of degree 3. Start at the top to find the value 692. It is larger than 315, so go to the right branch. It is between 458 and 792 so go down the middle. The bottom leaf points to the rest of the data. The bottom leaves also contain links to provide sequential access.

to the left. A value greater than the right-most key goes to the right. Anything between the keys follows the middle path.

B^+-Tree Strengths

The main strength of the B^+-tree is that it provides a guaranteed level of performance for access to the data. Every element can be found in the same number of searches—which is determined by the depth of the tree. The tree also provides fast sequential retrieval. The other power comes from the ability to add or delete elements from the tree. As in a linked list, adding to a tree new items is relatively easy. The process is a little more complicated in a tree, because the rules require the tree to be rearranged periodically as data is added. However, adding items to a tree is still relatively fast and efficient.

Overall, the B^+-tree approach provides the best general access to data. If you do not know anything useful about the data or how it will be used, you should always choose the B^+-tree method to store a table. It provides the best overall performance for typical data—for sequential retrieval, random lookup, and for changes to the data.

Direct or Hashed Access

Some situations require super fast random access to data. For example, in transaction situations you might need virtually instantaneous retrieval of some data items. When a grocery store clerk scans an item, the DBMS must retrieve the price immediately. A delay of even 5 seconds would be incredibly annoying and costly given the huge number of items that are scanned every day. In this example, the computer is given a unique bar-code number and needs to retrieve the matching data. It makes sense to optimize the search for this situation.

A **direct access** or **hashed-key** storage method solves this problem better than any other approach. The method works by first setting aside enough space to store all the key values you might need in numbered storage locations. Then the key value (bar code) is converted to a storage location number. Computer researchers have determined that a prime modulus function usually provides the best conversion. For example, you might have 100 elements with key values ranging from 100 to 999. You choose a prime number approximately equal to the number of elements. For this case, 101 is a good prime number. Then you divide each key value by the prime number and look at the remainder. As shown in Figure 9.16, a key value of 528 has

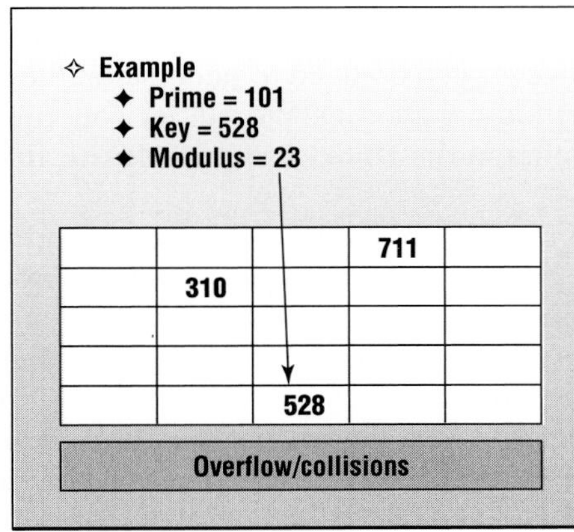

FIGURE 9.16 Hashed-key access. The key value (528) is converted directly into a storage location by dividing by a prime number (101). If two keys have the same remainder, one is stored in an overflow location.

a remainder (or modulus) of 23. Hence data for that key will be stored in location number 23. There is one catch—some keys might have the same modulus. The system sets aside an overflow area for these collisions, which it searches sequentially.

Uses

The hashed-key approach is extremely fast for finding and storing random data. The key's value is immediately converted into a storage location, and data can be retrieved in one pass to the disk. This method works best for transaction operations that require instantaneous retrieval of small amounts of data.

The hashed-key storage method requires you to know approximately how many items will be stored in the table. It also works best if the data does not change very often. It is acceptable to set aside enough space to add a few items. The method begins to deteriorate if key values are constantly being added to the table.

Drawbacks

One drawback to the hashed-key storage method is that it has little or no provision for sequential retrieval of data. It is possible to retrieve the data and sort it. Some order-preserving hash functions exist to keep the keys in a predefined order. However, sequential retrieval will be slower than with a B^+-tree index.

A second drawback is that the method sets aside storage space for the data, so you have to know how much space will be needed before you collect the data. If you add items to the table, they tend to end up in overflow storage, which is substantially slower. Performance can be improved by reorganizing the table—which creates more space and uses a new prime number. However, it takes time to reorganize the table, which should be done when the data is not being heavily used.

Bitmap Index

Some vendors (e.g., Oracle) provide highly compressed bitmap indexes for large tables. With a **bitmap index** each data key is encoded down to a small set of bits. The bitmap (binary) image of the entire index is usually small enough to fit in RAM. High-speed bit operations are used to make comparisons and search for key values. Hence the bitmap indexes are extremely fast. However, they are most efficient for small keys—such as integer data.

Comparison of Access Methods

All of these access methods are critical to computer scientists who create the DBMS. As an application developer, you do not need to know the gory technical details of the various methods. However, you do need to understand the strengths, weaknesses, and best uses of the methods. A good DBMS will let you choose how you want to store each table. At a minimum the DBMS will provide the ability to specify indexes for various columns.

To determine which method should be used to store and retrieve data, you need to know two things: the primary operations that will be performed on the table and which method best supports those operations. Figure 9.17 answers the second question by summarizing the comments from the previous sections.

In practice, you have only three choices. First, the B^+-tree is the best overall method to store and retrieve data. In almost any table the primary-key columns should be stored in a B^+-tree index to speed the join operations in queries. Second, hashed access should be used for tables that do not change often and the application re-

FIGURE 9.17
Comparison of access methods. The B^+-tree is the best overall method to store and retrieve data. Sequential is useful for large tables that do not change often and need only sequential access. Hashed is useful for rapid access to individual items.

OPERATION	SEQUENTIAL	B^+-TREE	HASHED
Read one	✓✓	✓✓✓✓	✓✓✓✓✓
Read next	✓✓✓✓✓	✓✓✓✓	✓✓✓
Read all	✓✓✓✓✓	✓✓✓✓	✓✓✓
Insert	✓	✓✓✓✓	✓✓✓✓
Delete	✓	✓✓✓✓	✓✓✓✓
Modify	✓	✓✓✓✓	✓✓✓✓
Reorganize	✓✓	✓✓✓✓	✓✓✓

quires fast retrieval or storage of data based on a key value. Third, sequential storage can be used if a table almost never changes and the application always retrieves data sequentially and in large chunks. Generally, your choice comes down to B^+-tree or hashed access. If you have tables that change often, you should consider removing indexes—which creates a sequential table.

STORING DATA COLUMNS

The previous section explored the various methods of storing and retrieving individual rows of data. The second issue in storing data is how to store individual columns of data. For basic business data consisting of numbers and short text, it rarely matters how individual columns are stored. However, business applications are being developed that need to store more complex data such as large amounts of text, graphics, sound, and even video clips. This data is relatively complex and requires significantly more storage space. Despite the declining cost of storage space, some of these objects are so large that you must be careful in how the database allocates storage for each item.

Fixed-width or positional storage is the simplest means of storing a row of data as shown in Figure 9.18. Each column is allocated a fixed number of bytes, and the data is stored in a set position. When the DBMS retrieves a row, it can find each column because the table definition lists the starting position of each column. The biggest drawback to this method is that at the start you must decide on the width of each column. Any data that does not fit into the assigned width will be truncated. This decision causes problems. For example, how much space should you set aside for a customer name? If you pick a small number, you risk throwing away part of a customer's name. If you pick a large number, the database sets aside that much space for every row of data—wasting space for most situations. This type of storage is used when you specify the domain as numeric or a CHAR column with a fixed width.

FIGURE 9.18
Fixed-width or positional-column storage. If data widths do not vary much, this method is a fast, efficient means to store columns. If descriptions can be short or very long, then you will have to allocate space for the longest possible description, which wastes space for the short descriptions.

ID	PRICE	QOH	DESCRIPTION
4	110.00		Dog Kennel-Extra Large
18	1.00	1874	Cat Food-Can-Premium
29	6.00	240	Flea Collar-Cat

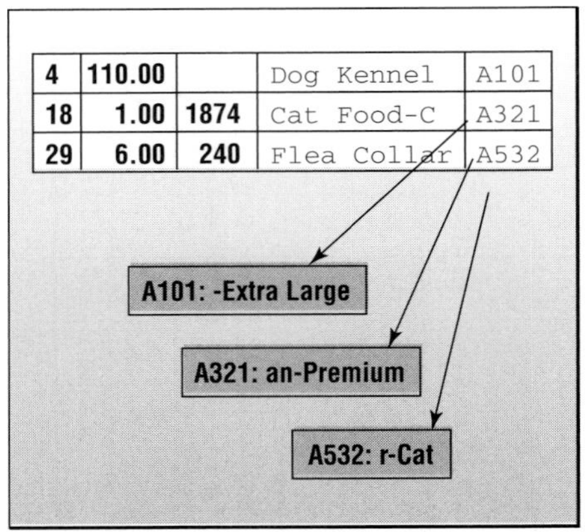

FIGURE 9.19 Fixed-with-overflow storage. Text columns that can be variable should be stored as variable width or overflow columns. The DBMS stores a pointer to the longer data that is stored in a pool.

The problem of deciding how much text space to allocate is common. Hence a solution was developed to accommodate text data that is highly variable in length. For example, descriptions, comments, and memos can be long or short. In these situations the best storage method to use is the **fixed-with-overflow** method, shown in Figure 9.19. In this case only a portion (or none) of the text is held in the actual row of the table. The overflow data is stored in a separate pool. The table then contains a pointer to the particular item stored in the pool. In SQL databases you specify this type of storage by selecting the **VARCHAR** column type. Some databases also use a memo or comment data type to implement this type of storage. For example, Access provides a Memo type, which can hold large chunks of text. The Memo type can hold up to 64,000 characters, whereas text columns are limited to 255. For most systems you should always use the VARCHAR instead of fixed-width CHAR to store a text column. The only exception is that some systems will not allow you to create indexes on VARCHAR columns and might limit your search capabilities.

A third method of storing columns is to create an index to each column on every row. Figure 9.20 illustrates the concept. Data for each column is stored as one long list. The starting point for the column is stored in an index, which is placed in the front of the row. When the DBMS retrieves a row, it uses the index to find the data for each column. This method does not waste space by saving empty data and is rel-

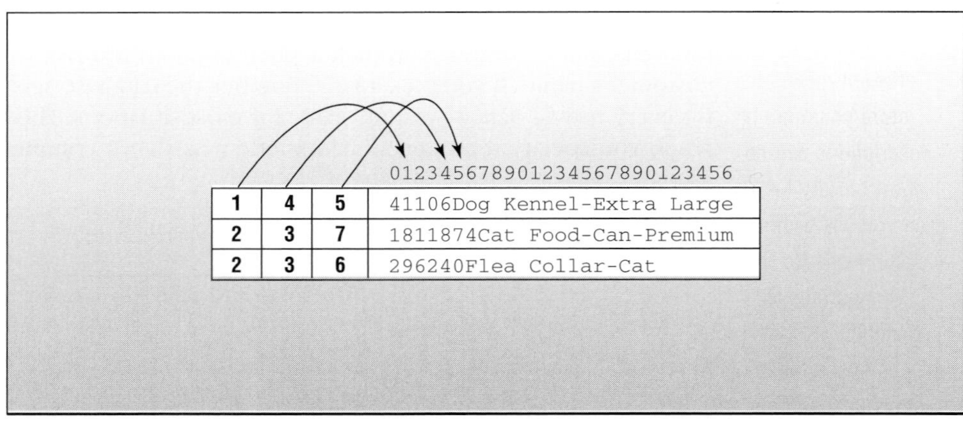

FIGURE 9.20 Indexed-column storage. The index at the start of each row tells the DBMS where to find data for each column.

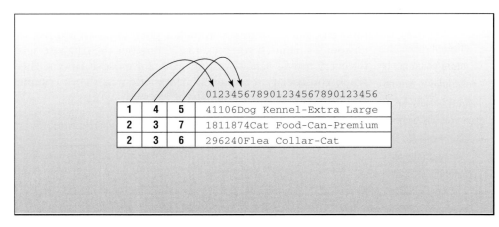

atively fast and efficient for most types of data. Microsoft Access uses this method for storing data, which means that all text columns use only the exact amount of space needed to store each character plus the pointer. This method does require extra space to store the index for each row. If you have a table with hundreds of short columns, indexed storage would not be very efficient. It might even double the storage requirements of a table.

Note that numeric data is almost never stored as characters. Instead, it is stored in binary format to save space. The numbers used in these figures are just for illustration. You rarely have to worry about the width of numeric columns; they typically use either 4 or 8 bytes of storage.

If you need to transfer data to a different database or a different application, you often have to use a delimited file. It is often called an ASCII delimited file because the table is converted to standard ASCII text characters (no binary numbers). As shown in Figure 9.21, each column is separated by a specific character or delimiter. A comma is a common delimiter. Because text data might contain commas or other special characters, all text columns are enclosed in quotation marks. Spaces are eliminated unless they are in quoted text columns. Missing data is simply not displayed, so if a column is missing, the data row would have two adjacent commas (e.g., 110,, "Dog . . . "). This technique is not very useful for permanent use within a database. Every time it retrieves a row, the DBMS has to search for the commas and interpret the quotes to find a particular column. However, it is a good way to transfer data between different systems. It is also good at saving space—particularly when many columns are missing.

In general, indexed storage is the best method for storing and retrieving data. By allocating space dynamically, each row uses only the space needed to store the actual data. In contrast, fixed-width columns waste space for most rows. The one advantage of fixed-width columns is that every row is the same width, so new rows can be placed into spaces where prior rows have been deleted. The indexed approach requires the database to be packed on a regular basis to remove and consolidate the spaces recovered from deleting rows.

Most current systems use a variation of indexed columns. However, they use an overflow approach for certain types of columns—such as memo and object data types. These data types are useful for large, nontraditional data. Most systems do not allow you to use them as primary keys, and you should avoid using them as join columns. You should also avoid trying to search them. If you do need indexed columns

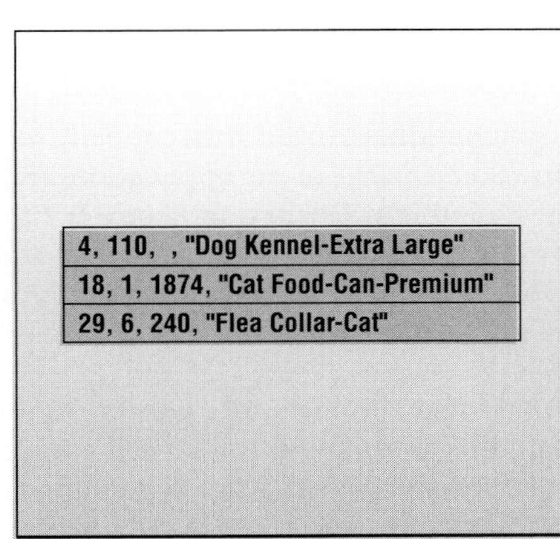

FIGURE 9.21
Delimited files. Each column is separated by a special delimiter character (,). Text columns are quoted to protect spaces and hide special characters like commas. This method is often used to transfer files to different databases or other applications.

for joins or searches, you can create a second column that contains a brief description, ID value, or keywords. This new column should be unique, it should be related to the data stored in the larger column, and it should be stored in a more traditional data type (numeric or short text).

One of the more challenging problems is storing variable-length string data, particularly when the lengths can vary widely, such as comments. If the system allocates a fixed amount of space, every row would be at the maximum value and most of the space would be wasted. On the other hand, if the system allocates space for each row dynamically, then some rows will be shorter than others. This approach saves space, but makes it more difficult to handle modifications of the data. If the new data is longer than the old row, the system cannot just overwrite the old row. Some systems (e.g., Oracle) solve this dilemma by allocating data blocks to hold a group of rows. Each block contains a certain amount of free space. The DBMS uses this free space to store modified data that is longer than the existing row. In Oracle, you can control the amount of free space through two parameters: PCTFREE and PCTUSED. If the current data block is fuller than the PCTFREE value, no new rows are added to the block. The remaining space is kept for expansion of existing rows. See the *Oracle Server Administrator's Guide* for details and suggestions on values for these parameters.

DATA CLUSTERING AND PARTITIONING

Another way to improve database performance is to control the location of individual components of the table. For example, some parts of your application may always be retrieved together, so performance might improve if the two sets of data are retrieved together. On the other hand, sometimes you collect data that might not be accessed very often. It is still worthwhile to keep the data, but it might be better to store it on cheaper, slower drives. A third technique exists to speed up access to data by spreading it across several disk drives. All three situations are related in that they involve partitioning data and controlling where it is stored to improve performance. The key to understanding these methods is to remember that mechanical disk drives are slow. Every access to the disk that can be avoided will improve the application's speed.

Data Clustering

To improve general system performance, most computers retrieve data in chunks. They try to anticipate the next demand and read ahead of the current request. If the system guesses correctly, the next data request can be filled from RAM, which is substantially faster.

Database systems designers have used this concept to improve performance of database applications. Some parts of an application are generally used at the same time. Consider the example presented in Figure 9.22. Generally, when users look at order items, they also want to see the related data stored in the order table. By storing all the data for Order 1123 in the same data block, the data can be retrieved in one pass. The application will run faster because it avoids a second trip to the disk drive.

If you are using a DBMS that supports data clustering, you can improve performance by identifying data that is commonly accessed together. To create a cluster, you need to specify the tables involved and the key columns that link those tables. The DBMS then automatically stores and retrieves the related data in the same cluster. Only some of the large transaction-oriented database systems support cluster-

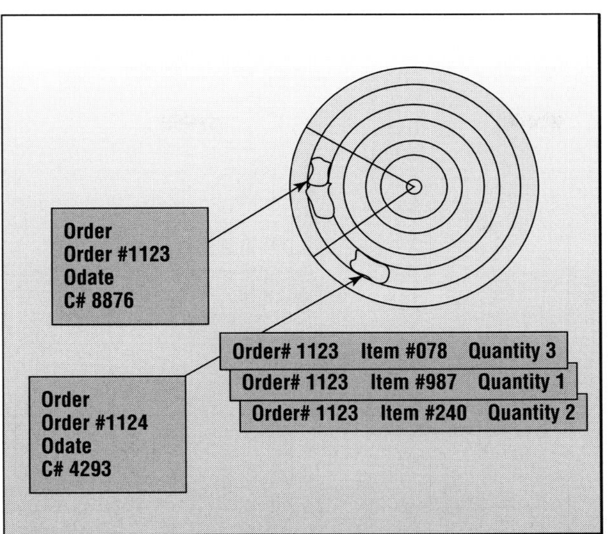

FIGURE 9.22 Data clustering. Order and OrderItem data are usually needed at the same time. By storing them close to each other, the computer can retrieve them in one pass. Clustering the data improves application speed by reducing the number of disk accesses.

ing. For example, Oracle has a CREATE CLUSTER command to define the tables and key columns.

Data Partitioning

Another situation that commonly arises in business applications is that some data is used more frequently than other data. Even in the same table, you might collect data that is used only occasionally. For example, a basic customer table could contain information on customers who have not placed orders for several years that the marketing department wants to keep. Because the data is rarely used, it would be nice to move it to a cheaper storage location.

As shown in Figure 9.23, this situation would involve a **horizontal partition.** Some of the rows (currently active customers) will be stored in one location, and other rows (inactive customers) will be stored in a different location. The active data

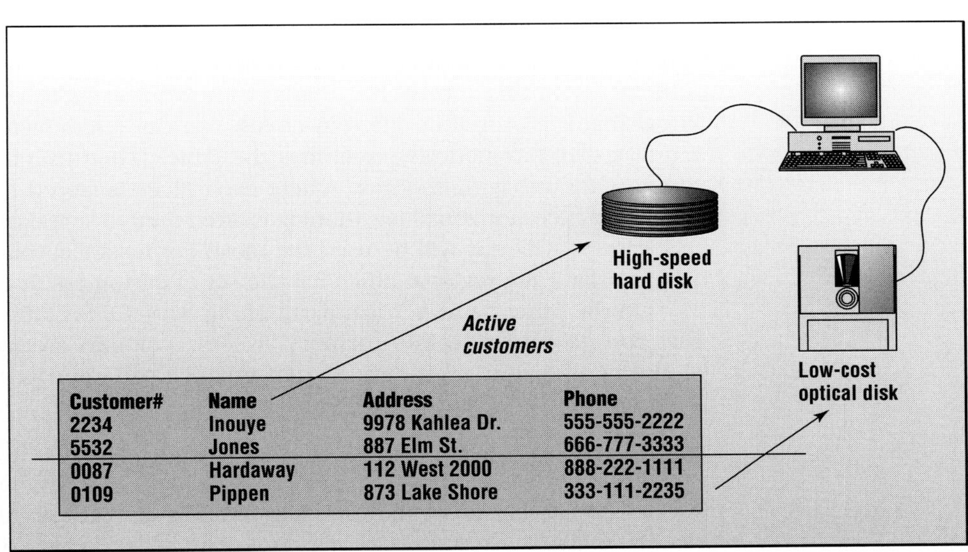

FIGURE 9.23 Horizontal partition. Data for currently active customers is stored on high-speed drives. Older data is moved to cheaper, slower optical drives. The user does not need to know about the split because the DBMS automatically retrieves data from either location.

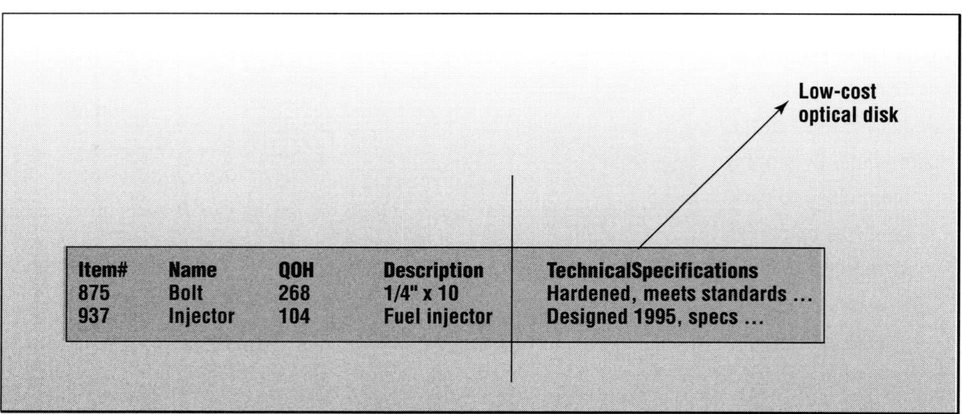

Low-cost
optical disk
Item# Name QOH Description TechnicalSpecifications
875 Bolt 268 1/4" x 10 Hardened, meets standards ...
937 Injector 104 Fuel injector Designed 1995, specs ...

FIGURE 9.24 Vertical partition. Technical data and images that are not accessed very often can be stored on a high-capacity, low-cost, but slower optical drive.

will be stored on high-speed disk drives. In extreme situations, some of this data could be stored on solid-state RAM drives, which hold all data in semiconductor RAM. On the other hand, the less-used data can be placed on slower-speed optical drives. The optical drives can hold huge amounts of data at a low cost; however, their access speeds are somewhat slower.

The key to making this approach work is that after you set it up, a good DBMS automatically retrieves the data from the appropriate drive. The user does not have to know that the data is stored on different drives. A single SQL query will retrieve the data—wherever it is stored.

Vertical partitioning uses the same logic. The only difference is that with vertical partitioning, some columns of data are stored on a faster drive, whereas others are moved to cheaper and slower drives. Figure 9.24 shows how a product table might be split into two pieces. Basic business data used in transactions is stored on a high-speed disk. Detailed technical specifications and images are stored on high-capacity optical disks. Most day-to-day operations will use the basic data stored on the high-speed drive. However, the detailed data is readily available to anyone who needs it. The only difference is that users will wait a little longer to retrieve the data on the slower drive.

In theory, data can be partitioned using any DBMS. Simply define two tables that can be joined by a common key. Then store each table on the appropriate drive. The difficulty with this approach is that anyone who wants to use the data will have to know that it is stored in different tables. You can circumvent this issue by building a query that automatically combines the tables. Then users can pull data from the query without having to know where each piece is stored.

In practice, horizontal partitioning is often used to split data so that it can be stored in locations where it will be used the most. For instance, you might split a customer table so that each regional office has the set of customers that it deals with the most.

On the other hand, vertical partitioning is useful for limiting the amount of data that you need to read into memory. If some columns are rarely used, they can be stored in a separate table. Overall performance will improve because the DBMS will be able to retrieve more of the smaller rows.

Disk Striping and RAID Storage

A relatively recent innovation in disk drives is dramatically improving the capabilities of DBMS. The system is known as a **redundant array of independent drives**

(RAID). Instead of using one massive drive, RAID technology stores several smaller drivers in one container. When the DBMS transfers a table to the RAID system, the rows of data are automatically split and stored on separate disks. As shown in Figure 9.25, this process can be envisioned as a **data stripe** that is written across the drives.

The primary advantage to storing data on separate drives is that each drive can store or retrieve data at the same time. This parallel processing can significantly improve the overall system performance. A second advantage to the system is that it can automatically duplicate each portion of the data and store it on a different disk. If one of the disks is destroyed, all of the data is still available on the other disks and can be recovered automatically.

RAID storage devices are continually being improved. There are also several different levels of RAID storage. Even in their current state, RAID storage devices are substantially faster and safer than traditional disk drives. The advantages of parallel retrieval and storage are particularly useful for huge databases and systems that are intensively used by many people. The other nice feature of RAID storage is that from the standpoint of a developer (or user), the systems are automatic. For example, Windows NT provides native support for several RAID levels, which means that with the proper disk drives, you can use a RAID system with minimal effort.

EXISTING DATABASE MANAGEMENT SYSTEMS

Each vendor provides different methods to monitor and control database performance. These tools are a major selling point for each vendor. Smaller systems like Microsoft Access provide only limited control over the physical storage of data. System developers generally use the storage methods that are appropriate for the most general situations (B^+-tree and indexed columns). You have some control over which columns are indexed but rarely have more sophisticated storage controls. Column storage is determined by the data type you assign.

Larger systems like Oracle provide a variety of tools to help evaluate and manage the performance of the database. For example, Oracle sets clustering and provides hashed access with the CREATE CLUSTER command. Indexed files can also be partitioned and clustered. Oracle database performance can also be tuned with various parameters. For example, the PCTFREE and PCTUSED options specify how tightly

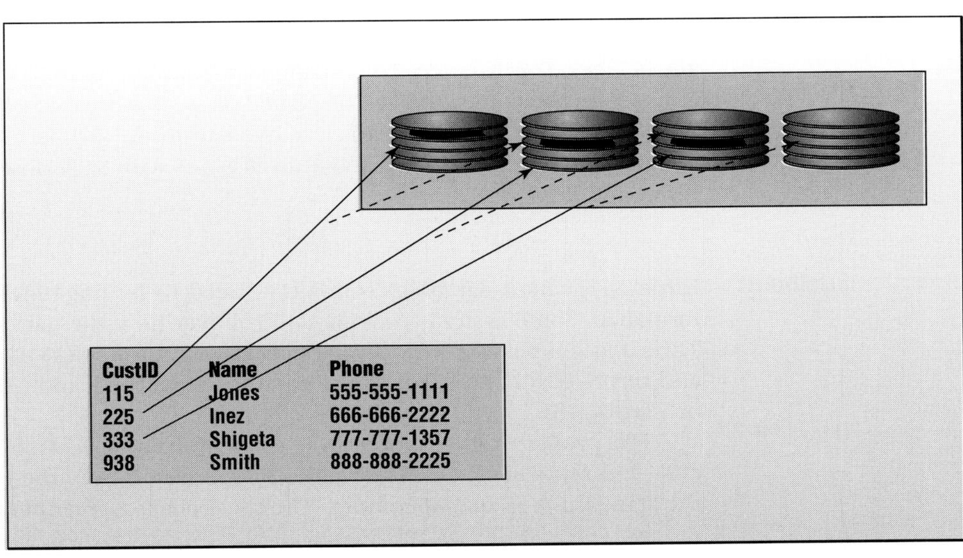

CustID Name Phone
115 Jones 555-555-1111
225 Inez 666-666-2222
333 Shigeta 777-777-1357
938 Smith 888-888-2225

FIGURE 9.25 Redundant array of independent drives (RAID). The table is automatically split and stored on separate drives (striping). Compared to systems that use a single drive RAID technology can store and retrieve data faster. Data can also automatically be duplicated for backup.

the data should be packed into the defined space. Various STORAGE parameters specify how the database should be expanded as it grows. Tables and indexes are stored in tablespaces, which are areas that the database administrator allocates on a drive. By specifying the location of the tablespaces, you can allocate data on specific drives. You can improve performance by storing each element in a tablespace on a different drive. For example, large databases should store transaction and recovery logs and main data on different drives.

SALLY'S PET STORE

At the start the Pet Store database should have few performance problems. Beginning in one store, an ambitious system might store the database on a central computer, which is connected to three or four other computers in the store. Reasonably up-to-date personal computers should be able to handle the initial database. As accounting functions are added, or if the system needs to expand beyond a single store, then the system would have to be reevaluated.

At the current time, there should be few concerns about performance tuning. However, to improve performance, all primary keys should be indexed. Microsoft Access generally defines these indexes by default, but you should examine each table to be sure. Be careful when assigning indexes to columns that are part of a concatenated key. The index on a partial key must allow duplicates.

One potential area for problems is the City table. This table currently holds basic data on cities throughout the United States. Performance could be improved by reducing the number of cities—on the assumption that most customers would come from the surrounding communities. However, if you choose to keep the data, you can improve performance by thinking about how the table will be accessed. In particular, it is often searched by ZIP code. Similarly, because users often want a sorted list of the cities, it would be useful to index the City column. Are there too many indexes for one table? You could test the performance of retrievals before and after adding the indexes. However, note that the City table is predominantly used for retrieval and rarely used to add data. Hence building additional indexes makes sense.

The same situation probably exists for the Merchandise table. Most applications and users will retrieve data from the Merchandise table, with few updates, deletions, or insertions. Hence you might build additional indexes on that table.

For now, partitioning and clustering are not warranted. Over time, as the business expands, you might want to move some of the older data to less expensive storage devices. For instance, data on animals sold more than 5 or 10 years ago will probably not be used often and can be placed on slower drives. Similarly, inactive customer data and older order data can be moved from the primary tables. The exact dates will depend on the cost of storage, discussions with Sally, observation of retrieval patterns, and legal needs.

SUMMARY

Large application databases sometimes need to be fine-tuned to improve their performance. Some systems provide control over how the data is stored and retrieved. Three basic types of controls can be used to determine (1) how table rows are stored and retrieved, (2) how individual columns are stored, and (3) how data is clustered or partitioned.

The primary choices for storing rows of data are B^+-tree indexes, hashed-key access, and sequential files. The method depends on how the data is used in terms of the standard database operations. The most challenging operations are searching for random entries and adding new data to the table. The B^+-tree approach is the most common because it provides the best overall access for a variety of situations. In particular, it provides reasonably fast random access, good sequential retrieval, and good performance for inserting and deleting rows of data. In contrast, the hashed-key approach provides high-speed random access to any data element, but it is poor at retrieving data sequentially. Sequential files are rarely used, because although they use a minimum of space, they provide weak access to random rows of data.

Most databases provide some control over how individual columns can be stored. The most common feature enables developers to control the storage of text data. Large text columns should be stored in varying-character (or overflow) columns instead of fixed-width columns. Another alternative is to provide an index to the columns of data in each row. The indexed approach provides fast retrieval, can automatically handle variable-width columns, and is relatively efficient with missing data. You should also be familiar with using delimited files for transferring data to different systems.

Some systems can cluster data in common locations on the disk drive. This approach improves performance by enabling the disk drive to retrieve related data in one pass. Another useful technique is to partition data so that data that is used less often can be moved to less expensive, slower disk drives. RAID systems provide another performance gain by splitting data and storing it on independent disk drives within the same system. The RAID drives can store and retrieve data substantially faster than a single disk drive can. RAID drives can also provide automatic backup by storing each component on two different drives.

Be careful when attempting to improve the performance of an application. Changes that help one area can adversely affect other operations. This trade-off is important when creating indexes for columns in a table. Indexes tend to improve data retrieval but slow down the processing when data is added to the table.

A DEVELOPER'S VIEW

As Miranda's problems indicate, database performance can become an important issue. Performance problems should be anticipated and solved as early as possible in design and development. You do not have to be intimately familiar with how the DBMS stores data. However, you do need to know which options are available to you. With many systems, the most important control you have is in choosing which columns to index. Sometimes you can choose the exact storage method. You need to understand the strengths and weaknesses of the various methods so that you can choose the method that best fits your application's needs. For your class project, you should identify the columns that should be indexed. You might have to generate sample data and compare processing time for various operations.

KEY WORDS

binary search, 332
bitmap index, 338
cylinder, 330
data stripe, 345
degree, 336
depth, 335
direct access, 337
drive head, 330
fixed width, 339
fixed with overflow, 340
hashed key, 337
horizontal partition, 343
index, 331
leaves, 335
node, 335
offset, 330
pack, 327
platter, 330

REVIEW QUESTIONS

1. What basic data operations are performed on tables?
2. What are the primary data storage methods?
3. What are the strengths and weaknesses of sequential storage?
4. What are the strengths and weaknesses of indexed (B^+-tree) storage?
5. What are the strengths and weaknesses of hashed (direct access) data storage?
6. How does data clustering improve database performance?
7. How does data partitioning improve database performance?
8. What is a RAID system and what are its benefits in a database application?
9. What types of applications can benefit from each storage method?

EXERCISES

1. If you have access to a DBMS that enables you to control the data storage method, create three copies of a table—using three different methods. Put sample data in the table (several hundred rows—write a short program to generate data). For one table at a time, write four SQL statements: (a) insert a row into the table, (b) delete rows, (c) retrieve one row, (d) change one value in the row. Write a short program to perform these functions in a loop. Time each program as it operates on the three tables. Record and analyze your results.

2. Create two new tables with three or four columns. Add several hundred rows of sample data (Hint: Copy it from a Rolling Thunder table). Write a short program that tracks through the joined query and totals one column of data. Time the procedure for three different situations:
   a. Define the primary key column (and link column) as long integer.
   b. Define the primary key column (and link column) as currency.
   c. Define the primary key column (and link column) as text.

3. Study the documentation of a DBMS (e.g., Oracle, SQL Server, or DB2) and list the various storage methods available to improve performance. Briefly describe the purpose of each method.

4. Create a B+-tree (degree 3). Show each final tree.
   a. The base tree holds the following key values: 1583, 2593, 2890, 3563, 4111, 5982, 6872, 7452, 7782, 8925, and 9152.
   b. Add the key value 1655.
   c. Add the key value 1105.
   d. Add the key value 1355.
   e. Add the key value 2441.
   f. Delete the key value 7452.

5. Draw a linked list.
   a. Start with the following key values: 252, 553, 773, and 987.
   b. Show how to insert the key value 673.
   c. Show how to delete the key 773.
   d. Outline the pseudocode needed to insert an item into the list.

6. Create a hashed storage example. Use a prime number of 67 but allocate only 20 main storage positions. Show the storage of the following numbers: 147, 287, 350, 945, 410, and 348.

7. Using vendor documentation and Internet resources, identify the steps needed to store a database on a RAID system with your DBMS. (Hint: SQL Server on Windows NT provides specific documentation for RAID.) What problems are you likely to encounter?

Sally's Pet Store

8. Remove all indexes from the City table in the Pet Store database. Build a combo box that retrieves the data from the City table, sorted by City. Compare the performance of the combo box both with and without the indexes. Write a short program to randomly retrieve 1,000 cities based on the CityID (use the Rnd function). Time this routine when the table is indexed and when it is not indexed.

9. Make copies of the Sale and SaleItem tables. Remove all indexes. Write a procedure to add 4,000 rows to the Sale table and 12,000 rows to the SaleItem table. (Hint: You can randomly select items, pick one customer, and one date.) Record how long the routine takes (use the Timer function). Now index every column in the table and time the routine again.

10. Use the two tables created in the preceding exercise and write a short procedure in which a query computes the sum of Price*Quantity for each item ordered. Time the operation of the query. Index the key columns in the two tables and time the operation again. If there is no substantial difference, add more rows to the tables until you get a measurable difference.

Rolling Thunder Bicycles

11. Make a copy of the Rolling Thunder database. Write SQL statements to perform the following operations on the Bicycle table: (a) add a row, (b) delete a row, (c) select all rows, and (d) write a program to change one value in every row. Write four short programs to perform these operations in a loop that repeats at least 100 times. Run the programs and record the time it takes to perform the operations. Next, index every column in the Bicycle table and rerun your tests. Record and analyze your results.

12. Examine the tables and the usage of each table in the Rolling Thunder application. Identify the primary uses of each table in terms of the table operations described in this chapter. Use this list to identify desired indexes and appropriate storage methods for each table if the database becomes large.

13. Examine the tables in Rolling Thunder and identify which tables should be clustered. Which tables could gain from partitioning? If the application is expanded, what new data could be added that might gain from partitioning?

WEB SITE REFERENCES

Site	Description
http://www.disktrend.com	Market research source on disk drives.
http://www.ciprico.com/raid.html	Tutorial on RAID storage.
http://www.baydel.com/tutorial.html	Tutorial on RAID storage.
http://www.broadbase.com/	Data warehouse vendors rely on optimizing physical data storage and retrieval.

ADDITIONAL READING

Dunham, J. *Database Performance Tuning Handbook.* Berkeley: McGraw-Hill, 1997. [In-depth treatment of improving your application's performance.]

Helman, P. *The Science of Database Management.* Burr Ridge, IL: Irwin, 1994. [A more formal treatment of databases and in-depth treatment of data storage.]

Loomis, M. *Data Management and File Processing.* Englewood Cliffs, NJ: Prentice-Hall, 1983. [In-depth treatment of data storage issues such as B-trees.]

Database Administration

CHAPTER 10

WHAT YOU WILL LEARN IN THIS CHAPTER

OVERVIEW

Miranda: *Finally, everything seems to be running well.*

Ariel: *Does that mean you finally got paid?*

Miranda: *Yes. They gave me the check yesterday. They even liked my work so well, they offered me a job.*

Ariel: *That's great. Are you going to take it? What job is it?*

Miranda: *I think so. They want me to be a database administrator. They said they need me to keep the database running properly. They also hinted that they want me to help their existing programmers learn to build database applications.*

Ariel: *Wow! That means you'll get more money than the programmers.*

Miranda: *Probably. But I'll have to learn some new material. I'm really starting to worry about security. The accounting manager talked to me yesterday and gave me some ideas of problems that I might expect with the sales application.*

INTRODUCTION

The power of a DBMS comes from its ability to share data. Data can be shared across many users, departments, and applications. Most organizations build more than one application and more than one database. Large organizations might use more than one DBMS. Most companies have several projects being developed or revised at the same time by different teams. Imagine what happens if you just turn developers loose to create databases, tables, and applications any way they want to. It is highly unlikely the applications would work together. Just using a DBMS is not enough. An organization that wants to build integrated applications must have someone in charge of the data and the databases.

Data administration consists of the planning and coordination required to define data consistently throughout the company. Some person or group should have the responsibility for determining what data should be collected, how it should be stored, and promoting ways in which it can be used. This person or group is responsible for the integrity of the data.

Database administration consists of technical aspects of creating and running the database. The basic tasks are performance monitoring, backup and recovery, and assigning and controlling security. Database administrators are trained in the details of installing, configuring, and operating the DBMS.

Database security is a subset of computer security topics. However, because of the goal of sharing data, security is a crucial issue in database management. Also, some interesting twists in database security should be studied by all application developers and database managers. If database security is assigned properly, it has the ability to reduce many types of fraud. If database security is ignored or performed poorly, major assets of the company could be manipulated or stolen from any computer in the world. It pays to understand the security issues and handle security properly.

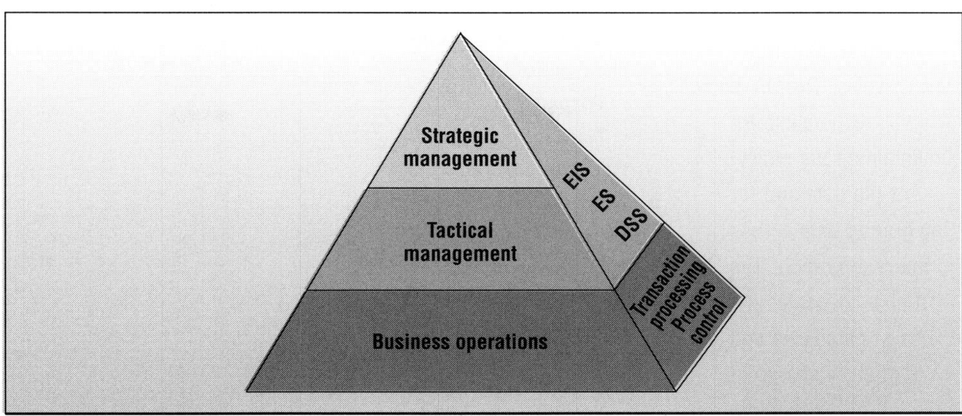

FIGURE 10.1
Decision levels. Data is an asset to the company and is used to make decisions at many levels, including day-to-day operations, middle-level tactical management, and strategic decisions to provide a competitive advantage.

DATA ADMINISTRATION

Data is an important asset to companies. Think about how long a modern company would survive if its computers were suddenly destroyed or all the data lost. Some organizations might survive as long as a few days or a week. Many, like banks, would be out of business immediately.

A company should not have to lose any of its data before it recognizes the value of the information contained in the data. As indicated by Figure 10.1, data is used for several purposes: business operations and transactions, tactical management, and strategic management. Business operations involve the day-to-day management of the firm—often collecting data involved in transactions such as sales and purchases. This data provides a foundation for managers throughout the company to make decisions. Tactical management involves analyzing the data to make improvements to the operations without completely restructuring the company. For example, a company might alter its marketing tactics if managers see sales slipping in a particular area. Managers also use data to make strategic decisions involving the long-term future of the firm and its competitive approach. Both internal and external data are used to make these decisions.

Over time, organizations build many different databases and applications to support their operational, tactical, and strategic decisions. Each application is important by itself, but when the applications and databases can coordinate and exchange data, managers receive a complete picture of the entire organization.

Despite the power and flexibility of database systems, applications built at different times by different people do not automatically share data. The key to integrating data is to put someone in charge of the data resources of the company. In most companies the **data administrator (DA)** fills this position.

As summarized in Figure 10.2, the primary role of the DA is to provide centralized control over the data for the entire organization. The DA sets data definition standards to ensure that all applications use consistent formats and naming conventions. The DA coordinates applications and teams to ensure that data from individual projects can be integrated into a corporatewide information system. If disputes occur among developers or managers, the DA serves as the judge, making decisions to ensure compatibility across the organization. The DA also monitors the database industry and watches trends and technologies to advise the company on which database systems and tools to consider for long-term benefits.

FIGURE 10.2 Data administrator roles. The DA is responsible for maintaining the quality of the data and for integrating data across the organization. The DA also advocates the use of databases and is often in charge of security.

- Provide centralized control over the data
  - Data definition
    - Format
    - Naming convention
  - Data integration
  - DBMS selection
- Act as data and database advocate
  - Application ideas
  - Decision support
  - Strategic uses
- Coordinate data integrity, security, and control

The DA plays a crucial role as an advocate. Most managers and many developers are not aware of the power and capabilities of modern database systems. By understanding the managerial tasks and the database capabilities, the DA is in a position to suggest new applications and expanded uses of the existing data.

Ultimately, the DA is also responsible for the integrity of the data: Does the data contained in the DBMS represent a true picture of the firm? Does the firm have the proper systems and controls in place to ensure the accuracy and timeliness of the data?

The DA position is largely a management job. The DA tasks consist of organizing and controlling the design aspects of application development. Control is maintained by setting standards, monitoring ongoing development and changes, and by providing assistance in database design as needed. The DA also spends time with business managers to evaluate current systems, monitor business trends, and identify future needs. The person hired for this position usually has several years of experience in designing databases and needs a detailed knowledge of the company. The DA also needs technical database skills to understand the various storage implications of the decisions. The DA must also be able to communicate easily with technical managers and business managers.

DATABASE ADMINISTRATION

A DBMS is a complex software package. Installing, running, and upgrading a DBMS are not trivial tasks. Even with personal computer–based systems, these tasks can require the services of a full-time person. Every database requires the services of a **database administrator (DBA).** The DBA position is generally staffed by a specialist who is trained in the administration of a particular DBMS. In smaller companies, instead of hiring a specialist, one of the lead developers may be asked to perform DBA duties.

DBA Tasks

The DBA role is relatively technical. As highlighted in Figure 10.3, the DBA is responsible for installing and upgrading the DBMS. Additional tasks include creating user accounts and monitoring security. The DBA is also responsible for managing backups. Although the actual backup task may be performed by a system operator, the DBA is responsible for setting schedules and making sure the data backups are safe. The DBA also monitors the performance of the databases and plans upgrades and additional capacity. The DBA must stay in contact with the DBMS vendor to keep track of system problems and notification of changes. As new utilities, tools, or information are provided, the DBA functions as a liaison to gather this knowledge and make it available to developers. The DBA has complete access to the data in the application. In many organizations the DBA is in charge of security for each database. Larger companies might appoint a special security officer to specify policies and procedures and to help with the monitoring. However, the DBA is generally in charge of carrying out the technical details of assigning security privileges for the database.

Data allocation and storage are an important part of the daily tasks of the DBA. Most large database systems require the DBA to preassign a space on the disk drive for each database. Oracle allocates physical space by creating datafiles. A set of datafiles is called a **tablespace,** which is a logical collection of space where data can be stored. SQL Server allocates space through a **data device.** Access does not require this step.

Separate space is usually allocated for the data tables, the indexes, and the transaction logs, and the DBA must accurately estimate the size of each component. If the DBA allocates too little space, performance will suffer; on the other hand, allocating too much space means that the company will waste money on unneeded disk drive capacity. Most systems provide tools to add space later, but it is best to get good estimates up front. The data volume estimates from Chapter 3 provide crucial information in determining the space requirements. For tables, the main concept is to determine the size of an average row (in bytes) and multiply by the expected number of rows in the table. Note that each DBMS stores data slightly differently, and some add bytes per row of storage. The documentation will provide details for each DBMS. A more accurate solution is to set up a temporary database, create a few rows of data in each table, and then use the actual average space to estimate future needs. Space required for the indexes and rollback log depend on the specific DBMS and the computer system. If you need highly accurate estimates, you will have to consult the documentation and support tools for your specific DBMS. Space for indexes and logs also depends on the number and length of transactions defined in the applications. For example the transaction log in a database used for transaction processing will have to be substantially larger than the log in a database used primarily for decision support and data retrieval.

DBA Tools

Many DBA tasks can be performed with SQL commands. However, the SQL commands utilize system tables and require detailed knowledge of how the particular DBMS stores internal operating parameters. Recently, vendors have simplified the management tasks by creating visual tools that enable the DBA to perform basic management tasks by selecting objects with a mouse. Each DBMS has its own set of management tools. For example, Oracle's Enterprise Manager provides performance mon-

FIGURE 10.3
Database administrator roles. The DBA tasks are fairly technical and require daily monitoring and changes to the DBMS.

- Install and upgrade DBMS.
- Create user accounts and monitor security.
- Manage backup and recovery of the database.
- Monitor and tune the database performance.
- Coordinate with DBMS vendor and plan for changes.
- Maintain DBMS-specific information for developers.

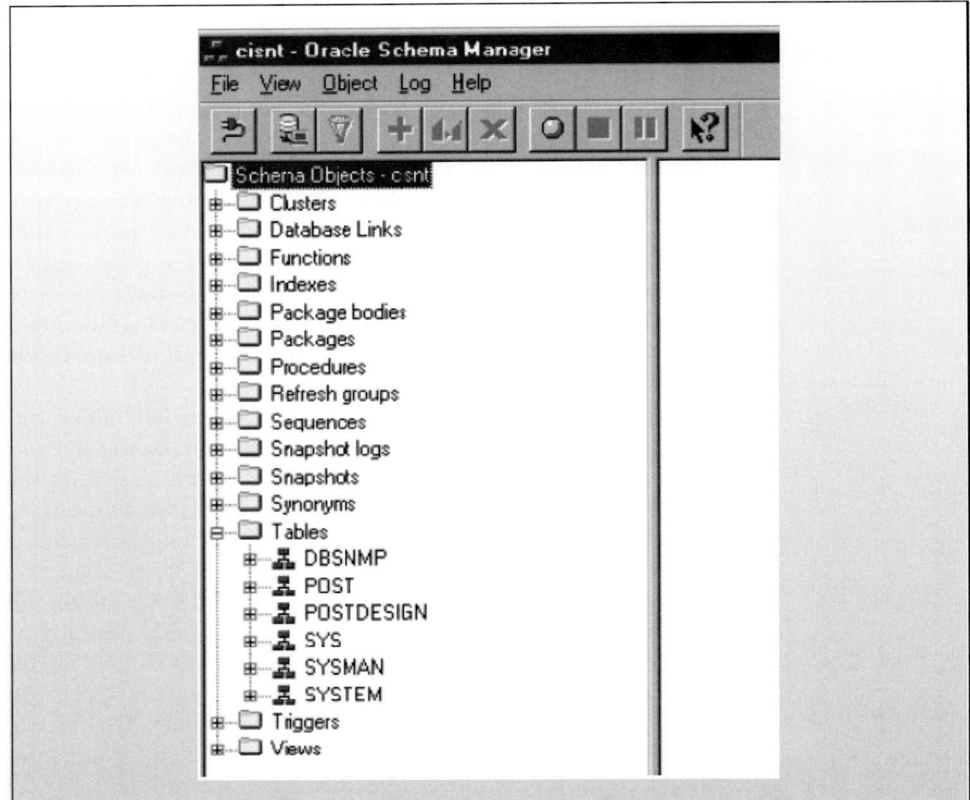

FIGURE 10.4 Visual DBA tools. Visual tools make it easier to manage a database. By selecting objects, the DBA can perform basic tasks like creating databases and tables and assigning security access rights.

itoring, security control, and database definition tools. Run from the DBA's computer, these tools can be used to monitor and control any Oracle database in the organization. Microsoft provides a similar tool (also called an Enterprise Manager) that enables the DBA to use visual tools to control SQL Server databases.

Some of the tasks that can be performed with these tools include creating a new database, creating tables, creating user accounts, assigning access rights, backing up and restoring the database, and setting database parameters. Figure 10.4 presents some of the choices available from the Oracle Schema Manager (which is part of the Enterprise Manager). Microsoft SQL Server Enterprise Manager is similar to this tool.

Compare the Schema Manager to the familiar introductory screen of Microsoft Access shown in Figure 10.5. Although the layout is different, many of the features are similar (although Oracle has many more features). Both systems provide visual access to the tables, views, forms, and procedures.

Performance Monitoring and Tuning

An important task of the DBA is to monitor the ongoing performance of the database. As indicated in Chapter 9, several techniques can be used to improve an application's performance. The catch is that you have to know that performance is lagging and you have to be able to track the source of the problem. Hardware bottlenecks also arise sometimes as the number of users increases. By knowing exactly which components are creating the problem, you can more wisely determine which ele-

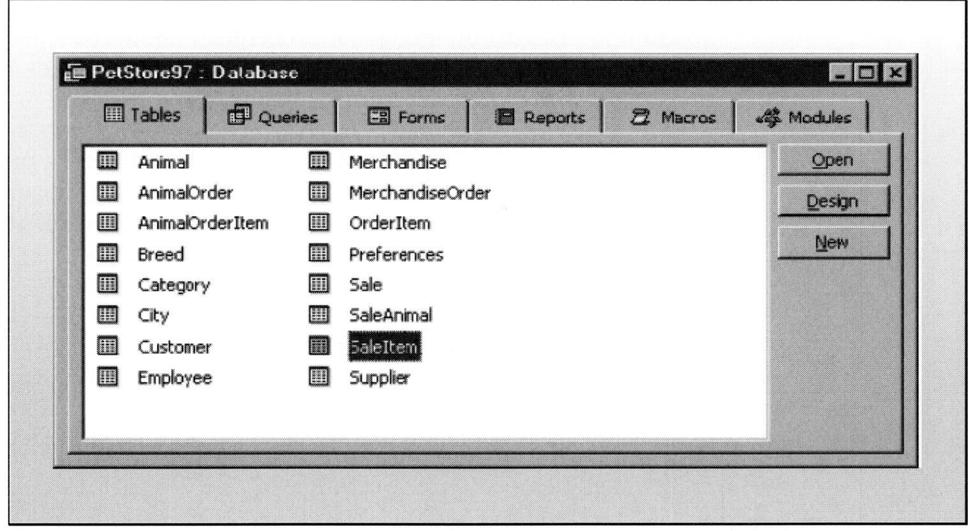

FIGURE 10.5 DBA in Microsoft Access. The main Access screen is similar to the visual DBA tools provided by Oracle and SQL Server.

ments need to be upgraded or modified. Figure 10.6 shows a few of the performance characteristics that can be continually monitored by Oracle. Each choice brings up a graph that displays the selected parameter. Microsoft SQL Server has a similar system that integrates with the Windows NT performance monitor.

Key items to watch are disk space, free space left for tables, number of users, memory usage including disk swapping, and I/O performance of the disk drives. An important ongoing task is to monitor the usage of the disk space allocated to each database to make sure there is sufficient space for the next week or month. Performance can be improved by placing these files on different disk drives or by placing index and rollback data in locations other than the main table data. Each component should be monitored for free space and usage.

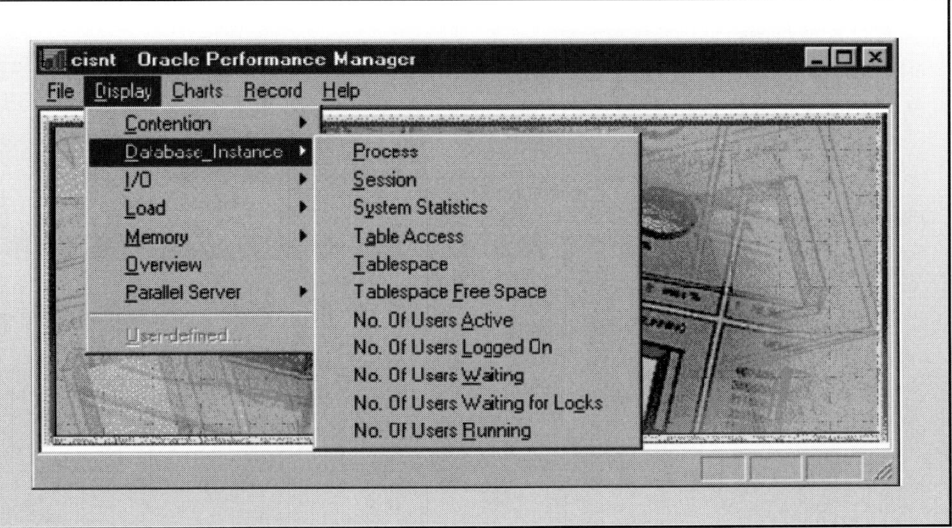

FIGURE 10.6 Performance monitoring. Several characteristics can be continuously monitored. Performance monitors enable the DBA to spot hardware and software bottlenecks and to predict the need for upgrades.

The performance tools can also monitor usage by individuals and can trace data access and changes by individual procedures. Monitoring individual processes and users helps to isolate the cause of problems. Also, if a deadlock situation arises or a system hangs and does not release resources, the DBA can manually stop processes, release locks, log off users, or free up resources. Of course, these steps should be taken only if the DBA learns from monitoring that there is a problem—closing a user process without notifying the user can cause serious problems for the user.

Microsoft Access does not provide monitoring tools that enable you to watch the ongoing actions of the database. If the DBMS is running on a Windows NT system, you can use the NT monitors to observe general disk and processor performance. Microsoft Access provides a different approach to performance tuning. From the Tools menu, you can ask the DBMS to analyze the performance of your database. Figure 10.7 shows the main screen. Access uses a set of rules to suggest changes that should improve the performance of your application. This performance analyzer is particularly good at identifying the need for additional indexes.

DATABASE TASKS BY DEVELOPMENT STAGES

Whichever development methodology you follow (e.g., traditional systems development life cycle, rapid development, or prototyping), certain database tasks are required at each step. Most of the tasks are performed by the application developers. Some involve coordination with the DA. Many require communication with the DBA, both to get advice and to provide information to help the DBA set up the databases.

Database Planning

During the feasibility and planning stages, you will have to make an estimate of the data storage requirements. These initial estimates will be rough, but they will help determine the size and capacity of the hardware needed to support the application. For example, if you are building a simple database to track materials that will be used by five people, the database might require less than 100 megabytes of storage and run on a personal computer. If the initial size estimates start to exceed a few hun-

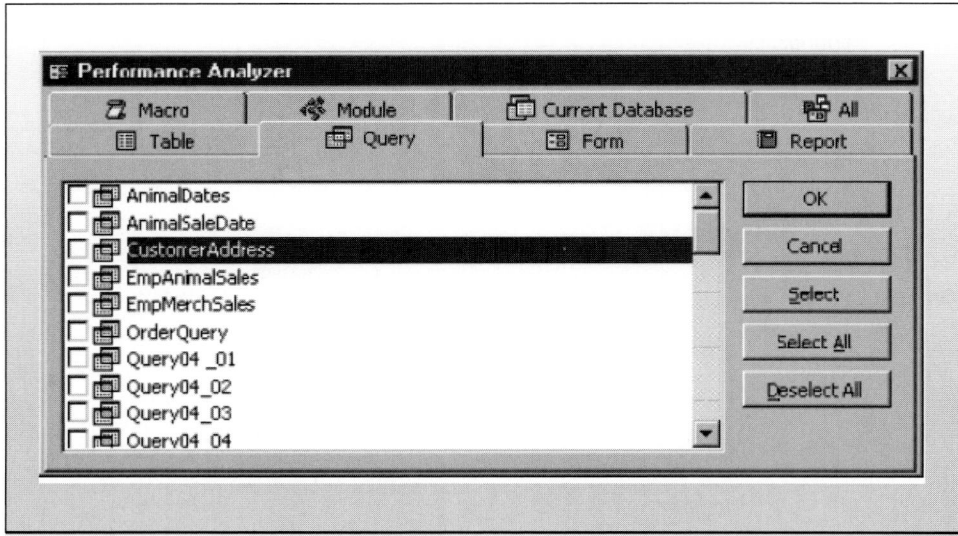

FIGURE 10.7
Microsoft Access performance analysis. Access uses a set of rules to suggest improvements to the design of your tables, queries, forms, and modules.

- Teamwork
  - Data standards
  - Data repository
  - Reusable objects
  - CASE tools
  - Networks / communication
- Subdividing projects
  - Deliver in stages
    - User needs / priorities
    - Version upgrades
  - Normalization by user views
    - Distribute individual sections
    - Combine sections
    - Assign forms and reports

FIGURE 10.8 Managing database design. Database design requires teamwork and standards to ensure that individual components can be integrated into a complete application. CASE tools and networks improve communication through a centralized repository of design data.

dred megabytes of storage, a file server with high-speed disk drives might be more appropriate. As the database estimates approach gigabytes or terabytes, you should investigate special database hardware and parallel-processing systems.

The initial investigation should also provide some idea of the number of forms and reports that will be needed, as well as their complexity. These numbers will be used to estimate the time and cost required to develop the system. An experienced DBA can provide estimates of space requirements from similar projects. Company records on other projects can provide estimates of the average time to develop forms and reports.

Database Design

The basic goal of the design stage is to identify the user needs and design the appropriate data tables. Data normalization is the primary database-related activity in this stage. The final table definitions will also provide better estimates of the storage requirements.

Teamwork coordination and project management are important administrative tasks at this stage. As highlighted in Figure 10.8, teamwork is supported with data standards as defined by the DA. Projects can be split into pieces and assigned to each team member. The ability to integrate the pieces into a complete application is provided through standards and communication. Communication is enhanced through a shared data repository, networked tools, e-mail, and **computer-aided software engineering (CASE)** tools. Leading CASE tools include Oracle Designer/2000, Rational Rose, IEF, and IBM's Visual Age. These tools provide a centralized repository for all project work, including diagrams, data definitions, and programming code. As team members work on their portion of the project, they can see the rest of the project. In an OO project, they can use the objects created by other teams.

From the perspective of data design or normalization, the project is often split by assigning forms and reports to individual team members. Each person is then responsible for identifying the business assumptions and defining the normalized tables needed for the assigned forms. Periodically, the individuals combine their work and create a centralized list of the tables that will be used in the database. This final list must follow the standards established by the DA.

Database Implementation

The primary database tasks required for implementation are listed in Figure 10.9. Development of the application and user interface are the major steps. Management and organizational tasks largely entail determining the overall look and feel of the application. Once the overall structure is determined, programming standards and testing procedures facilitate teamwork and ensure quality.

Another important management task is to assign ownership of the various databases. Owners should be from business management. Data owners are responsible for identifying primary security rules and for verifying the accuracy of the data. If the DBA has any questions about access rights or changes to the data, the DBA can obtain additional information and advice from the data owner.

Backup and recovery procedures have to be established and tested. If any component fails, the database logs should be able to fully restore the data. Backups are often handled in two forms: full backup at predefined checkpoints and incremental backups of changes that have occurred since the last full backup. Complete backups are easier to restore and provide safer recovery. However, they can be time-consuming and require large amounts of backup space. For small databases, full backups are not a problem. For large, continually changing transaction databases, it may only be possible to perform a full backup once a week or so.

Users and operators also have to be trained. No matter how carefully the user interface is designed, there should always be at least an introductory training session for users. Similarly, computer operators may have to be trained in the backup and recovery procedures.

Database Operation and Maintenance

Once the database is placed in operation, the DBA performs most of the management tasks. The primary tasks are (1) monitor usage and security, (2) perform backups and recovery, and (3) support the user.

Monitoring performance and storage space is a critical factor in managing a database. Monitoring is used to fine-tune the application performance and to estimate growth and plan for future needs. Security access and changes are also monitored. Security logs can track changes to critical data. They can also be specified to track usage (both read and write) by individual users if there is a suspected problem.

Monitoring user problems as well as performance provides useful feedback on the application. If users consistently have problems in certain areas, the design team

FIGURE 10.9
Implementation management. The user interface must be carefully chosen. Programming standards and test procedures help ensure compatibility of the components and provide quality control. Business managers should be assigned ownership of the data, so they can make final determinations of security conditions and quality. Backup and recovery plans have to be created and tested. Training programs have to be created for operators and users.

- Standards for application programming
    - User interface
    - Programming standards
        - Layout and techniques
        - Variable and object definition
    - Test procedures
- Data access and ownership
- Loading databases
- Backup and recovery plans
- User and operator training

should be encouraged to improve those forms. Similarly, if some users are running queries that take a long time to execute, the design team should be called in to create efficient versions of the queries. For example, do not expect a user to recognize or correct a correlated subquery. Instead, if the DBA sees users running complex queries that take too long to run, the team should add a new section to the application that stores and executes a more efficient query.

Similarly, if some people are heavily using certain sections of the database, it might be more efficient to provide them with replicated copies of the main sections. If the users do not need up-to-the-minute data, a smaller database can be set up on a server and updated nightly. The users end up with faster response time because they have a smaller database and less communication time. The rest of the database runs faster because there are fewer heavy users.

DATABASE APPLICATION TYPES

Database administration, maintenance, and performance tuning depend on the purpose and usage of the database. Several applications have become so common that vendors now sell specific hardware and software configurations to support each type. Two important classifications are **on-line transaction processing (OLTP)** and **on-line application processing (OLAP).** Each application type faces specific demands and constraints.

On-Line Transaction Processing

OLTP uses a database system that requires high throughput of transaction data. It intensively uses updates and inserts. The amount of data can be huge, and it grows constantly; hundreds or thousands of transactions might be performed at the same time. Classic examples include airline reservation systems, banking, and retail sales. The goals are to provide high-speed responses, full-time availability, data integrity support—particularly with concurrent access—and recoverability if something crashes.

Meeting these goals depends on (1) the size and location of rollback segments; (2) indexes, clustering, and hashing; (3) defining transactions carefully in the application; (4) storage and free space mechanisms for row data; (5) carefully defined applications and SQL statements; and (6) constant performance monitoring.

In many cases the databases become too large to risk running on one computer. Performance, integrity, and security can all be improved by splitting the database and operating on several computers. Chapter 11 investigates the potential power of the client/server approach.

On-Line Application Processing

OLAP is different from OLTP in one major respect. Whereas OLTP concentrates on storing new data—usually in small increments—OLAP focuses on retrieving data—usually through detailed analysis and complex queries. That is, OLAP generally focuses on using existing data—typically for decision support activities. OLAP is often performed by managers or researchers, who are looking for information or new patterns in the data. The key goals are to provide acceptable response times to queries, maintain and monitor security rights, and to make it easier for users to find the information they need.

Meeting the first goal is accomplished through (1) optimization by the query processor; (2) indexes, clustering, and hashing; and (3) parallel processing of the queries—particularly with RAID storage.

The important point to remember about OLTP and OLAP is that they result in different patterns of usage. Hence optimizing the DBMS for one approach can cause problems with the other type of usage. For example, indexes can substantially improve query performance in OLAP. Yet the more indexes you place on a table, the slower the performance for insertions and updates for OLTP.

Data Warehouses and Data Mining

The underlying conflict with performance tuning for OLTP and OLAP has not been solved. The catch is that managers need access to the transaction data, yet the business profitability hinges on the performance and reliability of the transaction system. The current solution chosen by many organizations is to maintain two separate systems: a system for transaction processing and a system dedicated to high-performance data analysis and retrieval. The transaction system generally consists of the legacy (existing) hardware, software, and databases. These systems have been configured and tuned over time to provide the desired level of performance and security. Then a new system is created that extracts the basic data from the transaction system and indexes it for analysis by the managers. This new system is often called a **data warehouse.** The data warehouse might contain only a subset of the transaction data, but it is highly optimized for retrieval and analysis.

A more important feature of the data warehouse is that all of the data is consistent. To search and analyze data, managers require that all data be consistent. For example, if they want to compute sales by city—then every entry for a city must be spelled the same way or provided with a unique key. Similarly, a product's name must be entered the same way, or the query will treat the entries as different products. Unfortunately, most legacy systems were built over several years—often across different divisions or regions—and generally created and revised by different programmers. Most companies are unlikely to have data that is "clean" and consistent. Hence a major factor in transferring data to a data warehouse is the need to clean up the data.

Once the data warehouse is established, many tools are available to search it. Some people might use basic SQL queries and gradually refine their search. Others might use spreadsheets to extract and analyze the data. More sophisticated approaches use data mining techniques. **Data mining** consists of using automated tools to search for hidden patterns in the data. Some tools include statistical methods (e.g., regression, discriminant analysis), pattern recognition (e.g., neural networks), and database segmentation (e.g., k-means, mixture modeling, and deviation analysis). A description of these tools is beyond the scope of this book. However, the key point is that they generally require substantial computing power and extremely high-speed data retrieval. Even with current high-speed systems, many of the techniques would need days or weeks to analyze some of the large datasets that exist. The point is that if users want to work on this type of analysis, the databases will have to be configured and tuned to their specific needs.

BACKUP AND RECOVERY

Perhaps the most critical database management task is backup. No matter how well you plan, no matter how sophisticated your security system, something will go wrong. Database managers and developers have an obligation to plan for disasters. The most critical aspect of planning is to make sure that a current copy of the database is easily accessible. Any type of disaster—fire, flood, terrorist attack, power failure, computer virus, disk drive crash, or accidental deletion—requires backup data. Given the low cost of making and storing backup copies, there is no excuse for not having a current backup available at all times.

As shown in Figure 10.10, database backups provide some interesting challenges—particularly when the database must be available 24 hours a day, 7 days a week (abbreviated to **24 x 7**). The basic problem is that while the database is making a copy, changes could still be made to the data. That is, every copy of the database is immediately out of date—even while it is being made. A related issue is that the DBMS copy routines might have to wait to copy portions of the database that are currently in use (possibly creating a deadlock situation).

Fortunately, the larger database systems provide many tools to solve these problems. In most cases the DBMS takes a **snapshot** of the tables. The snapshot represents the status of a table at one instant in time. Then the database maintains a transaction log of every change made since the last snapshot. The catch is that the DBA must decide how often to perform an incremental (partial) backup and how often a full backup (snapshot) is needed. A partial backup is faster to create and requires less storage space but takes longer to restore in the event of a disaster.

If there is a problem, the database has to be restored from the backup tapes. First the DBMS loads the most recent snapshot data. Then it examines the transactions. Completed transactions are **rolled forward,** and the changes are rewritten to the data tables. If the backup occurred in the middle of a transaction and the transaction was not completed, the DBMS will **roll back** or remove the initial changes and then restart the transaction. Remember that a transaction consists of a series of changes that must all succeed or fail together. The DBMS relies on the application's definition of a transaction as described in Chapter 8.

Backups have to be performed on a regular schedule. Occasionally, the schedule will have to be revised—particularly if the database records many changes. Remember that every change since the last backup is recorded in a journal or transaction log. The DBA has to watch the space on the transaction log. If it becomes too full, a backup has to be run earlier than scheduled. If these unexpected backups happen too often, the schedule should be changed.

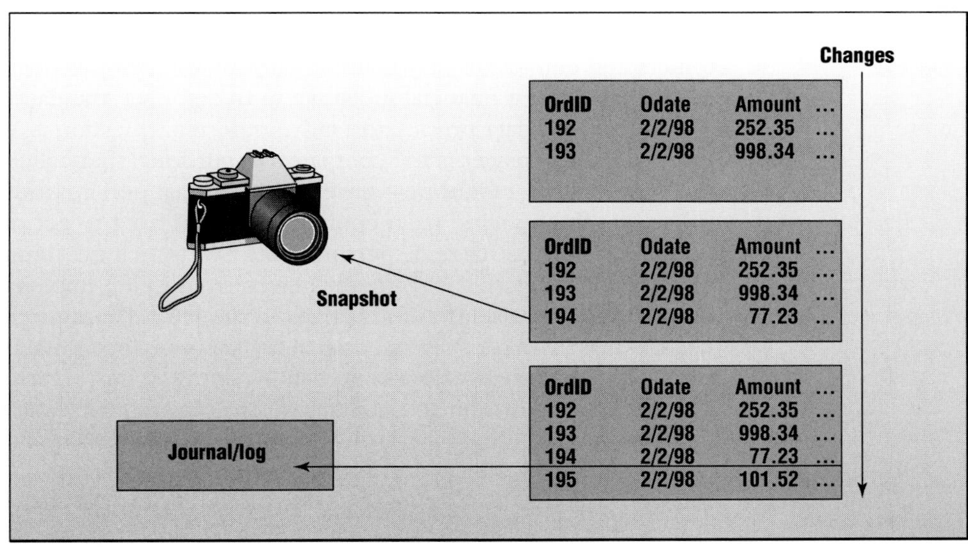

FIGURE 10.10
Backup of a changing database. Backup takes a snapshot at one point in time. New changes are stored in the journal or log. Recovery loads snapshot and adds or deletes changes in the journal.

Backup tapes must be stored offsite. Otherwise, a fire or other disaster, might destroy all data stored in the building. Snapshot and journal logs should be copied and moved offsite at least once a day. Networks make it easier to transfer data if the company is large enough to support computer facilities at more than one location. Several companies provide disaster-safe vaults for storage of data tapes and disks. In extreme situations, it might pay to have duplicate computer facilities and automatically mirror changes from the main database onto the secondary computer in a different location. Then when something goes wrong, the secondary computer can immediately pick up the operations. However, even in this situation, you should make physical backup copies.

SECURITY AND PRIVACY

Computer security is an issue with every company today, and any computer application faces security problems. A database collects a large amount of data in one location and makes it easy for people to retrieve and change data. In other words, a database is a critical resource that must be protected. Yet the same factors that make a database so useful also make it more difficult to secure. In particular, the purpose of a database is to share data. In a security context, you want to control who can share the data and what those users can do with it.

There are two basic categories of computer security: (1) physical security and (2) logical security. **Physical security** is concerned with physically protecting the computing resources and preparing for physical disasters that might damage equipment or data. **Logical security** consists of protecting the data and controlling access to the data.

Data Privacy

Privacy is related to security but with a slight twist. Companies and governmental agencies collect huge amounts of data on customers, suppliers, and employees. Privacy means controlling the distribution of this data and respecting the wishes of these external people. The concepts of keeping data accurate and limiting who has access to it are the same for security and for privacy. The differences lie in the objectives and motivation. In terms of security, every company has a self-interest in keeping its data safe and protected. In terms of privacy—at least in the United States—there are few regulations or limitations on what a company can do with personal data. Hence customers and employees may want a company to keep personal data private, but companies may have a financial incentive to trade or sell the data to other companies.

In terms of data privacy, the most important question is, Who owns the data? In most cases the answer is the company or individual that collects the data. Some people—particularly in Europe—have suggested that perhaps individuals should be considered as the owners. Then companies would have to get permission—or pay for permission—to use or trade personal data. So far, technical limitations have prevented most of the suggested payment schemes from being implemented. However, companies must pay attention to changes in the laws regarding privacy.

Database workers have an ethical obligation in terms of data privacy. Many times, you will have access to personal data—regarding customers and other employees. You have an obligation to maintain the privacy of that data: You cannot reveal the data to other people. In fact, you should avoid even reading the data. You should also not tolerate abuses by other workers within the organization. If you detect privacy (or security) violations by others, you should report the problems and issues to the appropriate supervisors.

Threats

What are the primary threats to computer security? What possible events cause nightmares for database administrators? Is it the outside hackers or crackers that you see in the movies? Is it tornadoes, hurricanes, or earthquakes (also popular in movies)?

No. The primary threat to any company comes from "insiders." Companies can plan for all of the other threats, and various tools exist to help minimize problems. However, you have to trust your employees, consultants, and business partners. For them to do their jobs, they need physical access to your computers and logical access to your database. Once you are committed to granting access, it becomes more difficult to control what they do. Not impossible, just more difficult.

Another, more insidious threat comes from programmers who intentionally damage data. One technique is to embed a time bomb in a program. A time bomb requires the programmer to enter a secret code every day. If the programmer leaves (or is fired) and cannot enter the code, the program begins deleting files. In other cases programmers have created programs that deliberately alter data or transfer funds to their own accounts. These examples illustrate the heart of the problem. Companies must trust their programmers, but this trust carries a potential for considerable damage or fraud. It is one of the reasons that companies are so sensitive about MIS employee misconduct. As a developer, you must always project an image of trust.

Physical Security

In terms of physically protecting the computer system, the most important task is to make sure you always have current backups. This policy of backups also applies to hardware. In case of a fire or other physical disaster, you need to collect the data tapes and then find a computer to load and run them. Instead of waiting until a disaster happens, you really need to create a disaster plan.

A **disaster plan** is a complete list of the steps that the IS department will take if a disaster hits the information system. The plan details who is in charge, what steps everyone will take, lists contact numbers, and how you will get the systems up and running. One popular method of finding an alternative computer is to lease a hot site from a disaster planning company. A **hot site** consists of a computer facility that has power, terminals, communication systems, and a computer. You pay a monthly fee for the right to use the facility if a disaster occurs. If there is a disaster, you activate the disaster plan, collect the data tapes, load the system, load your backup tapes, and run the system from the hot site. A slightly cheaper alternative is to lease a cold site. A **cold site** or **shell site** is similar to a hot site, but it does not have the computer and telecommunications equipment. If a disaster occurs, you call your hardware vendor and beg for a new computer. Actually, vendors have been very cooperative. The catch is that it can still take several days to receive and install a new computer. Can your company survive for several days without a computer system? For smaller computers, some of the disaster recovery companies can deliver a truck to your site and run the system from your parking lot.

A more interesting problem arises with personal computers. First, it is more challenging to back up data on many individual computers. If they are connected to a network, the data can be transferred to a central file server and copied from there. If there is a fire, at least the data can be recovered. Now, what about the computers? If you lose 5 or 10 computers, you can easily buy replacement units at your local computer store. If you lose several hundred computers, it will be a little more diffi-

- Backup data
- Backup hardware
- Disaster planning and testing
- Prevention
    - Location
    - Fire monitoring and control
    - Control physical access

FIGURE 10.11 Physical security controls. Backup data is the most important step. Having a place to move to is a second step. Disaster plans and prevention help prevent problems and make recovery faster.

cult to replace them. One creative solution is to help employees purchase computers for their use at home. If there is a problem, they can work from home while you rebuild the central computer systems and replace the personal computers.

As summarized in Figure 10.11, prevention is another important step in providing physical security. Computer facilities should have fire detection and protection systems. Similarly, computer facilities should be located away from flood plains, earthquake faults, tidal areas, and other locations subject to known disasters. Physical access to computers, network equipment, and personal computers should be limited. Most companies have instituted company badges with electronic locks. Access by visitors, delivery people, and temporary employees should be controlled.

Managerial Controls

Because the major threats to data security come from insiders, traditional managerial controls play an important role in enhancing security. For example, one of the most important controls begins with the hiring process. Some firms perform background checks to verify the character and trustworthiness of the employees. Even simple verification of references will help to minimize problems. Similarly, firms have become more cautious when terminating employees—particularly MIS employees with wide access to databases. Even for routine layoffs, access rights and passwords are revoked immediately.

Sensitive jobs are segmented. For example, several employees are required to complete financial transactions. Transactions involving larger amounts of money are routed to higher-level employees. Similarly, outside institutions like banks often call back to designated supervisors to verify large transactions. Transactions are often monitored and recorded in terms of the time, location, and person performing the operations.

In some cases security can be enhanced through physical control over the hardware. Centralized computers are placed in locked and guarded rooms. Employees are often tracked through video monitors. Security badges are also used to track employee access to locations and computer hardware.

Consultants and business alliances also raise security concerns. Generally, you have less control over the selection of the consultant and partnership employees. Although you have control in the selection of a consulting firm, you have little control over the specific employees assigned to your location. These risks can be controlled by limiting their access to the data and restricting their access to physical locations. In some situations you may also want to pair an internal employee with each consultant.

Logical Security

The essence of logical security is that you want to allow each user to have some access to the data, but you want to control exactly what type of access the user will have. You also want to monitor access to the data to identify potential problems.

FIGURE 10.12 Logical security problems. Each situation can cause problems for the company, including financial loss, lost time, lost sales, or destruction of the company.

- Unauthorized disclosure
- Unauthorized modification
- Unauthorized withholding

Figure 10.12 notes the three basic problems that you want to avoid: unauthorized disclosure, unauthorized modification, and unauthorized withholding of information.

Some information needs to be protected so that only a select group of users can retrieve it. For example, the company's strategic marketing plans need to be protected so that no competitor can retrieve the data. To be safe, only a few top people in the company would have access to the plans.

Some information is safe to display to users, but you do not want the users to change it. For example, an employee should be able to check the human resource files to verify his or her salary, remaining vacation days, or merit evaluations. But it would be a mistake to allow the employee to change any of this data. No matter how honest your employees are, it would be a dangerous temptation to allow them to alter their salary.

The third problem is subtle but just as dangerous. Consider what would happen if the chief financial officer needs to retrieve data to finalize a bank loan. However, the security system is set incorrectly and refuses to provide the data needed. If the data is not delivered to the bank by the end of the day, the company will default on several payments, receive negative publicity, lose 20 percent of its stock price, and risk going under. The point is that withholding data from authorized users can be just as dangerous as allowing the wrong access to other people.

Assuming you have a sophisticated computer system and a DBMS that supports security controls, two steps are needed to prevent these problems. First, the computer system must be able to identify each user. Second, the owner of the data must assign the proper access rights to every piece of data. The DBA (or a security officer) is responsible for assigning and managing user accounts to uniquely identify users. The application designer and data owners are jointly responsible for identifying the necessary security controls and access rights for each user.

User Identification

One of the major difficulties of logical computer security is identifying the user. Humans recognize other people with sophisticated pattern-recognition techniques applied to appearance, voice, handwriting, and so on. Yet even people can be fooled. Computers are weak at pattern recognition, so other techniques are required.

The most common method of identifying users is by accounts and passwords. Each person has a unique account name and chooses a password. In theory, the password is known only to the individual user and the computer system. When the user enters the correct name and matching password, the computer accepts the identity of the person.

The problem is that computers are better than people at remembering passwords. Consequently, people make poor choices for passwords. Some of the basic rules for creating passwords are outlined in Figure 10.13. The best passwords are

FIGURE 10.13 Password suggestions. Pick passwords that are not in a dictionary and are hard to guess. The catch is, Can you remember a convoluted password?

- Do not use real words.
- Do not use personal (or pet) names.
- Include nonalphabetic characters.
- Use at least six characters.
- Change it often.

long, contain nonalphabetic characters, have no relationship to the user, and are changed often. Fine, but a user today can easily have 10, 20, or more different accounts and passwords. Almost no one can remember every account and the convoluted passwords required for security. So there is a large incentive to either write the passwords in a convenient location (where they can be found by others) or choose simple passwords (which can be guessed).

Passwords are the easiest system to implement at this time. Some work is being done at storing passwords in a central security server (e.g., Kerberos), where a user logs into the main server and all other software verifies users with that server. Another approach is to use password generator cards. Each user carries a small card that generates a new password every minute. At login, the computer generates a password that is synchronized to the card. Once the password is used, it is invalidated, so if an interloper observes a password, it has no value. The system still requires users to memorize a short password just in case a thief steals the password card. Of course, if you lose the card, you cannot get access to the computers. Encrypted software variations can be loaded onto laptop computers, which then provide access to the corporate network.

Other alternatives are being developed to get away from memorizing passwords. Biometric systems that measure physical characteristics already exist and are becoming less expensive. For example, fingerprint, handprint, iris pattern, voice recognition, and thermal imaging systems now work relatively well. The advantage to biometric approaches is that the user does not have to memorize anything or carry around devices that could be lost or stolen. The main drawback is cost, since the validating equipment has to be installed anywhere that employees might need access to a computer. A secondary problem is that although the devices are good at preventing unauthorized access, many of them still have relatively high failure rates and refuse access to authorized users.

After individual users are identified, most systems enable you to assign the individuals to groups. Groups make it easier to assign permissions to users. For example, by putting 100 employees into a clerical group, you can grant permissions to the group, which is much faster than assigning the same permissions 100 times.

Access Controls

After users are identified, they can be assigned specific permissions to any resource. From a database perspective two levels of access must be set. First, the user must be granted access to the overall database, using operating system commands. Second, the user must be granted individual permissions, using the database security commands.

Remember that the DBMS is just another piece of software that runs in the environment of the computer. It stores data in files that are controlled and monitored by the operating system. Before anyone can get access to the data controlled by the DBMS, the computer must give that person permission to access the entire database directory and its files. This situation also requires users to be identified twice: once by the operating system and once by the DBMS. On some systems (e.g., Windows NT), the DBMS might accept the user identification directly from the operating system. On operating systems that have no security provisions (like personal computer–based Windows), the DBMS is responsible for providing all security.

Operating system permissions consist of permissions at the directory level (read, view, write, create, and delete). Similar permissions apply to individual files (read, write, edit, and delete). On larger systems the DBMS logs in as a separate user. The DBA grants this DBMS user full directory and file permissions to its own files. If you

- Read data
- Update data
- Insert data
- Delete data
- Open / run
- Read design
- Modify design
- Administer

FIGURE 10.14 DBMS privileges. These privileges apply to the entire table or query. The first three (read, update, and insert) are commonly used. The design privileges are usually granted only to developers.

are running a personal computer-based system (e.g., Microsoft Access) over a network, you will have to use the network operating system to give users access to your file (*.mdb). For example, users should be given read access to the directory where you store the file. They should also be given read and write permissions on the specific file and on the lock file (*.ldb). Avoid giving them delete permission to any files. A disgruntled user with delete permission could delete your entire database—even if he or she cannot change individual items. Of course, you have a backup, but the delay in finding the problem and restoring the database can be annoying to users.

When the operating system user has access to the overall files, you can use the DBMS security system to control access to individual tables. In most cases the DBA will have to create user accounts within the DBMS to identify each user. In some situations this technique means that users will have to log in twice: once for the operating system and once for the database.

The privileges listed in Figure 10.14 apply to the entire table or query. The most common privileges you will grant are read, update, and insert. Delete permission means that a user can delete an entire row—it should be granted to only a few people in specific circumstances. Privileges that are more powerful can be granted to enable users to read and modify the design of the tables, forms, and reports. These privileges should be reserved for trusted users. Users will rarely need to modify the design of the underlying tables. These privileges are granted to developers.

With most database systems the basic security permissions can be set with two SQL commands: **GRANT** and **REVOKE.** Figure 10.15 shows the standard syntax of the GRANT command. The REVOKE command is similar. SQL 92 provides some additional control over security by allowing you to specify columns in the GRANT and REVOKE commands, so you can grant access to just one or two columns within a table. However, the privilege applies to every row in the table or query. Microsoft Access does not support the GRANT and REVOKE commands. However, similar security capabilities are provided through the Security options on the Tools menu. Other database systems provide a similar visual-oriented procedure to assign and re-

```
GRANT privileges
   ON objects
   TO users

REVOKE privileges
   ON objects
   FROM users
```

FIGURE 10.15 SQL security commands. Most systems also provide a visual tool to assign and revoke access rights.

FIGURE 10.16 Security using queries. You wish to let all employees look up worker phone numbers. But employees should not be able to see salaries. Define a query that contains only the data needed and then give employees access to the query—not to the original table.

Employee(ID, Name, Phone, Salary)

Query: Phonebook
SELECT Name, Phone FROM Employee

voke security. The visual approach makes it easier to see exactly which privileges are granted to each user on every table. The SQL commands are most appropriate for batch commands that install or modify application packages.

Queries as Controls

The basic security commands are powerful but somewhat limited in their usefulness. For example, until SQL 92, there was no direct way to assign privileges to individual columns. In fact, most systems do not yet support this feature. Instead, the security commands apply to an entire table or query.

The true power of a database security system lies in the ability to assign access to individual queries. Consider the example in Figure 10.16. You have an Employee table that lists each worker's name, phone number, and salary. You want to use the table as a phone book so employees can look up phone numbers for other workers. The problem is that you do not want employees to see the salary values. The solution is to create a query that contains just the name and phone number. Remember that a query does not duplicate the data—it simply retrieves the data from the other tables. Now, assign the SELECT privilege on the Phonebook query to all employees and revoke all employee privileges to the original Employee table. If you want, you can also choose specific rows from the Employee table. For example, you might not want to display phone numbers of the senior executives.

Chapters 4 and 5 showed you the power of queries. This power can be used to create virtually any level of security that you need. Virtually all user access to the database will be through queries. Avoid granting any access directly to a table. Then it will be easier to alter the security conditions as the business needs change.

The basic process is to confer with the users and determine exactly which type of access each user needs to the data. In particular, determine which users need to add or change data. Then create the users and assign the appropriate security conditions to the queries. Be certain to test the application for each user group. If security is a critical issue, you should consider assigning a couple of programmers to "attack" the database from the perspective of different users to see whether they can delete or change important files.

Division of Duties

For years, security experts have worried about theft and fraud from people who work for the company. Consider a classic situation that seems to arise every year. A purchasing manager sets up a fake supplier. The manager then pretends that shipments arrive from the company, and authorizes payments. Of course, the manager cashes the payments. Some of these frauds run for several years before they are caught.

The standard method to avoid this type of problem is to divide the duties of all the workers. The goal is to ensure that at least two people are involved in any major financial transaction. For example, a purchasing manager would find new suppliers and perhaps issue purchase requisitions. A different person would be in charge of receiving supplies, and a third person would authorize payments.

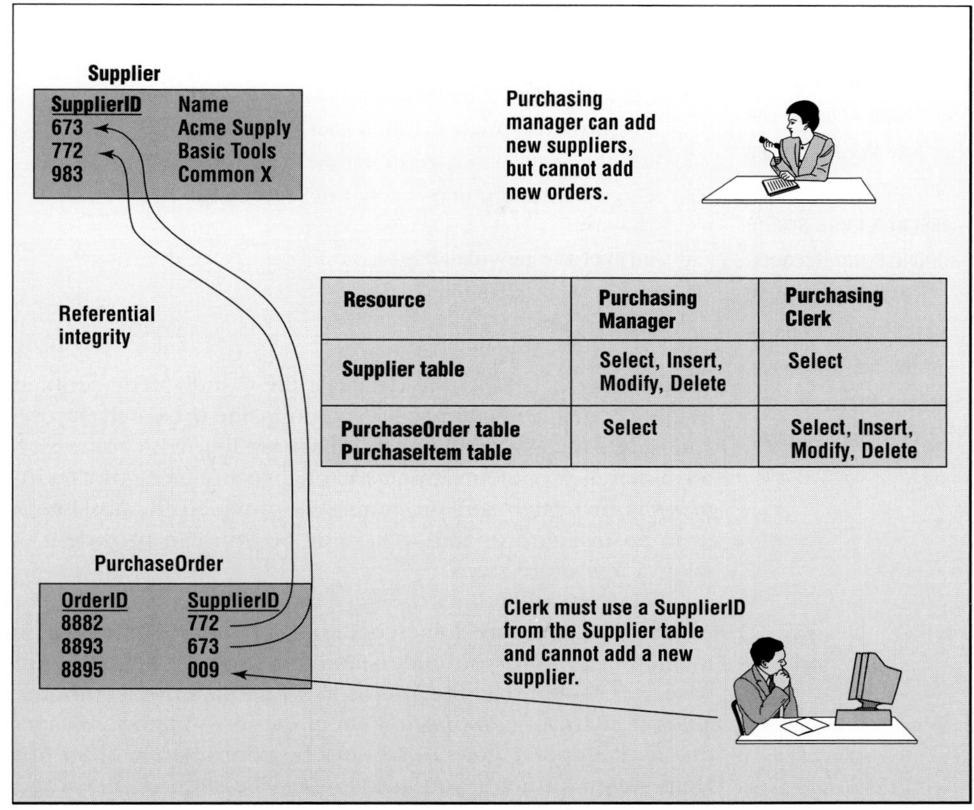

FIGURE 10.17 Separation of duties. The clerk cannot create a fake supplier. Referential integrity forces the clerk to enter a SupplierID from the Supplier table, and the clerk cannot add a new row to the Supplier table.

The goal of separating duties can be challenging to implement. Companies try to reduce costs by using fewer employees. Business picks up, and someone takes advantage of the confusion. It is impossible to eliminate all fraud. However, a well-designed database application can provide some useful controls.

Consider the purchasing example shown in Figure 10.17 in which the basic tables include a Supplier table, a SupplyItem table, a PurchaseOrder table, and a PurchaseItem table. In addition, financial tables authorize and record payments. The key to separation of duties is to assign permissions correctly to each table. The purchasing manager is the only user authorized to add new rows to the Supplier table. Purchasing clerks are the only users authorized to add rows to the PurchaseOrder and PurchaseItem tables. Receiving clerks are the only users authorized to record the receipt of supplies. Now if a purchasing clerk tries to create fake orders, he or she will not be able to create a new supplier. Because referential integrity is enforced between the Order table and the Supplier table, the clerk cannot even enter a false supplier on the order form. Likewise, payments will be sent only to legitimate companies, and a purchasing manager will not be able to fake a receipt of a shipment. The power of the database security system is that it will always enforce the assigned responsibilities.

MICROSOFT ACCESS AND SECURITY

Because Microsoft Access was designed to run on personal computers, there are a few twists to creating a secure database. The main problem is that simple personal computer operating systems (e.g., Windows and Windows 95) do not have a security system. So the operating system does not identify the user, and it is difficult to

FIGURE 10.18
Creating a secure database with Microsoft Access. The Security Wizard copies the entire database to assign a more secure administrator account. You must assign permissions to users in the new database. Be sure to encrypt the final database.

1. Set up a secure workgroup.
   Create a new Admin user.
   Enable security by setting a password.
   Remove the original Admin user.
2. Run the Security Wizard in the database to be secured.
3. Assign user and group access privileges in the new database.
4. Encrypt the new database.
5. Save it as an MDE file.

control user access to the database file (*.mdb). The problem caused by this shortcoming is that no matter what you do inside the database, users still have read, write, and delete access to the overall database file. With some technical knowledge, a determined user could examine and change any piece of data in the database. The good news is that Microsoft programmers provided for possible attacks on the database from an insecure operating system. So you can provide a secure database—it just takes a few more steps.

Figure 10.18 outlines the steps required to create a secure database with Microsoft Access. The steps are somewhat complicated, so Microsoft provides additional documentation to help you understand the process. Before attempting to secure a database, you should read the Microsoft white paper on computer security, which is available on Microsoft's Web site. One of the most important aspects to Access security is that each step in Figure 10.18 must be performed in order. You should use the Access Help system to guide you in following the steps in the proper order.

Step 1 in securing an Access database is to define a new administrator user and turn on security by assigning a password. All user account information is stored in a workgroup database file (system.mdw for Access 97; system.mda for older versions). You must remove all access to the Admin user, or your database can be opened by anyone who creates a new workgroup file that has an Admin user.

Step 2 is to run the Security Wizard. The wizard copies all database items to a new database and assigns the owner and administrator privileges to the new user you created in step 1. Without the wizard, this step is painful and time-consuming.

Step 3 is to assign the user and group privileges in the new database. As long as you know what permissions to assign, the visual tools make this step relatively easy. You should periodically review the permissions to make sure they are correct and support the current business operations.

Step 4 is sometimes performed automatically by the Security Wizard; however, it can be done separately. You must encrypt the final database. Encryption creates an internal, hidden encryption key and stores the database so that only someone who knows the key can read it. Of course, no one ever knows the key, so the only way to read the objects in the database is to use the DBMS. In other words, no one can use special disk tools to open and read the contents of the database.

Microsoft added another option in Access 97. You can save the database as an MDE file. An MDE file is automatically encrypted. More important, Access compiles all of the modules and removes the source code. Hence no one can retrieve or alter your custom programming. Even if you do not set additional security conditions, you should seriously consider distributing your applications as MDE files. Just be sure to save the original (MDB) database. There is no way to convert back from an MDE file.

ENCRYPTION

Encryption is a method of modifying the original information according to some code so that it can be read only if the user knows the decryption key. Encryption can be used to transmit information from one computer to another. Information stored on a computer also can be encrypted. Without the encryption key, the files are gibberish. Encryption is critical for personal computer-based systems that do not provide user identification and access controls. Encryption is also important when transmitting data across networks—particularly the Internet.

There are two basic types of encryption. Most methods use a single key to both encrypt and decrypt a message. For example, the **data encryption standard (DES)** method uses a single key. Although DES is a U.S. standard, versions of it are available throughout the world. The DES algorithm is fast, but it is older and can probably be cracked by a **brute force attack** that tries all possible key values. Figure 10.19 shows a basic use of the DES encryption method.

A second method uses both a **private key** and a **public key.** Whichever key is used to encrypt the message, the other key must be used to decrypt it. The **Rivest-Shamir-Adelman (RSA) algorithm** is an example of a method that uses two keys. RSA protection is available on a variety of computers. RSA encryption works because of the properties of prime numbers. In particular, it is relatively easy for computers to multiply two prime numbers together. Yet it is exceedingly difficult to factor the resulting large number back into its two component parts. The security of the RSA approach relies on using huge numbers (128 digits or more), which would take many years to factor with current technology.

Methods that use two keys have some interesting uses. The trick is that everyone knows your public key, but only you know the private key. Consider a situation where Takao wants to send a database transaction to Makiko across the Internet. Takao looks up Makiko's public key in a directory. Once the message is encrypted with Makiko's public key, only her private key can decrypt it. No one else can read or change the transaction message. However, someone might be able to destroy the message before Makiko receives it.

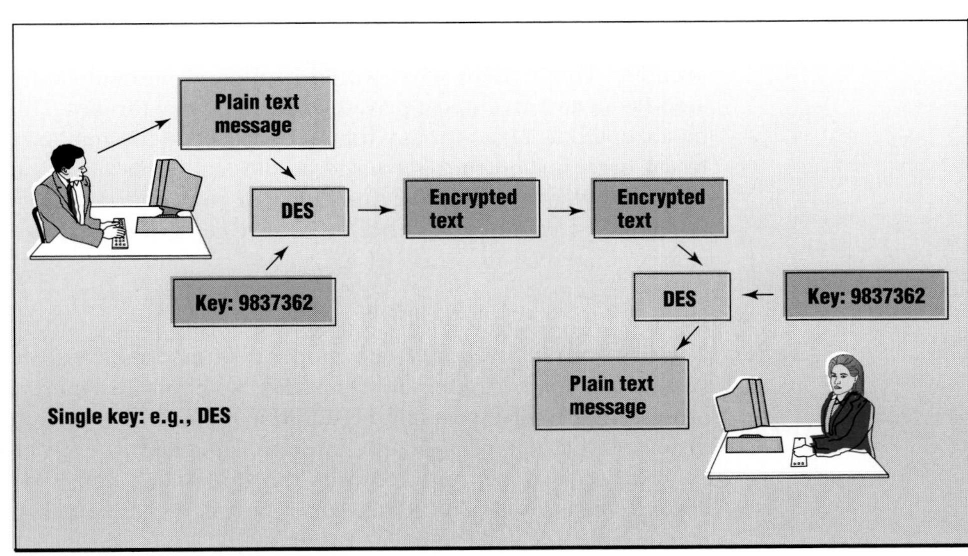

FIGURE 10.19
Single-key encryption. The same key is used to encrypt and decrypt the message. Distributing and controlling access to keys becomes a major problem when several users are involved.

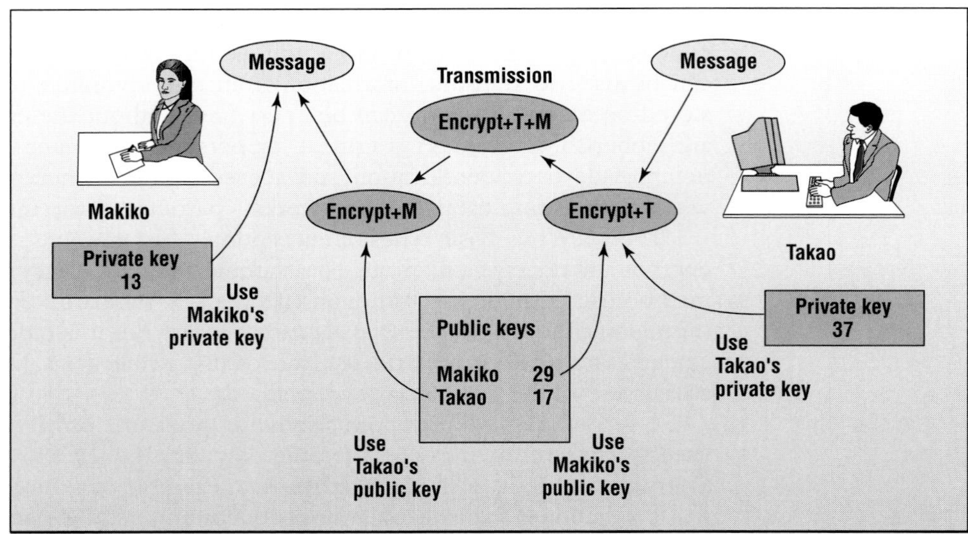

FIGURE 10.20 Dual-key encryption. Takao sends a message to Makiko. By encrypting it first with his private key, Takao authenticates the message. By encrypting it next with Makiko's public key, only Makiko can read the message.

There is a second use of dual-key systems called **authentication.** Let's say that Takao wants to send a message to Makiko. To make sure that only she can read it, he encrypts it with her public key. However, he is worried that someone has been sending false messages to Makiko using his name. Takao wants to make sure that Makiko knows the message came from him. If Takao also encrypts the message with his private key, it can be decrypted only with Takao's public key. When Makiko receives the message, she applies her private key and Takao's public key. If the message is readable, then it must have been sent by Takao. This situation is displayed in Figure 10.20.

Modern encryption schemes are powerful tools. They can be used to automatically ensure safe storage and transmission of data—even in open networks like the Internet. Keep in mind that all encryption schemes are subject to a brute force attack. As computers get faster, older encryption schemes become risky.

Dual-key encryption systems are useful in all aspects of information communication. They do have one complication: The directory that lists public keys must be accurate. Think about what would happen to authentication if someone impersonated Takao and invented a private and public key for him. This interloper would then be accepted as Takao for any transaction. Hence the public keys must be maintained by an organization that is trusted. Additionally, this organization must be careful to verify the identity of anyone (individual or corporation) who applies for a key. Several companies have begun to offer these services as a **certificate authority.** One of the early commercial firms is Verisign.

SALLY'S PET STORE

The first step in assigning security permissions for Sally's Pet Store is to identify the various groups of users. The initial list is shown in Figure 10.21. As the company grows, there will eventually be additional categories of users. Note that these are groups and that several people might be assigned to each category.

The second step is to identify the operations that various users will perform. Separate forms will be designed to support each of these activities. Figure 10.22 contains a partial list of the major activities.

FIGURE 10.21
Initial list of user groups for Sally's Pet Store.

MANAGEMENT
Sally/CEO
SALES STAFF
Store manager
Salespeople
BUSINESS ALLIANCES
Accountant
Attorney
Suppliers
Customers

The user and group accounts need to be created within the operating system and within the DBMS. After the tables, queries, and forms are created, the DBA should make sure that no group has any permissions on the base tables or queries. In other words, only the DBA should be able to read or modify data.

Now go through each operation and identify the queries and tables needed to perform the operation. You should list the permissions for each user group that are required to complete the operation. Figure 10.23 presents the permissions that would be needed to purchase items from suppliers. Notice that only the store managers (and the owner) can order new merchandise (add permission on the MerchandiseOrder and OrderItem tables). Also note that only the owner can add new suppliers. Remember that a referential integrity constraint is in place that forces the MerchandiseOrder table to use only Suppliers already listed in the Supplier table. Hence a store manager will not be able to invent a fictitious supplier. Also note that we would like to permit store managers to add items to the OrderItem table, but

FIGURE 10.22
Primary operations at Sally's Pet Store. All of these transactions will have forms or reports built in the database.

PRODUCTS
Sales
Purchases
Receive products
ANIMALS
Sales
Purchases
Animal health care
EMPLOYEES
Hiring/release
Hours
Pay checks
ACCOUNTS
Payments
Receipts
Management reports

FIGURE 10.23

Permissions for purchases. Notice that only the owner can add new suppliers, and only top-level managers can create new orders.

Purchase	Purchase Query				PurchaseItem Query	
	Merchandise Order	Supplier	Employee	City	Order Item	Merchandise
Sally/CEO	W/A	W/A	R: ID, Name	R	W/A	W/A
Store manager	W/A	R*	R: ID, Name	R	A	R
Salespeople	R	R*	R: ID, Name	R	R	R
Accountant	R	R*	R: ID, Name	R	R	R
Attorney	—	—	—	—	—	—
Suppliers	R	R*	—	R	R	R
Customers	—	—	—	—	—	—

*Basic supplier data: ID, Name, Address, Phone, ZipCode, CityID.

R = Read; W = Write; A = Add.

they should not be able to alter the order once it has been completed. The DBMS might not support this restriction, and you probably have to give the managers Write permission as well. If available, the distinction would be useful. Otherwise, a manager in charge of receiving products could steal some of the items and then change the original order quantity. If Sally has enough managers, this problem can be minimized by dividing the duties and having one manager place orders and another manager record the shipments.

Also note that Sally wants to record the identity of the employee who placed the order. For this purpose, you only need read permission on the EmployeeID and Name columns. This privilege can be set by creating a separate EmployeeName query that only retrieves a minimal number of columns from the Employee table. Then use this query for purchases instead of the original Employee table.

SUMMARY

Several steps are involved in managing a database. The DA performs management tasks related to design and planning. Key priorities are establishing standards to facilitate sharing data and integrating applications. The DA also works with users and business managers to identify new applications. In contrast, the DBA is responsible for installing and maintaining the DBMS software, defining databases, ensuring data is backed up, monitoring performance, and assisting developers.

Each stage of application development involves different aspects of database management. Planning entails estimating the size and approximate development costs. Project management skills and teamwork are used in the design stage to split the project and assign it to individual workers. Implementation requires establishing and enforcing development standards, testing procedures, training, and operating plans. Once the application is operational, the DBA monitors performance in terms of space and processing time. Physical storage parameters and other attributes are modified to improve the application's performance.

Backup and recovery are key administrative tasks that must be performed on a regular basis. Backup is more challenging on systems that are running continuously. The DBMS takes a snapshot and saves the data at one point in time. All changes are saved to a journal, which is also backed up on a regular basis. If the system has to be recovered, the DBMS loads the snapshot and then integrates the logged changes.

Security is an important issue in database management. Physical security consists of problems that involve the actual equipment, such as natural disasters or physical theft of hardware. Data backup and disaster planning are the keys to providing physical security. Logical security consists of protecting data from unauthorized disclosure, unauthorized modification, and unauthorized withholding. The first step to providing logical security is to create a system that enables the computer to identify the user. Then application designers and users must determine the access rights that should be assigned to each user. Access rights should be assigned to enforce separation of duties.

Encryption is a tool that is often needed to protect databases. Encryption is particularly useful when the operating system cannot protect the database files. Encryption is also used when data must be transmitted across networks—particularly open networks like the Internet.

A DEVELOPER'S VIEW

Miranda will quickly see that the tasks of a DBA are different from those of a developer, yet the developer must work closely with the DBA. As a developer, you need to understand the importance of data standards. You also need to work with the DBA in planning, implementing, and maintaining the database application. Before implementing the application, you need to establish the database security rights and controls. For your class project, identify all users and determine their access rights. Use queries to give them access only to the data that they need. Test your work. Also, run any performance monitors or analysis tools.

KEY WORDS

24 x 7, 363
authentication, 374
brute force attack, 373
certificate authority, 374
cold site, 365
computer-aided software engineering (CASE), 359
data administration, 352
data administrator (DA), 353
data device, 355
data encryption standard (DES), 373
data mining, 362
data warehouse, 362
database administration, 352
database administrator (DBA), 354
disaster plan, 365
encryption, 373
GRANT, 369
hot site, 365
logical security, 364
on-line application processing (OLAP), 361
on-line transaction processing (OLTP), 361
physical security, 364
private key, 373
public key, 373
REVOKE, 369
Rivest-Shamir-Adelman (RSA) algorithm, 373
roll back, 363
roll forward, 363
shell site, 365
snapshot, 363
tablespace, 355

REVIEW QUESTIONS

1. What is the role and purpose of a data administrator?
2. What tasks are performed by a database administrator?
3. What tools are available to monitor database performance?
4. What aspects of a database should be monitored to avoid performance problems?
5. How does the DA facilitate teamwork in developing database applications?
6. How do CASE tools help developers design and create large applications?
7. What are the primary security threats to a business?
8. How is a hot site used to protect the business applications?
9. What are the three problems faced by logical security systems?
10. What basic methods are available to identify users in a security system?
11. What are the basic database privileges that can be assigned to users?
12. How do queries provide detailed access controls?
13. How does a good DBMS application provide for division of duties?
14. What are the basic steps involved in securing a Microsoft Access database?
15. Why is encryption an important step in securing databases?
16. How does a dual-key encryption system provide for security and authentication at the same time?

EXERCISES

1. Extend the example in Figure 10.14. Add Title to the Employee table. Now create two phone books. One is accessible to all employees and lets them see phone numbers for anyone without the word *Executive* in his or her title. The second book is for executives and lists phone numbers of all employees.
2. A DBMS is halfway through recording a transaction with several related updates, and someone trips over the computer's power cord. Describe the steps the DBMS uses to protect and restore the database.
3. Briefly describe how you would protect a computer system from the following problems. Estimate how long it would take for your solution to get the system operational.
   a. Lightning strikes a tree, and your facility loses power for 3 hours.
   b. A floodwall fails, and your data center is flooded.
   c. Teenage mutant hackers from Europe attack your computer over the Internet, trying to break the login accounts of your users.
   d. Data entry clerks keep mistyping the item codes in orders.
   e. You suspect one of your employees is leaking information to a competitor.
   f. A purchasing department employee created fake supplier accounts and redirected company payments to his own accounts.
   g. A disk drive fails and loses all of its data.

h. A low-level worker acquires a user's password; the worker then transfers money to her bank account.

i. Someone on the Internet acquires a password from one of your salespeople by monitoring the Internet traffic passing through a router.

4. Get permission from your network administrator to perform the tests in this exercise. If you have access to a good DBMS with system monitoring tools, set up the monitoring tools. Then have other students perform various tasks and record the effects on the system. Start with one user and add users to examine the effect.

5. If you have access to a CASE tool (e.g., Oracle Designer), use a team of students to create a class diagram. Try having everyone work on the project at the same time and at different times. How does the CASE tool support teamwork? What procedures would you establish to improve the use of the tool?

6. Explain why 24 x 7 access to a transaction database makes it more difficult to provide backup and security.

7. What are the current U.S. laws on data privacy? What are the current European rules concerning customer privacy? What steps should a database administrator take to ensure privacy of data?

8. You have the following tables:
   Customer(<u>CustomerID</u>, . . .)
   Items(<u>ItemID</u>, . . .)
   Sale(<u>SaleID</u>, . . .)
   SaleItem(<u>SaleID</u>, <u>ItemID</u>, . . .)
   Purchase(<u>PurchaseID</u>, . . .)
   PurchaseItem(<u>PurchaseID</u>, <u>ItemID</u>, . . .)
   You have several types of users (management, shipping clerks, sales clerks, accounting checks, and purchasing clerks. What access rights should you give to each user category? What other logical security precautions should you take?

9. Employees and other insiders present the greatest security problems to companies. Outline basic policies and procedures that should be implemented to protect the computer systems. (Hint: Research employee hiring procedures.)

Sally's Pet Store

10. Devise a security plan for Sally's Pet Store. Identify the various classes of users and determine the level of access required by each group. Use the Access Security Wizard to make a secure copy of the database. Create the users in the Access security system. Assign the appropriate permissions to each group. Create any queries necessary to provide the desired security.

11. Create a list of tables and processes that might cause problems as the store and the database become larger. Explain how you would monitor the system to identify potential problems.

12. Create a backup and recovery plan that will be used at Sally's Pet Store. Identify the techniques used, who will be in charge, and the frequency of the backups. Explain how the process will change as the store and the database grow larger.

Rolling Thunder Bicycles

13. Devise a security plan for Rolling Thunder Bicycles. Identify the various classes of users and determine the level of access required by each group. Use the Access Security Wizard to make a secure copy of the database. Create the users in the Access security system. Assign the appropriate permissions to each group. Create any queries necessary to provide the desired security.

14. Devise a backup and recovery plan for Rolling Thunder Bicycles. Be sure to specify what data should be backed up and how often. Outline a basic disaster plan for the company. Where are security problems likely in the existing application? How should duties be separated to improve security?

WEB SITE REFERENCES

Site	Description
http://www.dama.org	Data Management organization
http://www.aitp.org	Association for Information Technology Professionals organization
http://www.acm.org/sigsac	Association for Computing Machinery: Special Interest Group on Security, Audit, and Control
http://www.for.gov.bc.ca/isb/datadmin/	Canadian Ministry of Forests data administration site, with useful information on data administration
http://www.securityserver.com	Links to information on computer security
http://www.capacityplanning.com/	Explores issues in capacity planning
http://www.benchmarkresources.com	A related site that explores issues in benchmarking and performance
http://swynk.com	Consultant/author with many links and on-line full-text SQL Server book
http://www.rational.com	A major CASE tool vendor
http://www.sterling.com	A major CASE tool vendor
http://support.microsoft.com/download /support/mslfiles/WX1051.exe	Microsoft's original white paper on Access 2.0 security; still one of the better explanations

ADDITIONAL READING

Castano, S., ed. *Database Security.* Reading, MA: Addison Wesley, 1994. [Collection of articles from Association of Computing Machinery ACM.]

Fayyad, U. "Diving into databases." *Database Programming & Design,* March 1998, pp. 24–31. [Good summary of OLAP, data warehouses, and future uses of databases.]

Loney, K. *Oracle8 DBA Handbook.* Berkeley: Osborne, 1997. [One of many Osborne books on Oracle.]

Oracle7 Server Administrator's Guide. Oracle, available on CD-ROM with the oracle DBMS. Berkeley, 1996. [Appendix A describes the technique used to estimate space required for tables, indexes, and rollback logs.]

PART 5

Distribution and Integration of Data

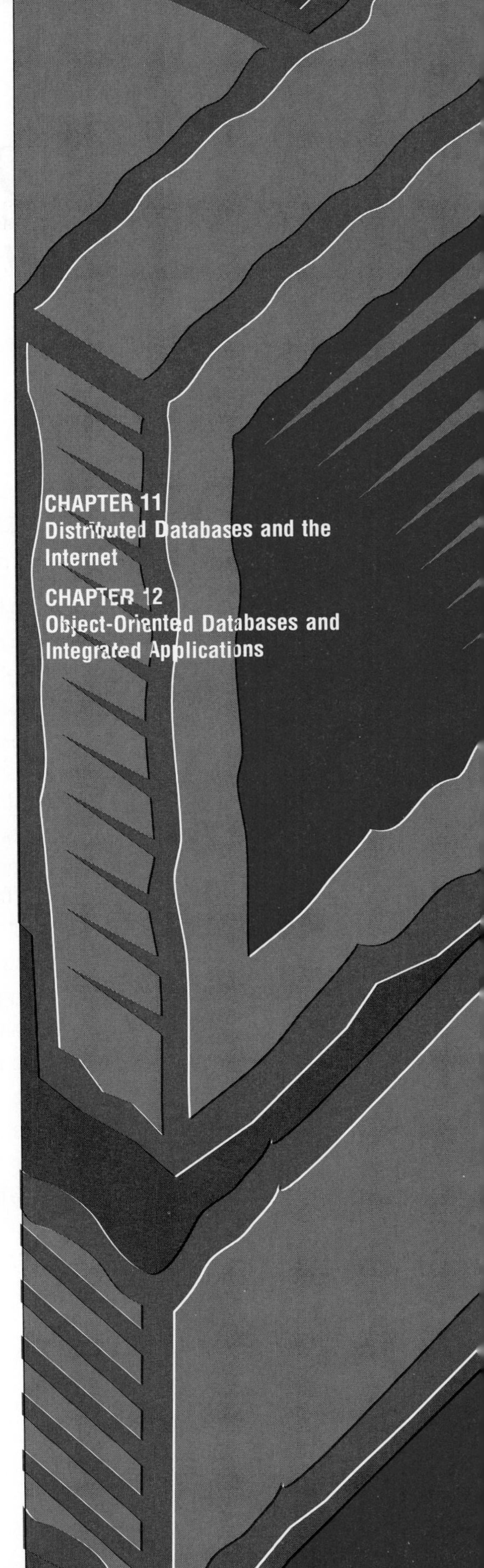

Businesses are increasingly expanding their use of databases and computers. Additionally, competitive pressures are creating a need for increased flexibility. Businesses are meeting this challenge through decentralization of many functions. Computers are distributed throughout the organization, and databases have followed. You increasingly need to build client/server applications that can handle data in many geographic locations. The Internet is also a powerful force for client/server applications and brings the need to support databases on your Web site. Chapter 11 discusses some of the challenges, options, and solutions to handling distributed databases and the Internet.

Chapter 12 discusses the increasing importance of object-oriented databases and the additions to SQL3 that may change the way you build databases. It also examines the techniques for integrating different application objects into your database system. With integrated tools you can create and use spreadsheets and word processing documents from within your database application.

CHAPTER 11

Distributed Databases and the Internet

WHAT YOU WILL LEARN IN THIS CHAPTER

- Why do companies need distributed databases? 384
- What problems are created or exacerbated with distributed databases? 391
- What are the strengths and weaknesses of a client/server application? 394
- What standards are available to provide connectivity between database systems? 397
- How does a three-tier client/server application provide flexibility in an application? 398
- What are the capabilities of an Internet Web client? 400
- How do you use databases on Web servers to build interactive Internet applications? 402
- How is Oracle PL/SQL related to other programming languages? 412

OVERVIEW

Ariel: *How is the new job going, Miranda?*

Miranda: *Great! The other developers are really fun to work with.*

Ariel: *So you're not bored with the job yet?*

Miranda: *No. I don't think that will ever happen—everything keeps changing. Now they want me to set up a Web site for the sales application. They want a site where customers can check on their order status and maybe even enter new orders.*

Ariel: *That sounds hard. I know a little about HTML, but I don't have any idea of how you access a database over the Web.*

Miranda: *Well, there are some nice tools out there now. With SQL and a little programming, it should not be too hard.*

Ariel: *That sounds like a great opportunity. If you learn how to build Web sites that access databases, you can write your ticket to a job anywhere.*

INTRODUCTION

Today even small businesses have more than one computer. At a minimum they have several personal computers. More realistically, most organizations today are taking advantage of networks of computers by installing portions of their database and applications on more than one computer. As companies open offices in new locations, they need to share data across a larger distance. Increasingly, companies are finding it useful and necessary to share data with people around the world. Manufacturing companies need to connect to suppliers, distributors, and customers. Service companies need to share data among employees or partners. All of these situations are examples of distributed databases. Many applications can take advantage of the network capabilities of the Internet and the presentation standards of the World Wide Web.

Building applications that function over networks and managing distributed databases can be complicated tasks. The goal is to provide location transparency to the users. Users should never have to know where data is stored. This feature requires a good DBMS, a solid network, and considerable database, network, and security management skills. However, a well-designed distributed database application also makes it easier for a company to expand its operations.

The Internet and the World Wide Web are increasingly used to share data. One of the fundamental strengths of the Internet is the set of standards that define how users connect to servers and how data will be displayed. By developing applications to run on a Web site, you ensure the widest possible compatibility and accessibility to your system. Building applications that use a database on the Web is similar to building any database; you just have to learn to use a few more tools and standards.

SALLY'S PET STORE

Now that the database is operating in Sally's store and the store is making money, she wants to expand. She is talking about adding a second store. She is also pushing for creation of a Web site, so that customers can order products, check on new animals, and get some help on caring for their pets. As a first step you have decided to talk to Sally about making your job a full-time position. She needs someone to manage the computers on a regular basis, modify the programs, and train other workers.

Sally's request to expand the database to a second store raises many questions. Does she need "instant" access to the sales data from both stores all the time? Do the stores need to share data with each other? For example, if a product is out of stock at one store, does Sally want the system to automatically check the other store? Will the stores operate somewhat independently—so that sales and financial data are maintained separately for each store—or will the data always be merged into one entity? How up-to-date does data need to be? Is it acceptable to have inventory data from yesterday, or does it need to be up-to-the-minute?

The primary design question we need to answer is whether one central database should handle all sales or separate, distributed databases should handle each store. The answer depends on how the stores are managed, what type of data is needed, the network capabilities and costs, and the capabilities of the DBMS.

In many ways, initially the cheapest solution is to keep the second store completely independent. Then there is no need to share data except for some basic financial information at the end of each accounting period. A second advantage of this approach is that it is easy to expand—since each new store is independent. Similarly, if something goes wrong with the computer system at one store, it will not affect the other stores.

However, at some point Sally will probably want a tighter integration of the data. For example, the ability to check inventory at other local stores can be a useful feature to customers, which means that the application will need to retrieve data from several databases, located in different stores. These distributed databases must be networked through a telecommunications channel. There are many ways to physically link computers, and you should take a telecommunications course to understand the various options. Once the computers are physically linked, you need to deal with some additional issues in terms of creating and managing the distributed databases.

The Internet has rapidly become a leading method to contact customers and share information. Connecting a database to a Web site is a powerful method of providing up-to-date information and enabling customers to find exactly the information they need. To understand how to link a database to a Web site, it is helpful to first understand the details of distributed databases.

DISTRIBUTED DATABASES

A **distributed database** system consists of multiple independent databases that operate on two or more computers that are connected and share data over a network. The databases are usually in different physical locations. Each database is controlled by an independent DBMS, which is responsible for maintaining the integrity of its own databases. In extreme situations the databases might be installed on different hardware, different operating systems, and could even use DBMS software from different vendors. That last contingency is the hardest to handle. Most current distributed databases function better if all of the environments are running DBMS software from the same vendor.

In the example shown in Figure 11.1, a company could have offices in three different nations. Each office would have its own computer and database. Much of the data would stay within the individual offices. For example, workers in the United States would rarely need to see the daily schedules of workers in France. On the other hand, workers in France and England could be working on a large international project. The network and distributed database enable them to share data and treat the project as if all the information was located in one place.

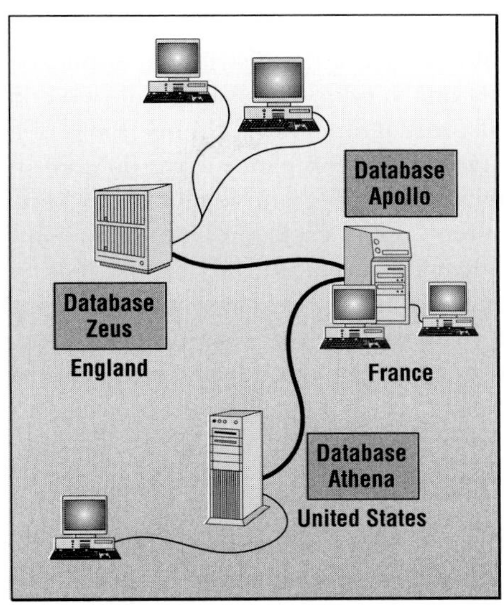

FIGURE 11.1
Distributed database. Each office has its own hardware and databases. For international projects, workers in different offices can easily share data. The workers do not need to know that the data is stored in different locations.

Distributed databases can be organized in several configurations. The most popular method today involves a client/server approach. In a **client/server** system, the server computer is more powerful and provides data for many clients. The client computers are usually personal computers with a graphical user interface. The role of the client is to provide the interface to the user, collect and display data, and return the data to the appropriate server.

Goals and Rules

It is difficult to create a DBMS that can adequately handle distributed databases. (The major issues are addressed in later sections.) In fact, early systems faced various problems. Consequently, a few writers have created a set of goals or rules that constitute the useful features of a distributed DBMS. C. J. Date, who worked with E. F. Codd to define the relational database approach, lists several rules that he feels are important. This section summarizes Date's rules.

In anyone's definition of a distributed database, the most important rule is that the user should not know or care that the database is distributed. For example, the user should be able to create and run a simple query just as if the database were on one computer. Behind the scenes the DBMS might connect to three different computers, collect data, and format the results. But the user does not know about these steps.

As part of this rule, the data should be stored independently of location. For example, if the business changes, it should be straightforward to move data from one machine and put it in a different office. This move should not crash the entire application, and the applications should run with a few simple changes. The system should not rely on a central computer to coordinate all the others. Instead, each computer should contact the others as needed. This separation improves system performance and enables the other offices to continue operations even if one computer or part of the network goes down.

There are additional, somewhat idealistic goals. The DBMS should be hardware and operating system independent so that when a newer, faster computer is needed, the company simply transfers the software and data to the new machine and everything runs as it did before. Similarly, it would be nice if the system were independent of its network. Most large networks are built from components and software from a variety of companies. A good distributed DBMS should be able to function across different networks. Finally, it would be nice if the distributed application did not rely on using DBMS software from only one vendor. For example, if two companies merge, it would be great if they could just install a network connection and have all the applications continue to function—even if the companies have different networks, different hardware, and database software from different vendors. This idealistic world does not yet exist. However, some systems, like Oracle, provide many components of these goals.

These features are desirable because they would make it easier for a company to expand or alter its databases and applications without discarding the existing work. By providing for a mix of hardware, software, and network components, these objectives also enable an organization to choose the individual components that best support its needs.

Advantages and Applications

The main strength of the distributed database approach is that it matches the way organizations function. Business operations are often distributed across different locations. For example, work and data are segmented by departments. Workers within each department share most data and communications with other workers within that department. Yet some data needs to be shared with the rest of the company. Similarly, larger companies often have offices in different geographical regions. Again, much of the data collected within a region is used within that region. However, some of the data needs to be shared by workers in different regions.

There are three basic alternatives to sharing data: (1) have one central computer that collects and processes all data, (2) have independent computer systems in each office that do not share data with the others, and (3) use a distributed database system.

The second option is a possibility—as long as the offices rarely need to share data. It is still a common approach in many situations. Data that needs to be shared is transmitted via paper reports, fax or telephone calls, or possibly e-mail messages. Of course, these are ineffective methods for sharing data.

Some early computer systems used the first option. However, routing all transactions to a central computer has several drawbacks. In particular, transferring the data to one location is expensive. And if the one computer is unavailable, everyone suffers.

Figure 11.2 illustrates several advantages of the distributed database approach. First, distributed systems provide a significant performance advantage through better alignment with the needs of the organization. Most updates and queries are performed locally. Each office retains local control and responsibility for the data. Yet the system enables anyone with the proper authority to retrieve and integrate data from any portion of the company as it is needed.

A second advantage to distributed databases is that, compared to centralized systems, they are easier to expand. Think about what happens if the company is using one large, centralized computer. If the company expands into a new region, requiring more processing capacity, the entire computer might have to be replaced. With a distributed database approach, expanding into a new area would be supported by adding another computer with a database to support the new operations. All existing hardware and applications remain the same. By using smaller computer systems, it is easier and cheaper to match the changing needs of the organization.

Because the distributed database approach can be tailored to match the layout of any company, it has many applications. Two common categories are transaction processing and decision support applications. In a transaction processing system,

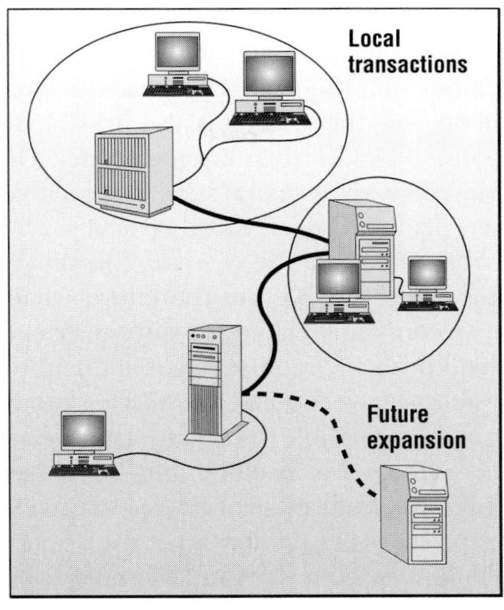

FIGURE 11.2
Distributed database strengths. Most data is collected and stored locally. Only data that needs to be shared is transmitted across the network. The system is flexible because it can be expanded in sections as the organization grows.

each region would be responsible for collecting the detailed transaction data that it uses on a daily basis. For instance, a manufacturing plant would have a database to collect and store data on purchases, human relations, and production. Most of this data would be used by the individual plant to manage its operations. Yet as part of the corporate network, summary data could be collected from each plant and sent to headquarters for analysis. As another example, consider a consulting firm with offices in several countries. The workers can store their notes and comments in a local database. If a client in one country needs specialized assistance or encounters a unique problem, the local partners can use the database to search for similar problems and solutions at other offices around the world. The distributed database enables workers within the company to share their knowledge and experiences.

Creating a Distributed Database System

The basic steps to building a distributed database are similar to those for creating any database application. Once you identify the user needs, the developers organize the data through normalization, create queries using SQL, define the user interface, and build the application. However, as shown in Figure 11.3, a distributed database requires some additional steps. In particular, a network must connect the computers in all the locations. Even if the network already exists, it might have to be modified or extended to support the chosen hardware and DBMS software.

- Design administration plan.
- Choose hardware, DBMS, and network.
- Set up network and DBMS connections.
- Choose locations for data.
- Choose replication strategy.
- Create backup plan and strategy.
- Create local views and synonyms.
- Perform stress test: loads and failures.

FIGURE 11.3
Additional steps to create a distributed database. After the individual systems and network are installed, you must choose where to store the data. Data can also be replicated and stored in more than one location. Local views and synonyms are used to provide transparency and security. Be sure to stress test the applications under heavy loads and to ensure that they handle failures in the network and remote computers.

Another crucial step is determining where to store the data. The next section examines some of the issues you will encounter with processing queries on a distributed database. For now, remember that the goal is to store the data as close as possible to the location where it will be used the most. It is also possible to duplicate heavily used data so that it can be stored on more than one computer. Of course, then you need to choose and implement a strategy to make sure that each copy is kept up-to-date.

Backup and recovery plans are even more critical with a distributed database. Remember that several computers will be operating in different locations. Each system will probably have a different DBA. Yet the entire database must be protected from failures, so every system must have consistent backup and security plans. Developing these plans will probably require negotiation among the administrators—particularly when the systems cross national boundaries and multiple time zones. For example, it would be virtually impossible to backup data everywhere at the same time.

Once the individual systems are installed and operational, each location must create local views, synonyms, and stored procedures that will connect the databases, grant access to the appropriate users, and connect the applications running on each system. Each individual link must be tested, and the final applications must be tested both for connections and for stress under heavy loads. It should also be tested for proper behavior when a network link is broken or a remote computer fails.

Operating and managing a distributed database system is considerably more difficult than handling a single database. Identifying the cause of problems is much more difficult. Basic tasks like backup and recovery require coordination of all DBAs. Some tools exist to make these jobs easier, but they can be improved.

Remember the rule that a distributed database should be transparent to the user? That same rule does not yet apply to DBAs or to application developers. Coordination among administrators and developers is crucial to making applications more accessible to users.

Distributed Query Processing

The challenge with distributed databases comes down to physics and economics. As illustrated in Figure 11.4, data that is stored on a local disk drive can be transferred to the CPU at transfer rates of 10 to 20 megabytes per second (or higher). Data that is stored on a server attached to a **local area network (LAN)** can be transferred at rates from 1 to 10 megabytes per second. That is, the average speed of a LAN can

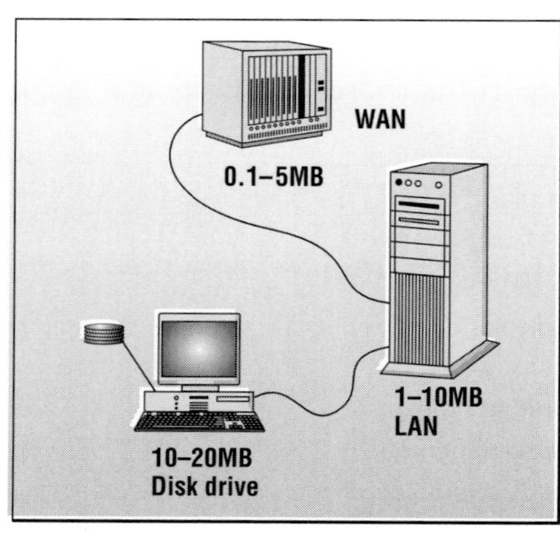

FIGURE 11.4
Network transfer rates. Transfers from disk drives are faster than LAN transfers, which are faster than WAN transfers. High-speed WAN transfers are much more expensive than other transfer methods.

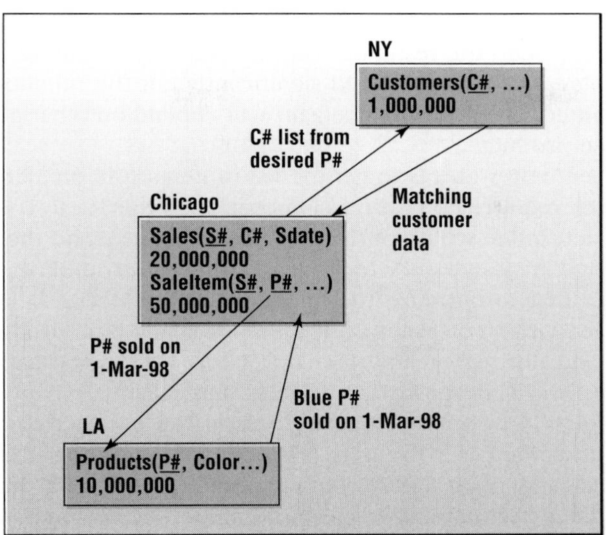

FIGURE 11.5 Distributed database query example. List customers who bought blue products on 1-Mar-98. A bad idea is to transfer all data to Chicago. The goal is to restrict each set and transfer the least amount of data.

be 10 times slower than a direct disk transfer. Using public transmission lines to connect across a **wide area network (WAN)** provides transfer rates from 0.01 to about 5 megabytes per second. To get that 5 megabytes per second (on a T3 line), your company would probably have to pay at least $20,000 a month. As technology changes these numbers are continually improving, but the comparative relationships tend to hold true. That is, transfer to a local disk drive is faster than to transfer across a LAN, which is faster than to transfer across a WAN.

The goal of distributed processing is to minimize the transfer of data on slower networks and to reduce the costs of network transfers. Part of this goal can be accomplished through design—developers must carefully choose where data should be located. Data should be stored as close as possible to where it will be used the most. However, there are always trade-offs when data is used in several locations.

Another issue in transferring data arises in terms of query processing. If a query needs to retrieve data from several different computers, the time to transfer the data and process the query depends heavily on how much data must be transferred and the speed of the transmission lines. Consequently, the result depends on how the DBMS joins the data from the multiple tables. In some cases the difference can be extreme. One method could produce a result in a few seconds. A different approach to the same query might take several days to process! Ideally, the DBMS should evaluate the query, the databases used, and the transmission times to determine the most efficient way to answer the query.

Figure 11.5 illustrates the basic problem. Consider tables on three different databases: (1) a Customer table in New York with 1,000,000 rows, (2) a Production table in Los Angeles with 10,000,000 rows, and (3) a Sales table in Chicago with 20,000,000 rows. A manager in Chicago wants to run the following query: List customers who bought blue products on 1-Mar-98.

There are several ways this query could be processed. Consider a bad idea. Transfer all of the rows to Chicago, then join the tables and select the rows that match the query. This method results in 11,000,000 rows of data being transferred to Chicago. Even with a relatively fast WAN, anything less than 30 minutes for this query would be amazingly fast.

A better idea would be to tell the database in Los Angeles to find all the blue products and send the resulting rows to Chicago. Assuming only some of the products are blue, this method could significantly cut the number of rows that need to be transmitted. The performance gain will depend on what percentage of rows consist of blue products.

An even better idea is to get the list of items sold on March 1 from the Chicago table, which requires no transmission cost. Send this list to Los Angeles and have that database determine which of the products are blue. Send the matching CustomerID to the New York database, which returns the corresponding Customer data.

Notice that to optimize the query, the DBMS needs to know a little about the data in each table. For example, if there are many blue products in the Los Angeles database and not very many sales on March 1, then the database should send the Sales data from Chicago to Los Angeles. On the other hand, if there are few blue products, it will be more efficient to send the product data from Los Angeles to Chicago. In some cases the network also needs to know the transfer speed of the network links. A good DBMS contains a query optimizer that checks the database contents and network transfer speeds to choose the best method to answer the query. You still might have to optimize some queries yourself. The basic rule is to transfer the least amount of data as possible.

Data Replication

Sometimes there is no good way to optimize a query. When large data sets are needed in several different places, it can be more efficient to **replicate** the tables and store copies in each location. The problem is that the databases involved have to know about each of the copies. If a user updates data in one location, the changes have to be replicated to all the other copies. The DBMS uses a **replication manager** to determine which changes should be sent and to handle the updates at each location.

Developers and database administrators can tune the performance by specifying how the database should be replicated. You can control how often the changes are distributed and whether they are sent in pieces or as a bulk transfer of the entire table. The biggest difficulty is that sometimes a network link might be unavailable or a server might be down. Then the DBMS has to coordinate the databases to make sure they get the current version of the table and do not lose any changes.

Figure 11.6 illustrates the basic concepts of replication. Marketing offices in each location have copies of Customer and Sales data from Britain and Spain. Almost all updates are based on data in the local country. Managers probably do not need up-to-the-minute data from the other countries, so the tables can be replicated as batch updates during the night. The data will be available to managers in all locations without worrying about transfer time, and the company can minimize international transmission costs by performing transfers at off-peak times.

Transaction processing databases generally record many changes—sometimes hundreds of changes per minute. These applications need to have fast response times at the point of the transaction. It is generally best to run these systems as distributed databases to improve the performance within the local region.

On the other hand, managers from different locations often need to analyze the transaction data. If you give them direct access to the distributed transaction databases, the analysis queries might slow the performance of the transaction system. A currently popular solution is to replicate the transaction data into a data warehouse. Routines extract data from the transaction processing system and store it in

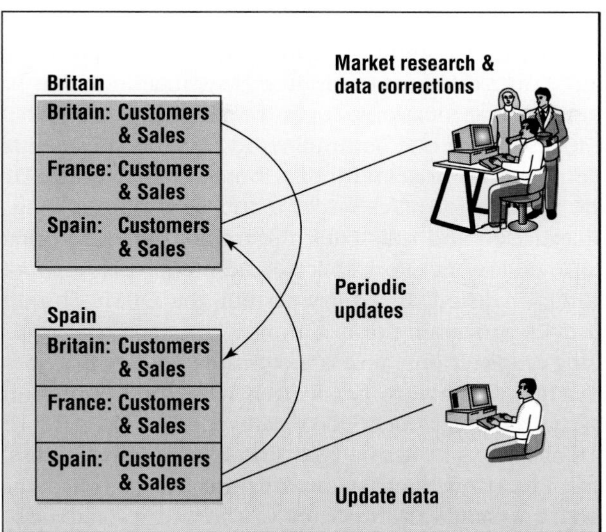

FIGURE 11.6 Replicated databases. If managers do not need immediate data from other nations, the tables can be replicated and updates can be transferred at night when costs are lower.

the data warehouse. Managers run applications and build queries to retrieve the data from the warehouse and analyze it to make tactical and strategic decisions. Because the managers rarely make changes to the underlying data, the data warehouse is a good candidate for replication. The underlying transaction processing system retains its speed, and the raw data is not shared. Managers have shared access to the warehouse data.

Concurrency, Locks, and Transactions

Concurrency and deadlock become complex problems in a distributed database. Remember that concurrency problems arise when two people try to alter the same data at the same time. The situation is prevented by locking a row that is about to be changed. As shown in Figure 11.7, the problem with a distributed database is that

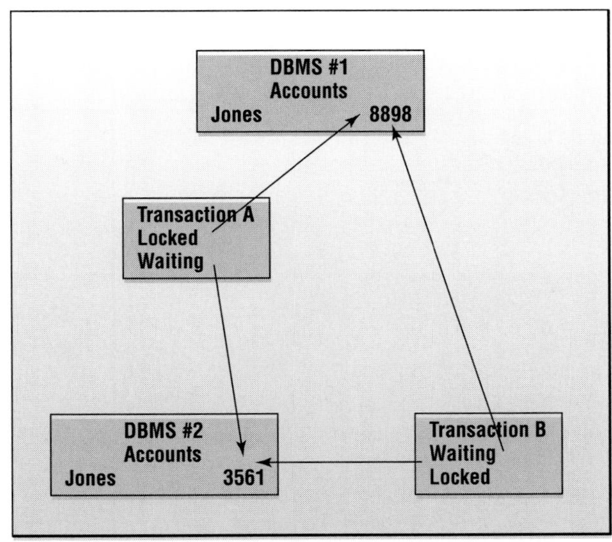

FIGURE 11.7 Concurrency and deadlock are more complicated in a distributed database. The deadlock can arise across many different databases, making it hard to identify and resolve.

the application could create a deadlock that involves different databases on separate computers. One user could hold a lock on a table on one computer and be waiting for a resource on a different computer. Now imagine what happens when there are five databases in five locations. It can be difficult to identify the deadlock problem. When the locks are on one computer, the DBMS can use a lock graph to catch deadlock problems as they arise. With distributed databases the DBMS has to monitor the delay while waiting for a resource. If the delay is too long, the system assumes a deadlock has arisen and rolls back the transaction. Of course, the delay might simply be due to a slow network link, so the method is not foolproof. Worse, the time spent waiting is wasted. In a busy system, the DBMS could spend more time waiting than it does processing transactions.

Handling transactions across several databases is also a more complex problem. When changes have to be written to several computers, you still have to be certain that all changes succeed or fail together. To date, the best mechanism for verifying transactions utilizes a **two-phase commit** process. Figure 11.8 illustrates the process. The database that initiates the transaction becomes a coordinator. In the first phase it sends the updates to the other databases and asks them to prepare the transaction. Each database must then send a reply about its status. Each database must agree to perform the entire transaction or to roll back changes if needed. The database must agree to make the changes even if a failure occurs. In other words, it writes the changes to a transaction log. Once the log is successfully created, the remote database agrees that it can handle the update. If a database encounters a problem and cannot perform the transaction (perhaps it cannot lock a table), it sends a failure message and the coordinator tells all the databases to roll back their changes. A good DBMS handles the two-phase commit automatically. As a developer, you write standard SQL statements, and the DBMS handles the communication to ensure the transaction is completed successfully. With weaker systems you will have to embed the two-phase commit commands within your program code. If you know that you are building an application that will use many distributed updates, it is generally better to budget for a better DBMS that can handle the two-phase-commit process automatically.

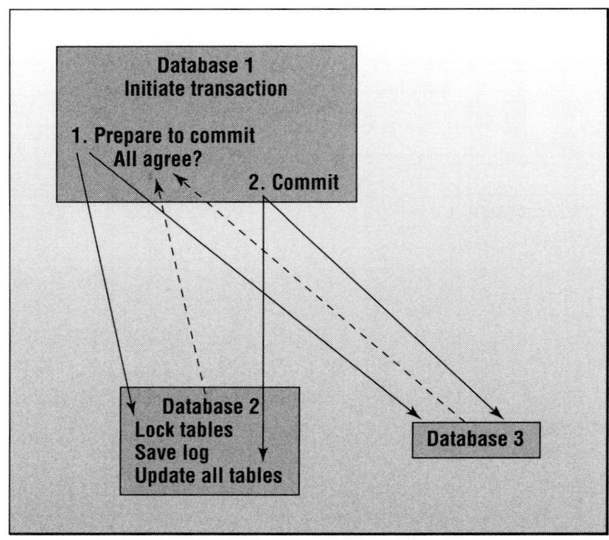

FIGURE 11.8
Two-phase commit. Each database must agree to save all changes—even if the system crashes. When all systems are prepared, they are asked to commit the changes.

FIGURE 11.9
Design questions. Use these questions to determine whether you should replicate the database or provide concurrent access to data across the network. Transaction operations are generally run with concurrent access. Decision support systems often use replicated databases. However, the exact choice depends on the use of the data and the needs of the users.

QUESTION	CONCURRENT	REPLICATION
What level of data consistency is needed?	High	Low-Medium
How expensive is storage?	Medium-High	Low
What are the shared access requirements?	Global	Local
How often are the tables updated?	Often	Seldom
Required speed of updates (transactions)?	Fast	Slow
How important are predictable transaction times?	High	Low
DBMS support for concurrency and locking?	Good-Excellent	Poor
Can shared access be avoided?	No	Yes

Distributed Design Questions

Because of the issues with transmission costs, replication, and concurrency, distributed databases require careful design. As networks gain better transfer rates, database design will eventually become less of a problem. In the meantime you need to analyze your applications to determine how they should be distributed Figure 11.9 lists some of the questions you need to ask when designing a distributed database. The main point is to determine what portions of the databases should be replicated. If users at all locations require absolute consistency in the database, then replication is probably a bad idea. On the other hand, you might have a weak DBMS that poorly handles locking and concurrency. In this situation it is better to replicate the data, rather than risk destroying the data through incomplete transaction updates.

Distributed Databases in Oracle

Oracle provides one of the most complete approaches to distributed databases, so it is worth examining in more detail. If all the distributed database systems you use are from Oracle, there are some additional methods to connect and share data. First, any user or application can refer to a database anywhere on the network by using the full name of the database. The name is specified as Schema.Table@Location. The *schema* is a collection of tables stored as one database. The location name depends on the type of network, but it is commonly specified by its Internet address. Oracle provides support for database synonyms. A **synonym** is a short name for the full database path. An advantage of the short name is that it is easy to remember; in addition, the user never needs to know where the data is located. A stronger advantage is that if everyone uses the synonym, DBAs can easily move the server databases to different locations. Simply change the definition of the synonyms, and all of the applications will work as before.

Figure 11.10 shows three methods of linking distributed databases. Each method has a different effect on security. The synonym just provides a shorter name for the database and does not affect permissions or control over the database. All access is controlled by the DBA of the original database. Another approach is to create a view on the local computer and assign open permissions to that view. Security responsibilities are transferred to the DBA of the local machine through local permissions assigned to the view. A third approach is to create stored procedures on the server database. User permissions are then assigned to the procedure and not to the original database. This method provides strong control by specifying exactly which tasks users can perform and is particularly useful for DELETE operations. Rather than give users full DELETE permissions on a table, you can write a limited query that they can run. The query deletes the data for the users, but gives them no additional permissions.

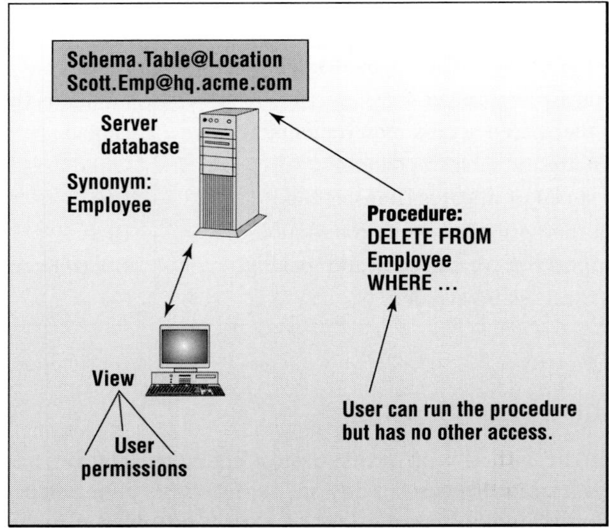

FIGURE 11.10 Oracle options. A synonym makes it easier to move a database. A view can enable local DBAs to control access to the data. A stored procedure directly limits what tasks the user can perform.

CLIENT/SERVER DATABASES

The client/server approach is currently the most popular system of distributing data (and computers) on networks. With this system powerful machines with multiuser operating systems function as servers. Smaller computers—usually personal computers—operate as clients. The servers hold software and data that will be shared by the users. Individual client computers hold data that is used by the individual using that machine.

The client/server approach was driven largely by the limited capabilities of personal computer operating systems. Early operating systems could not support multiple users and provided no security controls. Hence powerful operating systems were installed on servers that handled all the tasks that required sharing data and hardware. The client/server approach is also somewhat easier to manage and control than monitoring hundreds of PCs. Any hardware, software, or data that needs to be shared is stored in a centralized location and controlled by an MIS staff. With the client/server approach, all data that will be shared is first transferred to a server.

As indicated by Figure 11.11, a client/server database operates the same way. The actual database resides on a server computer. Individual components can be run from

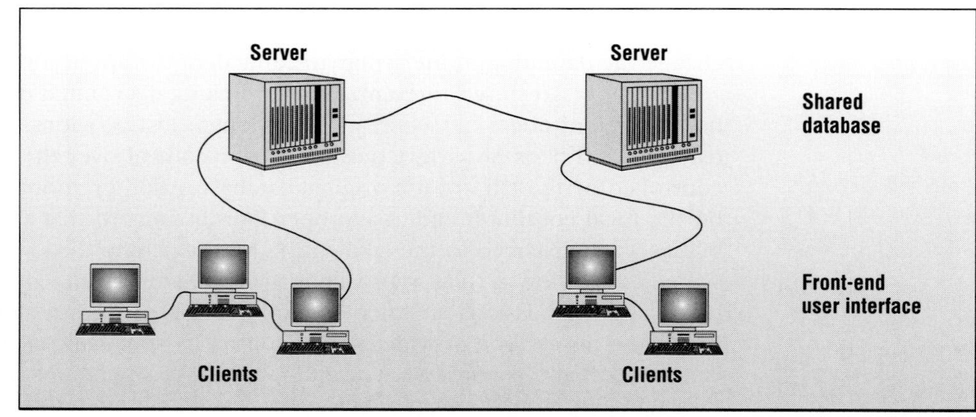

FIGURE 11.11 Client/server system. The client computers run front-end, user interface applications. These applications retrieve and store data in shared databases that are run on the server computers. The network enables clients to access data on any server where they have appropriate permissions.

client machines, but they store and retrieve data on the servers. The client component is usually a front-end application that interacts with the user. For example, a common approach is to store the data tables on a server but run the forms on personal computers. The forms handle user events with a graphical interface, but all data is transferred to the server.

There are a few important concepts you need to understand to design and manage client/server databases. Like any distributed database, where you store the data and how you access it can make a substantial difference in performance. This section also demonstrates some of the tools available to build a client/server database application.

Client/Server versus File Server

To understand the features and power of a client/server database, it is first useful to examine a database application that is not a true client/server database. Initial local area networks were based on file servers. A file server is a centralized computer that can share files with personal computers. However, it does not contain a database. The basic Novell network is a common example of this type of system. The file server stores files, but to the personal computers it appears as a giant, passive disk drive. The sole purpose of the server is to provide secure shared access to files. The client personal computers do all of the application processing.

Figure 11.12 illustrates the basic problem. The database file (e.g., MyFile.mdb) is stored on the file server. Security permissions are set so that each user has read and write permission on the file. When the application is run, the forms and your code are downloaded to the client computer. The problem arises when your application runs a query. The processing of the query is done on the client computer. That means that the personal computer has to retrieve every row of data from the server, examine it, and decide whether to use it in the computation or display. If the database is small, if the network connection is fast, and if users often want to see the entire table, then this process does not matter. But if the table is large and users need to see only a small portion, then it is a waste of time and network bandwidth to transfer the entire table to the client computer.

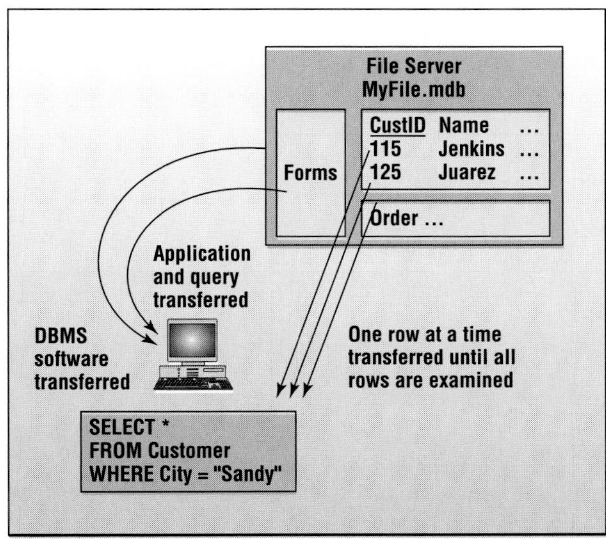

FIGURE 11.12
File server problems. The file server acts as a large, passive disk drive. The personal computer does all the database processing, so it must retrieve and examine every row of data. For large tables, this process is slow and wastes network bandwidth.

Some tricks can be used to improve the performance of databases running on a file server. First, split the application into two parts: (1) The data tables are stored in one database on the file server, and (2) the application forms and code are stored on a separate database that is installed and run from each client. This split improves the loading time and operation of the application, but it does nothing to improve the transfer of data. A second performance tip is to make sure that all major queries are supported by indexes. The indexes must also be retrieved from the server, but because they are smaller, the transfer time is reduced substantially. A third possibility is to replicate some of the data to the client computers. It will be challenging to keep the client copies up-to-date, so this technique works only for data that does not change very often. For example, tables with data on cities or perhaps well-defined customer or product data could be stored on each client computer.

None of these tricks truly solves the problem of transferring huge amounts of data when the application needs only some of the data. The client/server database approach was designed to solve this problem. With a client/server database, the binary code for the database actually runs on the server. As shown in Figure 11.13, the server database receives SQL statements, processes them, and returns only the results of the query. Notice the reduction in network transfers. The initial SQL statement is small, and only the data needed by the application is transferred over the network. This result is particularly important for decision support systems. The server database might contain millions of rows of data. The manager is analyzing the data, and often wants summary statistics, such as an average. The server database optimizes the query, computes the result, and transfers a few simple numbers back to the client. Without the server database millions of rows of data would be transferred across the network. Remember that even fast LAN transfer rates are substantially slower than disk drive transfers.

Of course, the drawback to the server database approach is that the server spends more time processing data. Consequently, the server computer has to be configured so that it can efficiently run processes for many users at the same time. Fortunately, processor speeds have historically increased much more rapidly than disk drive and network transfer speeds. The other drawback is that this approach requires the purchase of a powerful DBMS that runs on the server. However, you rarely have a choice. Only small applications used by a few users can be run without a database server.

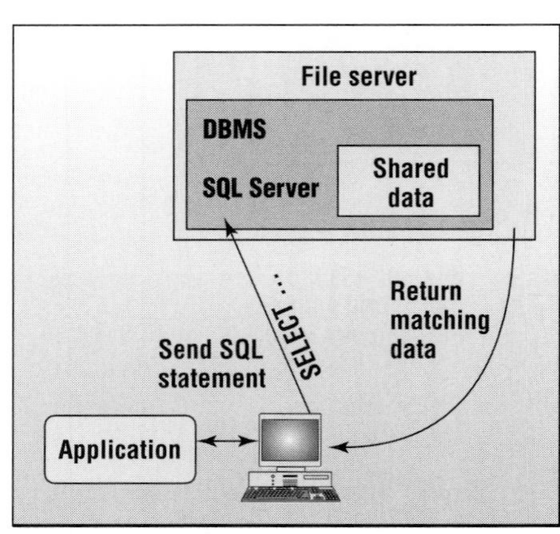

FIGURE 11.13 Database server. The client computer sends a SQL statement that is processed on the server. Only the result is returned to the client, reducing network traffic.

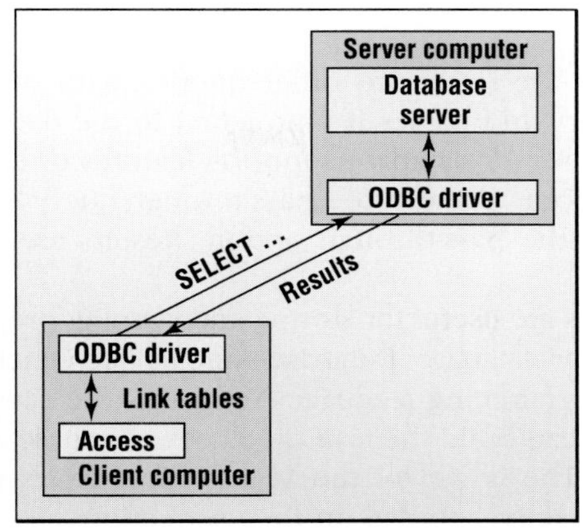

FIGURE 11.14 Open database connectivity (ODBC). The ODBC driver acts as a buffer between the client software and the server database. In many cases you can change the server database without altering the application by replacing the ODBC driver.

The Front End: Microsoft Access

Microsoft Access is a DBMS that was designed to run on personal computers—it can be used as the client side of a client/server database. Using Access as a client is different than using it in a file server approach. In a file server approach, you store one Access database on a file server. On the other hand, a client/server approach requires at least two databases: The shared data is stored on the server, and the application forms are run from a second database on the client computers. The client database links to the tables on the server.

A similar approach is to use Microsoft Visual Basic (VB) to handle the front-end tasks. VB is similar to the forms and reports features provided by Access except that VB is designed to create stand-alone applications. Therefore, users do not need to purchase their own copy of Access. In addition, the application can be compiled to machine language so that it runs considerably faster.

Open Database Connectivity

Figure 11.14 shows the technique for connecting to a database server to build larger applications. In this case separate database engines run on the server (e.g., SQL Server) and the client (e.g., Access). The client database needs to know how to connect to the server. Microsoft has created a method called **open database connectivity (ODBC)** to perform this function. You install an ODBC driver on the client and server computers. This small piece of software connects to the appropriate database, converts and sends the SQL command, receives the results, and feeds them to the client software. Once the server database is running and the ODBC drivers are installed, you can link the client Access database to the server through the ODBC driver. Now the queries will be processed on the server instead of on the client.

ODBC has some additional advantages. First, it is often possible to change the server database without changing the application. Simply install a different ODBC driver. Likewise, if the server database is moved, you can simply alter the ODBC definition without affecting the client application. A second strength is that other client applications can use the same link to retrieve data. For example, if Access is too slow or you need more control over the user interface, you can write the application in VB, or Visual C++, and still have access to the data using SQL commands that are routed through the ODBC driver.

Pass-through Queries

Pass-through queries are similar to other queries with one twist: Access completely ignores the query and passes it untouched to the database server. This feature is useful when the server database supports features or extensions to SQL that are not supported by Access. You create a pass-through query like any other query—just be sure to specify the pass-through option. Results are stored in a snapshot query in Access.

Pass-through queries are useful for storing and running programming statements and triggers on the server database. Database systems like Oracle extend the SQL approach by adding a programming language. You can store these commands on the server database, or you can build them in the Access database and pass them to the server to be executed. The power of the Access approach is that your application can build the code interactively based on the user actions.

The Three-Tier Client/Server Model

The **three-tier client/server** model has been suggested as an approach that has some advantages over the two-tier model. The three-tier approach adds a layer between the clients and the servers. The three-tier approach is particularly useful for systems having several database servers with many different applications. The method is useful when some of the servers are running legacy applications.

As shown in Figure 11.15, one role of the middle layer is to create links to the databases. If necessary, the middle layer translates SQL requests and retrieves data from legacy COBOL applications. By placing the access links in one location, the server databases can be moved or altered without affecting the client front-end applications. Developers simply change the location pointers, or alter the middleware routines.

Another important role of the middle layer is to host the business rules. For example, creating identification numbers for customers and products should follow a standard process. The routine that generates these numbers should be stored in one location, and all the applications that need it will call that function. Similarly, common application functions can be written once and stored on the middle-layer servers.

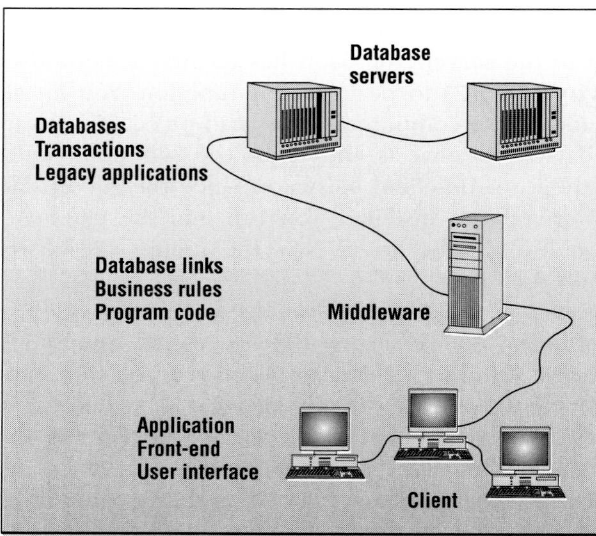

FIGURE 11.15
Three-tier client/server model. The middle layer separates the business rules and program code from the databases and applications. Independence makes it easier to alter each component without interfering with the other elements.

This middleware system is well suited to an object-oriented development approach. Common objects that are used for multiple business applications can be written once and stored on the middle servers. Any application can use those objects as needed. As the business rules change or as systems are updated, developers can alter or improve the base objects without interfering with the operations of the applications on the client side. The three-tier approach separates the business rules and program code from the databases and from the applications. The independence makes the system more flexible and easier to expand. Some recent programming tools, like the enterprise edition of VB, facilitate development of the middle layer. These tools provide naming conventions that enable applications to find code and execute it on any server.

The Back End: Server Databases

Server databases are available from many companies, and the various products have specific strengths and weaknesses. Some must run on certain brands of computers; others will run on several machines. Fortunately, most of the leading DBMS vendors support some version of SQL. Hence defining the database and building queries will follow the steps you already know. Of course, the database vendors also add new features that you will have to learn.

Server database systems tend to be considerably more complex and require more administrative tasks than personal computer–based systems. The server environment also provides more options, which makes administration and development more complicated. Server computers use more sophisticated operating systems to support multiple users. The DBA must work closely with the system administrator to set up the software, define user accounts, and monitor performance. Some of the administrative tasks and tools are described in Chapter 10.

Server database systems also support programs that are run on the server. These programming languages tend to be different for each vendor. The appendix presents the approach used by Oracle. Many of these concepts are being formalized in the proposed SQL3 standard. Sometimes you have no choice about where to write your application code. Other times, you will have to analyze the performance and test an application by running code in multiple locations: on the server, on the client, or on a middle-layer computer.

One rule of thumb is to write user-interface code for the client computers and to write data manipulation and control programs to run on the server. Middle-layer programs are used to encode business rules and provide data translation and database independence. The primary objective is to minimize the transfer of data across the network. However, if some computers are substantially slower than others, you will have to accept more data transfers in order to execute the code on faster machines.

THE WEB AS A CLIENT/SERVER SYSTEM

The **World Wide Web** was designed as a client/server system. The objective was to enable people (physicists and researchers) to share information with their colleagues. The fundamental problem was that everyone used different hardware and software—both for clients and for servers—and the solution was to define a set of standards. These evolving standards are the heart of the Web. They define how computers can connect, how data can be transferred, and how data can be found. Additional standards define how data should be stored and how it can be displayed. The clients run **browser** software that receives and displays data files. The servers run Web server

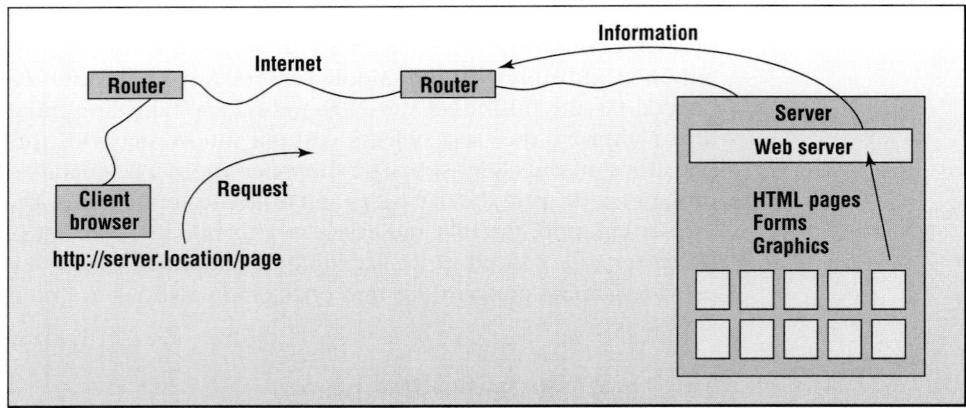

FIGURE 11.16 Web servers and client browsers. Browsers are standardized display platforms. Servers are accessible from any browser.

software that answers requests, finds the appropriate files, and sends the required data. Both the clients and the browsers are becoming more sophisticated but the essence of the method is presented in Figure 11.16.

HTML Limited Clients

Today the Web server can be tied to a database. The database can hold traditional data, or it can hold complex graphics and other objects that can be retrieved with browsers. To build applications in this environment, you must understand and follow the rules to display data on the browsers.

The basic rule of browsers is that they only know how to display certain types of data, such as text and graphics. Each type of data must be created in a predefined format. For the most part, you are not allowed to create new formats or new types of data. The browser capabilities are continuously being expanded to handle new types of data, such as sound and video. However, your application and the database must follow the standards for the new data types. Also, there are differences in the ways the various browsers display information. If you want a wide audience for your data, you have to be careful to avoid the incompatibilities.

Hypertext markup language (HTML) is the foundation of the display system for browsers. It is a simplified page description language. For maximum compatibility, all information sent to browsers should be sent as an HTML page. Several sources for learning HTML are available on the Internet, and many tutorial books are available to help you learn the language. For the basics you control the page layout and text attributes with tags. A *tag* is just a short term enclosed in brackets, such as <B>. HTML uses pairs of tags; for example, to boldface a word, you surround it with a start tag and an end tag, like <B>my text</B>. A simple example of HTML is shown in Figure 11.17 with the output in Figure 11.18.

Database applications often use two special sets of tags: one set to create tables and another to create forms. Tables display output from the database, whereas forms collect data for the database and get parameters from the users to build queries. You should learn more about these basic tags if you want to build database applications on the Web. Fortunately, several tools exist to help automate the creation of HTML pages, so you do not have to memorize the HTML syntax. Most word processors today can store documents such as input forms in HTML format. Microsoft Access provides tools that generate HTML output pages for a query, including the basic table definitions.

Graphics are a little more restrictive. You need to store images in one of three formats (GIF, JPEG, or PNG). Modern graphics software can perform the conversion. Because of the limitations in displaying graphics and data, you should consult with a graphics designer when developing applications for the Web.

Hypertext links are an important feature of the Web. Each page contains references or links to other pages. The basic format of a link uses the **anchor tag** (<A>). For example: <A HREF="newfile.html">Text to display </A>. Typical static pages have fixed links so that each person sees exactly the same page and the same links. A database enables developers to create more interactive pages and links. The links (and the text) can be stored in a database table. Based on the actions of the user, the application can retrieve the desired data from a table and build a page with links for any situation. A common example is an order form. The user can select a category, and the application will retrieve a list of items in that category. In addition to displaying the list, each item will be linked to a description page and a picture. Users who want more information can click on the links. The key is that the category and link information are stored in a database—which makes the list easier to search and easier for product managers to change. Your application simply needs to retrieve the data and format it with the <A> tag.

Browser capabilities and standards continue to improve rapidly. Browsers now support an object model that you can use to create applications. Much like a database form, the browser records user events and enables you to attach code to these events. This client-side code can record user choices, manipulate the display, and interact with your server. Similarly, server-side code can retrieve data from databases, track user connections, and maintain transaction integrity. When coupled with a server-side DBMS, the Web can be used to create client/server applications. The main advantage to using the Web is that users can access your applications from anywhere in the world, using a variety of client computers.

FIGURE 11.17
Typical HTML page. The tabs set the page layout and control text formatting. Database applications often use tags to create tables to display results. Forms tags are used to collect data to interact with the server.

```
<HTML>
<HEAD>
<TITLE>My main page</TITLE></HEAD>
<BODY BACKGROUND="graphics/back0.jpg">
<P>My text goes in paragraphs,</P>
<P>Additional tags set <B>boldface</B> and
<I>italic</I>.
<P> Tables are more complicated and use a set of tags
for rows and columns.</P>
<TABLE BORDER=1>
<TR><TD>First cell</TD><TD>Second cell</TD></TR>
<TR><TD>Next row</TD><TD>Second
column</TD></TR>
</TABLE>
<P> There are form tags to create input forms for
collecting data.
But you need CGI program code to convert and use the
input data.</P>
</BODY>
</HTML>
```

FIGURE 11.18
HTML output.

My text goes in paragraphs.
Additional tags set **boldface** and *italic.*
Tables are more complicated and use a set of tags for rows and columns.

First cell	Second cell
Next row	Second column

There are form tags to create input forms for collecting data. But you need CGI program code to convert and use the input data.

Web Server Database Fundamentals

There is no standard mechanism for connecting databases to the Web server. Consequently, the method you use depends on the specific software (Web server and DBMS) that you install. Most of the methods follow a similar structure, but vary in the details. The details discussed here are based on using Microsoft's Windows NT Web server. There are simpler methods (e.g., Cold Fusion), but Microsoft's current approach offers significantly more power and flexibility. With a Windows NT server computer and ODBC, you can connect to any database system that runs under Windows NT. Three common examples are SQL Server, Oracle, and Access. However, Microsoft does not recommend using Access as a database engine on a Web server except for small projects with a limited number of concurrent users.

Figure 11.19 shows the basic process of connecting a DBMS to a Web server. The numbers indicate the three basic steps that take place. Remember that there are two perspectives of these actions: the client and the server side. (0) You first have to create a form, which is requested by the client. (1) Then the user receives the form and enters data. The data might be constraint values for a condition in a query. For example, a user might select an animal category and color. (2) This data is returned to the Web server in the form of a **common gateway interface (CGI)** string.

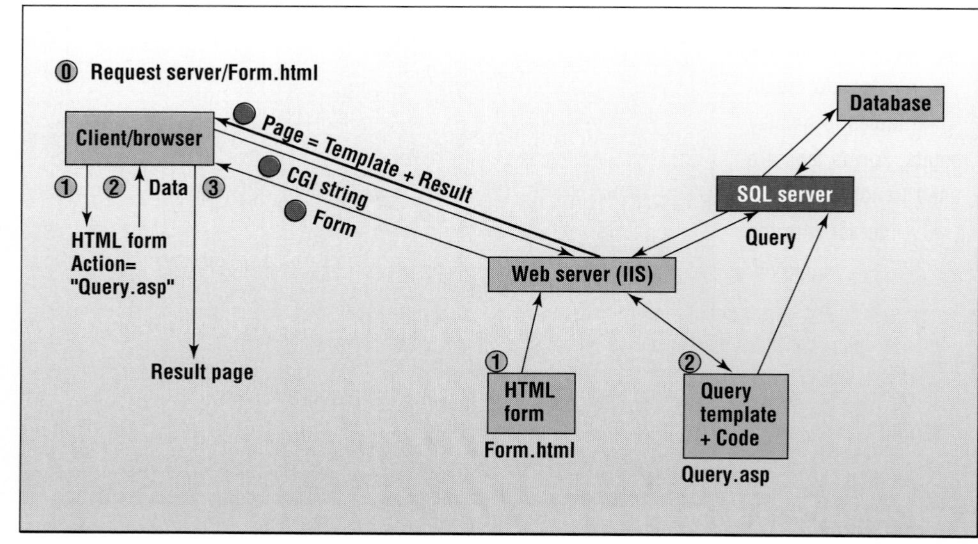

FIGURE 11.19
Web server database fundamentals. The developer builds the initial form, the query, and a template to display the results. The Web server merges the input data with the query and passes it to the DBMS (SQL Server). The query results are merged into the template and sent to the user as a new page.

CGI specifies the format of data that is transmitted between computers. The data also tells the Web server which file to open and transfer the data to. (3) A new page is constructed and returned to the user.

Client Perspective

On the client browser the user will see a simple sequence like the forms shown in Figure 11.20. Once someone chooses a search option, the AnimalSearch form is displayed on his or her browser. The user chooses a category and enters a color. When the search button is clicked, the choices are sent to a new page on the server. This page retrieves the data and formats a new page. The data is generally stored in a table, similar to the one shown in Figure 11.19. The user never needs to know anything about the DBMS. Users see only forms and new pages. Each new page should provide additional choices and links to other pages.

Server Perspective

Microsoft has created a powerful technique to retrieve data using a Web server. The goal was to make it easier to create interactive pages. Your Web pages consist of program code as well as text. The program code is used to respond to user requests. Connecting to ODBC databases is a powerful component of these **active server pages (ASP).** The **active data objects (ADO)** approach used by ASP is similar to the recordset programming described in Chapter 7. The logic is identical, and even the syntax is similar. The ADO techniques are slightly more complex, and you have to be careful with the syntax, but you gain detailed control over how the data is integrated into your form.

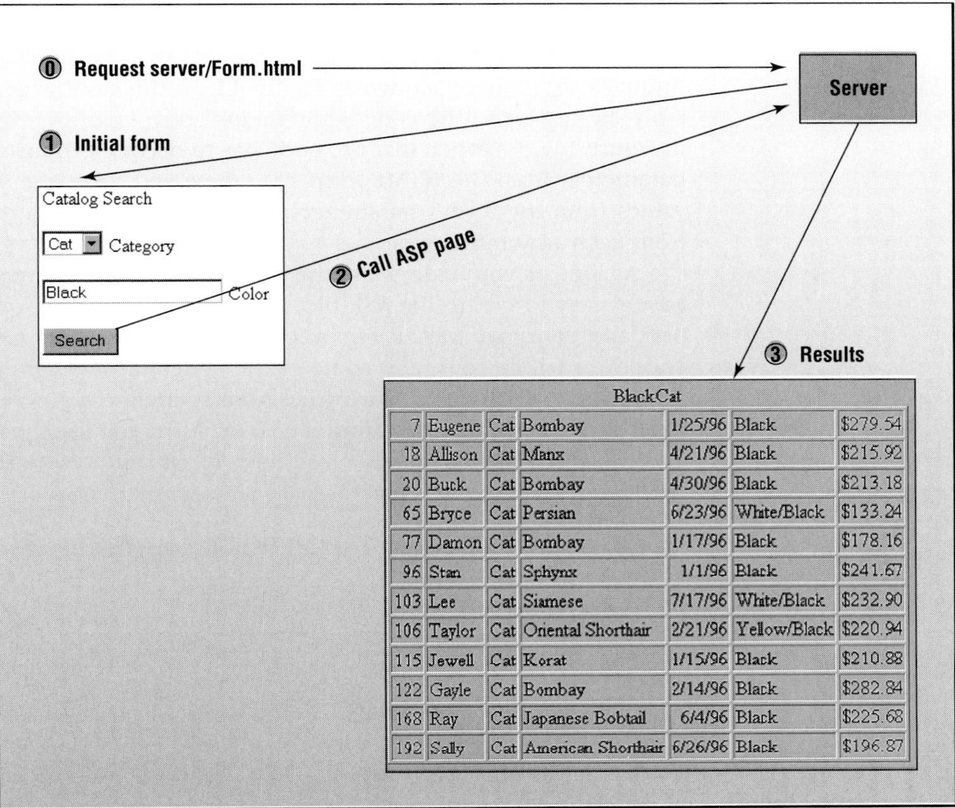

FIGURE 11.20
Client perspective. The client enters data into a form. Clicking the search button sends the data to a server page. The server page retrieves the matching data from the DBMS and formats a new HTML page. This table is returned to the user, along with additional choices.

```
<HTML><HEAD><TITLE>Catalog Search</TITLE></HEAD>
<BODY TEXT="#000000" BGCOLOR="#ffffff">
<FORM ACTION="PetStoreSearch.asp" METHOD="Put">
<P>
<SELECT NAME="Category">
<OPTION SELECTED VALUE="Cat">Cat
<OPTION VALUE="Dog">Dog
<OPTION VALUE="Fish">Fish
</SELECT> Category</P>
<P>
<INPUT TYPE="TEXT" NAME="Color" VALUE="Black">Color</P>
<P>
<INPUT TYPE="SUBMIT" VALUE="Search" NAME="Submit"></P>
</FORM></BODY></HTML>
```

FIGURE 11.21 Initial HTML form. The form can be generated by Microsoft Word. To use the automated system, the next box should be named Data. There is also a hidden text box named Param with a value of the column to be matched (SerialNumber).

Figure 11.21 presents the HTML code for a form that Sally's Pet Store might use. The company wishes to set up a Web site so customers can search for specific animals, send requests, and check genealogy and health data. Figure 11.20, which asks for the animal category and color, shows the simplest form that might be used. In actuality, you would add more graphics and more choices.

In addition to any text and graphics, three elements appear on this form: (1) a select (combo) box, (2) a text box, and (3) the Search or Submit button. The form can be created with any HTML generator, such as Microsoft Word, or with a simple text editor. The underlying HTML code is shown in Figure 11.21.

The Submit button connects the HTML data-entry form to a new page: AnimalSearch.asp. As shown in Figure 11.22, this new page does most of the work. Only the outline of the code is shown in Figure 11.21. A few more details are shown in Figure 11.23. Notice that the code has to do three things: (1) get the values of the parameters from the HTML form, (2) create and open the SQL query, adding in the values from the form's parameters, and (3) track through the query and place data from each row into a table.

As long as you understand the basic operations that must be performed, it is relatively easy to create the ASP file. First, design a suitable query in Access. Then export the query as an ASP file. Access will automatically generate most of the ASP code. You will have to edit some of the code, but it is generally easier to edit a few lines than to create the entire page from scratch.

To retrieve parameters from the HTML form, you use the Request object and specify the name of the parameter you wish to examine. Note that all code must be en-

```
Connect to the Database      ②
Create the SQL
Connect to the Database/Recordset
Loop through the Recordset
   Get a Field
   Display it
   Move to the next row
End Loop
```

FIGURE 11.22 ASP code structure. These steps are used in almost every ASP database page. The syntax is provided in Microsoft documentation.

closed in angle brackets and percent signs; for example, <% code goes here %>. Any number of lines can appear between these markers. You can also use a <SCRIPT> tag.

You use string operations to build a query the same way you did with the basic programs examined in Chapter 7. Just add the parameter values to create the appropriate WHERE clause.

FIGURE 11.23 ASP code to retrieve data. The initial page was created automatically by Microsoft Access from a standard query. There are three parts to the program: (1) connect to the ODBC database, (2) build and open the query, (3) step through the rows of the query and place the results data in a table.

```
<HTML><HEAD><TITLE>Animal Search Results</TITLE></HEAD>
<BODY>
<%       ' Connect to ODBC database
   Set objConn = Server.CreateObject("ADODB.Connection")
   objConn.open "PetStore","",""
      ' Build sql query from form data
   sql = "SELECT AnimalID, Name, Category, Breed, DateBorn, Color, ListPrice "
   sql = sql & "FROM Animal WHERE (Category = '"
   sql = sql & Request.Form("Category") & "') AND (Color LIKE '*"
   sql = sql & Request.Form("Color") & "*')"
         ' Open the recordset
   Set rst = Server.CreateObject("ADODB.Recordset")
   rst.Open sql, objConn, 3, 3
%>       <! Build the table with captions !>
<TABLE BORDER=1><CAPTION><B>ASPSearch 1</B></CAPTION>
<THEAD><TR>
<TH>AnimalID</TH>  <TH>Name</TH>       <TH>Category</TH>
<TH>Breed</TH>     <TH>DateBorn</TH>   <TH>Color</TH>
<TH>ListPrice</TH>
</TR></THEAD>
<TBODY>
<%       ' Put each retrieved row in the table
   On Error Resume Next
   rst.MoveFirst
   do while Not rst.eof
%>
<TR VALIGN=TOP>
<TD><%=Server. HTMLEncode(rst("AnimalID"))%>         <BR></TD>
<TD><%=Server. HTMLEncode(rst("Name"))%>             <BR></TD>
<TD><%=Server. HTMLEncode(rst("Category"))%>         <BR></TD>
<TD><%=Server. HTMLEncode(rst("Breed"))%>            <BR></TD>
<TD><%=Server. HTMLEncode(rst("DateBorn"))%>         <BR></TD>
<TD><%=Server. HTMLEncode(rst("Color"))%>            <BR></TD>
<TD><%=Server. HTMLEncode(rst("ListPrice"))%>        <BR></TD>
</TR>
      rst.MoveNext
   loop
   rst.Close
   objConn.Close
   Set rst = Nothing
   Set objConn = Nothing
%>
</TBODY></TABLE></BODY></HTML>
```

Similarly, VBScript (or JavaScript if you prefer) is used to track through the rows of the query. Note the standard "do while Not rst.eof," "rst.MoveNext," and "loop" statements. Retrieving data from the query is straightforward but follows a slightly different object syntax. To retrieve data, you use a statement like rst.Fields("CustomerID"). This command provides the value from the CustomerID column in the current row. However, when you want to display data on an HTML result page, you have to add a step. The raw data might contain some characters that do strange things to a Web browser. To handle these situations, you should always display data using a special function that corrects raw data. This special function is called with the command Server.HTMLEncode( ).

You can include many other types of program code within an ASP page. For example, you might change the display based on the value of the data being retrieved. If a certain type of data appears, you might want to extend the table or add a form button that the user can click to get additional data. The details are explained in some of the references and in Microsoft's documentation, but usually it will take only a few additional statements.

Now, before you panic and decide that developing Web applications is too hard, you should know that virtually all of the forms and code for this example were created automatically by Microsoft tools. The initial HTML form was created using Microsoft Word, which enables you to add the text boxes and Submit button by clicking icons. Amazingly, the ASP query file was created by Microsoft Access. Simply create the base query—without any constraints. Then export the query as an ASP file and modify the SQL string to incorporate the values entered by the user on the original HTML form.

Even if your database tables and application are created in SQL Server or Oracle, you can still use Access to create the ASP code. Just create a temporary database in Access and attach all of the tables from your database using an ODBC connection. Then create your queries in Access and export them to an ASP format. You can even export forms in an ASP format, and the forms will run as Web pages. However, you will have to make some changes to indicate the proper location and names of tables and variables.

You can save many hours of time by using these tools to automatically build the initial version of your forms and queries. One of the main advantages is that you will now have sample code to follow—so you do not have to spend hours looking up the syntax for each function.

Every day companies are making more information accessible to customers on the Internet. The brief introduction in this section should get you thinking about the many possibilities. Unfortunately, it is not possible to cover all of the information you might need to create these sophisticated Web pages. However, using this foundation and a few hours of reading and experimenting, you should be able to integrate your database applications with a Web site. Keep in mind that Web tools and techniques are changing every day. No matter which system or vendor you use, you will have to work hard to stay up-to-date with the changes. However, the Web provides exciting jobs and enables you to create applications that can be used by millions of people.

This section has barely touched on the power of ASP for building Web sites that utilize databases. For example, the Session object is an important feature of ASP. This object automatically uses a cookie to track individual sessions. A *cookie* is a small text file that is sent by the server to be stored on the client's computer. When the client returns, it retransmits the cookie, so the server knows the identity of the client. ASP even includes a timer to automatically cancel a session if a user does not return within a set time. The power of ASP is that these actions are handled automatically. As a developer, you can concentrate on building the best possible application.

SUMMARY

As organizations grow, distributed databases become useful. Distributed databases enable the company to expand individual departments without directly affecting everyone else. Distributed databases also give individual departments increased control and responsibility for their data.

However, distributed databases, with independent database engines running in different locations, increase the complexity of developing and managing applications. One of the primary goals is to make the location of the data transparent to the user. To accomplish this goal, developers and DBAs need to carefully define the databases, networks, and applications.

Some of the major complications generated by distributed databases are query optimization; data replication questions; and support for transactions, concurrency controls, and deadlock resolution. These issues become even more complex when multiple databases are involved. Network transfers of data are substantially slower than transfers from local disk drives. Transfers over wide area networks can be slow and costly. These factors imply that developers must carefully design the applications and the data distribution strategy. The applications also have to be tested and monitored for performance and cost.

One of the major strategies in designing and controlling distributed databases is to replicate data. Instead of maintaining one source, it is often more efficient to replicate data that is heavily used in multiple locations. Of course, replication requires additional disk space, along with periodic updates and transfers of the data changes to each copy. Replication saves time by providing local access to data. It reduces costs by reducing the need for a full-time high-speed connection. Instead, bulk data is transferred at regular intervals—preferably at off-peak communication rates.

Client/server networks and client/server databases are a common means to design applications and distribute databases. Clients usually run applications on personal computers, and most of their power is devoted to the user interface. The data is maintained on a limited number of database servers, which are more efficient than simple file server transfers. With a server database, the client sends a SQL query, and the server processes the request and returns only the desired data. With a file server, the client computer performs all the processing and must retrieve and examine all the data. Microsoft supports several server databases through ODBC drivers.

Larger, object-oriented applications are being built using a three-tier client/server architecture. The additional layer is in the middle and consists of business rules and program code (business objects) that execute on servers. The middle layer is also responsible for pulling data from the database servers and reformatting it for use by the client applications. Separating the three layers makes it easier to modify each component without interfering with the other elements.

The World Wide Web is becoming a popular mechanism to create client/server applications. The clients have limited capabilities, but standards make it easier for everyone to get access to the applications and data. Capabilities of all Web tools are increasing rapidly, making it easier for developers to extend the reach of their applications.

A DEVELOPER'S VIEW

Like Miranda, most developers understand the importance of the Web. The client standards make it easier to distribute data and connect with users around the world. Additionally, as applications expand, it becomes necessary to create distributed databases to improve performance and to support different regions. Distributed databases can significantly complicate application development. First be sure the application runs on one computer. Then get the best software you can afford. As much as possible, let the server databases perform the data manipulation and computation tasks. Use the client computers to display the results. Learn as much as you can about the Internet—it changes constantly, but it will become increasingly important in your applications. For your class project, you should identify where the company might expand, and where you would position distributed computers to support it. Explain how the database design would change in a distributed environment.

KEY WORDS

active data objects (ADO), 403
active server pages (ASP), 403
anchor tag, 401
browser, 399
client/server, 385
common gateway interface (CGI), 402
data replication, 390
distributed database, 384
FETCH, 416
hypertext link, 401
local area network (LAN), 388
open database connectivity (ODBC), 397
pass-through query, 398
replicate, 390
replication manager, 390
synonym, 393
three-tier client/server, 398
two-phase commit, 392
wide area network (WAN), 389
World Wide Web, 399

REVIEW QUESTIONS

1. What are the strengths and weaknesses of a distributed database?
2. Which features are needed to make the distributed database transparent to the user?
3. Why might a query on a distributed database take a long time to run?
4. When would you want to replicate data in a distributed database?
5. Why is concurrency a bigger problem with distributed databases than with standalone databases?
6. How does the two-phase commit process work?
7. Why is a client/server database more efficient than a database on a simple file server?
8. Which tools exist to help connect databases from different vendors?
9. What are the advantages of the three-tier client/server approach?
10. What are the basic components of Oracle's PL/SQL?
11. What are the capabilities of an Internet Web client?
12. How do you use databases on Web servers to build interactive Internet applications?

EXERCISES

1. Research software that can be used to build three-tier client/server applications. Describe the capabilities of the software. Explain how components are assigned to each tier. For example, consider VB enterprise edition.

2. Describe how to create a distributed database in Oracle. If you have access to Oracle, build a small example with two tables on each machine.

3. You have the following distributed databases:

LOCATION	LINK SPEED	TABLES	SIZES
Seattle	33Kbps	Inventory(ItemID, Quantity, . . .) Shipments(ItemID, Date/Time, Q, . . .) Purchases(ItemID, Date/Time, Q . . .)	1,500 rows 3,000,000 rows 300,000 rows
Dallas	56Kbps	Inventory(ItemID, Quantity, . . .) Shipments(ItemID, Date/Time, Q, . . .) Purchases(ItemID, Date/Time, Q . . .)	1,000 rows 2,000,000 rows 200,000 rows
Miami	128Kbps	Sales(SaleID, Sdate, CustomerID, EID, . . .) SaleItem(SaleID, ItemID, Q, warehouse . . .)	5,000,000 rows 15,000,000 rows
Chicago (HQ)	local	Customer(CustomerID, . . .) Employee(EID, . . .)	500,000 rows 1,000 rows

   Write an application that runs from Chicago to solve a basic problem. A customer calls and wants to know when to expect a shipment. You have to find which warehouse (Seattle or Dallas) was supposed to ship the product. If the item is out of stock in that warehouse, you need to check the other warehouse. Optional: If neither warehouse has the item in stock, check the purchases against the shipments to determine which warehouse has already ordered the desired item. Be sure to optimize the queries to handle the slow transfer speeds.

4. In Oracle create a small database with a table of customers that includes a home and a work phone number. Write a PL/SQL procedure to count the number of customers whose home area code is different from their work area code.

5. In Oracle create two tables: Transaction(TransID, Tdate, ItemID, Amount, . . .) and Security(ItemID, Quantity). Transactions are normal updates (e.g., sales). The Security table is used to count the number of times a negative value is entered for Amount in the Transaction table. (Too many negative values on a particular item signifies a problem.) Write a trigger procedure that updates the Security table whenever a negative value is entered into the Transaction table. Start with an empty Security table. Your procedure should add a new row if necessary; otherwise, just increment the Quantity counter for the appropriate item.

6. Create a simple Web page that displays a small data table. The headings of the table should be in a different font than the body.

7. Create a small Web site that lets users select a product and use the database to see whether it is in stock, e.g., Inventory(ItemID, Quantity, . . .).

Sally's Pet Store

8. Sally is planning to add a second store. Write a plan that describes how the data will be shared. How will you control and monitor the new system? Which tools will you add?

9. Sally wants to connect to some of the breeders so that she can get up-to-date information on their animals—including health and genealogy records. Explain how you would set up a system to enable this sharing of data.

10. Create a Web site to provide basic information on Sally's Pet Store and her philosophy. You should include a page that encourages potential customers to register by providing their name, address, phone, and e-mail address.

11. Create a Web site so Sally can let potential customers search for a particular animal.

12. Create a Web site so that potential customers can enter various characteristics and the system will suggest a type of animal that meets the requirements.

Rolling Thunder Bicycles

13. Rolling Thunder is planning to expand to a second location across the country. How should the database be distributed? Where should each table be stored? Which tables should be replicated, and how should the data changes be reconciled?

14. Transfer the data portion of Rolling Thunder to a server database. Use ODBC to connect the client-side code to the server database.

15. If you have a three-tier client/server system, describe which components you would store in each location (client, server, middleware). Justify your choices and examine options.

16. Build a Web form that enables customers to check on the progress of their bicycle orders.

WEB SITE REFERENCES

Site	Description
http://www.microsoft.com/sitebuilder	Microsoft Web help (site builder network)
http://www.w3.org/	Web standards body
http://home.netscape.com	Netscape Web support
http://www.microsoft.com/vbasic ado20/techmat/whitepapers/	Microsoft ADO and RDO white paper
http://activeserverpages.com	Consulting group with comments and links on building Windows NT Web sites with databases

ADDITIONAL READING

Corey, M., and M. Abbey. *Oracle Data Warehousing.* Berkeley: Oracle Press, 1996. [Introduction to data warehouse concepts and challenges.]

Date, C. J. *An Introduction to Database Systems.* 5th ed. Reading, MA: Addison-Wesley, 1991. [In-depth discussion of distributed databases.]

Fortier, P. J. *Database Systems Handbook.* Burr Ridge: McGraw-Hill, 1996. [Technical discussion on building applications using multiple database systems.]

Hillier, S., and D. Mezick. *Programming Active Server Pages.* Redmond: Microsoft Press, 1997. [A summary of how to use ASP to build Web sites, including database connections, sessions, and issues in scaling up your site to hundreds of users.]

Jones, E. *Developing Client/Server Applications with Microsoft Access.* Berkeley: Osborne, 1997. [Details on building client/server applications.]

Ladd, E., and J. O'Donnell. *Using HTML, Java, and CGI.* Indianapolis: Que, 1996. [One of many books on building Web sites.]

Signore, R. P., J. Creamer, and M. O. Stegman. *The ODBC Solution: Open Database Connectivity in Distributed Environments.* Burr Ridge: McGraw-Hill, 1995. [Technical discussion of ODBC.]

Simon, E. *Distributed Information Systems: From Client/Server to Distributed Multimedia.* Burr Ridge: McGraw-Hill, 1996. [General but technical discussion on building distributed systems.]

Yazdani, S., and S. Wong. *Data Warehousing with Oracle: An Administrator's Handbook.* Englewood Cliffs, NJ: Prentice Hall, 1997. [Introduction to data warehouse concepts and challenges.]

APPENDIX

Introduction to Oracle PL/SQL

Distributed database applications require programming control over the distributed databases. Because Oracle is one of the leaders in distributed databases, this section describes the fundamentals of writing programs in Oracle's extensions to SQL. To provide additional programming control over the database, Oracle extended SQL by adding programming commands within the SQL statements. Oracle also has a separate PowerObjects product for front-end application development; this product behaves much like Microsoft's VB. However, this section describes the PL/SQL extensions to the primary Oracle database. One point to remember is that each PL/SQL statement must end with a semicolon. Another feature you should know with any new language is how to mark comments. Oracle uses two forms: (1) two hyphens (--) for one-line comments or for comments on the same line as the code and (2) the C language convention (/* comments */) for multiple-line comments.

The purpose of this appendix is to provide a brief introduction to the PL/SQL language. If you intend to write complex applications in Oracle, you should obtain an additional book that explains the syntax and options in detail. You can also use the Oracle Help system and CD-ROMs to read more about each topic.

Variables and Data

The common data types are all available in PL/SQL. Oracle also derives several additional types, and the data types have changed over time, so you can expect to see variations in code written by other programmers. However, you should be able to write most application code using just the data types shown in Figure 11.1A. The ranges on the numeric data types are different than for Microsoft Access. For example, a numeric data type can have up to 38 digits of precision. Oracle also supports user-defined data types, so developers can build complex types from these primary types.

Oracle supports arrays of data, but calls them tables. However, a table or array is just a sequence of data that is held internally. It is not the same as a database table.

Scope of Variables

All variables must be defined within a DECLARE section—usually at the top of a routine. If you include the keyword CONSTANT when you define a variable, then the assigned value cannot be changed. Any code block can have local variables. A block is a section of code enclosed between BEGIN and END statements. It is also possible to create packages that contain several different procedures. A package can have variables that are global and accessible to all procedures within that package.

FIGURE 11.1A
Primary Oracle PL/SQL data types. Variations of these types are also available.

```
Number(precision, scale)
  Precision: number of digits
  Scale: round-off point
  NUMBER(7,4): 123.4567
INTEGER
BOOLEAN
  Yes/No
CHAR
  Fixed-length string
VARCHAR2
  Variable-length string
LONG, LONG RAW
  Binary data
DATE
```

Computations and Functions

To minimize confusion, Oracle does not use the equals sign (=) to assign values. Instead, it adds a colon to produce statements like (X:=3). As shown in Figure 11.2A, standard mathematical operators are similar to other languages. However, note the use of ** for exponentiation (e.g., 2**3=8). Although only one version is shown in Figure 11-2A, Oracle actually supports three versions of the inequality sign (!=, ~=, and <>). Note that you can use the pattern-matching operator (LIKE) in any conditional statement. Oracle supports the SQL standard characters for wildcards: percent (%) to match any number of characters and underscore (_) to match one character. To append strings, use the concatenation operator (e.g., FirstName || LastName). Remember that any operation involving a NULL value will return a NULL value.

Oracle supports the usual mathematical functions as well as several functions to convert data and manipulate date variables. For example, Oracle ABS returns absolute values of numbers, ROUND rounds off a computation, and SUBSTR examines portions of strings or character variables.

In some situations you need to examine summary data from the database tables. For example, you may need to use the average or standard deviation of a numerical column in a statistical computation. A slight modification to the SELECT statement retrieves this data and stores it in a program variable. For example, the statement SELECT AVG(Salary) FROM Employee INTO varSalary; computes the average value of the salary and stores it into the program variable (varSalary), which must already be declared.

FIGURE 11.2A
Common arithmetic operators in Oracle. Primary differences include ** for exponentiation, !=for inequality, and the ability to use SQL commands LIKE, BETWEEN, and IN for all conditional statements.

OPERATOR	OPERATION
**	Exponentiation
*, /	Multiply, divide
+, −, ||	Add, subtract, concatenate
=, !=, <, >, <=, >=,	Comparison
IS NULL, LIKE, BETWEEN, IN	
NOT, AND, OR	Logical operators

FIGURE 11.3A
Oracle uses an ELSEIF statement to handle a variable with many possible values. For safety and quality control, always include the final ELSE condition.

```
IF (ACCOUNT = 'P') THEN
   --do personal accounts
ELSEIF (ACCOUNT = 'C') THEN
   --do corporate accounts
ELSEIF (ACCOUNT = 'S') THEN
   --do small business
ELSE
   --handle error
END IF;
```

Conditions

The IF . . . THEN . . . ELSE condition is common to most languages, including PL/SQL. Oracle uses an ELSEIF variation instead of a switch or case statement. As shown in the example of Figure 11.3A, a bank might wish to perform different computations based on the type of account. The ELSEIF clause identifies each account type. As a quality control step, you should always include a final ELSE clause in any switch statement. Even if there are currently only three types of accounts, think about what will happen if a new type is added later and someone forgets to update your statement.

Note the use of the semicolons in Figure 11.3A. Position of semicolons is an issue of syntax, but it can be frustrating when you first learn a new language. First, note that the IF-THEN-ELSE structure has a semicolon at the end, after the END IF statement. Second, there are no semicolons after the THEN line. Instead, each of the action statements would have semicolons (except that in the example they are all comments).

Loops

Oracle provides several similar versions of loops. The main difference lies in how they start and end. As shown in Figure 11.4A, the LOOP and END LOOP commands are the common features. There are three choices for the statement to start the loop.

1. No start condition at all. In this case the loop is always executed, and you must provide an EXIT or EXIT WHEN statement or the loop will never finish.
2. A WHILE statement. For example, the statement WHILE (x < 10) LOOP repeats until the condition becomes false (e.g., x >= 10).
3. A FOR loop that repeats for each element in a list. For example, the loop beginning FOR i1 IN 1 . . . 10 will be executed 10 times.

FIGURE 11.4A
Foundations of a loop. The starting condition can be missing, it can be WHILE (condition), or it can be a fixed loop based on a FOR condition.

```
(Start statement)
Loop
. . .
EXIT;
EXIT WHEN (condition);
. . .
END LOOP;
```

Subroutines

Subroutines or procedures break the application into smaller pieces. Modularity makes it easier to create programs, modify them, and assign multiple developers to a large project. It is often possible to change the way a procedure operates without affecting the rest of the application.

Figure 11.5A shows a short procedure to remove old accounts from the main system table. It uses a parameter from the calling program to identify "old" accounts. That is, any account that has not placed orders since the given date will be copied to a backup table and removed from the main table. The procedure is then called by using its name and passing it the value of the parameters. In the example the calling command is DropOldAccounts(1/1/97). If you are concerned about date formats, you can use the TO_DATE function and specify exactly how the parameter should be converted from text into a date variable. Functions have similar definitions, but they return a value. The RETURN statement is used to signify the value being returned.

If a function or a procedure has several parameters, you should name each parameter when you call the procedure; for example: DropOldAccounts(CutDate=>1/1/97). Naming parameters makes it safer to change the procedure. If you use the traditional positional method, the DBMS assigns the values to parameters in the order they are listed by the procedure definition. If someone adds a new parameter to the middle of the procedure list, developers will have to go through every line of code that might call that procedure and change the calling parameters. Naming the parameters when you call a procedure ensures that the values are always assigned to the correct parameters even if the procedure is changed.

Pass-by-value and pass-by-reference are handled with the IN and OUT modes. Specifying a parameter as IN means that the calling program ignores any changes made to the parameter within the procedure. The OUT mode returns values to the calling program. Consider the following declaration: PROCEDURE NewBalance (Penalty IN NUMBER(5,2), Balance IN OUT NUMBER(15,2)). The Penalty parameter can be used within the procedure, but its value cannot be changed—it is essentially a constant. On the other hand, the Balance parameter can be changed (e.g., add the Penalty to it). Also, the new value will be returned to the calling program.

FIGURE 11.5A Procedure example. This procedure is called by a developer or user with a cutoff date. Accounts with no activity after that date are moved to a backup table and removed from the main system.

```
PROCEDURE DropOldAccounts (CutDate DATE) IS
   --Local variables are defined here
BEGIN
   --First copy the date to a backup table
   INSERT INTO OldAccounts
   SELECT * FROM Account WHERE AccountID NOT IN
      (SELECT AccountID FROM Order WHERE
      Odate>CutDate);
   --Copy additional tables . . .
   --Delete from Account automatically cascades to others
   DELETE FROM Account WHERE AccountID NOT IN
      (SELECT AccountID FROM Order WHERE
      Odate>CutDate);
END DropOldAccounts;
```

SQL Cursors

Many of your procedures will need to track through database queries to examine or change one row at a time. Because SQL operates on an entire set, it has to be modified slightly to enable program code to examine individual rows. Tracing through a query one row at a time uses a cursor. There are three basic steps to using cursors: (1) Declare the CURSOR and specify the query with a SQL statement; (2) OPEN the cursor, loop through the query, and **FETCH** the data for that row into memory; and (3) CLOSE the cursor.

Figure 11.6A shows the basic steps, along with a few twists to make programming easier. First, you would never use the sample program as it stands; to compute a total, the SQL SUM statement would always be more efficient. However, a simpler program is a better teaching tool.

The cursor is defined in the DECLARE section of the procedure or function. It simply defines the SQL statement. In practice, you would usually include a parameter to specify the WHERE clause of the SQL statement. For example, the program might pass in a department name and the procedure would perform the computation for the specific department. Now carefully examine the way the varTotal variable is declared. It uses an Oracle trick so that it is automatically defined with the same data type as the column in the original Employee table. The beauty of this trick is that if someone decides to change the type of data in the Salary column of the Employee table, the program code will automatically be redefined. Obviously there are limits—if someone changed the table's data type to CHAR, the computations would fail.

The next step is to open the cursor, which tells the DBMS to allocate some internal buffer space, locate the table, and set any necessary locks. Whenever you open a cursor, you should immediately type the corresponding CLOSE statement. A program will run if you forget the CLOSE statement, but if you do not close a cursor, the program might leave the buffers and memory space open. Eventually you will run out of space. Always type the CLOSE statement right after you type the OPEN statement—so you do not forget.

Now you need a loop to track through each row of the query. The program needs a loop, and it needs a place in memory to store the data that it retrieves. The simplest method to accomplish these two tasks is to use a FOR loop. The version of the FOR loop shown in Figure 11.6A automatically creates a new record variable (recEmp) that matches all the columns of data. Then it loops through each row in

FIGURE 11.6A
SQL cursor example. The CURSOR statement sets the query. Note the use of the %TYPE statement to automatically match the data types declared in the table. The FOR loop automatically creates a memory variable that matches the data in the query columns. The FETCH statement in the main loop retrieves one row of data and moves the cursor to the next row.

```
DECLARE
   CURSOR c1 IS
      SELECT Name, Salary, DateHired FROM Employee;
   varTotal Employee.Salary%TYPE;
BEGIN
   varTotal = 0;
   OPEN c1;
   FOR recEmp in c1 LOOP
      varTotal := varTotal + recEmp.Salary;
   END LOOP
   CLOSE c1;
   --Now do something with the varTotal
END;
```

the query, fetching one row at a time into the memory record variable. Any statements needed for computations or changes are entered within the FOR loop. Note that individual column values are retrieved by referencing the record variable and the name of the column (e.g., recEmp.Salary).

If you want to change the data in the table, you need to use an UPDATE command with a WHERE clause that specifies the exact row that you want to change. The CURRENT OF statement makes this process easier. For example, if you want to alter the salary of an employee, you could use a statement like UPDATE Employee SET Salary=Salary*1.10 WHERE CURRENT OF c1. If you want to change data, there are two other modifications you should make. First, the SELECT query should tell the DBMS that you are going to be changing the data. Just add the words FOR UPDATE to the end of the cursor's SELECT statement. Second, be sure to use a COMMIT statement to tell the DBMS when you are finished changing the data for one transaction, which usually occurs in the last statement before the END LOOP command. If necessary, you can fine-tune the transaction controls for performance by using the SET TRANSACTION command.

CHAPTER 12

Object-Oriented Databases and Integrated Applications

WHAT YOU WILL LEARN IN THIS CHAPTER

- How can you store complex objects and multimedia clips in a database? 420
- Can you store custom objects in a database? 421
- What object-oriented features are being added with SQL3? 423
- Can object-oriented programs store and share persistent objects in a database? 426
- What do you gain with integrated applications? 427
- How do you store commercial software objects in a database? 430
- How can a database application utilize other tools (e.g., spreadsheet or word processor)? 431

OVERVIEW

Miranda: *Hi Ariel. I haven't seen you in a while.*

Ariel: *That's because I got a new job.*

Miranda: *That's terrific. What will you be doing?*

Ariel: *Well, this company hired me to build an application for use by cities. The managers want to track the location and condition of all the utility lines, zoning ordinance boundaries, and so on.*

Miranda: *Wow! That sounds like a big project—and hard.*

Ariel: *It will be a big team, so I don't have to do everything myself. The fun part is that they want to use state-of-the-art object-oriented tools. They said they need me to design the database so that the applications can share data.*

Miranda: *Well, your experience with using the GPS to plot mountain-bike trails for your bike club should come in handy.*

Ariel: *Sure, that part should be easy. Now I have to spend some time learning how the new database management systems handle object-oriented data.*

Miranda: *Yes, I guess there's always something new to learn in this field.*

INTRODUCTION

Originally, business databases dealt with numbers and short text elements. DBMSs were designed to provide good performance for this type of data. Just look at the types of data that can be stored and at the commands available to manipulate that data. Because most business applications were transaction-oriented, this focus worked well. Businesses were content to store simple items such as account balances, product numbers, names, and dates.

In the last few years, computers have been asked to handle increasingly complex types of data, including images, sound, and video. At this point most of these objects are handled as separate files, with individual programs to create and manipulate this type of data. In a sense the industry is back at the program-and-file stage of data storage for these more complex objects. Because relational databases are so good at handling basic data types, it is natural to ask whether databases can also improve the storage, searching, and manipulation of more complex objects.

The next step involving complex data objects is to determine whether it is possible to create a true object-oriented DBMS. That is, can a DBMS store and manipulate entirely new objects that are defined by the developer? Storing objects is one step; manipulating and searching the objects is more difficult.

Another powerful use of objects lies in their ability to create integrated applications. Today most business applications are built using a single tool, such as a DBMS, a spreadsheet, or a separate programming language like C++. On the other hand, managers use a variety of tools every day, including spreadsheets, word processors, scheduling systems, and e-mail. Increasingly, managers need applications that cross these boundaries and can integrate and share data with each of these tools. For example, a monthly report might pull data from the DBMS, analyze it and create graphs within a spreadsheet, and then format the output using a word processor. Developers can take advantage of two aspects of this new world: (1) They can create applications that use features from all of these tools, and (2) the objects created with these tools (e.g., a spreadsheet) can be stored within the database. Remember that databases are designed to share data among many users—features like security and concurrency control can be valuable for sharing complex objects like reports.

DATA TYPES AND OBJECTS

The fundamental data types are shown in Figure 12.1. Note that before the computer can store and process data, it must be reduced by input devices to binary format. Output devices return the binary data to a form that humans can handle. Each data type can have many different subtypes. For example, numbers can be classified as integer or real. Text may look simple, but it becomes more complex when you need to store alphabets from different nations. Date and time data can be considered as text, but it is best to treat it as a separate data type. Images can be stored in any of a hundred different formats, split between bitmap and vector images. Similarly, there are many ways to store sound and video clips.

Difficulties with Complex Data Types

There are two basic complications with handling complex objects. First, they require considerably more space. For example, a detailed image can easily take several megabytes of storage space. Sound and video absorb huge amounts of space because every second generates more data. As an example, even with compression, a high-resolution video clip with sound can fill 2 gigabytes of storage in 10 minutes. These large objects present problems for database systems that were optimized to store millions of rows of short pieces of data.

The second problem presented by complex objects is that they cannot be manipulated by traditional commands. For example, there is no obvious way to sort a table of sound clips. Yes, you can sort on other attributes, such as length or volume,

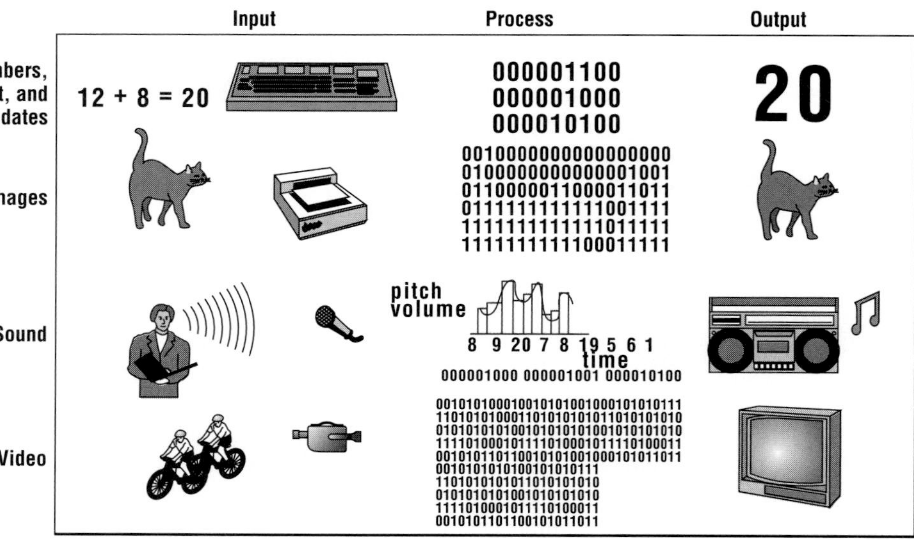

FIGURE 12.1 Base data objects. Databases commonly support many variations of numbers and text, including dates. Some database systems can store complex objects like images and sound. Few provide the tools to manipulate the more complex objects.

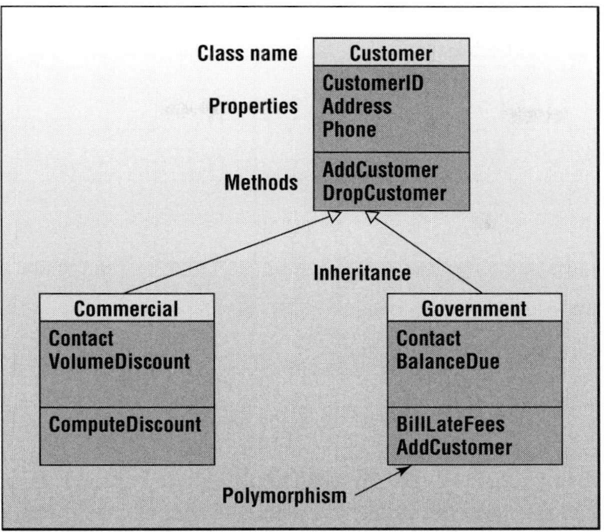

FIGURE 12.2
Object definition. Objects have properties and methods. New objects can be defined from existing objects, and they will inherit the properties and methods of the earlier classes.

but comparison of the sound itself is difficult. Similarly, what does it mean to search an image or a video clip? Some work has been done on creating computer systems that can search images or videos for specific items—for instance, list all pictures that contain horses. However, much of this work is on the leading edge of artificial intelligence research and is not reliable enough for everyday use.

The bottom line is that it is difficult for a database to handle complex objects. Even conceptually, there is no clear answer on what the database system should be able to do with these objects. For now, most systems are content to simply store and retrieve the objects. Most systems provide a data type specifically designed to hold large, undefined chunks of binary data. For instance, Microsoft Access refers to them as *objects,* and Oracle uses a LONG RAW data type; other systems call them **binary large objects (BLOBs)**.

Custom Objects

Complex, base objects like images, sound, and video have standard definitions, and these objects are used by many organizations. Hence there are industry-standard definitions of the objects, and there are relatively standard methods for storing and displaying the objects. Even commercial software objects like spreadsheets or word processor documents are predefined. What if developers need to create and store their own objects?

Recall that objects have properties and methods. Properties are the same as database table attributes, which makes it straightforward to store a portion of the objects in a relational database. Simply create a table with columns as the properties of the desired object or class. Of course, it is not really that simple.

As shown in Figure 12.2, a true OO approach enables you to define objects in terms of other objects, where properties are inherited from the earlier definitions. In the example a base customer class defines the properties and methods that are used by all types of customers. When special classes of customers are needed, they are derived from the existing definition, and designers simply add the properties and methods that are unique to the new class. For instance, commercial customers have a separate contact and they are given a volume discount.

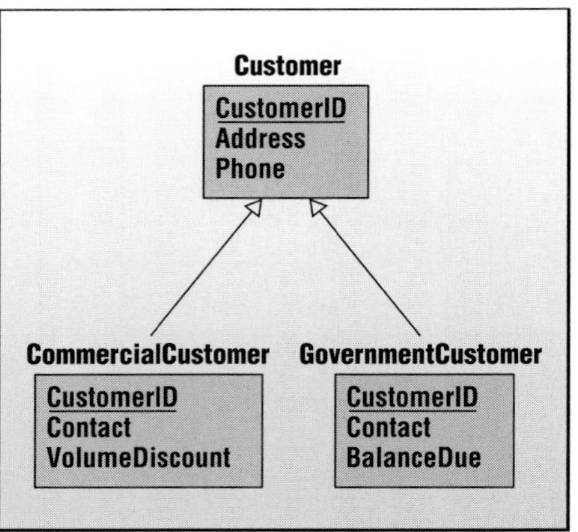

FIGURE 12.3 Storing objects in a relational database. Each subclass is stored in a separate table. The tables are connected by using the same primary key.

The first problem is that it is difficult to work inheritance into a typical relational database. As explained in Chapter 3, you have two basic choices: (1) create one large table that contains all the attributes for all classes of customers or (2) create separate tables for each class and link the tables together with a common primary key. If there are small differences between the classes, then the first method might be more efficient. In general, the second method is preferred—especially if there are many classes or many differences in attributes. However, this technique makes it a little more difficult to create new objects—the developer has to write code to add rows and store data in several tables. Nonetheless, as shown in Figure 12.3, this technique does work, and it provides an efficient means to store and retrieve objects.

The most difficult problem with objects arises from the methods. Each class definition contains methods, which are functions or procedures that carry out some task for the object. The problem lies in storing, retrieving, and executing program code for these methods. The greatest difficulty lies in where the code will be executed. If the code is executed on the same machine that holds the database, it is not too difficult to create a DBMS that can retrieve code from a database table and execute it. If the code will be executed on different computers, the task is considerably more difficult.

Consider the network of personal computers attached to several database servers illustrated in Figure 12.4. The workstations might have different processors than the server. Almost certainly, they have different operating systems and different tools available; in addition each personal computer could have a different environment. Procedures written to run on one system will probably not function on the others. Although a DBMS might be able to store and retrieve the code, the difficulty arises in sharing the code across different computers. Transferring code across a network also presents problems because of low transmission speeds. Running the database application on a single computer resolves many of the problems, but what is the point in using a DBMS if the application does not need to share data? One possible solution to the compatibility problem is to define a virtual machine with its own language environment. Procedures or methods written to this standard should be able to run on any machine that retrieves data. Recent developments for the Internet might help resolve these issues. In particular, the **Java** language was designed to run on any supported computer. If methods were written in Java, they could be stored in a table and the DBMS could transfer and execute methods on any machine as needed. However, there is a performance penalty for this approach. The penalty is incurred from transferring the code and because the code is interpreted instead of being compiled to a native program.

OBJECT-ORIENTED DATABASES AND SQL3

There are two basic approaches to handling true object-oriented data: (1) extend the relational model so that it can handle typical OO features or (2) create a new object-oriented DBMS. Vendors are working with both of these approaches. At this point both approaches have strengths and weaknesses, and there is no dominant solution.

The approach that adds OO features to the relational model is best exemplified by The American National Standards Institute (ANSI). In conjunction with DBMS vendors, ANSI is working on a new version of SQL to be called **SQL3.** SQL3 is designed to add object-oriented features to the SQL language. In 1997 the SQL3 development group merged with the Object Database Management Group (ODMG). Three features are suggested to add OO capabilities: (1) abstract data types, (2) subtables, and (3) persistent stored modules. SQL3 is not completely defined, and DBMS vendors have only started to implement some of the features. Even the theories behind OO database systems have not been completely defined. Consequently, the concepts are constantly changing. The following discussion is based on the working draft for SQL3, which will be somewhat different from the final version. Nonetheless, this chapter presents the foundations required to understand the topics. Also, some vendors have started to incorporate these features into their products (e.g., Oracle 8).

Object Properties

The first issue involves defining and storing properties. In particular, OO programmers need the ability to create new composite properties that are built from other data types. SQL3 creates **abstract data types** to enable developers to create new types of data derived from existing types. This technique supports inheritance of properties. The type of data stored in a column can be a composite of several existing abstract types. Consider the example shown in Figure 12.5 which shows part of a database for a **geographic information system (GIS).** The GIS defines an abstract data type for location in terms of latitude, longitude, and altitude. Similarly, a line segment (e.g., national boundary), would be a collection of these location points. By storing the data in tables, the application can search and retrieve information based on user requirements. The database also makes it easier to share and to update the data. In the GIS example, the database handles the selection criteria

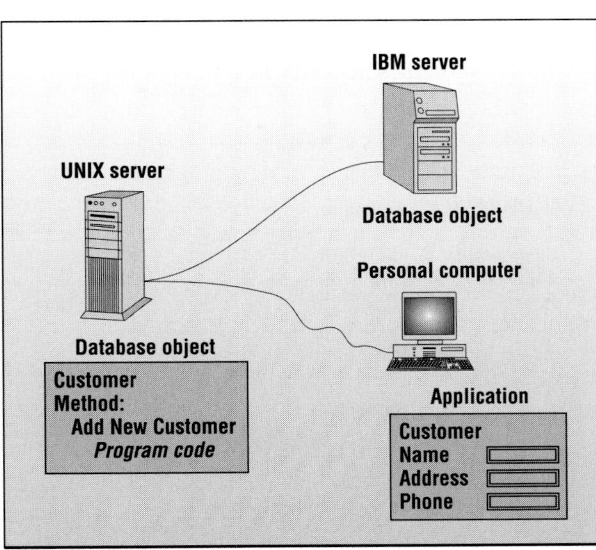

FIGURE 12.4 Difficulties with OO methods. How can a method (program) run on different computers, which use different processors? Either store code for each processor or use an interpreted language like Java.

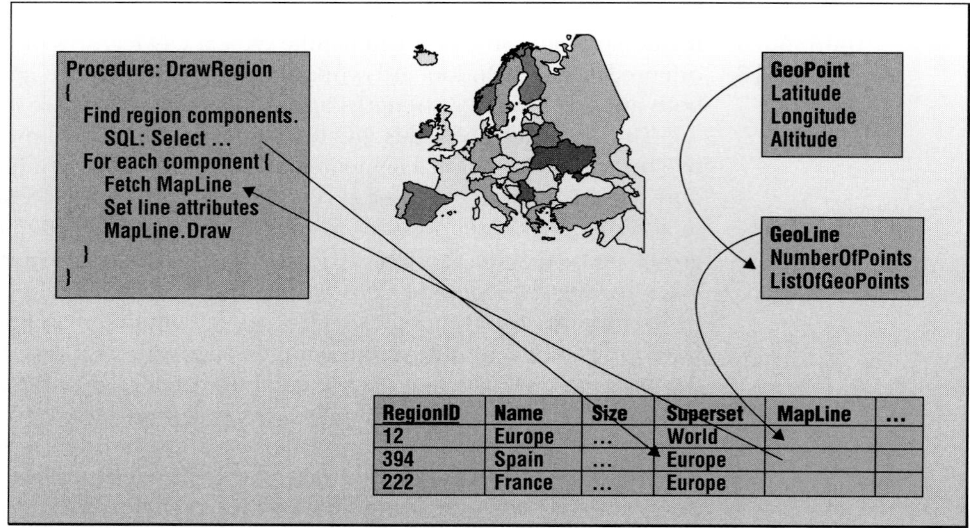

FIGURE 12.5 Abstract data types or objects. A GIS needs to store and share complex data types. For example, regions are defined by geographic line segments. Each segment is a collection of points, which are defined by latitude, longitude, and altitude. Using a database makes it easier to find and share data.

(Region=Europe). The database can also match and retrieve demographic data stored in other tables. The advantage to this approach is that the DBMS handles the data storage and retrieval, freeing the developer to concentrate on the application details.

The abstract data type enables developers to create and store any data needed by the application. The abstract data type can also provide greater control over the application development. First, by storing the data in a DBMS, it simplifies and standardizes the way that all developers access the data. Second, the elements within the data type can be encapsulated. By defining the elements as private, application developers (and users) can only access the internal elements through the predefined routines. For example, developers could be prevented from directly modifying the latitude and longitude coordinates of any location by defining the elements as private.

SQL3 provides a second method to handle inheritance by defining subtables. A **subtable** inherits all the columns from a base table and provides inheritance similar to that of the abstract data types; however, all the data is stored in separate columns. The technique is similar to the method shown in Figure 12.3, which stores subclasses in separate tables. The difference is that the OO subtables will not need to include the primary key in the subtables. As indicated in Figure 12.6, inheritance is specified with

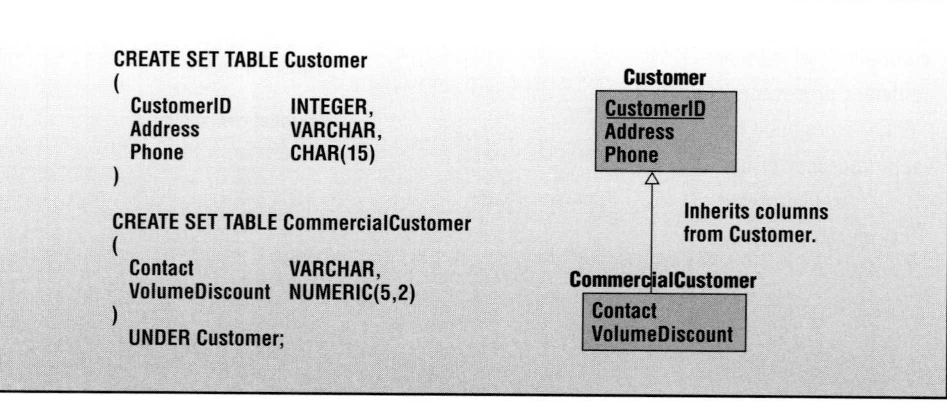

FIGURE 12.6 SQL3 subtables. A subtable inherits the columns from the selected supertable. Queries to the CommercialCustomer table will also retrieve data for the CustomerID, Address, and Phone columns inherited from the Customer table.

an UNDER statement. You begin by defining the highest level tables (e.g., Customer) in the hierarchy. Then when you create a new table (e.g., CommercialCustomer), you can specify that it is a subtable by adding the UNDER statement. If you use the unified modeling language (UML) triangle-pointer notation for inheritance, it will be easy to create the tables in SQL3. Just define the properties of the table and then add an UNDER statement if there is a "pointer" to another table.

It is important to understand the difference between abstract data types and subtables. An abstract data type is used to set the type of data that will be stored in one column. With a complex data type, many pieces of data (latitude, longitude, etc.) will be stored within a single column. With a subtable the higher-level items remain in separate columns. For example, a subtable for CommercialCustomer could be derived from a base Customer table. All the attributes defined by the Customer table would be available to the CommercialCustomer as separate columns.

Object Methods

Each abstract data type can also have methods or functions. In SQL3 the routines are called **persistent stored modules.** They can be written as SQL statements. The SQL language is also being extended with programming commands—much like Oracle's PL/SQL extensions described in Chapter 11. Routines are used for several purposes. They can be used as code to support triggers, which have been added to SQL3.

Persistent routines can also be used as methods for the abstract data types. Designers can define functions that apply to individual data types. For example, a GIS location data type could use a subtraction operator that computes the distance between two points.

To utilize the power of the database, each abstract data type should define two special functions: (1) to test for equality of two elements and (2) to compare elements for sorting. These functions enable the DBMS to perform searches and to sort the data. The functions may not apply to some data types (e.g., sound clips), but they should be defined whenever possible.

SQL3 also provides a more direct interface between the DBMS and a programmer's code. SQL3 provides two methods to use the database from external programs: (1) **call-level interface (CLI)** and (2) embedded SQL. Both methods consist of commands that are added to OO programming languages (e.g., C++). With embedded SQL your compiler needs to analyze SQL statements and provide libraries to communicate with the database. With CLI the database provides the communication libraries and handles much of the data exchange itself. From a programmer's standpoint, the commands are similar. You build SQL statements to store and retrieve data. Database cursors are used to track row-by-row through a table. The CLI approach requires a few extra programming steps, but provides more control over the communication with the database, particularly in terms of identifying and controlling errors.

Figure 12.7 shows the difference between SQL3 persistent stored modules and externally hosted programs. External programs provide the developer with more control over the application and the environment. For example, C++ or Visual Basic programs provide complete access to the personal computer Windows interface. Because they are compiled to machine code, external programs generally run faster as well. On the other hand, persistent modules stored within the database are accessible to anyone who uses the database—regardless of the machine used. Additionally, by integrating the modules into the object definitions, the objects are easier to modify and applications are easier to create.

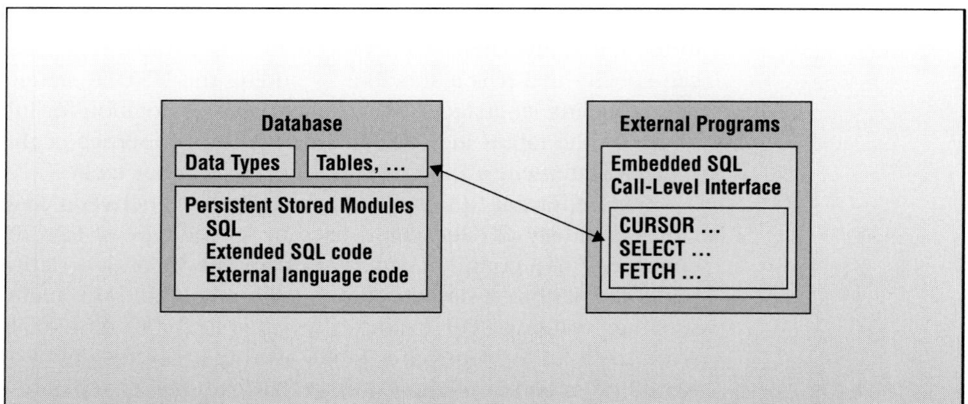

FIGURE 12.7 SQL3 persistent stored modules and external programs. On the left SQL3 modules are stored and executed within the DBMS. On the right embedded SQL and CLI functions run from an external program and establish communication with the DBMS. Externally compiled programs give the developer more control over the environment and generally execute faster by compiling the code.

Object-Oriented Languages and Sharing Persistent Objects

The development of true OODBMS models was initiated largely in response to OO programmers who routinely create their own objects within memory. They needed a way to store and share those objects. Although the goals may appear similar to the modified-relational approach, the resulting database systems are unique.

Most OO development has evolved from programming languages. Several languages were specifically designed to utilize OO features. Common examples include C++, Smalltalk, and Java. Data variables within these languages are defined as objects. Each class has defined properties and methods. Currently, developers building applications in these languages must either create their own storage mechanisms or translate the internal data to a relational database.

Complex objects can be difficult to store within relational databases. Most languages have some facility for storing and retrieving data to files, but not to databases. For example, C++ libraries have a serialize function that transfers objects directly to a disk file. There are two basic problems with this approach: (1) it is difficult to search files or match data from different objects, and (2) the developer is responsible for creating all sharing, concurrency, and security operations. Essentially, this approach suffers from all of the problems described in Chapter 1 because data is now intrinsically tied to the programs.

Essentially, OO programmers want the ability to create **persistent objects,** that is, objects that can be saved and retrieved at any time. Ideally, the database would standardize the definitions, control sharing of the data, and provide routines to search and combine data. The basic difficulty is that no standard theory explains how to accomplish all these tasks. Nonetheless, as shown in Figure 12.8, several OODBMS exist, and users have reportedly created many successful applications with these tools.

The key to an OODBMS is that to the programmer it simply looks like extended storage. An object and its association links are treated the same whether the object is stored in RAM or shared through the DBMS. Clearly, these systems make development easier for OO programmers. The catch is that you have to be an OO programmer to use the system at all. In other words, if your initial focus is on OO programming, then a true OODBMS may be useful. If you started with a traditional relational database, you will probably be better off with SQL3 or a relational DBMS that has added OO features.

FIGURE 12.8
OODBMS vendors and products. Each tool has different features and goals. Contact the vendors for details or search the Web for user comments.

- GemStone Systems, Inc.
- Hewlett-Packard, Inc. (OpenODB)
- IBEX Corporation, SA.
- Illustra (Informix, Inc.)
- Matisse Software, Inc.
- O2 Technology, Inc.
- Objectivity, Inc.
- Object Design, Inc.
- ONTOS, Inc.
- POET Software Corporation
- UniSQL
- Unisys Corporation (OSMOS)
- Versant Object Technology

In theory, the 1997 agreements between ANSI and ODMG were designed to bring the SQL3 and OODBMS models closer to a combined standard. In practice, it could take a few years and considerable experimentation in the marketplace. For now, if you are serious about storing and sharing objects, you will have to make a choice based on your primary focus: OO programming or the relational database.

INTEGRATED APPLICATIONS

For the last few years most commercial software packages have been created from an OO perspective. Microsoft applications in particular have emphasized the use of objects. To users, the most noticeable result is the emphasis on setting properties of application objects. For example, the right mouse button is used to set colors and styles for drawing objects. However, the emphasis on OO programming offers even stronger capabilities to developers building business applications. As shown in Figure 12.9, modern commercial applications expose the object properties and the object methods to developers. Hence developers can directly manipulate objects in different applications.

Increasingly, managers need applications that utilize a variety of tools. Data is pulled from a database and analyzed in a spreadsheet. Graphs and tables are created and inserted into a word processing document that formats the final report. Common

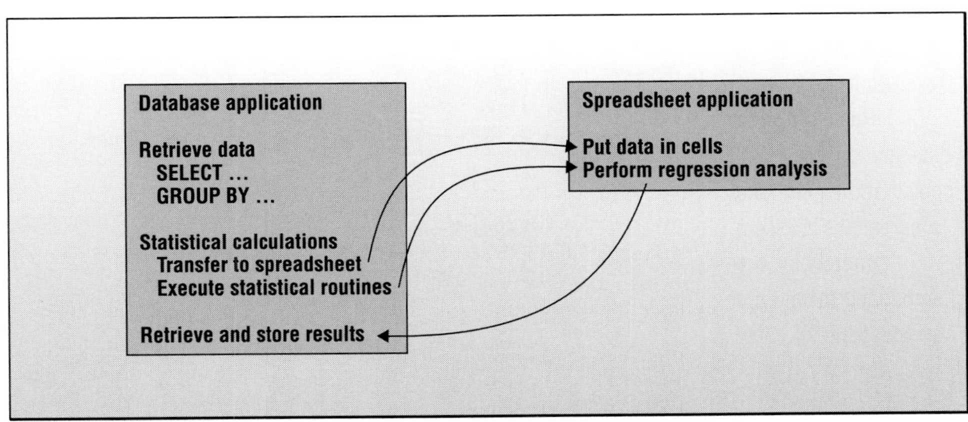

FIGURE 12.9
Integrated applications. Code in the DBMS can activate a spreadsheet application. It can then use the predefined spreadsheet objects to transfer data and perform calculations.

software tools include a spreadsheet, word processor, graphics package, and a DBMS. Many managers also use a personal information manager that includes facilities for scheduling, communication, note taking, and storing data on business and personal contacts.

Useful applications can be built by utilizing the capabilities of these commercial tools. At a minimum developers can create and transfer objects—automating the process of combining the tools. An even greater level of automation and integration can be achieved when the vendors expose the object properties and methods within the tools. In this situation a developer can use an external program to alter objects in any of the tools. The main application can also execute the functions provided by the individual objects.

Consider a situation where a manager needs to produce and evaluate a weekly report that compares sales for different divisions and products. A base application can call the DBMS to retrieve the desired data and transfer it to a spreadsheet. Various financial formulas can be inserted and graphs built on separate pages. The manager can then alter the formulas or examine additional details. Completed graphs and tables can be linked or copied to a word processor and formatted automatically. Once the manager has made final changes, the document can be automatically e-mailed to people on a distribution list.

The key to integrating applications is to understand that each application has strengths and weaknesses. The goal is to use the best tool for each task. For example, a DBMS is good at storing, retrieving, and sharing data, but it is weak at computations. A spreadsheet performs complex computations and analyses, but is not good at sharing data with simultaneous users. Word processors do an excellent job at formatting text and creating final reports. When the tools can be integrated, you can create a better application with less work.

Object Linking and Embedding

The first step in integrating applications is to transfer data across applications. Windows provides a tool for this step known as **object linking and embedding (OLE).** OLE is a Microsoft Windows standard that describes how applications should exchange data and communicate with each other. From a user's perspective, data is transferred using the Edit/Copy and Edit/Paste commands. There are two basic choices when transferring data: static copies and dynamic links. As shown in Figure 12.10, when a static copy is made, the new copy is independent from the original. Changes made to either version will not affect the other.

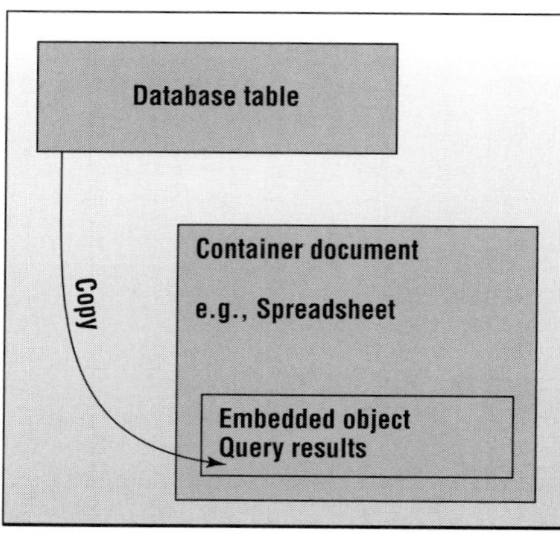

FIGURE 12.10 Static OLE copy. Results from a database query can be copied and pasted into a spreadsheet. Like a photocopy, the embedded results are an independent copy.

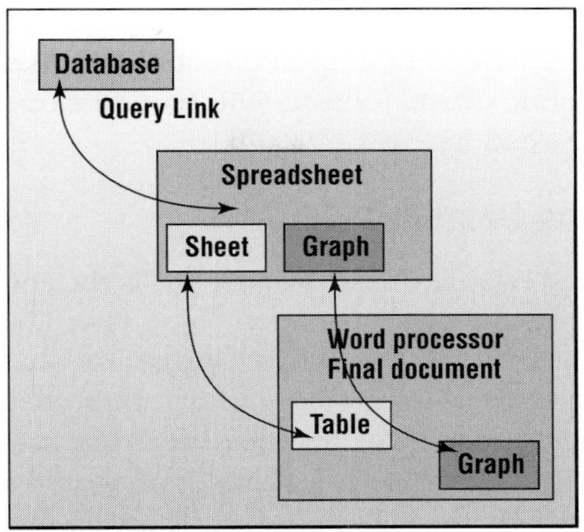

FIGURE 12.11 Dynamic OLE links. When the data changes, the new values are sent to the spreadsheet, which recalculates and redraws any graphs.

A second method of transferring data is to create a dynamic link. With a dynamic link the current data is copied, but the applications also establish a communication link. If the data changes in the original, a message is sent to the container application and the new data is transferred. When a container application opens an existing file, it checks all the dynamic links to get the most recent data. Figure 12.11 shows several levels of links. Dynamic links are also created through the Edit menu. The difference is that you use the Paste Special command and select the Paste Link option.

Microsoft Access supports static copies directly. Users simply mark the desired items, copy them, and paste them into an application. Access also supports dynamic links—but only through queries. You first build a query and then copy and paste it as a link—usually into a spreadsheet.

Microsoft COM and CORBA

To facilitate the integration of applications within the Windows environment, Microsoft created the **component object model (COM).** COM is a technique for defining objects so that they can be shared by applications running in a Windows environment. Applications that use the COM model use Windows features to transfer data and manipulate objects in other applications. Microsoft sells several tools (such as Visual C++) that help developers incorporate COM principles into applications.

A consortium of other vendors, led by IBM, is attempting to define a similar technique for use on a variety of machines. The technique is known as the **common object request broker architecture (CORBA).** Compared to COM, the goals of CORBA are more ambitious and consequently more difficult to achieve. The challenge with the CORBA goal is the desire to manipulate objects stored on different computers and diverse operating systems.

The strength of the Microsoft approach is that it is integrated into the Windows operating systems, which makes it easier for developers to use. However, the applications must run in a Windows environment to share object methods.

The COM model is being converted to other systems (notably UNIX), but it is too early to know if COM will be accepted and used outside the Windows environment.

The CORBA initiative was designed to share data across larger applications running on centralized servers. Historically, it has been difficult to share data among these products. Simple text and numeric data can usually be shared today. Sharing and activating internal objects is rarely done. For example, it might be useful for a large Oracle database application to activate complex statistical processing in an SAS application running on a different computer. Techniques like this example might be possible at some point, but sharing objects will require close cooperation by several hardware and software vendors.

Storing Objects in the Database

A useful feature provided by many database systems is the ability to store large binary objects. You can use this data type for common objects like images or sound. Microsoft documentation provides examples of storing images as objects. A more interesting business application is to store objects created by other commercial software.

Have you ever had to search for a spreadsheet file because you could not remember what you called it or where you stored it on your hard drive? Now consider a management team working on a large project. There are dozens of analyses for the project. Everyone shares the files, making changes, updates, and comments. Even with a LAN, it is hard to determine who has the current file or who made the last changes. If there are related files, it is hard to keep them together.

This situation should sound much like the problems presented in Chapter 1 involving traditional programs and files. The only difference is that the data involves more complex spreadsheet objects (or documents, graphs, etc.). A DBMS can solve some of these problems. The key is to store the spreadsheet in a separate column in a table.

As shown in Figure 12.12, the spreadsheet is accessible from a common form. When users double-click on the worksheet, the spreadsheet software is activated and they can modify the spreadsheet. It is automatically resaved into the database. Different spreadsheets can be displayed on different forms (different rows in the database). With a little code, revisions can be automatically stored as new rows in the database. By activating the Track Changes option within the spreadsheet software, the spreadsheet will highlight changes by color—based on the individual who made the changes.

Programming Links

One way to build relatively complex applications is to link data to a spreadsheet and then to a word processor. However, the true power comes from using programming code to build links, modify data, and generate applications that are customized for each situation.

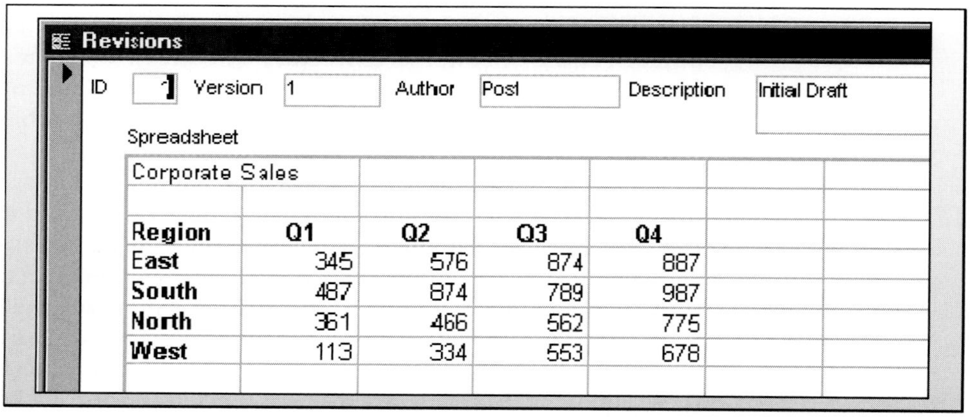

FIGURE 12.12
Storing objects in the database. Spreadsheets can be stored as a column in the database. Managers can edit the spreadsheet on the main form. Code can be added to automatically track modification times. By centralizing the storage, the DBMS makes it easier to share and control access to the data.

Revisions

ID 1 Version 1 Author Post Description Initial Draft

Spreadsheet

Corporate Sales				
Region	Q1	Q2	Q3	Q4
East	345	576	874	887
South	487	874	789	987
North	361	466	562	775
West	113	334	553	678

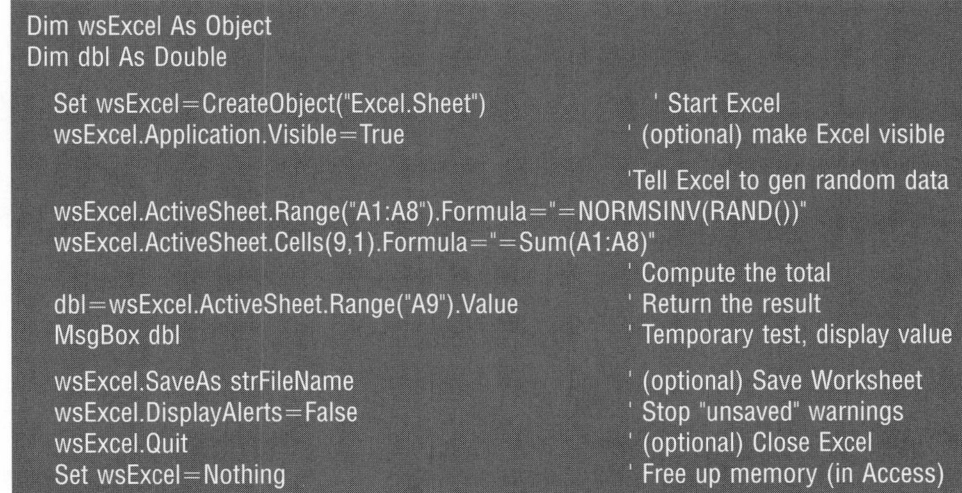

```
Dim wsExcel As Object
Dim dbl As Double

  Set wsExcel=CreateObject("Excel.Sheet")              ' Start Excel
  wsExcel.Application.Visible=True                     ' (optional) make Excel visible

                                                       'Tell Excel to gen random data
  wsExcel.ActiveSheet.Range("A1:A8").Formula="=NORMSINV(RAND())"
  wsExcel.ActiveSheet.Cells(9,1).Formula="=Sum(A1:A8)"
                                                       ' Compute the total
  dbl=wsExcel.ActiveSheet.Range("A9").Value            ' Return the result
  MsgBox dbl                                           ' Temporary test, display value

  wsExcel.SaveAs strFileName                           ' (optional) Save Worksheet
  wsExcel.DisplayAlerts=False                          ' Stop "unsaved" warnings
  wsExcel.Quit                                         ' (optional) Close Excel
  Set wsExcel=Nothing                                  ' Free up memory (in Access)
```

FIGURE 12.13 Programming with objects. From Access this program starts Excel, enters formulas into the worksheet, and retrieves the computed value. A business application would contain more sophisticated formulas, but the principles are the same.

All the applications in Microsoft Office support **Visual Basic for Applications (VBA).** VBA is the code examined in Chapter 7. The other important feature of the applications is that they have many predefined objects. Each of these objects has properties that you can read and set. The objects also have methods that you can execute. A simple example is shown in Figure 12.13. The basic structure is to create an object in the target application (e.g., an Excel worksheet). You can then assign properties or activate methods of that object. Both properties and methods use a dot notation. Remember that objects are hierarchical, so Excel contains worksheets, which contains cells. When you are finished, you should close the target application, unless you want to leave it open for the user to make changes. Finally, you should clear the object variable in the host application.

Virtually any command that can be executed by a user can also be executed using the object methods. These objects and methods can be activated from other languages (such as C++ or Visual Basic), which means that any program can control these other applications. There is only one catch: You have to know the names of the objects, their properties, and the methods available. The documentation for Microsoft products is readily available in help files. However, there are hundreds of objects, properties, and methods. It takes a while to learn the object system. The VBA debug window is also useful—particularly in conjunction with the **object browser.** As shown in Figure 12.14, by starting the object browser within the desired application, you can get a list of all the objects, their properties, and methods.

Examples

There are many business situations in which linking data into a spreadsheet would be useful. Analysis of data is an important management task—particularly at the tactical and strategic management levels. A decision support system (DSS) is designed to help managers make these decisions. A DSS provides three levels of support: (1) data collection, (2) modeling and analysis, and (3) presentation—particularly graphical. Different tools are generally required to provide these three features. A DBMS retrieves data (probably from a data warehouse), a spreadsheet performs computations and creates graphs, and a word processor or graphics package produces reports and presentations.

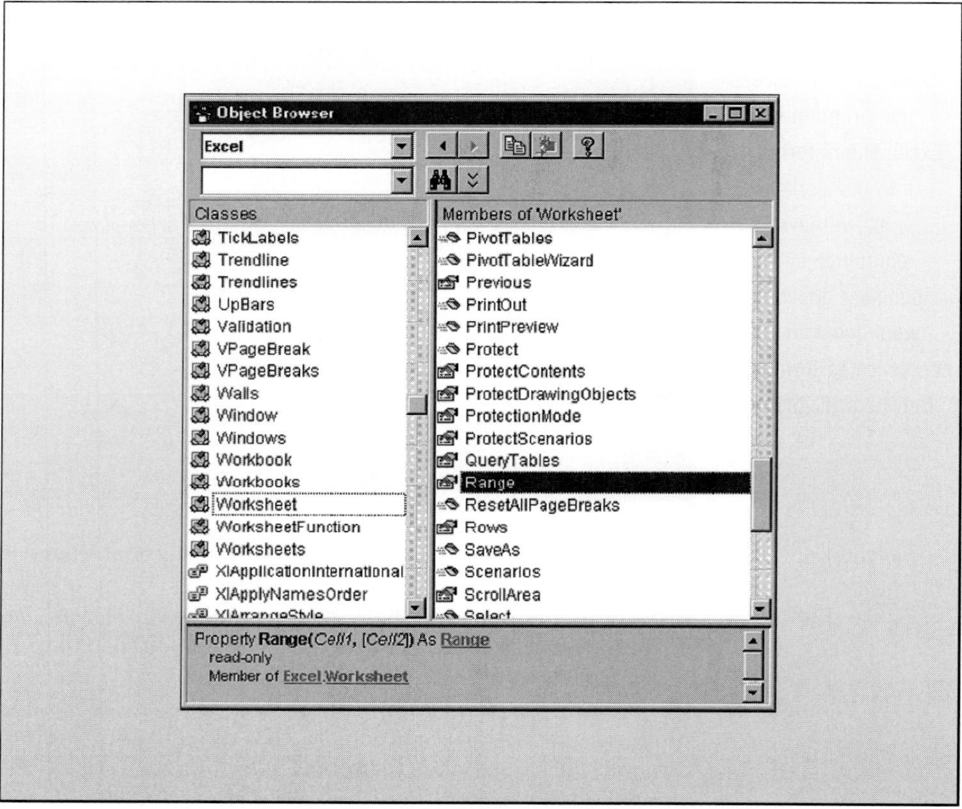

FIGURE 12.14 Microsoft object browser. The object browser provides a list of all of the objects, properties, and methods available in accessible software packages (e.g., Excel).

Enterprise information systems (EIS) can benefit from integrating applications. An EIS provides a model of the overall company. It uses a graphical interface to present a picture of the company. Managers then click different icons to receive current information on sales, costs, production, or any other aspect of the company. This data is usually displayed graphically. With an integrated application the requested data can be moved into a spreadsheet for further analysis. Similarly, graphs can be transferred to a graphics package where they can be annotated or enhanced for a presentation.

Financial Planning

Projecting financial statements is a common tactical step in financial analysis. The different financial statements (e.g., balance sheet, income statement, cash-flow statement) have their own forecasting techniques, but the overall approach is similar. The projected statement begins with the existing statement. Then individual items are forecast—based on historical data or estimates from various departments. Some item forecasts depend on others—for example, costs are generally related to sales.

The objective is to use the historical transaction data to forecast the individual items. The financial report is built as a spreadsheet, which enables the manager to examine the effect of different assumptions and to compare the results in graphs. Figure 12.15 shows that the basic accounting data can be linked into a spreadsheet to create the basic balance sheet and income statement. Similarly, a crosstab query is linked into the spreadsheet to forecast the values for the next quarter.

This example is straightforward. It requires no programming, and the links can be placed manually. However, one important catch illustrates the complications encountered when integrating applications. The main challenge is to place the values from the database into the appropriate cells in the spreadsheet. One solution is to build separate queries for each individual cell. But it takes time to create the queries. Also, it is inefficient for the system to process multiple small queries. A more efficient solution is to link the query into a separate worksheet and then copy the values to the appropriate spreadsheet cells. The drawback to this second approach is that you should avoid assuming the data will always be in the same location. If items are added to the query, it might shift the order of the values in the linked data. A spreadsheet lookup command can handle this problem. The key is to watch for this potential problem whenever you use a dynamic link.

Report Formatting with a Word Processor

Another useful integration trick is to send database reports to a word processor. There are two main advantages. First, you have all of the control of the word processor available to perform formatting. By building the report from code, you have full control over the output. Second, users can modify or add information to the report. Users are familiar with word processor documents, so less training is needed for them to customize their reports.

If you do not need to control formatting, you can use standard OLE tools to copy a report into a word processor document. However, you do not gain much with this approach, and the resulting report is difficult to modify. Another approach is to write a program in the database that retrieves the data items and places them into a document. Chapter 8 illustrates the basic process of generating a report using program code. The next step is to use the word processor controls to control the formatting of the report.

Two useful tricks will help you build reports in a word processor. First, turn on the macro recording feature and create parts of the report manually. The macro recorder saves your keystrokes as program code. You can copy and paste much of this code into your program. With a few modifications you can retrieve data from the queries and insert it into the macro code to produce the main report.

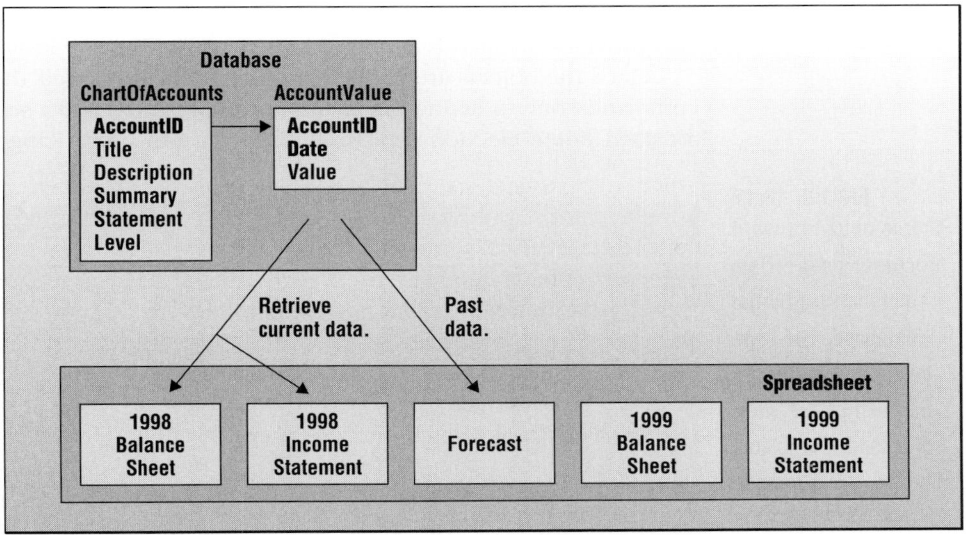

FIGURE 12.15 Financial planning. Accounting data is retrieved from the database to build a current balance sheet and income statement. Historical data is used to forecast values for the next quarter.

```
Start Word.
Add a document.
Set tab stops.
Open query.
   Read each row.
   Format and "Print" to Word.
End loop.
Close query.
Define footer.
Save and Close Word document.
Clear variables.
```

FIGURE 12.16 Outline for building a report that will be produced in Microsoft Word. The report retrieves and formats three columns from a query. A footer is printed on each page. The code could be written inside any application (Access, Word, or Visual Basic).

The second useful trick is to use templates and style formats as much as possible. A *template* specifies the primary formatting for a document; all you have to add is the text. *Styles* are important to ensure consistency across the report. Instead of setting attributes for each word, you assign attributes to a named style and then apply the style to the text. For example, all section headings could be assigned to the Heading1 style, and detail rows in a table could be assigned to a TableDetail style. The main strength to this approach is that users can reformat the entire document by changing the style formats. For example, to squeeze data into a tighter space, users could reduce the point size of the TableDetail style. This change would affect every table in the document, ensuring consistency.

The basic steps to build a report are shown in Figure 12.16. A portion of the report is displayed in Figure 12.17. This example is deliberately simplified to highlight the main steps. It uses a simple query and prints only three columns. A real report would generally contain more data, more conditions, and a more complex layout. However, the key to programming is to start simple, get it to work, and then add details later.

Figure 12.18 shows the code used to create the report. The basic process is to create an object for Word. You then set the properties and call the methods of this object. The catch is that you have to know what properties and methods to use. If you set Tools, References to include word objects, then the object browser will show you the choices for each object. The Help system provides additional details. Microsoft also provides detailed reference material on its Web site at www.microsoft.com.

Once the objects are defined and the query is opened, the report uses two basic commands: one to define the layout (with tab stops) and a second to display the text for each line (Selection.TypeText). You can also use a Range.InsertAfter command.

10	Current Assets	$136,886.00
15	Fixed Assets	$45,673.00
20	Current Liabilities	$98,963.00
25	Long Term Liabilities	$14,982.00

Footer
6/15/99 Accounting Summary

FIGURE 12.17 Sample output of word processor report. Data formats are set by the database. The page layout and footer are controlled by the word processor. Templates and styles provide consistency across the document.

FIGURE 12.18
Basic code to build a simple report in Microsoft Word. The code relies on properties and methods of predefined objects within Word. The object browser in the Visual Basic editor lists the properties and methods. A more complex report would expand the code inside the loop.

```
Dim objWord As Word.Application
Dim dbs As Database
Dim rst As Recordset
Dim rngfoot As Variant

If (Task.Exists("Microsoft Word")=True) Then
   Set objWord=GetObject(, "Word.Application")
Else
   Set objWord=CreateObject("Word.Application")
End If
objWord.Visible=True

objWord.Documents.Add
Set dbs=CurrentDb()
Set rst=dbs.OpenRecordset("Query5")

' Set the tabs for the columns
Selection.ParagraphFormat.TabStops.Add Position:=InchesToPoints(0.5), _
   Alignment:=wdAlignTabLeft, Leader:=wdTabLeaderSpaces
Selection.ParagraphFormat.TabStops.Add Position:=InchesToPoints(3), _
   Alignment:=wdAlignTabRight, Leader:=wdTabLeaderSpaces

' Read all of the data rows and put them into the document
Do While Not rst.EOF
   Selection.TypeText Text:=rst!AccountID & vbTab & rst!Title _
      & vbTab & Format(rst!Value, "Currency")

   Selection.TypeParagraph
   rst.MoveNext
Loop
rst.Close
' Add a footer for each page with File name and creation Date
Set rngfoot=objWord.ActiveDocument.Sections(1). _
                      Footers(wdHeaderFooterPrimary).Range

With rngfoot
   .Delete
   .Fields.Add Range:=rngfoot, Type:=wdFieldFileName, Text:="\p"
   .InsertAfter Text:=vbTab & vbTab
   .Collapse Direction:=wdCollapseStart
   .Fields.Add Range:=rngfoot, Type:=wdFieldCreateDate
End With

objWord.Documents.Save
objWord.Close
Set objWord=Nothing
```

The code also illustrates the power of Word's page footer (or header) feature. Any text, including a set of predefined values, can be placed in the page header or footer.

Visual Basic for Applications provides two useful commands for dealing with objects: **With . . . End With** and **For Each . . . Next.** Remember that objects are defined in hierarchies. For example, Word holds documents, which have sections, which have footers, and so on. The With statement provides a simple way to specify several properties of an object at a lower level and makes the code easier to read. You define the full object one time and then specify only the properties or methods inside the With . . . End With grouping.

The For Each command is useful when you need to repeat a command on a group of similar items. A common situation is when you want to affect a range of cells in a spreadsheet. The For Each statement sets up a loop that applies to every cell in the selected range. Any commands inside the loop are applied to each cell.

With Microsoft Office the code for these examples could be written inside any of the major applications. Each application has its own objects and methods, so you can manipulate objects in any of the other applications. Another option is to use the separate VB package to host the primary application. Then you can use objects from any application as needed. VB has the additional advantage of using compiled code for faster applications.

SALLY'S PET STORE

To help her understand the current financial condition of the store, Sally wants to be able to create basic accounting statements from the database. You thought about building a complete accounting system into the database, but some important data is not currently collected by the database. Building a complete data entry and accounting package within the database would require several months of work, and you need a faster alternative.

Consider the basic income statement shown in Figure 12.19. Sales and purchase totals can be retrieved from the database. Operating costs, administrative costs, miscellaneous income or expenses, and taxes will be provided by the accountant.

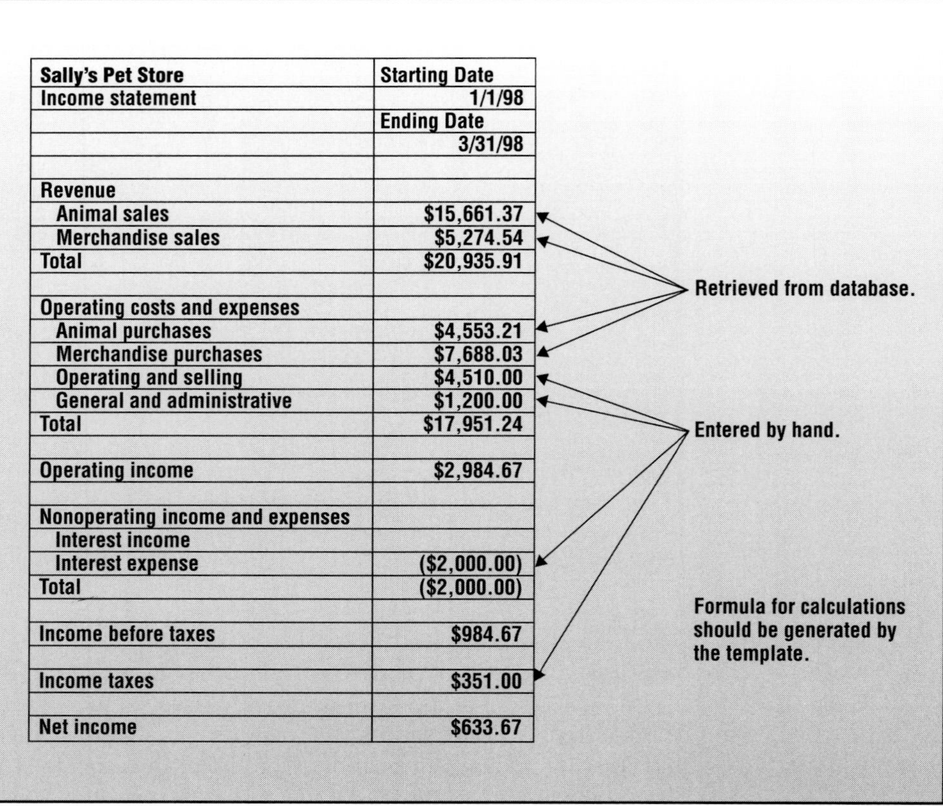

Sally's Pet Store	Starting Date
Income statement	1/1/98
	Ending Date
	3/31/98
Revenue	
Animal sales	$15,661.37
Merchandise sales	$5,274.54
Total	$20,935.91
Operating costs and expenses	
Animal purchases	$4,553.21
Merchandise purchases	$7,688.03
Operating and selling	$4,510.00
General and administrative	$1,200.00
Total	$17,951.24
Operating income	$2,984.67
Nonoperating income and expenses	
Interest income	
Interest expense	($2,000.00)
Total	($2,000.00)
Income before taxes	$984.67
Income taxes	$351.00
Net income	$633.67

FIGURE 12.19 Basic income statement. An Excel spreadsheet is generated by code within Access. The user selects the starting and ending date and then enters the data that is not available in the database.

FIGURE 12.20
Code to open Excel. The GetObject command tells you if Excel is already running. If not, the New Excel.Application statement opens Excel if it can. The hourglass cursor should be on because some machines might be slow to start an application.

```
Dim goExcel As Excel.Application
Public Function OpenMSExcel() As Variant
On Error Resume Next
' Subroutine that checks to see if Excel is open
' If not, start it up
  DoCmd.Hourglass True

  Set goExcel=GetObject(, "Excel.Application")
  If (goExcel Is Nothing) Then
    Set goExcel=New Excel.Application
  End If

  If (goExcel Is Nothing) Then
    MsgBox "Can't start Excel", , "Unexpected Error"
    OpenMSExcel=False
  Else
    If (Not goExcel.Visible) Then
      goExcel.Visible=True
    End If
    OpenMSExcel=True
  End If
  DoEvents
  DoCmd.Hourglass False
End Function
```

To make the application easy to use, the income statement is created as a spreadsheet in Excel. To make it even easier, the spreadsheet is automatically created by code within Access. All Sally has to do is enter the additional data from the accountant. Starting from a form in Access, Sally simply chooses the starting and ending dates; programming code automatically opens Excel, creates the basic template, and fills in the data that is available.

The first programming step is a subroutine that determines whether Excel is already running. If not, the subroutine starts Excel. Then the code sets a global object variable (goExcel) so that you can execute commands in Excel. The subroutine is shown in Figure 12.20. You can use this routine in any program you need. Just be sure to declare the global variable. You can easily alter this function to open other applications (such as PowerPoint).

The main code to build the spreadsheet calls the function to open Excel. Once Excel is open, you create a new workbook. Then you can place text and computations into each cell. You can also set column widths and format any cell. Any command you can issue in Excel, you can put into code. When working with Excel in Access, Excel objects must be activated inside Access. From any code window, select Tools, References from the menu and be sure that Microsoft Excel is selected. To carry out complex Excel operations, you should start in Excel, turn on the macro recorder, and perform the steps using typical Excel mouse operations. Then you can copy most of the code generated by the macro recorder into your Access program.

Portions of the code to generate the Sally's income statement are shown in Figure 12.21. Some of the repetitive steps are dropped to save space. For example, many of the labels and formula are not included in this listing. Likewise, only one of the

FIGURE 12.21 Code to create the income statement inside an Excel worksheet. Some of the code has been omitted to save space. Also, be sure to put the complete strSQL statement on one line. Here, the ON section was placed on a new line to make the listing fit on the page.

```
Private Sub cmdIncome_Click()
   Dim dbs As Database
   Dim rst As Recordset
   Dim strSQL As String, strWhere As String
   If Not OpenMSExcel() Then       ' Open Excel if we can
      Exit Sub
   End If
   On Error GoTo Err_cmdIncome_Click
   goExcel.Workbooks.Add       ' Create a new workbook
   With goExcel.ActiveSheet       ' Which sets a default sheet
      .Cells(1, 1).ColumnWidth=30.5       ' Set up the basic template
      .Cells(1, 1).Value="Sally's Pet Store"
      .Cells(1, 1).Font.Bold=True
      .Cells(2, 1).Value="Income Statement"
      .Cells(1, 2).Value="Starting Date"
      .Cells(2, 2).Value=[StartDate]
      .Cells(8, 2).Value="=B6+B7"
      .Cells(15, 2).Value="=SUM(B10:B14)"
      .Range("B6:B28").Select       ' Format the cells
      goExcel.Selection.NumberFormat="$#,##0.00;($#,##0.00)"
      .Range("B2,B4").Select
      goExcel.Selection.NumberFormat="m/d/yy"

      ' Now build the queries to get the totals, using the dates from the form
      strWhere="Between #" & [StartDate] & "# And #" & [EndDate] & "#);"
      ' First do the Animal Sales
      strSQL="SELECT Sum(SaleAnimal.SalePrice) AS SumOfSalePrice"
      strSQL=strSQL & "FROM Sale INNER JOIN SaleAnimal
                              ON Sale.SaleID=SaleAnimal.SaleID"
      strSQL=strSQL & "WHERE (Sale.SaleDate " & strWhere
      Set dbs=CurrentDb()
      Set rst=dbs.OpenRecordset(strSQL, , dbReadOnly)
      rst.MoveFirst
      .Cells(6, 2).Value=rst!SumOfSalePrice
      rst.Close
   End With
Exit_cmdIncome_Click:
   Exit Sub
Err_cmdIncome_Click:
   MsgBox Err.Description, , "Unexpected Error"
   Resume Exit_cmdIncome_Click
End Sub
```

four retrievals is shown in the SQL code. The entire listing can be found in the actual Pet Store database.

When working with multiple software packages, be sure to document your code. As new versions of the applications are released, you will undoubtedly have to rewrite your code. It is much easier to change if you have good notes to explain what the code is supposed to do.

Another solution to generating complex reports is to build a pivot table inside an Excel spreadsheet. A ***pivot table*** retrieves data and enables the user to interactively change sort order, filter criteria, and select subtotals or other computations. Figure 12.22 shows a pivot table for the Pet Store that enables managers to examine monthly or quarterly sales by employees for animals and merchandise. You can even use VBA code to create the base pivot table. Once the data is selected and the table created, it is relatively easy for users to point and click to examine the data in different layouts and groupings. Additionally, they will have a familiar spreadsheet interface to create graphs and create their own specialized reports. The power of the pivot table is that with a little training, users can quickly create custom reports.

			Quarter	Month			
			Quarter 1	Quarter 2	Quarter 3	Quarter 4	Grand Total
Last Name	Employee	Data					
Carpenter	8	Sum of Animal	1,668.91	606.97	426.39	7.20	2,709.47
		Sum of Merchandise	324.90	78.30	99.00	128.70	630.90
Eaton	6	Sum of Animal	522.37		341.85	562.50	1,426.72
		Sum of Merchandise	30.60		54.90	107.10	192.60
Farris	7	Sum of Animal	5,043.36	1,059.70		796.47	6,899.53
		Sum of Merchandise	826.92	188.10		306.00	1,321.02
Gibson	2	Sum of Animal	4,983.51	1,549.83		2,556.10	9,089.44
		Sum of Merchandise	668.25	238.50		450.90	1,357.65
Hopkins	4	Sum of Animal	4,131.30	811.54	372.65	128.41	5,443.90
		Sum of Merchandise	595.71	134.10	121.50	7.20	858.51
James	5	Sum of Animal	3,282.77	2,373.08	437.88	150.11	6,243.84
		Sum of Merchandise	505.89	693.45	99.00	99.00	1,397.34
O'Connor	9	Sum of Animal	2,643.69	180.91	510.12		3,334.72
		Sum of Merchandise	263.70	83.70	55.80		403.20
Reasoner	3	Sum of Animal	4,577.43	625.74	812.60	2,500.24	8,516.01
		Sum of Merchandise	762.30	89.10	153.90	396.90	1,402.20
Reeves	1	Sum of Animal	1,120.93				1,120.93
		Sum of Merchandise	263.88				263.88
Shields	10	Sum of Animal	1,008.76		162.15		1,170.91
		Sum of Merchandise	62.10		22.50		84.60
Total Sum of Animal			28,983.03	7,207.77	3,063.64	6,701.03	45,955.47
Total Sum of Merchandise			4,304.25	1,505.25	606.60	1,495.80	7,911.90

FIGURE 12.22
Excel pivot table. First create the ODBC link. Then build a query to retrieve the data needed. Next create the pivot table by selecting which data is displayed as rows and columns. Monthly data can be grouped into quarters. Users can instantly get quarterly or monthly totals by double-clicking on the column heading.

SUMMARY

Like most other computer applications, database systems initially concentrated on handling typical business data—columns of numbers, short text, and dates. With the advent of powerful and affordable multimedia computers, people increasingly need databases to store more complex objects. Typical objects include graphics, sound, and video clips. For some applications, like geographic information systems and computer-aided design, developers need the ability to define their own objects.

Storing objects involves two aspects: storing data for their properties and storing and activating their methods. The first part—storing properties—is relatively easy. In a relational database, the properties become columns.

There are two major complications with storing objects in a database. First, objects are usually derived from other objects, leading to a hierarchical structure. Second, methods are difficult to store—particularly when many different computers are involved.

Relational databases can be adapted to handle objects. The proposed SQL3 standard is an attempt to reconcile the difficulties. One of the main components is the ability to define new data types. These data types are treated as objects, and they can inherit properties from other data types. Some support is being provided for defining methods, but the issue of multiple computers is not yet resolved. One approach is to use an external language (e.g., Smalltalk or C++) to handle the methods and the processing and then to connect to the database to store and share the objects.

Many commercial applications are created using OO methodologies. The Microsoft Office suite is a primary example of this approach. By exposing the internal object properties and methods, developers can use the applications to create complex, integrated business applications. Your applications can use all the features of a spreadsheet, word processor, or graphics package. Through object-linking it is relatively easy to create complex decision support systems. Through the use of object programming, you can transfer data and utilize the internal functions of any of these applications. Linking data from the database into a spreadsheet is a popular way to build applications that analyze data—such as financial projections. Similarly, custom reports with sophisticated layout controls can be generated by writing the report into a word processor.

A DEVELOPER'S VIEW

Remember Miranda's comment: There is always something new to learn. Get used to spending time (and money) at your favorite bookstore. Much of the programming world is moving to OO techniques. Relational databases today can store the attributes of the objects. The problem currently lies with handling the methods. SQL3 offers some new ideas in handling inheritance, but it is not yet standardized. You need to work on integrating your database applications with other software—especially spreadsheets and word processors. You can incorporate many powerful features, and give users more flexibility, without too much additional work. For your class project you should write a routine that transfers data to a spreadsheet to perform additional computations or to a word processor for formatting.

KEY WORDS

abstract data types, 423
binary large object (BLOB), 421
call-level interface (CLI), 425
common object request broker architecture (CORBA), 429
component object model (COM), 429
For Each . . . Next, 435
geographic information system (GIS), 423
Java, 422
object browser, 431
object linking and embedding (OLE), 428
persistent objects, 426
persistent stored modules, 425
SQL3, 423
subtable, 424
Visual Basic for Applications (VBA), 431
With . . . End With, 435

REVIEW QUESTIONS

1. What are the basic problems with storing objects in a database?
2. How are custom objects different from predefined commercial or multimedia objects?
3. How can you store object-oriented data in a relational database?
4. What is the purpose of the abstract data type in SQL3?
5. How are subtables different from abstract data types in SQL3?
6. What are the advantages of storing commercial software objects in a database?
7. What is the difference between static and dynamic linking of objects?
8. How can you use spreadsheet tools from within a database application?
9. What are the advantages of creating a database report inside a word processor?

EXERCISES

1. Find a current SQL3 description or DBMS and list the syntax for creating an abstract data type and a subtable.
2. Find three database systems that support objects and describe their features, strengths, and weaknesses.
3. You have to develop a database using an object hierarchy that describes automobiles and trucks as shown in the accompanying figure.
   a. Define the relational database tables you would use for this database.
   b. If an OODBMS is available, create the tables and enter some sample data.

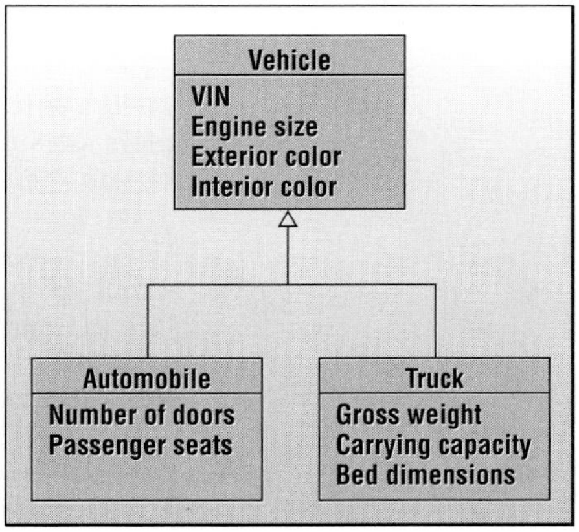

4. Create a database that has an Employee table. This table should include a column for storing a photograph of each employee. Build a form that displays basic employee data along with the photograph. Make it easy for the user to add new employees—using images from a scanner, digital camera, or from a file.
5. Create a database for storing versions of a spreadsheet. The spreadsheet is stored in the database. When users make major revisions, store the new spreadsheet in a new row of the database. Include data on when the spreadsheet was changed, who changed it, and a description of the changes.
6. Modify the application shown in Figure 12.12. Use a spreadsheet to generate a table of 50 random normal data points. Display the results in a graph on a database form.

Sally's Pet Store

7. Each animal category has unique health requirements. For example, each has special requirements for vaccinations (different shots and different times). Define the subtables needed to handle health records for the animals at the Pet Store.

8. Sally wants to create a Web site to help people choose the best animal for their lifestyle. She wants to store characteristics of each type of animal that she carries and then match the animal's requirements to each lifestyle. For example, reptiles and fish require less day-to-day care than mammals. Dogs require more attention and energy than cats. Some breeds of dogs are better with children and so on. Create initial abstract data types that can be used to store the data for this application.

9. Sally wants to forecast sales for the next 3 months. Write a spreadsheet application to dynamically total animal and total merchandise sales by month. Use a spreadsheet forecasting method (moving average or regression) to forecast the two sales totals for the next 3 months.

10. You remembered from your production management class that you can use an economic order quantity (EOQ) model to monitor the level of inventory items. Add two columns to the Merchandise table: OrderPoint and OrderQuantity. Find the formula for the EOQ model. Write a database program that evaluates each merchandise item to find the optimal OrderPoint and OrderQuantity. Use spreadsheet statistical methods to estimate the demand parameters of the EOQ model.

Rolling Thunder Bicycles

11. Write a database program to create a sales report for monthly sales and transfer the data directly into Word. List all the bicycles sold in each month by type of bicycle and print the totals quantity and total value of the sales for each category for each month.

12. Build a spreadsheet application that analyzes sales by city. Link to a query that displays sales of bicycles by city (ZIP code). Include total quantity and value for each bicycle type. Use the spreadsheet's GIS capabilities to display sales by region or state.

13. Create a new SalesForecast table that will display marketing's forecast for the next 2 months by bicycle type (quantity and value). Now create an application that transfers the current sales data to a spreadsheet and uses the spreadsheet's forecasting functions to predict sales for the next 2 months. Transfer these forecasts back into the SalesForecast table. Hint: First build a test spreadsheet by hand.

14. Describe how an object-oriented approach could be used to improve the Rolling Thunder application. What objects would be defined (include properties, methods, and hierarchy). What advantages would be gained? What are the potential drawbacks?

WEB SITE REFERENCES

Site	Description
http://www.omg.org/	OMG and CORBA
http://www.odmg.org/	ODMG (OODBMS)
http://www.objs.com/x3h7/fmindex.htm	SQL3
http://www.jcc.com/sql_stnd.html	SQL3
http://www.odbmsfacts.com	Barry and Associates consulting firm site with comments on existing OODBMS products

ADDITIONAL READING

Bahrami, A. *Object-Oriented Systems Development.* Burr Ridge, IL: Irwin/McGraw-Hill, 1999. [A good introduction to OO design and UML.]

Brown, D. *Object-Oriented Analysis: Objects in Plain English.* New York: Wiley, 1997. [One of many introductions to object-oriented design.]

Forsyth, D., J. Malik, and R. Wilensky. "Searching for digital pictures." *Scientific American*, June 1997, pp. 88–93. [An interesting discussion of searching visual images.]

Jain, R. et al. *Communications of the ACM* 40, no. 12 (December 1997), pp. 31–80. [Five articles on searching and storing visual and multimedia images.]

Microsoft Office 97/Visual Basic Programmer's Guide. Redmond: Microsoft Press 1997. [All the details on syntax and integrating applications.]

Sheriff, P. "Integrate Visual Basic and Excel." *Access-Office; VB Advisor,* January 1998, pp. 34–45. [Examples with code for integrating applications using VBA.]

APPENDIX

Database Projects

OVERVIEW

To truly learn how to build business applications, you need to work on a database project. The projects described in this appendix are generally simpler than real-life projects but complex enough to illustrate common problems that you will encounter.

The projects are designed to be built throughout the term. Students should demonstrate a completed database application at the end of the term. Preliminary questions or assignments are given for each project to get you started. However, the most important aspect of the case is to build the final, complete application. To provide additional feedback, the instructor should also evaluate the projects at two intermediate stages: (1) the list of normalized tables and (2) some initial forms and reports.

The most important advice to the students is that you must begin work on the project as soon as possible. Do not put the project off until the end of the semester. To have any chance at completing the project, most students will have to put in 20 to 40 hours of time. The project will reinforce the concepts discussed in the chapters—particularly data normalization and application design. If you work on the project throughout the semester, you will gain a better understanding of the topics and you will finish most of the project before the end-of-term crunch.

Class projects are slightly different from real-world applications, but they have many features in common. One of the most challenging aspects is that any project contains a level of uncertainty and ambiguity. When you start a real-life project, you never know exactly what the project is going to involve. As you talk with users, you encounter contradictions, uncertainty, and confusion over terms and goals. In real-life, you resolve these problems through experience and discussions with managers. With class projects, you do not have direct access to the managers and users. The instructor can answer some questions, but students will need to make their own decisions and interpretations.

When you first read the case, try to focus on the big picture. Identify the environment, goals, and objectives of the proposed system. You should take notes on the company and jot down additional questions. Additional research of the industry and similar firms will help identify terms, goals, and potential problems. When you begin to analyze the individual forms and reports, you need to identify the overall purpose of each form. The Nevasca case is particularly challenging in this respect. You should be able to describe the purpose of each form in one sentence. Avoid using the form's title—describe its purpose in your own words. For any of the cases, you should make this list and keep it handy so you always remember the overall purpose of the application.

Remember that you will probably have to rework the normalization several times before the project is complete. Remember that every time you change the primary keys, you first have to delete relationships. Try to develop a good normalized list before you begin creating forms and reports, but leave yourself enough time to go back and change the tables if you find problems.

In many cases it pays to start small and add tables and features slowly. Start with an initial set of tables and keys that you are certain are correct. Then begin building forms. Add columns and tables as you need them. If your initial tables are correct, you should be able to add new columns and tables without altering the existing design. For the final project, it is usually better to complete half a project where everything works, instead of a large mess where nothing works.

One final word of advice: backup. Always keep a backup copy of your project on a different disk. Two or three copies are even better. Disks are cheap.

Nevasca Production

Nevasca Production manufactures basic appliances. It started 30 years ago with refrigerators and gradually expanded into other kitchen appliances. Today the company sells more than 200 different products and 20 models of refrigerators. It generates revenue of $800,000,000 with profits last year of $15,000,000. The firm has assets of about $750,000,000 and almost 5,000 employees. Most of the employees are lower-level manufacturing workers paid hourly wages.

In the last few years sales have been slipping. Competition has increased, and discounters like Circuit City have pressured manufacturers for large discounts. Earnings per share last year were about $1.50, which was a 25 percent drop from the prior year.

Some high-priced consultants have suggested that Nevasca could improve its sales by expanding its marketing efforts in two areas. First, it needs to create innovative products and make continual improvements to existing products—particularly in the form of new features. Second, the company needs to expand its promotional campaigns to improve its brand image. The ultimate goal is to identify target groups, find out what features they want, create products targeted for that niche, and use advertising to convince people to ask for Nevasca products by name.

You have been hired to design and build a system that will enable the company to monitor and evaluate various marketing promotions. The company managers are a little uncertain about exactly what they want the system to do. A member of your team has interviewed employees of the company and identified several areas that could benefit from a database system.

ADVERTISING MEDIA

The consensus is that managers need better access to information about various promotional options and the different advertising media. Upper management is a little naive about viewer/reader characteristics and target marketing. Several basic types of advertising channels are available: direct mail, telephone solicitation, newspaper and magazine, radio, and television. Each category has many options. The company can choose among hundreds of newspapers, magazines, and radio or television stations. Radio and television stations have additional options in terms of time of day and program content. Each option tends to cater to a different category of viewer or reader. Each media type also has a different reach—some are national, some are regional, and some are strictly local.

Most publishers provide basic readership statistics. These statistics often fill many pages. Various organizations audit the numbers and verify their accuracy. However, the main listings are detailed and not really needed by general management. Instead, management wants to track some of the primary categories for the main advertisers.

Along with the basic readership data, managers also want an estimate of how much it might cost to run an advertisement. There are two types of costs: the cost to develop the advertisement and the display cost to run the ad. For example, designing a newspaper ad requires the skills of an artist, photographer, and a writer. Then the company must pay the newspaper or magazine to run the ad.

FIGURE 1

PROMOTION OPTION SUMMARY

Prepared by: Name, Title, Date
Basic option (Newspaper, Direct mail, Phone, Radio, Television, Other)
Title
Publisher
Contact Title Phone
Publication frequency
Region

Development/Production

Fixed cost	
Variable cost	Unit of measure
Average time to develop	
Management time	Management costs

Modification

Size	Time	Cost
major	fast	...
major	slow	...
...		
minor	fast	...
minor	slow	...

Display

Fixed Cost	Marginal	Unit	Cost per Viewer	Cost per Target

Audience

Age	Number	Pct	Income	#	Pct	Special	#	Pct
<13			<10K			Sports		
13–18			10–20K			Animals		
18–25			20–30K			Family		
...			...			...		

Both costs tend to have fixed and variable components. In development the fixed costs generally outweigh the variable costs. However, as a campaign becomes larger, the costs increase—for instance, a 1-minute video spot costs more than a 20-second spot. On the other hand, variable costs predominate in the display costs. The more often you run the spot, the longer the ad, or the larger the display, the more the company will have to pay. Figure 1 lists some of the basic data that the company wants to collect for the primary advertising option. The new marketing manager currently has data on about 500 options. However, the manager is hoping to obtain more detailed breakdowns (e.g., by television show) in the next year or so, eventually leading to about 2,000 entries.

NEW PRODUCT PROPOSAL

All employees in the company are encouraged to submit ideas for new products. In practice, most of the ideas are submitted by the engineers and salespeople. Sometimes a line worker will bring an idea to an engineer. Most of these suggestions are minor changes in the existing products—often to improve the manufacturing processes. Ideas from customers are submitted by the salespeople. These suggestions are usually new features or slight redesigns that might be appealing to customers. Occasionally, there are ideas for entirely new products.

When an item is first proposed, anyone involved with the new product (engineers, marketers, mangers, etc.) can add to the basic description. Everyone also contributes to a list of potential benefits and features. Marketing also researches competitors to see whether they are offering any of the proposed features. In a good year Nevasca employees and customers generate about 1,000 new product ideas. Most of them never get produced—some are incorporated into other ideas. The firm produces maybe 30 new products a year. Existing products are redesigned on a regular basis—usually twice a year. The products generally receive three to five new features each time.

Product ideas often involve options. Like automobiles, appliances are built from a few basic patterns. Then different features or options are added. The more features—the higher the price. For a while the company thought about manufacturing products to custom specifications. Customers would fill out a sheet at the retail store to choose a size and indicate exactly which options should be added. After a short investigation the company decided that it would be too expensive to collect this data, build the thousands of different products, and get the appliances to the proper destination. Instead, the marketing team picks a combination of features and offers them as a "package" on a new model. In designing a new product, the marketing team likes to list all of the possible options along with approximate costs and the price it thinks the company can charge for each option. The options are then rated in terms of importance. For example, an ice maker is more important on a refrigerator than having a wide range of colors.

Once the basic product has been outlined, an engineer coordinates with purchasing to identify the basic components needed to produce the appliance. The team locates potential suppliers and estimates the cost of the various components. Some specialized components have to be manufactured, and it will take time for the supplier to build or modify the facilities to create the custom pieces. This order lead time is important for planning purposes. When all the necessary component and supplier data is collected, the engineering department produces a more accurate estimate of the production cost. Engineers also examine current production schedules to determine how long it will take to make modifications and begin production of the new product. Factoring in distribution and marketing delays yields the estimated time before the product will hit the market.

All other departments work backward from estimated market date to determine their schedules. For example, marketing managers devises a sales promotion to coincide with the release date. They also schedule training for the sales force. Finance takes the design, marketing, and production schedule estimates to determine cash flow needs. Accounting modifies the record system so that shipments can be tracked and costs are properly attributed to the new product line.

Figure 2 shows a sample form that the company wants to use to collect and display the basic data on new products. Additional information such as blueprints and supplier contracts will be maintained in paper files. This summary sheet is designed for quick reference and communication with management.

PROMOTION DEVELOPMENT

Once management has given permission to produce the product, the marketing department begins developing a promotional campaign. New campaigns are also developed for existing products.

Following the advice of the consultants, each campaign is targeted to a specific market segment of consumers. However, because many different types of people buy the products, each promotion can be aimed at multiple targets. Once the basic consumer profile is established, the type of media (newspaper, radio, etc.) is chosen. The various media choices are examined for their target reach and the costs. One of the first things the marketing department produces is a list of the suggested media, the

FIGURE 2

NEW PRODUCT PROPOSAL
Suggested Name

Employee	Date	Estimated retail price

Product category ____________________
☐ New product
☐ Modification of existing product. (Product ID__________)
Description
Dimensions Height_____ Width_____ Depth_____ Weight_____
Target market(s)

Options

Description	Importance	Estimated Cost	Estimated Price
...	...	...	...

Components

Source	Estimated Cost	Order Lead Time
...	...	...

Key Feature/Benefit List	Competition List

Estimated production time
Estimated production cost
Estimated time to hit market

Contact List

	Name	Phone	Office
Lead engineer			
Lead marketer			
Lead finance			

target audience, and a brief description of the goals for each promotion. For example, the company might choose ads in *USA Today* to reach educated, young adults across the nation. The goal might be to sell a certain quantity of small refrigerators—suitable for small apartments.

Development of the promotion takes time. For each suggested ad, the marketing managers estimate the development schedule in stages. Each stage has estimated costs, and a marketing employee is placed in charge of monitoring the production schedule, ad development, and costs. Each stage can produce different outputs. For example, a video production might be broken into stages for (1) developing ideas, (2) negotiating contracts, (3) developing storyboards and initial plans, (4) shooting, (5) editing and revising, and (6) producing the master. Each stage would have different outputs. For example, the initial stage would produce sketches, ideas, and tentative schedules. Some items are developed in-house; others are contracted to outside companies. The most important step is to track the schedule—in terms of estimated dates, deadlines, and actual delivery dates. An initial tracking form/report is shown in Figure 3.

Development of the promotion produces many items such as storyboards, preprints, and video tapes. Figure 3 lists only the basic schedule data. Nevasca needs to track considerably more information on the individual items. One of the biggest problems is that many people are working on the promotional campaign. Any of these people might be using a particular item, and other workers need to know who has each item. Because much of the work is performed by outside contractors, the company also needs to worry about tracking shipments of the items. Most shipping

FIGURE 3

PROMOTION DEVELOPMENT

Prepared by			**Date/time**
Estimated run date	**Start/end**		
Estimated budget			

Goals

Media Type	Target Audience	Suggested Media	Goals
Newspaper	Young Adult	USA Today	
	Investors	WSJ	

Production Schedule	***Outputs***				
Start End Category/Stage Description Employee in charge Estimated costs	Item	Description	Employee	Department	Estimated Date ... ...
Start End Category/Stage Description Employee in charge Estimated costs	Item	Description	Employee	Department	Estimated Date ... ...

companies provide tracking numbers and enable workers to track each package using an Internet connection. The catch is that it is hard to know who shipped each item and when it is supposed to arrive.

Team members also need to identify changes to each item so they can monitor the progress and avoid duplicating the work. Managers also want to track which employee (or contractor) made the revisions.

At some point in the future, it might be nice to convert each item to digital form and store it in the database. However, the company and its contractors do not yet have the hardware and software to handle advanced digital audio and video formats. Figure 4 presents the basic format of the information Nevasca needs to track the status of changes and the location of the various items developed for marketing promotions.

PROMOTION CAMPAIGN

After the marketing items have been developed, Nevasca contracts with various publishers to run the ads. Each contract specifies the number of times the ad is displayed, the size or length of the ad, and the basic charges. Costs are generally based on a per viewing schedule; however, some publishers charge fixed up-front costs as well.

Schedule changes and errors often arise in publishing and advertising. Hence the marketing department assigns someone to verify each ad. (College interns often perform this task.) Print ads are relatively straightforward, but errors sometimes arise from printing the ad on the wrong page, the wrong size, or from printing errors that make portions of the ad illegible. Radio and video ads are much more sensitive. Sometimes a station does not run an ad; sometimes it runs at the wrong time. Other

FIGURE 4

ITEM DEVELOPMENT

ItemID **Description**
Format/media
Primary responsibility (employee) **Telephone**

Size

Print	***Audio***	***Video***
Width	**Length**	**Length**
Height	**Format**	**Format**
Number of colors	☐ **Tape**	☐ **US/broadcast**
	☐ **CD**	☐ **PAL**
	☐ **Digital**	☐ **SECAM**

Revisions

Date/Time	**Version**	**Person**	**Firm**	**Description of Changes**
...				
...				

Location

Checkout Date/Time	**Person**	**Shipping**	**TrackingID**	**Reason**	**Check-in Date/Time**
...					
...					

times an ad might be surrounded by a negative image. For instance, imagine the problems created if an ad for refrigerators runs immediately after a news segment on landfill problems. It's hard to sell appliances when the last image the viewer sees is a grunge shot of old rusting refrigerators in a landfill. All of these problems are cause for rebates and compensation by the publisher. Often the compensation takes the form of additional free ads run at new times.

The catch is that the advertiser usually has to report the problem to the publisher within a certain time frame. With hundreds of products and ads running in different locations, keeping track of the problems and verifying all the placements can be a challenge. Figure 5 illustrates a basic report that marketing managers use to record various problems. The student employees who verify the ads might use a simpler version of the form.

FIGURE 5

PROMOTIONAL CAMPAIGN

Media type
Title **Publisher**
Advertising manager **Phone** **Fax** **Account#**
Their contract number for this campaign
Campaign authorized by

Start date/time **End date/time** **Number of ads**
Fixed cost
Additional cost per ad
Estimated total cost
Estimated total viewers

Rebates

Date/Time	**Reason**	**Estimated value**	**Description**	**Contact**
...				

Verification

Date/Time	**Employee**	**Lead in**	**Trailer**	**Comments**
...				

FIGURE 6

PROMOTION COSTS

Promotional campaign
Product
VP in charge
Supplier   Accounting contact   Phone   E-mail
Category (Development, Management, Advertising, Royalties, ...)

Supplier invoice number   Date received

Items

ItemID	Category	Description	Units	Cost/Unit	Cost	Discount	Net
...							

Category: Development, Management, Advertising, Royalties, ...

PaymentID   Total payment amount
Received by (may be blank)   Total disputed amount

Method of Payment

EDI	*Check*
Our bank	Bank
Our account	Account
Supplier bank	Check#
Supplier account	Amount
Date/time	Authorized/signed by
Amount	Date Date cleared
Authorized by	Mail method

Itemized Payments

Item	Description	Billed Amount	Amount Paid	Disputed Amount
...				

Of course, advertising campaigns carry costs that must be paid. The accounting department controls funds by requiring all suppliers to send invoices. Basic supplier information must already be on file with the accounting department before any money is transferred. Additionally, individual items are randomly verified by internal auditors to make sure that suppliers provide the items listed in the invoices.

Nevasca has had problems with some suppliers in the past. Some listed items are not received, or a shipment might contain fewer items than the quantity listed. In these cases Nevasca wants to pay only for the items received. In a few other instances, there have been disagreements over the price. Nevasca purchasing agents claim one price was set, whereas the supplier insists on a higher price. In these cases the accounting department pays the smaller amount but sets aside the disputed amount until the actual payment can be negotiated with the vendor. Figure 6 presents an itemized payment report that illustrates these issues.

The method of payment depends on the arrangements with the vendor. To save money, Nevasca prefers to use electronic data interchange (EDI) transfers directly between the banks. Each transaction is recorded in case the supplier complains. Nevasca still has to write checks for vendors that cannot handle EDI transfers. In this case it is hard to verify that the supplier received the check. The best we can do is record when and how the check was mailed and then record when the check was cleared by the bank. In major disputes a copy of the cleared check can be obtained from the bank.

SALES TRACKING AND PROMOTION EFFECTIVENESS

The entire purpose of a promotional campaign is to improve sales. During each promotional campaign Nevasca looks at sales in the various regions. Data is collected from sales scanners, sales calls to retailers, survey calls to customers and potential customers, and purchased data from market analysis firms.

By running different types of promotions in different regions, the marketing staff can determine the effectiveness of the various campaigns by comparing sales in the regions. Small promotions can be used to check the effect on the target market. After the strategy is fine-tuned, it can be used for nationwide promotions.

Marketing managers use the summary sales report in Figure 7 to gauge the effectiveness of the promotion campaigns. However, the marketing department would also like a spreadsheet that can perform statistical analyses on the data to compare the effectiveness of the various promotions. The department would also like graphs to compare the original projections against the survey data for the target markets.

As much as possible, sales data is tracked by individual stores. However, it is rarely possible to track target audience purchases at the store level. In surveys customers rarely remember exactly where they shopped. Instead, stores are grouped into regions, and target audience data is collected from regional surveys. Sales data is also aggregated into regions because promotions generally affect several stores in a region. The regions are defined by the top management group. Currently, there are 20 regions, and sales are tracked for almost 1,000 stores. However, the individual stores and regions change—as stores go in and out of business.

FIGURE 7

SALES SURVEY

Time period (day, month, quarter, year)
Method (scanner data, salesperson, phone survey, service firm)
Start date End date

Sales

Store / Location	Item	Dept	Category	QtySold	Revenue
Store **Location**	...	...	...	...	...
Classification (upscale, typical, small)	...	...	...	...	...
Store manager...	...	...	...	...	...
Region **Regional manager** **Address** **Phone, Fax, Pager**					
{next store}					

Target Audience Purchases

Age	Saw Ad	Bought	Income	Saw Ad	Bought	Special	Saw Ad	Bought
<13			<10K			Sports		
13–18			10–20K			Animals		
18–25			20–30K			Family		
...			...			...		

PROJECT HINTS

The main assignment is to create a database application that helps Nevasca monitor and evaluate its marketing promotions. The basic steps to building the application follow the textbook. First, you identify the user needs and collect documents. Then you create normalized data tables. Next, you build input forms and reports. Finally, you tie all the forms and reports together to make a completed application.

Of course, no project is that simple. Every project has some ambiguity: You do not have exact definitions of each concept; users can have conflicting opinions; and you need to plan for the future, but no one seems to know what will happen tomorrow. These issues always present problems because finding an "expert" to answer your questions can be difficult. As much as possible, try to find realistic answers—study a marketing textbook, share ideas with your classmates, beg a marketing professor for insight. When in doubt, improvise—but be ready to change the design later.

Understand that this case can become quite complicated. Even an experienced developer might require 40 to 50 hours to build a relatively complete application. Get started early.

Do not let the size of the project intimidate you. Use the spiral (or evolutionary prototype) model of software development. (See McConnell: *Rapid Development.)* First, be absolutely certain that the data tables are normalized. Then build a few forms; keep them small and make sure they store and retrieve data correctly. Next, improve the forms—think about the user tasks, make the forms easier to use, and add some code to automate basic steps. Find some users (perhaps some marketing students) to work with the forms and get some feedback. Then improve the forms. Now go back and build new forms and reports.

Be sure to design a solid framework or organization to hold the forms and reports. Avoid creating 150 forms and reports and tying them together with a basic menu. Instead, think about individual tasks and build a set of integrated forms and reports to make that task easy to perform.

EXERCISES

1. Create a list of all of the forms and reports that Nevasca might use.
2. Create a normalized list of tables for each form and report.
3. Create an integrated list of normalized tables for the entire application. Draw the corresponding class diagram.
4. Create the basic tables in a DBMS (e.g., Access), along with all necessary relationships and integrity constraints. Enter a few rows of sample data into the tables to test your design.
5. Create a process (or collaboration) diagram of the main processes. Identify important events that need database triggers.
6. Evaluate the normalized tables and estimate the size of the database—both current size and estimated size in 3 years.
7. List the initial security conditions for the data tables. Create a list of user groups and identify their basic access needs.
8. Design the overall structure of the application. Outline the overall structure and the primary forms. Select a design scheme, including layouts, effects, and colors.

9. Build three initial input forms.
10. Build three initial reports.
11. Improve the forms and reports to make them easier to use.
12. Test your forms and reports with sample users.
13. Build additional forms and reports. Improve all of them. Test all of them.
14. Connect all the forms and reports into an application. Test all the links. Test the forms and reports. Check for consistency.
15. Add security, backup and recovery, and other management features to the application.
16. Move the data tables to a centralized server, leaving the application to run on a client. Build the necessary links and retest the application.
17. Move the entire application to a Web server. Build the forms so that they run on a Web browser.
18. Create a spreadsheet to perform additional data analysis. Link the data so that the spreadsheet is updated automatically.
19. Write code to generate a report into a word processor document.

Hungry Waters Golf Club

Hungry Waters is a mid-priced private golf club. In addition to golf, the club offers members a swimming pool, tennis courts, and a full-service dining room. A pro shop carries typical golf articles (clubs, balls, and so on). It also carries a limited selection of clothing. Many of the items carry the club logo—and are not available elsewhere.

The golf course is the primary reason members join. It is a modern, challenging layout. With strategically placed traps and many water hazards, weaker golfers tend to avoid the course. Consequently, the members are mostly better golfers, and they take pride in the course. To keep the course in good shape and to ensure that members can play when they want, the club restricts the number of members and tries hard to keep tee times available. Figure 1 shows the basic scorecard and course ratings.

Currently, Hungry Waters does not make much use of computers. The accountants have a basic accounting package that prints standard accounting reports. It also handles basic payroll and tax functions. After considerable discussion, the club has decided to hire you to help automate some additional tasks. Members are somewhat concerned about the price, so they would like an initial estimate of the costs and possible benefits after you examine the basic ideas.

Several members have also raised the idea of using the Internet to make it easier for members to communicate with the club. For example, one of the most important tasks that needs to be automated is handling tee times (reservations). Several members have indicated that they would like to be able to check the club's Web page for openings and book their own reservations.

TEE TIME RESERVATIONS

To minimize crowding, the club sends out foursomes at intervals of 7 or 8 minutes. A shorter interval would cram too many people on the course at one time. Reservations are taken over the phone (or in person), and they are entered onto a daily reservation sheet. For busy days golfers sometimes spend 10 to 15 minutes talking with the reservation clerk to find an open time slot that they want. The process becomes even more painful when someone cancels a reservation. Because reserva-

Course Layout

	1	2	3	4	5	6	7	8	9	10	11	12	13	14	15	16	17	18	
Par	4	4	5	3	4	3	5	4	4	5	4	4	3	4	5	3	4	4	72
Tee/yards																			
Blue	424	436	582	198	417	210	537	403	418	567	398	435	215	402	524	185	416	436	7203
White	401	427	558	189	405	203	525	389	412	543	378	418	192	378	510	159	403	422	6912
Red	357	387	510	146	357	167	510	327	356	498	327	338	170	323	451	127	339	363	6053

FIGURE 1

Course Ratings			
		Rating	Slope
Blue	Men	73.6	121.8
	Women	80.1	133.3
White	Men	72.3	117.1
	Women	78.5	129.9
Red	Men	68.4	103.2
	Women	73.7	117.7

Note: Rating names and formulas are owned and controlled by the USGA.

tions can be made a week in advance, many people need to alter their reservations. By the end of the week, the daily reservation sheet is full of cross-outs, corrections, and side notes. Once in a while the process is so messy that a clerk accidentally schedules two foursomes for the same time slot. Some of the members get really mad when that happens. Last year two clerks were fired for making too many of these mistakes. With about 80 reservations per day and 7 days of reservation sheets open at once, it can take a while to find the proper location and record the basic data. A full-time clerk is employed to handle the reservations. On busy days the pro shop employees often help answer the phone, find open slots, and take requests. Of course, it is confusing and error prone to have three people work on the same reservation sheet at the same time.

Complicating the process even further, some of the members can make standing tee times. Members who have been in the club long enough and who pay extra fees, as well as some influential members, can obtain a level 5 membership. At this level they can make one standing tee time that is automatically entered each week. Many rules govern this privilege, but for now you only have to keep track of the reservations requested. Members with this privilege fill out a card indicating approximately when they want their tee time. The rules committee assigns a priority to each of these tee times in case of conflicts. Lower values get first choice. Figure 2 illustrates the basic card for standing reservations.

FIGURE 2

Standing reservations by level 5 members

Day of week **Time (±30 min.)**
Start date **End date**
Approved by __(manager)__________
Priority number__________

Foursome is required. Primary (level 5) member listed first.
Member ID __________ **Name** __________
Member ID __________ **Name** __________
Member ID __________ **Name** __________
Member ID __________ **Name** __________

FIGURE 3

Daily reservations

Date ____________ **Day of week** ____________
Weather
Events
Course conditions

Time	Member	#Players	#Carts	Callback phone	Member priority	Date/Time/Employee
6:00 AM 6:07 6:15 6:22						
6:30 AM 6:37 6:45 6:52						
7:00 AM 7:07 7:15 7:22						

All members in good standing are allowed to reserve tee times. However, tee times can be reserved no more than 1 week in advance. Also, special events such as tournaments sometimes restrict the number of slots available. Each day someone creates a new reservation sheet for the day 1 week in advance. Figure 3 shows a portion of a sample sheet. The employee fills in any special events and crosses off the appropriate tee times. The employee then goes through the card file of standing reservations and copies the appropriate data to the daily reservation sheet.

When each reservation is made, the employee taking the reservations enters the appropriate data and records the date and time the reservation was made. Not all members are equal. If all slots are filled within a certain hour, members with higher priority levels are asked whether they want to bump a lower priority member. To prevent abuses, members are not allowed to bump reservations more than twice a month. If someone is bumped, the employee taking the new reservations calls back the first member and asks whether the person wants to reschedule. The rules committee has talked about creating a new rule that no member can be bumped more than once a year. However, committee members have not figured out how to implement the rule because they are concerned that it would take the employees too long to find the data and make the correct decision.

SCORE TRACKING AND HANDICAPS

On completing a round, players record their score. Every week the scores are sent to an outside company that uses a computer routine to compute the player's handicap based on the USGA system. The resulting printout is made available to the members so that they can accurately identify everyone's handicap. Because of the costs and delays, the club would like to incorporate handicap generation within the new system. Entering scores is relatively straightforward. If members play a different course, they can incorporate that score into their handicap—however, they have to know the course rating. The course rating depends on the tees—longer tees receive higher ratings. At a minimum the club wants to store the member's scores and their handicap data. Since handicaps change over time, the club wants to keep the current value and the value at the end of each month for each player and the rounds within the current year (but always keep the last 20 rounds when you delete a prior year's data). Figure 4 shows the basic form that members fill in to record their scores. The figure also shows the standard form of the handicap report.

The club leaders have talked about saving money by computing the handicaps in-house, but the cost of creating and maintaining the handicap software seems prohibitive. If you are interested, the procedures are available from the USGA at http://www.usga.org. You should read the procedures for two reasons. First, you should provide an estimate of the costs of incorporating the handicap computation into your system. Second, you need to be aware of the rules and procedures for dealing with handicaps—particularly the posting of scores and restrictions on the use of the handicap system and submission of data. A member of the club's handicap committee noted that as of 1998, the USGA does not seem to understand the use and value of the Internet as a communication system.

CHEMICAL APPLICATIONS

Golf courses require careful maintenance. Members expect the course to be in top shape at all times. Greenskeeping requires large amounts of chemicals—fertilizers, herbicides, and pesticides. Various state and federal regulations must be followed in terms of applying chemicals, following safety procedures, and notifying employees and customers. For example, employees must be notified of the location of all hazardous chemicals and hazardous material data sheets that list the chemicals, potential hazards, safety precautions, and how to treat injuries must be available. Additionally, all employees who apply the chemicals must take educational courses and hold a chemical license issued by the state. Figure 5 shows the basic form used to track the training classes and licenses or certifications of each of the employees. This

FIGURE 4

Score Recording

			Hole-by-Hole Score																	
Member Course/Rating/Slope	Date/Time Tournament?	Score	1	2	3	4	5	6	7	8	9	10	11	12	13	14	15	16	17	18

Member USGA Handicaps

Date

Name	Handicap	Average	Best 10 Average	Last 20 Rounds																			

FIGURE 5

Employee Chemical Certifications

Name
Job title
Home phone
Address
City, State, ZIP
Date of birth Gender

Date	Education Course	Provider	Grade	Cost

Date	License# and type	Chemicals or Actions Covered

data is used to fill out standard reports to the various agencies, including annual license reports and incident reports when there is a spill or accident.

Customers and members need to be notified about which chemicals have been applied each day. The pro shop maintains a board behind the counter at the sign-in station. Each day the lead greenskeeper writes down the basic chemicals that were applied that day. Some of the members who are sensitive to certain chemicals have suggested that a schedule be made available ahead of time so that they will know which chemicals are going to be applied when they make their reservations. The greenskeepers are fighting this proposal because they say that it is hard to know precisely when a chemical will be applied. Some chemicals need the right weather, some pests appear randomly and require immediate treatment, and sometimes chemicals need to be applied more than once. Various governmental agencies also have to be notified about the type and location of the chemicals stored on site. Figure 6 shows

FIGURE 6

Chemical Application

Date Time Employee Certification level

Chemical brand name Manufacturer ProductID

Category *(fertilizer, herbicide, pesticide, multipurpose)*
Application method *(spray, spread, hand, pellet, other)*

LotID	Size	Amount Used	Disposal Method	Storage Location

Location Applied	Reason	Amount	Runoff Controls

the basic form that is currently used by the greenskeepers to track the use and location of the various chemicals.

MEMBERS

All potential members must be sponsored by an existing member. An existing member can sponsor no more than four potential members a year, and someone must be a member for 2 years before he or she can sponsor a new member. As indicated on Figure 7, members must submit basic credit references. Applications are considered by the membership committee, which meets once a month. The basic decisions are to accept the member, deny membership, request additional information, or defer the membership until an opening arises. The club wants to limit the number of members so that the course does not become congested. Memberships are occasionally offered to some businesses. But this type of membership is rarely used anymore—except when the club needs money or wants assistance from a specific firm.

The applicant has the option of purchasing a single or family membership. Even with the single membership, the spouse and children can use most of the facilities of the club (pool, dining room, pro shop, etc.); however, only the original applicant has access to the golf course. The main member does have the right to bring guests occasionally, but there are limits on the number of guests and on how often a guest can return. For example, a member cannot bring a spouse as a guest every day.

Members make several payments to the club. First, there is an initial one-time fee to join the club. Some of this money can be returned if a member moves and a new

FIGURE 7

Membership Application

Application Data	Fees
Application date Sponsored by Decision	Type (single, spouse, family, business) Application fee Membership purchase

Personal	Children		
Name Date of birth Spouse Address City, State, ZIP Home phone Job title Employer Work phone	Name	Date of Birth	Gender

Credit References

Name	Account
Type (bank, credit card, broker, ...) Address, City, ZIP Phone Contact	

member is brought in. There is also an annual membership fee, which is used to cover operating expenses. This fee can change each year, and the fees committee sets it. Members have an option to pay the fee at the start of the year or to pay in monthly installments. The monthly installment payments are slightly higher—the number is determined by adding a 5 percent surcharge to the fee and then dividing by 12.

To ensure profitability of the dining room, members are also required to spend a minimum amount of money each month in the clubhouse—either in the dining room or the bar. Management keeps a running tab of each member's expenditures, and they are billed at the end of the month. Members are always billed at least the minimum amount. Some members have suggested that they should be allowed to carry over higher totals from prior months, that is, to use an average expenditure instead of a fixed minimum each month. Members argue that they often take monthlong vacations and cannot spend the minimum during those months. The clubhouse management committee is resisting the idea because it would be too hard to track the data and the process is too complicated. Employees are also worried that they might be fired if they make a mistake with this more complicated system.

Members can also charge costs from the pro shop. Common items include merchandise, golf lessons, and greens fees for guests. Currently, the pro shop has a small computer that runs an off-the-shelf retail sales program. The clerk enters the product ID number into the computer, and the computerized cash register looks up the price, computes taxes and totals, and prints a receipt. The system works well, but because it is a proprietary system, it cannot be integrated into any other systems that you might create.

Currently, the accounting staff handles all of the billing and payments. Most of the data collection is done by hand. The members sign a credit slip or bill. The next day all of the credit data is entered into their account. The accounting staff keeps an electronic spreadsheet for each member and enters the total and the location of each bill. Payments are similarly recorded. The spreadsheet is printed and mailed to the member at the end of each month. Total costs and payments for all members are computed and entered into the club's basic accounting package.

YOUR MISSION

You need to create a database application to solve at least some of the issues raised by the Hungry Waters Golf Club. You should first put together a proposal that spells out (1) what the application will do, (2) what problems it will solve, (3) what the benefits will be, and (4) how much it will cost and how long it will take you to create the application. You do not necessarily have to include every project in the initial application. However, you should indicate how the additional pieces could be added later. When you receive approval for the project, you will then create the application.

EXERCISES

1. Create the feasibility study (initial proposal).
2. Create a list of all of the forms and reports that the club might use.
3. Create a normalized list of tables for each form and report.
4. Create an integrated list of normalized tables for the entire application. Draw the corresponding class diagram.

5. Create the basic tables in a DBMS (e.g., Access), along with all necessary relationships and integrity constraints. Enter sample data into the tables to test your design.
6. Create a process (or collaboration) diagram of the main processes. Identify important events that need database triggers.
7. Evaluate the normalized tables and estimate the size of the database—both current size and estimated size in 3 years.
8. List the initial security conditions for the data tables. Create a list of user groups and identify their basic access needs.
9. Design the overall structure of the application. Outline the overall structure and the primary forms. Select a design scheme, including layouts, effects, and colors.
10. Build three initial input forms.
11. Build three initial reports.
12. Improve the forms and reports to make them easier to use.
13. Test your forms and reports with sample users.
14. Build additional forms and reports. Improve all of them. Test all of them.
15. Connect all of the forms and reports into an application. Test all the links. Test the forms and reports. Check for consistency.
16. Add security, backup and recovery, and other management features to the application.
17. Move the data tables to a centralized server, leaving the application to run on a client. Build the necessary links and retest the application.
18. Move the entire application to a Web server. Build the forms so that they run on a Web browser.
19. Create a spreadsheet to perform additional data analysis. Link the data so that the spreadsheet is updated automatically.
20. Write code to generate a report into a word processor document.

Hungry Waters Golf Course Pro Shop

The pro shop at Hungry Waters golf course is an important source of revenue for the club. Members are encouraged to make all of their golf purchases at the club. The pro shop is somewhat independent from the rest of the club. It has its own manager and makes its own decisions about products and prices. Based on member preferences, the pro shop focuses on top-quality merchandise—in both golf products and clothing. There are several discount stores in the city, so the pro shop tries to keep prices down.

The club's golf professional receives a portion of the profits from the sales in the pro shop. He also receives a salary and all of the money from lessons. Any profits remaining are returned to the club. The money is generally used to make improvements in the shop and clubhouse. A few years ago the pro (whose tenure is usually a few years) was completely in charge of the pro shop. He would pay a "lease" fee to the club, but then he could order any products and keep all profits. Several problems arose, including complaints about prices, lease payments not being made by the pro due to "losses," and general mismanagement. The problem seemed to be lack of management experience by the pros. Consequently, the club members (mostly businesspeople) have taken a stronger role in the management of the pro shop.

SALES SYSTEM

To make it easier to track inventory, simplify checkout, and impose financial controls, the club purchased an off-the-shelf retail sales system. It runs on a single personal computer that serves as an automated cash register. The clerk basically enters the product ID number into the computer and the computerized cash register looks up the price, computes taxes and totals, and prints a receipt. The system works well, but this proprietary system cannot be integrated into any other systems that you might create. The basic screen appears in Figure 1.

One important limitation of the existing system is that it prints receipts only at the time of the sale. It does not keep sale information for each member. This limitation is important because members usually charge purchases to their account. Members would like to get a complete printout of their purchases at the end of the month when they are billed. Currently, accounting clerks take the total values and write them in a ledger the next day. Members get a list with total values—not the items. Figure 2 illustrates the type of report that the club would like to be able to generate.

The monthly bill includes items from the pro shop as well as from other areas of the club, for example, dining charges and guest fees. The Category column lists the source of the charge. At some point the club wants to put a computer terminal in the dining area so that charges can be entered immediately. For the moment the plan is to continue with the cash register and paper bills—in part to collect the member signatures. Member charges will be entered into the system the next day.

FIGURE 1

Hungry Waters Pro Shop Sales

Date/time **Clerk**
Member name

Item	Description	Price	Quantity	Extended

Subtotal
Tax
Total

PAYMENTS Members are required to pay their entire monthly bill on time. If they do not, an interest charge is imposed on the unpaid balance. If members let a balance accumulate for two or more months, the payments committee starts an investigation. Depending on the circumstances, the committee can allow the debt to continue, forgive the debt (e.g., health problems), or even expel the member.

When payments are received, the accounting department cashes the checks and records the payment on its computer. The existing stand-alone system is designed for simple accounting reports and only tracks total payments. One of the features the department wants to add is the ability to record disputes over costs. For example, a member might occasionally challenge a charge for a certain item. In these situations the department wants to mark each disputed charge so that it will not be included in the past-due totals. The department also wants to print out lists of disputed charges—by time frame (e.g., month), by member, and by area or department.

FIGURE 2

Member name **Statement date**
Address **Account#**
City, State, ZIP
Previous balance
Amount paid
Balance past due
New charges **Interest charge**

Total due **Date due**

Date/Time	Item	Category	Description	Price	Quantity	Value

page# **Total**

FIGURE 3

Payments in Dispute			5-30-1998
Month	Newly Disputed	Old Disputes Collected	Old Discharged
January	$ 521.52	$ 637.18	157.34
February	215.79	172.32	59.17
March	1154.82	118.94	132.57
April	837.15	735.18	318.92
May	315.92	453.12	315.78
Total	3045.20	2116.74	983.78

Total disputed payments as of 1-1-1998	$978.15
Total disputed payments as of 5-30-1998	922.83
Net change	$-55.32

FIGURE 4

Member Payments in Dispute			5-30-1998
Member	Start of Month	Change	End of Month
1713 Jones	$ 289.32	$ 75.15	$364.47
2783 Guerra	357.18	−117.32	239.86
1152 Branigan	0.00	192.13	192.13
...			
1739 Smith	279.15	−279.15	0.00
Total	$1375.81	$ −452.98	$922.83

FIGURE 5

Payment Disputes by Area			5-30-1998	
Area	End of Month	Start of Month	Change	Pct
Pro shop–clothes	$217.84	$ 352.19	$-134.35	−38.1
Pro shop–golf eqp.	119.57	253.28	−133.71	−52.8
Dining room	198.73	312.87	−114.14	−36.5
Bar	278.13	412.34	−134.21	−32.5
...				
Other	17.34	68.15	−50.81	−74.6
Total	$922.83	$ 1375.81	$ −452.98	−32.9

Figures 3 through 5 provide sample reports that the accounting team wants. These reports are generally printed each month. The third report (Payment Disputes by Area) needs to be created as a form. The accounting manager wants to be able to sort the data on any column. Printing is optional, but the depart-

FIGURE 6

Order #	Purchase Order Hungry Waters Golf Course	Date issued Date invoiced Date paid
Supplier Contact Phone Fax Name Address City, State, ZIP		Employer ID Name Title Authorized by Authorized date

Item	S_Item	Description	ListPrice	SalePrice	Quantity	Extended

Total

ment will probably want to print at least one variation of the report when the analysis is complete.

With Figure 3 the accounting team wants to select the starting and ending dates. So far, the team always wants the data listed by month but wants to specify which months should be included in the report. With Figure 4 (Member Disputes), the accounting manager wants the list in descending order of the current (end of the month) totals.

The three forms/reports should use the same basic data. The real difference is in the organization and in some of the computations. Because they use the same data, make sure that the totals match across all three reports. Also, the accounting manager is picky, so make sure that you get the layout to match the samples as closely as possible.

To monitor profitability, the club members closely watch the purchases by the pro shop. The club pro has some leeway to select vendors and products; however, all invoices are verified by the accounting manager. Several of the club committees review total purchases and sales throughout the year. Each purchase is recorded on a purchase order form shown in Figure 6.

You will need to produce a report listing the total purchases and total sales for each month and for each quarter for the pro shop. The members are not picky about the layout—just be sure you have the data they need to analyze the sales and costs for the pro shop.

EXERCISES

1. Create a list of all of the forms and reports that might be used in this case.
2. Create a normalized list of tables for each form and report.
3. Create an integrated list of normalized tables for the entire application. Draw the corresponding class diagram.
4. Create the basic tables in a DBMS (e.g., Access), along with all necessary relationships and integrity constraints. Enter sample data into the tables to test your design.

5. Evaluate the normalized tables and estimate the size of the database—both current size and estimated size in 3 years.

6. List the initial security conditions for the data tables. Create a list of user groups and identify their basic access needs.

7. Design the overall structure of the application. Outline the overall structure and the primary forms. Select a design scheme, including layouts, effects, and colors.

8. Build three initial input forms.

9. Build three initial reports.

10. Improve the forms and reports to make them easier to use.

11. Test your forms and reports with sample users.

12. Build additional forms and reports. Improve all of them. Test all of them.

13. Connect all of the forms and reports into an application. Test all the links. Test the forms and reports. Check for consistency.

14. Add security, backup, and recovery features to the application.

15. Move the data tables to a centralized server, leaving the application to run on a client. Build the necessary links and retest the application.

16. Move the entire application to a Web server. Build the forms so that they run on a Web browser.

17. Create a spreadsheet to perform additional data analysis. Link the data so that the spreadsheet is updated automatically; for example, export the data needed to create the Disputed Charges by Area form.

Jackson, Smith & Majors Engineers

INTRODUCTION

Jackson, Smith & Majors is an engineering and design firm that was established in the early 1970s by three partners. The firm designs buildings and civil engineering projects for medium-size businesses and state and local governments. It has developed a reputation for projects that highlight environmental issues, such as parks, greenbelts, and wildlife areas. The firm also tries to incorporate environmentally friendly elements into all of its buildings and designs.

The firm has grown to a staff of 10 partners and 40 associates. The company is still controlled by the three original partners. Associates eventually hope to become partners, but promotion to partner occurs only when employees generate enough new clients to support the growth of the firm. About 100 employees make up the support staff that performs clerical, research, and drafting tasks.

Initially, the three partners concentrated on the design and engineering efforts in the company. Now they are spending increasing amounts of time with basic administrative tasks like employee evaluation and making sure that clients pay their bills on time. Five years ago, the firm came close to going under when two major clients deferred their payments for 6 months. The incident prompted the partners to formalize their billing and payment system. They created a set of procedures and forms to handle common business tasks. Now they want to move most of the forms and management to a computer system.

PROJECTS

The firm bids on commercial and governmental contracts. When it wins the bid, a new project file is created to hold the basic management data. Projects are located in many different states and occasionally in other nations. A managing partner is assigned as the in-charge partner (usually based on which partner obtained the client). The in-charge partner is responsible for scheduling and making final decisions on the design. Additional team members are assigned based on the demands of the project, the skills of the employees, and the existing workload.

The number of open projects depends on the size of the projects. The firm sometimes works on only two or three large projects in a month. More commonly, there are 30 to 40 open projects a month, with a completion rate of between 200 and 400 projects a year.

Once the project is defined, a project schedule is created. The schedule lists the basic project data and any comments or discussion by the in-charge partner. The team breaks the project into a set of activities that consist of various tasks. An initial time frame and cost structure is created for each step. In a design or construction project, tasks and activities often depend on earlier steps. For instance, a building frame cannot be started until the foundation is complete. This dependency is noted on the project schedule by indicating the percentage of a task that must be completed before beginning a new task (required %). For example, the task of framing might require that the foundation be 100 percent complete. On the other hand, walking paths might be installed when plumbing is 50 percent complete (where the 50 percent represents installation of exterior water pipes). A sample project form is presented in Figure 1.

The partners have thought about moving the project scheduling to specialized project management software. However, they feel it is more important to be able to share the project data with team members. The partners also want to produce reports that analyze many projects at the same time. For example, they would like to create reports that show the average time spent in each activity category across all projects. By comparing the time and cost performance across teams and over time, they hope to gain a better understanding of where they might cut costs and development time. The partners have talked about integrating Microsoft's project management system with customized reports built in Access, but they want to develop the basic management applications first.

Most medium-size projects are divided into 50 to 70 activities consisting of an average of 19 tasks each. Activities are assigned to various categories (such as initial site preparation, foundation work, framing, finishing, and landscaping).

ASSOCIATE TIME AND PROJECT COSTS

Project costs are divided into three categories: associate (and partner) time, subcontracted work, and charges for material items. Associates and partners bill their time directly to clients and must keep track of the hours spent on each project. Each associate has a billing rate that represents the base hourly rate charged to clients. On some projects this rate is modified based on negotiations with the client. For taxa-

FIGURE 1

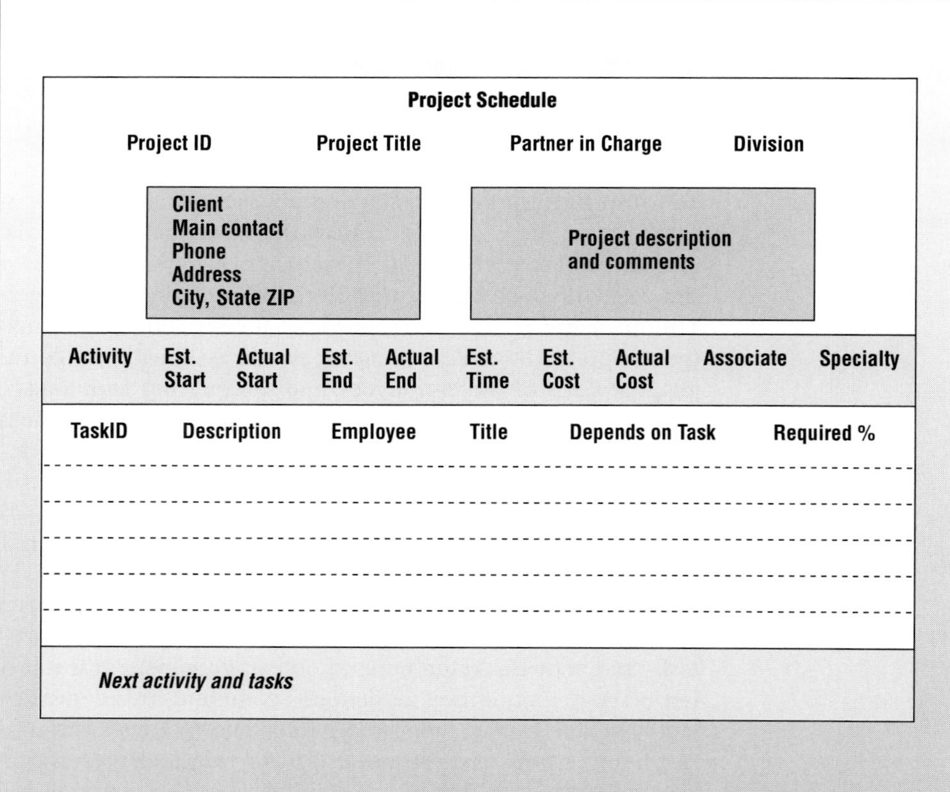

FIGURE 2

Associate Time and Costs

Associate **Office** **Phone**
Salary level

Start date **End date** **Project** **Bill rate**

Date/Time	Task	Description	Project	Activity	Comments	Hours	Extra/Discount	Extended	Associate total

Subcontract

Date/Time	Contractor	Supervisor	Address	Our Cost	Bill Rate	Extra/Discount	Total	Subcontract total

Item charges

Item	Description	Quantity	Price	Extra/Discount	Total Extended	Item charges

Total charges

tion purposes the firm keeps track of both the fixed billed rate and the final amount billed to the client. In a few situations (such as emergency work or special overtime compensation), the final charges might be higher than the base billing rate.

Associates are also encouraged to keep track of time that is not directly billable. For example, administrative tasks such as filling out internal forms cannot be billed to a project. These hours are maintained on a separate form that lists only the associate's name and the number of nonbillable hours for the week. The partners want a monthly report that shows the number of billable and nonbillable hours for each team (and the firm overall), along with a report indicating the total amount of billed revenue for that month. Similar reports for each individual (monthly and annually) are also useful when evaluating employees each year. Figure 2 shows the basic form that the partners use to record time and cost data.

Partners often work on two or three projects at a time and typically put in 60 hours a week, with 45 to 50 billable hours a week. Most projects have one or two tasks performed for each activity, and sometimes an entire set of activities is outsourced to a contractor. Item charges depend on the task, but rarely exceed 50 items for a given task on one bill.

CLIENT BILLING AND RECEIPTS

The project cost data is used to generate client bills, which contain an abbreviated form of the data. Over time, the partners have noticed that clients tend to argue over portions of the bill. Partners would like to keep track of these disputes by recording payments separately for each item. If the dispute is resolved in favor of the client, the billed amount is reduced, but this change can be entered only by an authorized partner.

The partners would like a monthly report that illustrates the percentage of bills that are paid within a month and a chart showing the percentage of total bills that are disputed. They also need a report that indicates the age of the outstanding bills. For example, they want a report that shows the dollar amount (and percentage) of bills that have not been paid for 1 month, 2 months, and so on. Most bills are paid within 2 months, and almost all of them within 6 months, but sometimes a bill will not be paid for as long as 2 years.

It is important to record the client's bank and the check number. So far, there have been few problems with bad checks, but the partners are worried that the problem might increase if they start working on smaller projects. The accountants have also suggested that any computerized-billing system should also maintain data on audits. For example, when internal auditors verify a particular check, they want to be able to record that fact. An initial form for a client bill is presented in Figure 3. Most of the time only two or three items on a bill are disputed. Every once in a while, a client disputes the entire bill.

PAYMENTS TO VENDORS

On some projects Jackson, Smith & Majors purchases construction material directly and bills the client. Additionally, supplies used in the design process are often billed directly to the client. Some services such as blueprinting are also purchased from outside vendors and billed to the client.

A few years ago, the firm experienced problems from one of the payment clerks. The clerk was creating invoices from fake vendors and cashing checks for supplies

FIGURE 3

Client Bill and Receipt

Receipt#	Date/time	Employee	Client name	Total due	Total paid	Disputed
Bill#	Date billed		Client branch		Check# and bank	
	Project	Percent complete				

Activity	Start date	End date

Task	Associate	Hours	Extra/Discount	Total	Paid	Authorization

Subcontractor	Description	Amount	Paid	Authorization

Item	Description	Price	Quantity	Extra/Discount	Amount	Paid	Authorization

Next activity and detail.

FIGURE 4

Payments to Vendors

Payment#	Date/Time	Amount	Employee Employee verify/audit	Authorization level Date/time
Check#	Account	Bank	Paid to	
Description	Comment		Name / TaxID / Invoice#	
ProjectID	Activity	Task	Address	
Disputed/Not Paid			City, State, Country, Postal Code	

Supplier ID	Amount	Description	Reason for Dispute	Our Contact	Their Contact	Resolution	Date/Time

Next supplier/dispute.

that were never provided. The clerk was fired, but most of the money was lost. With more than 200 vendors, an average of 35 vendors per project, and approximately 110 major payments a month, it can be time-consuming to analyze every payment. Consequently, the firm would like to separate the vendor payments function from ordering and receipt of products. For example, clerks and partners who authorize payments should not be able to create new vendor accounts. It would also be nice if the system would at least match the vendor payment to the value on the corresponding vendor invoice. A sample vendor-payments form is illustrated in Figure 4.

PROJECT COSTING AND TEAMWORK

Almost all work performed at Jackson, Smith & Majors is done with teams of workers. Each team is led by a partner; other members are chosen from partners for their specialties. Staff workers are assigned to teams based on the needs of the team. There is some rotation among team members—and some substitution or trading when workers are away on vacation or assigned to overseas projects.

Consequently, the lead partners are interested in including some aspects of a groupware system, where key documents can be shared by various team members. The database should also keep multiple versions of the documents and track individual changes and comments. Team members can refer to prior documents, and project leaders can assess the progress of the team.

Project cost estimation is a key process for the firm. Initial estimates are used to bid on projects. The estimates are revised as the design and construction progresses. When the project is complete, the actual costs are recorded. Partners compare the initial estimates to the final costs to help them create accurate bids on future projects.

Figure 5 illustrates a simple version of a spreadsheet template that is used to estimate initial costs. The three categories of costs (associate time, subcontractors, and material items) are listed on separate worksheets. The main worksheet presents a summary, along with the subtotals and a graph.

To track the revisions, the partners want to store each revision of the project spreadsheet in the database. Team members should be able to retrieve the worksheets, modify them, and store the new version. Basic change information should

FIGURE 5

Sample Worksheets for Estimating Costs

Project Activity Partner	Task Design time Descriptions	Estimated Time	Estimated Rate	Estimated Cost
	Total	0	0	0

Total Estimated Costs	
Time	0
Subcontract	0
Items	0
Total	0

Subcontractors Job	Type of job	Estimated Time	Estimated Cost
Total			

Items	Quantity	Estimated Price	Estimated Cost
Total	0	0	0

also be stored with the worksheet so team members can identify changes and search for particular spreadsheet versions.

As workers make changes, they are asked to list the estimated impact on the schedule and on costs. Workers should also enter a list of team members who should be notified of the changes. The base list might include all of the team workers on the project but could also include various partners and possibly vendors. Some partners have expressed an interest in having the system automatically send out e-mail notices to workers on the list.

The base estimation form is shown in Figure 6. Cost estimates tend to change on a weekly basis. Project time frames depend heavily on the size of the project, with small projects lasting 4 to 8 weeks, medium projects up to a year, and large projects lasting anywhere from 6 months to 2 years. Activity and cost impacts generally include 5 to 10 items, but the partners are trying to convince workers to be more detailed in their assessments.

EMPLOYEE EVALUATIONS

All partners and associates are evaluated on a quarterly basis. When team members are overseas, evaluations are sometimes skipped. In addition to formal evaluations, senior partners often receive comments from clients about various workers. Sometimes the comments are good, sometimes bad. Although partners value these comments, they understand that some clients can be overly sensitive about some topics and might be overly critical. Additionally, some comments might be hearsay or rumors. Although the partners want to record most of these comments, the partners also want to note the believability, source, and context of these messages. For example, oral comments mentioned in passing are considered less reliable than written statements or detailed comments on specific actions.

In quarterly evaluations employees are rated on various categories, such as the ability to meet deadlines, the quality of their work, and attention to detail. The firm is creating comprehensive job descriptions that contain a list of categories for each job. The lists will contain general attributes like those described, as well as specific attributes (like typing speed) that apply to individual jobs.

In the quarterly meetings employees are given the opportunity to review the comments and ratings. They can also write a response, which is stored in their records. A similar procedure is followed for client comments. Figure 7 presents a sample form to record basic employee data, promotions, and evaluations.

The partners are interested in producing reports that summarize employee evaluations, perhaps listing employees based on their ratings and number of client comments (net positive comments). When they begin to evaluate associates for promotion to partner, senior partners also find it useful to examine a list of the candidates sorted by the amount of money they brought in (total value of projects where they were in charge). Other lists sorted by title, salary, and number of employees they supervise would also be helpful.

SUMMARY

Your job is to build a database to provide the basic features desired by the partners at Jackson, Smith & Majors. Note that some features might be deferred for future versions if they are too complex to include in the initial product. In that case, you should provide a list of potential features and enhancements.

The system should be complete including all help files and documentation. You should also provide an estimate of the total database size with an indication of the hardware and software that will be needed to provide adequate performance. The system should be easy to install and use with minimal training. Security issues should be addressed as much as possible within the database. Additional security procedures (e.g., backup) should be documented.

FIGURE 6

Costing and Revision Notes

Item **Date/time** **Employee** **E-mail address** **Machine/userID** **Version#**

Project **Activities** **Tasks**

Reason for change **Description of change** **Authorization: internal client**

Time Impact

Activity	Task	Start Change	End Change

Notification List

Name	E-mail	Office Address	Cell Phone

Cost Impact

Activity	Task	Initial Est.	Change

Spreadsheet/object

FIGURE 7

Employee Evaluations

Employee ID **Date hired** **Title** **Supervisor**
Name **Date released** **Salary base**
SSN

Office
Phone
Home address
City, State, Country
Postal Code

Promotions

Date/Time	Title	Level	Salary	Bonus	New Supervisor	Approved

Evaluations

Date/Time **Evaluator** **Title**

Category	Rating	Comments	Response
Timeliness			
Quality			
...			

More evaluations ...

Customer Comments

Client **Phone** **Importance**
Person **Date/time** **Project**
Message type **Good/bad**
Context

Received by
Probablity of belief

Comment	Response	Notify employee (Date/Time, Who, How)	Response resolution

Also, keep track of time spent on the project so that you can adjust your billing for future projects.

EXERCISES

1. Create a list of all of the forms and reports that might be used in this case.
2. Create a normalized list of tables for each form and report.
3. Create an integrated list of normalized tables for the entire application. Draw the corresponding class diagram.
4. Create the basic tables in a DBMS (e.g., Access), along with all necessary relationships and integrity constraints. Enter sample data into the tables to test your design.
5. Evaluate the normalized tables and estimate the size of the database—both current size and estimated size in 3 years.
6. List the initial security conditions for the data tables. Create a list of user groups and identify their basic access needs and limits.
7. Design the overall structure of the application. Outline the overall structure and the primary forms. Select a design scheme, including layouts, effects, and colors.

8. Build three initial input forms.
9. Build three initial reports.
10. Improve the forms and reports to make them easier to use.
11. Test your forms and reports with sample users.
12. Build additional forms and reports. Improve all of them. Test all of them.
13. Connect all the forms and reports into an application. Test all the links. Test the forms and reports. Check for consistency.
14. Add security, backup, and recovery features to the application.
15. Move the data tables to a centralized server, leaving the application to run on a client. Build the necessary links and retest the application.
16. Move the entire application to a Web server. Build the forms so that they run on a Web browser.
17. Create the spreadsheet needed for Figures 5 and 6 and build the Access form to store it in the database.
18. Build a small project management system in Microsoft Project. In Access create queries and reports that extract the data to compare on-time totals for each associate. The report should list the individual projects for each associate, show the amount of time they are behind (or ahead of schedule), and show the difference between budgeted and actual expenses. It should compute these totals for each associate.

The Regional Epidemiology Center

To improve public health services, several local and state governments banded together and formed the Regional Epidemiology Center. Its mission is to track diseases, look for trends, and research potential causes of major diseases. The center also provides research services to the state legislatures by analyzing changes in legislation.

DISEASE REPORTING

One of the most important tasks is to collect data on several contagious diseases from physicians. All of the states require certain diseases to be reported. The center collects and analyzes this data. The analysis is shared with several other agencies, but personal histories are generally confidential. There are some exceptions—certain highly contagious diseases are reported, and people who might have become infected are contacted and tested. The basic reporting form is shown in Figure 1. Note that this case has been highly simplified for classroom use.

Location is a key element in tracking the diseases. To produce the reports needed later, the center wants to identify every location as precisely as possible. For example, each physician, clinic, and hospital address is identified by its geographic coordinates (latitude and longitude).

The center is also careful to track which employees enter data. For privacy concerns, it is also interested in security systems that automatically monitor who retrieves individual records.

For most diseases the center also asks physicians to interview patients (and family members) to identify where the patient has been in the last month. As much as possi-

FIGURE 1

Disease Incidence Report

Date/time

Patient name Age Gender Address City, State ZIP	Reporting physician Address City, State ZIP Phone, Fax Location

Disease name
Diagnosis probability

Observed Symptoms

Symptom	Severity	Length of Time

Center Use Only

Date/time received
Date/time recorded
Employee who entered data
Date/time disease confirmed

FIGURE 2

Patient Tracking

Patient ID
Occupation

Category	Location	Time		Person	Relation	Address	Contact

ble, researchers want to track patients by geographical location. Most addresses can be converted into latitude and longitude by existing databases. Some diseases such as venereal diseases require listings of other people. These people are then notified of the potential infection and asked to report for a test. Figure 2 shows a basic form used to collect this data. Patient locations are listed by basic categories (home, work, shopping, and so on). The patient is asked to estimate the amount of time spent at each location per week. Recent travels to other states or other countries are particularly important. Contact with other people is recorded—particularly close contacts. Each contact is listed by a predefined set of categories (such as same room, handshake, kissing, and sexual).

TEST RESULTS

Diagnosing some diseases is difficult. Patients may have complications from several different diseases at once, and people show different varieties of symptoms. For important cases the center tries to track all tests performed on the patient. Tests are categorized by basic type (blood, skin, observation, and so on). Most tests have numeric results, and these values are compared to benchmarks for healthy people. Figure 3 shows the basic form used to record the test data. The numeric results of each test have a specific measure (e.g., milligrams/milliliter). The center also has a list of most of the clinical and research labs in the region. The physician records the lab on the list, and the database contains basic information about the lab, such as location, phone, name of the owner, and type of facilities.

FIGURE 3

Test Results

Patient ID
Ethnic background
Physician

Date	Lab	Test Name	Type	Measure	Result	Benchmark	Interpretation

FIGURE 4

Basic Disease Description

Name
First discovered
Discovered by
Source ❍ Bacterial ❍ Viral
Germination period

Symptoms

Description	Severity	Percent Cases	Time to Appear

Transmission Mechanisms

Category	Probability of Transfer	Comments

DISEASES The center keeps basic information about highly contagious diseases. Researchers are particularly interested in maintaining a list of typical symptoms. This list is available on-line to physicians in case they need to research the disease. As shown in Figure 4, symptoms are listed by severity and by the percent of the cases in which they appear. Some symptoms do not show up for extended periods, so a time factor is also included. Where appropriate, death is listed as a symptom (although it is more of a consequence, it is important information).

The disease is described by its transmission mechanism (air, surface, sexual, and so on). Physicians use this list when they question patients about their movements and actions over the last few weeks.

REPORTS Center researchers produce many reports and charts to help analyze the data. One of the most important reports is a geographical display of the disease rates. A GIS is used to help plot the data; however, a nongraphical version shown in Figure 5 is also generated. In this report the regional deviation is important—it is the percentage difference in total cases from the mean: (count—mean)/mean.

FIGURE 5

Geographical Dispersion Report

Disease
Time period

Region	Population	New cases #	New cases %	Total cases #	Total cases %	Region Deviation

FIGURE 6

Multiple Disease Correlation

Disease Time period Region description Number of patients	Disease	Count	Percent
Ethnic – 1		_____	_____
	Subtotal:		
Ethnic – 2		_____	_____
	Subtotal:		
Ethnic – 3		_____	_____
	Subtotal:		
		_____	_____
	Grand total:		

Researchers are also interested in the incidence of multiple diseases. One basic report is shown in Figure 6. For a given disease (e.g., HIV), the report lists all other diseases recorded by those patients (e.g., tuberculosis and Karposi's sarcoma). The report is often broken down into categories, such as an analysis by ethnic background or geographic region. You should give researchers a choice in how to present the report.

Researchers also want to create a GIS report that displays multiple disease reports on a map. They want two initial alternatives: (1) if the diseases were contracted by the same person, or (2) total incidence of the diseases regardless of the patient. In both cases the researchers will supply a list of diseases, and your system should display the totals graphically on a map.

EXERCISES

1. Create a list of all of the forms and reports that might be used in this case.

2. Create a normalized list of tables for each form and report.

3. Create an integrated list of normalized tables for the entire application. Draw the corresponding class diagram.

4. Create the basic tables in a DBMS (e.g., Access), along with all necessary relationships and integrity constraints. Enter sample data into the tables to test your design.

5. Evaluate the normalized tables and estimate the size of the database—both current size and estimated size in 3 years.

6. List the initial security conditions for the data tables. Create a list of user groups and identify their basic access needs and limits. Discuss how you will monitor database usage and maintain patient privacy.

7. Design the overall structure of the application. Outline the overall structure and the primary forms. Select a design scheme, including layouts, effects, and colors.

8. Build three initial input forms.

9. Build three initial reports.

10. Improve the forms and reports to make them easier to use.

11. Test your forms and reports with sample users.

12. Build additional forms and reports. Improve all of them. Test all of them.

13. Connect all of the forms and reports into an application. Test all the links. Test the forms and reports. Check for consistency.

14. Add security, backup, and recovery features to the application.

15. Move the data tables to a centralized server, leaving the application to run on a client. Build the necessary links and retest the application.

16. Move the entire application to a Web server. Build the forms so they run on a Web browser.

17. Create a prototype of the GIS reports using Microsoft Excel. Automate as much of the data transfer as possible. You will have to enter sample location data in a format supported by Excel (e.g., national or state data, unless you have the city or regional databases for Excel's mapping system).

Glossary

24 × 7: Operation of an application or database 24 hours a day, 7 days a week. Because the database can never be shut down, performing maintenance is a challenge.

Abstract data types: In SQL3 the ability to define more complex data domains that support inheritance for storing objects.

Accessibility: A design goal to make the application usable by as many users as possible, including those with physical challenges. One solution is to support multiple input and output methods.

Active data objects (ADO): The objects used in Microsoft's Web server pages to access databases from the Internet. Similar to DAO programming, these objects provide row-level access to the database.

Active server pages (ASP): Microsoft's Web pages that enable you to run script programs on the server. Useful for providing access to a server database for Internet users.

AddNew: VBA programming command to add a new row of data to a table.

Aesthetics: An application design goal, where layout, colors, and artwork are used to improve the appearance of the application—not detract from it. By its nature, the value of any design is subjective.

Aggregation: The generic name for several SQL functions that operate across the selected rows. Common examples include SUM, COUNT, and AVERAGE.

Aggregation association: A relationship where individual items become elements in a new class. For example, an Order contains Items. In UML, the association is indicated with a small open diamond on the association end. Also see composition.

Alias: A temporary name for a table or a column. Often used when you need to refer to the same table more than once, as in a self-join.

ALL: A SQL SELECT clause often used with subqueries. Used in a WHERE clause to match all of the items in a list. For example, Price > ALL (. . .) means that the row matches only if Price is greater than the largest value in the list.

ALTER TABLE: A SQL data definition command that changes the structure of a table. To improve performance, some systems limit the changes to adding new columns. In these situations to make major changes, you have to create a new table and copy the old data.

Anchor tag: The HTML tag that signifies a link. Denoted with <A>.

ANY: A SQL SELECT clause often used with subqueries. Used in a WHERE clause to match at least one of the items in a list. For example, Price > ANY (. . .) means that the row matches as long as Price is greater than at least one item in the list.

Application: A complete system that performs a specific collection of tasks. It typically consists of integrated forms and reports and generally contains menus and a Help system.

Application design guide: A standard set of design principles that should be followed when building applications. The standard makes it easier for users to operate new applications, since techniques they learn in one system will work in another.

Application generator: A DBMS tool that assists the developer in creating a complete application package. Common tools include menu and toolbar generators and an integrated context-sensitive Help system.

Association: Connections between classes or entities. Generally, they represent business rules. For example, an order can be placed by one customer. It is important to identify whether the association is one-to-one, one-to-many, or many-to-many.

Association role: In UML the point where an association attaches to a class. It can be named and generally shows multiplicity, aggregation, or composition.

Attribute: A feature or characteristic of an entity. An attribute will become a column in a data table. Employee attributes might include name, address, date hired, and phone.

Authentication: Providing a verification system to determine who actually wrote a message. Common systems use a dual-key encryption system.

Autonumber: A type of data domain where the DBMS automatically assigns a unique identification number for each new row of data. Useful for generating primary keys.

B^+-tree: An indexed data storage method that is efficient for a wide range of data access tasks. Tree searches provide a consistent level of performance that is not affected by the size of the database.

Base table: A table that contains data about a single basic entity. It generally contains no foreign keys, so data can be entered into this table without reference to other tables. For example, Customer would be a base table; Order would not.

BETWEEN: A SQL comparison operator that determines whether an item falls between two values. Often useful for dates.

Binary large object (BLOB): A data domain for undefined, large chunks of data. A BLOB (or simple object) type can hold any type of data, but the programmer is often responsible for displaying, manipulating, and searching the data.

Binary search: A search technique for sorted data. Start at the middle of the data. If the search value is greater than the middle value, split the following data in half. Keep reducing by half until the value is found.

Bitmap index: A compact, high-speed indexing method where the key values are compressed to a small size that can be stored and searched rapidly.

Boolean algebra: Creating and manipulating logic queries connected with AND, OR, and NOT conditions.

Bound control: A control on a form that is tied to a column in the database. When data is entered or changed, the changes are automatically saved to the data table.

Boyce-Codd normal form (BCNF): All dependencies must be explicitly shown through keys. There cannot be a hidden dependency between non-key and key columns.

Browser: A software package on a client personal computer used to access and display Web pages from the Internet.

Brute force attack: An attempt to break a security system by trying every possible combination of passwords or encryption keys.

Call-level interface (CLI): A set of libraries that enable programmers to work in a language outside the DBMS (e.g., C++) and utilize the features of the DBMS. The DBMS provides the communication libraries and handles much of the data exchange itself.

Cascading delete: When tables are linked by data, if you delete a row in a higher-level table, matching rows in other tables are deleted automatically. For example, if you delete Customer 1173, all orders placed by that customer are also deleted.

CASE: A SQL operator supported by some systems. It examines multiple conditions (cases) and takes the appropriate action when it finds a match.

Certificate authority: A company that ensures the validity of public keys and the applicant's identity for dual-key encryption systems.

Check box: A square button that signifies a choice. By the design guide, users can select multiple options with check boxes, as opposed to option buttons that signify mutually exclusive choices.

Clarity: The goal of making an application easier to use through elegant design and organization that matches user tasks so that the purpose and use of the application is clear to the user.

Class: A descriptor for a set of objects with similar structure, behavior, and relationships. That is, a class is the model description of the business entity. A business model might have an Employee class, where one specific employee is an object in that class.

Class diagram: A graph of classes connected through relationships. It is designed to show the static structure of the model. Similar to the entity-relationship diagram.

Class hierarchy: A graph that highlights the inheritance relationships between classes.

Client/server: A technique for organizing systems where a few computers hold most of the data, which is retrieved by individuals using personal computer clients.

Cold site: A facility that can be leased from a disaster backup specialist. A cold site contains power and telecommunication lines, but no computer. In the event of a disaster, a company calls the computer vendor and begs for the first available machine to be sent to the cold site.

Collaboration diagram: A UML diagram to display interactions among objects. It does not show time as a separate dimension. It is used to model processes.

Combo box: A combination of a list box and a text box that is used to enter new data or to select from a list of items. A combo box saves space compared to a list box since the list is displayed only when selected by the user.

Command button: A button on a form that is designed to be clicked. The designer writes the code that is activated when the button is clicked.

Common gateway interface (CGI): With Web servers, CGI is a predefined system for transferring data across the Internet. Current scripting languages hide the details, so you can simply retrieve data as it is needed.

Common object request broker architecture (CORBA): A model developed largely by the IBM and UNIX communities to enable objects to communicate across networks. Goals include support for diverse computers, operating systems, and database systems. Also see component object model.

Component object model (COM): The Microsoft standard that supports data transfer among programs that run under the Windows operating system. The DCOM variation (distributed COM) is designed to share objects across networks. See common object request broker architecture for a competing approach.

Composite key: A primary key that consists of more than one column. Indicates a many-to-many relationship between the columns.

Composition association: A relationship in which an object is composed of a collection of other objects. For example, a bicycle is built from components. In UML, it is indicated with a small filled diamond on the association end.

Computer-aided software engineering (CASE): Computer programs that are designed to support the analysis and development of computer systems. They make it easier to create, store, and share diagrams and data definitions. Some versions can analyze existing code and generate new code.

Concatenate: A programming operation that appends one string on the end of a second string. For example, LastName & ", " & FirstName could yield "Smith, John".

Concatenated key: See composite key.

Concurrent access: Performing two (or more) operations on the same data at the same time. The DBMS must sequence the operations so that some of the changes are not lost.

Consistency: The goal of making an application easier to use by using the same features, colors, and commands throughout. Modern applications also strive for consistency with a common design guide.

Constraint: In SQL a constraint is a rule that is enforced on the data. For example, there can be primary-key and foreign-key constraints that limit the data that can be entered into the declared columns. Other business rules can form constraints, such as Price > 0.

Context-sensitive help: Help messages that are tailored to the specific task the user is performing.

Context-sensitive menu: A menu that changes depending on the object selected by the user.

Control break: A report consisting of grouped data uses control breaks to separate the groups. The break is defined on the key variable that identifies each member of the group.

Controls: The generic term for an item placed on a form. Typical controls consist of text boxes, combo boxes, and labels.

Correlated subquery: A subquery that must be reevaluated for each row of the main query. Can be extremely slow. Can often be avoided by creating a temporary table and using that in the subquery instead.

CREATE DOMAIN: A SQL data definition command to create a new data domain that is composed of existing domain types.

CREATE SCHEMA: A SQL data definition command to create a new logical grouping of tables. With some systems it is equivalent to creating a new database.

CREATE TABLE: A SQL data definition command to create a new table. The command is often generated with a program.

CREATE VIEW: A SQL command to create a new view or saved query.

Cross join: Arises when you do not specify a join condition for two tables. It matches every row in the first table with every row in the second table. Also known as the Cartesian product. It should be avoided.

Crosstab: A special SQL query (not offered by all systems) that creates a tabular output based on two groups of data. Access uses a TRANSFORM command to create a cross tabulation.

Cursor: (1) The current location pointer in a graphical environment. (2) A row pointer that tracks through a table, making one row of data active at a time.

Cylinder: Disk drives are partitioned into cylinders (or sectors), which represent a portion of a track.

Data Access Objects (DAO): Microsoft's cursor-level programming for tracking through a table one row at a time. You retrieve and alter data using predefined methods and properties of the objects.

Data administration: Planning and coordination required to define data consistently throughout the company.

Data administrator (DA): The person in charge of the data resources of a company. The DA is responsible for data integrity, consistency, and integration.

Data definition: A set of commands that are used to define data, such as CREATE TABLE. Graphical interfaces are often easier to use, but the data definition commands are useful for creating new tables with a program.

Data device: Storage space allocated to hold database tables, indexes, and rollback data. See tablespace.

Data dictionary: Holds the definitions of all of the data tables and describes the type of data that is being stored.

Data encryption standard (DES): An older but standard method for encrypting data. It is a single-key technique.

Data independence: Separates the data from the programs, which often enables the data definition to be changed without altering the program.

Data integrity: Keeping accurate data, which means few errors and means that the data reflect the true state of the business. A DBMS enables you to specify constraints or rules that help maintain integrity, such as prices must always be greater than 0.

Data manipulation: A set of commands used to alter the data. See INSERT, DELETE, and UPDATE.

Data mining: Searching databases for unknown patterns and information. Tools include statistical analysis, pattern-matching techniques, and data segmentation analysis.

Data normalization: The process of creating a well-behaved set of tables to efficiently store data, minimize redundancy, and ensure data integrity. See first, second, and third normal form.

Data replication: In a distributed system, placing duplicate copies of data on several servers to reduce overall transmission time and costs.

Data stripe: Used in RAID storage systems, where portions of the data are stored on different drives.

Data type: A type of data that can be held by a column. Each DBMS has predefined system domains (integer, float, string, etc.). Some systems support user-defined domains that are named combinations of other data types.

Data volume: The estimated size of the database. Computed for each table by multiplying the estimated number of rows times the average data length of each row.

Data warehouse: A specialized database that is optimized for management queries. Data is extracted from online transaction processing systems. The data is cleaned and optimized for searching and analysis. Generally supported by parallel processing and RAID storage.

Database: A collection of data stored in a standardized format, designed to be shared by multiple users. A collection of tables for a particular business situation.

Database administration: The technical aspects of creating and running the database. The basic tasks are performance monitoring, backup and recovery, and assigning and controlling security.

Database administrator (DBA): A specialist who is trained in the administration of a particular DBMS. DBAs are trained in the details of installing, configuring, and operating the DBMS.

Database engine: The heart of the DBMS. It is responsible for storing, retrieving, and updating the data.

Database management system (DBMS): Software that defines a database, stores the data, supports a query language, produces reports, and creates data entry screens.

Datasheet: A gridlike form that displays rows and columns of data. Generally used as a subform, a datasheet displays data in the least amount of space possible.

DBEngine: The top-level object in Microsoft's Data Access Objects. Rarely used by itself.

Deadlock: A situation that exists when two (or more) processes each have a lock on a piece of data that the other one needs.

Decision support system (DSS): A system that collects data, analyzes models, and presents the results in a manner to help managers make decisions. From a database perspective the demands that analysis and presentation place on the system are different than those of a transaction processing system.

Default values: Values that are displayed and entered automatically. Used to save time at data entry.

Degree of a tree: The maximum number of children that can fall below any node. Choosing the degree determines how fast the database can find any particular item.

DELETE: A SQL data manipulation command that deletes rows of data. It is always used with a WHERE clause to specify which rows should be deleted.

Deletion anomaly: Problems that arise when you delete data from a table that is not in third normal form. For example, if all customer data is stored with each order, when you delete an order, you could lose all associated customer data.

DeMorgan's law: An algebraic law that states: To negate a condition that contains an AND or an OR connector, you negate each of the two clauses and switch the connector. An AND becomes an OR and vice versa.

Dependence: An issue in data normalization. An attribute A depends on another attribute B if the values of A change in response to changes in B. For example, a customer's name depends on the CustomerID (each employee has a specific name). On the other hand, a customer's name does not depend on the OrderID. Customers do not change their name each time they place an order.

Depth of a tree: The number of nodes between the root and the leaves. It represents the number of searches required to find any item in the tree.

Derived class: A class that is created as an extension of another class. The programmer need only define the new attributes and methods. All others are inherited from the higher-level classes. See inheritance.

DESC: The modifier in the SQL SELECT . . . ORDER BY statement that specifies a descending sort (e.g., Z . . . A). ASC can be used for ascending, but it is the default, so it is not necessary.

Direct access: A data storage method where the physical location is computed from the logical key value. Data can be stored and retrieved with no searches.

Direct manipulation of objects: A graphical interface method that is designed to mimic real-world actions. For example, you can copy files by dragging an icon from one location to another.

Disaster plan: A contingency plan that is created and followed if a disaster strikes the computer system. Plans include off-site storage of backups, notifying personnel, and establishing operations at a safe site.

DISTINCT: A SQL keyword used in the SELECT statement to remove duplicate rows from the output.

Distributed database: Multiple independent databases that operate on two or more computers that are connected and share data over a network. The databases are usually in different physical locations. Each database is controlled by an independent DBMS.

Dockable toolbar: A toolbar that users can drag to any location on the application window. It is generally customized with options and buttons to perform specific tasks.

DoCmd.RunSQL: The Microsoft command used to execute a SQL statement. The SQL statement is generally built as a separate string based on user choices. This command causes the SQL to execute.

Domain-key normal form (DKNF): The ultimate goal in designing a database. Each table represents one topic, and all of the business rules are expressed in terms of domain constraints and key relationships. That is, all of the business rules are explicitly described by the table rules.

Drag-and-drop: A graphical interface technique where actions are defined by holding down a mouse key, dragging an icon, and dropping the icon on a new object.

Drive head: The mechanism that reads and writes data onto a disk. Modern drives have several drive heads.

DROP TABLE: A SQL data definition command that completely removes a table from the database—including the definition. Use it sparingly.

Dual-key encryption: An encryption technique that uses two different keys: one private and one public. The public key is published so anyone can retrieve it. To send an encrypted message to someone, you use the person's public key. At that point, only the person's private key will decrypt the message. Encrypting a message first with your private key can also be used to verify that you wrote the message.

Edit: The Microsoft DAO command to alter data on the current row.

Encapsulation: In object-oriented programming, the technique of defining attributes and methods within a common class. For example, all features and capabilities of an Employee class would be located together. Other code objects can use the properties and methods but only by referencing the Employee object.

Encryption: Encoding data with a key value so the data becomes unreadable. Two general types of encryption are used today: single key (e.g., DES) and dual key (e.g., RSA).

Entity: An item in the real world that we wish to identify and track.

Entity-relationship diagram (ERD): A graph that shows the associations (relationships) between business entities. Under UML, the class diagram displays similar relationships.

Equi-join: A SQL equality join condition. Rows from two tables are joined if the columns match exactly. Equi-join is the most common join condition. Rows that have no match in the other table are not displayed.

EXCEPT: A SQL operator that examines rows from two SELECT statements. It returns all rows from one statement except those that would be returned by the second statement. Sometimes implemented as a SUBTRACT command. See UNION.

Expert system (ES): A system with a knowledge base consisting of data and rules that enables a novice to make decisions as effectively as an expert.

Feasibility study: A quick examination of the problems, goals, and expected costs of a proposed system. The objective is to determine whether the problem can reasonably be solved with a computer system.

Feedback: A design feature where the application provides information to the user as tasks are accomplished or errors arise. Feedback can be provided in many forms (e.g., messages, visual cues, or audible reminders).

FETCH: The command used in SQL cursor programming to retrieve the next row of data into memory.

First normal form (1NF): A table is in 1NF when there are no repeating groups within it. Each cell can contain only one value. For example, how may items can be placed in one Order table? The items repeat, so they must be split into a separate table.

Fixed-width storage: Storing each row of data in a fixed number of bytes per column.

Fixed-with-overflow storage: Storing a portion of the row data in a limited number of bytes and moving extra data to an overflow location.

Focus: In a window environment, a form or control has focus when it is the one that will receive keystrokes. It is usually highlighted.

For Each . . . Next: In VBA an iteration command to automatically identify objects in a group and apply some operation to that collection. Particularly useful when dealing with cells in a spreadsheet.

Foreign key: A column in one table that is a primary key in a second table. It does not need to be a key in the first table. For example, in an Order table, CustomerID is a foreign key because it is a primary key in the Customer table.

Forms generator: A DBMS tool that enables you to set up input forms on the screen.

Fourth normal form: There cannot be hidden dependencies between key columns.

FROM: The SQL SELECT clause that signifies the tables from which the query will retrieve data. Used in conjunction with the JOIN or INNER JOIN statement.

FULL JOIN: A join that matches all rows from both tables if they match, plus all rows from the left table that do not match, and all rows from the right table that do not match. Rarely used and rarely available. See LEFT JOIN and RIGHT JOIN.

Function: A procedure designed to perform a specific computation. The difference between a function and a subroutine is that a function returns a specific value (not including the parameters).

Generalization association: A relationship among classes that begins with a generic class. More detailed classes are derived from it and inherit the properties and methods of the higher-level classes.

Geographic information system (GIS): Designed to identify and display relationships among business data and locations. A good example of the use of objects in a database environment.

GRANT: The SQL command to give someone access to specific tables or queries.

Graphics interchange file (GIF): One standard method of storing graphical images. Commonly used for images shared on the Internet.

Group break: A report that splits data into groups. The split-point is called a break. Also known as a control break.

GROUP BY: A SQL SELECT clause that computes an aggregate value for each item in a group. For example, SELECT Department, SUM(Salary) FROM Employee GROUP BY Department; computes and lists the total employee salaries for each department.

Hashed key: Direct access storage of a row of data, where the key value is converted to a physical storage location.

HAVING: A SQL clause used with the GROUP BY statement. It restricts the output to only those groups that meet the specified condition.

Heads-down data entry: Touch typists concentrate on entering data without looking at the screen. Forms for this task should minimize keystrokes and use audio cues.

Help system: A method for displaying, sequencing, and searching help documentation. Developers need to write the help files in a specific format and then use a help compiler to generate the final help file.

Hidden dependency: A dependency specified by business rules that is not shown in the table structure. It generally indicates that the table needs to be normalized further and is an issue with Boyce-Codd or fourth normal form.

Hierarchical database: An older DBMS type that organizes data in hierarchies that can be rapidly searched from top to bottom, e.g., Customer — Order — OrderItem.

Horizontal partition: Splitting a table into groups based on the rows of data. Rows that are seldom used can be moved to slower, cheaper storage devices.

Hot site: A facility that can be leased from a disaster backup specialist. A hot site contains all the power, telecommunication facilities, and computers necessary to run a company. In the event of a disaster, a company collects its backup data, notifies workers, and moves operations to the hot site.

Human factors design: An attempt to design computer systems that best accommodate human users.

Hypertext link: Hypertext (e.g., Web) documents consist of text and graphics with links that retrieve new pages. Clicking on a link is the primary means of navigation and obtaining more information.

Hypertext markup language (HTML): A display standard that is used to create documents to be shared on the Internet. Several generators will create HTML documents from standard word processor files.

Icon: A small graphical representation of some idea or object. Typically used in a graphical user interface to execute commands and manipulate underlying objects.

IN: A SQL WHERE clause operator typically used with subqueries. It returns a match if the selected item matches one of the items in the list. For example, WHERE ItemID IN (115, 235, 536) returns a match for any of the items specified. Typically, another SELECT statement is inserted in the parentheses.

Index: A sorted list of key values from the original table along with a pointer to the rest of the data in each row. Used to speed up searches and data retrieval.

Indexed sequential access method (ISAM): A data storage method that relies on an index to search and retrieve data faster than a pure sequential search.

Inequality join: A SQL join where the comparison is made with an inequality (greater than or less than) instead of an equality operator. Useful for placing data into categories based on ranges of data.

Inheritance: In object-oriented design, the ability to define new classes that are derived from higher-level classes. New classes inherit all prior properties and methods, so the programmer only needs to define new properties and methods.

INNER JOIN: A SQL equality join condition. Rows from two tables are joined if the columns match exactly. The most common join condition. Rows that have no match in the other table are not displayed.

InputBox: A predefined simplistic Window form that might be used to get one piece of data from the user. But it is better to avoid it and create your own form.

INSERT: Two SQL commands that insert data into a table. One version inserts a single row at a time. The other variation copies selected data from one query and appends it as new rows in a different table.

Insertion anomaly: Problems that arise when you try to insert data into a table that is not in third normal form. For example, if you find yourself repeatedly entering the same data (e.g., a customer's address), the table probably needs to be redefined.

Internet: A collection of computers loosely connected to exchange information worldwide. Owners of the computers make files and information available to other users.

INTERSECT: A set operation on rows of data from two SELECT statements. Only rows that are in both statements will be retrieved. See UNION.

Intranet: A network internal to a company that uses Internet technologies to share data.

Iteration: Causing a section of code to be executed repeatedly, such as the need for a loop to track through each row of data. Typical commands include Do . . . Loop and For . . . Next.

Java: A programming language developed by Sun Microsystems that is supposed to be able to run unchanged on diverse computers. Originally designed as a control language for embedded systems, Java is being targeted for Internet applications. The source of many bad puns in naming software products.

JOIN: When data is retrieved from more than one table, the tables must be joined by some column or columns of data. See INNER JOIN and LEFT JOIN.

Leaves: The bottom nodes of a tree. They hold pointers to the actual data. In a B^+-tree, leaves are linked sequentially.

LEFT JOIN: An outer join that includes all of the rows from the "left" table, even if there are no matching rows in the "right" table. The missing values are indicated by Nulls. See RIGHT JOIN and INNER JOIN. Left and right are defined by the order the tables are listed; left is first.

Lifetime: The length of time that a programming variable stays available. For example, variables created within subroutines are created when the routine is executed and then destroyed when it exits. Global variables stay alive for all routines within the module.

LIKE: The SQL pattern-matching operator used to compare string values. The standard uses percent (%) to match any number of characters, and underscore (_) to match a single character. Some systems (e.g., Access) use an asterisk (*) and a question mark (?) instead.

List box: A control on a form that displays a list of choices. The list is always displayed and takes up a fixed amount of space on the screen.

Local area network (LAN): A collection of personal computers within a small geographic area. All components of the network are owned or controlled by one company.

Local variable: A variable defined within a subroutine. It can be accessed only within that subroutine and not from other procedures.

Logical security: Determining which users should have access to which data. It deals with preventing three data problems: (1) unauthorized disclosure, (2) unauthorized modification, and (3) unauthorized withholding.

Loop: Each loop must have a beginning, an end condition, and some way to increment a variable. See iteration.

Menu: A set of application commands grouped together—usually on a toolbar. It provides an easy reference for commonly used commands and highlights the structure of the application.

Metadata: Data about data, typically stored in a data dictionary. For example, table definitions and column domains are metadata.

Method: A function or operation that a class can perform. For example, a Customer class would generally have an AddNew method that is called whenever a new customer object is added to the database.

Modal form: A form that takes priority on the screen and forces the user to deal with it before continuing. It should be avoided because it interrupts the user.

Module (or package): A collection of subroutines, generally related to a common purpose.

Monolithic program: A common programming technique before event-driven, object-oriented interfaces. Each program was self-contained and was written as one large block of code.

MsgBox: A predefined method in Windows for displaying a brief message on the screen and presenting a few limited choices to the user. Because it is modal and interrupts the user, it should be used sparingly.

Multiplicity: The UML term for signifying the quantities involved in an association. It is displayed on an association line with a minimum value, an ellipses (. . .), and a maximum value or asterisk (*) for many. For example, a customer can place from zero to many orders, so the multiplicity is (0 . . . *).

N-ary association: An association among three or more classes. It is drawn as a diamond on a UML class diagram. The term comes from extending English terms: un*ary* means one, bin*ary* means two, tern*ary* means three; so N-ary means many.

Naming conventions: Program teams should name their variables and controls according to a consistent format. One common approach is to use a three-letter prefix to identify the type of variable, followed by a descriptive name.

Nested conditions: Conditional statements that are placed inside other conditional statements. For example, If (x > 0) Then . . . If (y < 4) Then . . . Some nested conditions can be replaced with a case statement.

Nested query: See subquery.

Network database: An older DBMS type that expanded the hierarchical database by supporting multiple connections between entities. A network database is characterized by the requirement that all connections had to be supported by an index.

Node: The element of a data storage tree that holds the key values and pointers to other nodes.

Normalization: See data normalization.

NOT: The SQL negation operator. Used in the WHERE clause to reverse the truth value of a statement. See DeMorgan's law.

NotInList: An event corresponding to a combo box in Access. It is triggered when a user enters a value that does not yet exist in the selected list. Often used to add new data to a table, such as new customers.

Null: A missing (or currently unassigned) value.

Object: An instance or particular example of a class. For example, in an Employee class, one individual employee would be an object. In a relational environment a class is stored as a table, and an individual row in the table contains data for one object.

Object browser: A tool provided within Microsoft software that displays properties and methods for available objects.

Object linking and embedding (OLE): The technique used in Microsoft Windows to transfer data among various software products. Dynamic linking can be used to automatically transfer data to other tools.

Object-oriented database management system (OODBMS): A database system that holds objects, including properties and methods. It supports links between objects, including inheritance.

Object-oriented programming: A programming methodology where code is encapsulated within the definition of various objects (or classes). Systems are built from (hopefully) reusable objects. You control the system by manipulating object properties and calling object methods.

Offset: A location within a sector on a disk drive that indicates where a piece of data is stored.

On Error: A visual basic statement used to set up an error-handling routine. This line describes what to do if an error arises. Typically, it routes the processor to a separate routine.

On-line application processing (OLAP): The use of a database for data analysis. The focus is on retrieval of the data. The primary goals are to provide acceptable response times, maintain security, and make it easy for users to find the data they need.

On-line transaction processing (OLTP): The use of a database for transaction processing. It consists of many insert and update operations and supports hundreds of concurrent accesses. High-speed storage of data, reliability, and data integrity are primary goals. Examples include airline reservations, online banking, and retail sales.

Open database connectivity (ODBC): A standard created by Microsoft to enable software to access a variety of databases. Each DBMS vendor provides an ODBC driver. Application code can generally be written once. To change the DBMS, you simply install and set up the proper ODBC driver.

Option button: A round button that is used to indicate a choice. By the design guide, option buttons signify mutually exclusive choices, as opposed to check boxes.

ORDER BY: The clause in the SQL SELECT statement that lists the columns to sort the output. The modifiers ASC and DESC are used to specify ascending and descending sort orders.

Outer join: A generic term that represents a LEFT JOIN or a RIGHT JOIN. It returns rows from a table, even if there is no matching row in the other table.

Pack: A maintenance operation that must be periodically performed on a database to remove fragments of deleted data.

Package: A UML mechanism to group logical elements together. It is useful for isolating sections of a design. Packages can provide an overview of the entire system without having to see all the details.

Page footer: A report element that appears at the bottom of every page. Often used for page numbers.

Page header: A report element that appears at the top of every page. Often used for column headings and subtitles.

Parameter: A variable that is passed to a subroutine or function and used in its computations.

Pass-by-reference: A subroutine parameter that can be altered within the subroutine. If it is altered, the new value is returned to the calling program. That is, the subroutine can alter variables in other parts of the code. Usually a dangerous approach. See pass-by-value.

Pass-by-value: A subroutine parameter that cannot be altered within the subroutine. Only its value is passed. If the subroutine changes the value, the original value in the calling program is not changed.

Pass-through query: SQL queries that are ignored by Access on the front end. They enable you to write complex SQL queries that are specific to the server database.

Persistent objects: In object-oriented programming, the ability to store objects (in a file or database) so that they can be retrieved at a later date.

Persistent stored modules: In SQL3 a proposed method for storing methods associated with objects. The module code would be stored and retrieved automatically by the DBMS.

Physical security: The branch of security that involves physically protecting the equipment and people. It includes disaster planning, physical access to equipment, and risk analysis and prevention.

Platter: Disk drives contain multiple platters or surfaces to hold data. Each platter has two sides.

Pointer: A logical or physical address of a piece of data.

Polymorphism: In a class hierarchy each new class inherits methods from the prior classes. Through polymorphism you can override those definitions and assign a new method (with the same name) to the new class.

Primary key: A column or set of columns that identify a particular row in a table.

Private key: In a dual-key encryption system, the key that is never revealed to anyone else. A message encrypted with a public key can be decrypted only with the matching private key.

Procedural language: A traditional programming language that is based on following procedures and is typically executed one statement at a time. Compared to SQL, which operates on sets of data with one command.

Procedure: A subroutine or function that is designed to perform one specific task. It is generally wise to keep procedures small.

Property: An attribute or feature of an entity that we wish to track. The term is often applied in an object-oriented context. See attribute.

Prototype: An initial outline of an application that is built quickly to demonstrate and test various features of the application. Often used to help users visualize and improve forms and reports.

Public key: In a dual-key encryption system, the key that is given to the public. A message encrypted with a public key can only be decrypted with the matching private key.

Query by example (QBE): A fill-in-the-form approach to designing queries. You select tables and columns from a list and fill in blanks for conditions and sorting. It is relatively easy to use, requires minimal typing skills, generally comes with a Help system, and is useful for beginners.

Rapid application development (RAD): A systems design methodology that attempts to reduce development time through efficiency and overlapping stages.

Recordset: The object in Microsoft's DAO that represents a query or a table. Setting a Recordset enables your code to track through the data row by row.

Redundant array of independent drives (RAID): A disk drive system that consists of multiple drives with independent controllers. There are several levels of RAID offering different features. The goal is to split the data to provide faster access and automatic duplication for error recovery.

Referential integrity: A data integrity constraint where data can be entered into a foreign key column only if the data value already exists in the base table. For example, clerks should not be able to enter an Order for CustomerID 1173 if CustomerID 1173 is not in the Customer table.

Reflexive association: A relationship from one class back to itself. Most commonly seen in business in an Employee class, where some employees are managers over other employees.

Reflexive join: A situation that exists when a table is joined to itself through a second column. For example, the table Employee(EmployeeID, . . . , ManagerID) could have a join from ManagerID to EmployeeID.

Relational database: The most popular type of DBMS. All data is stored in tables (sometimes called relations). Tables are logically connected by the data they hold (e.g., through the key values). Relational databases should be designed through data normalization.

Relationship: An association between two or more entities. See association.

Repeating groups: Groups of data that repeat, such as items being ordered by a customer, multiple phone numbers for a client, and tasks assigned to a worker.

Replication manager: In a distributed database that relies on replication, the manager is an automated system that transfers changes to the various copies of the database. It has to handle conflicts if two people changed the same data before it was replicated.

Report footer: A report element that appears at the end of the report. Often used for summary statistics or graphs.

Report header: A report element that appears only at the start of the report. Often used for title pages and overviews.

Report writer: A DBMS tool that enables you to set up reports on the screen to specify how items will be displayed or calculated. Most of these tasks are performed by dragging data onto the screen.

Resume: A VBA error-handling operator that tells the processor to return to a new location and continue evaluating the code. Resume by itself returns to the line that caused the error. Resume Next returns to the line immediately following the error. Resume <label> sends the processor to a new location.

REVOKE: The SQL command used to remove permissions that were granted to certain users.

RIGHT JOIN: An outer join that includes all the rows from the "right" table, even if there are no matching rows in the "left" table. The missing values are indicated by Nulls. See INNER JOIN. Left and right are defined by the order the tables are listed; left is first.

Rivest-Shamir-Adelman (RSA) encryption: A dual-key encryption system that was patented in the United States by three mathematicians. See dual-key encryption.

Roll back: A database system transaction feature. If an error occurs in a sequence of changes, the preceding changes can be rolled back to restore the database to a safe state with correct data.

Roll forward: If an error occurs in processing transactions, the database can be restarted and loaded from a known checkpoint. Then partially completed transactions can be rolled forward to record the interrupted changes.

Root (of a tree): The first entry point in a tree structure. Usually shown at the top.

Row-by-row calculations: The way that SQL performs in-line calculations. For example, the statement SELECT Price*Quantity AS Extended goes through each row and multiplies the row's value for Price times the matching value for Quantity.

Schema: A collection of tables that are grouped together for a common purpose.

Scope: Refers to where a variable is accessible. Variables defined within a subroutine can typically be accessed only by code within that subroutine. Variables defined within a module are globally accessible by any code within that module.

Scroll bars: A common graphical interface feature used to move material horizontally or vertically.

Second normal form (2NF): A table is in 2NF if every non-key column depends on the entire key (not just part of it). This issue arises only if there is a concatenated key (with multiple columns).

Sector: Disk drives are partitioned into sectors (or cylinders), which represent a portion of a track.

SELECT: The primary data retrieval command for SQL. The main components are SELECT . . . FROM . . . INNER JOIN . . . WHERE.

Self-join: A table joined to itself.

Shell site: See cold site.

Single-row form: An input form that displays data from one row of a table at a time. The most common input form, since the designer has full control over the layout of the form.

Snapshot: In a constantly changing database, you can take a snapshot that provides a copy of the data at one point in time.

SQL: A standardized database language, used for data retrieval (queries), data definition, and data manipulation.

SQL3: A proposed new version of SQL. SQL3 is largely designed to add object-oriented features to the SQL language.

Subform form: A form that is displayed inside another (main) form. The data in the subform is generally linked to the row currently being displayed on the main form.

Subquery: Using a second query to retrieve additional data within the main query. For example, to retrieve all sales where price was greater than the average, the WHERE clause could use a subquery to compute the average price.

Subroutine: A separate section of code designed to perform one specific purpose. A subroutine can use parameters to exchange data with the calling routine.

Subtable: In SQL3 a subtable inherits all of the columns from a base table. It provides inheritance similar to that of the abstract data types; however, all data is stored in separate columns.

Switchboard form: A form that is used to direct users to different parts of the application. Often used as the first form to appear. Options on the form should match the tasks of the users.

Synonym: A short name for the full database path. Advantages of the short name are that it is easy to remember and the user never needs to know where the data is located. In addition, if everyone uses the synonym, database administrators can easily move the server databases to different locations just by altering the synonym's properties.

Syntax: The specific format of commands that can be created in a program. Programs consist of logical steps, but each command must be given in the proper syntax for the compiler to understand it. Compilers generally check for syntax and prompt you with messages.

Table: A collection of data for one class or entity. It consists of columns for each attribute and a row of data for each specific entity or object.

Tablespace: In Oracle a tablespace is disk space that is allocated to hold tables, indexes, and other system data. You must first know the approximate size of the database.

Tabular form: An input form that displays data in columns and rows. It is used when there are few columns of data or when the user needs to see multiple rows at the same time.

Third normal form (3NF): A table is in third normal form (3NF) if each non-key column depends on the whole key and nothing but the key.

Three-tier client server: A client/server system with a middle layer to hold code that defines business rules and consolidates access to various transaction servers.

Toggle button: A three-dimensional variation of the check box. It is used to signify a choice of options.

Toolbar: A small object in applications that can hold buttons and text menus. Users can execute commands with one or two mouse clicks. Used to hold frequently used commands, and commands that are used across the entire application, such as printing.

Tooltip: A short message that is displayed when the user moves the mouse cursor over an item on the screen. Extremely useful for identifying the purpose of icons.

TOP: A SQL SELECT clause provided by Access that restricts the displayed output to a specified number of rows. You can set the number of rows directly or use a percentage of the total number.

Track: Each platter on a disk drive is divided into concentric tracks. The drive head must be moved to reach a different track.

Transaction: In a database application a transaction is a set of changes that must all be made together. Transactions must be identified to the DBMS and then committed or rolled back (if there is an error). For example, a transfer of money from one bank account to another requires two changes to the database—both must succeed or fail together.

Transaction processing: Collecting data for the purpose of recording transactions. Common examples include sales, human resource management, and financial accounting.

Trigger: An event that causes a procedure to be executed. For example, clicking a button can be a trigger, as can a change in a data value.

Two-phase commit: A mechanism for handling concurrency and deadlock problems in a distributed database. In the first phase the coordinating DBMS sends updates to the other databases and asks them to prepare the transaction. Once they have agreed, the coordinator sends a message to commit the changes.

Unicode: A standard method of storing and displaying a variety of character sets. Almost all current world character sets have been defined, as well as several ancient languages. It uses 2 bytes to represent each character, enabling it to handle over 65,000 characters or ideograms.

Unified Modeling Language (UML): A standardized modeling language for designing and documenting computer and business systems.

UNION: A SQL clause to combine rows from two SELECT statements. Both queries must have the same number of columns with the same domains. Most systems also support INTERSECT and EXCEPT (or SUBTRACT) operators.

UPDATE: A SQL data manipulation command that changes the values in specified columns. A WHERE clause specifies which rows will be affected.

User interface: The look and feel of the application as it is seen by the user. Graphical interfaces are commonly employed in which users can manipulate icons and data on the screen to perform their tasks.

Validation tables: Simple tables of one or two columns that contain standardized data for entry into other tables. For example, a list of departments would be stored in a validation table. To enter a department name into an Employee table, the user would be given a choice of the rows in the validation table.

VARCHAR: A common method for storing character data. It stands for variable characters. Each column of data uses the exact amount of bytes needed to store the specific data.

Variable: A location in memory used to hold temporary values. Variables have a scope and a lifetime depending on where they are created and how they are defined. They also have a specific data type, although the Variant data type in VBA can hold any common type of data.

Vertical partition: Splitting a table into groups based on the columns of data. Large columns or columns that are seldom used (e.g., pictures) can be moved to slower, cheaper storage devices.

View: A saved query. You can build new queries that retrieve data from the view. A view is saved as an SQL statement—not as the actual data.

Virtual address: A computed location on a disk drive. More useful than a physical location because it is easier to move the data to different drives.

Virtual sequential access method (VSAM): A data storage method that uses virtual addresses instead of physical locations in the index. A true VSAM technique also provides multilevel indexes and other storage features. It has largely been replaced by B^+-tree indexes.

Visual Basic (VB): A stand-alone programming language sold by Microsoft and used to develop applications for the Windows environment. The professional version supports database connections. The program can be compiled into a stand-alone executable file.

Visual basic for applications (VBA): The programming language that underlies almost all of Microsoft's tools, including Access.

Volume: The name of a data storage device. Often used to represent a different physical drive, but it can be applied to an entire system of drives.

Volume table of contents (VTOC): A design tool that can be used to outline the overall structure of an application. It generally shows a sequence of interrelated menus.

WHERE: The SQL clause that restricts the rows that will be used in the query. It can also refer to data in subqueries.

Wide area network (WAN): A network that is spread across a larger geographic area. Parts of the network are often outside the control of a single firm. Long-distance connections often use public carriers.

With . . . End With: In VBA a shortcut for examining or altering several properties for a single object. Once the object is specified in the With statement, you simply refer to the properties inside the "loop."

World Wide Web (WWW): A first attempt to set up an international database of information. Web browsers display graphical pages of information. Hypertext connections enable you to get related information by clicking highlighted words or icons. A standard method for displaying text and images on client computers.

Organizations Index

Subject Index

B

C

D

E

F

G

H

I